Workforce Diversity Management

Challenges, Competencies and Strategies

Bahaudin G. Mujtaba

Llumina Press

© Bahaudin G. Mujtaba (2007). Workforce Diversity Management: Challenges, Competencies and Strategies

Published by: Dr. Bahaudin G. Mujtaba
         Nova Southeastern University
         3301 College Avenue
         Fort Lauderdale, FL 33315-3025 USA.
         Phone: (954) 262-5000 Or (800) 672-7223
         Email: mujtaba@nova.edu

ISBN: 1-59526-548-1

Printed in the United States of America by Llumina Press

Library of Congress Control Number: 2006930381

* * * Dedication * * *

This book is dedicated to those who make good use of
diversity as well as those who promote fairness,
justice, and equity for all. May the
force be with their heads,
hearts, and
habits.

✲
✲
✲
✲
✲
✲
✲
✲

Table of Contents

Foreword

What comes to mind when you hear the word *diversity?* Have you ever asked yourself, what does the word diversity mean, in the context of business or organizations? What does it mean when you hear or read the phrase, *we must value diversity?* What personal quiet thoughts are invoked? Or, what controversial "water cooler" conversations occur? In some organizations, working with diverse people and respecting their cultures, at a minimum, mean following work rules established by the human resource department (and the attorneys) in order to avoid lawsuits. In the *Workforce Diversity Management* book, the author encourages the reader to explore these questions or topics and much more at a personal level and as a professional in the workplace in order to go above and beyond the organizational and legal requirements.

Webster's dictionary defines *diversity as* "differing from one another." How many of us are truly comfortable with embracing someone we believe is distinctly different from us? It is in our nature, as Homo sapiens, to initially, fear or at least become uncomfortable with people and ideas that are not similar to our own. The author also uses the word *tolerance* as he invites leaders to T.A.P. into a new model for managing diversity through such concepts as tolerance, awareness, and personal development. Webster's 3rd edition of the American Heritage Collegiate dictionary defines *tolerance* as the "capacity to endure hardship or pain." Rarely do we look forward to *tolerating* anything or anyone, particularly if it painfully removes us from our zone of comfort, security, and familiarity!

In some respects, this book is not really about diversity or tolerance! This is a treatise on understanding that we are alike in so many ways. It is a call to learn and understand how similar our workplace values are indeed! In this book are lessons that teach how best to build relationships upon a bedrock of congruent values and goals rather than struggle with our collective fears.

We all want the universal promise of life, liberty, and the pursuit of happiness. Oh yes, and the opportunity to become millionaires! Although we may have differing ideas on how to reach these goals, great leaders will be able to channel the best of what we have to offer individually toward achieving the organization's vision and mission in a just manner. She or he will value quality and teach others to embrace excellence as well. The *Workforce Diversity Management* book will be of great assistance in this endeavor.

Dr. J. Preston Jones, Executive Associate Dean
H. Wayne Huizenga School of Business and Entrepreneurship

Preface

Diversity is a reality of life and a stimulating concept. The subject of diversity requires examining one's own beliefs and values as well as learning the skills of dealing appropriately with those whose personal beliefs and professional values may be very different. Understanding, mastering, and applying the information in this *Workforce Diversity Management* book can help professionals and managers deal with today's diverse workforce more effectively in order to attract and retain productive associates in a very competitive global economy. The book can also help managers create a pleasant work environment where all employees of diverse beliefs and values are respected and treated with dignity.

Managing differences throughout a country or organization, according to systems thinking, is like managing a diverse group of people in a small department. You have to understand each individual and let people freely voice their opinion in order to maximize their efficiency and productivity toward the department. Likewise, it is important to have representatives from all relevant departments, sub-departments, suppliers, buyers, and customers that are working concurrently toward the same objectives for the organization. It means working with everyone in the department and organization to serve all customers in a quality manner. Everyone in the department and organization must be able to adjust and adapt to the changing circumstances and needs of diverse customers at each moment.

In 1988, while working as a first time Manager in the bakery department at the Altamonte Store of Publix Super Markets in Central Florida, we were all waiting for the founder of our company to visit the store. We did not get to see him often since his office was in Lakeland, and this was a privilege to actually see the founder of the organization for a quick visit. As managers and employees, we synergistically worked to get the store to look very nice and neat for the visit. While he was in the store, an elderly customer asked to speak with the manager, and I ended up spending over fifteen minutes answering her questions and completing her order. She was about eighty years of age, and since she was European, she did not speak English fluently. While answering her questions about a specific birthday cake for an upcoming party, I noticed that Mr. George Jenkins, the founder of Publix, made his visit to the Bakery Department and shook the hands of several employees. Since he was not able to walk comfortably, he was sitting in a wheelchair thanking everyone for doing a good job at Publix. At that moment, I was disappointed for not having the opportunity to personally speak with him while he was in my department. When he asked "who is the Department Manager", he was told that the manager was the one helping the customer. Ten minutes later, and after making his rounds throughout the store, he decided to come back to the Bakery Department to personally say hello to me. When I saw him, he said "Thank you for serving customers and your employees." I said "I am sorry about earlier when you came through the department as I could not walk away from the customer since she did not speak English well and she was not able to speak fast due to her breathing challenges. So, the order-taking process took a little longer." He said, "No need to be sorry. I saw you were helping an elderly customer while adapting to her pace, instead of rushing her. Adapting and being flexible with people is a sign of effective management and leadership. You did a good job." Mr. George Jenkins, as a leader of a Fortune 100 Firm and an experienced practitioner, was reinforcing the essence of diversity management by complimenting me publicly for helping the elderly customer and adapting to her pace. I still have not forgotten his statement about assisting the customer at her pace instead of mine. Adapting, of course, is one aspect of diversity management in today's workforce, and all organizational leaders and managers need to act like Mr. George Jenkins by reinforcing the expected and positive behavior with regard to various dimensions of diversity. I am sure many of you, as practitioners, managers and leaders, are always reinforcing good behaviors in your organization when you see it. Keep it up.

As a practitioner and educator, I understand that you are not necessarily reading this material because you have diversity problems. You are reading because you, as an individual or as a team, have diversity opportunities which can be converted into a competitive advantage through respecting each other's differences and capitalizing on each other's strengths.

Thanks for reading this material on *Workforce Diversity Management*. First of all, let me congratulate and commend you in your efforts toward diversity awareness and integration in the workforce. Second, I want to thank you for acquiring this book to be a part of your reading, training, library, and development program. Diversity management is a topic that is very near and dear to my heart personally and professionally both from an academician and a practitioner's perspective. Third, I understand that as an author I am at a disadvantage when it comes to knowing your internal operations. So, please bear with me during the various exercises and discussions on diversity, and try to link the material to your current workplace. Throughout the book, I'll be presenting the topic of diversity from a general perspective with a management flavor to it.

For some readers, this material will only be a reinforcement of the good practices they are already doing. For others, it will be more of an awareness session. The overall purposes of this material on *Workforce Diversity Management* are to increase one's sensitivity and awareness regarding diversity and interpersonal productivity in the workplace.

Workforce Diversity Management book is not about becoming an expert on the laws of the United States. *Workforce Diversity Management* is about increasing one's cultural competency, understanding people as individuals rather than groups, and building productive human relationships in the workplace. A balloon sales person once said that "it's not the color or the size of the balloons that matter or make a difference. It is what is inside that makes them go up." *Workforce Diversity Management* is about applying the principles implied in what this balloon salesperson was saying. It is the content of our character rather than our race, gender, body size, or ethnicity that makes a difference in our performance on the job.

The author and contributors have used the concepts discussed in this book both nationally and internationally with academic and practitioner audiences to help increase their awareness of diversity and different cultures. It is also acknowledged that, initially, the author and his colleagues learned and used this material at Publix Super Markets to help managers become culturally more competent. The concepts, cases and exercises have been gleaned from a variety of sources and professionals in the United States and others around the globe. The experts in the area of diversity, including the author and trainers at the National Multi-Cultural Institute (NMCI), have taught many of these concepts and thoughts with thousands of managers in the United States and abroad. As such, the concepts, cases, and exercises are very relevant to today's work environment, and thus can easily fit most diversity management or cultural competency courses, seminars, and employee development workshops. Diversity management trainers, corporate universities, colleges or professors wishing to adopt this book or any of its chapters may contact the publisher or the author request the available supplementary facilitator's materials such as the electronic Power Point files for presentation, chapter summaries for usage with lectures and online postings, test questions for discussions or exams, and/or other supplementary material for exercises. The Instructor's CD (resources) come electronically using Microsoft Power Point, Word, and Excel files; as such, they can be adjusted by each educator and facilitator for his or her lectures, training and presentations.

Mohandas Gandhi said that "Happiness is when what you think, what you say, and what you do are in harmony." Therefore, I wish you harmony in your head (thoughts), heart (feelings), and habits (behaviors).

Bahaudin

****
"We are led to believe a lie - When we see with and not through the eye."
"When I die, I shall sour with the angels. But if I die an angel, you cannot imagine what I'll become."
****

Acknowledgements

Special thanks go to my family members, colleagues and friends for their guidance and valuable input in the review of this material. In particular, I thank and acknowledge the following individuals for generously sharing their thoughts, suggestions, writings, and other contributions on diversity, culture, management, internationalization, and leadership related issues in this book.

1) Abiodun Raimi
2) Alma M. Sierra
3) Anisa Brockington
4) Ann (Goldie) McKernan
5) Anthony (Amp) Stevens
6) Barbara Dastoor
7) Bebe T. Frisbie
8) Betty Varela
9) Bina Patel
10) Bryan Monaghan
11) Brian Quier
12) Carletha Toote
13) Claudette Chin-loy
14) Dan Austin
15) Dawn Rohicki
16) Denice Ford
17) Donovan McFarlane
18) Ebony Thomas
19) Eleanor B. Marschke
20) Frank Cavico
21) Fred Barron
22) Gerraldine Ippolito
23) Ismary Rodriguez
24) Ikwukananne I. Udechukwu
25) J. Preston Jones
26) Jack Snow
27) James Artley
28) Jean McAtavey
29) Jennifer Severe
30) Joseph Dolcine
31) Juliett Reid
32) Kimberly L. Caleb
33) Lauren Niles
34) Larry Lelah
35) Lisa Mujtaba
36) Macie E. Dawkins-Hanna
37) Maria Carla Garces
38) Mary Toledo
39) Michael Sithole
40) Michelle Newton
41) Monica Nino
42) Nicole A. Pirone
43) Phil Rokicki
44) Reccia N. Charles
45) Regina Harris
46) Robert Preziosi
47) Rohini Anand
48) Roscoe Dandy
49) Simone Maxwell
50) Terrell Manyak

I first became a diversity student, and eventually a trainer, when I was a department manager with Publix Super Markets. As demonstrated by the life of Mr. George Jenkins, founder of Publix, Publix Managers were expected to see their employees and customers as their most important and mission-critical resources for success in the twenty first century work environment. As such, managers were expected to learn their business, adapt to their customers' (both internal and external) changing needs, and lead by example in each location and community. As a manager, I attended many workshops and became an avid advocate of fairness and justice as well as personal, professional, and cultural diversity discussions. I owe much appreciation and gratitude to Publix Super Markets, trainers at Publix, and diversity experts from the National Multi-Cultural Institute (NMCI) that helped me understand the complexity and benefits of diversity and cultural competency. Some of the practical concepts discussed in this book have been applied by, and/or facilitated with, thousands of managers and workers at such organizations as Publix Super Markets, Denso Manufacturing, Nova Southeastern University, University of Phoenix - Tampa Campus, Lawrence Reagan Communication Conferences, as well as medical professionals in hospitals, managers in manufacturing facilities, police officers, political administrators, and teachers in the United States, Jamaica, Bahamas, and Afghanistan. I thank all managers and workshop participants in the aforementioned organizations for their "feedback" and application of these concepts.

According to Mohandas "Mahatma" Gandhi, "The best way to find yourself is to lose yourself in the service of others." Thank you for helping with this material which can assist others better "serve" humanity.

Bahaudin

"No longer are Americans rising and falling together as if in one large national boat. We are, increasingly, in different smaller boats."
Robert Reich, Secretary of Labor - Clinton Administration

"We are a nation of many nationalities, many races, many religions—bound together by a single unity, the unity of freedom and equality. Whoever seeks to set one nationality against another, seeks to degrade all nationalities. Whoever seeks to set one race against another seeks to enslave all races. Whoever seeks to set one religion against another seeks to destroy all religions."
Franklin D. Roosevelt,
American President – Address in New York, 11/1/1940

"To put the world right in order, we must first put the nation in order, to put the nation in order, we must first put the family in order; to put the family in order, we must first cultivate our personal life; we must first set our hearts right."
Confucius

Part I

Perspectives on Diversity

Diversity: What Is It?

D iversity is a subject that can be very powerful and emotional for everyone who deals with it either directly or indirectly. Diversity topics deal with issues of being different and alike, inspiration and perspiration, sadness and gladness, privilege and lack thereof, culture and religion, tolerance and justice, and hatred and animosity. Diversity challenges and opportunities impact all nations around the world to one extent or another. Today, in the years 2006 and 2007, issues of cultural identification, religious protection, ethnic cleansing, racial supremacy, oppression of minority groups, unfair compensation to various groups of people based on their minority status or gender, and other such critical issues impact various nations around the world. For example, countries such as the United States of America and Russia are suffering from racial conflicts caused by groups of individuals claiming "white supremacy" and privilege.

There are hundreds of hate groups in the United States (as well as around the world), such as the Klu Klux Klan (KKK), that are active in promoting hatred and animosity toward minorities. As a matter of fact, there are at least 500 "hate group" websites on the internet spreading the message of hate and racism. As reported by the Good Morning America Show of ABC (June 11, 2006), the internet seems to be a growing tool for hate groups to spread their message and attract new members. ABC showed videos of KKK members demonstrating on June 10, 2006, yelling and screaming that they want Mexicans, Jews, and illegal immigrants out of the United States. The *"Intelligence Report,"* from spring 2006, which is published by the Southern Poverty Law Center, states that "hate groups are up 33% over the last five years." The report goes on to say that "For almost 30 years, the National Socialist Movement was a forgotten bit player on the neo-Nazi scene, overshadowed by groups like the National Alliance and Aryan Nations. But as other groups collapsed, NSM has exploded, launching a new white power music label and adding a plethora of new chapters." The report talks about "Books on the Right," stating that "After a sympathetic portrayal of a key neo-Nazi leader, a tenured professor at the University of Vermont's latest books celebrates white nationalism." The section about Updates on Extremism and the Law" report that a white supremacist, who is also known for yelling racial epithets, was arrested on October 2005 for imprisoning, torturing and sexually assaulting two black women. This person, according to police officers, kept the women locked up in a shipping container in his back yard near Philadelphia (Intelligence Report, 2006). Such forms of blatant discrimination and illegal behaviors seem to be commonplace today by some groups of individuals with extreme views in certain nations around the world. For example, there were many minority individuals killed during 2006 in the former Soviet Union by groups of white individuals who felt threatened by the diversity in their country. One racist Russian, interviewed on May 2006 by the Public Broadcasting System (PBS), said that he is the leader of one group and will continue severe hate crimes because he feels as though all the opportunities for him and "his people" have transitioned to minorities since they now own most businesses in "his" country. Similarly, Germany has seen a rise in their cases of racism and hatred of non-Whites in the last two years. In 2006, several non-White individuals were targets of racism, vandalism and beatings by some Germans that belong to various groups that encourage racial divisions. Racial and religious divisions among various groups of people in Iraq have been on the rise during the occupation of that country by the American and British soldiers. To increase cultural sensitivity among the foreign military forces in Iraq, all American soldiers are now required to complete a cultural sensitivity training to increase their awareness of diverse cultures and the people of Iraq. After a thorough investigation of American soldiers allegedly killing 24 innocent men, women and children in one Iraqi village, the 130,000 soldiers stationed there, as of July 2006, are now required to also complete a standardized training in the areas of legality, ethics and morality so they can be better prepared to treat people with respect and dignity in all circumstance.

As can be seen from these brief statements thus far, diversity is a major local, national and international challenge and an opportunity for every human being if we are to live in a peaceful and healthy world. Of course, differences and its perceptions are not always so extreme that they lead to innocent individuals being abused, injured or killed. For examples, differences can exist in the compensation of individuals in different ranks, or as per their gender. Males tend to earn more annual income than many female employees who are performing the same jobs in various industries. Upper management usually tends to earn more money than lower level employees. According to a study by the Federal Reserve in 2005-2006, chief executive officers' salaries in the United States are now about 170 times greater than the average worker's pay, up from about 40 times greater recorded in the 1970s. In the United Kingdom, for the chief executive officers' salaries, the multiple is 22, and in Japan it is about 11 when compared with non-management workers. Such differences in compensation can also be issues of diversity, equality, fairness, and the effective management of a firm's human resources. Overall, understanding diversity is about feeling comfortable and maximizing productivity in an interdependent or in an interrelated society where each workplace is a microcosm of the world's demographics.

The subject of diversity requires examining one's own beliefs and values as well as learning the skills of dealing appropriately with those whose beliefs and values may be very different. Diversity, like communication, is a fact of life. It is natural, irreversible; and its tolerance is a necessity of life if one is to function effectively in this universe. Diversity has made our lives more interesting, attractive and less monotonous. Simultaneously, it has made our lives more complicated, challenging and unpredictable. It is not uncommon to become offended by people's actions, sayings, thoughts, and overall behaviors in diverse teams and general group settings in today's workforce. Some of these comments, thoughts and actions may make us uncomfortable because they challenge our beliefs and values that have been embedded into our subconscious minds for years and decades since childhood.

Some of the material in this *Workforce Diversity Management* (WDM) book will move you intellectually (impacting the *head*), some may move you emotionally (impacting the *heart*), and others may move you physically (impacting the *habits*). Regardless of whether you are impacted intellectually, emotionally, or physically, this material will serve as a "primer." It is a "primer" because learning about diversity is a continuous process and not necessarily a destination. It is a continuous process because individuals change, grow and develop, thereby changing their personal set of beliefs and values. Consequently, in order to make decisions that are good for our friends, co-workers, managers, suppliers, customers, and associates, we need to get to know them continuously.

Because of many diversity dimensions, our unique backgrounds, religious beliefs, societal norms, and cultural differences, we may view the same situation in two different ways. For example, many people see a hard working manager who is always working late, meeting deadlines, and constantly "pushing" his/her people to do more each and every day as proactive, assertive and energetic individuals. On the other hand, the same manager could be seen as egotistical, self-centered, pushy, materialistic, and rude by others from different cultures or backgrounds. It is not that one view is right and the other is wrong; they are just different and appropriate under certain circumstances and conditions. The key is to understand what constitutes "normal," "acceptable," and "correct" behavior in each situation and environment. These different perspectives have existed in our societies for thousands of years in different regions. Since technology has made it easier to travel around the world in a matter of hours, the world has shrunk and has become smaller. This means that many different groups of individuals could be living in similar geographical locations.

Having a diverse workforce means that our associates, peers, customers, suppliers, and managers comprise people of various backgrounds, languages, cultures, values, and beliefs. Today's workplaces are not homogeneous anymore; however, they are highly heterogeneous. This heterogeneity has brought about many changes, and some traditional ways of doing business are being scrutinized and restructured on a daily basis. Understanding, mastering and applying the information in this *Workforce Diversity Management* book will help professionals and managers deal with today's diverse workforce more effectively in order to attract and retain productive associates in a very competitive global economy. The book can also help managers create a pleasant work environment where all employees are respected and treated with dignity.

Cultural, generational, financial, personal, and professional diversity have been part of humanity since the days of Adam and Eve. Diversity impacts every aspect of a person's life. Today's population is more diverse than ever before and the workforce population has been changing rapidly along with it. Such diverse workers and managers should be culturally competent and be able to effectively manage diversity if they are to work synergistically in today's competitive work environment. Becoming an effective diversity advocate or "manager" and learning to remain as such is a moral imperative for all leaders in today's global world. Being an effective leader or manager in a diverse environment requires expecting the same standards from all workers regardless of their race, gender, language, sexual orientation, age, and general background. Managers should not evaluate or rate workers differently because of their gender, nationality, or language, since such differences can have negative consequences as a result of the self-fulfilling prophecy. All workers must *earn* their evaluations based on actual performance and according to the formal evaluation criteria communicated. Managers and team leaders are obligated to treat each person fairly and expect high standards from them regardless of their gender, ethnicity/nationality, primary language, age, experience, disability, and other non-job related variables. Organizations should also provide reasonable accommodations, privileges, opportunities, incentives, and facilities to attract and retain diverse employees and customers.

As leaders, professionals, executives, and senior managers, you can do a lot of things to enhance the productivity of your people by being a role model, providing diversity training and development workshops, and by making sure people treat each other fairly. Regardless of your rank, position title or power, chances are high that you cannot erase years and centuries of cultural bias and personal opinions that exist in the society. However, what you can do is to consistently insist that your workplace is free of bigotry and full of opportunity for all individuals. Therefore, you must first understand and support cultural competency and diversity management concepts which are discussed in this book. *Cultural competency* is the continuous learning process that enables one to function effectively in the context of cultural differences. *Diversity management* is the process of becoming culturally competent by understanding the needs, wants, desires, strengths, weaknesses, beliefs, and values of each person, while providing him or her the opportunity to contribute to the collective genius of the whole. Diversity management is about creating synergistic results that are equal to or greater than the sum of the individual parts. Managing diversity is about enabling each member of the workforce to perform above and beyond his or her potential. Managing diversity is about making sure people are not led to believe a lie or stereotypes so they can be free of guilt and "live happily ever after."

Managers should and must avoid all issues that present a conflict of interest in their manager-employee relationships. For example, employees must not be placed in *"quid pro quo"* (which is a favor for a favor in return mindset), positions of doing things for managers as this could very well lead to cases of sexual harassment. Whether "quid pro quo" cases are intentional or unintentional, they must be avoided since they put employees in a challenging position, especially when their promotion or merit raises depend on the manager's perception.

The first few chapters of this book discuss diversity, its definition and dimensions, the basics and implications of the self-fulfilling prophecy concept as it is applied in the diverse work environment, diversity management concerns, and some foundational best practices for effectively educating adults. The suggestions, stated throughout this book, offer diversity management ideas so managers can be successful in achieving their stated outcomes synergistically. Many of the suggestions have been used by the author as well as trainers, managers, educators, and leaders throughout the world to create a productive and happy work environment for all. As stated by Mahatma Gandhi, "Happiness is when what you think, what you say, and what you do are in harmony." This book is about creating harmony in one's head (thoughts), heart (feelings), and habits (behaviors) about people of diverse backgrounds and cultures. It is fair to say that diversity and ethics related issues are likely to, and should, impact a person's head, heart and habits if they are to lead to long-term peace and prosperity in life.

> ➤ *Head.* Head implies continuous cognitive learning about each situation, thinking objectively based on current facts, awareness of universal principles, and knowledge generation.
> ➤ *Heart.* Heart implies the consistent controlling of one's feeling, basing it on objective facts, and aligning it with universal values. It means basing one's feeling for long-term impact, rather than short term satisfaction of personal desires that are linked to revenge, vengeance, payback, or retribution.
> ➤ *Habits.* Habits should be linked to one's objective feelings and universal principles. It means ensuring that one's day-to-day behaviors are aligned with one's universal principles of right and wrong, personal or professional values, and knowledge-based and goal-oriented feelings.

Diversity Means Differences

Diversity means "difference" or "variety." So the term "diverse workforce" refers to a workforce where the workers have a variety of different characteristics including but not limited to gender, disability, culture, ethnicity, religion, experience, body size, skills, etc. By becoming aware of today's diversity and its impact on managers, one can learn effective ways of dealing with these issues appropriately. *Workforce Diversity Management* book is not only designed to help current and prospective managers become aware of some of the major changes in today's workforce, but it is also designed to give workers and managers some of the skills needed to maximize productivity and gain a competitive advantage. By reading and applying the concepts discussed in this book, students, workers, and managers will have the foundation to:

- Define and discuss diversity,
- Understand culture and its influence on human behavior,
- Explain discrimination and eliminate discriminatory practices,
- Understand and value personal as well as cultural differences,
- Recognize biases and behaviors that hinder productivity,
- Work with a diverse workforce synergistically, and
- Create a work environment where all individuals can contribute to the mission.

Diversity and cultural competency require continuously learning about one's own and others' values, beliefs and cultures. Of course, learning is one of the most basic human needs and takes place from one's birth until death. Some things are learned consciously, while others are learned by osmosis during one's socialization process. Some things are learned because of what is said by others or heard from others, while other things are learned from observation of actions toward people or cultures even when nothing is said. Yet, there are things a person will never know and things that people want to know. Learning to work harmoniously with others is within most people's ability and a necessity that managers and professional workers cannot afford to ignore. Robert Fulgham, author of *Everything I really need to know, I learned in kindergarten*, said it well when he wrote:

All I really need to know about how to live and what to do and how to be, I learned in kindergarten. Wisdom was not at the top of the graduate-school mountain, but there in the sandpile at Sunday School. These are the things I learned: Share everything. Play fair. Don't hit people. Put things back where you found them. Clean up your own mess. Don't take things that aren't yours. Say you're sorry when you hurt somebody. Wash your hands before you eat. Flush. Warm cookies and cold milk are good for you. Live a balanced life---learn some and think some and draw and paint and dance and play and work every day some. Take a nap every afternoon. When you go out into the world, watch out for traffic, hold hands, and stick together. Be aware of wonder...Everything you need to know is in there somewhere. The Golden Rule and love and basic sanitation. Ecology and politics and equality and sane living. Take any one of those items and extrapolate it into sophisticated adult terms and apply it to your family life or your work or your government or your world and it holds true and clear and firm. Think what a better world it would be if we all--the whole world—had cookies and milk about three o'clock every afternoon and then lay down with our blankies for a nap. Or if all governments had as a basic policy to always put things back where they found them and to clean up their own mess. And it is still true, no matter how old you are--when you go out into the world, it is best to hold hands and stick together" (Pages 4 – 5, 1988).

While much of what we as human beings know is already within us, at times, our behaviors toward other individuals who are different from ourselves tend to be contrary to these intrinsic beliefs and knowledge. This is due to societal conditioning that human beings receive during their socialization process as young children, and which are further reinforced over one's adult years, thereby creating a vicious cycle reinforcing the same stereotypes until one or two "heroic" or transformational leaders, with help from thousands of others, are able to stop it. As can be seen, understanding diversity and diversity education becomes much more important than ever before in today's cross-cultural world of business. Companies focus and invest in diversity initiatives for various reasons, with the changing face of the workforce being one of the most compelling. During the past two decades and the coming few decades, women, minorities and immigrants have been a part of—and will continue to make up—a growing portion of new workers. Not only has this trend changed the face of the workforce, but also the faces of customers, suppliers, shareholders, regulators, and competitors.

Companies that are expecting their employees to help them increase or maintain quality products, services, productivity, flexibility, and innovation must understand and fulfill the needs and desires of their people. The needs and desires of most people have changed or shifted dramatically over the past few generations. What used to motivate people to get up in the morning and rush to work may not work anymore. Such dramatic changes in the workforce require dramatic adjustments in management and leadership styles throughout an organization.

In today's competitive global market place or market space, it is essential to gain the necessary skills in cross-cultural communication, negotiations, and in dealing with diverse individuals from different cultures. Nationally, many U.S. firms are attempting to increase their percentage of women and minority workers to better serve their diverse customers. Since the retention and upward mobility rates for most professional women, immigrants and minorities have been somewhat challenging, many firms find disparate representation of these groups within their organizations. Corporate leaders have come to the conclusion that simply focusing on Equal Employment Opportunity (EEO) laws are not enough to retain a diverse and competitive workforce. Therefore, many corporate leaders are personally championing diversity initiatives and training programs to strategically enhance their competitive advantage in today's global market place.

Many organizations are beginning, or continuing, their diversity training programs to maximize the well-being of their human resources. Most workers, who are each firm's human resources asset, have received conditioning from a society whose members do not always treat each other with respect; and such disrespectful thoughts and behaviors often carry over to the workplace. Poorly managed cultural, racial, gender, religious, ethnic or other diversity related conflicts can, and often do, have a negative impact on interpersonal relationships and eventually on productivity. Diversity education and training programs focus on creating an inclusive work environment where all individuals, as per their capabilities, can become as successful as they would like to be. Creating and maintaining such positive, supportive and fair employment practices allow all workers regardless of their race, sexual orientation, gender, age, disability, culture, religion, and other such characteristics to contribute to their fullest potential. In addition, a good understanding of diversity-related issues can better equip managers with an arsenal of useful skills that allow for timely and appropriate interventions when disagreements arise and friction escalates within the diverse workforce. Understanding and proactively managing diversity can be a strategic approach to avoiding a costly litigation and negative publicity that seem to be a corollary of most discrimination lawsuits. Also, organizations that do conduct diversity training with their managers and workers tend to save money through reduced recruitment costs, turnover rates, court costs, as well as from the disgruntled-employee sabotage and shrinkage.

Dr. Martin Luther King, Jr. once said, "We are faced with the fierce urgency of now…This may well be mankind's last chance to choose between chaos or community." So, it is each employee's responsibility to speak and stand up for inclusivity and fairness regardless of whether or not there are biases in one's peripheral view. It is best to remember that measuring individual guilt or innocence might be useful in legal situations, but may not be a valid yardstick for measuring the presence or absence of racism in a department, firm, community or society. As a matter-of-fact, racism, sexism, ageism, and other such discriminatory attitudes are often perpetuated by individuals who have no such intent in the first place. Overall, workers and managers should focus on diversity because it is the right thing to do morally, socially, economically, financially, personally, and professionally. One should also remember that racism or discrimination, both overt and covert, causes low employee commitment, a decrease in employee and customer retention, low morale, shrinkage, social loafing, bad corporate image, dissension, animosity, negative synergy, and a lack of competitive spirit or culture. While some of the intangible results might be difficult to quantify and measure, they can put a company out of business.

The corporate world is full of cases where managers have overtly (intentionally) and covertly (secretly behind the scenes) been discriminating against individuals because of their age, culture, gender, race, religion, sexual orientation, body size, disability, etc. For example, within the last few decades, Home Depot paid $104 million to settle a gender lawsuit; Coca Cola had to pay $192.5 million for racial discrimination; Denny's paid $54.4 million for their racial discrimination case; Cracker Barrel paid $2 million for settling their race discrimination case; the Boeing Corporation paid $7.5 million for their racial discrimination case; Mitsubishi settled their sexual harassment class action lawsuit at a cost worth as high as $30 million; Ford agreed to pay $7.5 million to settle their racial and sexual harassment lawsuit; Lockheed Martin agreed to pay $13 million and rehire 450 people in one of the largest age discrimination cases ever filed; and Texaco agreed to pay $200,000 each for two plaintiffs, $100,00 each for four others, $60,000 each for 1,340 remaining individuals in their race discrimination class action lawsuit. There are many other examples of large firms that have settled discrimination cases at high costs to their shareholders during the past decade. So, managers and professional workers have an obligation to be proactive as opposed to reactive when it comes to the true meaning of diversity which, at a minimum, is about tolerance, respect, understanding, and exploration of fair choices and alternatives. Managers and professionals should proactively work on always being in control of their heads (or thought process, knowledge acquisition and knowledge generation), hearts (or feelings, emotions, and "hot buttons") and habits (or behaviors and actions). In other words, everyone must work on managing his or her perceptions, words, non-verbal body language, behaviors, and take appropriate actions when noticing that an inappropriate comment or behavior is taking place in the work environment.

Changing Demographics and Trends

The population and increased influence of various minority people groups are growing rapidly. An understanding of the demographics of the customer base allows one to maximize changing market opportunities. Leaders and managers skilled in managing a culturally diverse customer base and workforce will be successful and instrumental in improving morale, employee commitment, productivity, customer satisfaction, and the overall competitive advantage of their firms.

The data presented in this section are some facts and trends compiled from studies by the U.S. Department of Labor statistics, the 1990 U.S. Census, and researchers in the field. For a number of very good reasons, a greater percentage of women and minority group members are being elected and appointed to major political leadership positions. By the year 2025, only about 9 percent of those entering the U.S. workforce will be white males, 42 percent will be white females, and the balance will be made up of African-Americans and immigrants. About 33 percent of the new entrants will be men and women of color. Physically and mentally challenged individuals comprise the largest *non-ethnic* people group in the United States and perhaps many other countries, about 60 million individuals in 2007. According to U.S. Department of Commerce, about one in five Americans have some kind of a disability. By the year 2010, American Latin Hispanics will be the largest minority in America. Their buying power in 1998 was around $279 billion and it will be about $940 billion annually by 2010.

In the year 2006, less than 15 percent of people entering the American workforce came from white males. The others were white females (about 32%), Hispanic males (16%), Hispanic females (12%), black females (9%), black males (7%), Asian and other males (5%), as well as Asian and other females (5%). By the year 2050, the average U.S. resident will trace his or her ancestry to countries such as Africa, Asia, the Hispanic and Latin countries, the Pacific Islands, and Arabia and not necessarily to a European ancestry. The median age of the workforce was 28 in 1970, and 37 in 1990; however, it had risen to about 41 in the year 2006. There were about 58 million people over the age of 45 working in the United States of America in the year 2006. Also, Americans 65 years old and over will make up about 20 percent of the total population by the year 2030.

Ethnic minority people groups along with new immigrants are major contributors to the population and workforce growth in the United States. For example, *American Latin Hispanics* represented 9% (24 million) of the population in 1992 and are expected to increase to 21% (81 million) by the year 2050 to become the largest minority people group in the U.S.A. *African Americans* represented 12% (32 million) of the population in 1992 and are expected to increase to 16% (62 million) by the year 2050. *Asian Americans* represented 3% (8 million) of the population in 1992 and they are expected to increase to 11% (41 million) by the year 2050. *Native Americans* represented 1% (2 million) of the population in 1992 and are expected to have a slight increase to over 1% (5 million) by the year 2050.

Defining Diversity through the Iceberg

The following whimsical witticism of common stereotypes is reported to have appeared on a plaque over the 20-foot-long dinner table at Podere Toreno, a bed and breakfast in Radda-Inn-Chianti, Italy:

> Heaven is a place where the lovers are Italian, the cooks are French, the mechanics are German, the police are English, and the Swiss run the government. Hell is a place where the lovers are Swiss, the cooks are English, the mechanics are French, the police are German, and Italians run the government.

Unfortunately, as humorous as they may sound, such stereotypes are common in today's work environment and they can impact individuals, their thinking, feelings, or behaviors negatively. To prevent the negative impact of such stereotypes and conditioning, it is best to understand diversity, cultural differences, stereotypes, the impact of stereotypes, and then make decisions consciously based on facts.

To understand the various dimensions or aspects of diversity, let us do an exercise. You can begin this interactive exercise by thinking of various characteristics that make each person a unique human being among billions of others. Then, on the diversity iceberg (Figure 1.1), write all the characteristics that are apparent about a person, "based on a first look," on top of the waterline. When looking at a large iceberg, the top part of it which is above the waterline is noticeable first; however, one must remember that the largest part, forming the foundation, is usually under the water and cannot be seen at first glance. Write those characteristics that are not apparent based on a first look (and require more communication with the person) on the bottom of the waterline. "First look" can be defined as the first second or two when a person sees another individual, for the first time, without even having said hello or having made an introduction. For example, a person's hair color is apparent based on a first look since it can be immediately seen with one hundred percent certainty through the naked eye; therefore, it would go above the waterline. Write as many characteristics above and below the waterline as you can think of before moving on.

Figure 1.1 – Diversity Iceberg

Now, if you do not already have any of the elements mentioned on the following list, then make sure to place each characteristic, category or dimension of diversity either above or below the waterline based on where *you think* they belong:

1. Skin color
2. Martial status
3. Appearance
4. Race
5. Hair color
6. Body size
7. Culture or cultural background
8. Ethnicity
9. Educational background
10. Disability
11. Profession
12. Religion
13. Personality type or temperance
14. Financial status
15. Age
16. Gender
17. Values
18. Intelligence
19. Hobbies
20. Work experience
21. Parental status, and
22. Sexual orientation

Reflect on why you think they go above or below the waterline. You will notice that individuals have more control over the characteristics on the bottom of the waterline which also tends to be more important to who people are as human beings. Unfortunately, many individuals in the society tend to make assumptions about these important characteristics based on what is apparent on the first look or first impression - the visible characteristics which people have little to no control over, and tend to be least important to who they are as human beings.

With regard to the various dimensions of diversity, specifically a ring on one's left finger, many people assume that a person who wears a ring is married as the ring might be associated with marriage. While wearing a ring might signify one's marital status in some cultures and customs, it is not true of all individuals and assuming that one is married may not be true. For example, in some other countries outside of the United States people wear a wedding ring on the right finger. In such cultures, people wear a ring on the left finger as a sign of engagement to be married, and once they are married the ring is switched to the right finger as a symbol that the relationship has strengthened. In another case on April 20, 2006 as shown on the Tyra Banks Show (UPN 33), a gay man who was previously married to a woman for over 20 years stated that he is married now to his male partner but wears a ring on his right finger because the left finger will always be a sign of his love, respect and devotion to his ex-wife and children from the previous marriage. In another case, while sitting next to a newlywed on the plane, the man said he was coming back from his honeymoon. When asked why he was wearing the wedding ring on the "wrong" hand (his right hand), he responded that it was because he just discovered that he has married the "wrong" woman. Then he explained that in his culture they wear the wedding ring on the right hand finger. Furthermore, other examples show that some single people wear a ring on the right or left hand (where often married individuals place the wedding ring) simply because they like it. So, the category of "marital status" would go on the bottom part of the diversity iceberg since one cannot tell with a high level of certainty whether or not a person is married simply by the presence, or lack thereof, of a ring. Just as people make assumptions about a person's marital status based on a piece of jewelry, many individuals are also conditioned to prejudge others based on clothing, skin color, height, body size, and hair color, which are often wrong. Therefore, one should be cautious and not make judgments on external characteristics which do not really define the character or human qualities of the person. Consequently, to get to know another person, one must "dig deeper" through effective communication and factual evidence in order to discover the information about characteristics which are below the waterline on the diversity iceberg.

Figure 1.2 – Dimensions of Diversity

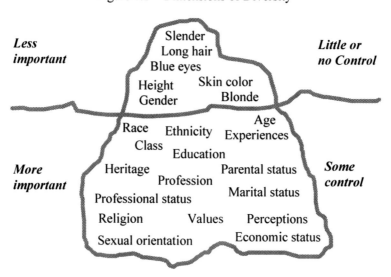

Having thought about the various dimensions of diversity, it is time to create an operational definition for the term diversity. In this sense and throughout this book, *diversity* describes the many unique internal and external qualities and characteristics that make a person similar to or different from others. Some of these characteristics might be apparent on the first look, such as skin color, hair color, body size, and general appearance. Other important characteristics, such as ethnicity, disability, religion, financial status, age, values, cultural background, and sexual orientation, may not be apparent based on a first look or a first impression. Diversity also encompasses the multitude of experiences, aptitudes and attitudes available in today's workforce. All these distinct dimensions of diversity tend to impact individuals differently. For example, the dimension of gender in a specific society might impact males very differently than females. In this case, males may receive favorable unearned privileges on their way to higher management ranks; whereas females may face the "glass ceiling" despite their superior experience and qualifications. Another reality is that many individuals in society are conditioned to make decisions about other people based on certain characteristics (being above the waterline on the iceberg) that are less important to the person's character, and characteristics over which they have little to no control. For example, with the exception of surgery or rapid weight loss, most people do not change their color of eyes, gender, height, and body size every few years. However, people do have more control over many of the more important characteristics such as their values, personal beliefs, professions, financial status, marital status, etc. (characteristics that fall way below the waterline as seen in Figure 1.2). So, in order to make better decisions, one must get to know others' values, hobbies, abilities, interests, profession, and desires.

Societal Conditioning

As people learn about the world, they receive information and misinformation from many sources. As children and adults, people receive lots of information, perhaps some misinformation, as they socialize and live within various communities. Usually, the misinformation is delivered without malicious intent, but often people receive this misinformation about people who are different from them. This misinformation is conveyed overtly, and sometimes in more subtle ways, at home, school, by the media, and peers. While people learn many useful and great things from the above sources they also receive misinformation either through what was said directly or its absence from the discussion. This misinformation may condition human beings to respond inappropriately to many individuals in the society. For example, while education is a major source of information, it may not always give the whole picture. The point is that no matter what time or geographical location, it is possible that the educational system may have had a built-in, somewhat slant (although subtle) toward whatever the prevailing culture was in each location.

Practically speaking, most educational institutions have had a major focus on the mainstream. For example, most school textbooks in the United States during the 1940's and 1950's talked about the dominant groups' accomplishments. So, the absence of discussion on the accomplishments of women, Asians, African-Americans, Hispanics, Native American, and other groups may give a student or reader the wrong impression of them. Maybe, the student will tend to believe that they really haven't done much in society, maybe they are incapable of making worthwhile contributions, and even worse the student may treat these individuals differently because of such perceptions and stereotypes. Of course, discussions of the dominant group's achievements in school books have not been limited to the books in the United States. Besides many other nations, discussions of the dominant groups in most books have also been the case in Afghanistan and the former Soviet Union over the last five decades of the twentieth century. On the other hand, school is also a good source of information. According to Peter Russell, author of *The Global Brain*, it is a human being's formal education and *consciousness* that enable him or her to generalize, learn, form abstractions, create technology and science, produce art, communicate fluently with people of diverse cultures, and do all that which differentiates him or her from other animals. Human brain cells are interconnected and work harmoniously to make the brain useful in one's day-to-day interactions. Similarly, human beings, who comprise of over six billion individuals, need to interconnect and work harmoniously as one race. According to research, over 80% of DNA is common in individuals of every race. As leaders and managers, people of all cultures need to overcome and replace conditioned influences and unintentional behaviors with conscious thoughts and rational decisions.

With regard to conditioning, as a person living in the United States, one can also say that media has influenced the population very much, and consequently, it can give one the wrong image about individuals from various cultures. For example, it is through the media that people have heard or seen images, stereotypes, and depictions of:

- Women as kind-hearted, teachers, nurses, home-makers, and care-takers,
- Latin Hispanics as short-tempered,
- Mexicans as drunk, illiterate, farmers, or construction workers,
- British people as intelligent, presumptuous, egotistical, and arrogant,
- Asians as exotic, cruel, martial art experts, and mysterious,
- Asian Indians as doctors, gas station owners, excitable, and/or "silly",
- African Americans as athletes, dancers, singers, violent, and criminals,
- Middle-easterners as swarthy, extremists, ravishing, and "crazed",
- Italians as gang members, Mafia-related, and pasta lovers,
- Pacific Islanders as fun-loving and lazy, and
- American Indians as drunk, barbarous, savage, and "noble."

Of course, these are not realities; and accordingly people shouldn't base their decisions on such stereotypes. The main point is that people receive lots of information and some misinformation, which tend to form their "mental tapes." The early learned stereotypes, also known as "mental tapes," can affect one's thoughts, feelings, and behavior. In other words, mental tapes affect how one responds to people who are different from him/her.

Ken Keyes, American writer and philosopher who founded Keyes College wrote, "We are not responsible for the programming we received as children. As adults, we are 100% responsible for changing it." While we could not do much about the conditioning we received as children, as adults we have the power to change those stereotypes and replace them with conscious and factual thoughts. This requires learning about diversity and making decisions based on facts rather than previous stereotypes or conditioning. Conditioning is a very powerful influence, and most people tend to receive it throughout their lives.

The objective of the following exercise is to demonstrate the power of conditioning. For this exercise, read the following statement in about 15 seconds to see how many "Fs" are in it. So, count the number of "Fs" in 15 seconds and then continue reading the next paragraph.

FOREIGN FILMS OF THE PAST FEW DECADES
FOCUSED ON FACTS THAT ARE OF MORE VALUE
THAN THAT OF NEW FEATURES

How many Fs did you get? Keep this number in mind or write it down. Most people get some of the "Fs" on the first try, but not all of them. Now, before moving on, go back and read the message again one more time in 30 seconds to see if your number changes. There are many reasons why people don't get all of them on the first attempt. Speed-reading training, capitalization of the letters, too little time, and not pronouncing the word "of" with the letter "f" sound are some of the obvious reasons for not seeing all of the Fs. Maybe you are one of the few who do see all nine "Fs" in the statement. If you did not get all of the Fs on the first attempt, go back and try to locate them. There are some key points associated with conditioning and the following represents a few of them:

1. Conditioning is very easy and can take place in even just a few seconds.
2. In conditioning exercises, in spite of knowledge to the contrary, many people give incorrect answers to simple questions after conditioning of only a few seconds.
3. Conditioning over a number of years is very powerful and can have a harmful effect on people's minds, thoughts, feelings, and responses.
4. With some conscious thinking and rational decision making based on facts, one can overcome the conditioning and respond more effectively.

In her book, titled "*The Tale of O: On Being Different in an Organization,*" Rosabeth Moss Kanter (1980) explains that organizations usually have at least two different kinds of characters. First, there are the Xs (people who represent the majority) and then there are the Os (people who are few in numbers). She also has a video with the same title (originally prepared in 1970s) which was reproduced in 1993. To get a better understanding of this concept, take a look at Figure 1.3 before reading further and reflect on what you notice in this figure. What do you see in the figure and what are some items that sort of "stick out" as you look at the picture?

Figure 1.3 – Being Different: The Tale of the Xs and the Os

```
                      X   X   X
              X   X   X   X   X
          X   X   X   X   x   X   X
          X   x   X   O   X   x   X
          X   X   X   o   X   X   X
          X   X   X   X   X   X   X
              X   X   X   X   X
              X   X   X   X
                  X   X   X
```

In both her video and book, Kanter explains that people are conditioned to and have a tendency to notice the Os more often than the Xs and give them special attention. Therefore, the Os normally feel like they are being watched more critically and are "walking on a tightrope" a majority of the time. She states that Os are often asked to generalize their thoughts regarding all of the Os as if they are proper representatives of all individuals in their group. Furthermore, Os are often given more attention than others, not necessarily because of their skills and knowledge, but because of their differences and uniqueness. As professionals, all leaders and managers need to overcome and replace conditioned influences and unintentional behaviors with conscious thoughts and rational decisions that are based on current facts.

Summary

Differences have existed both in the society and the workforce today and will continue to increase at a growing rate. There is a moral responsibility for each individual to become aware of these differences and respect each person as a unique human being. Valuing diversity and thereby becoming a diversity champion requires each person to tolerate differences, respect differences, understand differences, and to examine or explore those differences in order to maximize the productivity of the workforce and gain organizational competitiveness. Valuing diversity isn't just an idea that sounds good and promotes positive publicity for the firm. Valuing diversity and each person's genuine commitment to its thorough implementation are critical to one's success as an individual and to the company's survival. In order to be successful, workers and managers need to become culturally competent.

Dr. Martin Luther King, Jr. envisioned that someday people would be judged by the content of their character and not by the color of their skin, not by their gender, not by their ethnic backgrounds, and not by their disabilities. He also envisioned that all individuals would sit down together at the tables of brotherhood and sisterhood. Those tables are in the classrooms, conference rooms, boardrooms, cafeterias, restaurants, and manufacturing floors. Our responsibility and challenge are to not only take our seats at these tables, but to sit there with an open mind and unclenched fists. Shelby Steele, author of *The Content of Our Character* (1990), said "What is needed now is a new spirit of pragmatism in racial matters where 'disadvantaged minorities' are seen simply as American citizens who deserve complete fairness and in some cases developmental assistance, but in no case special entitlements based on minority status." The only individuals that should be given special accommodations in the workplace, as directed by the legal counsel or human resources specialists, are employees with legally recognized disabilities whose needs are communicated to managers from the outset.

Overall, Chapter One has pointed out the complexity and dimensions of diversity as well the impact of conditioning. The next chapter will expand on diversity, diversity management, and self-fulfilling prophecy as it relates to learners and educators in an academic environment.

The upcoming chapters further extend the topic of diversity and its various dimensions. As outlined in Figure 1.4, *Workforce Diversity Management* is designed to cover diversity management issues in Part One, cultural competency topics in Part Two, some of the strategies and skills needed to manage the workforce and cultural diversity in Part Three; and Part Four offers relevant cases and exercises that can be used along with various discussions or chapters.

Figure 1.4 – Outline of Workforce Diversity Management

Parts I & II		
Parts III & IV		

Parts I & II Diversity Awareness ↔ Cultural Competency

Parts III & IV Skills ← Cases → Exercises

Workforce Diversity Management

Discussion Questions

While you and your organization may have conscious, subconscious or formal protocols in place to make sure everyone is treated justly and fairly, the society may not condition everyone to act as such toward all individuals. It is best to consider one's total experiences when thinking of diversity dimensions, challenges, and opportunities. Reflect on the following questions individually, and then discuss them with your friends, teammates and/or colleagues. Answering the questions effectively may require more research on each topic by reading recently published articles, books, and/ore interviewing experts in the field. When possible, try to relate the questions and topics to your life, your organization, and today's society.

1. Define diversity in terms of your colleagues in the work environment.
2. What are some important dimensions of diversity that relate to teamwork?
3. How have the changing demographics impacted you during the past five – twenty years?
4. How will the demographics of your society and workforce change in the coming decades?

5. Who are your peers, as per your first impressions, and are they in the right fields, professions, and jobs? Given their backgrounds (as per your first impressions), would they be more effective in other jobs or professions? Think of one or two specific individuals and rationalize your reasoning to make sure it makes sense to you.

6. How can managers best appreciate and effectively use the diversity of their workers? Mention specific behavioral and verbal examples.

7. Sexual orientation is one dimension of diversity and many employers are now providing benefits to their gay and lesbian employees' partners. Find two companies that are offering such benefits and determine the outcomes.

8. While "sexual orientation" is the correct term, some literature and individuals still use the term "sexual preference." Discuss the differences and explain why "sexual orientation" is more accurate and accepted?

9. Is a person's marital status apparent based on a first look? Why or why not? Does wearing of a ring always signify a person's marital status in today's diverse work environment? Discuss.

10. One purpose of this book is to help readers relate diversity to their heads, hearts and habits. The chapter stated that managers and professionals should proactively work on always being in control of their heads, hearts, and habits. In other words, everyone must work on managing his or her perceptions, words, non-verbal body language, behaviors, and take appropriate actions when one sees that an inappropriate comment or behavior is taking place in the work environment. Discuss actual examples of how diversity relates to a person's head, heart, and habits. Provide real life examples and stories.

Diversity Management in Academia

C ultural, generational, personal, and professional differences as well as
unique motivational factors are characteristics of learners in today's academia. The student population of nearly all institutions has drastically
changed from what it was twenty and thirty years ago. Some institutions of
higher education have predominantly traditional students from 18 to 23 years
of age attending college on a full-time basis; while other institutions might
have all working adult students and/or a mixture of the two. It is apparent that
today's student populations are much more diverse in terms of their gender,
ethnicity/nationality, age, disability, and beliefs than they were twenty years
ago. Therefore, these student populations need diverse teaching skills, different experiences, and more facilitation abilities in order for them to learn best
as per their learning styles. One of the needed skills would be to acknowledge
their differences, and then actively incorporate their experiences into the
learning objectives of each session. This chapter provides an application of
diversity and cultural competency considerations in the education arena.

Diversity Management in Education

Globalization is an important dimension of diversity as it involves different cultures, countries, and people groups. Due to the importance of
globalization in today's work environment, most business schools have added
a focus on it to many of their courses or curriculums. However, many schools
have not gone as far as actually creating a comprehensive approach to understanding globalization and global education. In their June 2006 article,
entitled *"The Global Footprint,"* Ilan Alon and Craig McAllaster state that "A
business school must examine six essential components of its program to create an effective and ongoing globalization strategy." The six dimensions
include: faculty global experiences and cross-cultural diversity in faculty
(making up the Faculty dimensions); global curriculum and languages of instruction or learning (making up the Interface dimensions); and the cross-
cultural diversity in students and student global experiences (which make up
the Student dimensions). According to Ilon and McAllaster (2006), attracting
and admitting a diverse student body is still a challenge for many schools in
the United States and abroad. While some schools' student body is totally
homogenous, others are a bit more diverse in terms of gender, culture or ethnicity where no single nationality dominates the campus. Similarly, most
schools prefer their faculty members to be of diverse backgrounds and experi-

ences. For example, while most schools want their students to gain an international perspective from their curriculum, many of their faculty members do not bring personal experiences from abroad, and they are not encouraged to travel to foreign countries for professional or academic conferences. In such a case, experts believe that these schools are asking their student body to "do as they say, not as they do," which can be a difficult "sell." Just as it is for corporations and public agencies, diversity management issues can be a challenge for academic institutions as well. For an example, review and reflect upon the case of *"Graduation Speaker and Insensitivity,"* which is included in Part IV of this book. The case demonstrates that highly educated academicians can make major mistakes and be insensitive to their own students and faculty members. The case further demonstrates that diverse institutions must be extra-sensitive to the needs of their stakeholders and constituencies using a fair and just decision-making process.

Recognizing and understanding personal and professional differences in a student body are neither easy nor automatic, since they require conscious focus and a good level of "comfort" on the part of the faculty with cultural diversity issues. In order for educators and students to be successful, they thus need to become culturally competent. As previously mentioned, *"cultural competency"* for all practical purposes refers to the continuous learning process that enables both educators and students to function effectively in the context of cultural differences both in academia and in the workforce.

One method of becoming culturally competent in the academic arena is to learn about one's colleagues and each other. It is great to see that various institutions of higher education are actually celebrating their student, staff and faculty diversity. For example, Nova Southeastern University's College of Allied Health and Nursing hosted an "International Day" at their school to celebrate the cultural diversity amongst its students, employees and faculty members. This "International Day" event was held on May 5, 2006 from noon – 2:00 p.m. at the Health Professions Division-Terry Building, and they featured international food and a cultural/fashion show. Not only did everyone get to learn about each other's differences with regard to food and fashion, they also networked and learned more about their beliefs and values.

Besides informal gatherings and diversity celebrations, nearly all organizations and academic institutions have various forms of formal or mandatory training for their associates, faculty, and/or staff during their initial hiring stage and as an ongoing process annually. Much of this training is formally required to make sure employees of these institutions are aware that the organization expects them to treat everyone fairly. However, in many academic as well as corporate organizations, much of the training on diversity competency, ethics, and sexual harassment topics is not reinforced through effective continuous training and development. Oftentimes, employees are provided a handbook or a website to read the material, and then asked to sign a document that they have read the material. Furthermore, some organizations that do offer a formal face-to-face training session on such important topics tend to "brush through" the content to make sure the legal side is covered without making sure that the material is received, understood, fully comprehended, and the expected concepts or behaviors can be successfully applied by those who attended the session. Nonetheless, many of such training workshops and topics are professionally presented by experienced educators, and thus a review of them seems relevant for adult educators.

Today, there are very diverse student populations in terms of their background, abilities, age, language, body size, geographic location, culture, desires, learning styles, and cultural conditioning. Diversity, as mentioned in the definition, describes the many unique characteristics and qualities that make a person (or student in this case) similar to or different from others. Some of these characteristics might be apparent such as skin color, hair color, body size, and general appearance. While other characteristics such as ethnicity, disability, religion, financial status, age, values, cultural background, and many others may not be apparent based on first impressions. It is imperative that people do not judge others based on assumptions; and accordingly one must treat everyone fairly and equitably.

Diversity, as previously mentioned, also encompasses the multitude of experiences, aptitudes, and attitudes available in today's workforce. Diversity initiatives encourage leaders and educators to empower their associates and students as well as to tap into their wealth of differences in order to achieve synergistic results. In return, these students and associates will be ready to satisfy, excite and delight their diverse customers and achieve organizational effectiveness by delivering superior value as a result of diversity initiatives modeled in the classroom by the educators. Robert Reich, Secretary of Labor during Clinton's Administration, said, "No longer are Americans rising and falling together as if in one large national boat. We are, increasingly, in different smaller boats." So, classroom students, customers, organizations, and societies will become progressively more diverse and educators need to tolerate differences, respect them, understand their nature, and educate students about them so they can successfully work with their diverse organizations and customers. Eventually, this may lead to students' personal and professional success with hopes that they can be as successful as they so desire to be. What is success and who defines it?

According to Sophocles, "success is dependent on effort," and not necessarily physical characteristics or limitations. According to Brian Tracy, author and speaker, "One of the most important rules for success is this: Every great success is the result of hundreds and thousands of small efforts and accomplishments that no one ever sees or appreciates." In the summer issue of Nova Southeastern University's *Foresight* publication (2001), Dr. Randolph Pohlman, Dean of School of Business and Entrepreneurship at Nova Southeastern University, wrote, "In this final issue…we strive to get at the core of what is success. By sharing with you the thoughts of various leaders, educators, and entrepreneurs, we hope to help our readers define for themselves what is success." The same is true for students; therefore, success should be defined by students based on their desires, abilities, goals, and efforts. At his primary school, Malcolm X (African-American leader) was told by one of his (white) teachers that he should not dream of becoming a lawyer since he could not be very successful in that job and should pursue something that requires the use of his hands. Unfortunately, due to strong biases and stereotypes, such incompetency may still exist in the American education system and educators need to do everything possible to ensure it does not happen in their schools or to current students. It is not the place of the faculty member to determine how successful a student can or should be based on his/her first impression of the student or based on the student's physical/personality characteristics.

Ralph Waldo Emerson said, "What is success? To laugh often and much; to win the respect of intelligent people and the affection of children; to earn the appreciation of honest critics and endure the betrayal of false friends; to appreciate beauty; to find the best in others; to leave the world a bit better, whether by a healthy child, a garden patch, or a redeemed social condition; to know even one life has breathed easier because you have lived." Simply put, success can be practicing what you preach, progressively realizing predetermined goals/ideals, and doing one's best to make worthwhile contributions to society. It is a moral imperative and obligation for educators and faculty members to (assume and) proceed as though limits to students' abilities do not exist, unless objective evidence tells otherwise.

Recognize and Respect Diversity in the Class

Educators need to encourage students to think critically, add value to the class by participating, and to synergize as teams or as a whole class. Appreciating, understanding, and valuing personal differences in each individual student or team member can eliminate "groupthink" both in the classroom as well as in the boardroom. *Groupthink* is a pattern of faulty and biased decision making that occurs in groups whose members strive for agreement, among themselves, at the expense of accurately assessing information relevant to a decision. Groupthink is not a desirable objective in today's diverse and very sophisticated world of intermingled competition. This usually happens in homogeneous teams and groups because everyone's societal values tend to be similar. Research has shown that homogeneous teams are neither as creative nor as productive as heterogeneous teams when dealing with or solving complex problems. Diverse teams can achieve synergistic results if they appreciate, understand, and value their differences effectively. *Synergy* is where the whole is greater than the sum of its parts. Ultimately, synergy is the performance gains that result when individuals, teams and departments coordinate their actions toward the same goals. Synergistic teams, colleagues, peers, and departments tend to function more cooperatively and productively than if they were operating in isolation.

Synergy happens when two or more individuals working together produce more than their combined efforts individually. For example, a team of four students should produce a final project (product) that is much better than the combined results of each of the four students' outcome that is produced individually. Diversity awareness can help teams function harmoniously in the context of cultural differences and thereby produce synergistic results. On the other hand, lack of diversity awareness and lack of respect for diversity can lead to negative synergy. Negative synergy is when two or more people working together produce less than what they could produce individually. According Stephen R. Covey, author of *"The Seven Habits of Highly Effective People,"* negative synergy takes place when people do not respect and appreciate each other's differences.

Differences may exist in how male and female students relate to and understand material presented in the classroom. Using sports analogies to make a point in the classroom may not clarify the concepts or objectives to those who are not familiar with the rules of a specific game. This can apply to both males and females in the same way. Faculty members need to be aware of their audience and create an "inclusive learning environment." An *"inclusive learning environment"* is where all students and participants are actively involved in the learning process and can fully relate to the concepts being presented. In 1991, the Kinney Shoe Corporation realized that, gender differences (in orientation, communication, and behavior) seem subtle, yet they represent great dissimilarities in the ways that men and women function on a daily basis. Simply put, the differences can translate into an institutionalized tendency to work only within one's "comfort zone," men working only with men, and women working with women, unless this tendency is consciously acknowledged and avoided. Many firms have established gender-sensitivity training in order to create awareness and to eventually produce synergistic results among teams. It has been stated that females, in general, view work as a process while males usually focus on the end result and desire specific action plans. Researchers have concluded that many males were raised with a competitive nature, where power was the key. Furthermore, males have been found to have more of a succinct speaking style, similar to military speech, whereas females tend to communicate in a storytelling style. While many females prefer a circular style of group discussion so everyone can be heard, seen and acknowledged; most males tend to initially prefer the lecture style where the group is directed and the meeting can be brought to a closure in a timely manner. Females tend to put more focus on the process (how we get there), while males may focus more on the results (where are we going and when will we get there). Such differences may exist in the classroom as well and adult educators need to recognize and capitalize on such diversity appropriately as per their session objectives and learning outcomes. Understanding and respecting such differences can create an "inclusive learning environment" where groupthink is avoided and synergistic results flow infinitely, as learners think for themselves and stretch their abilities beyond their existing boundaries. Of course, there are many challenges and opportunities in teams, and each person should be aware of how to overcome possible conflicts and capitalize on possibilities.

When participating as a team member, remember that each person has something unique to bring to the discussion. Capitalize on the strengths of each person and build the weaknesses as a team. Remember that each person has a need for feeling significant; and such feelings are enhanced by clear, stretching expectations, and an empowering focus on strengths that he or she can offer to the team or department. So, focus on clarifying and setting challenging objectives for the team and stretching to achieve them. Ideal team size should be four to six diverse individuals with complementary skills. Having smaller or larger teams could be advantageous or the exact opposite depending on the group dynamics or the structure and the discipline exercised. For example, having a large team could be an advantage in that there's extra brainpower and/or diversity. It could also be a disadvantage in that it might be tougher to reach consensus. Personal experience shows that this advantage and disadvantage tends to even out to make a five-person team comparable with a six-person team.

Both small and large size teams are subject to "social loafing," just as we have social loafers at work and the community. *Social loafing* is the tendency of a team member to put less effort in a group environment than he or she would if he or she had to work individually on the project. Institutions have to create the infrastructure to reduce this to the minimal occurrence. In the real world, most peers or teams don't have a choice of whom they get to work with; and they cannot pick their colleagues as managers tend to do the hiring, although peer and team interviews are becoming more common in today's workplace. Nonetheless, often we don't have a choice of "firing" or "terminating" our colleagues' services or employment. So, the question or the challenge we are left with is: "How do we motivate our colleagues to put forward or contribute their best to the team?" Obviously, this is no easy task. This is why universities have been required to integrate more team projects into their curriculums. The majority of undergraduate business schools also have team projects in each course to help students build their teamwork skills.

The reality is that we all join teams (work and school related or when we come into a "marriage" relationship) with different abilities, motivations and desires. Sometimes, these differences don't match that of other team members and the challenge becomes more complex. The challenge is also posed for universities and instructors as they need to discriminate between those who do contribute and those who are social loafers. However, this needs to be done very carefully, as not to turn everything into a competition of individuality, because teamwork is meant to be representative of a team's outcome, thereby encouraging or building teamwork skills. So, it requires taking initiative and at times maybe sitting back and ensuring that others take a leadership role to see other paradigms surface. Expectations for teams are that the entire team makes contributions to each team project. In an academic project team, leadership roles, editing responsibilities, and providing the needed information should be rotated among the group as per everyone's agreement.

Pygmalion Effect: Self-Fulfilling Prophecy

A video titled *"The Eye of the Storm"* was filmed and released in 1970 in an actual classroom setting in Riceville, Iowa. Many diversity trainers and workshop participants, including thousands of managers at Publix Super Markets, have seen and benefited from the lessons offered in this documentary. The children were actual third grade students and not actors. Jane Elliot, their teacher, conducted an activity that allowed her students to experience the effects of conditioning and discrimination. This video also appeared on Frontline, which was conducted as a follow-up documentary by Judy Woodruff through Public Broadcasting Systems (PBS) titled *"A Class Divided."* The video is actually a follow-up of the first experiment, after fifteen years, with Jane Elliot and most of her third grade students involved in the original documentary. Jane Elliot and the students discuss the impact of the experiment on all the students involved. It appears to have had positive results on her students' lives.

The actual experiment demonstrates how discrimination and stereotypes can be created rapidly in a very short period of time. On the first day of the experiment, she gives special privileges to children with blue eyes (things like second lunches, taking longer breaks, going to lunch first, etc.), and explains to the class that blue-eyed people are better than brown-eyed people, since she along with many other intelligent people have blue eyes. Furthermore, she required the children on the bottom (brown-eyed children) to wear large collars that distinguished them from the smart kids. Jane Elliot kept reinforcing statements like "blue-eyed children are smarter than brown-eyed kids", "blue-eyed children learn faster than brown-eyed children", and "brown-eyed children are wasteful, forgetful and lazy." Pretty soon, the students started calling each other malicious names (brown-eyes, etc.) in a condescending and offensive way while treating the brown-eyed students as inferior, stupid and dumb. The superior group (actually about ninety percent of them) seemed very willing and helpful when it came to finding ways of punishing the inferior group if they got out of line and didn't follow the rules.

However, on the second day Jane Elliot told the class that she was wrong about the blue-eyed people being smarter. It is actually the opposite. So, the special privileges were taken away from the blue-eyed children, and given to the brown-eyed children and they were continuously reinforced to be the smarter group. The blue-eyed children wore the large collars and had to sit in the back of the class since they were the inferior group on this day. It was not long before the "brown-eyed" kids started treating the blue-eyed children as inferior and started acting more confidently as if they knew everything. The overall results showed that children responded to how they were treated, and thus became what they were expected to become. The children on top (smart and privileged) consistently did better on the exams and exercises than when they were on the bottom or inferior. When the children were wearing collars, the results were very negative. The results included:

- Loss of self-esteem and/or self-confidence. They lost confidence in themselves in about fifteen minutes of consistent conditioning by the teacher. Bryan, one of the third graders in class, had his head down on the desk and some children were actually crying since they were labeled as inferior. The facial expressions and body language exhibited by some of the children were very negative.
- Loss of performance. The children were not able to fully concentrate on schoolwork because they were unhappy about being inferior.
- Conflict among them. Fighting, acting-out, name-calling, and hitting each other were a few of the obvious results because they were labeled as inferior. Revenge, finger-pointing, blame, and anti-social behavior were some of the common responses by all the students who were in the inferior group.

These children had previously formed some stereotypes or "mental tapes" about people who were different from them and Jane Elliot was hoping that she could help them form new and more accurate pictures of people who didn't look like them. Jane Elliot said she learned more from the children when they were "on top" (considered superior). She learned that the superior group sought hierarchy, wanted revenge, and were delighted to be superior.

- The superior group wanted revenge. It was "survival of the fittest."
- The superior group liked superiority. The group was "delighted" to place the collars on the inferior group. Even the second day, when they knew how it felt to be treated badly, it was time to get even.
- The superior group sought hierarchy. "I am better than you because..." and "you are less than us because..." mentality existed. They even looked for ways to reinforce the hierarchy by locating the yardstick and asking the teacher to use it if the "inferior" kids get out of hand. They were also encouraging Mrs. Elliot to alert the cafeteria staff to help enforce the "rules" for the inferior group since some of them may have two or more lunches/servings.

Jane Elliot, the teacher who is considered to be one of the best facilitators of adult education, has now been facilitating her brown eyes/blue eyes exercise for nearly 40 years. In 1999, during a morning discussion with her in Washington DC at the National Multicultural Institute Conference (NMCI), she me that racial injustice is very much prevalent throughout our society and we have much work to do in order to eliminate this conditioning from the minds of children, students and employees in the workforce. As a conclusion to the video and a summation of what she has learned, she offers the following comment as a concluding remark that emphasized the critical role of the educator / faculty member: "It's not how "*they*" are...it is how *anybody* will become when treated in this manner." In accordance with self-fulfilling prophecy, what educators expect from their students is likely to be produced by those students. Therefore, expecting less from minorities or foreign students (whose primary language is not English) and evaluating them based on different standards would be unethical and unfair due to the concept of self-fulfilling prophecy. According to Dr. Dan Austin, professor of health administration, a teacher "has to be careful about making judgments and must work with students to help them find the pleasure of learning regardless of their level of passion." It is also a teacher's responsibility to help students find the pleasure of learning regardless of their nationality, race, gender or language. Because of the teacher's influence over students and/or because of the level of students respect for the teacher, it is expected that students will either live up to or down to the teacher's expectations. So, educators should avoid expecting less, or even expressing the perception that they expect less, from students based on preconceived notions and stereotypes associated with their gender, language, disabilities, place of birth, race, skin color, body size, sexual orientation, hair color, eye color, or other such characteristics. The educator should expect great commitment and high quality from all students.

Benefits and Solutions of Diversity: The TRUE Model

Through diversity training educators, managers and workers can become TRUE cross-cultural leaders that are able to work effectively in the context of cultural differences both nationally and internationally. Becoming a "TRUE" cross-cultural educator, manager and diversity champion initially requires:

- Tolerating differences,
- Respecting differences,
- Understanding differences, and
- Examining and exploring appropriate options.

The first step is usually the most difficult but a very important step in the process of becoming a TRUE diversity manager. For example, tolerance is a personal decision. It comes from an attitude that is learned. TRUE diversity management requires that people embrace the belief that each person on earth is a treasure who must be treated with respect. Human beings have the power to change their attitudes to overcome ignorance, and to influence their offspring, peers and colleagues positively. It begins with a personal commitment to consciously choose one's speech and thought patterns. As an initial step, one can stop labeling individuals with oppressive terms based on first impressions or physical appearance. Culturally competent individuals and TRUE diversity champions can stop the spread of offensive Polish, lawyer, gay, and other such jokes in order to create an inclusive work environment.

Becoming a TRUE manager will enable professionals and leaders to provide a supportive and inclusive work environment for all of their associates. This will result in fairness, equality, and a talented diverse workforce that can successfully compete in today's global world of competitive marketplace. Some of the common benefits of diversity initiatives and training programs can be a talented diverse workforce and satisfied customers, high morale and commitment, low employee recruitment and retention cost, better teamwork and increased productivity, and an inclusive as well as a supportive learning environment.

Working and teaching in a diverse environment require understanding and accommodating the various learning styles of students as well as the effective use of differences. One can and should become a TRUE cross-cultural manager, leader, and educator who would be able to work effectively in the context of cultural differences both nationally and internationally with diverse populations. Becoming a *TRUE* global manager, leader, educator, and true champion of diversity initiatives requires tolerating differences, respecting differences, understanding differences, and examining differences for the purpose of educating students and the workforce. So, be a TRUE diversity manager and educator, take "*The Educator's Challenge,*" and make a difference.

The Educator's Challenge

The challenge is to say something good about the people we see
    And to never ever let them settle for less than what they can be.
The challenge is not to shout "Raa Raa Ree, kick'em in the knee"
    But to believe in them and say "Let equality be, so we can all be free."
Imagine learning flowing harmoniously as the world and sea
    For that which is intrinsically imagined can most definitely be.
Personal success is a process hidden inside the leader in "me"
    It can be best achieved by serving others and contributing to "we."
The challenge is to say something good about the people we see
    And to never ever let them settle for less than what they can be.

Manage Differences

Understanding diversity and effectively managing it is imperative in today's rapidly changing global environment. It has been said that about two thirds of the world's immigration is coming into the United States of America, which also brings much global competition for the skills of students and workers. Immigration trends in the U.S. have greatly shifted during the past one hundred years. In the early 1900's, the majority of immigrants were from Europe; today, the majority of immigrants come from Central and Latin America, Asia, Africa, and the Middle East. Today, approximately one out of three American workers are African-American, Hispanic, or Asian; 6 out of 7 working age women are at work, and 1 out of 10 workers has some form of legally recognized disability. There are over 50 different forms of legally recognized disabilities and many of them are not apparent to the naked eye. English is soon expected to be a second language for the majority of Californians as well as those living in South and Central Florida cities.

In the mid 1980's, the Department of Labor commissioned the Hudson Institute to conduct a study on the demographic, sociological, economic, and political trends in America from post-World War II to the year 2000. The results, published in 1987 in a document titled *"Work Force 2000: Work and Workers for the 21st Century,"* indicated the following trends:

- More women are visible on the job and overall minorities comprise 1/3 of new workers. More immigrants are in the workforce and this trend is likely to continue.
- The pool of younger workers is decreasing and the average age of workers is rising.
- Service and information jobs are increasing and higher skill levels are required to compete effectively in today's global world of business.

As one can see, the challenges for businesses are immense. Educational institutions, governments, corporations, and communities are now recognizing the necessity of valuing diversity to remain competitive in today's complex global world of business. Since the current workforce is indeed demographically diverse, leadership and management techniques of inclusion are imperative. Creating an inclusive environment (and eliminating the exclusive world of bias and stereotypes) is necessary for an effective learning and working environment. As a faculty member or teacher of current and future leaders and managers, a professor with the assistance and cooperation of his or her audience must create an inclusive learning environment and educate all learners in this direction as well. The classroom is the laboratory for learning such interactions with diverse colleagues and eventually co-workers.

All leaders and educators need to understand that valuing diversity requires the creation of an open, supportive, and responsive environment where differences are accepted, valued, and managed effectively toward organizational synergy. Creating and encouraging such an open atmosphere in the classroom is the responsibility of the teacher. Valuing diversity means the management of a group of people with differences in such a way that all individuals perform at their maximum potential for the achievement of organizational goals by effectively using their unique skills, competencies, and talents. Each educator or faculty member can ask the following question and then apply the appropriate answers into his/her classroom sessions: In what specific ways, can I recognize and effectively manage diversity in the classroom to ensure a productive learning environment as well as to provide a superior educational value for students? The teacher along with his/her colleagues or students can "brainstorm" and mention specific strategies that are aligned with their vision, mission, and guiding principles that would benefit every one of the learners.

Respect and Involve Adult Learners

Successful and prepared faculty members and educators understand how adults learn best and accommodate the individual needs of diverse learners. Compared to young students, some adult learners have different needs and requirements that must be accommodated in order for them to learn best. Adults have different motivations than their young counterparts that energize them to learn. Adults are not "pushed" or "forced" into the school's class-rooms as is the case with many young children until they become conditioned. Adults choose to attend school and class voluntarily and have different expec-tations than elementary, middle school and high school children. Unlike children and teenagers, adults have many responsibilities besides learning. Because of these responsibilities that keep them away from learning at times, adults have barriers against participating in learning. Some of these barriers include lack of time, money, confidence, or interest, lack of information about opportunities to learn, scheduling problems, "red tape," and other challenges facing all adults. So, adults have a strong need to balance learning with their critical roles at work, community and families. On the other hand, we know that adults are willing to engage in learning experiences before, after, or even during life changing events. Once convinced that change is a certainty, adults will engage in any learning that promises to help them cope with the transition and/or accelerate their progress toward worthwhile and predetermined goals. Adults who are motivated to seek out a learning experience do so primarily because they have use for the knowledge or skill being sought. Learning is a means to an end, not an end in itself. Increasing or maintaining one's sense of self-esteem and pleasure are strong secondary motivators for engaging in learning experiences.

According to researchers, learning results from stimulation of the various senses[1]. In some people, one sense is used more than others to learn or recall information. Educators must present materials that stimulate as many of the senses as possible in order to increase learning and long-term retention. In the past, many faculty members used to provide only a mid-term and a final exam to assess and evaluate the understanding of their students. The first mistake with this strategy is that the faculty is not assessing the learning on a continual basis, but continues to lecture with the assumption that students are learning. The second mistake is that the students are not involved in the application of the material, but rather are studying to pass the exam in the course. The third mistake is that students wait to see what is likely to be on the exam and study those concepts to increase their chances of success. The fourth mistake with this strategy is that this method encourages students to study the week before the test so the material is fresh in their minds for the test. Oftentimes this leads to the traditional cramming session before the exam, which takes away from the real learning and long-term retention of the material. Unfortunately, there are some faculty members that still use such traditional methods of assessment

---

[1] This material is expanded upon in *Adult Education in Academia,* by Mujtaba and Preziosi (2006).

that used to be widespread in the educational arena. Luckily, there are many informed adult educators that use a good variety of assessment tools to actively involve adult students in the learning process so the material can be retained and reinforced for both immediate and long-term application.

Educators need to remember that students must retain the information in their memory for more than just a 24-hour period in order to benefit from the learning in the work environment. The educator's job is not finished until they have assisted the learner in retaining the information for long-term application. Long-term retention can come from being actively involved in the learning process. Retention is directly affected by the amount of thinking, application, and practice that takes place during the learning process. As previously discussed, many informed adult educators use a good variety of ways to involve and assess students' learning for long-term retention and application. For example, many faculty members use different forms of quizzes to assess current knowledge and to see if the students are reading the assignments. While objective quizzes and tests assess the understanding, they can also be used to reinforce learning. Other means of involving students and assessing their understanding can come from having students present specific topics orally, assigning them a team project, having students debate each side of a situation, completing case studies, preparing and conducting role-plays, as well as having mid-term and final exams, and asking students to prepare a term project. Having students complete a number of different projects (besides exams) takes time to grade and assess their learning, but it can also lead to involving them in meaningful projects that can raise their interest and result in better learning, better retention of the learning, and long-term transference of the learning in the workplace. *Transference* of learning is the desired result of education -- it is the ability to use the information taught in a new setting. This is the overall objective of each educator, and can happen when students become part of the learning process, and accordingly are offered many exposures and assessment tools to understand and reinforce the material in their minds.

Summary

Diversity exists in the workforce as well as in the educational arena today and will continue to increase at a growing rate. There is a moral responsibility for each individual to become a TRUE manager in today's workforce. Valuing diversity and thereby becoming a TRUE diversity champion requires each person to tolerate differences, respect differences, understand differences, and to examine or explore those differences in order to maximize the productivity of the workforce and gain organizational competitiveness. TRUE diversity means one should become culturally competent. Cultural competency refers to the continuous learning process that enables individuals to function effectively in the context of cultural differences.

Overall, this chapter discussed diversity, diversity management, and self-fulfilling prophecy as they relate to learners and educators in a diverse environment. It offered suggestions for adult educators and managers on how they can become TRUE diversity champions. The upcoming chapters further extend the topic of diversity and its various dimensions in terms of socialization and behavioral aspects of biases and stereotypes.

Discussion Questions

1. Is there diversity in the academic world? Can diversity management skills apply to the academic environment? If so, how?
2. How is the academic environment today different from three to four decades ago?
3. Do male and female students learn differently? Discuss.
4. Do people of different cultures have different learning styles? Discuss examples.
5. How have the teaching materials over the last few decades changed from what it was three to four decades ago?
6. What impact can such an experiment as Jane Elliot conducted with the third graders have on adults?
7. How can TRUE management make a difference in your organization or in this society?
8. Can the concept of TRUE diversity management be helpful in creating or producing synergy in a diverse work environment? If so, how, why, or why not?
9. How can educators be more effective role models of understanding, appreciating, and managing classroom diversity?
10. Is there diversity in the online work environment or in cyberspace? If so, discuss specific examples.
11. How can managers and educators appreciate and effectively use the diversity of their online workers and colleagues around the globe through the internet?

Chapter 3

Socialization and Stereotypes

Cultural influences, conditioned responses, and unfair work practices have been impacting individuals, teams, organizations, and businesses since the beginning of time. In many cases, the impacts of certain work practices, both in the society and workplace, have been negative, unethical and unfair to members of the minority group. This chapter discusses the various sources of information and stereotypes as well as their impact on behavior, and also how to make conscious choices when it comes to decision-making in a diverse workforce.

Sources of Influence and Information

Socialization is the process of growing up, forming one's beliefs, and becoming the character that one is destined to become. Thinking about the origin of one's personal beliefs and values is not always an easy thing to do because a variety of influences have helped shape these beliefs and values. Some of these influences were more impactful than others, and may have been culturally-based. These influences take place in the socialization process of young children at an early age. Socialization is about how one learns to fit in and get along with others in society. The discussion of socialization basically refers to one's character as a person, and how one becomes who he or she is as a result of growing up in a specific culture or many different environments. Some people are socialized to have an open mind about new cultures; whereas others are conditioned to be very cautious when dealing with other cultures. The socialization influences of such diverse conditioning can come from one's family, schooling or education, media, and peers.

The good news is that there is a large group of people who have not been socialized negatively in the society, and therefore do not need diversity training or cultural competency. However, the challenge is that they all reside in beds or hospitals throughout the land. In fact, they are newborns, perfect human beings who come into the world without any preconceived notions, biases, or assumptions. As the author's colleagues at Publix used to say, the main point is that *no human being is born needing diversity training or cultural competency*. In other words, an infant is not born with racist, sexist, or other oppressive attitudes. Denis Waitley, Psychologist, says that the secret of fulfillment is to look at life through the eyes of a child because a child looks at the world with a sense of wonder and freshness. Children are sort of like sponges, cameras, and tape-recorders, ready to welcome and experience every new natural phenomenon, sight, and sound they see, hear, or touch. They love to laugh and do so at an average of about four hundred times each day when given the opportunity. Children are curious about the world, about the future, and about possibilities which may exist within this universe made up of each and everyone of us. Therefore, they are always scanning the world with an unlimited imagination and an abundance mentality. Children know that the past is history, and thus deal with it in the same manner (by saying "it is *history,*" or a thing of the past), and they see the future as a bright vision that will be coming. However, most children understand and appreciate the wisdom of "smelling the roses" and living life to its fullest each and everyday because today is a gift from "up above," and that is why it is called present. Children enjoy life as it unfolds instead of worrying about the past, which has already happened, or thinking too much about the future, which may never come. They also enjoy everyone they come in contact with throughout their days without treating them as strangers, different, or unusual. To children, everyone is someone to play with, and everything represents an object to do something enjoyable with. Through their interaction with people and objects, they gain experience and form their thoughts regarding future dealings or transactions.

As children learn about the world, they receive information from many sources. Children receive lots of information, perhaps some misinformation, as they grow and mature. In other words, you and I receive lots of information and some misinformation as we socialize and live within our communities. Usually, the misinformation is delivered without malicious intent, but often children may receive this misinformation about people who are different from them. This misinformation is conveyed to them in an overt fashion or sometimes through more subtle ways.

Now, let us discuss some of the "major" sources of information and how they may have had a powerful effect on us as individuals from an early age. Reflect on this question: What are the "major" sources of information for young children as they learn to socialize and understand the world they live in? The major sources, as you may have already guessed, are *Family* (parents), *Education* (school), *Peers* (friends), and *Media* (television, newspapers, magazines, radio, and the Internet). There are others, but these constitute the major sources of information for the purpose of workforce diversity management practices.

Family

Let us look at the family first, since it is a very important aspect of each person's early socialization in life. It is certainly a very powerful influence on us at an early age. Many of us have perhaps thought of ourselves as a "chip off the old block." From a personal experience perspective, I am very much like my father in my actions, beliefs, and values. Often, when I answer my parent's telephone, people think they are talking to my dad because I sound so much like him. And my father is very much like his father, and so it goes on from generation to generation. I was taught to love, honor, and respect my parents, and learn through their wisdom. Therefore, their statements, messages, and sayings have had a great impact and influence on my thoughts, feelings, and behaviors. Sometimes, I think about the circle of friends my parents socialized with, but more importantly, I think about who was not included in this group. My dad, who is an engineer and was a university professor, mostly interacted with engineers, university professors, doctors, and researchers. This is called the principle of *social similarity* in social psychology. This is where we tend to interact with those who look like us, think like us and behave like us. This can result in groupthink and reduced diversity within the group, which can have major disadvantages when complex issues need to be resolved quickly. These professional engineers and doctors were mostly (or almost all) males, which reinforced the cultural view of males working outside the home and females inside the home. In my eyes, males were seen as the breadwinners and females as the homemakers. Consequently, my tendency was to act like those individuals we interacted with, think like them, play chess like them, and become an engineer like them, even though I had virtually no interest in technical occupations. My parents didn't interact with individuals who were singers, comedians, and athletes because most people in Afghanistan didn't think of their work as professions or respectable fields. A graduate student of the Indian background, who was born and raised in Kenya, said that when she lived in Gainesville and studied at the University of Florida many Indian families used to "look down" on her since she was studying business instead of being in the medical field. The reality for Afghans and people of many other developing countries is that comedy, singing, and playing sports have traditionally been considered as a "hobby" and "play" to fill idleness and remove boredom, which are not taken seriously. Realistically speaking, in most cases singers, comedians, and athletes weren't highly paid in Afghanistan. Therefore, they usually had other means and sources of income to make a living. As a matter-of-fact, one of the best and most respected Afghan singers (named Sawrbawn) was selling slippers in the streets of Pakistan when he escaped during the Russian invasion. I remember discussions with my parents about needing to study, going to school and becoming a professional engineer, lawyer, or doctor as opposed to playing volleyball and Tae Kwon Do after school hours. My mother said, "You can't make a living playing soccer; so grow up, get serious and don't hang around your friends who play sports." In these types of instances, and due to economic realities, my parents were just passing on to me whatever messages had been handed down to them from their parents and environments. The main point is that family members are major sources of information; and most often we tend to become like our parents and care-takers because they have a great influence on us.

While I interacted with people who were well educated and were focused on academics, I must have learned, subconsciously and by osmosis, that education and learning can open up opportunities and more doors to doing what one likes to achieve. So, the people my parents interacted with had many major positive influences on my life. On the other hand, my uncles on my mother's side did not have the same opportunities as my immediate family enjoyed. My mother's brothers, sisters and cousins lived in the country areas and were mostly farmers of their own land. Due to economic realities, most of them dropped out of school before completing third grade, therefore white-collar job opportunities were nonexistent for them. Unfortunately, without personal or professional education it is difficult to get a good job in Afghanistan or any country for that matter. So, they lived a difficult life of physical work and hard labor which they still do until this day. Perhaps this is why my mother, who never had the opportunity to attend school herself, was so strict about our study habits and educational performance. She often told us that "without education you will become like my brothers working on the farms." Now, I see that she meant well as she had personally experienced the hardships and frustrations of not having an education. During a visit to the Afghan refugee camps in Pakistan, my mother had asked her sixteen year old nephew why he didn't go to school that year. He responded by saying that he had completed two extra grades than any of his brothers or uncles in the family and that should be pretty good. My mother had slapped him in the face and told him that "you have only completed ninth grade! We have higher expectations of you than that." My mother said he is a teenager, and like most teenagers, he is unable to associate learning with greater ability, leadership, intrinsic fulfillment, and fascinating opportunities that lie ahead. Unfortunately, initially he was not able to break the family tradition, and consequently became a victim of self-fulfilling prophecy which exists deep in the mind because of continuous influences and reinforcements. Fortunately, there are many of my cousins who have now broken the cycle and are finishing various colleges and universities in Afghanistan.

My family always taught me to respect elders and the oldest person was always given the floor first. This mentality conditioned me to always think that I should address the oldest and the tallest people in a group first. When asking for direction, I usually ask the tallest person in a group of kids. Not knowing that s/he could be the dumbest in town.

Coming to America, I felt a different perspective. At times, I felt out of place and at other times I felt totally uncomfortable among my peers. For example, during my trip to the U.S.A., I got much attention on the plane because everyone was looking at my Afghan clothes. I also remember when the principal in Fort Myers High School called me because my sister, Anisa, was crying in her ninth grade homeroom class. This was our second week in the country and our first day attending school in the United States. She felt everyone was looking at her because she was different. The same perception was true for me as well. I stood out from the crowd because of the way I looked, the way I spoke, and the way I acted. I often received much unwanted special attention because of my physical appearance. Of course, much of the unwanted attention was about curiosity of other teenagers in the school from wanted attention was about curiosity of other teenagers in the school from the new foreign kids (my sisters and I) who did not speak much English. Unfortunately, there are millions of minorities throughout the world who experience actual biases everyday because of the way they look.

My "better half" and her family are from St. Clair, Michigan, and didn't have much interaction with foreigners before I met them. Some of their family information about Asians and Afghans were outdated and some of their family members tended to group all Asians and Afghans together, and thus stereotyped them based on limited information heard from media, neighbors and distant family members. Their circle of friends included mostly people from the prevalent American culture which at that time was "white." They lived in St. Clair which had "zero" Afghans, African-Americans, or Hispanics. Although, she mentioned that there were a small number of people from the Philippines who were mostly medical doctors. So, her primary schoolmates until the first year of college were all white individuals, which represented the mainstream in the United States. She graduated from high school in 1985, and had never lived in a city where African-Americans, Asian, Arabs, Native Americans, Afghans, or Latinos were part of the city or the school. Therefore, what they heard about African-American, Hispanics, and other people of different cultures were mostly stereotypical of what the mainstream had thought to be accurate. This was also the case with the Pushtoons and the Hazara tribes in Afghanistan. In most cases the Pushtoons didn't socialize or "hang out" with Hazaras and vice versa. By the way, such animosity and stereotypes are still causing much conflict in various provinces in Afghanistan. Therefore, Pushtoons and Hazaras didn't get to know each other, and consequently feared the unknown. As Dr. Martin Luther King, Jr. said, "People don't get along because they fear each other. People fear each other because they don't know each other. They don't know each other because they have not properly communicated with each other." So, family is a major source of information, and one should attempt to communicate the facts to each family member and friend.

Education

As demonstrated in the previous chapter, another major source of information is our educational (school) system. For example, I received most of my primary education in Afghanistan, and some of my high school education in Florida, where I took American History and other classes that were relevant to the American culture. I think about what I learned and didn't learn about the world from the information I received while attending school. There may have been some important information excluded from my education. Let us explore the possibilities! In Afghanistan, I learned about the Persian Warriors and heroes who had defeated their rivals (in most cases their neighboring countries) and ruled those countries for many years. I learned about the Egyptians, nomads, and their unorthodox ways from many years ago. I learned about Arabian countries, their customs, their philosophies of life, and their leadership styles. I learned about the Greeks, Greek mythology, the Greek gods and their medical advancements in the society from the prehistoric days. However, I didn't learn much about the customs, norms, and traditions of the Hazaras, Uzbeks, Hindus, and Badakhshanis who lived within Afghanistan in various states (provinces). Everything I learned about the traditions of these Afghans was "through the grapevine" and represented the views of my family members, friends, and the society at large. Unfortunately, most of these statements were biased, stereotypical, and not true. Furthermore, during the Russian invasion years in Afghanistan, I didn't learn much about the Europeans or Americans and their ways of life and philosophies. The schools didn't teach me about their forms of democracy and freedom of speech since the Communist concepts were being taught in school. I didn't learn about the American Constitution or the contributions of European scientists and other professionals who have done much research in virtually every field of study. Part of why the education system in Afghanistan focused on the topics taught at schools may have had to do with the prevalent beliefs, values, and cultures of its people at those times. And part of the reason may have been their lack of awareness and economic ability to invest in research about the Europeans, South Americans, and North Americans.

The classes taught me that it takes billions of atoms (approximately ten billion) to produce a living cell and about the same numbers of cells are needed in our brain to produce a conscious mind. The other major thing which primary school in Kabul taught me was to memorize information, guess what the teacher wanted to know, and fill the exam questions accurately based on what you think the teacher feels is right. This was my strategy for passing classes, and that is what I thought school was about, and not necessarily learning. This was like trying to learn how to play basketball and shooting the ball from the closest area under the basket and feeling good about making 100% of the free throws. I was able to pass my classes, but the knowledge had a way of going away after each test was over. This tendency wasn't unique only to my education because it happens in school systems throughout the world. Our education systems have a tendency to reward things other than learning, while hoping that students actually learn what is expected. Shelby Steele, author of *"The Content of Our Character"* and an English professor at San Jose State University, writes that "education is a troubled area in black communities for numerous reasons, but certainly one of them is that many black children are not truly imbued with the idea that learning is virtually the same as opportunity." Professor Steele said that he asked his mother at an early age "why don't the minority teenagers go to school like everyone else?' She made a profound statement, and said that "lack of discussion about minorities on the news and lack of political leaders or mentors to look up to can give minority teenagers the wrong impression about their opportunities in the future." Teenagers often think that regardless of their efforts they may or may not be able to succeed; therefore they cannot associate education with intrinsic satisfaction, opportunities, and a better life.

When you don't see role models who have been successful from your own culture in textbooks and in the society, then it may be more difficult to associate or link learning with opportunities at a young age when it is a critical time for education. On the other hand, the education systems often make something that is naturally fun and exciting, learning that is, related to grades and whether people can accurately guess what the teacher is thinking. Through History, Social Studies, and Science classes in the United States, most of the information I received was filled with the contributions of white, Anglo-Saxon people. The point is not what I was taught; it is what was left out! There was very little mentioned about the contributions of African-Americans, Asians, Hispanics, Native Americans, and others. David Taylor, a colleague who was born, raised and educated in the United States, used to say that "I remember a little bit about Eli Whitney, George Washington Carver, Marco Polo, and Mao Tse Tung, but little else." Unlike David, I completed my elementary and middle school education in Afghanistan, where the history, social sciences, and other classes focused much on the leaders of the world and not just the mainstream Afghans. While there were biases and dominant tendencies, in Afghanistan even poetry often involved many nations, many customs, and many points of views which taught people lessons about others who were different from the dominant cultures or customs. One of my friends said that he learned a lot of information about the American presidents and their leadership characteristics during his education in Japan. However, the same is not necessarily true of American books that were published many decades ago which mainly focused on the contributions of people in the mainstream.

In my undergraduate and graduate courses in Florida, I didn't have one single class that focused on diversity or understanding and accepting each other's differences and similarities. I studied much of the literature about management and leadership; however, to my knowledge very few of them were written by Asians, Native Americans, African-Americans, or Latinos who are a major part of today's workforce in the United States. Most of the authors were from the Anglo-Saxon background, which taught us how the dominant and prevalent culture sees leadership and management issues. Again, the principle of social similarity encouraged people to study one method and continue reinforcing the same research because they were completed by researchers who shared similar cultures and upbringings. In many cultures, management styles are very different than those of the American culture. Therefore, a manager who uses a participatory style of management, which is the usual way of management in Latin and Asian countries, may seem weak because s/he doesn't appear to be aggressive or decisive as a manager. In management education, I learned about Frederick Taylor, Frank and Lillian Gilbreths, Henry Fayol, Max Weber, Tom Peters, Ken Blanchard, Lee Iacoca, Mary Parker Follett, and other researchers and practitioners within the past century who came from similar backgrounds and traditions of management. While these are intelligent and highly creative individuals it may be very difficult, if not impossible, for them to see things from other people's perspectives without personal experience. An example of other perspectives and leadership styles might be Dr. Martin Luther King, Jr. or Mahatma Gandhi, who literally shook the world with their non-violent styles of leadership and got people's attention about other ways of dealing with autocratic and dogmatic leaders, rulers and governments. While education is a major source of information, it may not always give people the whole picture.

As stated before, what I'm asking you to consider is this: no matter what time or geographical location, is it possible that the educational system may have had a built-in, somewhat (subtle) slant toward whatever the prevailing culture was in your location, especially if you lived in the United States of America or the Former Soviet Union during the Cold War?

Peers

Let us look at our peers (friends) and how they influence our behaviors. As you may know, English is not my first language and probably can tell, during a short conversation with me that I have an accent, and have had accent improvement "opportunities" ever since I was five years old. I had the same problem when speaking my first language with people in Afghanistan because people in different provinces had different dialogues, accents, and used some words in different contexts. When I moved from Khoshie of Logar, the country area, to the city of Kabul in Afghanistan at age 5, the kids spoke differently, used words differently and at times with a totally different meaning and accent. Because of my accent and not knowing the local words, I was ridiculed by some children and constantly corrected by the teachers. I was often told that I spoke like Hazaras which, according to societal stereotypes, was a pejorative. The kids often made fun of me and called me inappropriate and offensive names due to the fact that I spoke differently. At other times, I was excluded from informal group interactions and participation. Imagine how it made me feel. As a young boy growing up, that "thing" called "peer pressure" was very real to me and many others.

Peer pressure seems to never go away and follows us throughout life. One of my relatives in the United States was ridiculed because he thought one of his co-workers' name was Dog and kept calling him Dog. It turned out that his name was Doug; however, he still hears about it. While learning English, I have mispronounced many words and one of the most memorable still today is the word "vague" which I pronounced as vagoo for two years. I still hear about it because my adult friends won't let it go. During my first few years in the United States, a friend (let us call him Kevin) always kept saying that he never paid too much for anything as he knows how to "jew people down." So, I assumed that "jewing" meant negotiating. One day in the twelfth grade, I used this word in the class by saying one needs to "jew the seller down" to get a good bargain. The teacher said what do you mean by that term? I said one needs to make sure he or she is not taken advantage of and one does not pay extra for any item…one should pay a fair price. The teacher pointed out to me that the word I was using was derogatory and inappropriate as it was based on stereotypes, wrongly associated with people of Jewish faith. She said the right term is "negotiation," and I began using the right term.

When working as a dishwasher during 1984 in the city of Cape Coral, there was a senior employee (let us call him Don M.) who used to tell me that "You are a good 'N…' and I am going to turn you into a good redneck since you are a hard worker." He continued to use this derogatory "N" word, per-haps assuming that I would not get upset since I was not black or the fact that I did not know what the term really meant. Apparently, nobody else in the department found it offensive either as nobody asked him not to use this term. There was no Black, Native American, Hispanic or African-American em-ployee working in the department. After several weeks of Don using the term with me, the manager asked if I knew what the "N" word really meant, and whether I was upset when Don used the "N" word with me. I said "no I do not know what the term means and I am not upset." The manager told me that the "N" word is commonly used by people in the United States to describe Black people. Of course, that description of the "N" word still did not tell me that this was a derogatory term. Don continued using the term for the coming weeks in the department by saying "Come here 'N….' let me show you how to get this new job completed." Every employee in the department heard and tolerated this offensive term. Don continued using the "N" word until the day another employee, who did not work in our department, heard it. We were outside the department and were supposed to bring the delivered supplies into the stockroom. Don was pulling the heavy load or pallet of supplies from the front toward the department and I, along with the truck driver, was pushing from the back. Don could not see that there were two people in the back of the supplies as the pallet was pretty high. In one area where the slope was high, the load became heavier as we were going up, Don yelled "Push 'N…,' push." The truck driver, a tall and muscular Black male, stopped pushing, called Don a "racist," as well as "stupid white trash," and left. Don was sur-prised, and so was I as I did not know why the truck driver got upset and left when I really needed his help. Although he did not have to assist us with the pallet, he was kind enough to come and help us push the pallet. Then sud-denly, he got upset and left. For all I knew, Don was speaking to me like he used to in the previous weeks. Don looked at me and said "why didn't you tell me that there was a Black man with you behind the pallet?" I said why would that matter…he was voluntarily helping us as the load was very heavy. Don said if I knew he was there, I would not have used the "N" word. That is when I understood that the "N" word was not a good term. Don assumed that since I was not African or Black, I would not get upset. That assumption was false since originally I did not get upset because I did not know what the term really meant. What Don and others like him should realize is that if a term is inappropriate, then it should not be used at all, regardless of whether the person impacted is present or not. Anyhow, eventually Don's employment was terminated with the company...perhaps because he was very consistent in using derogatory terms toward minorities despite the fact that he knew it was wrong. What is interesting is that although everyone in the department knew that the "N" word was derogatory and inappropriate, Don kept using this inappropriate word publicly...thereby reinforcing societal stereotypes. Maybe it was peer pressure that influenced everyone in the department to initially not say anything to Don or senior managers about the use of this inappropriate term. Before coming to our department as a senior and highly paid employee, Don had been a manager in other locations for a number of years with the company. Perhaps it was because of such attitudes and inappropriate terminologies that there were no African-American or Black employees in the department or in the surrounding departments despite the fact that there were many minority families in the neighborhood. Of course, why would one want to work in an environment where one is treated inappropriately through such derogatory terms?

There are examples of peer pressure in the movie *"Water-Boy"* where the football players are making fun of Adam Sandler, the water-boy, who has a mental disability and acts differently than everybody else. While only one person starts the thought of bothering the water-boy, everybody else goes along with the instigator for some cheap laughs. Another example of peer pressure and racial discrimination can be seen in the movie *"Dragon: The Bruce Lee Story,"* where Jason Scott Lee is called offensive names by one individual in the gym and everyone else seems to support it. In North Fort Myers High School, during the 1990's, students informally and overtly grouped themselves into different parties and each group was made up of and interacted with those similar to them. For example, there was the Latino group, the Asian group, the African-American group, and the "White" group. Each group socialized with others in a certain section of the school and drank from certain water fountains. If you belong to one of these groups then you cannot break the rules and drink from the "wrong" water fountain because you don't want to deal with peer pressure. Have you ever experienced this type of peer pressure before? If you have, then you probably remember it like it was yesterday.

While peers can cause much undo stress, they also serve as a primary source of information for most children and adults. For example, it was my friends who told me how to pronounce words accurately, how to study better, and how to score better on the exams. It was my friends who competed with me to become better and better. It was my friends who played volleyball and soccer with me. It was my friends who told me about the "birds and the bees." Most important of all, it was my friends who accepted me the way I was as an individual and that is why their messages had a great impact on my life. They were always nonjudgmental and empathic listeners. They seemed to understand my point of view and perspective. They made me feel important and a part of the team or group. Most people need to feel they belong to something or with someone. Even as teenagers, we want to belong and be with others; however often we lack the skills and courage to initiate contact. Do you remember the Junior High (Middle School) Friday night dances, in the United States, in the school gymnasium (Sock Hops)? There would be chaperons trying to get the boys and girls to dance together. Today, in many cases, the chaperons are trying to keep them apart! When teenagers come to me and tell me how difficult it is for them to deal with all the pressures in their lives, I often have a tendency to tell them "wait until you have to support your family, pay the bills, and put food on the table." Then, I pause and think about it and come to the realization that stress for them is very real as they attempt to "fit in" with their peers and be successful. I remember when one of my salespeople, who was a teenager, started crying while hearing a message from one of her friends on the sales floor. I took care of her customers at that time because she couldn't stop crying. I later discovered that the friend told her how her "boyfriend" had been seen with someone else and was planning to break up with her. That is when I concluded that, for some individuals in modern society, it is tougher to be a teenager than an adult.

Coworkers can and often do cause a great deal of stress in our adult lives. It is because of the existence of peer pressure in our work places that we strive to be the best that we can be. It was my coworkers who told me that the quickest way to the top (the "ladder of success" in the corporate world as understood in the prevalent culture) is to work more hours and devote much of life to work. So, I did. Until the day when my five year old nephew said "you are always busy at work." Then, he asked me "how much do you make an hour?" I said, maybe around twenty dollars an hour. He emptied his piggy bank and gave me about five dollars and said "I want a few minutes of your day to go to the park." His statement was so powerful that it made me think about my goals and definition of success as I had understood it from my peers. The main point here is that friends, coworkers, and peers in general are major sources of information and influence. Another major source of influence and conditioning seems to be the various forms of media.

Media

Now let us look at the media, television, and movies. The media includes radio, newspapers, magazines, and of-course television—otherwise known as the "legal narcotic." Specifically, let us draw our attention to television which is often used as baby-sitters, companions, and friends in most developed nations of the world. The reality is that the people I saw, or did not see, on television helped influence what I believed and valued. I would like you to take a trip down "memory lane" with me. Most of us watch television and some watch too much. An average 18 year old American is likely to have witnessed over one million commercials. If you lived in the United States during the 1960's and 1970's, then you probably watched some of the television

(TV) shows which I am familiar with. I am going to name some of the TV shows I have watched, many of which are still popular and can be seen through syndication today. Please, think back with me! Have you ever seen *"My Three Sons"* with Fred MacMurray? Or, *"Father Knows Best"* with Robert Young and Jane Wyatt? And you can't forget *"Happy Days"* with Richie and the Fonz! How about the *"Andy Griffith Show"*? Remember, Andy, Opie, and Aunt Bea! These were classics! And we can't forget *"Leave it to Beaver"* with Ward, June, Wally, and the Beav. Would you agree these television shows generally represented good family values to its audience? Most people tend to think so. Now, picture little me as a six-year old boy, if you can, watching and enjoying these shows night after night, day in and day out along with my family members. What do you think I learned about the role of "women" in the society I lived in? Remember, in the 1960's and 1970's, American women were generally portrayed as staying home, taking care of the family, cooking and cleaning. June Cleaver washed the dishes in high heels and pearls! Her husband made all the important decisions for the family. Perhaps, *"Leave it to Beaver"* represented stereotypical middle-class America. You know what that means: the husband worked, the wife stayed home, the 2.5 children, a dog, a white picket fence, and they all lived in the suburbs. One can ponder whether these shows represented what was real or the ideal in the minds of many citizens, writers, and directors of such shows.

Let us think about some of the other major dimensions of diversity and how Native Americans were portrayed on television and movie screens. While many of the baby boomers were growing up, cowboy and Indian movies were the rage. They made John Wayne a Hollywood icon. Think back to how the Native Americans were portrayed in these movies. They were often portrayed as law-breakers, savages, and violent. What about that scalping phenomenon, and the notion that Native Americans could not hold their liquor as a people group? Do these portrayals represent the truth? Well, of course not. Researchers have done some fact finding on this issue and found that out of approximately 482 treaties signed with the white people, the Indians broke none of them. And you know that scalping thing that has been attributed to the Native Americans, it was first done by buffalo hunters and only a few of the tribes were believed to have been involved in such an activity. And the observation is that if most people drink too much alcohol, they can get pretty crazy or sick. It is certainly not a cultural heritage or representation of Native Americans to get wildly drunk and intoxicated.

How about another dimension of diversity which represented the African-Americans? Most shows on television in the 60's portrayed African-Americans as maids, butlers, servants, and in other menial domestic roles. How about the African-American sitcoms of the 70's? Do you remember *"The Jeffersons"* with George and Weezie and *"Sanford and Son"* with comedian Redd Foxx? George was a successful business person, running a number of dry cleaning establishments; however, he was portrayed as only caring about money and wealth. Weezie represented the wife and homemaker, which was portrayed in most other shows of the time. I liked "*Sanford and Son*," but it was very stereotypical of the times. And we can't forget Archie Bunker in "*All in the Family*," the equivalent to *Sanford and Son*. Archie was about as biased and prejudiced as they come. Think about how he treated his wife, Edith, his daughter, Gloria, his son-in-law, Michael (also known as the meat-head, which initially made me think he was a meat department manager in the supermarket), and anyone else he came into contact with. One could call Archie as the equal opportunity offender since he didn't really like anyone who was different.

An often overlooked dimension of diversity is to see how individuals with disabilities have been portrayed in the media. For example, "*The Wonder Years*" television sitcom showed a positive story. "*Water-Boy*" is another example of learning that disability does not mean stupidity or lack of knowledge. "*Children of the Lesser God*" explains how deaf individuals feel about being biased and treated differently. A legally blind person was given the opportunity to be a contestant in the popular Jeopardy Show in the ABC television channel; and this contestant won and was asked to come back. The blind contestant commented that many individuals with various disabilities are unemployed; however, they can perform various jobs well without needing costly accommodations if they are given the opportunity.

Another dimension of diversity is to see how foreigners were portrayed in the media. Do you remember the "*I Love Lucy*" show with Lucille Ball and Desi Arnaz? Lucy's husband, Ricky, was a successful Cuban band leader at a popular night club. However, when Lucy caused him to get mad (which was on the average of about every five times an episode), he would yell at her in his native tongue, Aye Carrumba. Now what did that tell the six-year old child watching this show about Hispanics? Perhaps it communicated that you got to watch those Latinos, they've got hot tempers! Is it true that all Latin Hispanics have hot tempers? No, of course not; except, however, for my friends Jose, Rolando and Ricardo...just kidding guys. However, I can say that media has influenced us very much, and can give us the wrong image about individuals from various cultures. The main point is that we get lots of information and some misinformation from family members, education, peers, and media. The misinformation can become stereotypes or mental tapes which can subconsciously drive one's behavior toward people who are different. Furthermore, consistent reinforcements of misinformation and stereotypes can also lead to discriminatory practices in the workplace.

Stereotypes and their Impact[2]

The word stereotype comes from two Greek words: *stereo* meaning "solid" and *typos* meaning "a model." Initially the term was used to refer to metal plates that were used for printing pages of the same writing or diagrams.

---

[2] For more information, see "*Age Discrimination in Employment*," by Mujtaba and Cavico, 2006.

When applied to people, according to experts, it symbolized rigid, repetitive, and formalized behavior. Some writers have claimed that stereotypes are bad for a society because they are created or supported by cultures that are prejudiced and discriminatory toward various groups of people. Of course, the impact is that in adopting and using stereotypes, people can let their cultures do their thinking for them instead of using factual information or evidence as their guide.

Cultures often provide both accurate and faulty generalizations about people. According to experts, stereotypes become hurtful and ineffective when people use them to discriminate against a person or groups of individuals without considering the current facts or evidence. The word discrimination takes it root from the Latin word *discrimino*, which means "to divide or separate" into a division or category (Mujtaba & Cavico, 2006). While discrimination has its positive meanings, in most cases it is used to refer to making judgment about an individual's or people's behaviors solely based on their unique characteristics rooted on stereotypes or generalizations. Such is the case about appearance, age, gender, race, and disability discrimination which can negatively impact many workers in the twenty first century's environment.

Through personal observations and conscious thinking about employment practices, one can tell that it is not unusual to quickly find several headlines each week about employment discrimination cases through various genres and media outlets. Jeffrey M. Bernbach (1996), in his book entitled *"Job Discrimination: How to Fight, How to Win"* stated that "Job-related bias, unfortunately, is big news...and big business." Bernbach mentions that case of a secretary suing a large law firm who was awarded $7.1 million for sexual harassment; a pilot that blew the whistle on Tail-hook received an undisclosed settlement from the Navy and received $6.7 million in a sexual harassment case against a hotel chain; a salesperson who won $8.4 million from his employer for age discrimination; a woman that was awarded her job back along with $100,000 because she was fired for being "too fat"; and, of course, there are many other such cases currently that are keeping lawyers, law firms, and the court system busy as they attempt to bring about fair employment practices.

In an age increasingly dominated by the globalization of business, unique opportunities exist for international entrepreneurial endeavors and business expansion by organizations in the United States as well as foreign businesses. As trade and commerce become truly global, businesses outside the United States increasingly will view the United States as a key market, and thus seek access to a very large market composed of "first world" consumers. However, the U.S. business climate, due to its discriminatory practices and heavy government regulations, may be perceived as too anti-business or noncompetitive due to the legal environment; and thus certain foreign investors may conclude that it is not worth the time, effort, and money to embark on U.S. entrepreneurial ventures. At the very least, the foreign investor should be aware of the legal environment, especially the laws pertaining to labor and employment. In addition, the prudent foreign businessperson who seeks to invest in the U.S. and commence a business therein must be aware of U.S. cultural norms, which may be markedly different from those in the foreign business person's home country.

Mental Tapes

While watching television programs and learning from other sources, we absorb certain stereotypical subtle messages into our brain or our subconscious minds. It is like a video cassette recorder (VCR) tape - you push it in and it plays over and over again. That is why this section of the book is called "mental tapes." The early learned stereotypes become "mental tapes" which affect us on three levels: our thoughts (head), our feelings (heart), and our behavior (habits). In other words, mental tapes affect how we respond to people who are different from ourselves. Let me give you an example of a "mental tape." As a child, I was often told not to go out of the house because the nomads would kidnap me and take me with them to other countries, mostly to Pakistan. Then, they would sell me to strangers or rip my stomach apart to fill it with illegal drugs so they can smuggle them past the borders. I heard such statements about the two million Afghan nomads from most adults which became a stereotypical mental tape of these individuals in my mind. Therefore, I often thought of them as thieves, smugglers, poor, violent, malicious, and uneducated. Even as an eight-year old boy I was hesitant to talk with them. As an adult, I found them to be people like me who traveled either because of seasonal changes, because they were doing business, or because they were "snowbirds" who had relatives in different places. At one time, the nomads were the only link between people of different cultures, countries and villages that were very different from each other. They brought news, products, and knowledge with them from one place to the next.

The point is that people who are different are sometimes perceived by stereotypes and misinformation, rather than who they actually are as unique human beings. About five years ago, my mother was impacted by Bells Palsy and one side of her face including her right eye began wrinkling since there was no blood circulation and gravity was pulling the weight down. As a result, the right side of the face was being pulled down, and it appeared that she had no control over its muscles. This impacted the way she looked, the way she talked, how she ate her food, and how she was perceived by others. She was still the same intelligent, caring and capable person that she always had been; however, now she looked different and therefore was perceived to have a disability, especially if someone met her for the first time. What is sad about such diseases that impact a person is that the doctors don't know how they get started or when they will go away. Accordingly, there was no medication or cure for it. What is even sadder is to actually see a loved one in this condition, knowing that there is nothing one can do to make it better. Psychologically, it must have been rough to go through such a process as one's appearance is impacted…so the person would need positive reaffirmations from friends and family members. My mother's case lasted about two months and then, slowly, she started getting better. It took about six months for her to get back to a normal stage. During this process, she was able to do all her work as usual and kept going about her life as if nothing had actually happened to her. My mother is a very strong person, and she did an excellent job of not letting it "get to her." The key point is that a disability does not mean that a person cannot function well or do things as others. An individual who is impacted by a temporary or life-long disability or condition may very well be able to do many jobs without any accommodations. Therefore, they should be given opportunities to perform up to and beyond their abilities, instead of being defined by the disability.

Now, I would like to relay to you another story by Bonnie Bodilla, an actor, which has been shared by many diversity trainers. Bonnie was eating dinner in a restaurant with a friend of hers who had Multiple Sclerosis (MS). She observed a mother and her six-year old daughter eating at a nearby table. The daughter was watching her friend with MS as she was eating very sloppily (missing her mouth, smearing food on her face, and dropping food on the table). The daughter points this out to her mother who surveys the situation, sees that the lady is sick and tells her daughter to *hush up and not to stare*. If this type of behavior was repeated a number of times while the daughter was at an impressionable age, do you think that she might have gotten some sort of a negative message regarding people with serious disabilities? She might have assumed something is wrong - so she should ignore them! Children at a young age believe 100% of what they hear from their parents to be absolute truths and act according to what they are told. Experiments have shown that when children are told that they are stupid and lazy, it can be very damaging to their self-esteem. As stated in the previous chapter, Jane Elliot, a third grade teacher in Riceville-Iowa, told her students that children with blue eyes were dumber than those with brown eyes. Astonishingly, most of the class believed it and acted according to the teacher's expectations. The same is true for positive remarks and expectations which are properly communicated to children. Luckily, Bonnie's story has a happy ending! Bonnie observed everything at the dinner table and went over to the mother. She told her the lady's condition and that the lady would like to speak to her daughter. The lady explained about MS to the daughter and that she had a great deal of difficulty doing some things, but there were a lot of things she could do just fine. She let the daughter touch and hold her trembling hands and she was fine. The main point is that our early stereotypes become mental tapes which can affect our feelings, thoughts and behaviors. Consequently, mental tapes affect how we respond to people who are different from us. In other words, as a result of years of conditioning, one can be on "automatic pilot" in terms of his or her responses and behavior without considering the current facts or the individual differences regarding a person who is different.

Being on Automatic Pilot

So we've discussed the major sources of information influencing our beliefs and values and how we form mental tapes (unconscious responses). The next major point is the tendency to go on "automatic pilot." Simply put, going on automatic pilot is responding without thinking, without being conscious of why we do what we do. You go on automatic, just like when a baseball is hit right at you, you respond by catching it! Often, my class participants catch the *koosh* ball, which I pass or throw to them suddenly, without planning or thinking about it. They just respond and catch the ball automatically as most people would. We make assumptions and we interact with others based on our previously learned stereotypes. As adults, we may still be on automatic pilot, continuing to form new mental tapes and responding inappropriately to those who are different from ourselves.

As a manager, I had a tendency to predict what my associates were asking, and often answered their questions without fully hearing them. This can lead to bad communication habits and major communication problems, not to mention low morale and feelings of not being heard on the associates' part. The majority of the time I was accurate about their perspectives and questions; however, the problem was that they didn't always feel heard and in some cases fully understood. On the personal side, I did the same thing at home while communicating with my wife, parents and other family members. When my wife mentioned about her day at work, I would evaluate the situation and tell her how she could do better next time. I was constantly advising, probing, interpreting, and evaluating what was said, and did it very quickly. I thought that people always wanted answers from me because I was a manager and was required to know everything. I was trying to rush things and felt a sense of urgency to do everything quick and fast. I was conditioned as a manager to respond quickly because in the corporate world "time is money." I thought being fast and solving people's problems quickly meant productivity and leadership. Contrary to my beliefs as an inexperienced manager, I discovered that my paradigm was totally wrong and consequently not effective nor very efficient. While I still believe time is important and very precious, doing things fast without fully understanding the situation can be costly and damaging to a person physically, mentally, emotionally, and psychologically. Unfortunately, going on automatic pilot is a conditioned reality for many of us; fortunately, it can be avoided by being aware of our responses and conscious thinking when making decisions.

Coming Off of Automatic Pilot

Getting off automatic pilot is a necessity and a prerequisite for effective leadership. Remember, our goal is to gain more knowledge and skills and to use conscious thinking in making choices about our beliefs and values regarding diversity. We need to respond to others based on accurate information. We may not be able to completely erase these negative mental tapes, like we can a VCR tape, but we can record over them by having new experiences with positive outcomes. There is a two-step process to doing this. First, we need to become aware of our own thoughts, feelings, and behavior. Becoming aware sets us up, and allows us, to choose a response. So the second step is to exercise our freedom of choice and choose our responses based on conscious thoughts. We can do this by responding to differences in a logical, rational manner, and by analyzing the available facts.

I would like to give you an example of how this works. I would like to relate a story by a man named Tom Finn that is often mentioned in diversity workshops offered by Publix and the National Multicultural Institute (NMCI). He was visiting his home town of Newark, New Jersey with his family. While driving through a certain part of town, he locked his doors automatically. Later, he thought about what he had done. He remembered forty years ago as a young child in the 60s riding through Newark with his father. His father would always lock the car doors when they were passing through this part of the city. His father may have perceived a danger! The moral of the story is to think consciously about the current situation to see if there is a valid reason to lock the doors. Again, be aware and choose your response in a logical and rational manner. Lawyers and medical professionals do this very successfully. They ask questions and diagnose the situation from all perspectives before making a decision about possible strategies to resolve or attack the problem.

One can also get off of automatic pilot by being involved in good causes for ethics, diversity and equality. Similarly, organizations can involve their employees by being involved in important causes. For example, in their *2005* Highlights Report to Stakeholders, the Social Venture Network (SVN) mentioned their *"Inclusion and Diversity Efforts and Actions* (IDEA)." IDEA was initially created in 2001 to focus on three goals: to create a more inclusive culture at SVN; diversify the SVN network; and provide resources to help SVN members leverage diversity in their own organizations or institutions. Over a four-year period (2001-2005), SVN has increased their percentage of women and people of color in the SVN network by about 116%, and has assisted members enhance diversity efforts within their own departments or organizations through various training programs and diversity initiatives. In 2005, SVN further increased its diversity and inclusion initiative by including members of the Social Impact Leadership Coalition (SILC), which is a group of business networks that work on building economic justice.

As another example, let us look at a specific dimension of diversity, disability. Disability is one dimension of diversity, and it is important that people become of aware of the facts regarding various forms of disabilities. To assist in the development of building bridges and create awareness, on Tuesday (May 23, 2006), the U.S. Dept of Labor Assistant Secretary W. Roy Grizzard and Florida Senator Nan Rich (D-Sunrise) were keynote speakers at *"Building Bridges: Blueprints for Success,"* in a Disability Workforce Summit that was sponsored by Nova Southeastern University's Fischler School of Education and Human Services at the Seminole Hard Rock Hotel and Casino in South

Florida. According to NSU's SharkByte electronic newsletter, "The purpose of the Disabilities Workforce Summit was to create a change agenda for Florida's Workforce Disability Policy in the areas of competitive and self-employment of persons with disabilities in Florida." This NSU sponsored Summit brought together a host of professionals in the disability employment system to discuss key issues and develop an action agenda to better engage Florida employers and individuals with disabilities. The NSU sponsored Summit concluded with focus groups of disability employment system policy influencers, policymakers, and policy implementers, who discussed the key perspectives and developed priorities and recommendations for system change. Such involvement can be a great way to educate an institution's workforce about the various dimensions of diversity and the facts regarding each aspect of diversity so people can "operate" based on current information instead of mental tapes and stereotypes.

Summary

It is hoped that the above examples have helped you see how a variety of early influences may have helped to shape our beliefs and values. The messages we receive from misinformation may lead to forming stereotypes and perhaps some oppressive attitudes towards various groups of people. For example, we have a tendency to become like our care-takers and those we socialize with on a regular basis. Our education system may not have taught us much about individuals from non-dominant cultures. We learn that if we belong to one group then we don't belong in certain other groups. Through the media, we receive lots of information and some misinformation during our socialization. We all have some formal mental tapes which affect us subconsciously in our thoughts, feelings and behaviors. In other words, these mental tapes affect how we respond to people who are different from us. We have a tendency to go on automatic pilot and respond without thinking or knowing why we do what we do. We need to get off of automatic pilot by becoming aware of our thoughts, feelings, and behaviors, and by choosing our responses consciously, rationally and logically.

Stereotypes and biases impact management practices. Professionals should create a work environment that respects human beings and supports them by capitalizing on their unique qualities. This chapter has pointed out the impact of stereotypes and how it impacts a person's behavior.

Ken Keyes, American writer and philosopher who founded Keyes College, tells us that "we are not responsible for the programming we received as children. As adults, we are 100% responsible for changing it." The word "programming" very much relates to the conditioning which we receive both as children and as adults; it can be monitored and should be controlled through conscious thinking and rational decision making. Become educated about the facts, think for yourself and then it is easy to be yourself. Ralph Waldo Trine, philosopher and author, said that "There are many who are living far below their possibilities because they are continually handing over their individualities to others. Do you want to be a power in the world? Then be yourself."

Oftentimes, if we reflect and think deeply about a question or topic, our learning is at a deeper and more meaningful level. As a guide to help stimulate your thinking about some major points as seen at the conclusion of previous chapters, listed at the end of this chapter are some questions to reflect upon. Perhaps you can take some time now to reflect on what you have learned and make some notes regarding each topic. Remember, learning is not complete until it is applied, and learning does not produce anything without application. As an example, a few questions from this chapter are answered, based on the author's perspective, as follows and you may add your own personal answers to your notes:

1. Describe the impact of using *conscious thinking* as it relates to your personal level of cultural competence.

   Conscious thinking helps me make better and more rational decisions that are more effective and less biased. It can also help me respond in such a way that my thoughts (head), feelings (heart), and behaviors (habits) are aligned with my personal values and mission.

2. For many of us, there is a natural and strong tendency to make *assumptions* about people different than ourselves. In what ways will your future assumptions be affected by what you have learned from reading this material on Workforce Diversity Management issues thus far?

   I learned that not all of my assumptions are based on reality all of the times. Most of what is important seems to require getting to know the other person and long-term relationships. It is best to confirm any pre-determined assumptions before acting out upon them.

3. Thinking about the power and *influence of early conditioning* (stereotypes or mental tapes), list several ways that you could effectively form new mental tapes.

   a) *First of all, I have stereotypes and mental tapes as do most people due to their socialization in the society. The key is to become aware of my own mental tapes and how they impact my behavior toward others.*

   b) *I could think consciously about my decisions.*

   c) *Educating myself and becoming aware of the current facts is important aspect of being and becoming culturally competent.*

   d) *Choosing my responses by thinking rationally and logically is a must for effective decisions.*

   e) *Another important element for me is to ask question and seek to understand before speaking and deciding what to say or how to behave toward others.*

Discussion Questions

1. What are mental tapes?
2. What are the main sources of mental tapes and sources of information for people as they are growing up? Discuss two sources.
3. Describe the impact of using *conscious thinking* as it relates to your personal level of cultural competence.
4. For many of us, there is a natural and strong tendency to make *assumptions* about people different than ourselves. In what ways will your future assumptions be affected by what you have learned from reading this material on Workforce Diversity Management issues thus far?
5. Thinking about the power and *influence of early conditioning* (stereotypes or mental tapes), list several ways that you could effectively form new mental tapes.
6. How has the education system in your area and country influenced you in the area of diversity, stereotypes, and discrimination?
7. How has the media influenced you in the area of diversity, stereotypes, and discrimination?
8. How has your family influenced you in the area of diversity, stereotypes, and discrimination?
9. How has your peers influenced you in the area of diversity, stereotypes, and discrimination?
10. What are some ways in which today's media and television shows influence and condition children?

Discrimination in Practice

D iscriminatory practices have been part of society since the beginning of time. In many cases, the impacts of discriminatory practices, both in the society and the workplace, have been negative, unethical, and unfair to members of minority groups. This chapter discusses discrimination, stereotypes, harassment, and other such issues which managers should be aware of as they recruit, attract, hire, promote, and develop a diverse workforce.

Physical Appearance[3] and Body Size

As previously discussed, there are many forms of discrimination, including gender, body size, race, age, appearance, and many other dimensions of diversity. Appearance is a very widespread form of discrimination that impacts people of all backgrounds. Employers and customers in the business world regularly make decisions based on appearance. Yet, there is no law explicitly prohibiting the use of appearance as a consideration for hiring or other employment decisions. Nevertheless, appearance issues increasingly are arising in the context of conventional employment discrimination law cases. Employers realize that an employee with a professional, clean, and neat appearance may make the difference in making a big sale or securing an important deal. Employers assume that persons who do not look like they can take care of themselves will not elicit confidence that they can take care of a client's or customer's business.

Dress codes, grooming requirements, or other appearance-based employment policies generally are permitted under discrimination laws so long as they are enforced in a fair and even-handed manner. These policies, in order to be legal, must not have a disparate impact on any particular protected class, either on its face or in its application. Yet, some variations in requirements may be permissible. For example, in one case, a male employee was discharged for wearing an earring to work in violation of the employer's dress code. The federal district court rejected the employee's discrimination claim. The court explained that minor differences in appearance regulations that reflect "customary modes of grooming" do not constitute sex discrimination within the meaning of Title VII of the Civil Rights Act. In the court's view, so long as both men and women were held to similar standards of professionalism, gender-based differences in standards were not discriminatory,

---

[3] For more information, see "*Age Discrimination in Employment*" by Mujtaba and Cavico, 2006.

presuming they complied with traditional or customary practices. In another case, two men were fired when they wore ponytails after the effective date of a revised grooming policy that required hair to be clean, neatly combed, and arranged in a traditional style, and for men, no longer than mid-collar in the back. The terminated male employees asserted that because their former employer applied its hair length and style rules differently for men and women, they were discriminated against on the basis of their sex. The court, the New Jersey appeals court, relying on federal precedent, determined that hair length policies generally do not constitute sex discrimination under Title VII of the Civil Rights Act. In yet another case, this one by female Department of Corrections (DOC) officers, who filed a class action in federal court contending that the DOC's dress code policy of requiring men and women officers to wear trousers violated their First Amendment rights under the Constitution. In particular, the women claimed that their religious beliefs prohibited them from wearing pants. The court decision, affirmed by the U.S. court of appeals, rejected the women's claims, citing emergency and safety reasons for a rule prohibiting skirts, and also noting that the DOC should be given great latitude in determining the dress code for its correctional employees.

Similarly to the sex discrimination cases, the U.S. courts have held that grooming and dress code policies must also be fair and even-handed in their treatment and enforcement between majority and minority races. In one case, an African-American woman brought a racial discrimination case against her employer because it required her to seek prior approval of hairstyles she planned to wear at work. The policy also required hairstyles to be neat and well-groomed. When she wore a "finger wave" style, the employer revised its policy to prohibit "eye-catching" styles. The federal court allowed the woman's discrimination to proceed, on race discrimination grounds, because of evidence that Caucasian women were not subject to the prior approval or "eye-catching" requirements. In another appearance-race case, an African-American woman wanted to display her heritage through her choice of clothing by wearing African-styled attire and also by wearing her hair in dreadlocks and braids. The woman, however, was terminated; but she was replaced by another African-American woman. The terminated employee contended that because of her choice of clothing and hairstyle, she represented a subset of African-Americans whose claim of race discrimination could not be defeated by the hiring of another minority woman whose appearance was more typical of corporate America. The federal district court, however, refused to find that her claim was actionable, and stated that she had failed to provide sufficient evidence for a court to infer discrimination.

Even when employers do not have an established dress code or grooming policy, employers can still be subject to appearance-based lawsuits. In one case, a female employee wore skirts and blouses that, in the employer's opinion, were too tight, short, shear, and revealing. The employee was repeatedly counseled, especially by the firm's chief financial officer, a male, as to the inappropriateness of her clothing. The employee eventually was fired, and her appearance was a contributing factor in the termination decision. The employee sued for sex discrimination, but the federal appeals court upheld her discharge. The appeals court emphasized that there was no evidence that the chief financial officer had ever sexually harassed the employee or discriminated based on sex. Moreover, the court underscored that in addition to the CFO, two female supervisors had informally counseled the employee as to the inappropriateness and unprofessional nature of her attire, thus indicating that she had not been singled out by the CFO. In another case, an employee was fired for failing to cover a racially offensive tattoo on his arm. The employee was a member of the Klu Klux Klan, and the tattoo showed a hooded figure and a burning cross. The employee sued, contending religious discrimination, but lost. The court pointed out that even if the employee could show a sincere religious belief, it nonetheless would be an undue hardship for the employer to have an employee in the workplace with a racially offensive tattoo.

The U.S. cases indicate that the courts are reluctant to accept appearance as a legitimate basis for discrimination claims. However, if an employee can successfully tie appearance to a protected class, such as being an older worker, and there is evidence that the protected class is treated differently from the majority, such claims may be successful. Although employers are prohibited from unevenly enforcing their dress codes or grooming policies, such policies may reflect differences that are considered reflections of customary appearance standards.

Another issue that generates lawsuits in the U.S. is that of an employee's weight. Such cases often are tied to appearance or grooming standards, and thus can be the basis of a sex discrimination case, but weight cases can also be framed as a disability discrimination claim. An important initial point to underscore is that weight is not a protected class under Title VII of the Civil Rights Act, and thus discrimination based on weight alone is not illegal. To succeed in cases alleging sex discrimination based on weight, there must be evidence that the employer treated men and women differently based on their weight. In one case, a federal district court case, a woman who weighed 270 pounds was repeatedly passed over for an outside sales position. She sued when she learned that a "thin and cute" female with less experience had been promoted to an outside sales position. The basis of her suit was that the employer applied weight standards to women but not to men. The employer admitted that she was denied the promotion because of her weight, but denied any gender discrimination in violation of the Civil Rights Act. The court agreed with the employer, particularly because the employee could not identify one overweight male outside sales person.

In another case, the federal appeals court found United Airlines weight policy to be discriminatory on its face. Although both men and women were subject to weight restrictions, the court found that the airlines was imposing more burdensome weight restrictions on women by requiring female flight attendants to meet maximums for a medium-framed person, while men were allowed to reach maximums for larger-framed persons. The majority of weight-based discrimination claims in the U.S. arise as ADA claims. Accordingly, the employee must show that he or she has a substantially limiting impairment that limits one or more major life activities. The EEOC guidelines, however, state that the definition of impairment does not include physical characteristics, including height, weight, and muscle tone, that are in the "normal" range and are not the result of any physiological disorder. Moreover, the EEOC guidelines explicitly provide that obesity, except in rare circumstances, is not considered a disabling impairment. Consequently, unless an employee's weight problem is so serious as to rise to the level of "morbid" obesity that is caused by a physiological condition, the employee will not be able to use the ADA's protections as the basis of a lawsuit. The ADA, as one court emphasized, was designed to protect people who truly have a disability, and should not be used as a "catch-all" lawsuit for discrimination based on size, weight, and appearance. Employers, therefore, can make decisions based on an employee's weight; but the employer must be very careful to treat all employees in a fair and even-handed manner; and must ensure that weight, and not race, sex, religion, or disability, is the actual consideration.

Based on the foregoing legal considerations, employers in the U.S. can take precautions to prevent appearance-based lawsuits. If an employer does promulgate appearance and grooming standards as well as a dress code, the employer must make sure that discriminatory standards are not built into the policies. Most importantly, men and women, as well as the young and old, must be treated comparably. The exact requirements may be different, but they must be similar and fair. Any differences in the standards between men and women, as well as the young and old, however, must reflect what is considered customary in society.

Discrimination and Sexual Harassment

Over the last 50 years or so in the United States, employment has been considered to be "at will," and with some exceptions, most employments are still "at will." One must remember that "employment at will" does not mean that the employment contract is not enforceable. Therefore, each party (employer and employee) must do their part to honor the employment contract. Employment "at will" means that both the employer and the employee can end the employment at any time, and for any reason. However, there are some ways that a company can be limited in its ability to terminate employment "at will" and the following are some of them:

1. There might be a written contract between the employer and the employee.
2. There might be third parties involved with specific termination policies and rules in place. The best way to terminate an employee in such cases would be to have "just cause" for doing so.

3. There might be specific state or federal laws that limit employment terminations by the employer.

Managers should remember that the that laws prohibit Equal Employment Opportunity (EEO) laws make it unlawful to "discriminate" on the basis of certain categories. It is important to remember that EEO laws do not make "discrimination" itself unlawful since it is perfectly fair to "discriminate" on the basis of how well an employee does his or her job; or to "discriminate" against employees on the basis of attendance or tardiness records. Discrimination simply means treating people differently, which is not necessarily unfair or illegal. Discrimination does not necessarily mean being unfair, making quick decisions, getting angry, being foolish, being wrong about a situation, having an innocent misunderstanding, violating company policy, changing one's mind, changing a practice because of continuous improvement, taking action without proper documentation, or making a decision based on the precise situation at hand. So, "discrimination" means treating employees, customers, and one's colleagues differently. More specifically, *unlawful or illegal discrimination* means treating people differently on the basis of a protected category. There can be many kinds or types of illegal discrimination, including, but not limited to (Equal Employment Opportunity Training, 1998):

1. *Impact.* A business policy or practice that has a statistically adverse "impact" on a protected group, if the practice cannot be justified on the basis of a business necessity.
2. *Treatment.* Treating a person differently as a result of a protected category.
3. *Failure to accommodate.* Some laws require that a company make special "accommodations" to certain employees, and a company that fails to do so has, in effect, discriminated against that employee.
4. *Harassment.* The discrimination laws generally prohibit harassment, and harassment is a special category of discrimination.

Managers should think about the fact that a specific practice or situation can have many possibilities with regard to the different forms of discrimination, including: a) the situation can involve unintentional discrimination, b) it can involve intentional discrimination, c) it can involve a failure to accommodate, and d) it can involve harassment. There are some cases, under *Bona Fide Occupational Qualifications*, when an employer can ask for a specific gender for a particular position. For example, one can specifically recruit a male actor to play the role of James Bond or Mahatma Gandhi.

"Discrimination" is against the Equal Employment Opportunity laws when it is discrimination on the basis of one of the protected categories such as: race, color, national origin, age, sex, pregnancy, marital status (state of Florida), religion, disability, military status, union activity, and protected legal activity. It is also important to remember "discrimination" with respect to almost every condition of employment. For example, it is unlawful to discriminate in the process of:

⇒ Hiring,
⇒ Performance appraisals,
⇒ Selection and promotion decisions,
⇒ Work assignments,
⇒ Shift assignments,
⇒ Training,
⇒ Pay,
⇒ Granting time off,
⇒ Disciplinary actions, and
⇒ Termination of employment.

While most of the frequent laws that managers face and encounter tend to be the Equal Employment Opportunity laws (antidiscrimination laws), managers and corporate leaders should also be familiar with other employment laws, such as the Fair Labor Standards Act and Child Labor Laws as listed in Table 4.1 (upcoming pages in this chapter), that are appropriate in their industries.

It is important for twenty-first century professionals to familiarize themselves with the Equal Employment Opportunity (EEO) laws. The purpose of EEO laws is to ensure equal employment opportunity for all current and prospective employees without regard to race, age, gender, disability, or other such protected characteristics which are not job-related. The agency that enforces Equal Employment Opportunity laws is the Equal Employment Opportunity Commission (EEOC). In addition to EEOC, most states, counties and cities have created laws and agencies to enforce their local laws. For example, while most states prohibit discrimination on the basis of age for "older workers," those individuals who are 40 years old or above, the state of Florida also prohibits discrimination on the basis of "age" for those who are younger than the protected category. The state of Florida has further prohibited discrimination on the basis of "marital status."

Employers, managers and workers must avoid all illegal forms of discrimination and sexual harassment in the workplace in order to create an inclusive and healthy work environment for everyone. There are many types of sexual harassments in the workplace and two of them are "quid pro quo" and "environmental" or the existence of a "hostile work environment."

1. *Quid pro quo.* This can include threatening to injure or reward an employee in his or her job depending upon whether the subordinate complies with or refuses a request for sexual favors.
2. *Environmental (hostile work environment).* This is where the sexual content of the workplace, company, or department is so abusive, offensive, severe, and pervasive that it affects an employee's working conditions.

Harassment can be seen as inappropriate and repeated behaviors that are geared toward specific persons or individuals within an environment or department. *Sexual harassment* is oftentimes seen as behavior that is *unwelcomed* (the recipient does not want it), *unsolicited* (the recipient did not ask for it), and *repeated* (the behavior is not one isolated incident). A behavior can be considered sexual harassment when submission to such conduct is made a condition of the individual's employment; when submission to, or rejection of, such conduct by an individual is used as the basis for employment decisions (such as salary increases, promotions, etc.) affecting the individual; and when such conduct has the purpose or effect of interfering with the individual's work performance or of creating an unfriendly or offensive work environment. On the other side, *quid pro quo* is a condition created by the harasser in which the harassed submits to unwanted sexual and physical advances to either obtain a reward (such as a good grade without earning it through objective performance in the course) or to avoid a consequence. An actual act is not required to establish quid pro quo. Such situations must be avoided by using professional, consistent and fair treatment strategies for all students in the class and employees in the workplace. Also, adult educators should be aware of and eliminate the presence of a "hostile learning environment" in their classrooms.

A *"hostile learning environment"* can be described as a situation where inappropriate remarks consistently take place and it is not corrected by the teacher/faculty member. This is a situation where insensitive and inappropriate remarks should be addressed publicly by the faculty member so everyone in the class understands the ground rules and the fact that inappropriate/insensitive comments are not appreciated nor tolerated. Educators must also avoid and eliminate the presence of sexual harassment from taking place in the classroom while maintaining a faculty-student relationship. Tangible consequences such as a lowered grade do not have to occur to substantiate the existence of sexual harassment. If a student's emotional and psychological abilities are substantially affected, there may be enough proof that sexual harassment occurred. The same is true in the workplace between managers and their employees.

For any type of discrimination and sexual harassment cases, besides the employers, individual managers can also be sued personally. Sexual harassment can be unlawful when it is carried out by a manager, a co-worker, or a non-employee (such as a supplier, vendor, union representative, etc.) who harasses an employee. Laws that can apply in discrimination or sexual harassment cases can include, but are not limited to, the following:

1. Title VII of the 1964 Civil Rights Act (sex or gender discrimination).
2. The Civil Rights Act, 1991.
3. State fair employment laws.
4. State tort claims, including assault and battery, invasion of privacy, infliction of emotional distress, etc.

Remedies for violating the law can include reinstatement of the employee, back pay to the employee, injunction, paying attorneys' fees, etc. One should also remember that punitive and/or compensatory damages may be awarded; and that the law allows for jury trial. Remedies can also include damages for pain and suffering, embarrassment, humiliation, and appropriate punitive damages. Laws can vary from state to state; therefore, managers should consult their human resources' department and legal counsels.

Table 4.1 - Employment Laws (Equal Employment Opportunity Training, 1998)

Law or Statute	Purpose
FLSA--Fair Labor Standards Act	The Fair Labor Standards Act, and related laws, deal with the payment of a minimum wage, and with requirements to pay for overtime hours at overtime rates. The FLSA (wage and hour) laws also regulate what constitutes work time, deductions from pay (such as required uniforms) that might reduce an employee's wages below the minimum wage and so on.
Child Labor laws	These laws restrict the types of jobs that minors may perform, the hours minors may work and so forth. There are both federal (U.S.) and state (California, Florida, Georgia, etc.) laws regulating child labor. They have different specifics, and a company must comply with both.
ERISA: Employee Retirement Income Security Act	The Employee Retirement Income Security Act regulates employee stock ownership plans, pension and retirement plans, and other fringe benefits, such as group health insurance, severance pay plans, and so on.
OSHA	Occupational Safety and Health Act regulates workplace safety.
IRCA	IRCA regulates the employment of aliens and requires proof of work eligibility for individuals seeking a job.
Polygraph Protection Act	Regulates administration of polygraph examinations.
Veterans Reinstatement laws	Require the reinstatement of individuals who have entered military service under various conditions.
NLRA	The National Labor Relations Act regulates how a company must deal with unions and union members. It also regulates how a company must deal with job applicants and associates in some circumstances which have nothing to do with unions.
FMLA	The Family and Medical Leave Act regulates absences from work for family and medical reasons.
Discrimination laws	Discrimination laws in the workplace mostly deal with "discrimination" on the basis of race, sex, and other protected categories.

Experts, such as Raymond Deeny and John Wymer (1993) from the Institute for Applied Management and Law, offer the following guidelines for employers, managers, human resource specialists, team leaders, and workers:

1. Have a clearly defined policy against sexual harassment and sexual discrimination.
2. Investigate harassment complaints thoroughly, fairly, and involve only those who must be involved.
3. Protect the privacy and reputation of both the alleged victim and the alleged harasser.
4. Make sure to involve human resources professionals and/or the legal counsel from the outset as the complaint is made.
5. Protect the complaining victims from retaliation by the manager, employer or other workers in the department.
6. Respond to the complaint or the case based on the facts, not assumptions.
7. Take appropriate action, as per the findings of the investigation, which is commensurate with the seriousness of the harassing conduct.

Daily Indignities

Thinking back to your life experiences you will recall that we all, at some point in time, have undergone experiences when we were treated differently or discriminated against because of physical differences and other such characteristics. While we all have experienced unfair treatment at one time or another you will see how some individuals in society may be exposed to this type of treatment on a more consistent basis. In fact, some individuals may experience such unfair treatment on a daily basis. This unfair treatment is called *daily indignities*- the negative things that individuals do or say to or about one another on a continuous basis, because of their biases and perceived differences. These daily indignities are demonstrated in many different forms. Several documentaries have been created that show these various forms of daily indignities or discrimination. These documentaries depict various forms of discrimination in actual work and daily life situations. Typically, two people, called "testers," are used. They are equal in all characteristics except the chosen discriminatory one, like age, appearance, skin color, or gender. Usually the testers are sent to a location to check on public response to a diversity characteristic in real life settings such as applying for a job, buying a car or making a major purchase, getting a ride on a highway, asking for directions, using the services of various organizations such an employment agency, renting an apartment, and shopping in a store. A few examples of these documentaries are focused on age, skin color, gender, and appearance.

The Age and Attitude Documentary

The *Age and Attitude* video focused on discrimination based on age (ABC's Prime Time, 1994). In the "*Age and Attitude*" documentary, older job seekers were discouraged by the interviewers from pursuing the job by telling them that they would not enjoy the job nor do well since most of the employees are young people who are working in a "dog-eat-dog" world. Some of the interviewers told the older applicants that they are looking for someone with more specific experience, but told the younger applicants that they are looking for someone like them who can be trained to present an energetic image to clients/customers. There was one applicant (older worker) who actually spent over $10,000 in medical surgeries to make herself look younger, and therefore more marketable, since she believed (based on her personal observations in the job market) that most interviewers were looking for and felt comfortable with younger applicants. About six months after the surgery, she went back to the same employment agency that had previously told her there was nothing available for her and this time they sent her to six different job interviews, despite the fact that the economy had not changed much. Research showed that younger applicants were called back for second interviews and were offered jobs much more often than their older counterparts. Aside from general bias toward older workers, it is also believed that some managers do not hire older workers because they believe that older workers are difficult to manage – "it would be like managing one's parents." One manager believed that he hired the younger candidate, despite the fact that he had less qualification, because he looked more confident in his responses, when in fact both the younger and older candidates were the same individual (but made up to look different with different resumes). Whatever the reason, they all amount to age discrimination which can be very costly to an organization. Overall, data shows that age discrimination is such an integral part of American society that it is even more difficult to detect than either racial or gender discrimination. It is also a fact that older workers (over 40) usually require 64% more time to obtain employment than their younger counterparts. It should also be mentioned that discrimination did not occur every time in this *Age and Attitude* documentary; some of the discrimination might have been unintentional; and it is possible that some of the discrimination that occurred was not because of the particular characteristic being tested. Nonetheless, such forms of age discrimination are prevalent in the United States and possibly widespread in the workplace. A pattern of such discrimination could cost the company major losses in lawsuits.

Managers should be aware of age discrimination laws and the fact that older workers can be a great asset to an organization. "Days Inn" Corporation had a program to study the productivity of "older workers" and they found that "older workers" were more loyal, took less sick days off, and were more productive than their younger counter parts (*Age and Attitude*, ABC's Prime Time documentary aired on June 9th 1994). Older workers usually have plenty of experience and can relate to customers better which leads to an enhanced level of customer service. So, there are many benefits that come with aging, and managers need to use these benefits to their advantage instead of operating based on stereotypes and biases which can be very destructive to the organization.

The Ugly Truth Documentary

The Ugly Truth documentary depicts discrimination based on appearance. Let us discuss two instances from this documentary showing discrimination based on looks. In one instance, two actors were placed as defendants in separate court cases. The jury was unaware that the defendants were actors. One defendant was attractive, while the other actor was made-up to be less attractive. In both cases, the defendants were not required to speak as their tone of voice could impact one's perception. The cases ended with the "attractive" defendant being found innocent and the "less attractive" defendant being found guilty. When the jurors were interviewed, they all admitted that attractive defendants look innocent and appear to be honest. These assumptions are supported by factual data as well. In real life situations, attractive defendants are more likely to be found not guilty or receive less severe penalties than defendants who are perceived to be less attractive. In another setting, elementary school children were the target audience. Two teachers were sent in separately to present identical information. One teacher was considered attractive while the other was considered less attractive. When the learning experience was complete, the students were asked to rate the teachers. The attractive teacher was considered more intelligent and the overall best teacher. According to a study, completed at the University of Pittsburgh, tall people seem to be more successful than short people because of the *expectations* people place on tall individuals especially during their early childhood years. Generally, we expect tall people to be more successful; therefore, the positive expectation becomes a self-fulfilling prophecy for tall people; as a result, they try harder and expect themselves to deliver superior performance.

ABC's 20/20 Show on April 14, 2006, which focused on the topic of "Freak-economics" and whether "looks" mattered, reported that appearance does matter. They sent hired actors (females who looked very attractive and females who looked average based on societal standards) to make cold calls by going door-to-door to people's houses to collect money for an unknown charity organization. The actors had hidden cameras on them to record what people said and how they responded to each group of collectors. The results showed that the "attractive" individuals collected more money than the "average" looking representatives. Their conclusion was that people respond more favorably to attractive agents, since in this experiment they collected more money for the charity. They extended the study a bit further by changing the hair color of the representatives to "blond." The "blond" representatives collected three times more money than others, perhaps because there was a "pretty young girl" at the door. As matter of fact, "blonds" collected more money than all other groups. So, studies consistently show that looks do matter. Therefore, one should attempt to look his or her best at all times.

The Fairer Sex Documentary

The Fairer Sex is a film depicting discrimination based on gender. A female and a male tester are placed in various, but identical situations with very different results. The following are some of the scenarios from this documentary and what actually happened:

- *Golf Tee times;* a female tester entering first was unable to obtain a Wednesday tee time and was told that an afternoon start time was the only time available on Friday. The male tester entered shortly afterwards and was given a Wednesday tee time and an early morning tee time on Friday.

- *Employment opportunities;* when both testers applied for identical employment opportunities, the female tester was often offered secretarial positions, while the male was offered better paying positions, including entry level management opportunities. This all occurred with the female tester having better work qualifications on the resume.

- *Automobile purchases*; the female tester was not allowed to drive the vehicle off the premises. The male tester was given the keys. The female tester was quoted a higher price than the male for the exact same automobile. In fact, on the average, the man's starting price was $500 less than the female tester's final price! Other documentaries have shown that African-American females are often quoted higher prices for automobiles than white females.

Real world cases and scenarios show that gender discrimination does exist; sometimes they are intentional and, at other times, they could be unintentional. Many companies are changing their policies and hiring processes to avoid and in some cases eliminate gender discrimination in their work environment. For example, Saturn Corporation has created the "one price for all" strategy where the focus has been on serving customers, regardless of their gender, as opposed to getting a higher commission by negotiating extremely high monthly payments with women and other minority groups. Generally speaking, traditionally women have been quoted higher prices than males and are often taken advantage of by car dealers. However, Saturn has changed this mentality within their company, and as a result has gained a good percentage of loyal customers.

In the month of May 2006, the American Broadcasting Corporation (ABC) television network had a segment called *"Save $100 a Day in May"* on their Good Morning America episodes with Charlie Gibson and Diane Sawyer. On May 9, they aired specific savings associated with new car purchases and how females can get a fair deal. They also confirmed that the average price of a new car purchase for a female is about $500 higher than for males. Apparently, about 76% of women take a man with them when purchasing a car since they are afraid that they will be "taken advantage of" by the salesperson.

There, of course, are some suggestions and strategies for females (minorities and males) to make sure they get a fair deal on their next automobile purchase. For example, one should do his or her homework before going into the dealership. Newspapers and online shopping are good means of understanding the market and various pricing structures. To get a good deal, it is best to be the last person shopping for a car in a given day since the salespeople want to go home. The end of the month, the end of the quarter, and the end of the year are often good times as well to find a nice bargain as dealers are often trying to meet their projected quotas. Another strategy is to shop for a new car on a rainy day or when the weather is really bad. Also, be prepared to make a low initial offer so you can have plenty of room for negotiating. As a recommended strategy, your first offer should be about $1,000 below the invoice price (the invoice price is what the dealer paid for it; it is not the suggested selling price). Also, do not negotiate on making a specific monthly payment. Dealers will often ask "how much do you want your monthly payments to be?" If you go with this route, it means that they will probably get the highest price from you. Instead, negotiate the car's bottom price and do not worry about the monthly payments at this time. Once the final price is determined, then, you can work out the finances or monthly payments (sometimes it is better to get a bank to finance it instead of the dealer as the dealer's financing can become somewhat "tricky" at times). Also, once you have seen the car, negotiate the price away from the car so you are not constantly looking at it and "falling in love with what you don't own yet." Also, if you have a car that you can trade-in, do not mention it during the initial negotiation process. You can discuss the trade-in car once you have finalized the purchase price of the new automobile. As it will be determined by the dealer's offer and his or her estimate for the true value of your existing car, keep in mind that you can often get a better deal selling the car yourself. On the other hand, if you do not get a fair or satisfactory deal for your "trade-in" car, you can still walk away and go to another dealer.

The True Colors Documentary

True Colors is a documentary about discrimination based on skin color. Some people in the United States truly believe and claim that racial or skin color discrimination no longer exists in this country; however, the personal experiences of many individuals and the scenarios on this documentary demonstrate otherwise. The following are some of the results:

- The person of color was followed in a music store when he declined help and was not offered help in a shoe store. The clerk in the shoe store ignored the tester for over 5 minutes. Both stores promptly offered help to the Caucasian tester and left him alone when he declined. On the video, one could see that the testers were in the stores at the same time.

- The Caucasian individual was provided a master key to view apartments that the person of color was told were rented.
- The testers were quoted different prices, different down payments, and different financing rates by the same salesperson on the same car on the same day. The African American tester had higher prices and rates quoted. Studies indicate that, as a group, African-Americans pay 5 to 12% more for used automobiles than their Caucasians counterparts in the United States.
- The Caucasian tester was courteously offered help at an employment agency, while the African-American tester was treated rudely and told he would be "watched closely."

It should also be mentioned that discrimination did not occur every time in these documentaries; some of the discrimination might have been unintentional; and it is possible that some of the discrimination that occurred was not because of the particular characteristic being tested. Nonetheless, the scenarios do demonstrate how discriminatory practices can happen to a person as a result of various characteristics that are unique to him or her.

Unearned Privileges

What do you think was the first question asked when babies were born before the existence of sonograms? *Boy or Girl*? The second question might have been about the baby's health and his or her number of fingers and toes. Society begins separating children right away; and this is usually done based on external characteristics which the individual has little or no control over. People tend to form into groups with others who share some of the same basic characteristics. Some people call them groups and others call them cliques, clubs, clans, tribes, etc.; perhaps we can call them groups/clubs. If you are a baby boy, society automatically enrolls you in the men's club. If you are a baby girl, society enrolls you in the women's club. Keep in mind that nobody is asked if they want to join. It just happens as per society's traditions. This phenomenon continues into adulthood in the society. Many folks, probably most, are unaware of this tendency of being grouped into "clubs." Even the traffic signs are somewhat humorously discriminatory. There are signs which say *"Slow* Children at Play." Are these signs telling people to be careful because *"slow"* or *"emotionally challenged"* children are present? While these children change, grow and become adults, the traffic signs change along with them. However, the adult traffic signs become more gender biased because they often say *"Slow* Men Working." On the serious side, we can say that prejudice seems to exist and may always exist to some extent; however, its unfair impact can be prevented, should be prevented, and must be prevented in order for people to function productively and live harmoniously as one race - the human race.

Prejudice usually affects people of minority groups or clubs in the society; and many are not always aware of it as discussed in daily indignities. Besides blatant discrimination, people are also affected in ways that are very subtle. The term often used to refer to this concept is unearned privilege. *Unearned privileges* are advantages given to some individuals and withheld from others, without regard to their personal efforts or abilities, because of their perceived differences. The existence of unearned privilege leads to increased tension, stress, and frustration because it usually comes at a cost to someone else. Sometimes, the society automatically affords a person unearned privilege because he or she falls in the norm. On the other hand, one may have to work harder than those who fall in the norm because the society is not structured toward his or her needs. For example, traditionally society has structured everything for the right-handed persons, which means that left-handed individuals have to function in a right-handed world. The school desks, manufacturing machines, scissors, doorknobs, golf clubs, and other necessities of life are usually built for right-handed individuals since society, for one reason or another, has considered that to be the "norm." In this case, the right-handed individual has received "unearned privileges" simply because he or she falls in the norm. One can realize these unearned privileges by asking some basic questions: What do I receive simply because I fall in the norm? What privileges are afforded to me because of my gender, because of my age, because of my language, because of my height, because of my natural good looks or overall attractiveness, etc.?

Many individuals can think of some of their own characteristics that have earned them certain privileges without any effort or work on their part. For example, being a male can have certain advantages as well as certain disadvantages. Also, being short can have many advantages and at other times many disadvantages. It can be concluded that those who have unearned privileges are seldom aware that they have it; consequently, those who don't have the privilege are very aware that they do not have it. One should also remember that, unlike daily indignities, unearned privileges are very subtle. Many people that have unearned privilege may be totally unaware that they have unearned privilege. When people are unaware, it is often difficult to convince them they do, in fact, have privileges they have done nothing to earn. Those who do not have these privileges are very aware. What is certain is that the existence of unearned privileges in the workplace can create tension, stress, and frustration.

There is the old parable about the King and his son. The King and his six-year old son were watching the poor people of the country pass through their castle and yell bad things about the King because of the inflation and hunger. The son asked, "Dad, why are they on strike?" The King replied, "They are hungry and need bread so they can eat and survive." The son replied by confirming his understanding and making a suggestion to solve the problem by saying "well, if they are hungry and don't have any bread, why don't they eat cake and cookies?" While eating cake and cookies was the norm for the

King's son it is a colossal luxury for a person who cannot even afford to buy a piece of dry bread so that s/he can survive another day. The moral of this story is that when you are in the "norm" you think that is the way it is for everybody. However, in reality it may not be so regardless of how much we want things to be that way.

As stated before, the existence of unearned privilege leads to increased tension, stress, and frustration because it usually comes at a cost to someone else. Sometimes, the society automatically affords you unearned privilege because you fall in the norm; and sometimes you may have to work harder because the society is not structured toward your needs. For example, as referred to earlier, society structures everything for the right-handed persons, which means that left-handed individuals have to function in a right-handed world. Please ask yourself the following question and write your specific, thought-provoking, and personal examples in a notebook for as many variables as you wish.

I acknowledge that society accords me more or less privilege based on my _____ (body size, disability, gender, skin color, ethnicity, sexual orientation, etc.). Mention specific examples of where you have more or less privilege based on various dimensions of diversity that apply to you.

_____

_____

_____

Overall, many of us can think of some of our own characteristics that have earned us certain privileges without any effort or work on our part. Unearned privilege is a subject that requires deep and introspective thought. The concept is more difficult to understand for some than for others. One can conclude that those who have unearned privileges are seldom aware that they have it.

Become a Cultural Ally

As discussed above, those who don't have unearned privileges are very aware that they don't have it. So, refuse accepting privileges that you have done nothing to earn and become a "cultural ally" for those who are not in the norm. *Cultural ally* refers to those individuals, professionals, managers, and leaders who intervene or interrupt, as needed, to stop mistreatment or injustice from occurring to innocent persons in their vicinity. These interventions and interruptions can be in a work or societal setting. These interventions can be private or public, use whichever is the most appropriate medium. Sometimes when we think about the magnitude of the challenges and opportunities that do exist in our society, we may feel we can't make a difference. One way that we, as individuals, can make a difference is by becoming a cultural ally.

Companies expect their managers to be allies in the workplace. As you become more culturally competent, you will find more and more opportunities to be a cultural ally in the society. This process means that everyone can serve as a cultural ally; and when they see unfair behaviors in groups, teams, departments, and organizations, then can eliminate it by appropriately intervening and begin to truly synergize.

To better understand the terminology of "cultural ally," let us dissect it into its individual parts and further discuss its necessity in the workplace. According to a review of its synonyms, other words that are similar to "ally" and can replace it in the same context are: friend, helper, supporter, assistant, partner, and collaborator. The antonyms of ally are: enemy, opponent, adversary, foe, and rival. Still further research shows that According to Webster's New World Dictionary[4] of the American Language, an ally is someone "joined with another for a common purpose." Being an ally on common issues is the process of working together to develop individual attitudes, institutions, and culture in which groupings of people feel they matter. The synonyms for "cultural," on the other hand, are: educational, artistic, edifying, enlightening, enriching, civilizing, literacy, and intellectual. When put together, "cultural allies" form alliances to raise public awareness that they exist, that a certain practice is unfair, and/or a certain cause should be given proper attention. Overall, "ally" *(as a noun)* refers to someone who helps and supports someone else. The term "allies" *(plural)* describes a group united in support of a common goal or shared interests. An ally is any person who is informed about sensitive issues facing people at work, in study group, and within the community. An ally affirms the experience and rights of individuals and chooses to challenge the opinions and beliefs of others, thereby bringing personal awareness and support. An ally is a person, who supports marginalized, silenced, or less privileged groups without actually being a member of those groups. This person will often directly confront and challenge systems of oppression (Queen Land University of Technology, 2006). According to some experts (such as Yeskl and Wright, 1997), "An ally is someone who speaks up or takes action against oppression that is not targeted at them." An ally builds and brokers relationships, relates and shares information, advocates justice, validates experiences, and explains acceptable norms (Nakashima and Hickman, 1995). Most allies appear to operate from a fierce personal commitment as well as a vision of what is fair and just while showing compassion. Most cultural allies share common beliefs that others value, they seek to empower others, and see others as unique human beings (Regional Educational Laboratory, 2006).

For cultural allies, there are a number of things that can be done to stop insensitive remarks and decisions from taking place at the workplace. When an individual crosses the line by saying insensitive remarks, which goes against what a persons believes, it is offensive, and should be dealt with in an

---

[4] Coauthored with Denice Ford and Macie E. Dawkins-Hanna, Nova Southeastern University – Bahamas Campus.

appropriate manner and at an appropriate time. When insensitive comments are made, an employer or employee should be told that the comment was offensive and inappropriate. When a remark is not appropriate, supervisors should be informed of such comments. If management does not know that a situation exists, it may cause the scenario to escalate, which could be troublesome for that individual and possibly many others in the department. What happens next is crucial. The manager should approach the individual to give him or her a fair opportunity to explain what happened, and also to correct this behavior in the department (Overcoming Bias in Nursing, 2006). *Sensitivity* refers to the ability to understand others, their position on the issues, as well as understanding how best to communicate with and influence them. It is necessary to be able to correctly read others' behavior so that their reactions and levels of resistance or support can be understood. When trying to influence others it is useful to be able to understand people's concerns, and to know their interests and attitudes (Civil Society Empowerment, 2006).

If managers, supervisors and other employees refuse to be participative, that is being sensitive towards all individuals, then eventually the organization will suffer the consequences for these actions. Taking action against an insensitive remark will depend on whether or not managers and supervisors are following the stated organizational policies or refuse to follow the rules of the Equal Employment Opportunity Commission (EEOC) or the guidelines and policies set by the company (Civil Society Empowerment 2006). People have a right to take action against insensitive remarks especially if it is not true, discriminatory or offensive slurs; individuals have a right to protest. An example of this is the case filed against the Wal-Mart Corporation on February 17, 2005 where the company "unintentionally" permitted a female associate (who was eventually awarded $315,000) to be sexually harassed by the store assistant manager at the same store location where two women had been involved in a 2004 suit. In that case, the assistant manager who committed the harassment, interviewed, and hired the female associate in January of 2002. Shortly thereafter, he began sexually propositioning her, subjecting her to vulgar language and unwanted sexual comments, and touching private parts of her body. Despite a complaint or warning received by the store manager regarding inappropriate sexual conduct, nothing was done to stop the inappropriate behavior until the assistant manager was transferred out of that store for unrelated reasons (EEOC Publication, 2006). Sexual harassment and other insensitive or inappropriate remarks are real in today's diverse workplaces and they can be very painful; such comments and complaints are worthy of immediate attention and action to set an example that insensitive remarks and actions will not be tolerated in the work environment. Of course, cultural allies can take immediate action by appropriately voicing their opinions and views directly to the person or his or her superiors. How one goes about creating a better work environment may depend on his or her ability to speak publicly, stand for a just cause, relationship with others in the department, level of seniority in the organization, expertise and position power, and projected response from others. The key for each cultural ally is to assess the situation and take an appropriate action toward the creation of a healthy, inclusive, and fun work environment.

There are many ways that individuals and organizations can serve as cultural allies. The Southern Poverty Law Center has created helpful material for individuals and organizations to understand tolerance and fight hate. According to the information and *"A Call to Action"* material provided by the Southern Poverty Law Center, the following are some ways to promote tolerance and fight hate:

1) One can and should speak up when hearing inappropriate statements and slurs. Let your colleagues and employees know that biased speech is unacceptable (in the workplace). Keep in mind that apathy can be as dangerous as hate.

2) Encourage yourself and others to cross "social borders." Create opportunities to interact with colleagues who are different from you with regards to the major dimensions and characteristics of diversity.

3) Demand corrective actions from law enforcement. Demand that the local law enforcement officers and agencies identify bias-motivated criminal acts as hate crimes.

4) Create awareness. You can do this by complaining to media outlets when they promote stereotypes, and biased individuals or organizations.

5) Become conscious of your own biases and stereotypes. You can do this by discussing hot topics with experts and taking reflective tests. For example, you can take a confidential test at The Hidden Bias website (www.hiddenbias.org) for your current personal reflections.

Interacting with different individuals by crossing social borders, as stated above, is one way of getting to know others, gaining more friends, and becoming culturally competent. Sometimes people have difficulty differentiating between different persons within a group of individuals who share certain common characteristics (such as skin color, ethnicity, religion, etc.). This is especially true when one is seeing another person for a very brief period without much formal or informal discussion. For example, some individuals tend to mistake one Asian person with another who might have similar height, hair, and physical features. The same might be true of a Black male among many other males who share similar characteristics, or a Hispanic female among a group of females of the same age category and other features such as similar clothing or hair styles. The reality is that all African-Americans, Asians, Arabs, Hispanics, or all White males do not look alike in all dimensions as each person has his or her own unique characteristics. The key is to seek and see those unique dimensions of each person, talk about or observe the person's unique features when appropriate, relate the details to one's mental video camera recorder by honestly learning the facts, while taking a visual photograph of his or her unique features, and by probing for details in order to make a connection with the person on a deeper level. In other words, when meeting a person for the first time, one can *Seek, Talk, Observe, and Probe* (STOP) for more information in order to connect with each new colleague or customer in the workplace. To use the STOP strategy, seek new information when speaking to a colleague or customer for the first time, talk about the person's uniqueness (i.e., origins of his or her name, culture, etc.), observe other features that you can relate or link to your experiences on a mental level, and probe for more helpful clues that will assist you remember more about this individual in the future. An important part of effectively using the STOP strategy is that you must "stop" prejudging the person and be open to learning the facts and new information. The STOP strategy can also be used to socialize with others in the community and gain more friends. It can also be used to memorize or remember people's names, hobbies and occupations. Using the STOP strategy can help you find the truth about each person, store the information for long-term retention, and become a cultural ally when he or she is being treated unfairly based on misinformation or stereotypes.

When Bahaudin (the author) was a manager in Orlando with Publix Super Markets, he noticed an actual example of being a "cultural ally" demonstrated by a District Manager (DM), Mr. Frank Hernandez at the Lake Frederica Shopping Center in Orlando, Central Florida. The district manager was walking around the store when he noticed a customer was making inappropriate and offensive racial comments to the cashier who was an African-American. The customer refused to be waited on by an African-American employee and demanded to be served by another cashier who was not Black. The District Manager intervened and told the customer loudly, clearly and unequivocally that we do not tolerate any discrimination in our company and if she is not happy with the skin color of this associate then she can take her business elsewhere. As you can imagine, that District Manager was courageous, compassionate and a true cultural ally. He did what was right decisively and without any hesitation. It is difficult to tell a customer that s/he can take his or her business elsewhere when we often preach that customers are always right. The truth of the matter is that discrimination should not be tolerated in any way, shape, or form when it is based on someone's physical characteristics, appearance or other protected categories. Managers and cultural allies should always make sure that people are treated with respect and dignity just like the fact that this District Manager made sure his employees were respected and treated in a dignified manner by everyone in the organization (including customers) regardless of the person's skin color.

There are many organizations (such as the National Multicultural Institute and the Southern Poverty Law Center) that offer practical suggestions for everyone to become cultural allies and promote tolerance in the workplace. According to the Southern Poverty Law Center (2006), among many other great suggestions, the following are some ways to promote tolerance in the workplace (see their website at "www.tolerance.org" for more information):

1) Hold a "diversity potluck" lunch or dinner. Invite co-workers to bring dishes that reflect their cultural heritage.
2) Arrange a "box-lunch forum" on topics of diverse cultural and social interest.
3) Partner with a local school and encourage your colleagues to serve as tutors or mentors.
4) Sponsor a community-wide "I Have a Dream" essay contest.
5) Examine the degree of diversity at all levels of your workplace. Are there barriers that make it harder for people of color and women to succeed? Suggest ways to overcome them.
6) Give everyone a chance for that promotion. Post all job openings.
7) Fight against the "just like me" bias — the tendency to favor those who are similar to ourselves.
8) Value the input of every employee. Reward managers who do.
9) Avoid singling out employees of a particular race or ethnicity to "handle" diversity issues on behalf of everyone else.
10) Vary your lunch partners. Seek out co-workers of different backgrounds, from different departments, and at different levels in the company.
11) Start a mentoring program that pairs veteran employees with newcomers.
12) Establish an internal procedure for employees to report incidents of harassment or discrimination. Publicize the policy widely.
13) Ensure that your workplace complies with the accessibility requirements of the Americans with Disabilities Act.
14) Push for equitable leave policies. Provide paid maternity and paternity leave.
15) Don't close your door. Foster an open working environment.
16) Provide employees with paid leave to participate in volunteer projects.
17) Publicize corporate giving widely, and challenge other companies to match or exceed your efforts.

At the individual level, the following strategies should give you some specific yet practical ways in which you can be a cultural ally in the society and your company. These are ways that you can operationalize specific techniques in your daily work environment. You are welcome to add some of your own thoughts and suggestions to this list.

Communicate with Respect:

- Intervene and stop inappropriate language, racial slurs and jokes. They should not be tolerated.
- Listen, understand, think, and consciously respond to others. Use active and empathic listening techniques to understand others' paradigms and perspectives.

- Give speakers your undivided attention. Give people the benefit of the doubt.
- Watch and control your tone of voice. "Speak softly but carry a big stick."
- Do not condemn people; when called for, condemn only their inappropriate actions as necessary.
- Use conscious thinking and think before speaking or acting.

Manage Stereotypes:
- Be aware of your own hot buttons. Become aware of your own stereotypes and gain more knowledge of how it may be affecting others.
- Don't be judgmental. Avoid stereotyping and prejudice by finding the facts and relying on facts. Don't categorize or hypothesize based on one or few individuals' behavior about others of similar culture or background.
- Become involved with, and involve those who are different from you or those who may have different perspectives than you.
- Clarify the truth. Remember, honesty doesn't mean truth because one can be both honest and wrong. Have the courage to do what is right at the right time and for the right reasons. And always think for yourself by deciding based on current facts.
- Decide based on character and competence as opposed to race, skin color, height, age, religion, or other individual differences that aren't job related. Equal opportunity for all and fairness in the process should be exercised.

Think before Speaking:
- Avoid natural tendencies by getting off of automatic pilot, and respond based on conscious thinking in a logical and rational manner.
- Seek to understand what is being said and requested before speaking your opinion.
- Evaluate your humor to make sure it adds value and does not offend anyone, before presenting it to your friends or peers.
- Think synergy and strive to reduce groupthink.

Groupthink

Groupthink has been seen as a pattern of faulty and biased decision making that occurs in groups whose members strive for agreement among themselves at the expense of accurately assessing information relevant to a decision.

Groupthink is not a desirable objective in today's diverse and very sophisticated world of intermingled competition. This usually happens in homogeneous teams and groups. Research has shown that homogeneous teams are neither as creative nor as productive as heterogeneous teams when dealing with, or solving, complex problems. As a matter-of-fact, research conducted in the past few decades has concluded that the heterogeneous team which had diversity related training to help them build stronger relationships internally were as much as six times more productive than the homogeneous team. Other researchers have concluded that the sophisticated environment of global competition requires heterogeneous teams in order to be more responsive to the volatile and changing consumer markets. Heterogeneous teams tend to work more synergistically when they have appropriate resources and proper diversity training.

Synergy

Synergy is where the whole is greater than the sum of its parts. Ultimately, synergy is the performance gains that result when individuals, teams and departments coordinate their actions toward the same goals. Synergistic teams, colleagues, peers and departments tend to function more cooperatively and productively than if they were operating in isolation.

Synergy happens when two or more individuals working together produce more than their combined efforts individually. Diversity awareness and training can help teams function harmoniously in the context of cultural differences and produce synergistic results. On the other hand, lack of diversity awareness and respect can lead to negative synergy. Negative synergy, as stated previously, is when two or more people working together produce less than what they could produce individually. This tends to happen more when people don't respect each other's differences. Negative synergy can be seen in nations where the people are not working together toward the same ends.

Summary and Reflections

Illegal discrimination practices are likely to be around in various parts of the society for many decades and centuries to come. Professionals should create a work environment that respects human beings and supports them in capitalizing their unique qualities. This chapter has pointed out the impact of discrimination and harassment. This chapter also discussed some of the common discriminatory practices, daily indignities and unearned privileges as they relate to workers in a diverse environment. Furthermore, the chapter offered the "STOP" strategy for getting to know people and concluded by encouraging teams to "think outside of the box" and work synergistically to make their place of work as productive and competitive as possible.

Discussion Questions

1. What is discrimination? Is it always illegal? Discuss and provide examples.
2. What is harassment? What is sexual harassment?
3. What is quid pro quo? What are some examples of this concept in the workplace? What should managers and employees be aware of in order to make sure everyone is treated fairly?
4. Discuss some of the employment laws that managers must be aware of when they are hiring and developing employees. Why are these laws important?
5. Have you seen, experienced or heard about any daily indignities in your lifetime? Discuss specific examples.
6. Do you have any "unearned privileges" and/or can you think of specific examples where certain individuals are enjoying them?
7. What is a cultural ally? Have you seen a cultural ally in the past few decades? Discuss.
8. Have you ever used the STOP (*Seek, Talk, Observe, and Probe*) strategy when meeting new people? If so, what was the result? Is the STOP strategy helpful? What other strategies can you use to get to know individuals when you meet them for the first time?
9. Mention two ways that managers and professionals can become cultural allies in today's workplace. In other words, how can today's managers and professionals stop unfair policies and mistreatment from occurring in the workplace? Discuss.
10. What is groupthink? Should teams and departments always avoid groupthink? Why or why not?
11. What is synergy? Discuss an example of it from your personal or professional experiences.

Technology, Gender and Appreciative Inquiry

T he workforce of the twentieth century is likely to be much more hetero-geneous than any other generation in the past. The same is true of twentieth century organizations and their need to make good use of their available human resources asset. Effective use of an organization's human resources asset and modern technology in the twenty-first century can greatly enhance learning for all workers and managers, especially those with various forms of disabilities. Along with an introduction to the concept of appreciative inquiry, this chapter presents how computer-aided instruction is one method that can be used by leaders and educators to engage students and encourage learning. In most cultures, women make up about 50% of the population; consequently, they should represent 50% of the workforce, when they are provided fair opportunities to acquire education and contribute to society. However, women make up only a small percentage of senior management positions, due to various reasons including stereotypes and the impact of glass-ceiling in the workplace.

Women in Information Technology

Despite the assumptions to the contrary, women in Information Technology (IT)[5] face similar hiring and promotional barriers as those in other fields such as business, government, law, and healthcare. According to the U.S. Department of Labor, women make up about 47% of the labor force. The percentage of women in the workforce has increased by at least 20% in the last four decades. In the mean time, there has been about a 10% decline in the male workforce. Studies also show that in education there have been similar gains as women account for about 56% of the estimated 1.14 million students getting degrees on U.S. campuses. In comparison, the number of men getting degrees has decreased. In 2003, women in the United States received 54% of all Bachelor Degrees (11% increase from 1971) and 52.5% of all Masters Degrees (12% increase from 1971). According to the U.S. National Center for Educational Statistics (2000), in 1971 women received 13.3% of the Doctorate Degrees and this number was 48.9% in 2000. Due to

---

[5] - This material comes from *Cross Cultural Change Management* book, by Llumina Press in 2006; pages 257-281; co-authored with Susan Key, Philip F. Musa, LeJon Poole, and Margarida Karahalios.

the higher level of educational attainments, female professionals are increasingly represented in the workforce. Yet, at the senior management level of corporate America, female professionals are not as well represented as their male counterparts. According to 2002 data provided in Figure 5.1, females seem to make up less than about 15% of the senior management (Catalyst, 2002).

Figure 5.1 – Female in Senior Management, 2003

In most large corporations, women hold about 10-15% of board directorships and senior management positions. While some women have attained the position of chief executive officer level, many more female professionals have achieved the ranks of lower and middle management levels. Data demonstrates that there are changes and women have a greater role in the professional world today than they did a few decades ago. In 1975 and 2003, women comprised 26% and 27% of computer programmers respectively. Overall, there wasn't much change. Research shows that the median age of these women who hold senior positions in the field of computer programming is about 30 years of age. Due to stereotypes and myths, many employers believe that being young is an advantage to learning new skills and this might be one reason for the widespread use of age discrimination.

Research shows that about 90-95% of the computer industry's senior management is male, while about 30% of lower and middle management positions are actually being held by women. With a level playing field, one would assume that the small number of women currently in senior management in the computer industry provides a unique opportunity for advancement. While the opportunities do exist, there are many other factors that prevent women from reaching these senior management positions (i.e. stereotypes, glass ceiling, societal expectations of women, childbirth, etc.). So, there seems to be many factors that affect the rise of women to senior management in Information Technology. While discrimination is certainly one variable that prevents equal opportunities for promotion and advancement to senior management, the absence of mentoring, work-family challenges, and the structure of work environments can also contribute to the lack of equality for women. While there has been progress in the representation of women across most fields, the income differentials still seem to exist. According to Key, Musa, Poole, and Karahalios, such data and "statistics are disturbing because they reflect the lack of upward mobility of women, the clustering of women in entry-level, lower paying positions across industry and the academe, and the mysterious salary gaps which appear over time between men and women of equal tenure" (Mujtaba, 2006, p. 257).

Women made a median of 73.3% of men's median wages in 2000; which means that in about 50 years women's earning power has increased about 10% in comparison to men's. In the fields of computer science and IT, women earn about 85% of what men earn at top management positions, while earning about 91% of what males earn at the entry level positions. In the United States and perhaps many other countries, the female dominated occupations tend to be lower paying without regard to a person's intellectual or experience level. For example, as stated by professors Key, Musa, Poole, and Karahalios, in the American society, the traditional female workforce, such as school teachers and nurses, require much more academic preparation but pay less than typically male-oriented jobs such as carpentry, auto repair and plumbing.

Experts have suggested that the fact that women are more closely involved in a variety of roles-- spouse, mother, parental/caretaker-- throughout most of their working careers might be one factor that explains differentials in salary and promotions between professional men and women. According to Key, Musa, Poole, and Karahalios, the factor of variety of roles along with several others help to explain why women do not reach higher level positions, and such roles are ingrained in social institutional structures. Of course, the concept and notion that the structure of institutions works to limit opportunities is not a new one. Furthermore, Key, Musa, Poole, and Karahalios state that "These are cultural biases which incorporate both the internal view that women have of themselves (self-expectations), and the external view of women (stereotyping, for example) that is held by society in general; the role of mentoring; and the levels of experience that women bring to academe and the marketplace" (Mujtaba, 2006, p. 259). Overall, professionals must do everything they can to eliminate the impact of institutional and social biases that prevent females from "climbing the ladder" of success in the workplace.

Information Technology, when applied justly and equitably, can be a key determinant in transforming the economies of developing nations as well as nations in transition thereby, ensuring their place in a global economy. As IT affects these changes, nations are also transformed socially and politically. Negotiating this transformation within cultures that have existed for thousands of years requires balancing traditional values with Westernized values which accompany IT as well as interacting in a global economy. The inclusion of women in IT appears to be one of the most controversial issues in the transformation of these nations, because this transformation appears to require women to assume more Westernized roles that may violate established cultural roles. Yet, a closer examination of the lessons learned from women in IT in Western society shows that women can effectively be included in IT and support traditional existing cultural mores. Gender needs transcend cultural needs. Lessons learned from various cultures and countries provide examples of how the integration of IT has been effectively accomplished. Each nation should proactively define educational policies that embrace the female population in IT. The result is not only a generation of women that are IT literate and positive contributors to the growth and development of one's society, but also a generation that can serve as IT intermediaries for older women to help the latter become economically empowered.

Beyond including women, each nation needs to consider including individuals with disabilities as part of their development effort. Disabilities are increasing across the globe, with some disabilities such as autism, reaching epidemic trends. Rather than including this population in the development of nations, societies across the globe, in general, seem to dismiss the potential of such individuals to positively contributing to the society. Women with disabilities are an especially marginalized group who face even greater poverty and alienation. IT, especially computer-aided instruction, has the potential to remediate or mitigate the symptoms of disabilities. In doing so, it has the potential to train individuals with disabilities to perform skills that can be part of the reconstruction process for which they are most appropriately suited.

A characteristic of individuals with autism, for example, is that they like routines. As such, they are perfectly suited for repetitive work, whereas the typical population would become bored and not wish to perform such work. This section focuses on autism as a specific disability example because it is one of the most pervasive developmental disabilities. It affects every aspect of a person's life and does so throughout a lifetime. All this is provided in the context of American education as it delivers decades of lessons learned. Interestingly, it also shows, how across the globe, people face the same issues and challenges when attempting to integrate women and individuals with disabilities in education, specifically IT education, and society. We have a long way to go towards full inclusion of all populations within our societies, economies, and politics. IT can serve as a vehicle for accomplishing these goals, and each country can become a participant in the effort to do so.

Gender Disability and Technology

Autism is one of many disabilities impacting thousands of young children each year. The American Broadcasting Corporation (ABC) presented some new information on their World News Report on May 04, 2006, about the fact that autism might be more widespread than currently known. New research shows that four to six children out of every one thousand kids are likely to have the autism disability to some extent. They also acknowledged that it might be impacting more children than currently known since the symptoms are not easily known. Some children are mildly affected by autism and others might have an extreme case of it. While there is no cure for autism at this time, its early detection can get experts and parents to help children with certain behavioral patterns to assist them in effectively functioning in the education and work environments. ABC News stated that autism is more prevalent in boys than in girls. According to Professor Margarida Karahalios, autism is a neurobiological syndrome—a collection of characteristics—with heterogeneous and impaired behavioral expressions in three interrelated areas: (a) social interaction, (b) communication, and (c) activities and interests that result in disordered development. The fundamental basis for the success of computer aids in helping individuals with autism seems to rely on a complementarity of worlds: the world of the computer and the world of the individual with autism appear to be complementary. The world of the computer either shares the same characteristics as the world of the person with autism or satisfies some of the same needs. The world of the computer is objective, two-dimensional, lacking in social contact and cues, non-threatening, logical, repetitive, consistent, predictable, focused, infinitely patient, filled with an extraordinary depth and breadth of visuo-spatial cues, and requiring sensorimotor interaction. Furthermore, the computer world affords the individual with autism total control; the user determines when and how to interact with the computer. The computer world seems to mirror and complete the solitary world of the person with autism. The computer and the individual with autism seem to speak the same language.

Educational programs for learners with autism must be systematically developed to (a) be engaging and to provide, (b) be explicit in instruction, (c) be organized in manageable chunks of information, and (d) explicitly show the connections between the chunks of information to create a gestalt. Insofar as a large portion of learners with autism are visual learners, this information must also (e) be presented in visual form. Furthermore, since learners with autism require (f) intensive, (g) repetitive, and (h) individually paced intervention, the format of the educational program must meet these needs. Essentially, professor Karahalios claims, learners with autism require a well-designed explicit, structured, intensive, consistent, individually-paced instructional program. Interestingly, these are the same requirements for any population group—women, men, rich, poor—wishing to learn new skills, especially ones with low literacy.

Communicative and social deficits are at the core of the diagnosis and treatment of autism. Various factors such as attention and motivational deficits, stereotypic behaviors, resistance to change, and language delays impede the development of individuals with autism. Computer-aided instruction (CAI) appears as a viable tool to provide this type of education. It can be used to engage students in learning, increase attention and motivation, encourage language development, and effect positive behavioral changes (Panyan, 1984). Since their first use in the 1970's, computers have been seen as useful tools in attempting to overcome communicative and social deficits of individuals with autism: "Increasingly sophisticated computer technology can meet the needs of children with disabilities in ways that were only dreams until the advent of personal computers" (Hutinger, 1996, p. 105).

The promise of computers to help individuals with autism is, however, being compromised. Regardless of the reason for computer use; e.g. educational, social, or rehabilitative, the format of the interaction is generally based on an inherently male gender-based play motif. Since play is increasingly gender-differentiated as children grow, computer software seems to increasingly discriminate against the needs and wants of female children and, thereby, alienates them. As such, children of the female gender, including those with autism, are deprived of optimal opportunities to overcome the symptoms of their disorders as well as opportunities for potential skill development that could result in greater empowerment and autonomy. The female population with disabilities is subjected to double discrimination: sexism and disability bias.

Eradicating Gender and Disability Bias

In 1972, the U.S. Department of Education passed Title IX as an effort to reform gender inequality in schools. This amendment required that 'no person in the U.S. shall, on the basis of sex be excluded from participation in, or denied the benefits of, or be subjected to discrimination under any program or benefits of, or be subjected to discrimination under any program or activity receiving federal aid'. The following year, 1973, Section 504 of the Rehabilitation Act made it illegal to discriminate against anyone with disabilities seeking employment with federal contractors and grantees. In 1975, the Individuals with Disabilities Education Act (IDEA) mandated that all children with disabilities be educated in a least restrictive environment—placing them in regular classrooms as much as possible. In 1980, the Science and Engineering Equal Opportunities Act was passed. This legislation proclaimed that:

> It is the policy of the United States to encourage men and women, equally, of all ethnic, racial, and economic backgrounds to acquire skills in science, engineering and mathematics, to have equal opportunity in education, training, and employment in scientific and engineering fields, and thereby to promote scientific and engineering literacy and the full use of the human resources of the Nation in science and engineering (SEEOA, 1980).

As recent as 1990, The Americans with Disabilities Act (ADA) was passed to ensure equal opportunities to individuals with disabilities in the areas of employment, public accommodations, state and local government, transportation, and telecommunications. Regardless of all this legislation, states professor Karahalios, gender bias and disability bias still persist—in society, at large, as well as the educational system, in particular. Insofar as technology integration has been emphasized in K-12 in the last decade, these biases have materialized in a technology gender gap and gender bias. The "Title IX at 30: Report Card on Gender Equity" which reviews the progress we have made in gender equity in the thirty years after the passage of Title IX, reveals the different marks in different areas of gender equity, with technology and career education being the worst offenders (NCWGE, 2002).

Considering that gender and disability bias are acknowledged and that the federal government has passed legislation to address these biases, then why do these biases persist? Studies explore how and why females are discriminated and alienated by the computer field as well as what steps we can take to reverse this discrimination and alienation in the hope of providing fair access to what appears to be a promising tool for ameliorating the symptoms of disabilities as well as providing empowering, self-management opportunities.

Gendered Play and Preferences

Psychologists have defined four genders: male, female, undifferentiated, and androgynous. Each gender shares certain stereotypic characteristics. The male gender is defined by such characteristics as analytical and aggression. The female gender is defined as nurturing and emotional. The undifferentiated gender possesses few male or female stereotypic characteristics while the androgynous gender possesses some of both. Koch writes that "Although men and women can display characteristics of any of these four genders, in our society women are socialized to be of the female gender" (1994, p. 14). Research indicates that this socialization has the greatest impact on children's play preferences, learning abilities, and temperament; we teach children how to "act" like girls and boys.

The primary differences between the gendered play of boys and girls appear to be based on the genders' interactions with their environment, each gender's self-image, and society's gendered expectations. Boys are more aggressive than girls; they play competitively. Girls play cooperatively. Boys are more concerned with justice, following the rules, competition, autonomy, objectivity, and control. Generally, as stated by researchers, boys are not expected to become involved with people, but to be involved with things. Girls tend to follow a care approach where they are concerned with being fair, being supportive, nurturing, working together, being emotive, as well as using their intuition and personal experience. They like to work together collaboratively and cooperatively. They are socialized to be less aggressive and assertive. Young boys often choose to spend their "free time" running around, exploring, and experimenting, and these activities help them prepare for the world of science and mathematics. Young girls are not specifically encouraged to participate in these "boy" activities, and are more often encouraged to "be careful." When boys and girls play together, boys' play preferences tend to prevail. In a study, both males and females performed roughly equally in math. However, self-perceptions of skill and competence differed. Twenty-two percent of the boys and only 14 percent of the girls strongly agreed with the statement, "I am very good at mathematics." This self-image reinforces for girls that they do not belong in the "boys" domain. Young children tend to choose colors, toys, and activities that they feel are meant for their sex, and like to play with other children of the same sex. Children get approval from their peers when their play is appropriate to their sex. Those who play in cross-sexed activities tend to be criticized by their peers or are left to play alone.

Solutions and Recommendations

Numerous studies over the past several decades have attempted to understand the gender and technology gap. In addition to providing reasons for this gap, these studies also attempt to recommend strategies that we might use to minimize, if not eliminate, the gender technology gap. Professor Karahalios claims that a starting place is to acknowledge and accept that girls and boys are different. Get training in equity fair practices, and then develop strategic differentiation of educational practice based on such differences:

⇒ Girls' cognitive learning style is based on focusing on the task at hand, screening out irrelevancies, carrying out the tasks, solving problems under stress, and being proficient in motor skill activities. Boys' cognitive learning style is based on curiosity and risk taking.

⇒ In group settings, girls collaborate more; compete less. In general, girls respond better to collaborative projects rather than competitive projects; encourage collaborations and be alert to boys dominating the group.

⇒ Girls like to see what computers can do for them. They see computers more as a tool and less as a toy; create purposeful activities on the computer. Boys like to tinker, but girls like a purpose. For girls, it is important to encourage the use of computers as a tool: recommend girls to type their papers on the computer, show them how to write web pages, or teach them how to make a graph using a spreadsheet.

It is also a good idea to provide female role models at home. Female parents need to play with their girls and be seen using technology in fun ways as well as with work. Parents who do not have a computer can visit places such as local libraries and internet cafes where they are available. Girls who have parental support are more likely to continue developing their technology skills during school years. Another suggestion is to expose girls to technology as early as possible. For example, one can place the computer in a central location so that all family members can have equal access to the computer. Ensure that all family members have equal computer usage time.

Educators can encourage computer use across the curriculum and for a variety of purposes (research, design, and word processing) rather than integrating computers in traditionally male subjects, such as mathematics and science. School professionals can also physically locate computers in neutral areas, instead of predominantly male dominated locations.

Appreciative Inquiry and Empowerment[6]

Information Technology professionals and leaders in all fields facing gender challenges and opportunities need to discover new methods of establishing empowerment for attracting, developing and retaining more female employees. This section focuses on the application of Appreciative Inquiry as a unique approach for understanding the methodology of empowering professionals and managers to do more toward bringing about positive change in their departments and organizations. The section uses a positive language philosophy referred to as *appreciative inquiry*, which influences positive change in the areas of involvement, consistency, and mission within the area of empowerment.

Appreciative Inquiry can serve as the basis for formal transformation and cultural change toward better and fairer employment practices within any organization. Once it is apparent to all individuals that change is needed, a formal tool such as appreciative inquiry can be very effective to bring about the needed changes. *Appreciative Inquiry* (AI) is an organizational transformation tool that focuses on learning from past and current successes as opposed to focusing on deficits and problems. According to Cooperrider and Whitney (2005), "Appreciative inquiry is the cooperative, coevolutionary search for the best in people, their organizations, and the world around them" (p. 8). Cooperrider and Whitney further write that AI "involves systematic discovery of what gives life to an organization or a community when it is most effective and most capable in economic, ecological, and human terms." Using AI, managers can begin the change process with a rigorous, "organization-wide" search, discovery and analysis of the "positive core" or the root cause of success analysis (Cooperrider and Whitney, 2005). Cooperrider and Whitney define positive change as "Any form of organization change, redesign, or planning that begins with a comprehensive inquiry, analysis, dialogue of an organization's positive core, that involves multiple stakeholders, and then links this knowledge to the organization's strategic change agenda and priorities" (2005, p. 12). Through the making of simple managerial changes, sharing of information with more employees, and inviting employees to participate in the affairs of the organization, companies can be transformed (Cooperrider and Whitney, 2005). The Appreciative Inquiry strategy focuses

---

[6] The remaining topics in this chapter are co-authored with Larry James Lelah, University of Phoenix.

on discovering what works well, why it works well, and how success can be extended throughout the organization to further encourage change initiatives toward the vision. It is both the vision, and the process for developing this vision, that creates the needed energy to drive change throughout the organization (Johnson & Leavitt, 2001). Appreciative inquiry can be seen as a systematic discovery of what gives "life" to a living system when it is most alive, most effective and most constructively capable, in economic, ecological, and human terms. Appreciative inquiry involves, in a central way, the Socratic strategy and practice of asking the right questions that strengthen a system's capacity to comprehend, anticipate and heighten positive potential (Carr-Stewart & Walker, 2003).

Appreciative inquiry from the perspective of an educational institution is best understood as a strategy for initiating micro-level reform within a single institution; reform that is both affective and analytical. The process would reconnect teachers and administrators to their passion for teaching and to their sense of mission; for students the process can enhance school pride and foster recognition of the bonds that students have with peers and teachers alike. Moreover, AI's approach counteracts exclusive preoccupation with problems that all too often de-energize teachers, staff, and sometimes administrators themselves at educational institutions (Ryan et al., 1999). According to researchers, AI is about appreciating and valuing the best of what is, envisioning what might be, dialoguing what should be, and assuming that an organization is a mystery to be embraced (Cooperrider and Whitney, 2005, p. 13). Cooperrider and Whitney state that the AI process has four phases which include: discovery, dream, design, and destiny:

⇒ *Discovery* emphasizes the mobilization of the entire system by engaging all relevant stakeholders in the articulation of the department or firms' strengths, core competencies, and best practices.
⇒ *Dream* requires the creation of a clear result-oriented vision and purpose. This image of the future can and should guide everyone's behavior in the organization.
⇒ *Design* stage mandates that managers and the organization create "possibility propositions of the ideal organization." It should provide a roadmap that people can follow for realizing the dream.
⇒ *Destiny* involves the strengthening of the affirmative capability of the entire system, in the hopes of enabling it to sustain momentum for ongoing productive change and higher performance (2005, p. 16).

Economic, managerial, and social changes are influencing organizations to use alternative approaches to foster organizational excellence. Appreciative inquiry, as a positive-language process, continues to gain popularity as a focal point for social constructionism because the principle relates to organizational change and maturity (Van der Harr & Hosking, 2004). The inception of appreciative inquiry took place in the early 1980s. At that time, a young doctoral student, David Cooperrider, was studying organizational behavior at Case Western Reserve University. While working with his mentor, Suresh Srivastva, Cooperrider was involved in a project that addressed organizational change, and he noticed a correlation between the influences of specific organizational behaviors and positive inquiry. He named the germinal phenomenon that he noticed "appreciative inquiry." The positive dialogue of appreciative inquiry posits that issues experienced by organizations do not necessarily have to be addressed from a negative position. Cooperrider et al. (2001) suggested that organizations would benefit by seeking to resolve issues from a positive perspective.

The appreciative inquiry approach suggests that inquiries should be conducted with a positive mindset. This approach can help create new ideas and images and encourage empowerment for the future, thus enabling managers to achieve new levels of customer satisfaction. The methodology associated with appreciative inquiry also enables the application of positive thinking in order to create new patterns and innovative ways for managing change and improving business results. The objective of appreciative inquiry is not to eliminate the discussion of problems, but rather to avoid expending the unproductive energy and thought associated with the deficit-based approach to resolving issues (Whitney & Trosten-Bloom, 2003). Issues and problems are typically approached from a problem-solving viewpoint. The focus and emphasis of appreciative inquiry was placed on positive change and on the hopes and desires of better things to come. The application of appreciative inquiry engages individuals in a process of uncovering and overcoming self-limiting assumptions (Watkins & Mohr, 2001).

When used to determine strategies for the organization, appreciative inquiry proponents have suggested numerous designs for creating positive change (Easley & Alvarez-Pompilius, 2004). Some of these designs include using positive dialogue to describe a specific situation or problem, encouraging imagination and creativity, and communicating the benefits associated with the future to others (Cooperrider et al., 2003). Some representative skills that can be improved and enhanced using the philosophical underpinnings of appreciative inquiry include communications, personal/professional coaching, team-building, and leadership development (Whitworth, Kimsey-House, & Sandahl, 1998). During the application of appreciative inquiry, the leadership team, organization, and research participants are required to participate in developing positive change and initiatives (Watkins & Mohr, 2001). The future is explored and related to the present by examining and highlighting situations in which the desired future is discussed (Fitzgerald et al., 2003). Positive communications can encourage positive behavior. More specifically, in an organizational setting, the theory of facilitative leadership suggests that a leader's positive vision and purpose can result in innovation and the creation of an environment of empowered employees. For example, positive communications resulted in increased productivity and innovative flexibility (Pullen, 2001). These results are supportive of the facilitative leadership theory because innovative problem-solving can create self-worth and stimulate empowerment when developing strategies (Berne & Raviv, 2004).

Schein (1999), a well-known organizational developmental expert on process consultation, discussed the concept of dialogue extensively and believed dialogue to be a major component of the entire communication process that takes place during a change event. He differentiated communication that is information sharing from the more complex and highly variable communication which he termed dialogue. According to Schein (1997), problem-solving groups need to begin with a dialogue format in order to facilitate the building of sufficient common ground and mutual trust and to make it possible to determine what someone is really thinking. Cooperrider and Srivastva (2003) suggested that most corporations possess the resources necessary for promoting employee interaction, performing value-added work, and achieving hoped-for results—all of which can be used as benchmarks for enhancing the culture of an organization. The awareness of best-in-class performance and of positive change provide a vision of what is achievable by the employees participating in the determining of such initiatives. The five principles that provide the theoretical basis, which supports appreciative inquiry are: constructionist, simultaneity, poetic, anticipatory, and positiveness (Watkins & Mohr, 2001).

Constructionist Principle

Appreciative inquiry suggests that perception and reality are constructed through dialogue and the examination and study of patterns of thought (Whitney & Trosten-Bloom, 2003). Individuals' decisions are relevant to their abilities to interpret reality. This understanding is determined by past experiences, traditional values, and the intellect (Walker & Carr-Stewart, 2004). What people believe about the reality of an organization will affect their behavior and approaches for creating change in a system (Watkins & Mohr, 2001). The methodologies, theories, and paradigms accepted by individuals in the interpretation of their experiences play a significant role in influencing how the reality of those experiences is perceived (Fitzgerald et al., 2003).

In contrast, reductionism minimizes the complexity of the organization because the desired outcome is one of efficiency (Wrigley, 2004). Reductionism adopts a cause-and-effect view as opposed to a systems view. The objective is to minimize waste and expend the least amount of effort. Appreciative inquiry, in contrast, employs a systems-focused or more holistic view (Checkland, 1999). According to Checkland, the perspective of Descartes suggested that Western civilization approaches complexity in the traditional manner of breaking up the parts and analyzing each individually. This approach, however, is not the most effective way of coping with organizational challenges (Hueth, 2004). Conversely, systems thinking deconstructs Descartes' approach by questioning the principle of the component parts of the entire being remaining the same when separated (Midgley, 2004). The systems-thinking perspective addresses the framework that contains the parts itself, the related parts, and how the framework and parts work together as a whole (Best et al., 2003). The constructionist principle is similar to the philosophy of appreciative inquiry, whereas reductionism is a model that focuses on the parts and as such, does not lend itself to the appreciative inquiry view.

Simultaneity Principle

Whether an inquiry is approached positively or negatively will affect the outcome of that inquiry and the actions of individuals involved (Cooperrider et al., 2003). According to Mohr and Watkins (2002), inquiry is a process within which the types of questions individuals ask determine the area of change that is affected. Using positive inquiry, the nature of the language employed could convert an experience of deficiency and hopelessness to one of hopefulness and possibilities (Fitzgerald et al., 2003). Pullen (2001) noted that when participants shared stories about the extraordinary experiences from which they had benefited, they began to change their thought patterns by focusing on positive and innovative approaches when addressing issues and interacting with others, taking on new responsibilities and roles, and dreaming about new and more positive patterns in their interactions with others. Moreover, positive energy was focused on creative problem solving. The simultaneity principle enables the expansion of ideas when thinking about the possibilities and creatively imagining what could be (Cooperrider et al., 2003).

Poetic Principle

From a social constructionist perspective, organizations develop power and energy through the use of metaphors (Ricketts & Seiling, 2003). Mohr and Watkins (2002) arrived at the conclusion that in the life of an organization, many ways exist with which humans think and interact, all of which are subject to numerous interpretations. Case studies were analyzed in order to find support for the notion that constructing a positive and hopeful view of the organization and its future lead to increased productivity and boosted morale (Fry et al., 2002). It was discovered that corporate cultures that bred effective organizational leaders had a direct influence on how employees viewed their organizations (Miller et al., 2002).

Anticipatory Principle

The anticipation of a desirable future reinforces the theory that positive images of the future are generated by an individual's perception of self-fulfillment (Cooperrider et al., 2001). This review included broad studies, such as those that examined the placebo effect, the Pygmalion effect, learned helpfulness, and inner speech (Watkins & Mohr, 2001). Similar to the approach of appreciative inquiry, the placebo effect posits that the projected imagery of positive beliefs results in a healing response that can be as significant as traditional methods (Cooperrider et al., 2003). The Pygmalion effect comes into play the moment an individual is born and exists within each individual as a myriad of images and associated expectations of others, all of which are influenced by the environments in which the individual lives (White & Locke, 2000). Learned helpfulness and inner-speech also suggest that a positive thought process enhances self-learning and creates a dialogue that can lead to enhanced employee empowerment (Cooperrider et al.).

Positiveness Principle

Past initiatives associated with bringing about organizational culture change were, for the most part, focused on an organization's being deficient and in crisis (Schein, 1999). Resistance to change, according to Senge (1990), was manifested when individuals lacked confidence in their abilities to perform their jobs and were unwilling or unable to learn from one another. In the application of appreciative inquiry, participants are identified as high-level performers who are able to create a desired and inspirational vision of what the organization could become, thus enabling known best practices to continue (Mohr & Watkins, 2002).

A positive, optimistic individual with a perceived sense of ability and confidence has a greater sense of self-efficacy, is more adaptable and more resistant to stress and burnout, and applies greater effort in resolving issues (English, Fenwick & Parsons, 2003). According to the positiveness principle, individuals are more productive when they are inspired by positive images, exercise inspirational concepts, and undergo positive and self-beneficial changes (Fitzgerald et al., 2003). When individuals focus on their best past experiences, they can take what they have learned and apply that learning in developing their perceptions of a more hopeful future (Mohr & Watkins, 2002).

Appreciative inquiry has been implemented with teams of various sizes. Because of the specific planning required, appreciative inquiry is unique to a specific group and area of targeted improvement (Cooperrider & Srivastva, 2003). During its application, peak experiences are uncovered, best-in-class practices are explored, and a commitment to put these practices into place is focused upon. Extensive dialogue produces insights, thus enabling employees to share positive experiences and formulate a positive future. This sharing results in quality solutions being implemented (Whitney & Trosten-Bloom, 2003).

The questions posed in an appreciative inquiry intervention will assist in the definition and discovery phase of implementing quality solutions (Mohr & Watkins, 2002). Cooperrider and Srivastva (2003) contended that organizational culture was derived from focusing on the positive characteristics of the topic being addressed in the intervention and that the nature of the inquiry and dialogue would determine the outcomes of the change initiative. The implications for developing interventions could include items such as maintaining an ideal culture that would continue to support the implementation of quality solutions and lead to the generation of positive thought (Mohr & Watkins, 2002).

Appreciative inquiry topics can be generated from multiple sources, including interviews, research, and informally talking with people within an organization. Appreciative inquiry facilitation is crafted within a positive framework and focuses on all positive areas associated with the topic of choice. The process is generally administered by facilitators who are trained and experienced in appreciative inquiry (Watkins & Mohr, 2001). In addition to appreciative inquiry focusing on high or positive moments and the power of positive imagery, the dialogue associated with implementing quality solutions is important (Mohr & Watkins, 2002).

Dialogue Principle

Communities of people within organizations can be described as independent social systems (Sawicki, 2002). Within these communities, people share, articulate, interpret, and respond to thoughts that have been articulated (Campbell, 2000). Such communities communicate beliefs and values which are characterized by dialogue. If this dialogue is positive, the dialogue can lead to building strong and effective teams, thus creating enrichment and empowerment among individuals (Cavanaugh, 2001).

Maccoby (1996) suggested that dialogue could be used as a catalyst for accelerating change within an organization. The dialogue he referred to was different from traditional corporate language which may be described as one-way and directive. Interactive dialogue is considered to be harmonious in nature and is dialogue in which individuals seek congruence and alignment with one another. Maccoby's thinking included the notion that individuals who engaged in interactive dialogue trusted one another and had mutual respect for each other.

The principles of appreciative inquiry further define the effects of positive dialogue. These principles describe appreciative inquiry as the valuing of the act of identifying the best in people and affirming past and present strengths, successes, and potentials that bring about health, vitality, and excellence in living systems. In other words, appreciative inquiry supports the age-old Taoist principle of nourishing the good in people and systems (Grilley, 2003). The appreciative inquiry approach uses interactive dialogue and builds a "constructive bridge" between and among members of the organization, with an emphasis on the achievements, potentials, innovations, strengths, and visions of the valued and possible futures.

Gergen (2003), an authority on social construction, pointed out that peoples' conversations revealed their personal biases. He posited that, in order to overcome these biases, researchers needed to take a *bottom-up* rather than a *top-down* approach to a problem. Gergen suggested that with *bottom-up* approach, executive management levels establish the guidelines for interactive positive dialogue. Although he preferred to use interactive dialogue in a world that was socially constructed, Gergen acknowledged that he often found the dialogue difficult to manage. He suggested that the application of interactive, positive dialogue was worth the effort however. The ability to manage this form of communication would have a positive influence on the relationships and understandings of members of an organization. Another theory suggested that appreciative inquiry was similar to social constructionist. This theory of Shelton's and Darling's (2004) was based on the assumption that change occurred in a more effective and efficient manner when managers were focused on areas that were going well versus focusing on problems and issues.

A different view of appreciative inquiry dialogue suggests that the dialogue can be used for acquiring knowledge in order to resolve issues within a team environment. An organization's processes and performance may be able to provide ways for improvement through the use of strategic and positive dialogue (Topping, Campbell, Douglas, & Smith, 2003). Thinking of possibilities leads to dynamic change in organizational culture and processes (Kruppa & Meda, 2005). Similarly, appreciative inquiry has been used to overcome apprehension and fear regarding change through offering intelligent and insightful assumptions (Walker, 2005). Overcoming the fear of change can empower employees to face change and raise their confidence levels (Lee, 2001).

In contrast, another viewpoint suggests that some autocratic leadership styles promote a sense of entitlement, and that leaders make all the key decisions, thus making themselves accountable for the change that is implemented. Rather than teamwork at lower levels in order to make decisions, such leadership does not promote empowerment. This viewpoint also suggests that the higher levels of management and trickle can drive delegation and communication downward. The elimination of such autocratic leadership hierarchies is thought to reduce this type of behavior by promoting a positive and empowered culture (Harder, Robertson, & Woodward, 2004). Such thinking about leadership suggests that there are numerous approaches to accomplishing behavioral change (Kerfoot, 2004). One example is using dialogue as a tool for affecting behavior. If each employee shares a story that is positive, the ensuing dialogue can enhance personal and team growth. As a result of this positive dialogue, teams can begin to focus on the positive aspects of their jobs (Blair, 2003).

Leadership

A fundamental aspect of culture is leadership. Leaders are those people who have the ability to create, destroy, or modify cultures by applying the skills they possess (O'Toole, 1996). Schein's (1997) view regarding leadership suggests that leaders play a significant role in creating and establishing the culture of an organization, thus paving the way for change. Examples of how leadership can influence culture include empowerment, innovation, insight, entrepreneurship, dignity, and positive communications (Sankar, 2003).

Dimensions within the framework of leadership include providing employees with a clear sense of direction as well as goals and objectives and the resources necessary to perform the job. The net result of effective leadership can include the successful leveraging of skills and resources of an organizational team for demonstrating high levels of client satisfaction and, ultimately, promoting empowerment and enhancing corporate culture (Ahn et al., 2004).

From the 1980's to the present, the prevailing leadership models and theories were born out of what has been called the *new leadership approach*. A common theme permeating the new view of leadership included viewing "leaders as managers of meaning rather than in terms of an influence process" (Clegg et al., 2002, p. 280). It is important to note that post-modernism and the tenets of the emerging post-industrial paradigm influenced this leadership approach.

Organizational theories also contributed to leadership development. These theories attempted to explain the ingredients involved in effective leadership and in some cases, strove to study the emergence of leadership over a given span of time. With these theories having been applied, there has been some criticism of scholars that has emerged with respect to the weaknesses of such theories and the potential consequences involved with their application. The challenge is to understand the facts without distorting the truth. Bass (1990) supported this observation by stating, "Unfortunately, leadership theories sometimes obscure the facts" (p. 37). To address this theoretical viewpoint, further investigation is needed with closer attention being given to determining the applicability, relevance, and appropriateness of today's emerging leadership paradigm to diverse cultures and work environments.

Appreciative inquiry is designed by leadership to articulate and build on what is currently viewed as effective or exceptional within the organization. This can result in establishing a focus on appreciating and exploring pathways leading to greater efficiencies. Appreciative inquiry has seen many derivations because it has become more widely researched by scholars and more often used by practitioners. Practitioners of appreciative inquiry posit that issues within organizations should not be approached from a negative standpoint, but rather organizations should seek to reaffirm, from an appreciative and positive perspective, what is best (Dixon, 1996).

Empowerment

Empowered employees can do a better job of satisfying client needs. This is especially important for large technological and telecommunications firms because of the rapid technological advancements that occur within the technological and telecommunications fields. The theoretical lenses of appreciative inquiry can be applied within such organizations in order to enhance empowerment, thus enabling a strengthened culture for the organization. The result-ing positive culture would foster leadership that establishes a structure that brings about positive change and produces significant competitive advantages (Golembiewski, 1999). The process is cyclical; and empowerment may be helpful for complementing the methodologies that support appreciative in-quiry. Within an organization, the identification, dependence, and empowerment provided by a leader are often attributed to transformational or charismatic leadership (Campbell, 2000). Campbell's viewpoint suggested that leading in this manner would result in self-acknowledgement and growth, and the empowerment of self and others (Kark et al., 2003).

Literature regarding empowerment has emerged over the past 20 years within a large number of disciplines and professions because of enlightened corporate visions (Gragnolati & Stupak, 2002). The study of empowerment may provide a common base for understanding and analyzing the current cor-porate culture at Company Z. The theoretical framework surrounding empowerment is based on prior knowledge and experience with creating a culture that fosters change (Kark et al., 2003). One theory of empowerment suggests that empowerment assists with job redesign and changes in corporate culture. A key element in positive corporate change is the continued motiva-tion of the workforce through empowerment (Peccei & Rosenthal, 2001).

Another empowerment theory addresses the forces of discrimination and oppression as they impact individuals and groups. Problems arise because of society's failure to meet the needs of all its members. Empowerment refers to an individual's and group's ability to access and control resources and people (Gruss, McCann, Edelman, & Farran, 2004). Empowerment requires develop-ing a critical awareness of the forces of discrimination and oppression and engaging in effective action that is led by management practices (Speer, 2000). This can also lead to a heightened awareness of oneself. Further ex-amination of empowerment in the self-assessment process describes how one person's self-assessment can contribute to the good of the entire organization (Ahmed, Yang, & Dale, 2003). This awareness will result in a personal sense of power and self-efficacy that will ultimately contribute to the organization (Yoon, 2001). Another theory suggests that organizations with self-efficacy and team-oriented employees play an important role in the relationship be-tween empowerment and outcomes, such as team commitment and performance (Fetterman, 2002).

The meaning of power in empowerment practice also needs to be clarified in terms of a team environment. The ability to exercise power is not the same as having power. Team empowerment suggests that power can be exercised to assist the common good (Rough, 2002). The exercise of power can take place in an organization and in a team environment (Campbell, 2000). An organiza-tion that fosters empowerment enables the allocation of power to change the environment (Yoon, 2001). Denison (2000) posited that the key factors that affect organizational change are involvement, consistency, adaptability, and sense of mission.

Involvement, Consistency, Adaptability, and Mission

One theory that can be particularly helpful for understanding empowerment suggests that employees who perceive that strategic planning is taking place experience a higher level of satisfaction (Kim, 2002). Empowerment can drive positive attitudes regarding work and can reverse negative attitudes, resulting in employees becoming involved more deeply in their work. Involvement can create a sense of ownership and responsibility within an organization. From this sense of responsibility, individuals can make better decisions and better implement corporate initiatives. Involvement traits are closely related to empowerment, team orientation, and capability development (Lashley, 2000). Involvement can be accomplished by establishing a work environment that provides knowledge transfer and the opportunity to learn and which enables employees to accomplish tasks (Laschinger, Finegan, & Shamian, 2001). Employees tend to respond positively to factors such as responsibility to self and team, intrinsic rewards, and a sense of self-fulfillment. These areas, therefore, contribute to employees' ability to perform a better job and maintain a positive focus in conjunction with their work. It was found that focusing on items such as corporate policies and standard operating procedures lead employees to have negative attitudes and be less productive (Laschinger et al., 2001).

To create consistency within the workplace, leadership theory suggests that, in general, a mid-level manager will be more effective in motivating subordinates by addressing the quality of the work experience itself. A manager can accomplish consistency in several ways. One example is that of a manager empowering and encouraging a teaming environment by using people's unique contributions in order to motivate and stimulate other people (Buckingham, 2005). Consistency can create a highly productive culture based on values and beliefs within a corporate system. This area of empowerment enables employees to feel empowered to react in predictable ways, thus enabling consistency within an organization. Consistency traits are closely related to coordination, integration, agreement, and core values (Lamsa & Savolainen, 2000).

In contrast to the internal leadership theory, external leadership can result in the empowering of service employees on behalf of the customers they serve. This is an example of corporate adaptability in relation to both employees and clients (Chebat & Kollias, 2000). Focus, perception, and the ability to establish a set of behaviors conducive to an organizational environment are essential for delivering high levels of service and focus on building competitive advantage. Adaptability traits are also closely related to creating change, customer focus, and organizational learning. Adaptability creates a motivated and positive experience for the organization and its customers. Both employees and customers can share in creativity and positive thinking and can experience a cohesive relationship (Welford, 2002). The positive energy created in the relationship will contribute to employees appreciating each other's roles and responsibilities (Sumner, 2004). In addition, this theory suggests that due to this relationship, a basic self-awareness is created, and both parties are able to operate at more sophisticated levels (Buckingham, 2005).

From this awareness, tools that incite with the enhancing of the relationship between managers and customers are created in order to assist with accomplishing an organization's mission. For example, a customer survey that is customized solely to enhance a relationship with a customer creates a tool that contains meaningful data for each party. The survey communicates and highlights significant areas of business that are meaningful and can assist in generating positive dialogue (Peak & Sinclair, 2002). An organization's mission can define roles, responsibilities, and corporate goals. When a mission is established, empowerment can exist because a desired state for the future can be established and communicated to all employees. Mission traits are closely related to empowerment, team orientation, and capability development (Jones, Dixon & Umoja, 2003). Due to the relationship between empowerment and involvement, consistency, adaptability, and mission, this link strengthens internal management relationships and also external client relationships.

Culture

The culture of an organization fosters commitment and creates the basis on which individuals operate. In essence, personal values reflect the core makeup of individuals within the organization. Schein (1997) posited that cultural assumptions are closely related to value-based people and speak to their humanness. Denison (1996) used Schein's definition of culture as the basis for the Denison Organizational Culture Model (Denison, 2000), which was used as the research measurement instrument.

Schein (1997) provided a complex model for diagnosing culture and analyzing the values and assumptions of an organization. The importance of his model involves understanding the dynamics of organizational culture. In the empowering of employees, a link to financial performance exists, both internally and externally (Goldstein, 2003). Goldstein described the importance of employee development for managing service environments when high-dollar amounts are associated with contracts. Organizational culture and leadership are instrumental in creating a positive business environment.

Many theorists have used various cultural and diagnostic instruments to analyze the cultures of organizations in order to uncover the important features of those cultures and in order to determine cultural strengths and weaknesses in organizations. Organizational culture is a very complex phenomenon; and thus leaders must strive to understand it and ensure that it aligns harmoniously with their organizational structures (Applebaum et al., 2004).

Angoujard (2005) suggested that leaders focus their energies on such areas as behavior and attitude, because leaders would have the greatest influence in exceeding clients' expectations. As organizations continue to reduce expenses and implement downsizing, such actions pollute the workplace environment by negatively affecting all employees. The in-depth analysis of culture plays an important role in understanding how organizations adapt to change. An important assumption with respect to acknowledging this understanding is that a company will have the ability to explore tacit and explicit knowledge but needs the objectivity of outside assistance, such as that provided by consultants (Nonaka & Nishiguchi, 2001).

Technology

Technology is viewed as a tool within the context of Vogl's (2004) leadership philosophy. People in an organization choose the technologies that enable them to meet and exceed customer needs. Vogl's leadership philosophy focuses on the people and the technological elements of the organization. This interest was displayed when Vogl visited Harvard, "looking for a framework for negotiated hierarchies in organizations instead of a command-and-control or pyramidal hierarchy" (Vogl, p. 31).

The importance of bureaucracy in the post-industrial worldview has been downplayed. Enabling people to be free to engage in the work they are accountable for is a form of democracy rarely experienced in the workplace. Another theory suggests that hierarchy in management can be eliminated and that new processes and technology can be implemented via empowerment (LaBonte, 2003).

A technical environment inherently functions as a system, which is often comprised of a management hierarchy that does not always lend itself readily to the application of empowerment (Zigurs & Buckland, 1998). Within a company's management hierarchy, empowerment is generally perceived in relation to a given job level. The intervention attempted to change perceptions of empowerment among the customer relations managers by introducing a different lens through which daily responsibilities are more effectively accomplished. The intervention may help to determine whether increased empowerment can be expanded, regardless of the employees' management level.

Summary

The preceding pages presented the theoretical and conceptual context for the information related to empowerment, gender role in information technology, and appreciative inquiry. The theories of empowerment suggest that the proposed intervention may bring about emotional states that correlate to the performance and behaviors of employees (Lashley, 2000). Supportive evidence examined in the literature suggests that empowerment theories are significant in supporting the appreciative inquiry approach. The framework of appreciative inquiry can drive leadership and technology; it may also positively influence an organization's culture to implement quality solutions for dealing with stereotypes and biases in the workplace as well as with employee recruitment, hiring, development, and retention.

The introduction of technology is associated with increased employment opportunities and, thereby, a road out of poverty. However, for women and individuals with disabilities (e.g. autism), the potential of Information Technology (IT) is much more than that as it represents a way of more fully including them in mainstream life—socially, politically, and economically. IT can provide both groups information to improve their circumstances whether it be, for example, through farming information to learn how to best grow local crops or to mitigate the symptoms of their disabilities.

Information Technology, however, is neither gender neutral nor is it disability neutral. In order for IT to be effective, it must consider the needs of these population groups. The inherent characteristics of computer-aided instruction—consistency, regularity, availability, and on-demand stimulation without 'taking over' or making demands on the learner—address some of the individual needs of women and individuals with disabilities. Users have control over the learning situation. Users select what they learn, when they learn it, and the pace at which they learn. As such, CAI (computer-aided instructions) holds much promise as a tool in the education of women and individuals with disabilities. In improving the education of these groups, perhaps using appreciate inquiry concepts, each nation enriches its society and improves the potential of all persons to constructively contribute to the development of their own lives as well as the life of their nation and the world at large. Furthermore, because the recommendations transcend cultural boundaries to address gender needs, developing economies can implement them while at the same time respect its unique cultural heritage and diversity.

Discussion Questions

1. What is gender discrimination and does it still exist in the workplace of modern countries such as the United States, France, Germany, Canada, Italy, and others? Explain.
2. Discuss some of the challenges women face in climbing the ladder of success in today's workforce. What are three examples?
3. What is glass-ceiling and how can this concept prevent women and minorities from going into senior management positions?

4. How can technology be used to help individuals with disabilities make full use of their abilities and talents in the workplace?

5. Is there technology bias toward females in the workplace? Discuss and explain your answers.

6. Is there technology bias toward females in the education arena such as primary schools and university levels? Discuss and explain your answers.

7. How can technology be used by educators, parents, and technology experts in the workplace to make sure both males and females have equal access?

8. Besides the Information Technology field, what other fields seem to be facing a challenge in recruiting, promoting, and developing more females into senior management positions? How can they overcome such challenges?

9. What is appreciative inquiry? Can it be used to bring about equality and empowerment in the workplace? Discuss.

10. What is empowerment? Discuss why it is needed in a diverse workplace in today's environment.

11. What can leaders do to consistently involve their employees and colleagues in the decision making process?

Affirmative Action: United States and South Africa

*D*iversity is a reality in most countries and organizations. However, blatant forms of discrimination have also been one reality of some generations in the United States due to people's stereotypes and cultural differences. The United States usually is viewed as an enormous "melting pot," encompassing many different peoples with diverse backgrounds, desires, goals, and philosophies. Yet, a common objective shared by most people is to take advantage of the many opportunities afforded by the U.S. democratic, free-market system and to succeed. One key measurement of success is to attain a managerial or executive position within a firm. However, the attainment of such positions has had many challenges for minorities (including women) throughout the past few centuries.

As discussed by Cavico and Mujtaba (2005), a review of the history[7] of United States reveals that minority groups and women have been victimized and hindered by past discrimination and social stereotyping; in many instances. Unfortunately, minorities and women still are being harmed by both the cumulative and current effects of racial, ethnic, and sexual prejudice. These negative effects are especially apparent in the private employment sector where, despite some achievement of workplace equality, the ranks of upper-level managerial and executive positions remain noticeably underrepresented by women and minority group members. The continuing debate over achieving racial, ethnic, and sexual equality, therefore, frequently centers on business. In the business context, moreover, attempts to achieve equality and to remedy the effects of past discrimination and social stereotyping have substantial, far-reaching, and long-lasting ramifications. The public discourse on discrimination frequently treats the subject in moral terms. What moral choices should businesses make to help redress the effects of past discrimination and stereotyping and to achieve the societal goals of equality of opportunity, social balance, and social harmony? In seeking to resolve these issues, one confronts the division and the strain between the quest for equality and the desire to protect individual rights. This conflict between two basic "American" values renders the complex subject of discrimination particularly

---

[7] For more information, see "*Business Ethics: Transcending Moral Requirements through Moral Leadership*," by Cavico and Mujtaba, 2005.

difficult to solve. A corporation, for example, that strives to do the "right" thing may find itself thrown into disorder by clashing values and competing claims; and nowhere do these contentious issues come to a greater head than in the area of Affirmative Action (Cavico and Mujtaba, 2005).

Most large corporations in the United States have some type of a diversity program to make sure employees are treated with respect and dignity, and most companies do appear to feel morally obligated to implement some form of Affirmative Action. Yet, what type of an Affirmative Action program should a company adopt, and what is the moral propriety of so doing? These questions, as discussed by Cavico and Mujtaba (2005), present exceedingly difficult legal, moral, and practical problems for a firm. Accordingly, the purposes of this chapter are to examine and discuss Affirmative Action programs and practices.

Diversity and Affirmative Action Programs in the United States

One way to predict and move toward the future is to look at, and briefly study, the past. Historically, in most cultures, parents and older family members have been the storytellers who kept family members busy around dinner tables and during evenings and weekend about what happened, how it happened and what it meant for their lives. However, that is not the case today for most families as everyone seems to be "overcommitted" to school work, job, and other community or extracurricular activities. In this fast paced world, we do not always do a good job of reflecting on the past. Therefore, it is essential to formally, although very briefly, study the past five decades of diversity programs in the United States. Diversity has been part of American history as people have migrated to this country from all around the world. However, the last five decades are critical from the perspective of a transition from legal discrimination toward certain minorities to a point where such practices became illegal.

Lauren Niles, a consultant to Publix's *"Developing Cultural Competency"* Workshop and trainer through the National Multicultural Institute, used to present the "Four R" concept about the history of diversity in the United States. Lauren Niles' concepts along with an added R will be presented in this section to make "Five Rs." These concepts were presented to thousands of managers by NMCI consultants and Publix trainers such as Lauren Niles, Rohini Anand, Annisa Brockington, Jack Snow, Anthony Stevens (Amp), David Taylor (Gator Dave), Ruth Ferking, and yours truly. During the author's sixteen years of employment, Publix started and implemented many new diversity initiatives and this is probably one of the reasons that they have been ranked as one of the best places to work at in America. Besides managers at Publix, thousands of other managers and professionals in the workplaces around the United States have been hearing these concepts from various diversity trainers, managers and educators from across the globe.

In the 1960s, the Congress and the President of the United States attempted to put a stop to the practice of excluding some people from educational, employment, housing, use of public facilities and services, and other opportunities based on race, color, national origin, religion, and gender. The attempt was to create a level-playing-field for all citizens in the country. A series of Equal Opportunity laws were enacted, some of which were, *The Equal Pay Act of 1963, The Civil Rights Act of 1964, The Voting Rights Act of 1965, The Age Discrimination in Employment Act of 1967,* and others. These laws served to eradicate what up to that point had been widespread and in some instances, legal discrimination. The focus of the 1960's era could be summed up with the key word *rights.*

In the 1970's, some major developments occurred in the area of Affirmative Action. Affirmative Action as a concept, however, is not based in statutes or legislation. It has its origin in case law, i.e., decisions handed down by judges in court cases largely stemming from *Title VII of the Civil Rights Act of 1964.* In such cases, an employee sued her/his employer for some form of discrimination, often in the areas of hiring or promotion. An employer's poor history of hiring and/or promoting persons-of-color and women implied that discrimination had been present. It was in such cases that Affirmative Action requirements were often placed upon employers. The objective was to make the employer's workforce more representative of the general population in its geographic area. The focus of the 1970's era could be summed up with the key word *representation.*

In the 1980's, (in part due to Affirmative Action gains of the 70's), Americans began to see an improvement in the representation of previously under-represented groups in some areas of employment. What we often did *not* see was an improvement in cross-cultural interpersonal relationships between people who worked together. Because our previous focus had been on rights and representation from a legal and conceptual point of view, we had not prepared for the social and psychological effects on individuals in the improved, diverse workforce. Two phenomena often accompanied their new workplace environment: (a) the "revolving door," meaning newly represented individuals were not staying with their employers very long; and (b) they were not being fully integrated into the workforce, meaning few relationships crossed race, gender, or other cultural lines. People were neither working well together, nor necessarily trusting each other across cultural lines. In response to that challenge, corporations and governmental agencies began "diversity" training so colleagues could better associate with other's differences. The expectation was that if people could better "understand," be more "aware," and be more "sensitive" to others, they could get along better. The focus of the 1980's era could be summed up with the key word *relationships.*

The 1990's saw the introduction of the concept of managing diversity both at the individual and corporate levels. Diversity became widely recognized and accepted as an opportunity rather than a problem. The main goal of diversity management is to tap into the potential of all people; that approach does not necessarily mean that you treat all people the same way. The managing diversity concept recognizes that people are different and have differing needs. This concept is a multifaceted approach that addresses many issues such as under-representation, upward mobility, and equal opportunity. New systems, procedures, and training to enhance, support, and encourage opportunities for previously under-represented groups are necessary. Some corporate examples are:

- Voluntary Affirmative Action (VAAP) and Community Involvement Plans,
- The Minority Vendor Purchasing Programs,
- Minority recruitment activities,
- The appointment of Diversity Development Departments, and
- The establishment of awards for departments and managers that best meet equal opportunity goals, maintain a discrimination-free environment which values diversity, and demonstrate dedication to the dignity, value and employment security of associates.

Training in both diversity awareness and skills is only one part of the overall concept of managing diversity. Change is beginning to happen, and happen fast, in corporate America. CEOs realize that change occurs one person at a time and the responsibility for change regarding diversity must be implemented at the personal level. Individuals are now being held personally responsible and accountable for their behaviors. Additionally, managers are given much responsibility for the communication, support, and sometimes implementation of company diversity initiatives. Many companies have adopted mission or value statements and expect their associates to align personal values to them. The focus of the 1990's era can be summed up with the key word *responsibility*. More accurately, it can be referred to as *personal* responsibility. Perhaps, through continued and appropriate Affirmative Action programs and each person taking responsibility for his/her actions, Dr. King's dream will be achieved much sooner. In his speech that has brought a paradigm change into the minds of thousands and the society around the world, Dr. Martin Luther King, Jr. said:

I still have a dream. It is a dream deeply rooted in the American Dream. I have a dream. That one day, this nation will rise up, live out the true meaning of creed. We hold these truths to be self-evident that all men are created equal…And He's allowed me to go up to the mountain. And I've looked over, and I've seen the Promised Land. I may not get there with you. But I want you to know tonight, that we, as a people, will get to the Promised Land (Dr. Martin Luther King, Jr., April 3, 1968, Memphis, Tennessee).

Common Responses and Cultural Lens

While Equal Employment Opportunity laws and the Affirmative Action concepts have been very helpful in leveling the playing field in the workplace, some people are still experiencing discriminatory practices. When these individuals state their perceptions of receiving blatant or subtle daily indignities to their colleagues or bosses, at times they might hear certain common responses that sort of "spin" the events in another direction. Typically when people are confronted with information such as what has been shared about discriminatory practices (i.e. daily indignities), and it does not match their personal experiences they tend to question its validity. Using one's own reality as an example, one can take a "leap of faith" and begin to believe that one's own perceived reality is, in fact, the truth. There is a very strong tendency to think there can only be one "correct" reality. Therefore, the other reality must be incorrect. For example, if your reality does not match John's, then John is likely to try to explain away the differences in terms of his own experiences. John will likely say some things like the "common responses" heard in the society. The common responses which we hear in our societies and some possible responses to them may look something similar to the following common response statements. Remember, that the person from the other culture or perspective would make such responses and s/he is basing them upon his/her own perceived reality.

Common responses by the listener (and possible counter responses from the *speaker or victim*) can include:

1. It happens to everybody. *Possible response: And when it does it is still not right.*
2. Maybe the person is just that way. It's their personality—they're just rude. *Possible response: Not when all too often I see the same person treating other individuals with respect.*
3. Maybe you are just being paranoid. You know if you look for trouble, you will find it. *Possible response: It does not happen every time. You can be paranoid, but when it happens often enough to see a pattern, it is hard to ignore.*
4. Maybe you should wear some better looking clothes. *Possible response: I have and it still happens.*

Why would one say or make these common responses to someone who is describing his or her experiences, such as how he or she was blatantly discriminated against? Perhaps this is so because the listener's "truth" is being challenged or does not match the speaker's experiences and the listener is trying to reinterpret the speaker's "truth" in terms of his or her reality. How do you think someone would feel when one responds to him/her in this way with common responses? What particular feelings may this invoke to the speaker? It is probably making the speaker feel pretty badly or negatively. Some feelings experienced by the speaker may be mad, angry, disappointed, or even frustrated as he or she is not being believed, despite the fact that the person might be sharing a factual personal experience and his or her actual feelings.

What impact will these types of common responses have on the relationship between the two individuals? You might say what relationship? There probably will not be a relationship if this process of questioning and using common responses continue. If the speaker and listener are coworkers, how might this affect their working relationship? The relationship would be strained at the least, and consequently productivity would suffer.

So, the reality is that we all have biases and perceptual filters which screen certain information out and consequently affect our responses. *Cultural lens* are learned stereotypes that filter certain information in and other information out of one's awareness. For example, if I believe based on previously learned stereotypes that you and I are/should be different, then the information about you that makes it through my filters is about the ways in which we are different. The ways in which we are similar tend not to make it through my filters. On the other hand, if I believe that you and I are similar, then the information that makes it through my perceptual filters or cultural lens is all about our similarities. As presented in Figure 6.1, one's truth is often the result of his or her experiences and the way he or she perceives things to be (or his or her perceived reality). I tend not to "see" or "hear" the ways in which we are different. This concept closely relates to the *Reticular Activating Systems* (RAS), often discussed in psychology books, which serve as bodyguards and secretaries by helping a person gather useful information and warning one of prospective danger. Simply stated, RAS states that what you think about you will find. For example, if you are planning on buying a red Toyota next year, then for the next six months you are likely to notice cars that look like the one you are planning to buy and other relevant information that will help you in your search. This is because you subconsciously registered the information in your RAS and it alerts you when relevant information passes though it and gets filtered.

Figure 6.1 – My Truth and Your Truth

We are brought up in a society whose members don't always treat each other very well and those inappropriate behaviors sometimes carry over into the workplace. You may ask, what can professionals and managers gain from becoming aware of daily indignities that occur in today's society? Well, by becoming more aware of some of the ways in which society may discriminate, professionals can help themselves to form habits that will not be discriminatory and habits that will help develop an inclusive work environment in their companies. Overall, with regard to perceptions and realities, one can conclude the following:

1. We tend to see the "truth" based only on our perceived reality. Therefore, we tend to think that if our reality is "right" then somebody else's reality must be "wrong."
2. There may be "truth" in two different perceptions or realities.
3. Refusing to believe there may be truth in someone else's reality is a double indignity.
4. Over time, discriminatory practices such as daily indignities and unearned privileges can affect self-confidence and self-esteem, which affects a person's morale and level of productivity in the workplace.

Affirmative Action: Purpose and History

As one continues reading articles (classic or "current event" issues) to learn more about diversity, one will notice some of the patterns and historical trends as they relate to managing diversity. One historical trend on diversity initiatives dealing with Affirmative Action is discussed in the classic article republished in *HBR on Managing Diversity* (2001) titled "From Affirmative Action to Affirming Diversity" by Dr. R. Roosevelt Thomas, Jr. This article was originally published in *Harvard Business Review* in 1990. Dr. Roosevelt is very well known for his work in the area of managing diversity. The author met him a few times in the mid to late 1990's when working as a senior training specialist and an internal corporate consultant at Publix Super Markets and when attending professional conferences. In one case in the late 1990's, Dr. Roosevelt was invited to be the keynote speaker during a four-day Leadership Conference at Disney World of Orlando. Dr. Roosevelt did an excellent job of fueling, reigniting and energizing the organization's diversity initiatives and training. The organization had developed an excellent workshop for managers that focused on awareness of diversity issues and the existing individual and societal stereotypes that can impact one's behavior, and how more times than not such stereotypes may negatively impact those who fall in the minority side in terms of their difference.

In his HBR article, titled *"From Affirmative Action to Affirming Diversity,"* Dr. Roosevelt provides a good understanding of Affirmative Action, its original intention, current challenges, and solutions to effectively deal with these challenges toward providing equal opportunities to everyone, including white males. He goes on to say that while Affirmative Action sets the stage for a gender-blind, color-blind, and culture-blind workplace, larger percentages of minorities and women still tend to stagnate, plateau, or quit when they fail to move up the corporate ladder. As a result, everyone's dashed hopes lead to corporate frustration and a period of embarrassed silence, usually followed by a crisis and more recruitment. Some organizations may have repeated such a cycle three or more times in the past few decades of the twentieth century. The assimilation model of washing away differences (the American melting pot) is no longer useful nor valid. So, organizations are faced with the challenge of having to manage unassimilated diversity using strategies designed for a homogeneous work force to earn employee commitment toward quality and high profits. Dr. Roosevelt continues to say that the challenge for executives, leaders and managers of today's workforce is to work not merely toward culture and color-blindness, but also toward an openly multicultural workplace that taps into and energizes the full potential of every employee without artificial programs, standards, or barriers. This can be achieved by learning to understand and modify ineffective organizational assumptions, models and systems, which can be a laborious challenge.

Affirmative Action was originally started with the several premises in the 1960s. Five of them were:

1. Adult, white males made up the majority of the American business mainstream.
2. The American economic structure was a solid, unchanging institution with more than enough space for everyone.
3. Women, blacks, immigrants, and other minorities should be allowed into the workplace as a matter of public policy and common decency.
4. Widespread racial, ethnic, and sexual prejudice keeps minorities out of the workplace.
5. Legal and social coercion are necessary to bring about the needed changes in the workplace.

Dr. Roosevelt's article provides data on the fact that more than half of the U.S. workforce now consists of minorities, immigrants, and women. White men (natives) are becoming a minority as they made up only about 15% of the workforce in the year 2000. Minorities and women no longer need a "boarding pass" since the major problem is no longer having entry into the workplace. Rather, the major challenge is to make better use of their potential at every level, especially in middle management and leadership positions. Affirmative Action may not provide the solutions to the changing landscape of America. Affirmative Action, which focused on short-term solutions to a major problem, alone cannot cope with the challenge of creating a work setting geared toward upward mobility of all individuals, including white men. Affirmative Action is a red flag to every worker who feels unfairly passed over and a stigma for those who appear to be the beneficiaries of its policies. Dr. Roosevelt offered ten guidelines for learning to manage diversity.

1. *Clarify motivation.* Learning to effectively manage diversity will make you more competitive.
2. *Clarify vision.* Create an environment where everyone will do their best work.
3. *Expand focus.* Create an inclusive environment for all.
4. *Audit corporate culture.*
5. *Modify assumptions.*
6. *Modify systems.* Examine the process for promotion, mentoring and informal assignments.
7. *Modify models.* "Doer to Enabler."
8. *Help people pioneer.* Empowered change agents can try and discover the best solutions in their progression toward effectively managing diversity.
9. *Apply the special consideration test.* Will the system contribute to everyone's success?
10. *Continue Affirmative Action.* We still need a diverse workforce to deal with diverse challenges.

The purpose/goal of managing diversity has been and should be to develop everyone's capacity to accept, incorporate, and empower the diverse human talents in the organization, in the nation, and eventually in the world so everyone can be as productive as possible. Diversity is both a national as well as an international reality and we must make it our strength.

As defined by MSN Encarta, Affirmative Action is "policies used in the United States to increase opportunities for minorities by favoring them in hiring and promotion, college admissions, and the awarding of government contracts." Some will argue that Affirmative Action is "the only way to ensure an integrated society in which all segments of the population have an equal opportunity to share in jobs, education, and other benefits." Others will argue that Affirmative Action is "reverse discrimination" and showing favoritism to one group while the dominant group pays for the sins of their ancestors. Now, many managers and leaders trying to do the right thing are asking the following questions:

1. Does Affirmative Action enable or disable a manager who is looking for the best candidate for the job?
2. If Affirmative Action were reversed, what would the effects be?
3. Has Affirmative Action become more than it was intended to be?
4. What other means do we have or can we create to ensure that equality and diversity exist in the workplace?

Perhaps the answers to such questions can be best answered by each in-dustry and each organization depending on their hiring patterns in the history and their current workforce demographics compared to the population demo-graphics since it is assumed that each organization wants to be fair to all individuals. Being ethical, fair and attempting to have a diverse workplace require deep reflections and eventually doing what is right.

Affirmative Action and the Cycle of Oppression

Among many individuals who have been impacted by reverse discrimina-tion or its perception, there may be some dissent or negativity regarding the concept of Affirmative Action. Much misinformation exists that is widely accepted as fact in the American society. To help clarify misinformation, it is best to understand some actual facts about Affirmative Action and its objec-tives of creating a level playing field and eliminating the cycle of oppression. First of all let us make it clear that Affirmative Action is more of a concept than a law. According to experts, it is largely a product of litigation filed un-der *Title VII of the Civil Rights Act of 1964* and the resulting consent decrees. Affirmative Action does not support or require the promotion of any unquali-fied individuals in the workplace. The notion of quotas is not necessarily part of the Affirmative Action concept. The 1972 *Philadelphia Plan* was probably a political move that established quotas only for business done under govern-ment contract. Sociologists and other experts have estimated that it would take about seven generations for the representation of some groups to normal-ize without the proactive implementation of Affirmative Action concept. Affirmative Action was designed to help break what was (and still is) known as a "cycle of oppression" as presented in Figure 6.2.

The need for acceptable education, housing, and employment for all sec-tors of the population represents three fairly basic human needs in today's society. These needs are interdependent and in the case of oppression, com-prise a vicious circle that prevents some minorities from fairly accessing such opportunities. For example, one needs a quality education to obtain satisfying employment that will enable the purchase of housing located in an area with access to schools that will provide a quality education. Many people are able to break out of the cycle, but some give up trying because they are over-whelmed, or don't know how to proceed since they face many consistent biases and stereotypes. No matter where a society attempts to break the cycle, it is likely to cause pain to some individuals. So, where do we break it? The reality is that leaders must start somewhere to break the cycle of oppression in order to create an inclusive and healthy environment for all individuals in the society.

Figure 6.2 – The Cycle of Oppression

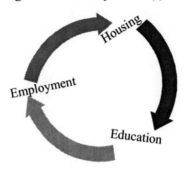

In modern society, the clashes of values and cultures have caused much violence, animosity and hatred among people of various nations and different governments. Wars have started and ended due to clashes of values and fears of the other (or the unknown). Unfortunately, this cycle of oppression and violence seems to continue "taking" and "using" so much physical and human resources throughout the world. These resources could be better used toward the well-being of humanity rather than war, destruction, and revenge. What leaders should remember is the fact that violence begets more violence and revenge can often legitimize war in the heads, hearts and/or habits of more people. It is important for everyone to remember, including government and military officers, that one should never resort to killing another person or living creatures (such as birds and animals) when other appropriate options are available. For example, killing a person who makes a major mistake (such as robbing or hurting innocent individuals) is a sad tragedy for all humanity. Such persons (be they thieves, thugs, gangs, or terrorists) must be "stopped" using "enough" force to prevent them from further harming others, but not more. In Tae Kwon Do, those who have achieved the prestigious rank of a black belt are expected to exercise good judgment when facing an opponent (be it a professional martial artist in a public event or a thug on the street). Black belt martial artists are likely to have "mastered" many skills or strategies for quickly breaking the arm of their opponent, thereby preventing him/her from further harming one. However, breaking the arm of one's opponent (or any other part of his or her body) may not be necessary to prevent him or her from causing damage to a person. The focus should be on "stopping" the person from harming others or "showing" one's superior mastery of skill. As a matter of fact, if and when a highly ranked martial artist uses his or her skills with excessive force to intentionally hurt his/her opponent in an official public fight, he or she is likely to lose points, be disqualified from the fight, and/or receive a warning from the referee as this is considered bad "sportsmanship." So, in martial arts, the higher ranked individuals are expected to exercise good judgment and use an appropriate strategy with their opponents (for example, exerting "enough" force to show mastery of skill but not more). Perhaps governments, military officers, and political leaders of all nations (especially the "strong and powerful" ones) should focus on using appropriate strategies to bring an end to the patterns of violence, insurgency, and terrorism which seem to be widespread in today's world. One must always remember that using excessive force or war with large groups of people or people of various cultures may further legitimize more violence and fighting. So, as can be seen from the struggles of Palestinians and Israelis, which have lasted many decades, war is not the solution to peace; however, education, communication and honest negotiations can be some of the best strategies to bringing an end to war and violence. Similar to the cycle of oppression, the cycle of violence and war must also be stopped using appropriate strategies in order for peace to become the norm throughout various nations in this world. It is the responsibility of all officials and leaders to exercise patience, discipline and good judgment to end the cycle of oppression and violence which are impacting people's heads (thinking), hearts (feelings) and habits (behaviors). Perhaps, Affirmative Action strategies that have been implemented in the United State and South Africa can be a "good means" for peacefully creating a fair and just society for everyone throughout the world through education, effective communication, and honest negotiations.

Affirmative Action in South Africa[8]: Decades of White Privilege

Most third world countries stand at the dawn of a bright future and massive transformation opportunities. Besides many other nations, Afghanistan is one such country that can embrace new technology and industry if its diverse people can stand together and work as a team toward a common goal. Many nations in the African continent seem to have similar opportunities as the world is willing to help them prosper. The international community's response to these countries' needs and massive financial infusion brings hope to people who are longing for a peaceful world. Liberation and democratization of traditionally authoritarian countries bring with it challenges including gender issues and ethnic equality. Countries such as Afghanistan, similar to South Africa, tend to be made up of people from diverse ethnicities and cultures. Furthermore, years of conflict and war has created divisiveness and animosity among some groups of people in Afghanistan. Such feelings of animosity can hurt minority groups in their education and equal access to jobs in the country. The examples and best practices from other developing economies and continents, such as South Africa, can provide a good learning experience for managers and leaders of both public and private sectors in developing economies.

---

[8] - This material is co-authored with Michael Sithole, College of the Southwest; Barbara Dastoor, Nova Southeastern University; and Gerraldine Ippolito, Globe Institute of Technology.

The challenges of ethnically diverse nations are similar to those of the Republic of South Africa. Ten years of freedom have ushered in a period of euphoria and hope to the previously disadvantaged Black majority. The government of President Nelson Mandela opted to embrace Affirmative Action as the vehicle for the transformation of the South African work force. This policy has been a resounding success in addressing the imbalances of the past. The authors believe that Affirmative Action strategies can play a similar role in the transformation of their societies to a fair and synergistic economy where people of all ethnicities can be equal partners and contributors.

According to the Department of Census and Statistics, South Africa has a Gross Domestic product of R2,300 per year. This places the country among middle income countries such as Chile, Mexico, Hungary, Thailand and Malaysia. The modern industrial and commercial economy gives the minority of the population, including most whites, a standard of living that is equivalent to Western Europe, but for the many who are wholly or partially excluded from the economy, incomes and lifestyles are characteristic of developing countries.

The apartheid heritage has left a strong connection between race and socioeconomic class. Under apartheid, from 1948 to 1994, a person's race influenced occupation, place of residence, education, choice of partner, freedom of movement, and use of facilities and amenities. This legacy will take decades to erase. In 1993, blacks made up 76 percent of the population but earned only 29 percent of the country's total income. Whites, who constituted only 13 percent of the population, accounted for 58 percent of total income. For Colored people the shares were 8 percent of the population and about 7 percent of the income; for Asians, 3 percent of the population and 5 percent of the income.

The first democratically elected South African Government in 1994 faced what appeared to be insurmountable obstacles on the employment arena. The previously disenfranchised majority suffered the disastrous effects of the Job Reservation Act of 1964 which prescribed what job categories were open to Blacks, Coloreds and Indians. Whites received the best education that prepared them for leadership roles in the industry. The Coloreds, Indians and Blacks received inferior education designed to perpetuate a glass ceiling that relegated them to serve their white masters.

The advent of freedom ushered in a period of euphoria and great expectations to the down-trodden majority. To these people, democracy brought hopes of opportunity and upward mobility on the work front. Some members of this group demanded retribution and redistribution of wealth, they demanded their proverbial pound of flesh. The white people demanded the maintenance of the status quo and bolstered their position with threats of a massive exodus to greener pastures with a concomitant brain drain. After all they owned most businesses and their disinvestments could have crippled the economy. The government of President Nelson Mandela opted for pragmatism in the face of pressure from the right and the left extremists, their policy was driven by the ruling party's declaration that "South Africa belongs to all who live in it." The government embraced Affirmative Action as the only pragmatic policy that could redress imbalances of the past. An examination of the government's plan clearly reveals their concerns for all the citizens of the country.

The government did utilize the huge Public Enterprises – including all seaports, railways, utilities to jump start the Affirmative Action plans. To underscore its commitment to the policy, top management positions in all these departments were awarded to suitably qualified (education and skills) though inexperienced Blacks, Coloreds and Asians. All government contracts were granted to institutions that included formerly disadvantaged groups as equity partners. Numerous consulting firms doing business with Blacks were registered and won government contracts. This set the stage for the implementation of the policy.

The South African Department of Census and Statistics conducted a national survey in 1996 and 2001. This paper utilized this information in exploring the success or otherwise of the government's Affirmative Action policy.

Historical Background in South Africa

The white minority government of South Africa passed a series of laws that discriminated against Blacks, Asians and Coloreds (mixed race) citizens. The Group Areas Act of 1950 prescribed where all the country's citizens could live, go to work, and associate with. The education system was designed to ensure white supremacy on the shop floor. There were separate education departments for Whites, Asians, Coloreds, and Blacks. The white education department received the highest funding per student and the Bantu Education Department, meant for the black majority, received the lowest funding per student. The quality of the education was also designed to ensure that blacks could not compete with whites on the shop floor. The government was not satisfied with these measures and added the Job Reservation Act of 1964. This law restricted the number of jobs that Blacks, Asians and Coloreds could be engaged in. Blacks, Asians and Coloreds could not attend to whites in their professional capacity, they could only serve as unskilled or semi-skilled workers. Blacks, Asians and Coloreds people could not rise beyond junior management positions. This glass-ceiling also affected females of all races as well.

The government of President Nelson Mandela opted for pragmatism in the face of pressure from the right and left extremists. Their policy was driven by the ruling party's declaration that "South Africa belongs to all who live in it" (Kliptown, 1955). The government embraced Affirmative Action as the pragmatic policy for the redress of imbalances of the past. An examination of the government's plan clearly reveals their concerns for all the citizens of the country:

⇒ Elimination of unfair discrimination; and
⇒ Implementing Affirmative Action measures to redress the disadvantages in employment experienced by designated groups, to ensure their equitable representation in all occupational categories and levels in the workforce.

The Employment Equity Act, 55 of 1998, prohibits unfair discrimination as it states that "No person may unfairly discriminate, directly or indirectly, against an employee in any employment policy or practice, on one or more grounds including race, gender, pregnancy, marital status, family responsibility, ethnic or social origin, color, sexual orientation, age disability, religion, HIV status, conscience, belief, political opinion, culture, language and birth." South Africa has effectively transformed the employment policies of the country through the vehicle of Affirmative Action. While the proponents of Affirmative Action hail it as a panacea for the redress of the imbalances of the past, the opponents perceive it as reverse discrimination. The South African government boldly declares in the Employment Equity Act, 55 of 1998 that, "It is not unfair discrimination to promote Affirmative Action consistent with the Act or to prefer or, exclude any person on the basis of inherent job requirement."

There is nothing discriminatory about an orderly transition towards the demographic representation of employees in the workplace providing that the beneficiaries of Affirmative Action have the necessary knowledge and skills. The subject of ability begs the question, if you have been effectively excluded from the process by discrimination and a glass-ceiling, how can you advance to higher echelons of management? What other vehicle does a government faced with a similar situation have to redress the imbalances of the past? When the maintenance of the status quo is inconsistent with the spirit of a non-discriminatory national constitution that South Africa has, Affirmative Action is the best vehicle for employment equity. This does not create room for quotas which would mean the promotion of ill-equipped candidates. The preference of previously disadvantaged groups with equal knowledge and skills remains the only answer. Quotas and retributive justice have no place in modern employment policies.

Literature Review of Affirmative Action

The origins of Affirmative Action in the United States go back to the Kennedy Executive Order 10925, March 6, 1961; the terms of this epic order was the creation of the Commission on Equal Employment Opportunity with the view to ensure that hiring and employment practices were free of bias.

This served as the impetus for the Civil Rights Act (July 2, 1964) signed by President Lyndon Johnson that prohibited all kinds of discrimination based on race, color, religion, or national origin. On September 24, 1965 Affirmative Action was enforced for the first time by Executive Order 11246. Government contractors had to take specific measures to ensure equality in their hiring practices. Affirmative Action spawned numerous reverse discrimination court cases (6/28/1978), Regents of the University of California v. Blakke (7/2/1980), Fullilove v. Klutznick (5/19/1986), Wygant v. Jackson Board of Education (2/5/1987), United States v. Paradise (1/23/1989), and City of Richmond v. Croson. These types of court cases still persist today with the Supreme Court upholding Affirmative Action in University Admissions. On June 23, 2003, Leiter & Leiter (2002) addressed the controversy on the application of Affirmative Action as a tool for combating discrimination based on race, national origin, ethnicity, and gender. The authors trace the roots of Affirmative Action, white supremacy, Title VII and employment issues, and possible future legal challenges facing the Affirmative Action policy. Landsberg (1995) addresses the history of Affirmative Action and its efforts to correct the effects of past discrimination, promote diversity, and endeavor to overcome the two-class society characterized by racial division. The authors also worried that the perception that Affirmative Action might lead to the assumption that Affirmative Action appointees are hired for reasons other than legitimate qualifications for the job (Northcraft, 1983). Pinkston (1984) commented that President Ronald Reagan's stance on Affirmative Action encouraged opposition and decreased the protections of law available to the people discriminated against. Davis (1998) made the point that some organizations establish glass ceilings, quotas and goals but use inappropriate practices to meet them. He further noted that some managers believe that there is no longer a need for Affirmative Action. Seltzer and Thompson (1985) made interesting conclusions in their empirical study. They noted significant differences in attitudes on Affirmative Action held by Blacks and Whites. The attitudes of high income Blacks differ from those of less-advantaged Blacks, White women are more supportive of Affirmative Action programs than White males. Well-educated Whites hold more liberal views on Affirmative Action than less-educated Whites. In a summary of papers on Affirmative Action presented at the United Nations conference in 1969, Greenberg (1984) notes that Malaysia, India, Israel, and the United States had Affirmative Action complying with the definition; Nigeria and Peru had arrangements that did not comply with the definition but were similar in purpose; Yugoslavia had Affirmative Action within regional minority areas; Sudan and West Germany had no Affirmative Action. Anonymous (2004) reports that the Indian government is contemplating the introduction of Affirmative Action – meaning quotas – to secure jobs for the poorer half of the population especially tribal groups and dalits – formerly called the untouchables. In a Wall Street Journal editorial, Guest (2004) argues that South Africa has the world's most extreme Affirmative Action program. He refutes the notion that all blacks in South Africa are poor; he further argues that Affirmative Action ends up helping well-off blacks, that the policy hampers productivity and fosters corruption and that Affirmative Action ends up hurting everyone even the purported beneficiaries. Scott, Amos, and Scott (1998) presented their empirical findings that include the following: that Affirmative Action programs for minorities are under fire in the U.S., but they are embraced in South Africa; the attitudes towards Affirmative Action become relatively unimportant once a career gets under way. Drogin (1995) reported that a 1991 South African survey revealed that there were only 30 black engineers vs. 17,840 white engineers, and 31 black pharmacists compared with 2,021 whites. In 1994, there were only 60 black chartered accountants and fewer than 20 black architects; blacks held only 3% of managerial positions in a country where blacks represent more than 80% of the population. McFarlin, Coster, and Mogale-Pretorius (1999) noted that, "The main issue is how to compensate for apartheid's negative legacy and bring large numbers of the previously disenfranchised black majority into the corporate mainstream. Achieving this goal will require South African firms to develop aggressive Affirmative Action programs and to embrace leadership and training approaches that better reflect African values." Human (1993) comments that in many South African organizations, the educational qualifications attached to certain jobs are often either arbitrary or too high which could constitute a subtle form of racism in itself. The author also argues that performance on the job is often related to competencies not encompassed in the entrance criteria.

Discussions and Implications

There can be no doubt that the South African racial discrimination policies of the white minority regime called apartheid were cruel and inhumane. The Group Areas Act prescribed where the different race groups lived; the Population Registration Act mandated that Blacks should carry identification documents on their persons at all times; the Job Reservation Act prescribed what jobs could be granted to which race group, effectively enforcing discrimination on the shop floor. Additionally, there were separate and unequal education systems aimed at ensuring that whites were better educated and ready for leadership positions in the workplace. While the system drew sharp criticism from the outside world, it persisted until the historic elections that brought President Nelson Mandela and his supporters to the helm of the government. The black majority agitated for swift changes, retribution, and redistribution of wealth. The white minority longed for the maintenance of the status quo and the preservation of their privileges. The newly elected government chose to adopt Affirmative Action as the only viable vehicle to redress the imbalances of the past. It would have been suicidal for the new government to maintain the status quo against the wishes of its electorate. It would have been equally imprudent to adopt a rapid Africanization policy – replacement of top management positions by inexperienced and poorly educated

Africans. The obvious results of rapid Africanization policy would have been chaos, lower expectations and productivity, and lower profitability. The government decided on a pragmatic Affirmative Action policy with the ultimate aim of having a South African labor force that reflected the demographics of the country. The Equal Employment Act describes the intentions and implementation process of the Affirmative Action policy. Firms had to draft and lodge their Affirmative Action programs with the Department of Labor. This department monitors the implementation of the policies by participating firms.

The implementation of Affirmative Action will always attract proponents and opponents anywhere in the world where such policies are adopted and South Africa was no exception. The perception that there are "winners and losers" with Affirmative Action assures conflict, more so in a country that experienced five decades of white privilege. Observers forget that blacks complained about white Affirmative Action (apartheid) just as whites are unhappy about Affirmative Action aimed at redressing the imbalances of the past. There was no doubt that the South African racial discrimination called for an immediate response from the incoming black majority government. The focus of this chapter is the evaluation of whether or not Affirmative Action is addressing the past imbalances as expected. The census data released by the government supports the effectiveness of Affirmative Action. The unmistakable increase in the ranks of previously disadvantaged groups in the managerial and professional groups cannot be ignored. The pragmatism of the government shines in the increase in the numbers of whites in the top echelons of the public and private sector. This appears to indicate a "win-win" situation.

One cannot ignore the volumes of research and concept papers that are highly critical of the South African Affirmative Action policy. The observation that Affirmative Action benefits affluent blacks merits a comment. Affluent blacks could afford better education in private schools that offered better quality education. Many expatriates graduated with business and other appropriate qualifications that confer some advantage in their search for employment opportunities. There is also a growing number of papers that indicate growing concerns about nepotism. Under no circumstances can nepotism be condoned. One has to accept that these concerns address process issues and not the Affirmative Action policy per se. Distributive justice is a virtue that all countries embrace.

Managerial Implications

The adoption and implementation of Affirmative Action demonstrates pragmatism by a government that faced an apparently insurmountable problem of apartheid. While opponents of the policy might fault it on process issues, they are yet to offer viable alternatives. There can be no malice in the implementation of a policy that seeks to redress the past imbalances with the goal of proportional representation of all race groups in the employment practices of South Africa.

Multi-National Corporations operating in South Africa need to familiarize themselves with the country's Affirmative Action policies that are highly unlikely to change. There is a huge reservoir of educated work seekers who need training, equal opportunity, fair performance appraisal, and upward mobility. The country did not embrace quotas and this is an encouraging development. The profitability of industries has not suffered because of Affirmative Action. South Africa is the engine of development in Sub-Saharan Africa with a growing potential for success. Similar regulations and policies can be helpful in the rebuilding of Afghanistan and other third world countries in order to ensure equality for all male and female employees of diverse ethnicities.

Summary

Diversity and blatant forms of discrimination has been one element of some generations in the United States and other countries throughout the world due to people's stereotypes and cultural differences. This chapter has discussed some examples of how people in the United States and in South Africa have overcome years of stereotypes and biases through formal Affirmative Action plans. While stereotypes and biases still exist in these countries, the negative impact of most blatant discriminatory practices have certainly been reduced and professionals now seem to have a much fairer "playing field" in reaching the ranks of management than ever before.

Discussion Questions

1. What is Affirmative Action? Discuss this concept and how managers can operationalize it in the United States or other countries within their firms.
2. Can Affirmative Action concepts be used to attract and retain a diverse workforce in large organizations? Explain your answers.
3. State several benefits of Affirmative Action concept to people in the United States.
4. Through research, find out what is meant by "reverse discrimination" and how such forms of discrimination can be eliminated.
5. What strategies have South African leaders implemented to eliminate blatant discrimination based on race?
6. What has been the result of Affirmative Action strategies in South Africa?
7. How different is the Affirmative Action strategy in South Africa from what has been implemented in the United States?
8. Can similar Affirmative Action strategies be implemented in other countries and culture? If so, where and how?

9. What are some of the negative consequences or "side effects" of Affirmative Action plans that employers must be concerned about?

10. What is the "cycle of oppression"? How does it impact minorities? Does such a cycle still exist in the United States or other parts of the world? Discuss.

11. How do the Affirmative Action plans in various countries impact multinational corporations that have office with local employees in these locations?

Part II

Perspectives on Culture and Organizations

Culture and Management

I t is assumed treating others the way one wants to be treated is sufficient for healthy interpersonal relationships and, perhaps this is true to some extent. When it comes to the diversity of cultures and different cultural practices, the "Golden Rule" (treating others the way one would like to be treated) may not always apply in each case and, thus, some have resorted to adopting the "Platinum Rule" in their workplace. The Platinum Rule states that one should treat others the way they want to be treated. Today's diverse situations and diverse cultures require flexibility in using whatever is relevant for the culture and time. As such, this chapter and section discuss cultural issues, organizational cultural issues, and international management concerns in today's global environment of business, using the healthcare industry as an example. As previously implied, *cultural competency* refers to the process of continually learning about diversity so one can effectively function in the contexts of national and international differences.

Managing Cultural Diversity in the Workplace[9]

Culture is one dimension of diversity in today's workforce and managers of today's organizations should effectively deal with it. *Culture*, as stated before, can be seen as a set of values shared by members of an organization that determine acceptable behaviors and attitudes. Organizational leaders need to be sensitive to multiple cultures, which can differ from the organizational culture. Diversity management is a way of coping with the increased cultural changes that affect organizations. Managing diversity helps promote equality and reduce conflicts in the workplace. Managing diversity can begin through an understanding of language and gender differences and stereotyping. It can originate from system thinking practices, where a broader sense of issues is better than having a single narrow minded perspective. The three core principles of tolerance, awareness, and personal development could help leaders develop a more comprehensive program to manage diversity in the organization.

Culture, according to Daft (2000), is defined as "the set of values, guiding beliefs, the understanding and ways of thinking, which are shared by members of an organization" (p. 368). An immediate image of an organization can be seen from its culture. Culture provides moral and social reasoning for em-

---

[9] - This material on culture is co-authored with Raimi Abiodun, University of Phoenix.

ployees, and it determines the behaviors and attitudes that are acceptable. Current debates on leadership emphasize cooperation and teamwork between leaders and followers (Ramamoorthy & Flood, 2004). Research has shown that for teamwork to be effective and meaningful in healthcare organizations and hospitals, hospital leaders must develop a "cultural orientation that meets the needs of a growing multicultural workforce and patient population" (Foley & Wurmser, 2004, p. 44). Hospital leaders need to be sensitive to the various cultures embedded in the organization. According to Schein (1992), most organizations have multiple cultures or subcultures within them. These can differ noticeably from the overall organizational culture.

Most managers have been schooled or trained in the importance of cultural diversity and how to use participation as a means of getting compliance from people. The current healthcare crisis of manpower shortage has created a diverse healthcare community and calls for a better management plan including initiatives on how to effectively manage this diverse cultural environment. The dialogue on healthcare management has shifted from providing equality of opportunities in order to maintain a functioning workforce and addressing social injustices make managing diversity less problematic for the organization to asking how leaders are providing a climate where all employees feel that they are valued by their contribution to the growth and survival of the organization.

Diversity management in organizations, especially in the healthcare industry, is a way of coping with the increased rapid cultural and sociological changes that affect organizations. To healthcare leaders, diversity management could be used as a vehicle for creating an environment where people are more comfortable, valued, and appreciated, while creating an external image of an industry that knows how to manage and respond to all the ongoing changes within the market industry. Healthcare organizations consist of different sets of professionals including physicians, nurses, pharmacists, laboratory technicians, social workers, and others who contribute to the care delivery. These professionals have their own sets of cultures and norms, and each member of these professions has a different cultural background, different educational background, and different life orientation.

The common denominator for these groups is the dominant interest each has for their professions rather than the hospitals that they work for and the care of the patients who unite them. A superior diversity plan can help healthcare leaders to better manage each diverse and unique working environment. Having a diversity plan will not only make it easier for the leaders to manage effectively, but will also help position the industry as one that is flexible and conscious of cultural changes. The healthcare system was created to meet the healthcare needs of the people. It must therefore be efficient, quality-focused, and customer-oriented. It must be able to integrate with other systems and form a collaborative relationship that brings a better life to the people it serves (Becker-Reems, 2001).

In their book, Noon and Ogbonna (as cited by Foster & Harris, 2005) stated that "managing diversity in both theory and practice offers a new challenge to conceptualizing and tackling the issues of equality, discrimination, and injustice in employment" (p. 7). Managing diversity helps promote equality and reduce the threat of social injustice and conflicts in the workplace. Because organizational culture might be a defining factor in recruitment and retention, leaders must also understand that better diversity management has the potential to position the organization as an inclusive place to work by promoting equal participation and involvement of all from every section of the organization. Research has shown that diversity management encourages the development of a more innovative and diverse workforce, which in turn helps build relationships and increases satisfaction of associates within the organization.

A good organization can find itself in a bad position if the interest of any members of the organization is in jeopardy. With the generational evolution of the healthcare industry, along with the industry's unique position of accountability to the government through laws and regulations, effects of poor diversity management can be overwhelming. It is important for health care organizations not only to learn how to cope with the changes and learn about competition, but they must also learn how to deal with different ethnicities within their organizational borders. The leaders of each organization must foresee the effects of diversity on its own needs and survival, including the result of organizational changes that occur in response to diversity.

In managing diversity, the leaders must understand the impact of several attributes (language, gender, and stereotypes) on how people perceive their relationship with others and their degree of involvement in decision-making within the organization. The first attribute is language. Managers or leaders in organizations must recognize that understanding the differences in languages people speak is often the first step in diversity management. Language understanding facilitates communication and information sharing. Understanding people's language or trying to put meaning into what has been said imparts clarity into one's intention or purpose.

Gender difference is another important attribute that managers and leaders must try to understand when developing a diversity management program. Men and women look at issues differently, automatically leading to different views and perceptions. For example, each gender uses conversation for different purposes. Some men find laughing and occasional jokes a lively and healthy event while others don't; some men tend to use talk to assert their status and accomplishment. Women often converse for the purpose of building and maintaining rapport, connection, and intimacy with others. Female socialization, according to Trice and Beyer (1993), encourages the development of selflessness, altruism, and self-sacrifice, contributing to the formation of female subcultures within the workplace. Understanding the differences between genders could improve relationships and serve as a catalyst to a better diversity management program for the organization.

Finally, the most important attribute is stereotype. Johnson and Johnson (2003) looked at stereotype as a product of the way the human mind stores, organizes, and recalls information. It is used to describe the differences among groups and to predict how others will behave. Stereotyping promotes unfairness and injustice in the organization. Organizational leaders must understand the potential problems related to stereotyping when developing a diversity management program. The leader must pay attention to the deep negative connotation stereotyping has on self-esteem and moral development. The leader must recognize stereotyping when it occurs and prevent it in order to foster a sense of community within the organization.

System Practice and Diversity Management

Managing diversity could be said to originate from system thinking practices, knowing that having a broader sense of issues related to the daily performance of the institute is better than having a single narrow-minded perspective. System practice teaches us that building a community is better than isolationism. A community is possible when leaders have a systematic outlook. System concepts within the organization give birth to a design that allows for a multidisciplinary team with different roles and perspectives and a common objective of working together in a collaborative environment.

According to Checkland (1999), general systems theory is a multidisciplinary approach that leaders can use to bring people together in an organization; through system practice, the leader challenges long-held assumptions and breaks through with new methods of solving problems. Understanding the interdependence and interconnections of systems within an operation can provide a more holistic atmosphere that embraces the new healthcare environment. The need for a collaborative healthcare system is very important to the overall quality of life and standard of living for the health care providers and the community that they serve.

Having common goals and a systematic approach will better serve the organization and allow different teams within the organization to complete the assigned tasks collaboratively by sharing information with each other. System practice is only possible in an organization that has confidence in open and socio-technical systems. An open system is one that appreciates the importance of soft system thinking to organizational problem solving. According to Checkland (1999), a socio-technical system rests on the principle that "organizations may be regarded as open systems and in such a system the technology, the sentiments of members as a social group, and the organization's environment are all interdependent: none is of prime importance over the others" (p. 33). This analogue helps put organizational decision-making and structural design into a joint basket in which every individual has a place, a room, and a part to play, both in the initial phase and in the implementation phase of the decision. Organizations that understand the importance of living together also recognize the principle of system practices and the importance of working together as a team to develop the organization.

Wang (2004) proposed that systems thinking in organizations transcends disciplined boundaries. Organizations must be seen as not having boundaries, but as open, organic, living systems that emphasize the dependence of the organization on a continual flow of energy and on resources located within the organization (Senge, 1990). Checkland (1999) stated that systems thinking theory helps shift the criterion from the parts to the whole. He believes that "living systems are integrated wholes, whose properties cannot be reduced to those of smaller parts" (p. 37). Organizational activities should be seen as the totality of connections among systemic elements used for the unification and interconnection of ideas among members of the organization.

The general system theory, as proposed by von Bertalanffy (as cited in Checkland, 1999), allows for systematic investigations into the nature of structure, organizational behavior, and the interdependencies between them. Systems thinking theory facilitates the comprehension of complex organizations by modeling them as united, as rule-governed, and as a comprehensive whole system. Systems thinking theory focuses on the interaction among the interdependent components of a complex organization, with a generality assumption, which states wholeness is better and more advantageous than the sum of its parts (Wang, 2004). When leaders look more closely at an organization's environment, they discover that the organization consists of various systems and subsystems interacting with their environments. The mutual relationships and understanding found among these systems or subsystems help bond people together into a whole.

Thornton, Peltier and Perreault (2004) reported that systems thinking should be a useful way to improve an organization. It is a helpful tool for initiating organizational change and maintaining continuous improvement in the organization. Decision-making in an organization is effective when all stakeholders are included in the process. Rausch (2003) alluded to participation by the whole as an important element of a decision, plan, problem, or opportunity. The best predictors of success or failure can be found in the social processes used during the decision-making process. These social processes include the degree of involvement and participation by stakeholders in the development of the solution (Vroom, 2003). When participation is used to foster decision implementation, there is usually a better outcome and higher success rate.

To be successful as a leader in today's working environment, the leader must believe in the collective efforts of all people and be ready to create and foster a culture wherein people have an opportunity to be heard, valued, and respected for their suggestions and contributions. When this occurs, the leader is said to recognize those values in diversity and to see diversity as a measure of unity in the organization and a process of bringing out the best in people. Working together as a body should be the centerpiece of organizational decision-making and a means of building a better community. When each individual feels the connectedness of working together as a united organization, they become more integrated as a group with common objectives and intentions. The result of this connectedness is body, soul, and mind of the individual coming together for the sake of the organization rather than being disconnected from the organization.

The leader's objective during decision-making should not be the effectiveness of the decision alone, but ensuring the decision will have the necessary support and commitment for effective implementation. Effective implementation depends on how far the leader goes in getting people involved during the initial phase of the decision-making process. Diversity management brings with it the following advantages to the organization: (a) a training ground in which people can think through the implications of decisions, (b) participation that serves as team building and fosters positive relationships among group members, and (c) alignment of the goals of individual members with the goals of the organization.

The desire of any leader is to achieve a stable and progressive organization; this is directly or indirectly, the long-term goal for survival and effectiveness of any organization. A systems approach is a proven way of achieving this stable and progressive state. This systems approach to organizational diversity can be accomplished through a set of interacting units with interrelationships among each unit. To be successful, an organization needs strong and effective relationships among its parts. Each member of the organization must be appreciated and their contributions seen as valuable. In hospitals, the nurse must appreciate the housekeeper doing the cleaning at the same time the physician values the contribution of the laboratory workers toward the final care of the patients. It is very important for the leaders to understand that people can be different in their thinking, values, and understanding, but united as a team because of their common goals and objectives and the synergy gained from their differences. Multiple studies have shown that when members of a team perceive a climate of justice, respect, and trust, they in return experience greater satisfaction and commitment to the organization.

A unified purpose is achieved when each member of the organization looks beyond his or her own personal needs and perspectives. Ultimately, in a systems approach, each leader and follower recognizes that no matter what his or her individual role is in the organization, each one cares about the patient and the organization's goals. From this perspective, all stakeholders can begin to work together as a team and attain all organizational goals, including unified team building.

Managing diversity means that all members of the organization are ready to live with the principle of oneness and equality. This is not accomplished through financial incentives. The successful implementation of organizational diversity occurs when all stakeholders allow the principle of diversity to reflect in their attitudes and behaviors, their interactions and communication with each other through daily practice. A stronger, more positive organizational relationship could be a final product for a well coordinated and managed diversity program in any organization.

Reinventing Core Principles of Diversity Management

Three core principles have emerged as a comprehensive model that could be used successfully by any manager when trying to reinvent diversity management in the workplace. These principles, identified by the acronym T.A.P., could help leaders and managers define, measure, and develop a more comprehensive program to manage cultural diversity in the organization:

1. Tolerance,
2. Awareness, and
3. Personal development.

Tolerance is significant when trying to manage cultural diversity in today's workplace. Since diversity means something different to every member of the organization, it is essential for the leaders to build a culture of tolerance in the organization; it should be considered a priority. Tolerance is about acknowledging the strengths and weaknesses of each member of the organization and being willing to accept them as they are. Tolerance eliminates destructive criticism, devaluation, and condescending attitudes while helping solidify diverse interests of different subcultures, beliefs, and understanding. Tolerance can provide the organization with basic functional knowledge and expertise about people and the ability to build a positive interdependence among various cultures. To be able to work together as a team, people must be willing to tolerate each other and create a cooperative environment in which positive relationships among diverse members are encouraged.

Awareness is the self-examination and exploration of one's knowledge about and understanding of the meaning of diversity. Leaders must encourage people to perform a self-examination of their own position, knowledge, and biases. Through self-examination, people begin to discover their own biases, prejudices, and assumptions about individuals who are different from them or share beliefs that are completely different from what they know or grew up to know. If there is no self-examination or awareness of one's position on diversity, the self-imposition of one's beliefs, values, and behaviors toward others will likely negate the principles of cohesiveness and team building in the organization.

Personal development through workplace diversity is possible because of the embedded knowledge that diversity brings to the organization. Spending more time to understand other people's cultures, beliefs, and what they bring to the team serves as a better way of understanding their worldview, which positively contributes to the self-enrichment of each individual. Knowing others' worldviews will help each individual understand how people interpret their relationships with others, and how this interpretation guides their thinking, their interactions, their associations, and their understanding of the work environment.

Managing diversity effectively includes personal growth and development of each member of the organization. Leaders must encourage members to devote time and resources to various aspects of learning to improve one's understanding of others and their cultures. Individuals need the skills to interact effectively with people from a wide variety of backgrounds. Through personal growth, individuals will be able to develop relevant diversity skills necessary for better relationships and team building. Individuals will be able to perform a better cultural assessment essential for team unification and to make more culturally sensitive issues less problematic to resolve. The more knowledge people are able to acquire on diversity, the better for the organization. It will help prevent stereotyping and conflicts while improving personal relationships among members.

Culture and Cultural Competency

It is common knowledge that each culture operates according to its own internal dynamic, its own principles, and its own laws, written and unwritten (Hall & Hall, 1987). However, there are some common threads that run through all cultures. *Culture*, according to some experts, can be likened to a giant, extraordinary complex, subtle computer. Cultural conditioning and programs, both consciously and subconsciously, guide the actions and responses of human beings in every walk of life. This process requires attention to everything people do to survive, advance in the world, and gain satisfaction from life. Furthermore, cultural programs will not work if crucial steps are omitted, which happens when people unconsciously apply their own rules to another system (Hall & Hall, 1987). Culture and cultural conditioning of people can affect technology transfer, managerial attitudes, managerial ideology, and even business-government relations. Furthermore, and perhaps most important, "culture affects how people think and behave" (Hodgetts & Luthans, 2003, p. 109). An example of observing the differences in cultures is when researchers and managers compare cultural values. Time and time again, it has been shown that there are difference in priorities of cultural values between the United States, Japan, and Arab Countries (Elashmawi & Harris, 1996, p. 63). For example while Americans often rank freedom as their first value, Japanese tend to choose belongingness and Arabs choose family security first. Of course, similar differences exist between the cultures of Jamaica, Turkey, Bahamas, Afghanistan, the United States of America and others which can impact employment practices among them.

From the comparison of cultural values by Elashmawi and Harris (1996), one can observe that freedom and independence are the two main priorities in the American culture; while in Japan it is belonging and group harmony; and in Arab countries it is family security and harmony. In the United States, the

Constitution stands for freedom and independence while in Arab countries, it is taught that family is the most important aspect of life. While "age" or seniority was ranked as fourth by the Japanese and Arab respondents, it did not even make the top ten list in the United States. Of course, such values and orientations toward age come from society; and society conditions human behavior which might lead to discriminatory decisions. Becker (2000) stated that "The technological innovations, demographic movements, political events, and economic forces have changed over time and are continuing to change human behavior in the future." As a matter-of-fact, one can say that "In today's increasingly competitive and demanding international free market economy, managers can't succeed solely on their domestic cultural understanding skills alone" (Becker, 2000, p. 1). It is very important for managers to understand the protocols of business operation in each particular culture / country, before making hiring, developing, and promotional decisions.

Harris, Moran, and Moran (2004) provided ten basic categories that are important for understanding culture and these categories can be useful when studying another culture. The ten categories offered by Harris, Moran, and Moran include (2004, p. 5):

1. Sense of Self and Space
2. Communication and Language
3. Dress and Appearance
4. Food and Feeding Habits
5. Time and Time Consciousness
6. Relationships
7. Values and Norms
8. Beliefs and Attitudes
9. Mental Process and Learning, and
10. Work Habits and Practices.

Culture, as stated before, and in its simplest form, is a way of life. For example, Afghans, and most other Muslims, often greet each other by saying "*Assalam-u-alaikum,*" which basically means "peace be upon you." In this respect, Afghan greeting is very similar to other practices or ways of life. For example, in the tribes of northern Natal in South Africa, they greet each other by saying "*Sawa bona,*" which means 'I see you,' and the other person would reply by saying "*Sikhona*" meaning "I am here." The concept is that by acknowledging that you are seeing the person, you bring him or her into existence. In Afghanistan, the proper reply for "*Assalam-u-alaikum,*" would be "*Wa`-alai-kum-Assalam*" which means "and peace be unto you." Afghans use this greeting because Afghanistan is an Islamic country and Islam is about the universal unity of every human being. As such, managers in Afghanistan are not allowed to discriminate based on race, culture, ethnicity, country of origin, or any other societal factors which one cannot change (when it is not a job requirement). In this case, Islam is a way of life as it has imposed a complete ethical code that expects honest, fair, generous, and respectful conduct and behavior from its members in all situations. This code also prohibits waste, adultery, gambling, usury, alcoholic beverages, and eating certain meats (such as pork). Each and every Muslim is responsible for his or her actions to a higher power, and are culturally conditioned to behave according to the societal norms.

While culture can condition individuals both positively and negatively, at times the conditioning can be stereotypical and lead to illegal or unethical discrimination. The word discrimination is synonymous with bias, making a distinction, taste, favoritism, bigotry, inequality, injustice, prejudice, unfairness, and intolerance. While many of these synonyms are negative, it is important to note that not all forms of discrimination are illegal or unethical. In society, a man may choose to discriminate against women who do not have a high school education when he decides to marry a woman; thus he may marry someone who has a college degree, while not even considering those who have not acquired this status. Similarly, a female might choose to marry a male who earns a comfortable salary and one who owns a house; as such, she may not even consider those who are unemployed, employed in low paying jobs, or those who have chosen to spend their money in other means versus owning a house. These forms of discrimination are based on personal values and preferences. However, such personal values and preferences do not always apply in the workplace when one is deciding who to hire, since hiring practices are based on one's ability to perform the job. Professionally, managers and leaders discriminate based on organizational values, educational qualifications related to the job, level of experience, and many others when looking for potential candidates in the workplace. However, these decisions do not always negatively impact candidates based on their age, gender, or race when practiced as intended by the organizational values and job qualifications. Yet, societal stereotypes and myths do lead some individuals to discriminate against others based on their gender, race, age or other such non-job related variables that are not necessarily indicative of a potential candidate's level of performance. These forms of discrimination are illegal in many nations and, certainly, highly unethical. Another important point is to understand that cultures do not discriminate, but people do in terms of their thoughts, words, actions, and behaviors. While cultures cannot be changed easily, people's thoughts, words, actions, and behaviors can be changed; and this change takes place best when it is intrinsically initiated through knowledge, education, awareness, critical thinking, and self reflection.

Overall, each person is likely to achieve fairness in hiring, development, and promotion of individuals as per his or her own efforts, education, self reflections, behaviors, and ability to effectively work with others. George Adams, philosopher, is reported to have said "There is no such thing as a 'self-made' man. We are made up of thousands of others. Everyone who has ever done a kind deed for us, or spoken one word of encouragement to us, has entered into the make-up of our character and of our thoughts, as well as our success."

Self-reflection about national and international issues is critical for personal growth and development as a global leader. Hopefully, all scholars of management, human resources management and global leadership do this often, and accordingly evaluate their actions and progress on a daily, weekly, monthly, and yearly basis. Of course, one way to answer the question of why study discrimination issues or global human resources management is to say that continuously getting more education in today's complex world allows for better leadership and upward mobility which can provide for a greater financial reward in today's changing environment. While these are good goals, oftentimes they are not the primary motivators for making the decision to such challenging endeavors. The opportunity to learn and grow personally tends to be the deciding factor for many individuals who choose to continue learning. As has been said many times, global knowledge can open many avenues and prevent many embarrassments. Overall, it is the vast amount of knowledge to be acquired in this world that continues to provide motivation and excitement for many people.

Today's world is an ever-changing place, providing avenues of learning at a pace that most people cannot keep up. These changes can only occur as a result of continued learning. It is the need to question that drives change. It is always easy to do it the way that it has always been done, but if one never looks past the obvious then how do we know what lies beyond. To truly learn, one must open his/her mind and try to put away preconceived notions. People must become and be critical thinkers in order to continuously learn and grow in understanding national and international human resource practices. The goal of a formal education program is to increase one's knowledge and insight. It allows people to increase their understanding of diversity management by expanding on subjects that were studied during the completion of a previous degree. A formal program allows one to take real life experiences and learn from them. The people participating in a formal program each bring a different background to the group, which allows for new perceptions to be shared and new interactions to occur. Such a program provides a support group to "bounce" ideas off of each other and gather encouragement from diverse perspectives.

With the current economic conditions, international firms are looking to fill vacant positions with people that have global experience and cultural sensitivity with regard to gender, age, local norms, and other issues related to hiring practices. They are looking for the candidate that has the "edge," the ability to understand and manage the business in a fair manner. Formal and informal education, especially in the area of international business, diversity management and human resources, provides the framework for these qualities. For those already with a company, senior management often sends the message that a degree is needed to move up the corporate "ladder." While promotion is a good reason to obtain a global awareness, sensitivity and education, the desire to accomplish one's tasks as a manager in a fair, just, ethical, and moral manner must come from a personal place – the inner-self. The opportunity for personal and professional growth should be a secondary accomplishment, not the primary.

Understanding cultural differences is a necessity for the growth and success of doing business with others throughout the world and serving each market in an effective and efficient manner. International expansions have been on the rise in the past few decades; and they present managers with new challenges on how to deal with the differences in culture. One of the benefits that such expansions offer is the access to new markets for economies of scale. With globalization of markets, competition and organizations, individuals increasingly interact, manage, negotiate, and compromise with people from a variety of cultures. Over a quarter of century ago, Hofstede (1980, 2001, 1993) identified five dimensions of cultural values: power distance (PD), uncertainty avoidance (UA), masculinity / femininity (Mas), collectivism/individuality (COLL), and long term-short term orientation (LTO) that characterize cultural differences among diverse countries or cultures. According to Hofstede, a country's position, on these five dimensions, allows predictions on the way societies operate, including the management principles that are applied. Other researchers have developed theories to explain the extent to which one culture can affect others as people migrate and interact in the global marketplace, including convergence, divergence and crossvergence (CDC). *Convergence* describes the merging of different cultures due to the influence of globalization and other factors that bring them into close contact with one another. *Divergence* is the extent to which distinctiveness is exhibited by a specific culture despite interaction with other cultures. Finally, *crossvergence* is the development of a new culture with its own characteristics that result from cultures interacting with each other over time (Dastoor *et al.*, 2005).

Many economies are shaping their management practices to model those of the United States and may, ultimately, transform their national cultures as well. According to some experts and writers, the export of U.S. management theories and practices through universities and management development workshops in other countries assumes that other countries are eager to become Americanized, that is, to converge with the culture of the U.S. Other researchers, however, think that there is a general lack of success in countries adopting the so-called western management practices to develop their economy (Hofstede, 1993).

Many third world and developing countries, including Jamaica, the Grand Bahamas, Turkey, and Afghanistan, have adopted Western management practices to achieve economic stability. Many foreign nationals work in the U.S. and many students study there as well. The diversity of the cultures within the U.S. presents opportunities and challenges as foreign students and workers are exposed to an entrepreneurial culture for a prolonged period of time. According to Dastoor, Roofe, and Mujtaba (2005), "when they return to their home country they sometimes discover that they no longer fit into the culture, and many end up returning to the U.S. on a permanent basis." Regardless of where people continue to work, international and cross-cultural management skills become important for today's professionals and diverse workforce.

Authors Hodgetts and Luthans (2003), in the textbook entitled *International Management: Culture, Strategy, and Behavior* defined international management as "the process of applying management concepts and techniques in a multinational environment" (p. 5). They further said that "culture is acquired knowledge that people use to interpret experience and generate social behavior." Of course, this acquired knowledge forms people's values, creates their attitudes, and influences their behavior in a predictable pattern (Hodgetts & Luthans, 2003, p. 108). Hofstede (1980) defined culture as the collective programming of the mind, through locally held value systems, which distinguishes one group of people from another. Today's managers, with diverse value systems, are global managers as they mostly manage people of diverse beliefs in an international environment. As such, understanding culture plays a critical role in workforce diversity management. For an organization to operate in several countries with different cultures, it is important for the management team to understand the culture of these countries in order to efficiently and effectively operate interdependently among them. The norms and practices of one culture may not be the norms and practices of another.

Culture Shock: Personal Stories of Coming to America

Culture is basically the way things are done at a specific place, department, organization, or country. Culture tends to reinforce the information or misinformation that people have learned in their earlier influences. Individuals form what is called a "cultural filter or lens" in their minds, which all information tends to pass through. The information is actually passing through an accumulation of all the stereotypes and prejudices that has been gained through socialization in the culture. In other words, the preconceived notions tend to strongly influence the filtering process. People tend to make assumptions based on these preconceived notions and then act on them as if they were fact. This is known as being ethnocentric. That is, a belief that "our" culture is the right one and anything different is suspect. *Ethnocentricity* is a trait that is especially true of members of dominant cultures, especially if there is a "superiority complex." The assumptions people make are influenced by the culture they were brought up in during their younger years.

Sometimes the behavior is strongly influenced by one's culture. Understanding culture can help professionals to keep it from being a source of conflict when they encounter people who see the world differently. Every culture is unique and has many elements that must be considered when learning about them. One needs to understand that folks from one culture may view an element very differently than folks from another culture. The diversity of views tends to often be a source of conflict in a diverse workplace. Understanding culture and its importance in shaping what is believed can help professionals avoid culture shock and to recognize when cultural differences are the cause of conflict.

Culture shock, a sense of psychological disorientation and discomfort one experiences, is a reality of life when one enters a new workplace, city, state, country, or culture. Some culture shock experiences can be severe and lead to sickness, while others can be minor despite the fact that they can cause discomfort or miscommunication among the people involved.

From a personal experience perspective, coming to America has given me many new insights about cultural perspectives and thoughts. For example, when coming to the United States of America, I was wearing my traditional Afghan clothes which are loose and baggy; as a result, I received much unwanted attention from people on the plane which made me very uncomfortable. On the plane, sitting next to me, there was a beautiful young lady with shorts and a T-shirt. Despite the fact that as a teenager I liked sitting next to her, I still felt uncomfortable due to my years of cultural conditioning because I felt as though I was sitting next to someone who was 'half naked." According to the Afghan culture women normally wear lots of clothes and fully cover themselves, while the western culture offers many different choices. This is not to say that one culture is right and the other is wrong, they are just different. Each culture sees things differently based on its own traditions and established norms. Accordingly, each culture must be respected in its own rights.

A week after settling in Fort Myers our neighbor invited us to her home for dinner on a Saturday. While sitting in her living room I noticed her dog came in the room and sat on the couch. I thought this is one brave dog and is probably going to get yelled at for coming into the room because in Afghanistan dogs don't come inside the living area. In most Afghan families, dogs live outside the living area or in the hallways. So, I immediately called the hostess and said "Becky, your dog just came into the living room and is making your couch dirty." She said "it's OK, she likes sitting on the couch." Even though I love dogs and, as a teenager, I have often had a dog or two in the house, I was surprised and shocked that they let the dog inside the living room. The dog ate in the same area as us and sat on the same couch as human beings. This is not to say that one culture is right and the other is wrong, they are just different. Each culture sees things differently based on its own traditions and established norms.

During dinner, at the neighbor's house, I noticed that one of Becky's children started eating pizza with her hands and Becky's husband held the chicken with his fingers as he was eating it. I was surprised, because I was told not to eat with my hands in the United States, and asked my Dad "aren't Americans supposed to eat food with forks and spoons?" He said "yes, however" he continued, "that there are certain foods (such as fried chicken, pizza, wings, hot dogs, hamburgers, etc.) that can be eaten with hands according to the American culture." In Afghanistan, most people eat with their hands since it is probably the cleanest "utensil" available and they have total control over its cleanliness. However, in the United States of America and most European countries people usually eat with forks and spoons. It is not to say that one culture's customs are right and the others are wrong, they are just different. Each culture sees things differently based on its own tradition and established norms. In Afghanistan, people use lots of oil and butter while cooking to keep hard working family members healthy. However, in the United States and most other developed nations, people attempt to reduce the amount of oil and butter in their food as they also want to remain healthy (or to avoid getting sick from obesity concerns). It seems like both cultures are concerned about the health of their people, yet they do things very differently due to the fact that the working conditions are different. I often tell my friends that I have always been a little overweight by choice -- because I have never eaten anything by mistake. But I am "working out" trying to go back to my original weight, nine pounds and two ounces. Then again, maybe…I'll just settle for being healthy and in good shape.

During my first few months in the U.S., I noticed that American men, in general, do not hold hands or kiss each other while greeting. However the opposite is true in Afghanistan. While in Afghanistan men traditionally don't touch or kiss women who are not related to them, American men often shake hands or kiss other women as a sign of appreciation, affection or thank you to the other person. This is not to say that one culture is right and the other is wrong, they are just different. Each culture sees things differently based on its own tradition and established norms. If you are not aware of these differences you can put yourself or others in embarrassing situations when going into a new culture or country. For example, an Afghan refugee brought his family to Miami and the local church personnel helped them find an apartment and home furniture that was donated by local people. As a favor to the community, his wife was one day involved in helping out and cleaning the church for some community activity and at the end the pastor came and thanked all of the ladies who had helped out. As he was thanking the women who had volunteered he was shaking their hands and kissing them on the cheek. When he approached closer to the Afghan wife to shake her hand and give her a kiss on the cheek she punched him in the face and broke his nose. The pastor needed medical assistance and received several stitches above his eyes. Most traditional Afghan women have very strong feelings about men who are not their husbands or immediate relatives kissing or touching them. In this case the pastor probably received a culture shock as did the Afghan wife. The truth is that in Afghanistan men generally don't kiss other women on the cheek, while in the United States this tradition seems to be okay with most families. This is not to say that one culture is right and the other is wrong, they are just different. Each culture sees things differently based on its own tradition and established norms. People now realize that when they are in Rome, they should not always have to do as the Romans when it comes to their cultural beliefs and mores. As such, they should be able to retain their own cultural customs.

Cultures can also change and alter, but they may do so very slowly. A friend who visited Afghanistan in 1999 after seventeen years said that he went shopping in the Kabul Bazaar and was surprised by what he saw. He noticed that a shop owner was not in his shop. However, the shop was left open. He observed that a customer went inside the shop, got five eggs, two onions, one tomato, and three loaves of bread, then he calculated the money, put the correct amount of money on the counter, and left. Throughout the next few minutes he observed similar situations in several other shops and found that people generally didn't take anything without leaving the correct amount of money, and shop owners felt comfortable leaving their shops unattended for a few minutes. In this time period of the late 1990's, people avoided stealing because the government in Afghanistan practiced strict rules when it came to stealing. In other words, thieves could lose one of their hands for stealing. These rules were made clear to the population and theft rates had essentially become obsolete. Can you imagine leaving your shop unattended on a street in Miami, Kingston, Nassau, Tokyo, London, Moscow or New York? You are probably not going to be in business for very long. This is not to say that one way is better than the other, they are just different. Each culture has its own traditions, customs, mores, and established norms. Accordingly, each culture must be respected for its customs and mores that have been communicated to its members.

Often individuals of dominant cultures tend to think that their culture and their way is the "right" way and anything different is suspect. As mentioned before, this belief or tendency is called ethnocentricity. Our assumptions are heavily influenced by our respective cultures and these assumptions need to be examined for accuracy. Dr. Susan Fisq, a sociologist from the University of Massachusetts, has been quoted as having said that "what separates a racist from a non-racist is whether your second thought is could my first impression be wrong?" We could substitute any other oppressive terms (*i.e.* sexist, ageist, etc.) with the term racist and ask the same question to make sure we are not making assumptions that are unfounded or based on misinformation. This can help professionals make better decisions when dealing with people who are different and see the world differently.

Benchmarking and International Management

Globalization has affected how people do business across the globe. Every day more and more businesses are moving toward organization-wide rationalization. Professor John Quelch describes a new style of management that is a mix between the U.S. model as a primary influencer and other countries around the world. The U.S. management style is focused on fast outcomes and results, although when needed it is very flexible and open to new ideas and people, learning the best practices from other countries and adapting (Emmons, 2005). Professor Deshpande has found that a company in order to be globally competitive and successful has some specific characteristics like an entrepreneurial culture that encourages and rewards risk, a large investment in customer insight, short period of time for the introduction to the market of new products and services and an organization with a strong commitment to the customer or customer-centric (Emmons, 2005). Professor Desphpande also suggests that the corporate culture of successful firms is often stronger than the national culture. As a global company implements a transnational strategy the decision making to accomplish this is stronger than the national influences and toward common practices shared by other top international firms (Emmons, 2005). Professors Khana and Palepu have found in the product and labor markets that there are similarities in international standards, although there is a limit and there are national influences that still remain powerful and distinct. However, in general, companies with global competition tend to benchmark themselves with global best practices and performance standards (Emmons, 2005).

Managers are finding common ground trying to find a balance between their culture and being open to other value systems, communications styles and decision-making processes. People are adjusting their behavior to facilitate work. According to Emmons (2005), Andy Klump describes an emerging international style that varies by company. Some companies like Dell in China have American attributes in the higher level management, although the department level management style is still ruled by the local culture. Aron Pempel describes the existence of universal standards in the workplace that are defined by large multinationals. In Mexico, for Nike employees, lunch time was reduced from two hours to one hour to resemble the American culture; this change altered lifestyles and customs for some employees, however the majority of employees voted to make the change (Emmons, 2005). Integration of the global economy is not allowing anyone to be insulated, the best practices of different countries are being leveraged worldwide by multinationals.

Globalization is making international companies more efficient. Multinationals are analyzing subsidiaries and branches and using the best practices and techniques of different countries of operation in a worldwide environment and applying them globally. In order to be competitive in the global marketplace, companies are not only looking at children and parent companies, they are also benchmarking the top performing organizations in the globe and adopting some of the methods. In order to be competitive companies are forced to comply with international standards and expectations.

There are some activities such as marketing that are kept local while others like the production process, quality assurance, human and workers right issues, and environmental matters are being adapted across international organizations from the most efficient operations. For example the Japanese manufacturing techniques have been benchmarked by many national and international firms around the globe. These techniques cause the system to look less American and more like a multinational.

The Significance of Effective Communication in Healthcare[10]

The changing demographics of the United States—especially with respect to its racial and ethnic diversity—have been widely published and highly publicized. According to the 2000 U.S. Census, approximately 30 percent of the population belongs to a racial or ethnic minority group. It is estimated that, by 2070, one in two Americans will be a member of a racial or ethnic minority group (Friedman, 2005). The Census Bureau further projects that, by the year 2100, non-Hispanic whites will comprise only 40 percent of the U.S. population. When populations change, health care is one of two sectors (the other is education) where the impact is felt immediately (Friedman, 2005).

According to Gardenswartz and Rowe (1998), the reality of health care in many areas of the country resembles Cigna's Grand Avenue Health Center in downtown Los Angeles, located near significant Latino, African American, and Asian communities, where both the patient population and the workforce are extremely diverse. Thirty-five percent of the staff is Latino, 20 percent is Filipino, 5 percent is Thai, and the remainder is Euro-American or Korean. More recently, Friedman (2005) reported that, in addition to the growing numbers of racial and ethnic minorities among the patient population, minorities and immigrants may well represent much of the potential health care workforce of the future.

The health component of every culture includes health preservation, prevention, illness, treatment, coping styles, and beliefs about death and dying; and culture determines illness behavior (Lassiter, 1995). In other words, an individual's worth and values are intrinsically ingrained, having been derived from one's culture of birth or habitation. The Institute of Medicine's landmark study, *Unequal Treatment: Confronting Racial and Ethnic Disparities in Health Care*, made public the cultural gap between the health care system and the huge number of racial and ethnic minorities it serves. The study found that U.S. racial and ethnic minorities experience a lower quality of health services and are less likely to receive, for example, routine medical procedures and appropriate heart medications; they are also less likely to be referred for kidney dialysis and transplants. Yet, they are *more* likely to receive less desirable procedures, such as lower limb amputations for diabetes and other conditions (IOM, 2002). Even when indexes of income, education, employment, and insurance levels are the same, these disparities persist. As the country becomes increasingly diverse, interpersonal communication, which is fundamental to *any* relationship and can be problematic even for individuals within the same culture, becomes increasingly challenging.

---

[10] -Coauthored with Roscoe Dandy, Former Commissioned Officer in the U.S. Public Health Service, and Dan Austin, Professor Emeritus, Nova Southeastern University.

Cultural competence, which is sensitivity to and respect for diversity in language, religion, customs, values, and traditions, is the foundation for effectively managing diversity; and effective interpersonal communication is crucial to cultural competence. Part of effective communication and cultural competency is about understanding the self and self-disclosure.

Self-disclosure has been investigated and researched for a number of years, because it is a useful strategy for sharing information with others. By sharing information, we become more intimate with other people and interpersonal relationship are strengthened. There are two models that have often used to illustrate self-disclosure, that is, the social penetration and the Johari Window.

1. *Self-disclosure* is not simply providing information to another person. Instead it is sharing information with others that they would not normally know or discover. One pair of researchers, Irwin Altman and Dalmas Taylor, developed a model of *social penetration* to illustrate how much and what kind of information we reveal in various stages of a relationship. The theory states that humans are like onions. While onions have layers and layers of skin, people have layers and layers of personality. You must first expose one layer before you can get to the next.

2. Joe Luft and Harry Ingham developed a conceptual model to help us understand what might be going on in interpersonal relationships. The name of their model is the *Johari Window*. The Johari Window Matrix, Figure 7.1, is a useful way of viewing self-disclosure. It is also a way of showing how much information you know about yourself and how much other knows about you. The window contains four panes, as shown below.

The *Public Self Pane* represents free and open exchange of information between others and one's public behavior available to everyone. The pane increases in size as the level of trust increases between others and self as more information – particularly personally relevant information – is shared. The *Blind Self Pane* includes information that others see in you, but you cannot see in yourself. You might think that you are a poor leader, but others think you exhibit strong leadership skills. The *Hidden Self Pane* contains information you wish to keep private, such as dreams or ambitions. The *Unknown Self Pane* includes everything that you and others do not know about you. You might have hidden talents for example, that you have not explored. Through self-disclosure, we open and close panes in the Johari Window so that we may become more intimate or effective in interpersonal communication with others. Overall, according to experts, the smaller the *open self* is, the poorer the communication. Self-awareness, therefore, is a way to understand and reflect on our *blind self* and to reduce the *hidden*. By definition, intrapersonal communication is internal, driven by our personality type.

Figure 7.1 – The Johari Window

	Known to Self	Not Known to Self
Known to Others	**Public Self:** *Known to self and others*	**Blind Self:** *Blind to self, seen by others*
Not Known to Others	**Private Self:** *Open to self, hidden from others*	**Unknown Self:** *Unknown to self and others*

Although numerous communication models have been developed, the model discussed here—*the Johari Window: A Model of Interpersonal Communication Processes*—measures interpersonal style in terms of communication awareness based on the interaction of two sources of information: oneself and others (Brown & Harvey, 2006). Following is a summary of each of this model's four areas of communication awareness (Brown and Harvey, 2006), followed by an example.

Public Area—Includes those thoughts, feelings, and behaviors known to both the person and to others. The area of both our public image and of interaction involves mutually shared perceptions. A basic assumption of the Johari Window Model is that there is a direct correlation between interpersonal effectiveness and the amount of mutually shared information. In other words, the larger the public area becomes, the more effective the communication will be. For example, if one chooses to let you in their public (open) area, more communication occurs and this free flowing atmosphere leads to better understanding, respect, value in what is being said, and trust in the sender of the communication.

Blind Area—Represents aspects of the self not known to oneself, but obvious to others. Such aspects include mannerisms and habits, of which one may be totally unaware, that are apparent to others. This is important in interpersonal communications because one often does not know whether another interprets their behavior as offensive or receptive. Unbeknownst to the sender of communication, the blind area (invisible signals) can lead to adversarial or engaging dialogue. There are unconscious reasons why A will not talk to B concerning duty assignments, reassignments, days off, and the like. Yet C can talk to A about the very same things and get positive responses.

Closed Area—Involves thoughts, feelings, and behaviors known only to oneself and not to others. This area, which includes feelings one perceives as possibly harmful to one's self-image, serves as the façade that protects one's ego. The closed area becomes a large part of people's interactions with strangers and in new situations, because they don't know much about each other; and trust is low. Disclosure is the only way for others to become aware of this area. As such, it can take years of knowing someone before gaining insight into it. Without trust, communication remains somewhat superficial or dormant. The closed area index can even build up with creeping signs of antagonism, resentfulness, and an inability to listen and behave within professional norms if, for example, the affected parties are in close proximity over long stretches of time doing stressful shift work. The guarded interactions sometimes result in mixed signals relative to organizational or team goals. Such signals can become further mixed if not clarified in oral instructions, printed materials, or engaging gestures of acceptance, helpfulness, and guidance.

Unknown Area—Involves feelings and behaviors that are inaccessible both to oneself and to others. Some psychologists believe that this is the area in which hidden aspects of the personality and unconscious, deeply repressed feelings and impulses reside (Brown & Harvey, 2006). Under certain circumstances, this unknown area can explode, based on provocation or precipitating events. For example, the supervisor continually tells the employee they smell alcohol on the person while, in actuality, the scent is more of a foreign smell to the supervisor. The employee, being from a different country than the supervisor is well acclimated to his/her body and, in fact, the supervisor's odor is also different to him/her.

Each cell in the Johari Window Model represents a specific area of knowledge about oneself and demonstrates the quality of the interpersonal communication process. The openness of communication leads to open relationships. Therefore, it is worth increasing the amount of communication in the public area by becoming more open, trusting, and risk-taking because, when this happens, others tend to react with more openness and trust, thereby enhancing the communication process.

Communication in Health Care

In the health care arena, there are two types of communication: one between health care workers and another between health care workers and patients. Although the two types are similar, there are unique differences. In communications between health care workers, the respect accorded the lead professional in America (for example, the physician on the ward or at the nurses' station, or the head nurse, if the doctor is absent) is very important.

The lead professional typically provides direction—that is, the treatment plan—and others on the team (social workers, physical therapists, dieticians, lab technicians, and so forth) are expected to abide by it. Brown and Harvey (2006), in the seventh edition of their book entitled *An Experiential Approach to Organizational Development*, provide a diagram which illustrates the diagnostic process from an organizational perspective which is also equally relevant from a clinical or health care perspective.

Problems frequently stem from the different roles that doctors and nurses are assigned in different cultures. Such problems are often accentuated by gender role differences. For example, male physicians from male-dominated countries tend to be even more authoritarian than American male doctors; and female nurses from such countries tend to be more submissive than American nurses (Galanti, 2004).

The patient's chart specifies the direction of the treatment modality to everyone involved in the patient's care. A breakdown in communications can occur when there is a lack of respect for the lead health professional or if the team member is from another country where the treatment plan might be implemented differently. Rather than communicate these differences or misunderstandings, health care workers of different cultures often associate negative patterns with persons they dislike or do not understand. Maintaining "battles" in the charting of the record and engaging in non-verbal battles seriously undermine productivity and do not foster a harmonious work environment. It has also been reported that Jamaican and African-American nurses clash over interpretations of what prejudice is and how it affects them. Unfortunately, they take it out on each other in work and social encounters provided by the health care setting. The issue to be addressed is: How do we resolve these communication barriers and move toward inclusive and healthy work behaviors? The solution is a paradigm in cultural education.

Strategies for the Health Care Diversity Manager

Galanti (2004) offers the following suggestions for easing tensions between racially and ethnically diverse staff members:

- Offer in-service training to foreign-born doctors on what to expect from American nurses. One of the nurse's important roles is to serve as an advocate for the patient. The nurse will not blindly obey a physician's order if it is believed to be detrimental to the patient.
- Instruct nurses to act in a less confrontational manner.
- Offer assertiveness training to those staff members who, by culture, tend to be submissive.
- Males from countries that lack sexual equality may refuse to take orders from a female supervisor. This issue should be openly discussed and, if change does not occur, termination should be considered.
- Offer an in-service workshop on the specific jobs expected of American nurses and the nature of the nursing culture.

- Offer in-service training on doctor/patient roles in different cultures.
- Offer sensitivity training to everyone.
- Establish clear rules concerning the speaking of native languages.
- Encourage openness in communication (for example, let someone know if your feelings have been hurt) to clear up misunderstandings.
- Require staff members to notify their supervisors when they have religious beliefs that interfere with some medical practices.

There are numerous opportunities for misunderstanding when the health care provider and the patient are of different ethnic backgrounds. For example, communication style and time orientation vary considerably from culture to culture, which can lead to confusion and annoyance for medical personnel. What is considered late in one culture may be within reasonable time limits in another culture. Pedro, whose head nurse reprimands him for being 20 minutes late, does not consider himself late and might respond with: What's the problem? Why are you picking on me? Another challenge is that people from different cultures might behave in similar ways, but for different reasons. Understanding why people communicate (or do not) in the way they do can alleviate health care workers' frustrations and potentially contribute to enhanced patient care (Galanti, 2004).

The communications between the health care worker and the patient involve a number of variables. In addition to language, which is a major barrier, age, race, gender, choice of words, body language, and tone of voice affect communication. Any of these variables can influence patient behavior and compliance; ultimately, they influence the outcome. The health care worker cannot be expected to always be conscious of all of the above variables and still focus on charting, medications, laboratory readings, vital sign variations, and referrals.

On the other hand, the patient often measures his/her care by the reduction of pain and by what the patient observes when the health care worker enters the room. Patients also observe and listen to how employees of varying backgrounds move through their tasks, communicate with each other, and address such clinical issues as wet beds, need for baths, medications, transfers for laboratory work-ups, and preparations for physical and occupational therapy exercises. It is in these settings that the patient exercises non-verbal communication with other patients to indicate how things are going. How the patient feels is a barometer of his/her interpretation of quality care and the hopes of getting better. Negative experiences in the health care setting may affect attitudes toward receiving care and impact further utilization of health care services (Shaver and Shaver, 2006).

There are other strategies that aid in communicating across language barriers. Before interacting with a patient, the health care provider should take time to imagine what the patient must be feeling. Figuratively walking in the patient's shoes is likely to make the provider more empathic. Gardenswartz and Rowe (1998) also offer the following suggestions:

- Use visual tools, such as pictures, symbols, and diagrams to make your point.
- Demonstrate, when possible; let the patient perform the required task with you observing.
- Whenever possible, use the patient's language.
- Speak slowly and pause between sentences to allow the patient time to process the information.
- Keep it simple. Avoid idiomatic expressions, medical jargon, and acronyms. Use simple words that are readily recognized.
- Repeat the message. Restate the information using different words.
- Expect confusion. Cultural influences that discourage giving a negative response make it difficult for some people to say no. Instead of relying on a yes answer, look for nonverbal signs of confusion or for behavior that indicates the person understands.
- Get help. If possible, obtain assistance from an interpreter who is fluent in both languages, but make sure the interpreter understands the concepts you are communicating.

Galanti (2004) also cites the following eight questions, developed by Arthur Kleinman et al. in a 1978 article on culture, illness, and care, which appeared in the *Annals of Internal Medicine*:

1. What do you call the problem?
2. What do you think has caused the problem?
3. Why do you think it started when it did?
4. What do you think the sickness does? How does it work?
5. How severe is the sickness? Will it have a short or long course?
6. What are the most important results you hope to receive from your treatment?
7. What are the chief problems the sickness has caused?
8. What do you fear most about the sickness?

These questions help the provider understand the patient's perception of his or her illness. Further, they contribute to the provider earning the patient's trust, thereby fostering the provision of more appropriate and more effective care (Galanti, 2004).

The growing diversity of the country's population, as well as that of its health care workforce, has raised communication to a new level of significance. To effectively manage diversity in health care organizations today requires communication skills that are, at minimum, clear, accurate, affirming, engaging, and sensitive to cultural variations. The acquisition of interpersonal skills and their appropriate utilization are imperatives for the success of the twenty first century health care manager dealing with an increasingly diverse health care workforce.

How the health care manager interprets cues, eye movements, clinical regimens, work styles, and social interactions between various cultures and ethnic groups working in the same setting is critical to his ability to move the team forward in achieving the desired outcome for the patient. A pre-requisite for the effective manager is exposure to different cultures and ethnic groups in both academic and clinical settings. The various elements of communication—tone, purpose, clarity, eye contact, and engaging persona—all play vital roles in constructive interactions that lead to productive outcomes with co-workers, patients, and patients' families. The effective manager should also encourage and coach employees in relating to patients and to one another, as well as serve as an example.

The health care manager is responsible for bridging gaps of confusion and for ensuring adherence to a steady course of quality clinical practices within an inclusive and harmonious work environment. The manager's communication style must further ensure that co-workers from various cultures share leadership roles relative to assignments (that is, determining who works the fast-paced medical wards and who works with the dialysis, respiratory, and nursing home patients), decision-making, and communicating with the various ethnic groups in the work setting.

Thus, a paradigm in cultural education via interpersonal communication skills is best learned in the work environment, or on-the-job training. Although academic learning serves as the baseline for internships, licensure, and certification, it is how the manager applies the book knowledge to a practicum setting that is critical to the survival, growth, and development of the health care organization. If, however, we move toward a new paradigm in cultural education, the classroom can be used as a quasi-work setting. Having taught graduate students for more than 25 years, one of the co-authors of this chapter has found that the classroom—that is, the classroom that includes role playing scenarios based on specific clinical issues, and that is also monitored and evaluated with proper training, coaching, case study materials, and peer evaluation—can serve as an excellent resource for the identification of a mix of potential problem areas in the workplace to aid in the development of the twenty first century health care diversity manager.

Summary

If we want to retain competent employees in our health care organizations, we must meet their needs of value, recognition, and inclusiveness and be aware of their sensitivities. One way to achieve this is to provide adequate training for health care managers, with a focus on how to communicate with persons from diverse cultures. Managing diversity in the health care system will require that equity be promoted and accountability maintained both in the social environment and within health delivery systems (Shaver and Shaver, 2006).

Culture is an important aspect of today's health care organizations, workforce and globalization patterns. Is globalization causing the development of a worldwide culture? Maybe! Some reflective thinking questions to consider are: Is it possible that globalization will cause a country's national identity to be lost as more international firms are incorporating management and operation styles from the developed nations to their business practices? While reflecting on such questions, one must acknowledge that cultures tend to regularize human behavior which can make predictability of behavior a bit easier for researchers and global employees.

Discussion Questions

1. What is culture? Describe some of the similarities and differences from two distinct cultures.
2. Do all countries have different cultures? Or, can different countries have similar cultural values? Discuss your thoughts and examples.
3. What is culture shock? Can you think of specific culture shock experiences that you or others that you know may have gone through? If so, list them.
4. What can firms, individuals, and managers do to reduce the impact of culture shock for those who travel abroad or to new cultures?
5. What are some effective methods of learning more about other cultures?
6. What is cultural competency? Is it necessary for international management?
7. Can a person become culturally competent on several cultures within a few short years?
8. What are the reasons why diversity management is essential for healthcare leaders?
9. What are some important steps for healthcare leaders to take in order to prevent misrepresentation and stereotyping among healthcare workers?
10. How will you create an effective diversity management program if you are a leader in a healthcare organization?
11. Is there any benefit for a healthcare organization with an effective diversity management program? If so, mention at least three.
12. How would you create a sustained diversity-training program in your organization?
13. How would you as a leader in a multicultural organization manage diversity?

14. How can diversity management and recognition programs help position your organization for the future?
15. Diversity management is about making the organization viable for the future. Can you explain further your understanding of this statement?
16. What are some communication challenges in the healthcare industry?
17. How can medical professionals use the Johari Window to become better interpersonal communicators with people of diverse cultures in the today's workplace? Discuss.
18. Gestures and non-verbal expressions can have different meanings in different cultures. For example, the circle made with thumb and forefinger in the United States, United Kingdom, most of Europe, and some other countries is a symbol of "A-OK," which means that everything is fine. However, this gesture for French people often says that "The person is a zero and should not be taken seriously." The same gesture means "Please give me change" in Japan. However, this symbol is a sexually obscene gesture in some Mediterranean countries and Afghanistan. Therefore, professional managers and global employees should be aware of such interpretations of their non-verbal gestures. What are some other non-verbal gestures that today's global workers should be aware of as they deal with people of diverse cultures and nationalities? Provide a list.

Generational and Spiritual Diversity

G enerational, religious, spiritual, and age diversity are realities of life and organizational leaders must be cognizant of these trends. This chapter discusses generational, spiritual and age related aspects of diversity as they relate to the workplace. This chapter also provides a review of the current literature concerning a serious problem facing current day organizations. It is one of a shrinking workforce that could happen because of the retirement of many older workers. This problem is exacerbated by the fact that many of the younger workers do not possess the skills and experience that the older workers have. The younger workers also have different moral and cultural values and different work ethics. According to an article on *Managing Workplace Diversity* by the Victorian Department of Education (2005), managing and:

> Valuing diversity is a key component of effective people management. It focuses on improving the performance of the organization and promotes practices that enhance the productivity of all staff. The dimensions of diversity include gender, race, culture, age, family/career status, religion and disability. Diversity also embraces the range of individual skills, educational qualifications, work experience and background, languages and other relevant attributes and experiences which differentiate individuals (Victorian Department of Education, 2005).

Generational and Age Diversity Management[11]

Donovan McFarlane describes aging from a medical point of view and states that it is the process of growing old or maturing, and also describes the gradual changes in the structure of a mature organism that occur normally over time and increase the probability of death (Mujtaba and Cavico, 2006). McFarlane states that the fear of aging is the fear of death which typifies the process across all cultures and societies. "Man" is forever searching for ways to escape his mortality and aging gives no comfort to him. Provided no other defects lead to death, aging eventually leads to death as the definition above communicates. Before departing this world, one is considered an "older worker," aging brings certain discriminatory practices when one is seeking employment.

---

[11] This material is co-authored with Peter T. DiPaolo, Nova Southeastern University.

As stated by Mujtaba and Cavico (2006), age discrimination has many causes and one of them seems to be cultural conditioning based on stereotyping of older workers. Schneider (2004) states that "Stereotypes have been accused of being bad because they are created or at least supported by cultures that are prejudiced and discriminatory." Of course, the impact is that in adopting and using stereotypes, people can let their cultures do their thinking for them instead of using factual information or evidence to be their guide. Schneider (2004) asks the question of whether stereotypes regarding age and other such characteristics are cultural products. The answer, according to many experts, is yes. Schneider (2004), states that cultures provide many "accurate generalizations and some really faulty ones as well." Stereotypes become bad, ugly, and ineffective when people use them to discriminate against a person or groups of individuals without considering the current facts or evidence. While discrimination has it positive meanings, in most cases it is used to refer to making judgment about an individual's or people's behaviors solely based on their unique characteristics based on stereotypes or generalizations. Such is the case about age discrimination, which negatively impacts many "older workers" in the twenty-first century's work environment.

Through personal observations and conscious thinking about employment practices, one can tell that it is not unusual to quickly find several headlines each week about employment discrimination cases through various genres and media outlets. Gregory (2001) states, that "Discrimination against middle-aged and older workers has long been a common practice of American business firms. Nearly all middle-aged and older workers, at some time during their work careers, will suffer the consequences of an age-biased employment-related action." Gregory continues to state that while the law prohibits age discrimination in the American workplace, workers over the age of 40 are "nevertheless subjected to adverse employment decisions motivated by false, stereotypical notions concerning the physical and mental abilities of older workers." As such, some older workers in the American workplace are often encouraged into premature retirements, denied developmental opportunities that can lead to promotions, denied deserved transfers or job promotions, terminated for causes that have little or nothing to do with their performance, and are excluded from long-term decision-making due to biases and assumptions. Gregory pointed out that "I can still state, without fear of contradiction, that age discrimination continues to be a common practice in the American business firms." Gregory ends with an optimistic view by stating that "isolated instance of enlightened thinking on the subject of age discrimination might very well be a harbinger of fairer days for older workers in the future (Mujtaba and Cavico, 2006). Of course, almost everyone would agree that the United States will be a better country once age discrimination, as well as other forms of illegal and unethical discrimination, in the workplace is eliminated.

Generational Differences

Generational differences cause many problems and therefore it is important that we know each generation and what they value. Pohlman and Gardiner (2000), in their book *Value Driven Management*, state that what people value drives their actions. Knowing this, organizations can now make decisions that help employees understand the reasons for their decisions and help balance the differences between the different groups. Defining and understanding some of the attributes of these different age-related work groups would help us to avoid any generational conflicts.

Table 8.1 – Various Generations in the United States (Mujtaba, 2006)

Generation Category	Birth Years	Population in the USA	Common Characteristics
Traditionalists	1900s-1945	75 million	Stability and security
Baby Boomers	1946-1964	80 million	Teamwork and human rights
Generation X	1965-1976	46 million	Empowerment and social responsibility
Generation Y	1977-1994	70 million	Technology and personal growth
Cyberspace Gen.	1995-Present	20 million	Globalization and internet
Total		290 million	

Currently, American corporate leaders, mentors and educators in the United States are dealing with a multi-generational workforce as they have four distinct generations working simultaneously. As can be seen from Table 8.1, the four generations currently in the American workforce are known as the traditionalists (or veterans), baby boomers, Gen X, and Gen Y individuals. Members of each generation tend to share certain experiences, events, and history that help shape their "generational personality" during their socialization in the society.

The characteristics discussed are generalities, and they do not necessarily all apply to each person and some of the characteristics described for one generation may very well apply to individuals of other generations as well. However, the characteristics described are likely to apply more often to individuals of the specified generation. As such, managers must be cautious and not stereotype specific individuals when it comes to hiring and evaluation solely based on these categories since each person is unique and may not necessarily fit the mold for the specified generation based on his or her place or time of birth. Nonetheless, understanding the various generational personalities can help managers and leaders build bridges in the work environment to create collaborative teams in today's learning organizations. Furthermore, this understanding may assist them to effectively recruit and retain diverse individuals by meeting the majority of their intrinsic needs in order to keep them loyal and committed to the organization. As one reads about the different generations, it is best to look for potential implications on one's own organizational systems and environments. As learning and wisdom increase, one can then appropriately use human systems (on an individual and organizational basis) to gain a true competitive advantage in the twenty first century work environment. Current leaders, like past leaders, can reap bottom-line benefits from using 'big picture' systems thinking to create user friendly cultures that accommodate the needs of a diverse generation of workers (Lancaster *et al.*, 2002). According to Lancaster *et al.* (2002), with the existence of four diverse generations of employees in the work system, misunderstandings might become a common everyday occurrence if teamwork and team learning is not encouraged. When generational collisions occur in the workplace, the results can reduce profitability, present hiring challenges, increase turnover rates, and decrease morale among all generations of employees in the department. Understanding the various generational personalities is essential in building bridges and creating new learning and development opportunities in the work environment.

According to Gomolski (2001), frequently, we detect differences in the complaints of managers who claim that younger workers have unrealistic promotion expectations and are unwilling to stick with something long enough to learn it well. Their young subordinates often frustrate baby boomer managers because they are trying to apply the same motivating factors that worked on them, and Generation X and Y workers are uninterested.

Economic Affects

Beyond the burdens to the economy of underutilizing older workers and supporting older non-workers, many economists are predicting a shortage of skilled workers resulting in a need to recruit and retain older workers who possess valuable skills. Labor Department reports indicate that falling unemployment could be causing the tightest labor market in many years (Steinhauser, 1999). According to Steinhauser, "From a practical point of view, companies are already becoming increasingly dependent on older workers. There are considerable bottom-line benefits in utilizing qualified older workers." Most studies report that older workers are reliable, thorough, conscientious, and dependable. Older workers tend to have fewer on-the-job accidents, miss less time than younger workers, and are very conscientious and careful in carrying out their assignments.

Myth versus Reality

Hard work is not age-specific. Neither are lifestyle changes which many times cross-generational lines. Younger workers, realizing that job security no longer exists, have less difficulty leaving an unhappy job situation without explanation than the older workers (Kennedy, 2004).

Kennedy claims that job dissatisfaction is universal. Falling out of love with a job is not age-related. What really is interesting is the length of time it takes for people to realize a job no longer fits. A Generation Y employee will likely decide in a week that a job has no future; older workers will suffer for years before facing this truth and acting on it (Kennedy). Kennedy also states that "priorities can shift at any age." According to the Kennedy:

> Expectations rather than age define workplace attitudes. It is true that real generational differences cluster around expectations of the role that work plays in life. Younger workers are less interested in careers and career planning and are more interested in working at an interesting series of short-term jobs. Many Boomers still yearn for long-term employment even if they have to give up fun and money to achieve it. Managers faced with motivating an age-diverse work group face enormous challenges. There is no universal motivation. More important, the age composition of the workplace is not stable. In the theoretical workplace models, there is a Bell curve of age distribution or even a skewing toward youth. Younger workers are cheaper to employ so when an older worker leaves the model says replace him/her with replace him/her with someone younger and probably less experienced" (Kennedy, 2004).

Managing Diverse Employees

As stated by Jones and George (2006), the latest data from the U.S. Census Bureau, shows that the median age of a person in the U.S. is the highest it has ever been, 35.3 years. The aging of the population suggests managers need to be vigilant in ensuring that employees are not discriminated against because of age. In addition, Jones and George state that it is important that managers educate themselves and their employees concerning the disabilities and capabilities. The Americans with Disabilities Act (ADA) prohibits discrimination against people with disabilities and requires employers to make reasonable accommodations to allow the disabled to effectively perform their jobs. A key challenge for all managers is to create an environment in which those needing special accommodations feel comfortable disclosing that need, while making sure that those accommodations are perceived to be fair by others in the department. Jones and George (2006) also state that there are two ethical imperatives to manage diversity effectively. The two moral principles that guide managers in meeting this ethical imperative to manage diversity effectively are distributive justice and procedural justice.

Distributive justice. The principle of distributive justice dictates that the distribution of pay raises, promotions, job titles, interesting job assignments, office space, and other organizational resources should be based on the contributions that individuals have made to the organization and not on irrelevant personal characteristics such as age, gender, etc. Statistics comparing employees in corporate America suggest that most managers need to take a proactive approach to achieve distributive justice in their organizations.

Procedural justice. The principle of procedural justice requires managers to use fair procedures to determine how to distribute outcomes to organizational members. Procedural justice exists when managers carefully appraise a subordinate's performance, take into account any environmental obstacles to high performance beyond the subordinate's control, and ignore irrelevant personal characteristics. Procedural justice is necessary to ensure ethical conduct and avoid costly lawsuits (Jones & George, 2006).

Experts suggest that mental preparation is very important for older workers when seeking employment in order to obtain a position that reflects all their skills and experiences. Apart from consideration of age, job hunting is highly competitive. Regardless of your professional field or discipline, in order to land the best employment opportunities, you need to be "on top of your game," as they say in sports. If you are over 40 and scouting the job market, be mentally prepared to compete with younger employers who (in many cases) represent a bundle of energy and enthusiasm, are willing to work for less pay, and are generally very savvy concerning the latest technology. Because the employment playing field is not altogether leveled, you will need to develop the mental resolve to compete and win as a serious contender. To accomplish this, mentally focus on the positive attributes of your age and experience. Think of what you offer an employer as a "more mature" job candidate: sound decision-making skills, experience in relating to a wide variety of people, broader perspectives on life, and mature judgment on business matters. Rather than defending your age, use it as an offensive strategy. What comes to mind is Ronald Reagan's retort to a presidential debate question concerning his age. With humor and finesse, he politely responded, 'I refuse to exploit my opponent's youth: age and inexperience.'

Think of yourself the same way. Age has given you valuable life and work experiences that contribute to you becoming a seasoned professional who has "been around the block a few times" and knows how to handle difficult people and challenges in the workplace. That is something to take pride in, not apologize for. Maintaining that mind set, you will be better equipped to compete, and win, in the job-search arena. In practical terms, during an interview mention specific instances in which you have made valuable contributions to the success of a company, offered solutions to vexing problems, trained others to perform at peak productivity, and so on. In that way, as explained by Bruce (2004), you can demonstrate (to use another metaphor) that "there's a lot of tread still on the tire."

Moral Maturity

According to a study by Mujtaba (1999), age has a direct affect on the moral maturity of employees. The general belief is that people's cognitive thought processes must be challenged with moral issues for moral maturity to develop. Mujtaba's 1999 study concerning moral maturity led him to two conclusions, which are supported by his research. First, that older age groups have a higher stage of moral reasoning than did younger groups. Secondly, older workers have stricter interpretations of moral/ethical standards than younger workers. Knowing these differences between the older employees and the younger employees will help management better understand the decision processes of their different employee groups.

In a book entitled *Generations at Work: Managing the Clash of Veterans, Boomers, Xers, and Nexters in Your Workplace* (by Ron Zemke, Claire Raines, and Bob Filipczak, 1999), the authors try to close this generational gap brought on by the different age groups in today's organizations. According to one of its reviewers, "Generations at work provides creative insights and solutions to issues of recruitment and motivation of the workforce, one of the biggest challenges in our industry today. It is clear that there is a new face to workforce diversity which organizations must recognize and respond to if they are to be successful in the new millennium. Generations at work will give you a tremendous advantage."

Age discrimination in the workplace is not only a problem in the U.S. but it is also becoming an international concern. In his article "*Awards Try to Tackle Age Discrimination,*" Barry Sion (2006) states that the government of WALES has an awards campaign trying to end age discrimination in the workplace. The government's Age Positive Awards 2006 Program aims at trying to reward individuals and employers who are tackling social prejudices about age in the workplace. The winning employers must show they have a positive attitude towards age diversity in their recruitment, selection, and training of current and future employees.

Dealing with Age Related Challenges

Management must continue to review organizational restructuring because current equal opportunity legislation is forcing them to understand the changes occurring in an aging workforce. Some of these changes could be downsizing or outsourcing, reduction of any autocratic management styles, and the impact of globalization and technology on current work practices. Any strategies for managing age diversity in the workplace must include individual development and performance, documenting and communicating any discrimination policies, and equip groups who face age barriers to employment to compete on an equitable basis (Victorian Department of Education, 2005).

Talley (2006) states that because there are now four different generational views of the work environment, many obstacles for the organization are now surfacing. These divergent approaches to work can cause loss of productivity, workplace conflicts, and recruitment and retention problems.

According to Steinhauser (1999), the challenges of motivating, managing and supporting an age diverse workforce can be broken down into the following steps.

- The first step is commitment at the top. That means diversity, AA/EEO, human resource and legal managers must see ageism as a major component of diversity, one likely to grow in significance and workplace conflict over the coming months and years. Too often, lack of time and resources, ambivalence about priorities and how aging relates to traditional and non-traditional victims of discrimination, sometimes even concerns about the extent of victimization by comparison with other groups and "potential wins and losses," may mean ageism gets only limited attention in diversity awareness programs.

- The next step is to talk to your employees. Do they feel valued? Do they feel there are issues in the workplace related to age that equate youth with success? Include focus group interviews with older employees and those who have left recently. Is the company environment considered a friendly environment for them?

- Offer age diversity workshops to all managers, supervisors and employees. Utilize trainers, either in-house or external, or both, who are thoroughly knowledgeable about age bias. Bringing out the best means using age diverse teams and the use of older workers as experts, specialists, and mentors in various fields.

- Using training programs and responding to "myths" about workers of all ages are critical but it's important to adjust negative attitudes throughout the workforce. For training to work, it requires a full-scale commitment. You have to look at these issues internally, from the top down. In addition, while addressing the issues, recognize that while there are real differences between Generation Xers and older adults, both are victimized by myths and stereotypes. and by being devalued and unappreciated. Managers who operate on the basis of stereotypes bring out the worst in both groups.

- Consider flexible work schedules to provide a variety of scheduling options. Understand that the shortage of technical talent may require employers to think about such "solutions" as a part-time pool of qualified retirees.

- Recognize and commit to the value of lifelong learning programs. Access to ongoing training is very important to attracting and retaining older workers. Many feel excluded from or not encouraged to continue with ongoing education. On-the-job training for older employees tends to be the most effective way of preventing obsolescence.

- Lastly, rethink insurance and wellness programs. Increasing life expectancy means companies have to deal with the fact that employees will be using benefits longer and more often. Concerns about health costs, pensions and other issues will need to be addressed. Older workers may be more interested in long-term care insurance or workplace wellness benefits. Encouraging people to maintain their health is increasingly important as they age and grow (Steinhauser, 1999).

Steinhauser (1999) also states that for resource assistance, tap into agencies and networks concerned with older adults, such as the National Council on the Aging (NCOA), American Association of Retired Persons (AARP) and the American Society on Aging's Business Forum on Aging (ASA). All these agencies and organizations have readily accessible on-line websites. Steinhauser further reports that these proactive and positive approaches can only benefit your company and all employees. Preventing age discrimination and successfully managing an age diverse workforce is a win-win for everyone and it has real bottom line implications. This new generation of older adults is fit, wise, dedicated, loyal, and ready for new growth and development. It is just this kind of productive, quality, age-diverse workforce that will take its place alongside new technologies and restructuring as we evolve into the new millennium.

Spirituality in the Workplace[12]

An evolving American culture and an unreliable business climate are driving the revitalization of the workplace through an infusion of spirituality. The need for a spiritual connection to carry over into the workplace is important to many partly because of an ongoing upheaval in organizational structure, which often results in feelings of insecurity regarding one's place in the system (Giacalone & Jurkiewicz, 2003). It is also important for people who perceive themselves as spirited beings to lead congruent lives by enacting their values in all areas of their lives. Thus, their sense of spirituality and commitment lead to their being energized through work. Spirituality in the workplace is about experiencing one's real purpose and meaning at work beyond paychecks and performance reviews. It involves people sharing and experiencing some common attachment, attraction, and togetherness with each other within their work unit and the organization as a whole (Harrington, 2004). It is a continuing search for meaning and purpose in life; an appreciation for the depth of life, the expanse of the universe, and natural forces which operate it; and, it is a personal belief system (Myers, 1990).

---

[12] - Co-authored with Eleanor B. Marschke and Barbara Dastoor, Nova Southeastern University.

What is Spirituality?

As the recognition of the spirit-to-work link is still in the early stages, articles on the topic have been mostly theory-based, addressing the changing work paradigm, the value of workplace spirituality to effective leadership and to organizational transformation. The importance of the workaday world has grown to the point where it has now become the central activity of our lives, with people either deriving great satisfaction from their jobs, or, conversely, wondering what is the value of what they are doing—"Why am I here?" Therefore, connecting personal spiritual values to work values has become a way to integrate your work with other aspects of your life.

The term spirituality means different things to different people. Webster's Dictionary defines spirituality as: of, relating to, consisting of or affecting the spirit; of relating to sacred matters; concerned with religious values; of, related to, or joint in spirit. The term "spirituality" comes from the Latin word *spiritus*, meaning vapor, breath, air or wind. Mitroff and Denton (1999) defined spirituality as the desire to find ultimate purpose in life, and to live accordingly. Still, there is no clearly agreed-upon definition of the term "spirituality" among those who are conducting research in this field.

The varying perceptions and definitions of spirituality in the workplace make this phenomenon as interesting as it is. In his article entitled "*An Exploratory Analysis of Definitions and Applications of Spirituality in the Workplace,*" Freshmen (1999) analyzed definitions and applications of spirituality in the workplace and found that:

1. Not any one, two or even three things can be said about spirituality in the workplace that would include the universe of explanations.
2. There is no one answer to the question, 'What is spirituality in the workplace?'
3. Definitions and applications of spirituality in the workplace are unique to individuals. One must be careful not to presuppose, otherwise. Therefore when planning any group or organizational intervention around the topic, again the suggestion is to derive definitions and goals from the participants themselves.
4. There are many possible ways to understand such a complex and diverse area as spirituality in the workplace (p. 318).

Recent scholars have moved towards defining spirituality in terms of purpose and meaning, community and an element of interconnectedness (Allegretti, 2000; Giacalone & Jurkiewicz, 2003).

Table 8.2 - Definition of Spirituality (Giacalone & Jurkiewicz, 2003)

Definition of Spirituality and Source
The personal expression of ultimate concern. Emmons (2000)
That which involves ultimate and personal truths. Wong (1998), p. 364
How the individual lives meaningfully with ultimacy in his or her response to the deepest truths of the universe. Bregman and Thierman (1995), p. 149
Our response to a deep and mysterious human yearning for self-transcendence and surrender, a yearning to find our place. Benner (1989), p. 20
A way of being and experiencing that comes about through awareness of a transcendent dimension and that is characterized by certain identifiable values in regard to self, life and whatever one considers to be the ultimate. Elkins et al. (1988), p. 10
A transcendent dimension within human experience . . . discovered in moments in which the individual questions the meaning of personal existence and attempts to place the self within a broader ontological context. Shafranske and Gorsuch (1984), p. 231
A subject experience of the sacred. Vaughn (1991), p. 105
A personal life principle which animates a transcendent quality of relationship with God. Emblen (1992), p. 45
That vast realm of human potential dealing with ultimate purposes, with higher entities, with God, with life, with compassion, with purpose. Tart (1975), p. 4
That human striving for the transforming power present in life; it is that attraction and movement of the human person toward the divine. Dale (1991), p. 5
Pertaining to the innate capacity to, and tendency to seek to, transcend one's current locus of centricity, which with transcendence involves increased knowledge and love. Chandler and Holden (1992)
The animating force that inspires one toward purposes that are beyond one's self and that provide one's life meaning and direction. McKnight (1984), p. 142

Allegretti defines spirituality as a kind of shorthand for the deepest urgings and impulses of the human self: that which gives meaning and depth to everyday life. The concept encompasses one's need for creativity, one's desire for self-expression, and a hunger for love and service. A spirituality of work refers to making work a part of one's spiritual life, finding opportunities for self-expression, bringing moral values into the workplace, standing up for what one believes, and developing a sense that all of life is sacred (Giacalone & Jurkiewicz, 2003). One view of spirituality is the idea that individuals hold sets of moral beliefs (distinct from religious beliefs) that inform their sense of right and wrong in the workplace. These beliefs and values generally center on a desire by the individual to be his or her best, to help others be their best, and to feel a sense of connectedness with one's work and coworkers. By acting upon these beliefs, individuals achieve a sense of sacredness in their actions and in the world (Giacalone & Jurkiewicz, 2003). For a variety of perspective and more information, see a series of definitions for spirituality in Table 8.2.

Three Aspects of Spirituality in the Workplace

There are at least three aspects of spirituality in the workplace, including:

- The spirituality movement of the twenty first century
- Spirituality's impact on the corporate bottom line
- A Model: The interaction of the spiritual component with the corporate body.

There is increasing evidence that a major transformation is occurring in many organizations (Ashmos & Duchon, 2000). In the so-called Spirituality Movement, organizations that have long been viewed as rational systems are considering making room for the spiritual dimension, a dimension that has less to do with rules and order and more to do with meaning, purpose, and a sense of community (Ashmos & Duchon).

Some corporate policies embrace spirituality and the value it can contribute to the company by enhancing organizational commitment and job satisfaction and by producing more effective leaders and managers. The surge of interest in spirituality in the workplace is evident from the many recent books and many articles from journals such as *The Journal of American Academy of Business, The Journal of Organization Change Management, Public Administration Review,* and *Journal of Business Ethics.*

A Google search of spirituality in the workplace returned in excess of 1,690,000 related subjects, and a search of spirituality in ethics produced in excess of 4,790,000. A search in Proquest provided 147 journal articles and 23 doctoral dissertations on the subject of spirituality, including psychology journals containing information about spirituality as it relates to constructs, methods, and measures for researching spirituality in organizations. Two foundational books, A *Spiritual Audit of Corporate America* by Mitroff and Denton (1999), and *The Handbook of Workplace Spirituality and Organizational Performance* by Giacalone and Jurkiewicz (2003) demonstrate current interest in the topic.

The Spirituality Movement of Modern Century

Ashmos and Duchon (2000) recognize that the world of corporate work is changing. Where Americans work, how they work, particularly since the advent of computer technology allowing telecommuting, bringing about the isolation and impersonal sense of detachment of those who work and communicate solely through computers—all of these factors contribute to a workplace ripe for embracing a connection, whether it be through spirituality or some other source. These changes are drastic, even revolutionary, and will affect every working American. According to Ashmos and Duchon (2000) and others, there are at least five reasons for corporate America's growing interest in spirituality at work, and they are:

1. The downsizing, reengineering, and layoffs of the past decade have turned the American workplace into an environment where workers are demoralized.
2. The workplace is being seen more often as a primary source of community for many people because of the decline of neighborhoods, churches, civic groups, and extended families as principal places for feeling connected.
3. Curiosity about Pacific Rim cultures and Eastern philosophies. Philosophies such as Zen Buddhism and Confucianism, which encourage meditation and stress values such as loyalty to one's groups and finding one's spiritual center in any activity, are finding acceptance.
4. As aging Baby Boomers move closer to life's greatest uncertainty—death—there is a growing interest in contemplating life's meaning.
5. The pressure of global competition has led organizational leaders to recognize that employee creativity needs a fuller expression at work (p. 134).

A 1999 issue of *U.S. News & World Report* reveals that in the past decade, more than 300 titles on workplace spirituality, from *Jesus CEO*, to *The Tao of Leadership*, have flooded bookstores. Indeed, at least thirty MBA programs now offer courses on this subject. It is also the focus of a recent issue of the Harvard School Bulletin. Signs of this sudden concern for the corporate soul are showing up everywhere: from boardrooms to company lunchrooms; from business conferences to management newsletters, from management consulting firms to business schools (Marques, 2005).

When spirituality made the front cover of *NewsWeek Magazine* in September 2005, the world took notice. *NewsWeek's* Special Report: *Spirituality 2005: In Search of the Spiritual*, cites significant facts and charts that can be a good source for researchers. A poll by *NewsWeek* and Beliefnet found that more Americans, especially those younger than 60, described themselves as "spiritual" rather than "religious." Almost two thirds of Americans say they pray everyday, and nearly a third meditate (Alder, 2005). Americans today are looking for personal, ecstatic experiences with God, and according to these statistics, they don't much care what Republicans or Democrats are doing about that. On matters of faith, the United States is still one nation, under God. In early August 2005, *Newsweek* and *Beliefnet* asked 1004 Americans how they worship and what they believe. For example, the study found that 55% of the respondents see themselves as "religious and spiritual" and 57% said they spirituality is very important in their daily lives. About 64% said they engage in religious and spiritual activities on a daily basis through prayers and 29% said they do this through meditation. Furthermore, 39% said that they practice religion to forge a personal relationship with God, about

30% do it to be and become a better person, and 17% do it to find peace and happiness. Others get involved in religious activities to connect with something larger than themselves (10%) and to give their lives meaning and structure (8%).

Dr. Judy Neal, founder and president of the Association for Spirit at Work, reports that managers often confuse spirituality with religion (Brandt, 1996). A person in corporate America can have a deepening meaning of spiritual experience at work without having people become upset with someone trying to convince them of a particular religious point of view. This phenomenon concerns employees who understand themselves as spiritual beings whose souls need nourishment at work; about experiencing a sense of purpose and meaning in their work, and experiencing a sense of connectedness to one another and to their workplace community.

According to Kroll (2003) in an article in *Forbes Magazine*, the Spirituality Movement of the twenty first Century must include America's mega-churches—defined as non-Catholic churches with at least 2000 members. Sometimes having a larger operating budget than companies in corporate America, mega-churches are corporations in themselves, where pastors often act as chief executives and use business tactics to grow their congregations. This entrepreneurial approach has contributed to the explosive growth of mega-churches with the purpose of spreading their faith to as many people as they can. Thus, particularly in the evangelical community, this growth has an impact on spirituality in the workplace. Those who come together view their faith as a lifestyle that has an impact on a corporation's integrity, values, and workplace culture.

Some believe that the spiritual movement of the twenty first century may be related to the way government is conducted in the White House. In his book, *The Faith of George W. Bush*, Steven Mansfield discusses the spirituality of the chief office in the United States. Mansfield describes the Bush brand of management as one distinguished by White House employees encouraged to bring their faith to work with them. Since 1997, federal regulations have allowed religious activities in government workplaces so long as the nonreligious were not harassed or pressured. Bible studies and prayer meeting in federal buildings have become commonplace, and nowhere more than in the White House itself (Mansfield, 2003).

Spirituality's Impact on the Bottom Line

How does spirituality in the workplace relate to the bottom line of a business? Some recent studies have focused on the relationship between workplace spirituality and organizational performance (Giacalone & Jurkieweiz, 2003). Earlier studies showed a strong correlation between corporate culture/core values and profitability. A Harvard Business School study examined 10 companies with strong corporate cultures and 10 with weak corporate cultures, drawn from a list of 200 leading companies. It found a dramatic correlation between an organization's spirited culture and its profitability and also that, in some cases, the more spirited companies outperformed the others by 400 to 500 percent in terms of net earnings, return on investment, and shareholder value (Marques & Dhiman, 2005).

University of Southern California's Marshall Graduate School of Business Professor Ian Mitroff indicates that organizations which identify themselves with spirituality have employees who: 1) Are less fearful of their organizations; 2) Are less likely to compromise their basic beliefs and values in the workplace; 3) Perceive their organizations as being significantly more profitable; and, 4) Report that they can bring significantly more of their complete selves to work, especially their creativity and intelligence. Many studies have indicated that what gives individuals the most meaning and purpose in their job is the ability to realize their full potential as a person (McCoy, 2001, p. 47.).

Companies that excel at engaging the hearts and heads of their people not only have values, they live them through their habits, thereby providing an element of spirituality in the everyday working environment. These spirituality elements expressed are core values — fun, fairness, integrity and social responsibility. Companies that focus on processes that include the spiritual element, such as bringing together employees for motivation at work and encouraging employees to find meaning in work, increase retention which has a decided impact on profitability.

McLaughlin (1998) emphasizes the relationship between spirituality and profitability by asserting, "A growing movement across the country is promoting spiritual values in the workplace and pointing to many examples of increased productivity and profitability" (p.11). According to McLaughlin, organizations that want to survive in the twenty first Century will have to offer a greater sense of meaning and purpose to people in the workforce. The author stresses, "In today's highly competitive environment, the best talent seeks out organizations that reflect their inner values and provide opportunities for personal development and community service, not just bigger salaries" (p. 11). McLaughlin further explains that the use of spiritual values as guiding principles has many positive financial effects on business. *Business Week* reported that 95% of Americans reject the idea that a corporation's only purpose is to make money. A study in *Management Accounting* found that companies committed to ethical business practices do better financially and have significantly greater representation among the top 100 financial performers than companies that don't make ethics a key management component. Furthermore, 39% of U.S. investors say they always or frequently check on business practices, values and ethics before investing. The *Trends Report of 1997* reported that three out of four consumers polled are likely to switch to brands associated with a good cause if price and quality are equal (McLaughlin, 1998, p. 11).

A credible way of demonstrating the correlation between a spiritual approach and corporate profitability is through case studies of companies. Thus, Milliman, Ferguson, Tricket and Condemi (1999) selected Southwest Airlines, justifying their choice for this company as follows:

> We selected Southwest Airlines (SWA) for our case study because it appears to have a strong sense of spiritual-based values guiding its organizational goals and practices. In addition, the company has an established track record of excellent organizational performance as well as high employee and customer satisfaction. In profiling SWA we certainly do not want to imply that it is a perfect example of living spiritual values; it has its problems and limitations like other firms. Despite this, there seems to be a genuine sense of spirit and affection in both SWA employees and customers (p. 221).

They identified the ways spirituality is manifested within SWA and assessed the impact of spirituality on SWA employees, customers, and organizational performance. One desirable outcome was that because of high employee satisfaction, SWA employees have one of the lowest turnover rates (6%) in the airline industry.

Spirituality is reflected through values such as making a contribution to humankind, considering the individual, and is expressed through human resources and other corporate employees in how they relate to corporate profitability and increased job satisfaction. In other words, it finds its expression through the interaction of the spiritual being with the corporate body.

Another researched case of profitability in a spiritually-led company is the Herman Miller Furniture Company. Max DePree, CEO of the Herman Miller Furniture Company, is recognized among the successful business leaders who demonstrate a spirituality that inspires good moral habits. According to the book, *Business as Unusual*, this company is described as problem-solving, risk-taking, committed to change, dedicated to quality, and the pursuit of excellence. It fosters an open climate of freedom in which people have the right and responsibility to contribute, to be involved, and to influence the design and manufacture of office and health care furniture. One of the ways to measure Herman Miller's successful performance is through the frequency in which this company is mentioned by a wide variety of authors on the topic of management excellence and outstanding organizational behavior.

The Interaction of the Spiritual Being with the Corporate Body

Marques and Dhiman (2005) studied spirituality in the workplace by interviewing six business executives in a qualitative study and developed a list of vital themes for spirituality in the workplace. The list of 19 themes that apply to a spiritual workplace are:

Ethics	Trust
Truth	Kindness (bonding, compassion)
Belief in God or a Higher Power	Team Orientation
Respect	Few organizational barriers
Understanding	A sense of peace and harmony
Openness	Aesthetically pleasing workplace
Honesty	Interconnectedness
Being self motivated	Encouraging diversity
Encouraging creativity	Acceptance
Giving to others	

The list of spiritual themes are all components a human being brings to the workplace and, when given the proper nurturing environment by management, allowing these traits to flourish has a decided impact on the profitability of a successful corporation. Based on the distinction of all these factors, Marques developed a model to display the process of the interaction of the spiritual person with the corporate body as presented in Figure 8.1.

Figure 8.1 - A Model: The Interaction of the Spiritual Being with the Corporate Body (Marques & Dhiman, 2005)

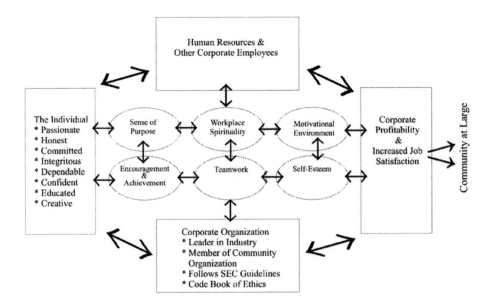

The model, provided by Marques, is a visual representation of the spiritual values a person holds as they interact with the corporate body, with the desired outcome that these spiritual values are a positive catalyst for the corporation to achieve leadership status in profitability, ethics, world citizenship, and philanthropy.

1. The model encompasses the individual, the human resources function, the corporate organization, and corporate profitability.
2. The human resource function, by nurturing applications of spirituality in the workplace, fosters a motivational environment supported by encouragement and recognition of achievement.
3. The individual's spiritual values lead him or her to be passionate, honest, committed, integritous, dependable, confident, educated, and creative. This, in turn, creates a dedicated, purpose-directed, member of the corporate organization, who possesses high self-esteem.
4. When workers are purpose-driven and dedicated, and when the human resource function recognizes achievement, working as a team to attain common goals will be productive and satisfying.
5. A corporate body composed of passionate, honest, dedicated, self-directed, achievement-oriented individuals with high job satisfaction will be accountable to its overseers, both corporate and governmental, and will attain increased profitability and productivity. It will use its resources, including its employees, to promote good citizenship to the larger community.
6. This organization will, in turn, continue to place value on nurturing spirituality among its workforce (Marques & Dhiman, 2005).

Apparently, interest in spirituality in the workplace is here to stay, reflected by the rising number of publications on the topic and the widespread interest in the topic. There is still a broad divergence in interpretations for the word spirituality as well as for the phenomenon "spirituality in the workplace." A spiritual mindset in the workplace can encourage the creativity and innovativeness of employees, which, in turn, enhances their productivity, leading to better overall performance for and by the organization.

Summary

Growth, age, spiritual, and generational diversity are realities of life in society and for leaders and managers in the workforce. This chapter discussed generational, spiritual and age related aspects of diversity as they relate to the workplace. This chapter also provided strategies for effectively dealing with age discrimination in the workplace. Furthermore, allowing the workforce to explore and fulfill their spiritual dreams and goals is about flexibility and the creation of a satisfactory work environment.

Discussion Questions

1. What is the definition of "older worker"? At what age is one considered an older worker and why?
2. What is a protected worker when it comes to age? In other words, what does "protected" mean when applied to various dimensions of diversity?
3. What is age discrimination? Discuss examples.
4. Is there age discrimination in today's workplace?
5. Is age discrimination a product of society, a product of myth, a product of stereotypes, a product of older workers, or simply a product of biases? Discuss.
6. What can managers do to prevent age discrimination?
7. Discuss two examples of firms that are currently benefiting from using older workers.
8. Are older workers more responsible and more ethical? Discuss and provide examples.
9. What are some common benefits associated with hiring older workers in one's firms or department?
10. What is spirituality? How does spirituality relate to diversity in the workplace? Discuss and provide examples.
11. How is "spirituality" different from a specific religion?
12. How can a person be "spiritual" and not necessarily "religious"?
13. How might a person's spirituality lead to increased organizational commitment?

Managing for Diversity in Public Agencies[13]

$\mathcal{P}$ ublic organizations tend to serve diverse consumers and most often some public agencies are staffed with diverse employees. Yet, one must acknowledge that the public sector in the United States is facing a dramatic number of retirements over the next 20 years. While exact figures are difficult to obtain, it is estimated that nearly three-quarters of the federal government's top executives are now eligible to retire. This same figure is probably reflective of state and local governments as well. Given these projections, how ready is government at all levels to replace this vast numbers of talented and skilled employees that will be leaving the public sector? While this question is daunting enough, the public sector is faced with another challenge that arises from the number of immigrants that will be entering this country in the coming decades. Will the public sector be able to transform itself to be reflective of this rapidly changing population?

A possible indicator of the public sector's transformational ability may be found in government's ability to create a diverse workforce. Knowing the public sector's past performance would help researchers and decision-makers decide if past recruitment and selection practices are sufficient or if new strategies are demanded given the dual challenges of the next two decades. This chapter looks at some of the facts surrounding diversity and how governments can prepare for this dramatic need for future employees. It further discusses how managers and employees can align their behaviors with the expectations of their agencies and departments.

As previously discussed, embracing private and public sector diversity is more than just tolerating people's differences; embracing diversity actually means welcoming and involving different individuals by developing a work atmosphere where it is safe for all employees to contribute to the final mission. Embracing diversity means actively seeking information from people of a variety of backgrounds and cultures in order to develop a broad picture of how to best involve and serve them. Despite sincere efforts on the embracing of diversity in the workplace, some people face discomfort unless all employees can put away their biases and keep an open mind. Diversity is an important aspect of every organization whether it is a private or public entity, states a colleague named Brian Quier (Personal Communication, May 18, 2006). As we discuss diversity challenges among government employees in this chapter, one should remember that public employees may face many challenges as it pertains to the working world. When talking about diversity in the

---

[13] This chapter is co-authored with Terrell G. Manyak, Nova Southeastern University, and Phillip S. Rokicki, Rokicki and Associates, Inc.

workplace, there are some differences between the private and public sector. Most of the diversity issues are probably the same, but it is how they are handled which can make a difference.

According to Brian Quier, a public sector employee in the United States, individuals who work in government jobs often make careers out of it and maintain a great benefit package. Mr. Quier states that since government jobs are generally looked at for long-term employment, public sector leaders should be aware that a large number of their aging workforce is approaching retirement. With the high rates of retirements and strategic planning, the government has an opportunity to bring new skills which can change how the government does business. The government will have a chance to compete with the private sector by offering job stability and decent salaries to attract and retain diverse individuals from across the country. However, the government is likely to have difficulty maintaining a balanced demographic profile in the public sector over the next ten years. Since the federal government is the largest employer in the nation with more than 1.8 million employees, it should be the most diversified, but yet it probably isn't at all levels due to the bureaucracy that can make it harder to diversify the workforce in a short span of time. In the public sector, there are many opportunities to move around into different positions for job enrichment and cross-functional training while working for the government. Such flexibility can assist public sector managers in developing and retaining some of the Baby Boomers, who are reaching retirement age, a few more years in their jobs.

The Aging Public Sector Workforce

Various generations of people comprise the United States and the American workplace; two of them are the Traditionalists and Baby Boomers. These two generations are somewhat different from younger generations as many of them are retired or are near retirement. *Traditionalists* (veterans) were born between the turn of the last century and the end of World War II (1900-1945) and they make up about 75 million individuals in the United States. Traditionalists, because of their experience, have learned to do without much participation, and the management style they learned came from the military (Lancaster *et al*, 2002). They were cautious, did not take much risk, spoke only when spoken to, and have been obedient to societal rules. They expect career security of life-long employment and do not appreciate job-hopping or downsizing jobs. Currently, many Traditionalists are working in large numbers at fast food locations and retail outlets such as various department stores, McDonalds, Wal-Mart, Home Depot, and many top Fortune 500 organizations. This generation prefers a learning environment that offers predictability, stability, and security. *Baby Boomers,* born between the years 1946-1964, number about 80 million individuals in the United States (Lancaster *et al*, 2002). They grew up in suburbs, had educational opportunities above their parents, saw lots of consumer products "hit" the marketplace (calculators, appliances). The television had a significant impact on their views of the world regarding equal opportunity and other human rights issues. Many members of this generation served in the military throughout the United States and around the globe. They enjoy perks that allow them to have more free time like errand-running service, car washes, food service, etc. The preferred learning environment of the Boomers is interactive and team activities.

Today as more *"Baby Boomers"* reach retirement age, pressure is mounting on public agencies at all levels to prepare for their anticipated exodus from the workforce. To understand the extent of the problem, the U.S. Census Bureau (2002) reported that over 21 million individuals were employed by federal, state and local governments in 2002. Out of this number, it is estimated that between 50 to 60 percent are age 45 or older and soon eligible for retirement (Office of Personnel Management, 2004). At the federal government level, the General Accounting Office estimates that 71 percent of the Senior Executive Service personnel are eligible to retire. This figure translates into a retirement rate that is 20 percent higher than in the previous decade (U.S. General Accounting Office, 2000). The concern of the GAO is echoed at the state level. For example, the state of Washington Department of Personnel projects that more than 50 percent of executive level and 30 percent of mid-level managers are now eligible to retire (Washington State, 2000).

Figure 9.1 – Country Immigration Trends

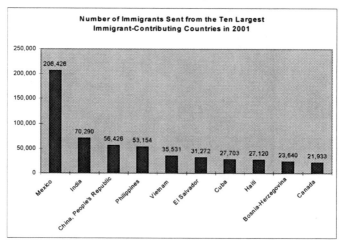

Both the GAO and the Department of Personnel reports challenge their respective government leaders to start succession planning now. In addition to identifying needs, government agencies need to streamline recruitment and compensation processes to facilitate replacing and retaining employees. They also need to develop proactive outreach efforts to be more competitive in recruiting in what will be an increasingly tight labor market.

Where are these replacement public employees going to come from if, as anticipated, the labor market does become tight? Given the past history of the public sector, a substantial proportion of these replacements will be women and minorities. The public sector has historically provided more opportunities for the disadvantaged than has the private sector. Both the federal and state levels of government report higher percentages of women and minorities working in technical, professional, and managerial positions than their private sector counterparts (Henry, 2004). As one observer noted, "In the aggregate, state and local governments are doing considerably better than the private sector in living up [to] the challenge of attaining sexual and racial-ethnic employment equity" (Dometrius & Sigelman, 1984).

There are many cities across the United States that have been greatly impacted by a diverse population and workforce. According to a colleague, Joseph Dolcine (Personal Communication; May 20, 2006), the city of Los Angeles has witnessed a huge boom in population growth, increasing from 7 million in 1970 to 8.8 million in 1990 (US Bureau of the Census). However, it is the dramatic change in ethnic and racial diversity of the population which has caught most observers' attention as it impacts the workforce, both public and private sectors. Dolcine states that Los Angeles has taken on a new form in terms of its racial diversity, moving from a biracial to a multiethnic setting since people of diverse backgrounds are now living there.

Table 9.1 - Projected Population Change in the U.S.A., Origin: 2000 to 2050 (US Census Bureau, 2004)

Change and race	2000 – 2050	2000 – 2010	2010 – 2020	2020 – 2030	2030 – 2040	2040 – 2050
NUMERICAL CHANGE						
TOTAL	137,729	26,811	26,869	27,779	28,362	27,908
White alone	74,078	16,447	15,634	15,102	13,959	12,936
Black alone	25,543	4,636	4,911	5,077	5,434	5,485
Asian Alone	22,746	3,557	3,747	4,592	5,412	5,438
All other races 1/	15,362	2,171	2,576	3,009	3,557	4,049
Hispanic (of any race)	66,938	12,134	12,000	13,299	14,530	14,975
White alone, not Hispanic	14,554	5,383	4,824	3,240	1,155	-48
PERCENT CHANGE						
TOTAL	48.8	9.5	8.7	8.3	7.8	7.1
White alone	32.4	7.2	6.4	5.8	5.1	4.5
Black alone	71.3	12.9	12.1	11.2	10.8	9.8
Asian Alone	212.9	33.3	26.3	25.5	24.0	19.4
All other races 1/	217.1	30.7	27.9	25.5	24.0	22.0
Hispanic (of any race)	187.9	34.1	25.1	22.3	19.9	17.1
White alone, not Hispanic	7.4	2.8	2.4	1.6	0.6	0.0

The non-Hispanic White population has declined from its 71 percent share in 1970 to a narrow numerical plurality of less than 41 percent of the county's population after the 1990's. Meanwhile, the Latino and Asian-Pacific population in Los Angeles witnessed a doubling – from 15% to 39% -- and nearly quadrupling from 3% to 11% of their population shares respectively. Meanwhile, African-Americans, while slightly growing numerically, were constant shares of the county population (11%) during this period. Thus, as can be seen from these numbers and the visual make up of the people, Los Angeles has one of the most ethnically diverse populations of any metropolitan area in the United States. This diversity calls for the reflection of public officials and leaders on several critical questions as they strategically plan for the future. Some of the questions to reflect upon, as stated by Joseph Dolcine in May 2006, could include but are not limited to: What does this ethnic diversity mean for multiethnic coalition building in the politics of Los Angeles County? Does the changing demography increase the opportunity for ethnic cooperation? Or, has the ethnic changes increased rather than decreased the prospects of interethnic conflict? By honestly answering such questions, leaders can more effectively and strategically plan their workforce needs and opportunities. Furthermore, they can integrate appropriate plans to prevent ethnic conflicts and riots from taking place and causing economic distress on the population.

The Impact of Immigration on Public Agencies

The success of the public sector in absorbing women and minorities will be challenged in future years by the need to absorb a rising tide of immigrants to the United States. The Center for Immigration Studies[14] estimates that immigration will account for about 63 percent of U.S. population growth over the next 50 years. Put another way, immigrants who have not yet arrived, but who will come to this country between now and 2050, will add the equivalent of the combined current populations of California, Texas, and New York State to the United States over the next 50 years.

The greatest number of "new immigrants" in 2001 came from three countries; Mexico, India, and China (see Figure 9.1). In addition, Figure 9.2 shows the percent of foreign-born population in this country is now on an upward trend (Gibson & Jung, 2006). This finding brings both opportunities and challenges for governments to respond to the dramatic need for new, trained, and skilled public employees (White & Rice, 2005). The challenge is to replace employees at all levels with competent new employees, while the opportunity is to bring a wider range of employees into public administration from different ethnic, racial and gender groups.

As noted above, the recruitment of a diverse work force has been a stated objective of the public sector for decades. While laudable achievements have been made, a significant question remains. How effectively has government

---

[14] The Center for Immigration Studies is an independent, non-partisan, non-profit research organization founded in 1985. It is the nation's only think tank devoted exclusively to research and policy analysis of the economic, social, demographic, fiscal, and other impacts of immigration on the United States.

utilized its diverse work force? The answer to this question will provide an indication as to how effective the government will be in absorbing and utilizing the skills of the growing immigrant population. The remainder of this chapter looks at some of the research findings on diversity and how the public sector can use this knowledge to prepare for its dramatic need to replace employees.

Figure 9.2 – Foreign-born Population

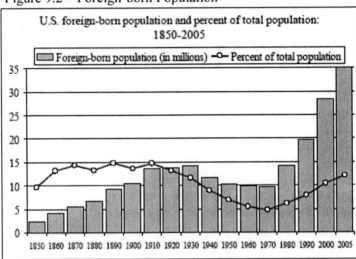

Source: U.S. Census Bureau; Passel (2005)

The Scorecard on Diversity in Public Administration

Several studies provide indicators that give us a partial answer to the question of just how well government has utilized its diverse workplace: the number of women that have attained upper management positions in government, how government deals with occupational segregation, and how it deals with the issue of equal pay for equal work.

Increasing the Number of Women in Upper Management Positions

Women in the government workplace have been an accepted reality for decades, but women still suffer from both the *glass-ceiling* and *glass-wall* effects. In a study of 23 U.S. cities over a nine-year period, Kerr, Miller and Reid (1998) researched the proposition that as women are elected to high-level positions and more women hold upper administrative positions this would actually increase the *"female share"* of the better-paying and more desirable city government jobs. The results of this study found that female administrators increased the female share of professional and protective service positions (e.g., child welfare, etc.). However, the study also found that having women elected to public office does not necessarily translate into an increase in the number of female job holders. This is especially true when data are aggregated across all city occupations. On a positive note, the study did find that female mayors do increase the female share of administrative positions in financial administration departments. The result of the study supports the belief that a glass-ceiling and glass-wall still separates women from their male counterparts in the public sector even as more women are elected or gain director-level status.

Policy Functions versus Occupational Segregation

Gender-based job segregation is still a fact of life in the public sector. For example, street workers are more often men than women, while finance departments often are staffed predominately by women. The question to be answered can be: is this gender-based occupational segregation connected to the policy functions of the government or to other reasons?

Using unpublished data from U.S. Equal Opportunity Commission, the authors of one study investigated gender-based city job patterns by separate functional policy areas (Miller, Kerr & Reid, 1998). The authors used Theodore J. Lowi's (1985) conceptual framework that suggests the *structures, processes, and relationships* associated with different policy types will affect the personnel practices in city governments.

After examining administrative and professional positions in U.S. cities from 1985 through 1993, Miller, Kerr and Reid (1998) found that even though cities have achieved gender balance in redistributive functions, such as in welfare and similar offices, women are dramatically underrepresented in distributive (e.g., purchasing) and regulatory agencies (e.g., code enforcement). Because salaries in redistributive agencies are, on average, less than those in distributive and regulatory agencies, the authors reported that "occupational segregation is still associated with salary inequities." They also found that while some evidence points to the erosion of glass-walls in the city distributive and regulatory agencies, the speed of this change has been indeed very slow.

Equal Pay for Equal Work

Governments were criticized in the 1980's and 1990's for not paying the same for equal work done by men and women. This *equal pay for equal work* movement impacted almost one-half of all of the states in the U.S. In response to this pressure, many governments passed comprehensive pay equity legislation that was intended to reduce the wage gap between men and women doing substantially the same type of work. Has this legislation been effective in achieving equity or has other factors, such as the concept of *"emotional labor,"* kept women from overcoming sex based hurdles in the workplace?

In a study of 47 states over a ten year period conducted by Kerr and Neuse (2000), the researchers wanted to determine if the pay equity measures adopted in the states actually reduced sex-based pay differences among administrative workforces. In the study the authors controlled for a number of factors that could also impact sex-based pay disparities, and, they used a pooled time series design to investigate the research question. The results of this study found that, on average, pay equity adjustments enacted by the states did not necessarily lessen sex-based salary differences among administrative workers. What the researchers did find was that pay differences between men and women in state governments were more likely to be impacted by the percentage of female administrators employed in the agency and the state's philosophy toward equal pay for equal work. The more female administrators that were hired and the more aggressively the state moved toward equal pay for equal work, then the smaller are the salary and wage differences between men and women.

Governments, even with a desire to pay equally for equal work, can be influenced by defining jobs in a way that reflects the type of actual or assumed duties the holder performs. For example, if the job requires the holder to use his or her emotion based skills, then it is often defined, either consciously or unconsciously, as a job for "women" rather than for men. In a study covering four states (Illinois, New Jersey, Oregon, and Florida) conducted by Newman and Guy (2006), the researchers attempted to answer the question, "Why do jobs identified as 'women's' pay less?" The researchers found that while dealing with emotions is essential for doing "*people work*;" and it is a legitimate occupational skill used on the job; "That it remains, for the most part, invisible and uncompensated." They also found that there is "a monetary penalty not only for being female, but also for holding a job that involves caring and nurturance" (p. 3).

The study reported that the reduced wages connected to women's "*emotional labor*" reflects a belief that caring is a *natural* activity for women that neither merits, nor requires, any credit in the salary and wage structure of state government. The research also found that when women work in what are defined as "*men's*" jobs, they sometimes come close to earning equal pay with the men also performing these functions. As an example, the researchers found the highest paid public occupation for men is being a physician paying $1,874 per week, but that women physicians were paid $896 less per week than male physicians. The highest paid occupation for women in state government is as a lawyer paying $1,255 per week, but still amounting to $455 less per week than was paid to male lawyers. Clearly, neither the "*emotional duties*" are fairly compensated, nor are women yet earning comparable salaries as far as this study found.

In summary, while this is not a complete look at diversity in public employment, the trends reported in these four recent studies suggest that public agencies have a distance to go before they truly utilize the skills and abilities of their diverse workforce. With this conclusion in mind, this chapter returns to looking at the challenges of the future. How can government replace the current thousands of retirees with an even more diverse employee population?

Challenge One – Lack of Benchmarking Data

Wise and Tschirhart (2000), in an Internet database study of research on public managers on diversity, found a scant 106 empirical studies on the outcomes of diversity for public sector managers. "The lack of empirical research on organization-level outcomes is troubling..." (p. 389). This shortage of empirical studies, which was also validated by the authors of this chapter, goes beyond just pragmatic studies on diversity. There appears to be a general lack of consistent reporting of diversity statistics by many public agencies at all levels.

In a random Internet review of states, counties and cities around the nation, the authors found no easily accessible data on the demographic, racial and ethnic background of public employees. While the units of government reported on the equal opportunity rules and appeals available to employees and applicants, none of these units actually reported the characteristics that would allow the researchers and others to compare the make-up of the unit of government against the make-up of the community it serves.

Rubaii-Barrett and Wise (2006), in their study of government websites, support this review. They found that only "A small number of states stand out for the diversity messages portrayed on the websites of their personnel agencies and may serve as benchmarks for other states" (p. 12). They found only eight state websites that promoted diversity as a core value of the state's recruiting activities. Even in these cases, the statements found on the websites reflected statements about diversity or pictures of a diverse workforce population, rather than statistics about diversity in the state's workforce. The researchers indicated that "The overwhelming majority of states do not include any diversity messages on their job listing website" (p. 8).

Why Is the Lack of Data Important?

The overall lack of data found on the Internet may not reflect the actual scarcity of information available to the local senior-level managers and decision-makers. Rather, it may actually indicate that units of government choose, for some reason, not to publish this information where it can be retrieved by researchers and others, such as job seekers, electronically. In our experience with governments, most report at least superficial information about the demographics of employees and applicants for open positions. This information, while reported to commissions, boards, etc., still does not appear to be widely decimated beyond the original report. What is lacking is a uniform set of benchmark figures that can be compared and contrasted between units of government, say from county to county or city to city. With a uniform set of data then comparisons would be possible, realistic benchmarks established, and progress measured from year-to-year for units of government in the United States.

This lack of comprehensive data has been overcome by a number of countries which realize that progress toward diversity can only be made when an adequate benchmark has been established.

Progress outside of the United States on Diversity Data

The Commissioner for Public Employment Supporting Material of South Australia noted that, "Diversity data provides valuable information for the development of government employment policies and service arrangements. The establishment of a comprehensive data set on the characteristics of the workforce enables a more responsive employment framework to be developed and targeted strategies to be identified" (South Australia, 2002, p. 4). The South Australia government created the *Workforce Profiling Project* with the objective of establishing a standardized set of core data to be used for monitoring and reporting on the diversity of the public sector workforce across South Australia. The Commissioner further noted that, "The project outcomes are essential to achieving a consistent, longitudinal approach to collecting and managing diversity data across the South Australian public sector" (p. 5).

The South Australian government wanted to measure the improvement of organizational and individual performance in the Australian public service. It also realized that it needed to create workplaces that "adapt rapidly to change and which identify and reward those staff who are creative and flexible" (p. 5). The Commissioner noted that, "A more diverse Australian Public Service workforce is central to the achievement of more innovative and productive workplaces" (p. 17).

What the Australian government realized is that in highly competitive organizations, diversity is a plus. Organizations, "whose cultures are based on the principles of inclusiveness, diversity and equity, where leadership is responsive to different views; and where the hierarchy does not constrain or dilute alternative views, are more productive and rewarding places in which to work" (p. 17).

The Type of Diversity Information Needed

Clearly, other countries have made the collection of and sharing of diversity data a priority. Governments at all levels should first ensure that data is collected, but equally important they should make it readily available on websites so that researchers and others can analyze the data. Such information can assist government decision-makers in setting achievable targets for diversity. The establishing of benchmarks and then the monitoring of progress toward achieving those benchmarks is an important first step in ensuring a diverse public employment workforce. Some of the types of data that should be collected and shared by governments are:

1. Age of employees by range.
2. Sex of the employees.
3. Educational attainment of the employees by categories.
4. Ethnicity of the employees by general categories (e.g., similar to those used by the US Census Bureau).
5. Experience in public administration or outside of government service.
6. General background information.
7. Tenure of the employee with the agency.
8. If the employee has a disability (by category).
9. If the employee is multilingual.

How to Use Diversity Data Collected

While there does not appear to be much consistently reported diversity data available across the United States, individual examples are available to show how governments could use this diversity information if it were available.

Using information from the Executive Office of the President as an example, one can look at data from the Senior Executive Service (SES). The SES is a separate personnel system covering most of the top managerial, supervisory, and policy-making positions in the executive branch of the federal government. Senior Pay Level (SPL) positions include the SES, Executive Service, Senior Foreign Service, and other employees earning salaries above Grade 15 in the General Salary Schedule. The SPL represents 1.05% of the total federal white collar workforce, the very top of the civilian federal employees. Diversity information from this report indicates that:

*   At the end of FY 2003, of the 15,308 SPL positions in the federal government, 7.09% were occupied by Blacks; 3.43% by Hispanics; 2.51% by Asians/Pacific Islanders; and 0.78% by American Indians/Alaskan Natives. By comparison, at the end of FY 1994, of the 13,385 SPL positions, 5.68% were held by Blacks; 2.18% by Hispanics; 1.35% by Asians/Pacific Islanders; and 0.60% by American Indians/Alaskan Natives. This information immediately shows that over a ten-year period the percentage of Blacks increased by slightly over 1 percent; that the number of Hispanics increased by 1.25 percent and the other minorities saw some slight increase. Now the question can be asked, "Is this a fair representation of minorities in senior levels given the racial makeup of the country?" An evaluation could then be made, targets set, and progress measured.
*   Women occupied 25.52% of SPL positions (up from 16.35% in FY 1994). With women making up slightly over one-half of the nation's

population, the logical question becomes obvious. Does this percentage, while an increase over the previous ten years, adequately reflects the percentage of women in the general population?

- The SPL participation rate for people with disabilities was 3.80%, while the participation rate for people with targeted disabilities was 0.42%. In 1994, the SPL participation rate for people with disabilities was 3.91% and for people with targeted disabilities was 0.37%. Again, with the data on people with disabilities, the agency and researchers can determine if there are an adequate number of individuals who have some recognized disability. The data in Table 9.2 shows the numbers of employees by category between 1994 and 2003.

With this type of data decision-makers can then establish benchmarks, monitor progress and take corrective actions to seek to recruit, train, and re-train underserved minority groups. Without this data progress will be slow or non-existent or worse, the government will never acknowledge that it has a diversity problem.

Table 9.2 - Senior Pay Level Representation

	FY 1994		FY 2003	
	Number	%	Number	%
Women	2,188	16.35%	3,906	25.52%
Men	11,197	83.65%	11,402	74.48%
Blacks	760	5.68%	1,085	7.09%
Hispanics	292	2.92%	525	3.43%
Asians/Pacific Islanders	181	1.35%	384	2.51%
American Indians/Alaskan Natives	80	0.60%	120	0.78%
Individuals with Targeted Disabilities	50	0.37%	64	0.42%

Professionalism: The Bridge to Harmony

Just like most other employees, public sector officials and managers can also face complex challenges when it comes to behavior alignment in the workplace, especially when their personal values are in direct conflict with the department's expectations. Public sectors professionals, as well as those in the private sector, must understand that there can be no question as to a manager's responsibility regarding fairness, diversity awareness and being culturally competent in managing a diverse workforce. As a professional manager or agent of an organization, one must treat people with respect and dignity and ensure that internal customers (associates and vendors) treat each other with respect and dignity. Mr. George Jenkins, founder of Publix Super Markets once said that "Some companies are founded on policy. This is wrong. Philosophy, the things you believe in, is more important. Philosophy does not change frequently—and is never compromised" (taken from The Publix Philosophy, 1982). There can be no question as to a manager's responsibility regarding being culturally competent when managing a multicultural workforce or interacting with a diverse customer base. An effective and competent leader and manager must create and maintain an inclusive work environment for all his/her employees. As can be seen from the Personal Inclination and Alignment Model (Figure 9.3), managers have a right to receive training in the area of diversity and understand the organization's expectations regarding cultural competency and behavioral alignment. Similarly, when one's personal values and the departmental expectations are in conflict, managers can use professionalism to meet the organization's expectations and to achieve the goals of having a fair and an inclusive work environment where the natural externalities are teamwork, synergy, and a productive workforce.

Figure 9.3 – Personal Inclination and Alignment Model

Today's associates come from diverse backgrounds and have a variety of experiences and personal values. Therefore, it is important to jointly discuss with everyone and emphasize the relationship between personal inclinations, professionalism and organizational expectations as well as what to do if there is a conflict between one's personal values and the department's expectations. As taught to thousands of corporate and public sector managers, the following definitions can be extremely helpful in understanding this concept:

- *Personal inclinations* are responses based largely on personal feelings and values.

- *Professionalism* (or the bridge between personal inclination and organizational expectations) is about having the requisite skills and experiences in a particular field, industry and profession.
- *Personal alignment* is about adapting one's personal behavior to be compatible with the character and values of the organization. In such a case, one is not required to change his or her values; however, one must align his or her behavior in the workplace to meet the standards established or expected by the organization or agency.

For example, let us say that a government manager, due to his or her personal inclinations tends to only believe in a marital relationship between a man and a woman, has attended a diversity workshop. As a result of this training or development, he or she does not have to change his or her personal values. However, since this public sector manager or employee is a professional in his or her field, he or she is expected to behave according to the needed industry standards and expectations to treat each one of his or her employees and colleagues with respect and dignity regardless of their sexual orientation or personal inclinations. In other words, this employee or manager would need to use professionalism as a bridge between his/her own personal inclinations and the expectations of the company when the two are in conflict. Regardless of one's personal view or inclinations, professionals and managers are expected to behave within the law, industry or departmental policies, and the boundaries of fair and ethical treatment of all individuals in the workplace.

Summary

The public sector of the United States is facing dramatic changes in the workplace through retirements and through immigration. How governments at all levels prepare for these challenges will depend in large part on the availability of data. Currently, the data that exists is inconsistent for governments. To correct this deficit, the writers propose a nationwide, standardized collection and publishing of data that allows for easy comparison of diversity statistics. To undertake this task will require the efforts of agencies such as the U.S. Census Bureau or the Bureau of Labor Statistics. The result of a comprehensive data collection process will encourage governments to establish accurate benchmarks by which they and all the citizens can measure progress toward a diverse public employee workplace.

Diversity will come to government in one way or the other. The question will be, "Will government be ready for the complexities of diversity and how will we know if it actually has a diverse workplace?"

Discussion Questions

1. What types of workforce diversity data are you able to find about your local government (select one department or one sector)?

2. Should all governmental units be required to publish annual reports on the Internet that provide statistical information on the status of their workforce diversity and goal achievement?

3. Do government agencies have a special obligation to recruit, develop and promote immigrants to the United States?

4. Should the goal of diversity for each governmental unit be to reflect as closely as possible the composition of the population it serves?

5. Should employers be obligated to include "emotional labor" as a compensable factor to equalize pay between traditionally female and male occupations?

6. Are special programs needed in the public sector to eliminate the "glass-ceilings" and "glass walls" that inhibit career opportunities for women?

7. Do female and minority executives have a special responsibility to promote the careers of other females and minorities in government?

8. Does the public sector have a special obligation to maintain a more diverse workforce than the private sector?

9. What programs could governmental units establish to manage the succession of new executives to fill the places of those who are or soon will be retiring from public service?

10. Will the political demand for recruiting immigrants into the public service inevitably lower the quality of service delivery?

11. Does diversity lead to improved or inferior decision making in the public sector?

12. What should a manager do when his or her personal values are in conflict with the organization's expectations or values? For example, let us say that a person believes that a mother should stay home with her children, should this manager preach this philosophy or personal believe to his/her employees in the workplace? Discuss.

Chapter 10

Organizational Learning and Knowledge

Knowledge management is a very important part of each organization's culture as well as each manager's responsibility. Accordingly, this chapter focuses on creating a culture of effectively managing knowledge and learning in today's diverse workplace.

Organizational learning and effective knowledge management practices are a necessity in today's global work environment where information becomes available and obsolete very quickly. Furthermore, managers are expected to have all of the information they need to make effective decisions regardless of whether they work at home or abroad. Yet, today's managers are constantly bombarded with more information than they can effectively absorb in a given day. As such, organizations are required to create organizational cultures where the right information is learned, retained and shared with all relevant parties. Thus, the study of managing knowledge and learning amid continuous change becomes critical. Overall, this chapter provides an overview of organizational culture, learning organizations and offers suggestions for effective knowledge management.

Organizations and Knowledge Management[15]

Sam Walton, founder of Wal-Mart, believed in getting extraordinary results from the work of ordinary people through effective knowledge and people management practices. The challenge for knowledge management and human resources experts seems to be in motivating and preparing ordinary employees to perform extraordinarily. As per Sam Walton's philosophy, "Retail is change" and continuous change seems to have become the law of operation at Wal-Mart Corporation. Proactive and positive change is taking place at Wal-Mart through the engagement of employees and the creation of knowledge workers since employees are the company's most important asset, according to John DiBenedetto who is currently serving as the Vice President of Learning and Development for this giant multinational corporation. Dr. DiBenedetto was a distinguished speaker at Nova Southeastern University on May 18, 2006 at the School of Business Entrepreneurship. According to DiBenedetto, one of the reasons their organization seems to get sued by their employers so often is because traditionally they have not had human resource professionals in each of their locations. Since a Wal-Mart Super Center can

---

[15] This chapter is co-authored with Claudette Chin-Loy, Nova Southeastern University.

have as many as 500 to 700 employees, their goal is to have at least one human resource manager in each location. This person can guide, train and monitor everyone's behaviors so all employees are treated with respect and dignity; consequently, this can eliminate or reduce unfair treatment of associates and/or its perception along with the unnecessary lawsuits. The average "calling-in sick" rate for a normal Saturday at Wal-Mart store can be up to about 30 percent in some locations. This has been changing with better learning and development opportunities for employees and managers. Dr. DiBenedetto discussed that Wal-Mart now has a slightly larger budget for their Associate Investment Model (AIM), which "aims" for the creation of an organizational culture that prepares everyone for higher performance through effective knowledge management and employee development programs.

Organizational culture is recognized as a major contributor to knowledge management as it represents a major source of competitive advantage for organizations to achieve their objectives (De Long & Fahey, 2000). Cabrera and Bonache (2001) contend that, clearly, knowledge management is of central importance to organizations. The latest revolution in business shows that instead of hoarding knowledge, there is an urgent need for managers to collaborate and share knowledge. The paradigm shift to knowledge management is pushing the efforts of many companies to manage knowledge as a competitive advantage in order to achieve their objectives; and there is a growing sense of urgency among executives about the practicality of leveraging knowledge within the organization (Cabrera & Bonache, 2001). Since the early 1980's, human resource practitioners have been urged to increase the competitive capacity of their organizations. These messages reflect the importance of developing a "strong" culture that supports the organization's competitive strategy. The current competition among businesses forces them to develop and manage systems to benefit from employees' learning, possession and development of knowledge; the way in which employees, who hold this knowledge, are managed can be an important source of competitive advantage.

The link between culture and knowledge has been the subject of much research. DeLong and Fahey (2000) suggest that their research on knowledge management initiatives shows that culture and knowledge are inextricably linked in organizations. Research suggests that intellectual capital generally is considered to be the stored knowledge possessed by an institution (Erickson & Rothberg, 2000). The underlying approach of knowledge management is that many companies have not achieved their objectives; and thus, there is a growing sense of disenchantment among executives about the practicality of trying to enhance organizational knowledge (DeLong & Fahey, 2000). Mellander (2001) proposes that no knowledge management initiate can succeed without first providing the right conditions for learning. DeLong and Fahey (2000) specify that organizational culture is increasingly recognized as a potential barrier to leveraging intellectual assets. They identified many ways in which culture influences the behaviors central to knowledge creation, sharing, and use.

The greatest challenge in knowledge management initiatives is the ability of managers to effectively establish, maintain, and link knowledge management and human capital to organizational culture. A company's prevailing cultural characteristics can defeat knowledge management efforts before they begin (Detert, et al., 2000). McDermott (1999) specified that the failures in implementing knowledge management systems often are blamed on the organization's culture. McDermott asserts that organizational culture is hard to change, that people change not because of policy or reward, but that change occurs by influence rather than by order. Organizational culture is related to transformation change theories as they apply to competencies including learning organization theories and research. Knowledge management initiatives are related to organizational benefits including the value of knowledge assets and considerations of the measurement of knowledge assets in a firm.

Organizational Culture Foundation and Framework

Culture is a pattern of norms, values, beliefs and attitudes that influences behavior within an organization (Schein, 1984, 1992, 1999). Schein's research on organizational culture analyzed culture at three levels: (1) Artifacts, are the visible organizational structures and processes which are difficult to define precisely; (2) Espoused values, the strategies, goals, and philosophies; and (3) Basic underlying assumptions, the unconscious, taken-for-granted beliefs, perceptions, thoughts, and feelings. Thus, there are a number of ways to conceptualize organizational culture.

This study follows the competing values model (CVM), because this framework has been used in this context before. Research supports that culture is shaped overtime by succeeding senior executives and other stakeholders within the organization. Lanegan-Fox and Tan (1997) state: "Organizational culture is a topic of current interest in management circles, with organizations adopting culture-based strategies such as total quality management and customer service in pursuit of the competitive edge." As we move into the 21st century, it is important to consider which key attributes in an organization's culture best support decision-making. "The concept of 'organizational culture' refers to the overall ethos of an organization. The characteristics include psychological and structural elements, which affect the perceptions and behaviors of employees (Fletcher & Jones, 1992)."

The area of organizational culture has been the focus of numerous research studies and has consistently been identified as an important independent variable in understanding employees' performance. De Long and Fahey (2000) indicated that culture dictates what knowledge belongs to the organization. Barlow and Batteau (2000) indicate that culture filters down through the organization, and is refined and modified by the day-to-day decisions of everyone in the business. Steven Feldman (1999) mentioned that culture is hierarchical because it creates a system of meaning where values are of central importance and other aspects are of secondary or marginal importance.

A strong culture may be an important factor in obtaining a competitive advantage. Cabrera and Bonache (1999) suggest that culture can be described as the characteristic way in which work is done in different organizations. The concept of organizational culture can most conveniently be operationalized in terms of either types or dimensions (Fletcher & Jones, 1992). According to Fletcher and Jones, the uses of types involve categorizing organizations on the basis of a range of evidence using a theoretical basis, for example, a bureaucratic culture. The use of dimensions identifies the position of the organization on a number of continua, each describing elements of importance to individual and organizational performance, such as how people perceive the quality of communication.

Ritchie (2000) refers to findings from many researchers supporting and suggesting that organizational cultures affect such outcomes as productivity, performance, commitment, self-confidence, and ethical behavior. His results suggest that organizational culture does have a positive effect on employee attitudes; the central focus of his study identified organizational culture as a powerful and positive force within an organization. He suggested that management should understand the relationship between a strong culture and positive organizational outcomes.

Cabrera and Bonache (1999) reported that if this manner of doing things is the most adequate for achieving success in a competitive environment, then the culture is an asset for the organization. On the other hand, if the culture does not encourage the behaviors necessary for the organization to compete successfully, then the culture is a liability.

According to De Long and Fahey (2000), to find the fit between the existing organization and knowledge management objectives, managers need frameworks to effectively identify how culture affects their unit's ability to create and apply knowledge. As De Long and Fahey emphasize, only then can they design strategies to either adapt to the culture or try to reshape it to support the firm's knowledge management objectives. As illustrated above, the concept of culture continues to be researched in the literature as a key variable in the success or failure of organizational innovations or initiatives. Hence, the theoretical framework and CVM of Quinn and McGrath (1985) provide the main focus of the literature in this field. This theoretical model, the competing values framework, provides a useful conceptual tool for understanding an organization's culture and thus to examine the relationship of culture to knowledge management.

The Competing Values Framework

The competing values framework is widely known to scholars and researchers as an efficacious way to measure and compare one culture to another. The competing values framework also has been used to organize the literature on organizational effectiveness, leadership, information processing, organizational change, organizational culture, and organizational decision-making. In a series of studies, Quinn and Rohrbaugh (1983) investigated the similarity and dissimilarity between pairs of organizational descriptors. The results of their numerous analyses are the competing value model of organizational effectiveness.

Quinn, et al. (1983) brought together four quadrants to form a model that illustrates the conflicts or competing values of organizational life. It depicts the organizations as adaptable and flexible, but also stable and controlled. They point out that the goals of the organization are to have growth, resource acquisition, and external support for tighter information management and formal communication, by emphasizing on the value of human resources and planning and goal setting. The two primary dimensions reflected preferences for either structural control or flexibility, and focus on either internal or external constituents. Crossing these two dimensions at their centers, therefore, identified four distinctive organizational types. Particular objectives and/or preferred processes for achieving objectives characterized each of the quadrants; the means-ends third dimension. The quadrants each had a conceptual polar opposite. Each implied values that appeared to be mutually exclusive. The competing value model has two axes, which defines four quadrants. The vertical axis ranges from flexibility to control; the horizontal axis ranges from an internal to an external focus. Each quadrant of the framework represents one of the four major organizational theories. In the human relations quadrant, one finds descriptors such as cohesion and morale, criteria suggesting the value of human resources and training. Horizontally contiguous to the human relations quadrant is the open systems quadrant, including descriptors such as adaptability, readiness, growth, resource acquisitions, and external support. The lower-right rational goal quadrant includes descriptors such as planning, goal setting, productivity, and efficiency. Last, the lower-right internal process quadrant includes information management and communication, stability, and control (Quinn, et al., 1991).

Each quadrant in the model has a polar opposite. For example, the human relations quadrant, emphasizing flexibility and internal focus, stands in contrast to the rational goal quadrant, emphasizing control and external focus. The open systems quadrant, characterizing flexibility and external focus, runs counter to the internal process where control and internal focus are valued (Quinn et al., 1991). As pointed out by Quinn and other colleagues, the parallels among the quadrants are also important. For instance, the human relations and open systems and rational goal quadrants have an external focus, which responds to outside change and production needs in a competitive market. Central to both the internal process and rational goal quadrants is the concept of control; whereas process and rational goal quadrants share a concern for the internal process and human relations quadrants share a concern for the human and technical systems inside the organization.

Quinn (1988) subsequently labeled the quadrants to refer to four types of organizational cultures. In the Human Relations culture, flexibility values and an internal focus describe the dominant value orientation, with group cohesiveness and morale providing the means to human resource development. In the Open Systems approach, flexibility values and external focus include innovation as a means to growth. In the Rational Goal culture, values for control and an external focus emphasize goal setting as a means to enhance productivity. Finally, in the Internal Process approach, values for control and an internal focus include formalizing communications and centralizing decision-making in order to achieve stability. Each cultural type seems tailored to meet the demands of particular constituents. Nonetheless, it is argued that all four approaches coexist in modem organizations, with some values more dominant than others (Quinn & Kimberly, 1984), and that the apparent oppositions exist only in our minds (Quinn, Hildebrandt, Rogers & Thompson, 1991).

The competing values framework also has proven useful for describing the dynamics of several organizational behavior phenomena. For example, Quinn and Spreitzer (1991) report on publications and research of Quinn and his colleague's application of the CVM to explicate concepts of organizational communications, leadership, organizational transitions, and organizational decision-making. Other empirical research lends indirect support for the CVM. Deshpande, Farley and Webster (1993), for example, reported associations among patterns of organizational characteristics and patterns of firm performance indices, which are consistent with the competing values approach. Ostroff and Schmitt (1993) also concluded that a balance of apparently competing characteristics was necessary in order for their subject organizations to achieve both efficiency and effectiveness, just as the CVM proposes.

Cameron and Quinn (1999) described each of the four culture types as Clan, Hierarchy, Adhocracy, and Market.

The Clan Culture: An organization that focuses on internal maintenance with flexibility, concern for people, and sensitivity to customers. The clan culture type organization provides a friendly place to work where people share a lot of themselves. The head of the organization and leaders are considered to be mentors or parent figures. The organization is held together by loyalty or tradition. Organizational commitment is usually high and the organization emphasizes the long-term benefit of human resources development. Great emphasis is placed on cohesion and employee morale. The success of the organization is defined in terms of sensitivity to customers and concern for people.

The Adhocracy Culture: An organization that focuses on external positioning with a high degree of flexibility and individuality. This culture type provides a dynamic, entrepreneurial, and creative place to work. It is a place where people stick their necks out and take risks. The leaders are considered innovators and risk takers. The glue that holds the organization together is commitment to experimentation and innovation. The organization places great emphasis on the leading edge. The long-term emphasis is on growth and acquiring new resources. Success means gaining unique and new products or services. The organization encourages individual initiative and freedom.

The Hierarchy Culture: An organization that focuses on internal maintenance with a need for stability and control. Cameron and Quinn identified that the hierarchy culture in an organization is one that is very formalized and structured. Procedures govern what people and the leaders pride themselves on being good coordinators and organizers who are efficiency-minded. Maintaining a smooth-running organization is most critical. Formal rules and policies hold the organization together. The long-term concern is on stability and performance with efficient, smooth operations. Success is defined in terms of dependable delivery, smooth scheduling, and low cost. The management of employees is concerned with secure employment and predictability.

The Market Culture: An organization that focuses on external positioning with a need for stability and control. The market culture type organization is result-oriented and the major concern is getting the job done. People are competitive and goal-oriented. The leaders are hard drivers, producers, and competitors. They are tough and demanding. The glue that holds the organization together is an emphasis on winning. Reputation and success are common concerns. The long-term focus is on competitive actions and achievement of measurable goals and targets. Success is defined in terms of market share and penetration. Competitive pricing and market leadership are important and the organizational style is hard-driving competitiveness.

The competing values framework portrays these oppositions as mutually existing in real systems. By implication, it suggests that these descriptors, and the values and assumptions they represent, are oppositions only in our minds; thereby reporting that the four organizational approaches are very different from one another, and may sometimes even be assumed to be mutually exclusive. Quinn and McGrath (1983) describe the competing values approach as a "meta" theory that emerged from their series of empirical studies and conceptual papers. They describe it as a theory of human information processing that assumes that all abstract knowledge is organized around a consistent framework of perceptual values and that the articulation of these values can do much to further human understanding.

The competing values model (CVM) describes organizational culture in what has been described as a mutually exclusive value dimensions (Howard, 1998). This model was first used by Quinn and Rohrbaugh (1983) to examine the relationship between culture and organizational effectiveness; and their work showed that differences among the many effectiveness criteria in the literature could be better understood when they were organized along two axes (Goodman & Zammuto, 2001). The competing values model has been used in subsequent research. For example, Quinn and Spreitzer (1991) used it for two studies to examine the impact of culture on executive well-being. The model was also used by them to identify alternative patterns of culture and to examine the impact of the patterns on various measures of life quality.

The CVM holds that there are four distinct dimensions of organizational culture – group, hierarchical, developmental, and rational. Drawing from descriptions provided by Harris and Mossholder (1996), the following is a summary of each of these dimensions. The group dimension represents an orientation based on values associated with affiliation and concern for people. The development of human resources, trust, teamwork, participative decision-making, and morale is emphasized in organizations whose cultures are high on the group dimension. The hierarchical dimension describes an orientation reflecting values associated with beauracracy. The developmental dimension represents an orientation permeated by assumptions of change. Finally, the rational dimension describes an orientation based on notions of competitiveness, performance, decisiveness, and goal achievement. The study of Harris and Mossholder of 245 managers and executives of large (Fortune 500) U.S. corporations revealed that "group" was the only culture dimension whose discrepancy was significantly related to outcomes. The group discrepancy also was significantly correlated with positive effect. This information is extremely useful to control for the potential influence of positive effect.

Several research studies used the competing values framework to examine the impact of culture on organizational issues. In their utilization of the Competing Values Framework, Goodman et al., (2001) examined the impact of organizational culture on the quality of work life and reported that the competing values framework is particularly useful in surfacing the existing culture; reporting that it incorporates numerous elements and creates a rich visual representation of an organization's culture. Harris and Mossholder's (1996) study on the affective implications of perceived congruence also utilized the CVM culture dimensions during organizational transformation. In a study to validate the CVM, Howard (1998) concluded that the CMV perspective provides a valid metric for understanding organizational cultures. He reported that it is a valuable tool to compare organizational cultures, and evaluate organizational cultures relative to other variables.

Organizational Culture and Change Theory

Schein's (1993) work had contributed much to psychological elements that inhibit or promote change. One of the primary focuses of his study was to help organizations find ways to change faster, in order to keep up with the rapidly shifting environment. His studies identified the abstract concept of learning, and also outlined a change management procedure that leaders can use to help their organizations change, and, ultimately, to develop perpetual learning organizations.

The idea of the learning organization has been around for quite some time, and it has been studied extensively. Rowden (2001) reported that "the learning organization" derives from Argyris' work in organizational learning. Its conceptual foundations are firmly based on systems theory (Senge, 1990); and its practical application to managing a business evolved out of strategic planning and strategic management. It also has roots in much of the quality improvement movement of recent years, with an emphasis on continuous improvement, and in Senge's application of learning organization concepts (Rowden, 2001).

Learning organization research shows that structural and cultural approaches to organizational learning can be institutionalized to systematically collect, analyze, store, disseminate, and use information that is relevant to the success of the organization (Popper & Lipshitz, 1998; Rowden, 2001; Salner, 1999). Schein (1993) states that most organizational learning theories focus on knowledge acquisition and insight, but instead should target behavior change. Organizational learning is important to the investigation of an organizational culture that traditionally hoarded knowledge and other assets believing that scarcity creates value. The organizational change theory can be useful to identify factors affecting organizational culture transformation and adaptation to knowledge management programs. The most difficult aspect of learning is overcoming bad habits and cultural rules (Schein, 1993). The strength of Lewin's (1947) theorizing lay not in a formal prepositional kind of theory, but rather in his ability to build models of processes that drew attention to the right kind of variables that need to be conceptualized and observed (Schein, 2000). This distinction is important because it lends to the concept of the different stages in the change process. Chris Agryris has shown in many ways that organizations are more effective when people are more open with each other when they solve problems, but it can be very difficult to get them to be open because of cultural rules about how to behave.

Organizational culture change has been considered broadly as having an influence on an organization's ability to successfully implement strategy. Management research has sought to explore the understanding of organizational culture for strategic change in organizational settings and to explore theoretical understanding of the links between changing organizational culture and management. Lanegan-Fox and Tan (1997) report that a recurring issue in the literature is the lack of universally accepted definition of organizational culture. What is the nature of the concept 'culture', and how can it be operationally defined? Lanegan-Fox and Tan (1997) cited a number of authors reporting that there appear to be four core issues underlying the many definitions of organizational culture: (a) it is stable and resistant to change; (b) it is taken for granted and less consciously held; (c) it derives its meaning from the organization members; and (d) it incorporates sets of shared understanding.

As a result of the complexity of organizational culture, researchers have focused on layers of culture as a way to understand this organizational phenomenon. Organizational culture change has been considered in an effort to transition the organization to one that will foster knowledge management. A flexible organizational culture is imperative to access and implement changes to the existing culture. Lanegan-Fox and Tan (1997) state that the fundamental assumption underlying these recommendations for culture-based strategies is that organizational culture enables positive economic consequences, such as increased employee commitment and cooperation, greater efficiency, improved job performance, and better decision-making. As such, culture must play a critical role when dramatic, significant change is mandated.

An introduction to change theory was developed in the mid 1900s by Kurt Lewin. His (1947) model of organizational change consists of two basic concepts. The first is that an organization's natural state is static or unchanging. He describes this state as being "frozen." When the organization is in a state of change it is malleable or it "thaws" then reverts to a static or "frozen" state. The second concept is that an organization can be successfully divided into two groups: one that seeks change, and one that opposes change. Lewin also identified three phases through which the change agent must proceed before the planned change becomes a part of the system. These stages include: unfreezing, movement, and refreezing. Unfreezing is where the change agent unfreezes forces that maintain the status quo, where people often become discontented and become aware of a need to change. Before change can occur, they must believe change is needed. Movement is where the change agent identifies, plans, and implements appropriate strategies. One must be sure that driving forces for change exceed restraining forces. Refreezing is the stage where the change agent assists in stabilizing the change in the system so that it becomes integrated into the status quo.

Bennett et al's (1994) model of stability and change address cultural alignment in response to strategies of organizational change. This model provides new considerations for a change framework. Bennett, et al. (1994) report two propositions for organizations when confronted with persuasion for significant strategic change: (1) either the existing culture appears complimentary to the changes imposed by the new strategy, or (2) some cultural change may be deemed necessary in order to affect and maintain organizational effectiveness. Their research proposes a generic model for initiating culture change. This change is viewed as a controlled process. The Bennett et al. (1994) model provides both theorist and practitioners with a guiding framework for understanding the actual change process. Their studies highlighted the following reasons for the organization to undergo significant strategic change:

- Poor performance.
- Environmental turbulence and uncertainty.
- Resource shifts.
- Risk reduction.
- Managerial preference.

According to Bennett, et al. (1994), regardless of the impetus for these types of changes, "the need to align all aspects of the organization with the new strategy is of vital importance to overall effective performance, as well as survival." McElyea (2002) states that "change is a functional characteristic of organizational existence."

Organizational Learning and Knowledge Management

The primary focus is on how people share knowledge. "Like people, organizations are unlikely to be successful unless they can learn from experience and their environment, transit that knowledge throughout the organization, and modify their behavior as needed in response to the knowledge gained" (Goh, 1998, p. 15). According to Peterson and Hicks (2000), in order to build a culture of learning and unleash talent, organizations need to enable the learning process.

Organizational learning has attracted considerable attention in the organizational literature. Argyris and Schon (1978) specifically devoted a lot of time and research on this topic focusing on the descriptive facet of organizational learning and its prescriptive facets. Kolb's (1984) model of the Learning Cycle, describes learning as a four-phase cycle that begins with experiencing and moves to reflection and conceptualization and then to experimentation, which restart the cycle. As the world changes, organizations must learn to adapt faster to survive and grow. The most urgent priority is learning to learn faster, organization must understand that learning is a necessity not a choice (Schein, 1993).

Senge (1998) reports that sharing knowledge occurs when people are genuinely interested in helping one another develop new capacities for action; it is about creating learning processes. Popper and Lipshitz (1998) present a two-faceted (structural and cultural) approach to organizational learning. The structural facet focuses on organizational learning mechanisms, which are institutionalized structural and procedural arrangements allowing organizations to systematically collect, analyze, store, disseminate, and use information that is relevant to their performance at the organization. The cultural facet focuses on the shared values, without which these mechanisms are likely to be enacted as rituals rather than as means to detect and correct errors.

Peter Senge (1990) articulates the reasons for transformation into a learning organization. He proposes a means to sustain the change as a learning organization. Senge outlines the process to achieve a learning organization and the core of learning organizations in system theory. McElyea (2002) states that the same open environment needed to facilitate the growth of knowledge to improve a competitive advantage can be argued as synonymous with the environment that facilitates organizational learning. Garvin (1993) states that, "A learning organization is an organization skilled at creating, acquiring and transferring knowledge, and modifying its behavior to reflect new knowledge and insights."

The aim of the learning organization approach is to implement organizational culture change as it relates to fostering an environment for strategic change for effective knowledge management. Mellander (2001) proposes that no knowledge management initiatives can exist or succeed in any environment without first providing the right conditions for learning. Stonehouse and Pemberton (1999) argued that by learning about the learning process itself, and by formalizing the processes and structures of knowledge management, organizations could shorten the time taken to learn and improve the quality and quantity of knowledge available.

Drew and Smith (1995) report that it is advantageous to link organizational learning strategies for restructuring and that such change can best succeed if the organization is ready. They developed a framework for conducting a type of "change audit." They further outlined the concepts of the learning organization and how it can be utilized to "change proof" the firm – to increase its capacity to withstand and exploit unexpected and rapid change. They also recommend combining implementation of a learning approach to strategy with successful, proactive change management.

The learning systems model, "change proofing," (Drew & Smith, 1995) consists of three essential elements – focus, will, and capability. Focus, will and capability may be interpreted as the organization's knowledge and awareness of potential change as described below.

1. *Focus*, which means a clear sense of direction and vision, arises from the strategic thinking, knowledge and understanding of the key decision-making groups and may be symbolized in clearly articulated strategic plans.
2. *Will* is the strength of strategic intent. With an inclination to set 'stretch' targets and face up to challenges, it characterizes groups and organizations with high levels of will. Will requires emotional commitment and high energy levels, which may be the result of tensions evoked by dissatisfaction with the status quo.
3. *Capability* is related to a limited number of learned competences, unique to the organization at a given time. Suggesting that capability is a characteristic of the top decision-making teams throughout the organization's history and culture. That capability also includes the ability to and freedom to take action.

Drew and Smith (1995) propose that the three-circle framework (focus, will and capability) has the benefit of conceptual simplicity and elegance. It has been extremely useful as a tool for simulating discussion of issues related to radical change. Further reporting that it is simple to grasp at an intuitive level, and can easily be linked to the characteristics of the learning organization. History shows that the consequences of failing to recognize and interpret change can be devastating. Senge (1990) wrote, reaction to change is significant because change is inevitable, and accepting change makes an individual part of the process and so he or she can survive.

Goh (1998) identifies five strategic building blocks, supporting foundations and specific strategic measurement and intervention processes that are the key factors in the learning organization archetype. They are:

1. *Mission and vision* -- Clarity and employees' support of the mission, strategy, and espoused values of the organization.

2. *Leadership* – Leadership that is perceived as empowering employees, encouraging an experimentation culture, and showing strong commitment to the organization.
3. *Experimentation* – A strong culture of experimentation that is rewarded and supported at all levels in the organization
4. *Transfer of Knowledge* – The ability of an organization to transfer knowledge within and from outside the organization and to learn from failures.
5. *Teamwork and Cooperation* – An emphasis on teamwork and group problem solving as the mode of operation and for developing innovative ideas.

Goh (1998) suggests that building a strong learning capability is crucial for knowledge-intensive organizations and for companies operating in a highly competitive environment. Although described as separate dimensions, these building blocks are interdependent and mutually supportive in a learning organization. It was further argued that "A learning organization is one where employees are empowered to act based on the relevant knowledge and skills they have acquired and information about the priorities of the organization" (Goh, 1998). Goh posited that skill and knowledge acquisition are obviously useless unless the employees can transfer them to the immediate job. Goh (1998) further proposed that it is even better if this knowledge can also be transferred to other parts of the organization to solve problems and energize creative new ideas.

In *The Fifth Discipline*, Senge (1990) states that in order to change what exists, the process must begin with identifying what he calls "the seven learning disabilities. Cathon (2000) reviewed Senge's seven processes, these consisted of:

1. I am my Position,
2. The Enemy is Out There,
3. The Illusion of Taking Charge,
4. The Fixation of Events,
5. The Parable of the Boiled Frog,
6. The Delusion of Learning from Experience, and
7. The Myth of the Management Team.

'I am my position'; people in general are trained to be loyal to their job. This becomes so ingrained that their job becomes part of their everyday identity. 'The Enemy is Out There' when focused only on one's self, one cannot see beyond his or her own actions. When a problem appears, the blame is placed on an external source. 'The Illusion of Taking Charge', often when an organization is faced with a problem, the feeling is that management needs to become more proactive. 'The Fixation on Events', learning cannot be sustained in an organization if people focus on short-term growth or on a single event. 'The Parable of the Boiled Frog', learning to see slow changes in a process requires one to step back from the everyday frantic pace and pay attention to subtle as well as the sudden. 'The Delusion of Learning from experience', the most powerful learning comes from direct experience. We learn best from experience but we never directly experience the consequences of many of the most important decisions. 'The Myth of the Management Team', often those in control who live by micromanagement theory supply the best example of skilled incompetence. These individuals become so aggressive in trying to control, they have no concept as to the process in which certain functions occur.

In order to make this change to a learning organization, Senge (1990) describes five disciplines. The five disciplines are (1) Personal mastery, (2) mental model, (3) shared vision, (4) team learning, and (5) systems thinking.

1. *Personal mastery* goes beyond competence and skills. It means developing one's life as a creative adventure. When personal mastery becomes a discipline, an active part of one's everyday way of life takes on two strong movements. One is clarifying continuously what is important, the second is continuous learning of how to see the new reality.

2. *Mental models* - one thing managers know is that many of the best ideas are never put into practice. More specifically, new insights fail to gain acceptance because they conflict with deeply held internal images that limit the individual to familiar ways of thinking and acting. Mental models are powerful in affecting what one does because they affect what one sees. That is why the management of mental models, of improving the internal picture, is a major step for building a learning organization.

3. *Shared vision* is not an idea; rather it is a force in a person's heart, a power. A vision is shared when more than one person has a similar picture and commits to having it. A shared vision is important for the learning organization because it provides the focus and energy for learning.

4. *Team learning* is the process of alignment and development of a team to create the results its members truly desire. It builds on the discipline of shared vision and personal mastery. Team learning has three critical areas; the need to think insightfully about issues, the need for innovative and coordinated actions, and the role of team members on other teams. Team learning requires practice.

5. *System thinking* binds the other disciplines together and it is essential that they develop as a whole for the learning organization to survive. It is the key to growing from a "me" to "we" mentality.

Pemberton and Stone (2000) describe the organizational learning context as consisting of three elements; (1) organizational culture, (2) structure, and

(3) infrastructure. Further, stating that these elements are the means by which an organization continuously increases the effectiveness and the efficiency of its learning and knowledge management processes and systems. As Stone and Pemberton notes, learning is treated as a cognitive process, with the organization 'learning about learning' and developing conditions which foster individual and organizational learning with emphasis placed on its knowledge assets and the supporting knowledge management systems. The first element, culture, was stated as the most important component of the learning organizational context.

The culture of the learning organization places great emphasis on learning and knowledge, creating an atmosphere of trust within which individuals feel empowered to experiment with new approaches to business, often resulting in the development of new core competencies. Pemberton and Stone (2000) defined the following as the components of a learning culture:

◊ A clear organizational vision.
◊ Leaders who are designers, teachers and stewards.
◊ A desire for continuous improvement.
◊ Attaches a high value to knowledge.
◊ Encourages questioning and experimentation through empowerment of individuals.
◊ Creativity, risk taking and tolerance of mistakes.
◊ Build trust to encourage sharing of knowledge within the organization and with selected partners.
◊ Emphasizes frequent contact and good communication.
◊ Encourages socialization and the development of a concept of community.
◊ Experiential learning of tacit knowledge.
◊ External vision to learn from the environment in which the business operates.

The second element, structuring for learning and knowledge management, requires flatter organizations with reduced cross-functional boundaries. Organizational knowledge must be holistic to ensure that specialist knowledge from related areas is fully integrated. Having a matrix structure is one way to promote a holistic view of knowledge. Pemberton and Stone (2000) stated that ultimately, network organizational structures are perhaps the most appropriate for supporting a learning culture, while having fewer hierarchical features and existing in a variety of forms. Pemberton and Stone further stated that while there is no single structure that uniquely supports learning, empowerment of the individual together with flat network structures, which foster cross-functional communication and where functional barriers are low, appear to facilitate knowledge management more effectively.

The third element, infrastructure and communication, is an integral part of building the learning organization. Developments in technology, and particularly those in information and communications technology (ICT), have played a vital role in providing the infrastructure needed to support network structures and organizational learning within. According to Pemberton and Stone (2000) ICT has transformed the ability of both the individual and the organization to augment their intelligence via accelerated learning. It has also increased the potential for sharing knowledge between collaborating organizations. The storage and communication of knowledge is also central to the way in which organization capitalizes on its knowledge base. Explicit knowledge is easy to store and communicate, with most media being effective. However, the intangible nature of implicit knowledge makes this a far more difficult proposition.

Pemberton and Stone (2000) describe the difficulties with storage and communication of knowledge, stating that the location base of knowledge is critically important. It is especially relevant in relation to implicit or tacit knowledge. Summarizing that systems and infrastructure go beyond the technology that supports them, training plays an important part in the process of knowledge diffusion. Ultimately, a learning organization gains sustainable competitive advantage by accelerating learning to develop superior intelligence and knowledge that, when harnessed, produces unique and durable competencies.

Knowledge Management

The study of knowledge management dates back to Plato and Aristotle. The various research and discussions surrounding knowledge management focus on the technology issue or the human issue. Today, knowledge management offers a unique concept considered by many in the industry as progressive and "soft" in application, primarily because of the intangible elements of knowledge (McElyea, 2002).

The literature proposes that it is imperative to have a better understanding of knowledge as the world change from a knowledge transition stage to a knowledge era. Lee (2000) writes that the latest revolution centers on an organization's ability to use intelligently the knowledge it already has within it, as well as the new intellectual capital created daily. Lee further went on to say that in this new paradigm, collaboration and sharing will replace knowledge hoarding, interested communities will provide the equipment necessary to maintain improvements, and technology will be positioned to ensure efficient knowledge transfer. For example, as De Long and Fahey (2000) suggested, the purpose of knowledge management is to enhance organizational performance by designing and implementing tools, processes, systems, structures, and cultures to improve the creation, sharing, and use of all three types of knowledge that are critical for decision-making.

As discussed by Lee (2000), information embedded and synthesized in the brain is knowledge. Communication of this intellectual capital is difficult to structure, much less capture, on machines or electronically. Lee further went on to show that knowledge by its nature is highly personal and extremely difficult to transfer with the richness as complete as the original holder of the knowledge understands it. Identifying that this difficulty in transfer exists is what often makes knowledge tacit as opposed to explicit.

As Berry (2000) claims, with effective knowledge management, managers will eliminate the barriers between the person who knows and the person who needs to know. He states that this is not an easy task, because one of the major impediments to successful knowledge management is changing the belief that "knowledge is power," and this should be hoarded, rather than shared freely. De Long and Fahey (2000) suggest that more and more managers and leaders are recognizing that organizational culture can be a major barrier to leveraging intellectual assets. Understanding how culture influences knowledge and its use are essential to finding a fit between culture and knowledge in any organization. As Hersey, Blanchard and Johnson (1996) so aptly state, "Culture influences how decisions are made, the style of management, and relations and behavior patterns in the organization."

Eisenhart (2001) states that, successful knowledge gathering and sharing cannot take place in an adversarial environment, where people are competing against each other, and where they feel they would be jeopardizing their own status and security by giving up knowledge. Eisenhart recommended that a company's overall knowledge management strategy should include managers actively encouraging sharing behaviors within and across the company, so that varying experts in the organization are willing to share what they know.

McDermott (1999) identified fundamental requirements for leveraging knowledge. Knowledge is different from information; accordingly, sharing it requires a different set of concepts and tools. He proposed that rather than identifying information needs and tools, we identify the community that cares about a topic and then enhance their ability to think together. More specifically, in order to leverage knowledge one must focus on the community that "owns" it and the people who use it, not the knowledge itself. De Long and Fahey (2000) discuss three related themes that are critically important to viewing culture as a lens to understand knowledge distribution. That is, who controls it, what knowledge and where they are located (De Long & Fahey, 2000). Elliot and O'Dell (1999) identify four enablers essential and critical to successful knowledge management (culture, technology, infrastructure, and measurement); they emphasize that all four are necessary to yield sustainable success.

According to Lambert (1999), it is evident that the emergence of understanding the complexity of knowledge management is a good indicator of business competitiveness in the knowledge era; intellectual capital becomes the primary asset, as the company's knowledge base continues to grow. Lee (2000) writes, "What distinguishes knowledge from its data and information brethren, is the inclusion of human contribution, and this adds more value to the transferee." As pointed out by Lee, the new business model of knowledge management is distinguished by the historical perspective, which is the closeness of knowledge to the application of its use. Klaila (2000) writes that knowledge management is about planning to change, revaluing our work, and changing the way we value work. She further stated that as a result of this change, there would be a shift in the way we work, and in the way we define leadership. Knowledge management is when executives get the insight they need to run their business and how they formalize that insight. Gupta, Iyer and Aronson (2000) state that, "Knowledge management is a process that deals with the development, storage, retrieval, and dissemination of information and expertise within an organization to support and improve its business performance" (p. 17)." They cite Nonanka and Takeuchi (1995) in identifying four processes that are commonly used in organizations for knowledge management:

1. *Socialization*: sharing of experiences through observation, imitation and practice. It generally occurs through workshops, seminars, apprenticeships, and conferences, as well as at the water cooler.
2. *Capture*: the conversion of tacit knowledge (e.g. what one learned at a workshop) into explicit form (e.g. written report).
3. *Dissemination*: the copying and distribution of the explicit knowledge.
4. *Internalization*: process of experiencing knowledge through an explicit source, i.e., one can combine the experience of reading the workshop report with previous experience.

Given the importance of knowledge management, researchers have looked for answers to the critical question: "What is the meaning of the growing importance of knowledge management?" With the emergence of knowledge management and intellectual capital as new concepts, more and more research is been done to examine knowledge management. Focusing on these relationships is important for theoretical and strategic reasons. Knowledge management is emerging as an important concept, and is often cited as an antecedent of innovation. While the need to effectively manage knowledge generally is accepted, knowledge management is still an elusive concept and much of the literature continues to explore issues of definition. Until a definition is widely accepted, measuring knowledge management and identifying its effect on outcomes such as innovation, growth, firm performance, and competitive advantage will be hard to determine.

Research suggested that knowledge is comprised of data, information and tacit and explicit knowledge; and that knowledge management is a process that deals with the development, storage, retrieval and dissemination of information and expertise within an organization to support and improve its business performance (Gupta, Iyer, & Aronson, 2000). The management function that creates or locates knowledge manages the flow of knowledge within the organization and ensures that the knowledge is used effectively and efficiently for a competitive advantage. When knowledge is used, learning takes place, which, in turn, improves the repositories of knowledge available to the firm. Therefore, a firm that effectively manages knowledge is also likely to be considered a learning organization (Mellander, 2001). Effective knowledge management has been presented in the literature as one method for improving innovation, productivity, and performance. More specifically, knowledge dissemination and responsiveness to knowledge repeatedly have been cited as the most effective way to a competitive advantage. Some authors focus on publications addressing the personalization of knowledge management practices primarily examining how people share knowledge. Ribiere (2001) identified two main approaches: codification versus personalization. The "codification approach" is intended to collect, codify, and disseminate information, which relies heavily on IT to manage explicit knowledge. Whereas, the personalization approach focuses on developing networks to link people so that tacit knowledge can be shared. Ribiere's study, on the characteristics of the personalization approach is summarized as follows:

1. *Competitive Strategy.* Provide creative, analytically rigorous advice on high-level strategic problems by channeling individual expertise.
2. *Economic Model.* Charge high fees for highly customized solutions to unique problems. Use small teams with a low ratio of associates to partners. Focus on maintaining high profit margins.
3. *KM Strategy.* Person-to-person; develop networks for linking people so that tacit knowledge can be shared.
4. *Information Technology.* Competitive strategy provides creative, analytically rigorous advice on high-level strategic problems by channeling individual expertise.
5. *Human Resources.* Hire graduates of a business program who like problem solving and can tolerate ambiguity. Train people through one-on-one mentoring. Reward people for directly sharing knowledge with others.

Ribiere (2000) also highlighted Stephen Denning's connecting dimension approach, which involves linking people who need to know with those who know, to develop new capabilities for nurturing knowledge and acting knowledgeably; and reported that it is a valuable tool to compare organizational cultures, and evaluate organizational cultures relative to other variables.

Summary

This chapter has provided sufficient evidence that effective knowledge management is critical to the success of twenty-first century organizations. Knowledge management is an effort to capture or tap into an organization's experience and wisdom and to make them available and useful to everyone in the organization.

The literature provided various perspectives on the emerging enthusiasm for knowledge management programs. Some researchers have supported that while knowledge management is technology based, it is not about computers, and for it to be effective it must be much more. For example, as the high positive correlations between organizational culture and knowledge management strongly suggest, organizational culture may be the "driving force" behind whether or not the organization achieved its objectives. Knowledge is considered to be one of the most important assets in the new economy. As such, it is vital to organizational benefits, such as competitive advantage, growth, and innovation.

The material presented on this topic supports the conclusion that as we move from an industrial era to one of knowledge, responsibility is placed on all national and global managers to better understand knowledge management systems. Studies also make clear that organizational culture should foster the concept that knowledge management is the tool to support an organization's strategic plan. It is evident that the evolution of knowledge management should incorporate technology solutions, content, process and all people involved in the value chain.

Discussion Questions

1. What is learning? Discuss.
2. What is knowledge? Discuss.
3. What is knowledge management? Why is knowledge management necessary in today's environment where most professionals in large firms seem to have access to modern computers, libraries, and people around the globe through various telecommunication technologies?
4. What is a "learning culture" as per your philosophy?
5. What is a learning organization? How does it vary from individual learning? Discuss.
6. How can knowledge management concepts be used to fairly, justly and equally develop people of both genders and all races?
7. Are firms that have diverse employees better off than firms that have a homogenous workforce? Discuss your thoughts and provide examples.
8. What can firms do to effectively manage the knowledge of their diverse staff?
9. Discuss one learning organization that seems to do a good job in the area of knowledge management? What makes them effective?
10. Create a list of some specific ways to make sure there is equal access to knowledge for everyone in the organization regardless of his or her gender, race, disability, age, etc.

Part III

Perspectives on Diversity Competencies and Skills

Power and Leadership

Successful leaders understand the skills of leadership, collaboration and teamwork with diverse employees, colleagues, suppliers, and customers to remain competitive. Using the concepts of leadership and *"Diversituation"* to effectively influence others, the chapter recommends using the skills of situational management and leadership with employees of diverse cultures and characteristics to help them develop progressively for more assignments and projects. So, effective diversity management requires understanding situational leadership styles and skills to gain power which can be used toward progressively influencing and developing others as per their level of readiness. While the diversity demographics discussed in this chapter may not necessarily be true of other economy's workforce, any country can benefit from the leadership and diversity management principles discussed in order to retain diverse teams that can quickly and effectively respond to today's diverse and complex global business challenges.

Leadership and Power Tactics[16]

The application of power and influence in virtually all settings continues to encourage spirited debate among scholars and captivates leading researchers. John French and Bertram Raven were the first to theorize that there were five bases of power in which people derive their ability to influence others. Subsequent studies by Raven, Kruglanski, Hersey, and Goldsmith formed two more power bases. David Kipnis added his belief that there were nine influence tactics which affected the behavior of targeted individuals. At the core of these theories is the idea that the effect of power and influence are the result of people's perceptions and interpretations of a particular situation. The situational leadership model developed by Hersey and Blanchard apply various types of power and influence strategies to advance people from one readiness level to another based upon task differentiation and appropriate leadership style. This chapter identifies the bases of power, influence tactics, and how they fit with the successful application of various leadership styles.

For centuries the definition and proper use of power has been the subject of wide debate and scholarly study. For example, Shakespeare's works often dealt with the acquisition and use of power, and Nicollo Machiavelli's book, *The Prince*, has been referred to as the "classic handbook on power politics" (Hughes, Ginnett & Curphy, 2002, p. 107; Baylor, 2005). Despite this exten-

---

[16] This chapter is co-authored with Regina H. Harris and Fred Barron, Nova Southeastern University.

sive work, the consensus definition of power remains elusive. House defined power as the "capacity to produce effects on others" (Hughes, Ginnett, et al., 2002, p.107). Hersey and Campbell defined it as "influence potential – the resource that enables a leader to gain compliance or commitment from others" (Hersey & Campbell, 2004, p. 234). Tjosvold, Andrews and Struthers defined power "as the capacity to make others do what they would not otherwise do or the ability to overcome resistance" (Tworoger, 2004). French and Raven viewed power in terms of influence and Kipnis agreed that influence tactics are the method by which a follower is moved towards the appropriate goal (Tworoger, 2004). Some view influence as kinetic power, just as power is potential influence (Bruins, 1999). In other words, power and influence are inextricably linked in terms of motivation.

Among varying opinions regarding the definition of power and the use of influence tactics, it is nevertheless agreed that motivation to perform is a function of three ingredients: the leader, the follower and the situation. This is the cornerstone of situational leadership. According to Hersey and Campbell (2004), the combination of power and influence, along with follower readiness and the appropriate leadership style for a particular situation has the greatest potential for producing the desired result.

An understanding of how power and influence play into follower movement is a prerequisite to effective integration of situational leadership model. Hersey and Blanchard believe that follower readiness determines the appropriate application of leadership style and power base (Baylor, 2005). Successful influence is dependent upon use of the right power base. Hersey and Campbell said that follower readiness is the function of demonstrated ability and willingness to perform a given task; there model provides four leadership styles which are aligned with four levels of readiness. Followers who are unable and unwilling to perform (i.e., readiness level one, R1) require high task and low relationship levels of supervision (i.e., S1). The second level of readiness pertains to people who are willing, but unable (i.e., R2). These followers require high levels of task and relationship orientation like those offered by leaders using an S2 style of leadership. Followers at readiness level three (R3) are able but often unwilling to perform new tasks. They tend to be better motivated by low task and high relationship supervision, which applies to a moderate level of readiness. This is referred to as an S3 leadership style. Finally, people who are ready, willing, and able are considered to be at the peak readiness level and require low task and relationship supervision. These R4s are at high levels of readiness to accomplish a specific task and work best under an S4 leadership style.

Once the appropriate readiness level is diagnosed, the leader can adapt his/her leadership style to suit the follower readiness level. Motivating anyone often requires influence that stems from a particular base of power. The variety of social power bases and influence tactics that may be applied to certain instances follows.

The Powers Behind Influence

Power, influence and leadership are inextricably intertwined. Although power is invisible, it is an ever present attribute in the influence one has on another (Hughes et al., 2002). In 1959, French and Raven identified five bases of power used to motivate and influence others in any situation. They categorized their power sources as expert, referent, reward, legitimate, and coercive. French and Raven hypothesized that certain applications of power produce greater force of influence. They found referent power has the greatest range. Coercive and reward power are dependent on the follower's conformity since coercive power breeds contempt while reward power encourages results. If coercive power, for example, is legitimate, there will be less resistance (Tworoger, 2004). French and Raven also theorized that some types of power are not applicable to all situations. It is left to the influencer to determine which behavior will have the greatest impact on the respondent.

Expert power comes from having knowledge and expertise in a given field. If a follower views his or her leader as being an expert in a situation, the follower will likely be better motivated (Bielous, 1995). It is also possible for followers to have more expert power than leaders in certain situations. Because expert power is attributed to another, it can help or hurt the leader. Losing credibility can irreparably harm the leader's reputation causing them to lose follower respect and expert influence. This type of power is largely a function of the person wielding it and the perception of the follower. When a follower has expert power, he/she requires little supervision (Hersey & Campbell, 2004).

Referent power is the influence one has over another due to the strength of the relationship or the oneness between the leader and follower (Hughes et al., 2002). When a follower views the leader as fair, confident and easily approachable, he/she will want to do a good job. Referent power must be developed over time and, if a meaningful relationship has not been established, attempts to influence in this way may be viewed as adversarial (Hersey & Campbell, 2004). Although referent power can be very strong, it can also hinder work productivity as leaders may be reluctant to discipline poorly performing followers (Hughes et al., 2002). This type of power is a function of both the leader and follower and is democratic in nature (Hersey & Campbell, 2004).

Legitimate power comes from organizational title and status induced by an internalized value. In essence, the follower must believe he/she is obligated to be influenced by another by virtue of position (Spring, 2002). Legitimate power does not equate to leadership and followers can counter with their legitimate power to influence leaders in certain situations. For example, conforming to union rules and job descriptions is a good use of legitimate power (Hughes et al., 2002). Often, disciplinary action is the only way to sanction those who do not abide by legitimate power.

Reward power is the ability to influence others using items of perceived value. In order for reward power to be effective, the reward must be aligned with something the respondent truly desires. This type of power induces superficial changes in the follower, as none of their beliefs, values or attitudes change (Bruins, 1999). Some believe this type of power increases with the size of the reward, but large rewards beget larger rewards and if the rewards regress, the expected behavior may erode. Rewards may be tangible or intangible, and is a combined function of the leader, follower, and situation (Hughes et al., 2002). This source of power can be problematic for a couple of reasons. First, it may encourage compliance without commitment, and employees may do only what is necessary to receive the reward without anything more (Hughes et al., 2002). Additionally, leaders can reduce their power by rewarding for one thing, but actually hoping for another alternative.

Coercive power is the use of negativity, sanctions, threats and punishment to influence others. It is a strong ability to enforce policies and procedures if performance is unacceptable (Bielous, 1995). This type of power is a function of the leader and situation, but it is also dependent upon what the follower perceives as punishment (Hughes et al., 2002). Some leaders are reluctant to use this type of power for fear of follower retribution. Coercive power must be exercised, or it will lose its magnitude (Hersey & Campbell, 2004).

French and Raven's theories have led to the creation of other power bases. More recently, scholars have identified new power bases such as information, connection, personal, and position power.

Information power constitutes a sixth power base and was discussed by Raven and Kruglanski in 1975 (Baylor, 2005). It is the possession or perceived access to useful information. Bielous (1995) agreed that employees will work harder for their supervisors if they can have access to important information. According to Hersey and Campbell (2004), information power is effective with followers in the above-average readiness levels, as they can use this information to improve performance. Further, this power references internalized and lasting changes in the follower's beliefs, attitudes and values (Bruins, 1999).

Found by Hersey and Goldsmith in 1980, *connection power*, or affiliation power, is based upon follower perception. People with strong connections are perceived as having the ability to get things done. This type of influence is useful in motivating followers with low readiness levels and may also induce compliance (Hersey & Campbell, 2004).

Hersey and Campbell define *position power* as the "extent to which those people to whom managers report are willing to delegate authority and responsibility down to them" (p. 236). Thus, this power flows down in an organization.

Personal power is "the extent to which followers respect, feel good about, and are committed to their leader and to which they see their own goals as being satisfied by the goals of their leader" (Hersey & Campbell, 2004, p. 237). Power base flows up in an organization and is not inherent to the leader. As Hersey and Campbell point out, this type of power can be given and taken away.

Based on French and Raven's research, the effective use of referent and expert power will lead to more motivated and satisfied subordinates (Hughes et al., 2002). Hersey and Campbell (2004) agreed with French and Raven, but also found that legitimate and expert power relates to compliance, while coercive power was associated with dissatisfaction. All agreed that it is best to exercise each power source to effectively influence desired behavior modification among followers.

Influence Tactics

People who hold power can use a variety of influence tactics to modify behavior and produce desired effects. Although "power is the capacity to cause change, influence is the degree of actual change in a target person's attitudes, value, beliefs, or behaviors" (Hughes et al., 2002, p. 108). Influence tactics refer to the mode used to change those behaviors.

Influence is an important motivator because it "concentrates on interpersonal contact and communication" (Bruins, 1999, p. 1). Contacts and communication can lead to belongingness, security, and social acceptance, as reflected in Maslow's research. A breakdown in influence can result in negative consequences such as lack of self-esteem and powerlessness (Bruins, 1999). French and Raven understood the connection between power and influence and created The Power/Interaction Model of Interpersonal Influence. This model describes the rational decision making process used by leaders who tend to weigh the costs and benefits of power bases before using one of them to influence a target individual (Bruins, 1999). Kipnis followed this research with the development of The Power Act Model. Simply stated, this model explains that the choice of influence is dependent upon the power bases one possesses, the willingness to use this power, against the expected resistance by using this influence tactic (Bruins, 1999). Before a tactic is applied, the leader must understand the reason behind possible resistance and diagnose which tactic to use. With such understanding, the leader can abandon, modify, or use a stronger influence tactic depending upon resistance (Bruins, 1999).

In 1982, Kipnis and Schmidt outlined nine influence tactics most often used by agents trying to affect change. The tactics included rational persuasion, inspirational appeals, consultation, integration, personal appeals, exchange, coalition tactics, pressure tactics, and legitimizing tactics. These tactics can be grouped into three categories: hard tactics which use authority and position power; soft tactics which rely upon personal power; and rational persuasion using logic (Thacker, 1995; Hughes et al., 2002).

Rational persuasion uses logical arguments and facts to influence others. Like expert and information power, it will appeal to followers who perceive data and knowledge as important factors in motivation. Thus, it can be used with any readiness level.

Inspirational appeals target emotions and are often used in religious situations. These appeals may work best with referent or legitimate power, but may backfire if people believe the influencer is taking advantage of the follower.

Consultation is used to collaborate on an activity. This tactic is best used with referent power and situations with high relationship affiliation. Empowered and encouraged individuals will display high performance. This tactic is beneficial with S2 and S3 leadership styles.

Integration is a tactic to get the follower in a good mood before making a request. It can be used at any readiness level by any leadership level and in any situation. It may be more effective with high levels of referent or connection power.

Personal appeals are favors requested based on friendship. This style would be more effective on those with high levels of referent and reward power and those with high relationship needs. Therefore, this tactic is best used by S2 and S3 leadership styles on R1 and R2 readiness levels.

Exchange targets trade of favors or information (Hughes et al., 2002). It can be used with almost any power except coercive. Thus, it can be used with all leadership styles and readiness levels. However, people at lower readiness levels may not have anything to exchange.

Coalition tactics are used to get a group of people to influence another's behavior. An example of coalition tactics could be an intervention for a compulsive gambler or an alcoholic. This tactic may require expert, legitimate, or position power to make others understand the significance of the event. Referent and personal power may appeal to the cause. The particular situation will determine which type of leadership style and readiness level is most appropriate for this tactic.

Pressure tactics relate to coercive power and use punishment and fear as motivators. These tactics will be effective on people with low readiness levels. However, these tactics will only prove effective on people who perceive the tactic to be punishing.

Legitimizing tactics occur when position power is used to influence. Some people will be motivated based on power and status. This tactic is best used on followers with moderate readiness levels.

Clearly, there are synergies between power bases, influence tactics, leadership styles and follower readiness. Kipnis and Schmidt determined that hard tactics like legitimizing or pressure are used when the influencer has the upper hand, when resistance is expected, or when the new behavior is not accepted by an organization (Hughes et al., 2002). Soft tactics like integration are used when the influencer is at a disadvantage, expects resistance or when the influencer will benefit. Rational tactics like exchange and rational appeal are often used when the leader and follower have equal power. Authoritarian and task oriented leaders use harder tactics, while democratic and relationship leaders often use softer tactics and rational appeals (Clark, 2000). To be sure, any tactic must be executed correctly in order to achieve the desired result. Further, the tactic, power base, leadership style, follower readiness, and situation are distinct areas that must be identified before any influence can be applied appropriately.

Applying Power and Influence to Leadership

In the situational leadership concept, the readiness of the follower directs the leader to apply a style of leadership that has the greatest likelihood of success. It is the readiness of the follower that determines the power base the leader should use in order to influence behavior and induce compliance (Hersey & Campbell, 2004, p. 315). In short, the effective leader will vary the power base chosen based on diagnosing follower readiness in order to maximize the probability of success or influence.

Coercive power is best used for followers at low readiness levels (R1) who need strong directive behavior in order to become productive. This is the telling stage when a leader needs to be assertive by telling, establishing, directing, forming, structuring, instructing, informing, and guiding. The leader must be perceived as having power to enforce sanctions, which may motivate the R1 followers to avoid punishment (Hersey & Campbell). Reward power is suited for followers at low to moderate levels of readiness (R2) who require high amounts of support. Also known as the selling stage, the leader needs to teach, mentor, convince, persuade, explain, coach, and train the follower. The leader should have access to rewards and must be willing to award achievement and small successes. If not, the follower will not be persuaded by this type of power. Legitimate power is most effective on followers with moderate levels of readiness (R2/R3). At this stage of readiness, the leader is able to induce compliance and influence behavior by virtue of organizational position (Hersey & Campbell).

The proper use of referent power has the most significant impact on followers at moderate to high levels of readiness (R3/R4). These followers require little direction, but crave high levels of communication and support from the leader. The role of the leader is to encourage and communicate, which includes collaborating, facilitating, and committing (Hersey & Campbell). Moreover, expert power has a profound effect on followers at a high level of readiness (R4) because these followers require little direction and support. These followers will only be influenced by leaders who have more expertise, skill and knowledge in an area where the follower is deficient. By using the S4 leadership style of assigning, delegating, observing, and entrusting, the follower will be influenced by the leader's use of expert power.

According to Hersey and Campbell (2004), there is no one best power base to use, but the proper combination of follower readiness, leadership style and power base greatly increases the potential to influence a person in a particular situation. However, people react to power and influence in various ways. Ratzburg (2005) theorized employee reactions to power bases will take one of three forms: resistance, compliance and commitment. Coercive power is often fraught with resistance because it is based on fear and ability to punish. Although rare in modern organizations, it can lead to dislike, rejection, anger, conflict, and resistance. Problematic because of the emotional side effects, coercive power can provoke considerable employee resistance. Reward and legitimate powers usually result in compliance. Unfortunately, in many organizations, managers have limited control over the nature of the rewards granted to employees and often rely on praise, compliments and flattery to motivate. However, when reward and legitimate power work together, supervisors are able to recommend raises and assign preferred tasks to follower. Expert and referent power usually result in commitment behavior. These leaders are often well-liked and possess skills that followers lack. As such, followers tend to be more committed to an intelligent friendly supervisor, and the relationship influence often extends across the organization (Lamb, 2004).

Lastly, power and influence tactics are best used to move people towards certain goals, and should not be used without conscious thinking or deliberation. As such, four guiding principles should be considered prior to exercising power and influence. It has been suggested that "People should influence others for the benefit of the team, not individual wants or needs; people should not be forced to do what others want but should be free to refuse them; people should not be seduced into compliance but should be told what is wanted of them; and people should be free to decide for themselves how they want to guide their lives" (Peak Experiences, 2005).

Analysis and Recommendations

All of the theories and concepts reflected thus far have stood the tests of time. Over 30 years ago, French and Raven outlined power bases that are just as applicable today. As they have matured over time, one can still see these powers applied in the corporate world, universities, and families. Influence tactics remain the vehicles by which power is asserted, and Kipnis' most utilized tactics are constantly displayed in virtually all environments. In fact, the majority of people do not even realize they are using the theories proposed by French, Raven and Kipnis in their daily activities. Despite being recognized by the psychological and behavioral science communities, power and influence are skills acquired as people develop. By virtue of getting what they want and the pleasure derived from achievement, people build on their power and influence skills from a very young age. Children learn they can get rewards for good behavior and punished for non-compliance. They understand that their parents have legitimate, expert and information power, and rely on them for guidance and direction. Kids also know how to use their influence to get what they want from their parents often by using inspirational appeals and exchange. As children mature into teenagers, their power lessens, but their tactics develop. Teenagers are often seen using personal appeals and integration to get a new pair of jeans or borrow the car. Peer pressure can be defined as a coalition tactic and rational appeals from one teen to another may result in illegal or irresponsible behavior requiring the parent to use the power of punishment.

These powers and tactics remain with individuals throughout their lives and adults continue to use the tactics found most helpful in earlier life. Age maturity gives adults the opportunity to modify and hone these skills and use them interchangeably as the situation permits. Human nature is such that people do not like to be manipulated and hard tactics and coercive power tend to be resisted at any age, but especially with adults. Perhaps these types of behavior modifications remind adults of their adolescence and the power wielded by their parents. The last thing an adult wants is to be scolded by a boss who sounds like his or her father. Hard tactics may trigger a deep and uncomfortable psychological response forcing the target person to become angry or lacking in self-confidence.

On the other hand, soft tactics and relationship oriented power bases encourage good feelings and create powerful mood enhancers. These tactics and bases join groups together to share in positive moments of cooperation, collaboration, and achievement. Again, these tactics are used throughout maturity and age levels, and are perfected over time.

It is clear that all of these power bases and influence tactics are used in situational leadership, whether it be professional or personal settings. For centuries past and days to come, all three elements will be used in daily living.

In sum, French, Raven, Kipnis, Hersey, Campbell, Blanchard, and other behavioral scientists have established real world theories and models with significant social implications. Because these research ideas permeate a wide variety of people, environments and situations, they survive and evolve long after these distinguished behavioral scientists have passed. Already widely accepted and used as the basis by which other theories and models are born, power bases, influence tactics, and situational leadership are valid models for continuous research that are consistently applied as influential modes of motivation and achievement.

As organizations evolve, so will the individual situations. This predicts a future with even more research to explore new power bases and additional influence tactics. Behavioral scientists should prepare to compare and contrast power and influence strategies in other countries and determine how these factors impact managers in a global economy. Perhaps a particular type of influence used in Afghanistan would not motivate a follower in the Bahamas and Jamaica or vice versa? Maybe hard tactics in one country would not only induce compliance but loyalty as well. Or, how will the combination of power and influence tactics be used in different settings around the globe as technology evolves?

Certainly, the study of power, influence and situational leadership are ripe for more exploration in diverse workplaces. Change is constant and the world is shrinking. Communication operates at lightening speed and people at a distance work together via a computer. The impact of these factors on power and influence ten, twenty even thirty years from now is undetermined. The same is true about the effect of expert and referent powers as people lack face to face communication. Information power may gain greater value in virtual settings. The determination of follower readiness with diverse individuals and cultures from a distance will challenge which leadership style is best.

Time will tell how these questions may be answered, but the validity of these theories and models have an indelible place in behavioral science and will continue to inspire others to pursue further research.

Diversity Management and Situational Leadership[17]

The ability to successfully integrate diverse employees into the organizational structure is relevant to all businesses and economies. In the past, assimilation to corporate culture was necessary for an individual to fit in. Nowadays, individuals are less likely to shed their cultural identity as a price of belonging. As differences are celebrated, multicultural acceptance becomes essential for business survival. Acculturation is the new practical concept and reality of the twenty-first century work environment. It is a change in the cultural behavior and thinking of an individual or group through contact with other cultures (Matsumoto & Juang, 2004). The necessity to acculturate the corporate environment makes the ability to manage diversity a critical competency for today's public and private industry leaders.

Diversituation is a term coined to represent diversity management combined with situational leadership skills in order to integrate objective criteria for the follower's development. Diversituation claims that the effective management of diversity should be approached based on the unique personal characteristics, values, beliefs, needs, desires, wants, and skills of each person. Diversituation provides one the structure and the ability to objectively treat individuals as respected human beings regardless of their race, ethnicity, gender, skin color, disabilities, religious affiliations, sexual orientation, body size, age, and other such characteristics. Using situational leadership styles of telling, selling, participating, and delegating, followers are analyzed and diagnosed based on their skills and levels of readiness for the specific task. With regard to promotions, hiring, and performance appraisals, one's employees or colleagues are not viewed in terms of race, ethnicity, skin color, gender, body size, sexual orientation, religion, or other non-job related factors. Employees are instead seen as unique individuals operating under a specific readiness level for each task. This readiness level is objectively addressed through applying the appropriate leadership styles of telling, selling, participating, or delegating as needed.

A diverse workforce poses both challenges and opportunities. It can offer an organization creativity, energy, and new approaches to problem-solving.

---

[17] This material is co-authored with Nicole A. Pirone, Nova Southeastern University. Originally published in *"Privatization and Market-Based Leadership"* book, Llumina, 2006

However, differences in backgrounds, values, and norms can also result in conflict, disruption, and lowered productivity. The outcome that results depends largely on how a team is managed. It is the responsibility of the leader to maximize the potential of each follower within a multicultural environment. To be effective in implementing that goal, leaders must be aware of their own values, accept limitations and mistakes, practice flexibility, and commit to constant learning (Simons, 1996). While leaders attempt to alter their personal perceptions of others, they are in dire need of a tool to get the ball rolling. The situational leadership model is an excellent resource for managers within any public or private industry. Followers' task and relationship behaviors are observed before appropriate actions are determined. Instead of lumping individuals into cultural classifications, four readiness categories can be used to predict behaviors. Using specific guidelines, managers then match their leadership style to the category or readiness level. Any leader can omit prejudiced methods of managing diversity by practicing this "tried and true" model of situational leadership. According to Dr. Hersey, effective performance in the workplace is the result of predictable, planned actions that can be learned and applied by almost everyone through situational leadership. The ability to overcome bias is a necessary skill if workplace tension is to be transformed into a powerful force toward collective synergy.

Diversity Relevancy

Personal affiliations with different groups are significant to individual life experiences. Cox (2001) defines diversity as the variation of social and cultural identities among people existing together. Dr. Roosevelt Thomas, Jr. (1996) sees diversity as any combination of individuals that are different in some ways and similar in others. Leaders require the ability to assume both macro and micro perspectives of this collective mix. A micro perspective views individuals and identify differences; a macro perspective views the team and acknowledges similarities (Thomas, 1996). Diversity can even be broken down into several layers. According to Gardenswartz and Rowe (1995) the first and foremost layer is *personality*. Next are the *internal dimensions* over which people have little or no control. These factors include age, gender, race, sexual orientation, ethnicity, and physical ability. The third layer consists of *external or social factors* such as education, religion, familial status, income, location, habits, and experience. Finally, *organizational factors* relating to work include position, seniority, department, field, management level, and division. All of these layers combine to form a person's unique filter for viewing the world (Gardenswartz & Rowe, 1995). It is people's unique views that dictate their behavior. In practical terms, as previously mentioned, *diversity* describes the many unique characteristics and qualities that make a person similar to or different from others.

Leaders embracing follower differences will discover positively unique resources. Substantial benefits range from social and economic to intellectual and emotional stimulation (Sonnenschein, 1999). Diversity provides different points of views. The decision-making process of the organization becomes enriched as status quo is challenged. Diverse groups offer a broader base of experience from which to approach a problem (Cox, 2001). Diversity is also directly connected to the bottom line. Corporate image, as well as employee morale effect productivity, profits, and progress. As product and service innovation rises, client needs are better met. Diversity helps to establish an organization in the global community (Sonnenschein, 1999). As differences create opportunities, they also create challenges.

Deficits often appear when handling change, working as a team, and maintaining interpersonal relations. Follower diversity can certainly contribute to these deficits. The mix of cultures, genders, lifestyles, and values often becomes a source for misunderstandings and conflict. Specific examples of conflict include resistance to collaboration, miscommunication, discrimination charges, limited social interaction, perceived favoritism, and insufficient participation. Improving management formulas is not the solution; a multicultural environment calls for quality leadership.

Leadership and Diversity

According to experts, "The fundamental purpose of management is to create value as perceived by the follower" (Hersey, 2000). Leaders, on the other hand, influence people. In general, leaders must be able to address conflict, tolerate uncertainty, manage diversity, embrace change, identify values, maintain accountability, use feedback, and balance power. Successful leaders also have a degree of charisma that makes people want to follow them. The key to successfully managing diversity is capitalizing on these human skills. Distinguishing characteristics associated with humanistic leaders include trustworthiness, sensitivity, and active listening. Most importantly, great leaders remind everyone "why it matters" by sharing a personal sense of purpose. Leaders can raise performance of their organization by demonstrating core values (Cox, 2001). Formal mission statements advocate fairness and respect for all people, but often lack substance. It is up to the leader to adopt the vision him/herself and influence followers to adopt it as well; however, this is easier said than done. Human beings have been conditioned to behave in certain ways, and all people are at times both perpetrators and victims of stereotypes. Ignorant assumptions lead to the creation of negative emotional reactions, misjudgment, and discrimination. In studying the influence culture has on one's own cognitive and behavioral traits, one may voluntarily agree to promote cultural awareness and sensitivity.

The underlying theme in effectively managing diversity within the workplace is coming to terms with personal attitudes, beliefs, and expectations about others. The leader must perceive the nature of cultural differences and understand both his / her own and others' cultural assumptions and behaviors. The leader must empathize with and appreciate different points of view, making a conscious effort to see individuals without labeling. This can be accomplished through initiating an ongoing strategy for improving cohesion. Personal dedication to improved interpersonal relationships through cultural awareness speaks volumes about a leader. The simple act of taking an interest in employees' culture can increase a leader's personal power.

Culture can be defined as a system of ordinances established to ensure group survival, involving subjective elements that are shared collectively, but harbored individually (Matsumoto & Juang, 2004). Culture affects many different aspects of life, influencing a broad range of activities, structures, behaviors, and events. The objective elements are tangible, observable things. This would include age, race, gender, etc. Categorized into domain and dimension, subjective elements are unobservable (Matsumoto & Juang, 2004). This would include values beliefs, attitudes, etc.

Within the workplace, there is a great need to develop cultural intelligence. One method of accomplishing this task is to build a mental almanac by documenting cultural similarities and differences (Matsumoto & Juang, 2004). Retrievable at any time, this reference guide will strengthen the ability to be culturally relative when interacting with people from diverse backgrounds. Although useful, this technique cannot thoroughly cover every culture encountered. It is possible, however, to become intimately familiar with a select number of cultures one frequently comes in contact with. In recognizing and appreciating cultural similarities and differences, one can better his or her interpersonal relationships and gain insight into a contemporary, civilized world.

In a world of different cultural norms and behaviors, leaders must possess the ability to shift perspective and influence others who are different in order to constructively achieve objectives. This involves broadening communication skills and resilience in the face of complex and challenging realities. Leaders often seek additional resources to supplement diversity management initiatives. Unfortunately, there is no universal method of doing things. It is the general idea that what works in one situation does not necessarily work in others, hence, a contingency theory is born. Hersey and Campbell (2004) found that a given style of leadership is contingent upon several internal and external factors. These authors state that "Situational approaches to leadership examine the interplay among these variables in order to find causal relationships that will lead to predictability of behavior." The effectiveness of a leader is dependent upon recognizing subordinate, group, and task variables, and applying the appropriate leadership style. It is recommended that "Leaders must become aware of each situation and be able to use the leadership style appropriate to that situation" (Hersey, 2000).

Integration of Situational Skills

Situational leadership skills can be used to influence any follower, regardless of his/her background, age, language, gender, ethnicity or religion. The three basic competencies of leadership are relevant when combining situational leadership with diversity management. *Diagnosing* would include assessing follower readiness and task; *adapting* would include modifying leader behavior to match follower readiness and task; and, *communicating* would include promoting understandable and acceptable processes (Hersey & Campbell, 2004).

To change the tendency of categorizing employees by race or gender, consider instead their readiness level. Readiness levels assess ability and psychological maturity. These factors, unlike race and gender, change. An individual may be at the readiness level one (an R1) in regards to one project, but at a readiness level four (an R4) at another. The goal of situational leadership is to facilitate the follower's capacity to a higher readiness level, thus empowering the employee. In familiarizing oneself with each readiness level and matching leadership style, a manager may condition his or her thinking. The situational leadership concept and skills could be used as a default method of categorizing followers. This is a black and white concept that once fully understood and practiced, can replace old stereotypes and assumptions. Instead of matching one's communication to the person's age or ethnicity, the appropriate style of communication would match their readiness level for performing the task. Whether consciously or subconsciously, people adjust their ways of communicating according to the person they interact with. If a follower is significantly younger, people often times use simple words or even slang. If a follower is a woman, one tends to use more sensitive language, offering reassurance and empathy. The situational leadership model provides managers with a valuable tool for managing diversity and promoting interoffice relationships instead of being driven by their stereotypes and assumptions. The application of this model departs from the traditional idea that treating people exactly the same is the most effective method for managing diversity. Instead followers' differences are analyzed to determine what style of leadership they need to become more productive and motivated. It is only their differences in readiness levels that are used, not cultural or racial factors.

In addition to assessing individual readiness levels, the situational leadership concept or model can be used to inspire cohesion in the corporate culture through assessing group readiness levels. A group at readiness level one (R1) may resist change, be unable and unwilling to work together, experience employee conflict, and leave tasks unaccomplished. A group at readiness level two (R2) might be unable to work together with others, but willing to take on the challenge. These members acknowledge the need for change, can see the big picture and are excited toward achieving harmony within the work setting. A group at readiness level three (R3) has demonstrated the ability to work together, but may have become unwilling to perform the task as required. Performance has decreased and motivation is low. A group at readiness level four (R4) has both the ability and willingness to get along with others. They are extremely productive and synchronized with each other. Techniques a leader would use to influence transition between the readiness levels remain the same. *Telling* would involve discussing what, how, when, and who regarding the diversity leadership initiative. Leaders would provide instruction and guidance on an incremental basis, keeping emotional levels in check. *Selling* would involve explaining why this is beneficial to the goal of the individual, the team, and the organization. Leaders would ensure member's understanding of the need for change and propose an optimistic outlook. *Participating* would involve encouraging members to provide feedback and actively listening to suggestions. Leaders could conduct a socialization assessment, facilitating two-way communication and staff involvement. Leaders could engage the staff in learning about culture, goals, similarities, and differences of their co-workers. *Delegating* would involve assigning the responsibility to each team member to follow-through and make a sincere effort to change behavior and thinking. There is little supervision, as leaders trust group members to maintain positive attitudes and reinforce them for continued high performance.

Summary

The value of human capital will always be associated with power and influence. French and Raven concluded there were five significant power bases used to move people from one area to another. Over time, additional power bases were framed by other scientists. Influence is the mode by which the follower moves from one area to another, and Kipnis and Schmidt noted nine different variations of usable tactics to pull it all together. The situational leadership concept clearly integrates the use of power and influence in follower readiness. Leaders diagnose the readiness level of the follower, apply the proper leadership style, choose their power base and finally their mode of influence to move followers to different levels of achievement. These three prongs of behavioral science culminate in a system of motivation that can be used in any situation, by any person, and at any age. These elements permeate society and offer keys to effective management and high performance in any environment. Because this system is user friendly, it can be effective in all areas of life. Various types of power and influence are available to people at all socio-economic levels, and not limited by gender or age. It can be used for good, evil, progress, or growth retardation. Power and influence are available to all people, but how they choose to use it, is their most important decision.

Leaders are responsible for understanding similarities and differences, and utilizing policies and procedures to promote harmony in the workplace. *Diversituation* represents diversity management combined with situational leadership. Followers are analyzed and diagnosed based on their skills and readiness levels to perform the task. This readiness level is addressed through applying the appropriate leadership style. Finally, communicating should mirror the leadership style while reflecting cultural intelligence. Leaders should take the time to know their followers' needs, wants, desires, beliefs, and values. Cultural awareness and sensitivity effectively integrated with situational leadership skills can enhance a leader's personal power, and improve team productivity in any economy or workplace. Such skills and capacity development of people in both the public and private sector of a country can go a long way in strengthening the government and preparing the culture for effectively reaping the benefits of a market-based economy.

Every professional has an obligation to make a positive impact on the lives of his or her colleagues and others in the community, the country, and possibly the world. This life is too short to let it go without making a positive difference in the life of at least one person who needs it most. Diversity management and championing fair treatment of all individuals is a great way to achieve this objective. Effective diversity managers and leaders are consistent and "walk their talk." Mahatma Gandhi, as stated earlier in the book, is quoted as having said that "Happiness is when what you think, what you say, and what you do are in harmony." Therefore, when it comes to diversity management, it is hoped that there is harmony in your thoughts (head), feelings (heart), and actions (habits).

Discussion Questions

1. What is power and how does it relate to diversity?
2. What are the best sources of power for influencing employees?
3. How is personal power different from positional power? Which should be used when and why?
4. What is situational leadership?
5. What are the various styles of situational leadership that professionals can use in the workplace to positively influence their employees toward high productivity?
6. How can professionals assess a person's readiness level for more responsibility or usage of different leadership styles?
7. What leadership styles are best when working with employees from developed nations versus employees in third world countries? Discuss and explain.
8. What are some uses for assessment of an employee's "readiness" level? In other words, what can a leader do once he or she knows the employee's readiness level? Discuss examples.
9. What is "diversituation" and how can it create an awareness of diversity related concerns?

10. Can the application of situational leadership concepts keep managers focused on the developmental needs of the employee rather than their own preconceived stereotypes and biases about the person?

Gender and Management Hierarchy

W omen throughout the world tend to face certain biases, stereotypes, and the glass ceiling in the workplace as they attempt to reach higher in the hierarchy of management. This chapter discusses gender differences as well as some of the challenges and possible means of combating various discriminatory practices that women face in the workplace. The author emphasizes coaching as one solution for women, minorities, and underachievers of all backgrounds. Coaching is a process that takes time, practice, planning, and collaboration with the employee. It is hypothesized that small successes lead to huge results, and underachievers can eventually have the self-confidence to achieve high level organizational goals, as well as significant personal achievements through effective coaching and fair development and promotion opportunities.

Common Gender Differences

Individuals at all levels of the organization are expected to deal with gender differences and solve problems generated by lack of understanding these differences. These gaps are often created by societal conditionings, lack of awareness, a not-caring attitude, and the changing environment in the workforce. While problems are often perceived as being negative, they can give rise to opportunities for restructuring or new methods of doing things better, faster, and more competitively.

As discussed before, society starts treating boys and girls differently from the time they are born. We dress them in different styles of clothes and in different color clothes; we sing different songs to them; we encourage them to take on different hobbies; and we treat them differently because of their gender. Therefore, they respond differently in their business dealings.

Gender research, similar to most others, is based on the bell-shaped curve which applies to most people and not necessarily to everyone. There will always be exceptions to generalities. The remarks in this chapter are generalized conclusions based on personal experiences and the surveys of other researchers as well as the author's survey of 602 individuals in the Central Florida region. The author, using John W. Clark's 1966 personal business ethics scores' instrument (PBES), concludes that gender is a factor in moral development. The PBES determines one's commitment level of personal integrity and honesty in business dealings and in the observance of the laws governing business. Males with no management experience (PBES=41.86) have significantly lower PBES mean than females (PBES=44.22) with no management experience. One possible explanation might be that males need more responsibility, accountability, awareness of laws and the justice system, and training in order to develop moral maturity, as compared to women. Carol Gilligan in 1982 stated that women emphasize sensitivity to others' feelings and rights, and show concern and care for others. While women approach ethical dilemmas from their "care" orientation, men approach ethical dilemmas from a "law and order" orientation, which could suggest that men need to know the facts based on laws, as opposed to their feelings and emotions, to make morally developed decisions.

The author's study also compared females under 26 years of age with males under 26 years of age, as well as females 26 years of age or older and with males who are 26 years of age or older. In both categories, the female population had higher PBES means; however they were not significantly higher. As mentioned previously, in the sample of males and females who did not have any management experience, the female PBES mean was significantly higher than that of males. This supports previous research that women are more caring, intimate, helpful, and relationship-oriented, as opposed to men who are more "law and order" oriented. This might be one explanation for the higher PBES mean for females with no management experience. Females with five or more years of management experience have a higher PBES mean than males with five or more years of management experience. However, the difference between their scores is not significantly higher (46.42 vs. 45.10).

Aristotle said it first over thousands of years ago, and the same principle and concept still holds true today:

> You get a good adult by habituating a good child to doing the right thing. Praise for truth-telling and sanctions for fibbing well, in time, make him or her "naturally" honest. Abstract knowledge of right and wrong no more contributes to character than knowledge of physics contributes to cycling (Michael Levine, NY Times, 1989).

The same habitual approach applies to adults as well as children, because learning and moral development does not stop at adolescence but continue throughout one's life regardless of gender. Formal as well as informal education and training in ethics and diversity, therefore, are critical in the business sector; and can make a difference in creating an awareness of sensitive ethical dilemmas and solutions which lead to and reflect moral behavior.

Males learn to compete (through competition in sports, their domineering personalities, etc.) which is related to conflict and one best method of doing things or one final winner. Whereas females learn to be compassionate and caring as they grow. Boys spend 50% of their time moving from one thing to another; they do something, learn from it and move on to something else. Boys do what they are told and when the coach asks to "go to the right," boys don't say "oh coach, I was thinking about going straight, what are your thoughts about it?" Most girls prefer to be involved in the entire decision-making process.

Men, as boys, learn how far to push people to get the job done before pushing becomes destructive. Boys learn to take risk which is often the best way to become successful in a competitive workplace. Boys learn not to cry and let their feelings get in the way. Boys learn that when the game is over, it really is over and after the game they go out celebrating and sometimes even with the members of the opposing team. While, for most women the end of the game is not really the end; the argument of the games can last a life time. While boys are goal focused, girls are process focused. Males assume that the president of a company needs to act like a president otherwise he or she will not be treated as one, while females may feel bad/guilty driving a brand new Mercedes when the rest of the employees are driving Hondas and Tercels.

Men behave according to the hierarchy while women behave according to a flat structure. For example, Dr. Pat Heim was giving a speech in Tampa Florida and was picked up in a nice limousine by a male driver who opened the back door politely for her and drove to the hotel without saying a word. He was polite and saw her in a position or rank above him in the hierarchy and treated her accordingly. This is based on the hierarchical structure and the driver did the right thing. When she got done a day later, a female driver drove her back to the airport. She called and said, "Are you Pat?" and Dr. Pat Heim said, "Yes, I am." The driver replied, "I am your driver. Would you like to act like a big shot and sit in the back or would you like to set in front with me?" So, Dr. Heim sat in front and 30 minutes later, they knew almost everything about each other. This female driver used the flat structure. Both the male and female driver did the right thing according to their approaches. Males often like to set up and structure meeting rooms by having the bosses and higher authority figures sit on top, while younger and lower level associates sit on the bottom. However, females usually prefer to sit in circles to make sure everyone can see each other and are able to share their thoughts without interrupting each other.

Girls learn not to take risks and be careful. They learn to avoid conflict and be nice. They learn to develop relationships. While women will talk to ten other people about a friend that they are not happy with because they did something wrong or unproductive, they often do not initially mention it to the person/friend which caused it because females, during their childhood years, have learned to develop a relationship and not destroy it. Boys will usually confront the person and get it over with regardless of future consequences to the person or the relationship. Generally, girls attempt to negotiate a win/win situation, while men attempt to get a win/lose situation.

From male superiors or bosses, most people take orders without any problems. But from a female superior, most people usually expect a little chit chat and small talk; otherwise we think she is upset or she is not treating us very well. For example, imagine the following statement by a male boss and then a female boss and imagine your response to it: "I need these papers and projects completed by three o'clock today." In general, some females will have difficulty with such statements, if not mentioned with some small talk, coming from females bosses. This is because females are expected to build the relationship and keep them that way. Males, sometimes, think that females waste a lot of time talking to people about irrelevant stuff; to most males this "small talk" is unproductive. While males think that small talk is a waste, females value and cherish this because it builds the relationship. On the negative side, when female bosses chit chat with male employees, the employees may not see the job as being important or requiring immediate attention.

Males go to the mall and get what they need and leave; while females go to the mall to buy a dress and they end up seeing or getting all types of other things with it. After hours of searching for a small size seven skirt, that barely fits them, they walk around and get matching shoes, socks, purse, jacket, earrings, and so on. Females would then want to eat lunch and see some other displays for the coming birthdays and holidays. Males are goal focused and do things according to that mindset. While females can and are able to do multiple tasks simultaneously, most males are not thrilled about doing many things at the same time. Males either watch television or talk; while females are able to hold the baby, cook food, answer the telephone, watch their favorite television show, and open mail at the same time. Females are interested in the process of getting there while males just want to get there and get it over with. While females prefer quality, males want quantity. While females prefer romantic dancing, communication and sharing; males usually want to get to the bottom line and perform their task as efficiently as possible in order to be the perfect "one minute manager" that they can be.

Males often answer with one word statements (such as yes, no, had a meeting, the day went fine, good, etc.), while females want to talk about what happened throughout the day in detail which at times may sound very boring to males. Females come home wanting to say every detailed activity that happened in their day, while males want to hear only the results. Females do not want to hear advice from men at all times; as matter of fact, most often females just want a listening ear. One time I made a mistake and gave advice to my own mother within the first minute of the telephone conversation because she seemed upset and I wanted to calm her down. It backfired on me and she started crying because I made her feel bad by giving her advice when she just wanted a listening ear. As males, we need to become the investigator and ask the other person "I am having a hard time understanding what you want from me. Do you want my advice or do you want me to just listen and hear you out?" Sometimes this would help eliminate misunderstandings and bad feelings. It has been said that men have the gift of advice, while women have the gift of understanding. As males, we do not hear people all the way through before we start giving advice. We make assumptions because we think we know what others want and we want to be helpful by jumping into conclusions and giving advice which is usually wrong if it is not based on accurate understanding. This is how males are conditioned as goal oriented individuals, whereas women are more process oriented. Both genders attempt to do their best, but they do so by different rules which may not seem right to the opposite gender because it may not be the usual way of doing things for them.

Males and females approach situations and solve problems based on what they are conditioned to throughout their lives. Males are authority and rank oriented, while females are process or involvement oriented. These approaches are right in some areas while not the best method or approach in others. But, since we are used to doing them according to only one approach, we keep doing them automatically and similarly in all situations thinking it is the best method. Just like time management, if you are used to doing things that are deadline driven, then you always do those deadline-driven things because they appear important and procrastinate on proactively preparing for things ahead of time.

In most societies, males and females are judged differently. Males are judged by masculinity and power, while females are judged by their level of intelligence and a caring relationship-orientation. Males can be tough which to most is acceptable behavior because they are males and they will be seen as strict or tough leaders; while strict or tough females are considered to be "witches" and people think that they are proving their manhood if they order and demand things from others. This tendency makes it difficult for women managers or leaders in a male-dominated world of business.

Males and females define "being a team player" differently. Being a team player to males means doing what it takes to do the job and following orders in any given situation. To males, being a team player means knowing your rank and being disciplined enough to obey authority. To females, this may sound mindless because one person gives orders and everybody else automatically follows without challenging the orders or having a discussion about it. Being a team player to a female means being involved, caring for one another, and helping each other. To some males this is not the most efficient manner of working in a team and may appear to be somewhat manipulative.

Males have friendliness while females have friends. To males, friendliness come and go as the situation fits, but to females, friends are friends unless they get into a major fight or disagreement about something. So, friendliness is very situational and temporary to males and not necessarily to females. In meetings, males of powerful behaviors (characters) attempt to dominate the conversation around their own ideas (dogmatic style), while females in general, want to share everyone's thoughts because they were conditioned to the word "share" as they were growing up. Research shows that females in general do not speak much in meetings and this is because they do not want to dominate the meeting; their general work ethic is to share and everyone should have their opportunity and turn to speak. Women tend to put their statements in the form of a question while males make statements of how it should be or what they should do. Males resist being influenced especially when others are present; while women smile and accept the facts as they come about or surface during the meeting. Males interrupt and females wait their turn to speak. To males the meetings take place outside the meeting (networking and politics), while females talk about things together in the meeting. Decisions, for males, are often made in the coffee room and hallways and the meeting is a ceremony or symbol to formalize the decision.

When selling a person a car, females have a tendency to tell you all the things that are wrong with the car before they tell you all the added extras or the good things about the car because to them this is honesty and relationship focused. Females use disclaimers, "this is what is wrong, but..." While males would tell you the best features of the car and focus on what works and may totally ignore to state what is wrong with the car. Both of these methods present different outcomes depending on the buyer's perspective and background.

For projecting future records, males and females may have different responses. Males have a tendency to make up future strategic financial numbers because in five years things will change and no one will remember the original numbers. Females would rather get all the facts and state an educated number rather than just making it up.

Women have a tendency to start essays with "I hope to accomplish...," while men have a tendency to start their letters or essays with "I will accomplish..." To most people, the males will accomplish it because they are positive and determined; while the female statements may appear somewhat weak and not very strong. We write and speak differently in regards to our genders. Males may call each other and say "you are an animal" and this often means that one is liked. While females would never call somebody an animal unless of course, somebody purposely wore the same outfit to make her look bad or when animosity exists between people. Males may say to each other, "you are fat and ugly, no girl is going to want to marry you" and this will be interpreted as a joke or as a part of the male bonding process. But females would not make such statements to their friends.

Males like to keep their emotions buried while females tend to show their sad faces. If a female has a sad face, it is best to ask her what is wrong; otherwise she may think that you are ignoring her and are not interested in her disagreement or discontent. Females like to talk to others while facing them; on the other hand males like to talk to each other standing side by side or while lying on the couch because facing each other represents conflict and competition. If you are not facing a female while she is talking, she may feel as though you don't care about what she has to say and are not interested. However, males interpret the face-to-face conversations as aggressive and competitive behavior.

Females nod because they are acknowledging the other person to say 'I hear you" but not necessarily agreeing; while males tend to nod because they agree with the other person. This is also true of cultural differences as well. For example, in Japan, nodding means they have heard you but not necessarily agreed with you. If males are not acknowledging females by nodding, which to males mean agreement, then females think that the male is neither interested nor listening. On the other hand, males think that females are agreeing with them because they are nodding and become really surprised when they find out that it is not so. Males think that the females are turning on them from agreement to disagreement. They may argue that you were agreeing with me earlier, what changed your mind or if I knew your discontent, then I could have explained it a little deeper; but you agreed, so I stopped talking, etc. We all have our gender and cultural differences which are not always known to us. We need to become aware of them and act accordingly.

The integration and understanding of female leadership traits can improve the ethical climate of a firm by bringing more sensitivity, caring treatment of customers, more creative approaches to problem solving, more effective relationship-building skills, creating greater trust in interpersonal affairs, and being supportive and understanding of supervisory style. Women in the workforce are often wrongly and stereotypically viewed as less decisive, slower to make decisions, or even naive at times. The best approach might be to combine the best traits of each sex at various levels of management in the organization to have a balance of both sides. This will enable individuals to help each other by developing strong solutions to their daily challenges; and they could learn from each other in the process.

Female Expatriate Managers

An article entitled "*An Evaluation of Female Expatriate Managers' Efficacy*" by Daspro[18] focuses on women in the role of expatriates to complete international assignments (2004). This section provides a summary of Daspro's thoughts about expatriate female managers in modern times. Many companies sometimes choose to not offer women international assignments because they believe that women carry too much baggage with them as they go on international assignments such as a spouse, children, or other marital woes (Daspro, 2004). When considering the term that is given of marital woes, one must question this thought process because there must be the point of reference to why there are considerations for male marital woes per se, and not for the women. One must believe, from this term, that women are generally more concerned about their family, and that there is something wrong with that, and also that women are less reliable to keep the focus of the task at hand; but this is simply not true. Several studies have been conducted where women have had equal success in their international assignments as men (Daspro, 2004).

Experience is Key

Female expatriates have long been trying to set their place in the expatriate world to have a level footing for international assignments as their male

---

[18] - Co-authored with Jennifer Severe, Nova Southeastern University.

counterparts. Many companies do not prefer female expatriates for international assignments because of the "attachments" that many of them have before leaving for the assignment, or might come to obtain during the assignment. Some companies even go as far as to question the competency of women to complete international tasks.

Women are sometimes thought to lack the authoritative role that needs to be attained through leading a company or a project, and because of this perception, there is little to no opportunity for international assignments. With this statement in mind, it must also be stated that women will not be able to attain these leadership roles without the chance to actually undertake international assignments. The experience and skills that these international assignments give to a person often lead to other international assignments and help to progress a person to a much higher executive position in the future; but if a woman does not have this experience, her growth and progression in the company is often compromised and stifled. Many different cultures look at the role of a woman as compromising when they see them in international assignments, and actually have difficulty attributing a woman to a role of authority. Common knowledge does exist that it is more likely to see a female expatriate in a Western nation, but there are some that even have the chance of going to some Asian nations, and predominately Muslim nations (Daspro, 2004).

Will She Be Effective, or Better Yet, Will She Be Efficient?

Efficiency and effectiveness is the primary goal of companies and their managers when setting out to be a part of international assignments. The number of female expatriates being chosen to undergo the experience of an international assignment is and has actually been gradually increasing over the past 20 years. Many employers are realizing the efficiency that a woman can bring to an international assignment, for many view women as more concerned about the family and situation of others; but one can truly say that it is not only the maternal insights that she carries that make her notable and able to complete her job, it is the fact that a female expatriate carries the knowledge and ability as well that is necessary for the fulfillment of her assignment. Sometimes female employees are kept from international assignments because of the concerns or prejudices of certain nations or individuals, but at times, even in Western nations, there is a problem with the advancement of females in executive positions as well (Selmar and Leung, 2003). The "place" of a woman is thought to be as more of a supporting, rather than an authoritative position, and with that, there comes the result of either employers not choosing a woman for international assignments, or, there is not more women requesting these positions. Indeed it will take consistently motivating work to have the past and present perceptions of a woman's effectiveness considered in an international assignment. The employers that allowed the female employees to complete an international assignment allowed them to complete a second, and then were offered regular international assignments; the efficiency of the female expatriate often surpasses the expectations of those male host nationals that expected less. Female employees are known to have rather effective human relation skills (Daspro, 2004) and sometimes see a perspective of the assignment that was not initially thought of in the commencement of the assignment. This shows that a woman does indeed have the ability to do just as good of a job as a male expatriate.

All of the material presented can indeed be utilized in today's work world. The idea of allowing a female to have a position of authority, as we see, is even a problem in the U.S. companies today. One would think that Western nations such as the U.S., Great Britain, Germany, etc. would be more liberal in choosing women for expatriate international assignments. Nevertheless, studies have shown that even amongst these Western giants, there is a sense of not wanting a woman to leave her "place" (meaning a more subservient position of support such as a secretary) in a company (Daspro, 2004). A woman's role is evolving as people's views therefore evolve, and with this comes an actual change—either for the better or worse.

Different, Yet So Similar

The view on a woman's role in society is one that has been thought of as just a caregiver and as more of just a supportive role rather than one of authority or leadership. With this view, there are similar thought patterns from around the globe, in different increments. From Nigeria to Japan, from Germany to Chile, from Turkey to the U.S., as different as many of these nations might be, all are somewhat similar with the views of a female's role in society (Selmer and Leung, 2003). Although the Western nations do have the opportunity for a woman to break the existing barriers that limit a woman's role in society (as women become lawyers, doctors, engineers, CEOs, CFOs, and presidents of companies), when surveyed, many of these Western nations also did not truly take a woman too seriously that was in an authoritative position because they would think of her more as having maternal affectations rather than a drive for serious executive success. This is a matter that is gradually altering as more women are given the chance to show what they are capable of achieving. Several examples of competent female executives are Martha Stewart, Oprah Winfrey, Hilary R. Clinton, Condoleezza Rice, and many other top-notch, highly competent females as active leaders of major agencies or their own self-made companies.

Can She Do it? Yes She Can!

Society needs to make sure that as we evaluate the challenges in which the world is going through, we keep the goals of the present and future at hand. Females can either wish or not wish to engage in an international assignment, and there are two reasons for that choice. One reason that a female might not wish to entertain the fact of being an expatriate is for the matters relating to one's family ties, and also because of the fear that they will not be treated as equal to their male counterparts, even though they have acquired and maintained the same, if not more knowledge than they do. Reasons why a woman might accept the challenge of an international assignment is the fact that they truly want the experience that these projects grant them in order to qualify for further advancement in their field of employment. Another variable might be the reason to prove that they are capable, and to even prove their male counterparts wrong about their lack of mental competency to complete anything that involves extensive brain activity. With the fact that a woman might complete her international assignment with success might leave the host national location surprised, or if not that, proven wrong, which would be sufficient for many women to view. The capability to change or at least make another reevaluate their position on a matter is what is occurring more and more everyday in the world, and is the attributing factor to what deciphers the growing companies to the stagnant ones. The growing companies will either adapt to the ever-altering methods of how business is evolving, or will either remain in their present state of steadiness or might eventually disappear. Change is something that will take time to process with differences in what others believe, but the perceptions of how a woman might or might not succeed can only be truly evaluated when she is given a chance to either prove herself to what might be perhaps one of the best changes to be made to a company.

Women in Management

Academic scholars have consistently stated that female leaders are often evaluated slightly less favorably than equivalent male leaders, and this difference is almost completely due to sex stereotype bias. Women are evaluated negatively when they adopt a stereotypically male leadership style and occupy traditionally male-dominated positions. Relatively more women are in management positions today in Western countries than there were ten years ago. However, there are still relatively few women in top management, and in some organizations, even in middle management. Even when women in Western countries do advance to top-management positions, special attention is often focused on the fact that they are women.

Research suggests male and female managers who have leadership positions in organizations behave in similar ways. Research further suggests that leadership styles may vary between women and men. Women tend to be somewhat more participative as leaders than men. Male managers tend to be less participative, making more decisions on their own. Female managers may be more participative as leaders than male managers because subordinates may try to resist the influence of female managers more than they do the influence of male managers, and because female managers sometimes have better interpersonal skills than male managers. The finding from research on leader behaviors is that male and female managers do not differ significantly in their propensities to perform different leader behaviors. Research suggests that across different kinds of organizational settings, male and female managers tend to be equally effective as leaders. As a matter of fact, women are rated higher than men on most leadership dimensions by employees, including the emerging leadership qualities of coaching, teamwork, and empowering employees. The increasing number of women in the workforce should result in a larger pool of highly qualified candidates for management positions.

Gail Evans, in her 2001 book titled *"Play Like a Man, Win Like a Woman: What Men Know About Success that Women Need to Learn"* mentioned that women account for over 46% of the total U.S. labor force. In 1999, only 11.9% of the 11,681 corporate officers in America's top 500 companies were women and in 1998 it was 11.2%. If this pace continues the number of women on top corporate boards will not equal the number of men until the year 2064. Also, out of the 500 Fortune companies only four had females appointed to the top chief executive officers' position. It is obvious that the business world and the world of management have traditionally been dominated by males. As such, the policies, rules, and "yardsticks" of success have been created by men as the rules for the game of business. So, now, women are stuck "playing the rules" made by men as they attempt to be effective competitors. Regardless of the culture, women will prosper when they are familiar with the rules and "play the game" better than their male counterparts. Evans claims that women do not need to follow the rules exactly as stated, but they do need to understand the rules of the game since it is part of the existing culture and the expected "yardstick" for measuring one's success in leadership.

The object of the business "game" is to simply feel great about what one does, because that is how a leader can feel fulfilled, and that is how one can influence the direction of the game leading to better performance. Evans states that there are four ground rules for women to play the business game in twenty first century management. First, remember that you are who you say you are. So, see yourself doing the job successfully. What would it feel like? What does it look like? Try to make your positive fantasies real. The first step to being successful is convincing yourself that you are successful and playing the part as such. Second, "one price does not fit all." You do not always need to follow the rules but you must be aware of the consequences. This will prepare you to respond effectively and it will eliminate any surprises. Third, work is not a sorority. Some women enter the workforce so they can form and maintain healthy and long-term relationships. "Playing the man's game" in the business world requires pretending that personal relationships are not always important. Fourth, women are always perceived to be a mother, daughter, wife, or mistress. Men in the workplace have a tendency to see women co-workers as a mother, daughter, wife or mistress, even when she is clearly not one of them.

One important aspect of success in the business game is learning the "playing field" well. Learn as much as you can about the company before you even go for an interview. Is there only one person to report to or are there many people? In which field would you rather work? Don't settle for anything, select a specific field of interest and one where you can excel. See if the company does something you can feel a connection with and find out if they have a good public image. Most women care about the totality of the "package," so if you are going to be successful you must feel comfortable with the organization and the people working there. Once you get the job, learn it well, and in due time set a vision that can be achieved. Evans states that a great career is seldom reached by a ladder of small steps. Combine good strategic planning with a vision that others can aspire to in joining you and your team for the realization of this ultimate mission. Goals stop possibility (unless one sets higher goals upon their realization), and vision creates possibilities for a brighter future. See the possibilities, and communicate this vision with others on your team and those managing the teams. Upon the achievement of small milestones and goals, keep score so you are given proper credit. When most people have done a good job they are usually satisfied if the boss praises the work and gives thanks and/or recognition. If women do not have the sense to ask for more staff, stock options, benefits, cars, club memberships, severance packages or guaranteed performance reviews, they probably will not get them. Some women tend to be shy about asking for such benefits when they deserve it, but they must overcome such modesty and ask for what they deserve so they are not overlooked.

Gail Evans offers fourteen basic suggestions as rules for success in playing the basic game in the business world and the following is a brief summary of her suggestions.

1) *Request what you want.* Make a request for what you want and deserve since asking is the only way to get what you want in the business world.
2) *Speak out.* If you don't talk, no one will know you exist or that you have ideas.
3) *Speak up with confidence.* You must speak in a convincing and unconditional manner.
4) *Toot your own horn.* Make sure everyone notices what you do. Kenneth Blanchard once said that if you don't toot your own horn, others may just use it as a spittoon.
5) *Don't expect to make friends.* Making friends is not an objective of a business situation. Treat everyone as professionally as possible and try to keep personal and professional transactions separate when possible.
6) *Accept uncertainty.* Have faith in your general ability to perform.
7) *Take calculated risks.* Individuals who take risks are people who have their fear under control. Remember, without fear it's not a risk.

8) *Be an "imposter."* It is fair to accept the fact that no one can honestly say that he or she knows everything about the job.
9) *Think one task at a time.* The cliché states that "a woman's work is never done" is not true so don't believe it. You can get the work done when you focus on each piece one at a time.
10) *Don't anguish.* If you feel like you can't complete a project on time then be honest about it and ask for help. Remember, you are not a "superwoman" and no one can fill this expectation.
11) *Follow the team leader.* Perform your assigned part to the best of your ability toward the vision or objective determined by the boss or the team.
12) *It is not always necessary to assume responsibility without authority.* However, offer your services only when the task is a career opportunity.
13) *Sit at the table.* It is not only the big shots that sit at the boss's table. Anyone who has something of quality to say should take her seat at the table and speak her mind.
14) *Laugh and enjoy your work.* Laugh at the appropriate attempts at humor even if it wasn't funny.

Most women think they can do it all, and many of them do it well, but one can not possibly do everything perfectly. If you are giving "your all" to everything for everyone, then you seldom have the time to take care of yourself. You don't have to live your life as though you only have one chance, do as much as you can, or as much as you want, and have fun in your own time. Remember, if you try to do it all, it won't be perfect so there is no reason to focus on perfection or satisfying everyone. Sometimes, it is perfectly acceptable to ask for help, and to say "no" to projects that you do not have time for at the moment. Overall, it is best to simply be yourself. Evans further suggests that you should "be a woman" in the workplace since by allowing the natural, nurturing part of oneself to be available, one can build genuine relationships with others. Finally, "be yourself," be true to yourself, and be your true self everywhere you go, including the office. Actions speak louder than words, and a leader's overall behavior will certainly communicate much about his/her character to others than anything s/he says. So, be the leader you are meant to be.

Summary

Women, like most other minorities in the United States, continue to face many biases, stereotypes, and the glass ceiling in the workplace. This chapter discussed some of the challenges and possible means of combating these types of challenges. Perhaps managers can consider coaching as one solution for assisting women and minorities in the workplace. Coaching is more than a job; it is a relationship between two committed people dedicated to the same goals of growth and development. Whether female, Hispanic or from "outer space," the foundation of the coaching process is established with trust, collaboration, and high levels of interpersonal communication. Using a variation of processes and techniques, managers can help underachievers determine what is important to them and what emotions and cultural norms may be holding them back from progress. It is not a process that occurs overnight, but one that takes time and commitment.

Discussion Questions

1. Are there management and leadership differences in styles based on one's gender?

2. How are men different from women in terms of how they approach teamwork and management?

3. Men and women are different. What do men need to know about women? What do women need to know about men?

4. What is coaching and how can it be used to develop employees in the workplace?

5. Are women more ethical than men? Discuss your thoughts and reasons.

6. What can managers do to provide female employees equal and/or more opportunities so they can reach their full potential?

7. Can men and women reach the top ranks of management using similar strategies? Discuss your thoughts, suggestions, and explanations.

8. Daspro's (2004) article looked at a woman's capability to complete an international assignment. The first question that would be of interest to pose is: A) if given the choice to choose a female or a male for an expatriate international assignment, which one would you choose? B) The second question would tie directly to the first in that why would you choose that specific gender? C) Another question for critical evaluation would be that of considering the many "excuses" or reasons that some employers give for not sending qualified females on international assignments, how viable do you find their thought of reasoning? D) While women having been fighting for equal rights in the workplace and other places for many years now, why are so many women still earning less than their male counterparts?

Teamwork and Synergy

T eams and teamwork are essential realities of developing a competitive advantage through a diverse workforce in the twenty-first century work environment. Teamwork and the synergy in each organization can bring about more efficiency and productivity in solving complex problems and being responsive to the needs of customers. This chapter discusses teams, teamwork and teambuilding skills to create efficiency, productivity, and a committed workforce.

While all functions of management are critical for productivity and efficiency, one indirect yet important function of managers is the building and organization of effective teams. High performing teams are made up of diverse members that make work fun and show camaraderie, and they can greatly enhance the long-term value of any department, organization, industry, and country. According to experts, high performing teams bring "talent," "difference," and "variety" to the mix, which, when managed effectively, can set the ground for creating a unique competitive advantage for an organization.

Teams and Teamwork

A *team* is a group of people who are mutually dependent on one another to achieve a common goal. Advantages of working in a team can include the results, how the job gets done, improved communication, organizational learning, and personal satisfaction. Disadvantages of being on a team can include time, individual performance, and conflict, to name but a few. *Teamwork* is the coordinated efforts of a *team* working toward a common goal because *T*ogether *E*veryone *A*chieves *M*ore! Of course, it is the performance of each individual that makes or breaks a team. Some say that there is no "I" in "team" and this can provide an inaccurate perception of the responsibility that goes with being a team member. Perhaps, it could be stated as *"Together every individual achieves more"* to emphasize the impact of personal or individual responsibility on the team. A team is different than a traditional group of people working together. A working group relies primarily on the individual contributions of its members for group performance. Working groups thrive in hierarchical structures where individual accountability counts the most, such as with individualistic cultures.

A team strives for "synergy;" a magnified impact that is incremental to what its members could achieve in their individual roles. Teams require both individual and mutual accountability. The choice, of remaining a working group or forming a team, depends largely on whether individual achievements can deliver the group's performance aspirations, or whether collective work-products, skills, and mutual accountability are needed. When compared to groups, teams have members who are totally committed to the goal and mission (that they developed or aspired to) for the project. Everyone in the team is accountable to each other. Teams usually have a culture of collaboration that leads to trust between the members. Team members agree on a common approach to achieve the performance challenge. Finally, leadership in a team is usually shared between all members and/or, at least those that are highly respected by everyone. Overall, key elements of a team are:

- Limited number of individuals with complementary skills,
- Commitment to a common purpose and performance goals,
- Commitment to an agreed upon strategy, and
- Mutual accountability.

It is estimated that in 2007 and beyond, about 90% of all large organizations will have some type of self-managed work teams. Some common forms of teams are functional teams, cross-functional teams, virtual teams, and self-managed teams. There is always a "learning curve" for each team member through which s/he must climb. However, learning is not enough to become a high-performing team. Each team member's behavior may need to change as well. Behavioral changes can be the most difficult part of teamwork, and it can be very uncomfortable at the outset. The "team performance curve" illustrates how well groups of people perform based on their approach and implementation plans. The following are possible variations of groups and teams shown on the team performance curve by Katzenbach and Smith (2005).

1. Working group
2. Pseudo-team
3. Potential team
4. Real team
5. High-performing team.

A potential team needs a unique blend of actions, events, and decisions in order to move up the curve and achieve high performance as a real team. Real teams do not emerge unless the individuals on them take risks involving conflict, trust, interdependence, and hard work. Real teams learn how to deal with such concerns through frank and open communication. Building the team's performance requires each leader (and team member) to:

1. Establish urgency and direction.
2. Select members based on skills and skill potential, not personalities.

3. Pay particular attention to first meetings and actions.
4. Set clear rules of behavior.
5. Set and seize upon a few immediate performance-oriented tasks and goals.
6. Challenge the group regularly with fresh facts and information.
7. Spend lots of time together.
8. Exploit the power of positive feedback, recognition, and reward.

"Team building" can give a powerful boost to the spirit and effectiveness of any group. Well designed and delivered team building programs can lead to better understanding, clearer alignment and much stronger motivation among members.

Great Teams

Great teams are consciously created to accomplish specific objectives. Great teams require development through various stages of forming, storming, norming, performing, and adjourning. Most researchers and leaders agree that great teams have certain common characteristics. The following are characteristics of great teams identified by Pat Williams, General Manager of the Orlando Magic Basketball team as he presented these characteristics at the *Excellence in Management* Conference (June 1998) in Chicago. According to Pat Williams, great teams have or exhibit the following character traits:

1. *Top talent.* Great teams consist of great talents. Each member of the team is talented in his/her vocation. Furthermore, each member of a great team must be teachable and inspired to learn.
2. *Outstanding leadership.* High performing teams have outstanding leadership. Leadership skills are learned through education, experience, and hard work. Bobby Bowdin, Head Football Coach at Florida State University, once said that "... No one is born a leader. Everyone must work in developing his/her leadership skills." Most researchers agree that leaders have:
   - A vision of the future for themselves and others.
   - Great communication skills and the ability to clearly communicate their thoughts.
   - An optimistic perspective on daily obstacles and situations.
   - Excellent motivation skills and are great motivators or cheerleaders in their organizations and communities.
   - Character traits of integrity, honesty, and a strong work ethic.
   - Competence in their vocation and avocation.

- Boldness and are able to make decisions based on what they know.
- A servant mentality and orientation.

3. *Total commitment.* High performing teams are totally committed to their cause, people, quality, and purpose. They are achievement-oriented and very competitive in nature, because they understand that competition brings out the best in each individual.
4. *Passion for the cause.* Great teams are passionate about what they do, their cause, and achievement. Team members are always upbeat, enthusiastic, and moving. They enjoy what they do and communicate their passion to others.
5. *Think teams.* Great teams have the philosophy of *"less me and more we."* Each member is willing to do what it takes to help the team achieve its purpose.
6. *Empower each other.* High-performing teams are able to feed and motivate each other to accomplish what may appear beyond their capability. Members of great teams constantly build people up. Abraham Lincoln once said "there is nothing stronger than quiet gentleness" and great teams are gentle to themselves and to others. They are also great with their children and family members. Research shows that people, specifically males, want to satisfy their fathers. Research with male prisoners have shown that majority of them have had some type of a dysfunctional relationship or problem with their fathers. Members of high performing teams are able to positively empower people, both in their personal and professional lives, in a gentle and caring way.
7. *Build trust and respect.* Great teams are constantly building trust among themselves and their colleagues, customers, suppliers, and community members. Team members respect each person as an individual and see something positive in everyone.
8. *Have members with strong character.* High-performing teams are made up of people with strong character who exhibit:
   - Faith in a higher power.
   - Integrity, honesty and maturity.
   - Humility.
   - Influence by positively affecting others.
   - Courage in their conviction.

High-Performing Teams

Price Pritchett (1992), in his little book, *Teamwork: The Team Member Handbook,* offers sixteen practical steps to building a high performance team that starts improving oneself and one's team members. The following are his suggestions with brief explanations that assist managers in applying the concepts toward building a high-performance team.

Push For High Quality Communication. Communication keeps teamwork alive. It is crucial to the coordination effort. No other factor plays such an important role in building and preserving trust among teammates. Everyone in the group needs to know what is happening and what is going to happen. The information network should connect all the individuals of the team. Teammates should meet, discuss and be involved in very open communication. Encourage members to give their opinions and to discuss their differences. This is the only way the team can achieve understanding, find out the best approach, and end up with "buy-in" by everyone. An individual needs to serve as a "relay person," helping to send information to teammates. Anyone who is left out, gets the information too late, or does not get it at all can destroy the coordination effort. Every member of the team needs to be a quality control person in the communication process, making sure that the data is accurate, up-to-date and meaningful. Any teammate that makes a move based on misinformation can ruin the group's efforts. Be sure to send clear and timely messages. Inaccurate and late messages can cause conflict and disorganization that can limit or damage the group's performance. Remember that accurate, timely communication is the key to high quality teamwork.

Bring Talent To The Team. The essence of teamwork is to be good at what you do. Teams need talented individuals. The more talent you have the more you can contribute. Improve your skills and you will be improving the team. "Strive for continuous improvement-the Japanese call it kaizen-so the team never stops growing." Keep improving your current skills and learning new ones and you can improve the team's scores. If you level off your learning, the potential of the group is not as high. If you are to be relied upon, you must be competent. Master the fundamentals of the job and bring your individual talent to the group. Never stop learning and improving. Give teammates good reasons to believe in you. Keep getting better at what you do.

Play Your Position. Find out the duties, standards of performance, time frames and deadlines you are supposed to meet. Know what is expected of you for your job and or your assignment. "Play your position." Teamwork, by definition, implies interdependence. Some people in the unit depend on you for their success; if you fail you may cause them to fail. If you are not at your own position, you may change the timing of the entire team. Your teammates may have to bail you out, abandoning their own assignments. Sometimes you may need to cover for teammates, however do not get in their way. It is best to support your teammates by playing your own position perfectly.

Turn Diversity to the Team's Advantage. In a team, differences can add depth, create strength, broaden the group and bring balance. Teams perform best when the team members bring a variety of abilities, experiences, personalities, and problem solving approaches. But for diversity to make a difference, you have to take advantage of it. Respect and use those individual differences to improve the team. Do not ignore the person who is "different"—whether that person is you or someone else. Do your part to help the team find the talents of each person and benefit from all of its members. Team members who are in the minority should not hamper the team by thinking that they should be treated differently. When someone decides that being "different" means special treatment, it creates controversy and conflict. Diversity can make teamwork seem more difficult at first, however it produces a more powerful team. Respect people's differences, and use everyone's uniqueness to benefit the team.

Back Up Others Who Need Help. Teamwork is helping one another to get the job done in the best possible way and in the shortest period of time. Thinking as a team will improve overall performance and build morale. Know your teammate's assignments and responsibilities. If you see that someone is having a problem, you should be able to back that person up. Being an effective back up means knowing other member's assignments and broadening your skills to cover for them. Cross training is very important to a team. In an emergency situation any team member can be used as a replacement of another. In a team an attitude of helpfulness is a necessity. Your teammates will be more eager to help you if you are willing to help them.

Practice. Practice is an important part of performance since it brings one closer to doing it perfectly. Practice gives you a chance to make errors and then find out what is the best way to correct them. You can learn new ways or more efficient ways of doing the job. The team can assess its weaknesses and its strengths by practicing together. Also, the team will be more able to meet challenging situations in the real world with a better understanding.

Be Prepared To Sacrifice For the Team. In any organization, there is always a question of "me versus we." This can sometimes cause conflict among team members, deciding whether the individual aspects of the team are the most important or the group as a whole. Sometimes an individual may have to sacrifice his/her own personal interest for the group. The choice may be a difficult one. Keep in mind your teammates will remember the choice you make.

Help New Teammates Make Entry. Life brings changes to us in many ways. We meet many people, some for only an instant. When new teammates appear, it is important to everyone that they succeed. If there is a high rate of turnover, it is because the team was not supportive enough. New teammates should be welcomed, supported, and taught their important role in the group. This will contribute to the success of the team.

Play Down Yourself and Build Up Others. Always point out the importance of the team members. Make it a habit to point out their strengths. Build up their confidence and you will bring success to the team. When someone compliments you, make sure you give credit to the team. If you are selfish in the accomplishments, the team will suffer. This will alienate the other team members. To keep team members feeling appreciated, you must make sure they feel important. Do not concentrate on you, but the team as a whole. Build up your team and they will praise you.

Spend Time With Your Teammates. Getting to know your teammates is necessary to form a cohesive unit. The more you work together as a unit the better your team will be. It is important to have togetherness for the group to be a real team. Set aside time to find out more about each other. This helps to understand each other better. You will be more able to back one another up if necessary. An informal atmosphere is more likely to increase bonding between teammates. So be sure to spend time with your teammates and you will find the togetherness that makes a real team.

Help Drive Discipline into the Group. Each member of a team needs to have self-discipline. The leader cannot be everywhere at once. He/she should not have to keep everyone in line. Individuals need to hold themselves to the highest standard. Discipline in your work is very basic. Doing what needs to be accomplished, living according to the rules, and making sure to follow the standards. Sometimes this may mean making sacrifices, but it will benefit the team. Coordination of a team needs discipline. Discipline helps the team to perform at the highest level, creating trust, reliability, and dependability. There is pride and accomplishment of a job well done in a team that has discipline.

Make Sure You Make a Difference. Making a difference is doing what counts. On a team it is important that everyone has an equal opportunity. Others on the team may be more talented than you, however if you try hard enough you may find that attitude is more important than talent. Meaningful results come from making a commitment to the team. Be someone who will be missed if you were not a part of the team.

Give Attention To The Group Process. There are always going to be problems when working with a team. Keep an eye on the team's effectiveness. Is the team using its resources efficiently? Are team members confused, or discouraged? If you find any of these problems bring them to the team's attention. Fix a problem when it is small before it becomes too large to handle. The team process has as much to do with its success or failure as does the talent of its members.

Help Create A Climate Of Trust. Trust is a key ingredient to teamwork. Every member of the team needs to be able to believe and rely upon one another. Your behavior is how the team members will know how much you are committed to the team. Be aware that even small violations of trust can destroy the cooperation within a team. Keeping your word, honoring your commitments, being consistent, and playing fair are ways that you can build the climate of trust.

Strengthen The Leader Through Good Followership. Good followers have initiative. They know what to do without being told and can think for themselves. They are able to lead themselves allowing the person in charge more time for other assignments. The responsibility of the follower is to support and strengthen the leader. A commitment to the team's common goals will support your leader. However, sometimes it may be necessary to argue your point, disagree with your orders or to challenge the leader if you feel they are abusing their power. You may need to do this for the good of the group, do not do it for your own personal gain. Do not blindly follow your leader, it is important to have enough knowledge and commitment to make sure your team is being led in a positive direction.

Be a Good Sport. Play fair and respect others. Forgive your team members' mistakes as they are bound to happen. Admit your own mistakes and do not take the criticism from your colleagues personally. When you are praised, share that praise with your team members. Do not lift yourself up at the expense of others. Teammates pay attention to your conduct and your attitude. Good sportsmanship creates harmony. Without harmony the team will not be a success.

Create and Lead a High-Performing Team

Today's leaders work in a fast-paced, competitive work environment and are asked to do more with fewer resources, and to do it better than before. The workplace is evolving and the individuals or teams that anticipate change, plan for it, and respond effectively will be the ones to survive. On the other hand, a low performing team can be less valuable than its individual members. Negative situations can have a slowing effect on productivity that directly affects bottom-line performance, making teambuilding more critical than ever before.

However, even the best leaders cannot do it alone. Leadership and teamwork is essential to the success of any organization. When leaders develop teams, they increase their performance and effectiveness. Synergistic teams become much more valuable than the sum of its parts. A true team shares common values and a sense of commitment among members. Teams set aside territorial issues and politics. They concentrate on the tasks and goals that need to be accomplished. This focused application of resources through "teamwork" breaks through barriers, identifies new opportunities and creates momentum that will add to a company's bottom line.

There are many different types of teams, ranging from cross-functional to self-managed, and they can be seen as either informal or formal. *Formal teams* often consist of a permanent staff with a defined purpose for their work. This type of team's purpose is usually continuous. *Informal teams* can develop on a per-project or shared interest basis, typically to perform work on specific projects. It is generally accepted that smaller teams consisting of five to ten people tend to be more successful than larger ones. Larger groups make it difficult to form ties and can lead to internal competition or delayed decision making.

Effective teambuilding and commitment leads to excellence, better problem solving, greater productivity, and more effective use of resources. In addition to these positive, business-focused results of effective teambuilding, there is also a group of softer benefits that greatly enhance the work culture. By working together in a safe environment, healthy teams will foster growth in team members. In these situations, individuals learn from one another and develop important skills at a faster rate than they would on their own. It provides a sense of purpose that is both motivating and fulfilling.

A group does not become a team by being labeled as one. A team is more than a group of individuals working together; it is the cohesiveness and cooperation between leaders and followers and their readiness and willfulness to strive towards common objectives.

Besides shared leadership, successful and effective teams have many other common characteristics and showing a high level of commitment is one of them. The very essence of a team is a shared commitment towards a common purpose. Without commitment, groups perform as individuals. With it, teams become a powerful force of collective performance. Successful teams invest a large amount of time and effort into shaping their purpose and direction (Katzenbach & Smith, 2005). This allows members to translate their purpose into performance goals and objectives. Clear performance goals give teams the opportunity to track their progress. Communication is paramount among team members as it helps members to stay focused on the mission. Every team member should know exactly what his or her needs are to accomplish and by what deadline (Belt, 1993). When teams are unable to accomplish performance objectives, members get confused and regress to mediocre performance. Effective teams meet their goals and build a momentum to become powerful production engines. A team requires a leader to closely monitor production progress and advocate to management, if necessary, on behalf of its members (Belt, 1993). Effective teams prepare and practice their skills to improve performance (Katzenbach & Smith, 2005). They analyze resources both inside and outside the organization to meet objectives and recruit new members with needed technical skill sets. A team relies on its members for individual contributions. High levels of cooperation and communication help minimize interpersonal conflicts among team members that often drain the team's energy and effectiveness (Hughes, Ginnett & Curphy, 2002). These unique characteristics define the overall success of a team.

As stated before, great teams are consciously created to accomplish specific objectives. Great teams require development through various stages of forming, storming, norming, performing, and adjourning. Although there is no set formula for building an optimum team, the following steps presents the most important principles shared by many successful teams. Building a high performing team[19] requires each leader (and team member) to follow the sex steps offered below:

1. Establish the core values.
2. Create an environment of effective communication and mutual respect.

---

[19] - Co-authored with Bryan P. Monaghan and Dawn Rahicki. Originally published in "*Privatization and Market-Based Leadership,*" by Llumina in 2006.

3. Analyze and respond to the needs of the team.
4. Communicate the vision and create the plan.
5. Set performance-oriented and achievable goals.
6. Provide fair and challenging rewards. Exploit the power of positive feedback and recognition.

Establish the Core Values

First, establish a strong foundation by clarifying the group's core values. These values are the principle foundation which holds teams together. They outline what the members truly stand for, motivate and guide the team during the decision-making process, and connect the members in a way a paycheck cannot. Successful teams have the following common values: communication, respect, integrity, accountability, and excellence. In this stage, basic ground rules relating to attendance, confidentiality, constructive confrontation, and contributions are established. These rules support members in reaching performance goals and create an environment of mutual respect within the team (Katzenbach & Smith, 2005).

A great team leader will live the organization's core values with integrity and act as a role model to inspire the team. Businesses that seek to align employee's values with the values of their organization are more successful than organizations that do not. Value-driven organizations focus on the needs of both the employees and their customers. As a result, these organizations tend to have fewer problems attracting and retaining a quality workforce. By comparison, organizations that are simply task-oriented and do not align their values with the team, tend to have stressful work environments and a difficult time retaining talented people for long periods of time.

Communicate and Respect Everyone

Successful teams communicate well with one another and take time to listen to each other. Team foundations are built on mutual respect or treating people the way one would like to be treated if the situation was reversed. While quality teams do not tolerate disrespectful treatment, they are not afraid of discussing challenges and differences of opinion openly in an effort to come to resolution. They know that a team is built on integrity, trust, and accountability. This integrity holds individuals open to sincere and high standards. When team members collectively decide on a specific task, then they commit to establishing a plan to achieve the objective. Effective teams share a common commitment and a sense of mutual accountability (Katzenbach & Smith, 2005). Great teams strive toward excellence. They are not satisfied with anything less than the very best.

Analyze and Respond to the Needs of the Team

An effective leader will analyze the needs of the project and develop a team with the skills, experience, readiness, willingness, and personality necessary to perform well together to meet the established vision, purpose, and performance objectives. Through effective questioning or interviewing and research, successful leaders choose people whose personality, experience, readiness, and skill set fit the image and culture of the prospective team. To avoid groupthink, the leader should choose followers with diversity of skills, ability, experience, and talent to fill the needed roles. While the diversity may lead to friction, at times it can also promote productivity and innovation. As discussed earlier, this friction can be resolved through open communication and mutual respect.

It is important that the leader creates a team with the right balance of personalities, skills, experiences, and values. Members should believe in and share the team's core values. The individual should have the ability to adapt to the environment, have strong skills and experience, be willing and able to learn additional skills, and be a positive addition to the team. Once a team is selected, the leader should observe their first meeting and pay particular attention to each member's interaction. Initial impressions go a long way and can be useful in determining which members have the most influence over others. This information is useful in organizing the team and assigning roles. Team leaders should establish a few challenging goals to start developing the team cohesiveness by obtaining results. As the team forms, storms, and norms, and the readiness of the members change, the leader should continue to assess the group's needs and steer them accordingly. By utilizing coaching, training, evaluation, two-way feedback, and mentoring, the leader can develop and motivate each member of the group. By promoting 360 degree evaluations, two-way feedback, and coaching across all lines of the organization, a leader can personally grow as well as motivate and train his or her team. This type of ongoing communication and coaching from the leader can assist in correcting the follower's behavior should one go off course.

Effective assessment and a situational leadership approach can also help the leader develop associates to potentially move them from one level of readiness to the next level of readiness. A leader who is able to lead people well through these changing situations will enhance the overall value of the team. Through effective mentoring and coaching by the leader, a team can mature to the point where they develop strong trust and open, respectful communication between the members. Leaders can accelerate evolution and enable their team to solve problems, seize opportunities, and apply theoretical principles to real-time situations by creating a culture of learning, coaching, and effective questioning. An enlightened leader is someone who participates in the process of learning and communicating without making others conscious of the effort (Preston, 2004).

'Leaderful' team designs produce effective outcomes because they engage the team members in mutual action. Individual talent is allowed to shine through and contribute to the team's greater good. As a team member, it is important for the leader to observe him- or herself before advising others. Once that degree of self-leadership is mastered, then the leader can begin to model self-leadership in others. At this point, one can encourage team members to go through self-discovery so they learn not only to take care of themselves, but to take care of one another as well.

Once the culture of learning and communication is established, the leader can encourage the team to hold one another accountable and constructively coach up, down, and across the organization without fear of repercussion. The leader should continue to analyze and respond to the needs and readiness of the team throughout the life of the team.

Communicate the Vision and Create the Plan

This process requires the leader to establish a clear vision with a realistic plan to accomplish the goals and objectives. The leader analyzes the team and establishes specific roles, responsibilities, and expectations of each member. Guidelines, responsibilities, and timelines are outlined and communicated to the members with an opportunity for the followers to offer their feedback and input. The specificity of performance objectives facilitates open communication and constructive conflict within the team. At this time, open discussion can clarify the steps needed to obtain or alter performance goals. When goals are ambiguous or do not exist, these discussions can be less productive.

Set Achievable Goals

Setting achievable goals for each individual which are in line with the team's overall vision, help team members maintain their focus on getting results. Performance goals allow team members the opportunity to achieve small victories. These wins help to motivate them and build their commitment and confidence. This will create a common purpose among the team members which coordinates their efforts for the good of the team. As the team is forming, the members will begin to understand their urgent and worthwhile purpose. The more meaningful and urgent the vision, the more likely a team will live up to its potential.

Reward and Recognize Good Performance

A cohesive, high performing team will begin to focus on the achievement of collective results. Leaders of these teams value and recognize outstanding performance and are quick to reward such performance. In the final phase, the members of the team are recognized for their individual and collective contributions and accomplishments. There are many ways in which the leader can reward performance. Besides compensation or gifts, a senior executive can speak to the team regarding his or her appreciation of the team speak to the team regarding his or her appreciation of the team successfully completing its goal. This important stage reminds the leader to appreciate the individual contribution of each member and to value them. The leader who takes the time to consistently support and value the team, celebrate victories and encourage fun in the process will build strong loyalty among members. Ultimately, the most cherished reward of many teams is the shared satisfaction of achieving more together than they ever could individually.

Training in Interpersonal Skills[20]

Modern teams that are made up of members from different cultures work more effectively when they have the requisite skills for the development of strong relationships. Of course, these skills are especially more important in a diverse workplace.

In their book entitled *Training in Interpersonal Skills: Tips for Managing People at Work* by Stephen P. Robbins and Phillip L. Hunsaker (2006), the authors offer many valuable tips and suggestions that are extremely appropriate for a diverse workplace. Twenty first century organizations are made up of people from around the globe; these people tend to best operate within a group or team environment and need effective interpersonal communication skills in order to successfully achieve their stated organizational goals and objectives with, and through, their peers. This therefore implies interdependent roles and relationships that are unified in the actions of individuals who make up the organization; therein lays the challenge for management to effectively communicate with their people. An effective manager is one who possesses the right skills and personality for a given position within the organization. However, almost all experts agree that successful managers will need effective communication and interpersonal skills in order for them to achieve their personal and professional goals. As such, understanding and acquiring effective interpersonal skills become very important for all managers if they are to successfully achieve their goals and compete in today's global economy. Today's workplace is full of many challenges and managing people through effective communication is one of them. Another one of these challenges is how individuals relate to one another in the workplace through meaningful discussions and dialogue. The population of many countries and industries today seems to be very diverse and this diversity presents a challenge especially in the area of communication for the workplace. Interpersonal communication requires specific skills that leaders and managers can master in order to effectively communicate with their employees, colleagues, suppliers, and superiors. However, before one can relate to another person, he or she would need to know him- or herself. Get-

---

[20] - Co-authored with Lisa M. Mujtaba, University of Central Florida.

ting to know oneself can be time-consuming and difficult at times. We do not always realize the consequences of our choices or decisions, and for managers this is a very important aspect of everyday work life.

The book by Robbins and Hunsaker (2006) is an excellent tool for improving and helping individuals as leaders and managers to relate to their co-workers, staff, vendors, and other stakeholders. The beginning six chapters focus on one's inner-self. Chapters one through three discuss a person's self-awareness and self-management. The style that each person uses as a manager affects all of the people around him or her. It is important to know oneself and one's strengths and weaknesses as a manager. Chapters four through six are all about various forms of communication, such as verbal, non-verbal and written communication. All these forms are a vital part of any organization. Communication is something every manager should strive to improve. There are so many ways things that are said or written can be misinterpreted between individuals and people working in various departments within a large organization. Sometimes, this miscommunication can affect people outside of the organization such as media, vendors, and suppliers. Some of such miscommunications can be very costly to the organization and its stakeholders. Therefore, it is important for leaders and managers to master the skills of effective interpersonal communication.

One of the ways that managers make a difference to the company is if they have the correct skills to motivate their co-workers. Chapters seven through nine focus on motivation, coaching, counseling, mentoring, goal setting, and empowerment skills. Managers must realize that it is very difficult for themselves and their employees to be motivated without a specific goal to achieve. As such, the setting of specific goals and its timely communication to all relevant personnel become extremely critical. The next section of the book is about leading people. Leadership style, managing change politicking, and persuading skills are discussed so managers and leaders can effectively use them as is appropriate with their people in the organization.

Throughout *Training in Interpersonal Skills: Tips for Managing People at Work,* there are either self-examination questions or exercises that can be done individually and in a group setting. The group exercises can be a great source for thought provoking discussions and for managers to realize that there may be more than one way to deal with a situation. These group exercises are scattered throughout the book. However, they are even more emphasized in chapters 14 through 20 which focus on working with teams, running meetings, diversity, ethical decision making, creative problem solving, resolving conflict, and negotiations. *Training in Interpersonal Skills* is an excellent source material book for a current manager or a new manager that is attempting to enhance his or her influence and communication skills. The content of the book is very relevant to today's diverse and global workforce. A manager's self-awareness, knowing how he or she affects his or her company and actual communication skills could create a success for the department or it could lead to failure and costly misunderstandings. This book is recommended for managers, upcoming managers, business students, management scholars, leadership specialists, and others who are interested in effective interpersonal communication skills. Faculty members and educators can use this book with adult learners in their workshops and classes. The book is also suitable for college students who work in teams or groups to complete course-related projects. Students can learn and apply effective interpersonal skills with their team members in the class and eventually use these skills with their peers in the workplace.

Summary

When diverse teams are working well, they create synergy by having multiple people with different skills and abilities, and converge on a specific problem or opportunity. Maximizing synergy gives the organization the opportunity to accomplish more with the same number of people.

It is the leader's responsibility to build a cohesive, productive, and healthy team through effective communication with them. By creating and sharing a long term vision, a leader begins to nurture a strong commitment to a common approach. Purposeful teams and exceptional performance are inseparable; a leader cannot always have one without the other. Teamwork represents a sense of shared values and beliefs that are encouraging to its members. It fosters open and healthy communication and active listening while providing support. It can promote continuous learning and development and holds members accountable for results. Teamwork promotes collaboration, cohesiveness, commitment, and recognizes achievement. Value-driven teams advocate both individual and collective performance. High performing teams often exceed an organization's expectations, setting them apart from other work groups. The very essence of teamwork is discovered in the shared commitment by members to care more about one another than for themselves, while respecting each other's differences as well as meeting and exceeding expectations.

Discussion Questions

1. What is a team?
2. What is teamwork?
3. What are the benefits of a diverse team when compared to a homogenous team?
4. What is synergy?
5. What are some common skills that team members need to become effective members of a team?
6. Why are interpersonal skills important for team members?

Listening and Conflict Management Skills

E ffectively resolving employee and interpersonal conflicts through proper communication are an important and mission-critical aspect of a manager's responsibilities. Effective managers are always focused on a balance of concern for people and production. As such, besides resolving conflicts, effective managers are performance-focused and developmental in their leadership and management styles as they are first and foremost concerned about the well-being and success of their employees. Besides appropriate diversity training and employee development practices, managers work toward first understanding and coaching employees in the "right" direction to meet acceptable professional and performance standards in the workplace. Furthermore, managers need to understand conflict and their own conflict management styles in order to discipline employees when needed and to develop an effective high-performing team in the department. The chapter emphasizes communication, listening, conflict management, and employee discipline as important aspects of effectively working with a diverse population.

Effective Communication

Communication takes place whether it is intended or not. Human beings have communicated for thousands of years and some major miscommunication experiences have been documented in books and cultural stories. Such experiences can teach human beings historical trends and their outcomes. The trends and outcomes will tend to show that most conflicts and challenges have been caused by misunderstanding and/or lack of effective communication to settle ideological or philosophical differences and disagreements around a table rather than battlefields. So, communication skills are extremely important for workforce diversity management. Communication is the process of exchanging information in ways that ensure a mutual understanding of content and feelings; this includes being heard and understood. Communication can also be defined as the transfer of information from one person to other(s), without the meaning being changed. Often communication takes the forms of speaking and listening. While speaking is done for the purpose of being understood, listening is the real tool for understanding, learning and growing. Being a good listener sets you apart and helps you become a much better communicator while speaking. Have you ever had someone describe you as "a very good listener?" If so, it's a compliment that says quite a bit about you. Remember, people are like fruit; therefore, human beings are either green and growing (learning and thriving), or ripe and rotting (suffering mental stagnation and atrophy). Living a life of continuous learning pays a wealth of dividends if people listen and use their learning effectively.

Every person without a hearing disability has been listening to what is said since before he or she was born. Yet, it is one of the most difficult skills of human interaction. Listening is not natural which means that people have to work at it; and furthermore, not listening, like communication, is irreversible. What you don't hear is gone and you may not get the opportunity to listen again. So, good listening skills are critical dimensions of effective communication.

Communication is simply exchanging information. *Effective Communication* is sharing information with others in such a way that they understand what you are saying. The goal of effective communication is mutual understanding. Of course, mutual understanding can be a challenge as words, phrases, connotations, denotations, and having different primary languages can make communication very complex. Imagine the following phrase and its meaning when speaking to a person whose first language is not English: It is best to "kill two birds with one stone," so we can "put out all the fires" quickly and not have to deal with the "can of worms" that seems to "pop up" consistently. Such sentences can confuse a person if he or she is not used to such a phrase or its meaning. Therefore, one must communicate effectively by asking questions and confirming understanding.

In a team and cross-culturally diverse work environment, the goal of effective communication is to make sure each team member is clear, concise, and credible in what s/he says to others. Getting one's point across and getting the results one wants requires that one build credibility, use logic and radiate positive emotional power. Using the power of asking effective questions is a good strategy for building credibility as an effective team member or leader in a diverse work environment.

Miscommunication through the Hierarchy

We can communicate vertically or horizontally in our organizations, communities, and families. However, there are some mishaps that can happen when communicating through letters and the chain of command. Carole M. Howard in 1998, at the *Excellence in Management Conference at Chicago*, presented one example of how something that was passed on from the city manager to an assistant manager was totally misinterpreted by the time it got to employees. The following is an example of what happened while communicating through the hierarchy:

1. *From city manager to assistant manager.* Next Thursday at 10:00 am, Halley's Comet will appear over this area. This is an event which occurs only once every 75 years. Call the department heads and have them assemble their staffs on the city hall lawn and explain this phenomenon to

them. If it rains, then cancel the day's observation and have the employees meet in the council chambers to see a film about the comet.

2. *From assistant manager to department heads.* By order of the city manager, next Thursday at 10:00 am, Halley's Comet will appear over your city hall. If it rains, then cancel the day's operation and report to the council chambers with your staffs where you will show films, a phenomenal event which occurs every 75 years.

3. *From department heads to supervisors.* By order to the phenomenal city manager at 10:30 next Thursday, Halley's Comet will appear in the council chambers. In case of rain over the city hall, the manager will give another order, something which occurs only every 75 years.

4. *Notice on the bulletin board.* Next Thursday at 10:30 the city manager will appear in our council chambers with Halley's Comet, something which occurs every 75 years. If it rains, the manager will cancel the comet and order us all out of our city hall.

5. *From employees to friends.* When it rains next Thursday at 10:30 over the city hall, the phenomenal 75 year old city manager will cancel all work and appear before the whole staff in the council chambers accompanied by Bill Halley and the Comets.

Listening Empathically

Empathic listening has been at the forefront of communication research since the 1960s and it was popularized by Carl Rogers. It has also been known as the Rogerian communication exercise and it is about understanding the other person. Dr. William James of Harvard University says, "The deepest need of every human being is to be understood." We often fail to take the steps necessary to really understand family members, associates, peers, and customers. To find out your listening tendencies, complete the Listening Scale Survey (located at the end of this chapter). Most individuals have a tendency to resolve the situation before making an accurate identification of the problem. If you have a tendency to solve problems before knowing the problem or its cause, then you're not alone. Sometimes our cultures condition us to listen, not with the intent to understand, but with the intent to respond. Therefore, it is best to fully explore empathic listening process and skills to help you reach a higher level of understanding so that you may always attempt to respond effectively and appropriately when interacting with others.

Empathy means compassion, understanding and emotional identification with the other person. While listening empathically you simply reflect the other person's feelings and sayings. *Reflect* means to think seriously about or contemplate something. *Empathic listening* is the process of listening to both the content and the feelings of a message. You reflect on the meaning and emotions of the message and then restate your understanding to the sender. The process of empathic listening gives you the opportunity to reach true understanding in communication. Empathic listening can be very effective in achieving mutual understanding among two or more parties. However, empathic listening is not a panacea for major problems or personality concerns. It is simply a process that can lead to better understanding of what is being communicated. There are many examples of empathic listening leads or phrases you may use when you are applying the process of reflective listening. Some of the listening leads can include the following:

- As I hear it, you feel as if...
- To me, it's as if you're saying you want...
- What it sounds like you're saying is, you need...
- If I'm hearing you correctly, you feel that...
- I'm not sure, but it seems as though you desire...

As you can see, empathic listening responses seek to understand the feelings and emotions of the sender along with the content meaning. Empathic listening process is especially useful when there are emotional topics being discussed.

Overall, *empathic listening* is the process of discovering the sender's perspective, thoughts, and feelings by encouraging the sender to self-disclose through active listening and/or empathy. Empathic listening involves listening with the eyes and heart for feelings and listening with the ears for facts, thoughts and views. Since performance discussions between colleagues, managers and employees can be emotional, it is best to master the skill of empathic listening. It is important that listeners are caring, gentle and understanding in such situations without losing focus of the performance issue. Effective listeners use the empathic listening skills which can be done by:

- Repeating the message.
- Summarizing the content of the message.
- Expressing or reflecting on the feelings of the message.
- Restating both the content and feelings of the message in your own words.
- Using good judgment with regard to determining which of the above steps are appropriate for each situation.

Benefits of Listening

Effective listening is not a passive activity nor easy. As a matter-of-fact, it is hard work, mentally draining and requires one 100% percent of one's attention. The following are some of the reasons one should commit to this hard work called *listening*.

1. *You can learn by listening.* You can learn about the subject being discussed and the person speaking if you consider his/her emotions, expressions, temperament, personality, word choice, reactions, pace, non-verbal, and so on.

2. *You can gain more friends by listening.* The speaker will appreciate you more for letting him/her talk and for listening actively or empathically to him/her while s/he expresses him/herself.

3. *Listening can reduce tension.* Giving the other person a chance to get his/her problem or viewpoint off his/her chest may help to "clear the air" of tension and hostility.

4. *Listening helps solve mutual problems and resolve disagreements.* You cannot agree or disagree intelligently with the other person until you understand his/her point of view. Remember, understanding the problem is often half of the solution.

5. *Listening leads to better work and cooperation from others.* When a person feels that you are really interested in him/her and his/her problems, thoughts and opinions, s/he respects you and is inspired to cooperate with you.

6. *Listening helps you make better decisions.* Through listening you can draw upon the experience of people who also work in the same area, thus helping you develop better judgment as well as to uncover additional facts.

7. *Listening can help you do a better job.* Try asking the people you work with, work for, or work alongside for suggestions as to how you can do a better job, and then listen. You may be surprised at the good ideas you can pick up by applying this suggestion.

8. *Listening can prevent major problems and catastrophes.* When we talk before we listen to the other person in a discussion, we stick our necks out, make decisions we later wish we could withdraw, state criticisms we later regret, or commit ourselves to actions we cannot or will not carry out. So, listen, understand, confirm and then speak if necessary.

9. *Listening can build self-esteem and self-confidence.* If you listen to and understand the opponent's arguments, you can be confident of accurate rebuttal. If you listen, you can spot "loopholes" in the other person's argument, and gain confidence in your own case.

10. *Listening can give you time to think.* The average person speaks about 150 to 250 words per minute and your capacity to listen is probably about 400 to 600 words per minute. You can use this extra time not only to improve your understanding of what is being said, but to think up answers, make decisions, and plan prospective actions, when appropriate.

Conflict Management[21]

Conflict is a reality of life, which everyone faces at one time or another. Leaders, managers, and team members thus need to understand the causes and effects of conflicts and how to respond in the best interest of all members concerned. Conflict is often a characteristic of change. Any attempt to adjust the status quo in an organization can result in conflict. If effectively handled, conflict can be a healthy way of airing differences. However, constant conflict can be anxiety-inducing, debilitating, and destructive. Conflict occurs within and between individuals, groups, teams, organizations, and societies. An effective conflict resolution process includes recognition, awareness, and choice.

Individuals react differently to conflict. Some people seem to thrive on conflict while others abhor it; yet, still a few other individuals can remain unruffled by the most conflicting situations. Individuals also deal with conflict in different ways, some people attack, while others tend to defend. However, most people are consistent in their individual responses to conflict, tending to react the same way over time, developing a behavior pattern.

Conflict often is assumed to be a contest, and it is not. Conflict is part of nature; neither positive nor negative, "it just is," said Thomas Crum (1987). People can choose whether to make conflict a contest, a game, which requires that some players become winners and some losers. Winning and losing are generally the goals of games, but not the goal of conflict management. Effective conflict management requires thinking "win-win" with the goals of jointly learning, growing, and cooperating. *Conflict* is the struggle that results when two or more individuals perceive a difference or incompatibility in their interests, values, or goals. Conflicts can arise from ambiguous roles and goals, stereotypes, biases, different procedures, distribution of resources, irreconcilable differences, perception of information and personalities, and the structures in place. In a diverse workplace, every interaction has a potential for conflict. Some conflict is good for team performance. Too much conflict causes team leaders to spend much time responding to it. *Conflict management* is the process of dealing with conflict in an effective manner. Positive conflict (conflict that is managed effectively) is great for team performance, and negative conflict can be very hurtful. Managers can manage individual conflict by:

Day-to-day challenges with employees, colleagues, and bosses serve as laboratories for you to develop conflict management skills. It prepares you to serve as effective leaders, managers, and workers in the workplace. Conflict is best resolved within/by the team itself or by individuals causing the conflict. The best way to resolve conflict is to seek cooperation from all parties involved and to create a win-win solution for everyone through collaboration and mutual problem solving. This way you can meet your needs and theirs. There are conflicts that can be ignored or avoided, but others must be dealt

---

[21] Originally published in "*Privatization and Market-Based Leadership*," by Llumina in 2006.

with appropriately. In order to determine the best response, one can conduct a conflict analysis by asking the following questions:

⇒ What is the nature of the conflict and what or who is causing it?
⇒ Whose progress is impacted by this conflict?
⇒ What are the relevant facts surrounding the conflict?
⇒ Whose feelings are being hurt by this conflict?
⇒ What do the conflicting parties want and under what conditions?
⇒ What is the consequence of ignoring the conflict?
⇒ What is the consequence of facing the conflict by forcing a solution on all parties?
⇒ What is the best strategy for resolving the conflict and what resources are needed for this approach?

No matter how hard one works to build a productive team, the behavior of some team members or employees can cause breakdowns and block team progress while hindering everyone's performance. Team members, managers, and team leaders need to recognize such behaviors and learn how to resolve conflicts that arise when diverse personalities are dealing with complex performance challenges. Quickly and effectively resolving such conflicts can speed up the team's progress toward achieving its purpose (performance challenge). When dealing with day-to-day conflicts, misconducts, and disagreements, remember to use the 4-F model by emphasizing the facts, feelings, future expectations, and following up.

➤ *Facts.* Stick with the facts and describe the behavior that is creating the problem or conflict. Avoid attacking the other person. Avoid using "you" statements.
➤ *Feelings.* State the impact of the problem or conflict, your feelings, the feelings of team members, and how the problem makes the team suffer. Use "I" statements by mentioning how the above mentioned problem or fact impacts you or your employees and colleagues.
➤ *Future expectations.* Clearly describe future expectations, norms, and rules of conduct.
➤ *Following up.* Managers should follow up with the parties involved to make sure employees are meeting the expected standards as agreed. If they are, then the manager has an opportunity to reinforce this good behavior. Otherwise, the manager will have another opportunity to start the process again (or take drastic actions as appropriate).

Most people tend to have one of the five conflict resolution approaches in the continuum of being assertive (meeting one's own needs) to being supportive (meeting others' needs): avoiding, accommodating, competing, compromising, and collaborating. To determine what your dominant style is, complete the conflict resolution survey (provided at the end of this chapter) and circle your two dominant style(s) in the diagram presented in Figure 14.1.

Managers are likely to have one or two dominant styles of resolving conflict. However, it is best to know one's natural tendencies and, if needed, improve upon them as desired. While in some cases "avoiding" might be an effective style for dealing with a conflict, other situations might require the use of collaborating or compromising in order to get things done with other team members. The situational variables should determine the best style. While situations do vary, a person should always keep his/her composure because objectivity and rational decision-making is critical for effective conflict resolution. Furthermore, effective conflict resolution process requires the use of excellent listening skills. While listening effectively, managers can use objective and open-ended questions to clarify further areas of interest for all parties involved.

Figure 14.1 – Conflict Management Styles

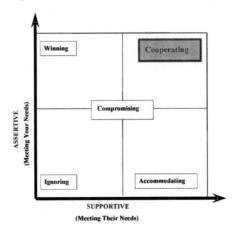

The essence of effective conflict resolution is to work together without offending anyone or being offended. Consequently, one should resolve all differences in a professional manner. It is also beneficial to remember that differences and disagreements can lead to better alternatives, better solutions, new ways of viewing each case, and opportunities for more quality communication. In each obstacle, there can be hidden opportunities. One needs to stay calm, stay "all together" in the face of disagreements, hear each other's differences and views, and then make sure one's views are heard by everyone on the team before agreeing on a final solution. In the case of performance-related conflict with employees, if the conflict resolution process does not resolve the situation, managers can then use a formal employee discipline strategy to correct the process.

One should remember that there is good conflict and there is bad conflict. In *positive conflict*, individuals of different views and personalities tend to show mutual respect for each others' thoughts and feelings in order to develop a strong partnership and eventually synergistic results. However, in *negative conflict*, people view each other as adversaries and are focused on "winning"; thereby, in negative conflict, people attempt to protect themselves, even if such a defense comes at a high cost to others. According to Murphy (1994), whether intentional or not, conflict that is not managed effectively can be a major barrier to one's personal and professional goal achievement. Therefore, managers should commit themselves to mastering an effective conflict management style or process. Murphy (1994) suggests that managers should master and use intellectual, emotional, interpersonal, and managerial skills for resolving conflicts. .

1. *Intellectual skills.* These skills and concepts can include such things as being analytical, learning ability, judgment, planning organization, perception, conceptualizing, objectivity, and flexibility.
2. *Emotional skills.* These skills and concepts can include such things as honesty, persistence, ambition, self-discipline, result-orientation, fast pace, initiative, assertiveness, and enthusiasm.
3. *Interpersonal skills.* These skills and concepts can include such things as persuasiveness, sensitivity, gregariousness, listening, communication, and writing.
4. *Managerial skills.* These skills and concepts can include such things as giving guidance, selecting competent people, motivating or creating a motivational work environment, terminating or demoting incompetent employees, delegating, and expecting professional behavior in the workplace.

Conflict management skills and techniques enable managers and leaders to reduce or eliminate those barriers that prevent individuals or a population group from achieving the results desired in the department or in the economy. One can summarize that conflict is simply a by-product of bringing about new developments, growth, innovation, and change toward a better work environment and culture. Just like change, conflict is inevitable. By understanding how to deal with conflict in a positive and performance-focused manner, and actually preventing small issues from becoming major conflicts, market-based leaders' behavior can serve as a model for others in the organization. According to Murphy (1994), leaders and managers can proactively sense and reduce/eliminate conflict by being visionary, giving feedback, getting feedback, defining expectations, and reviewing performance regularly with their employees. The benefits of conflict management can be better relationships with one's employees and colleagues, increased self respect, personal development and growth, increased efficiency and effectiveness, creative and innovative thinking in the department, and synergy or teamwork (Murphy,

1994). Jim Murphy, the author of *Managing Conflict at Work,* mentions that conflict resolution requires time, knowledge, as well as hard work, and suggests a five-step process for all employees and managers to successfully resolve conflicts. According to experts, in cases of conflict, one should:

1. Take responsibility for dealing with conflict.
2. Uncover, define, and discuss the real problem.
3. Ask questions and listen.
4. Set goals and create an action plan.
5. Follow up.

Overall, when it comes to day-to-day conflicts, managers have a choice to deal with the conflict, ignore the conflict, or leave the area or department that is causing the conflict. The best choice in many cases, according to experts, would be to proactively deal with the conflict in an effective manner. One always must focus on the issue while maintaining the relationship in trying to resolve the conflict. Of course, if conflict continues, managers can use a standard discipline process to correct inappropriate behaviors.

Employee Discipline Management[22]

Besides communicating and resolving conflicts, managers must also know about employees' rights as well as disciplining and effectively terminating employees as part of their managerial responsibility and authority. Fairness and consistency in communicating expectations to employees are extremely important in managing their performance and development, especially in a diverse workforce. Through the implementation of a consistent and fair process, managers and organizational leaders can achieve their organizational goals while gaining the trust and cooperation of employees. It also is clear that without a consistent and fair process for developing or disciplining employees, even outcomes that are favored by employees can be extremely difficult to achieve.

Fairly and caringly disciplining employees for misconduct, low performance, or not meeting the stated requirements in a timely manner can be one of the most difficult parts of a manager's job. Yet, a proper and systematic process can certainly make the job easier in order to benefit the manager, the employee, and the organization. Disciplining employees is a reality of life and most managers are likely to face it at one time or another. The purpose of discipline is to make sure employees are behaving according to the written, documented, and stated work-related rules and regulations. An initial step for both managers and employees is to understand that employees have rights and they must be given proper and timely feedback on their performance in the workplace. According to management experts, all employees and customers

---

[22] For more information, see *"Privatization and Market-Based Leadership,"* by Llumina in 2006.

in the workplace have rights, and are thus entitled to a fair, safe, respectful, and healthy work environment. This understanding can lead to respecting employees for their work, taking lessons about performance management and coaching employees, attending appropriate workshops, understanding the company's rules and policies with regard to discipline and termination, and being an effective manager.

Before moving forward with the discipline process, a manager must clarify the problem. The manager should make sure the performance problem or misconduct statement is clear. One must avoid generalities and never translate performance shortfalls and misconducts into attitudinal or personality problems. Managers should also make sure the problem description is specific, observable, documented, and factual. Also, it is important to proactively answer the "when," "what," and the "impact" aspects of the problem to clearly state the issue. The clearer the problem description, the easier it will be to communicate and discuss the issue with the employee.

Once the problem statement and its description is clear, one can begin resolving it. Overall, with regard to disciplining employees, it is best that managers not jump into making irrational decisions based on emotional outbursts. For effectively disciplining employees, managers should follow a progressive disciplining process in order to make employees aware of their shortfalls or misconducts, so they can immediately begin work on improving it. So, progressive discipline is about effectively communicating with employees about their performance, listening to their side, being fair to employees, and respecting their rights. It is important that managers and their firms give employees appropriate vehicles for allowing them to express their concerns, opinions, and frustrations without receiving or perceiving retaliation. Such a process can help managers gather the right information about improving the work environment for all employees, thereby creating an inclusive and safe workplace. One important element of a good work environment is fairness to all employees; or having an effective discipline process to deal fairly with problems and performance deficiencies. An effective discipline process must be perceived as fair by employees while allowing them sufficient opportunities to fix the problem.

Discipline without Punishment

Discipline is about correcting behavioral or performance-related problems and misconducts in the workplace. Most managers do not like to enforce discipline when employees are not performing or behaving as expected, and no one likes to be the target of it. This result is probably because most traditional discipline approaches require punishing the employee for behavioral problems. With punishment, some employees learn not to get caught by managers for doing what is disliked, instead of attempting to correct the problem and behaving as expected. While punishing the employee to correct a problem can lead to success in the short-term, it may only gain compliance to satisfy the boss and not necessarily commitment to doing a good job. With the practical "discipline without punishment" concept, managers understand and learn how to handle one of the toughest issues any manager faces in managing employees' behavior. Discipline without punishment is very much like using appropriate situational leadership styles where the manager provides either less or more direction to the employee depending on his or her level of readiness and maturity to perform correctly the specific task. In essence, situational leadership is about disciplining employees without punishment in order to take care of the task at hand, guide or develop the employee to correctly perform the task, and enhance the manager's relationship with the associate.

Every organization is likely to have employees that occasionally show "discipline problems." If these misconducts and problems are handled incorrectly, as explained by the concept of discipline without punishment, and "when discipline is equated with punishment, even a small problem with only one person can ruin the entire team's morale and productivity" (Discipline without Punishment, 2005). When discipline issues are handled incorrectly, discipline has the possibility of causing a "battle of wills," with anger and hurt on both sides. As experienced in the workplace, for long-term purposes, not much is gained with many of the traditional discipline approaches, because most employees do not respond progressively better when they are treated progressively worse for a performance issue or a misconduct.

Using modern approaches and respectful examples, the discipline without punishment scenario provides effectives ways to use discipline for a healthy department and long-term productivity. It should be understood that workers do not change their attitudes and personalities, but they can change their behavior in the workplace when asked by the organization and managers in a respectful and fair manner. Changing employee behavior is the essence of discipline without punishment since misconducts in the workplace tend to be a behavior problem. Discipline without punishment requires that managers first get the individual to admit there is a problem, and then coach the employee on how to solve his or her misconduct or performance-related problem. Discipline without punishment shows how managers:

⇒ Use the steps of focusing on the problem, gaining the employee's agreement to change, identifying strategies for improvement, and following-up to make sure the behavior is changed to discipline employees for lasting improvements in the workplace.
⇒ Prevent a discipline problem from turning into an attitude problem for the employee, and a morale issue for the rest of the workers in the department.
⇒ Keep personality differences, which often have nothing to do with the problem at hand, out of a discipline situation.

⇒ Handle discipline respectfully so self-esteem and feelings of self-worth are kept intact because the employee's long-term growth and development are important for productivity and healthy relationships.

⇒ Delegate the responsibility for taking care of the problem on the shoulders of the problem owner, the employee. *Discipline without punishment* requires that managers put the responsibility for a discipline problem right where it belongs—on the shoulders of the employee.

There are many situational variables, such as the employee, the manager, the problem, the environment, the culture, the relationship of the employee with the manager, and other such factors that must be considered when disciplining employees. While considering the situational variables, one should follow a standardized process to help the employee improve his or her behavior and performance in the workplace without hurting morale or causing negative or ill feelings. Discipline without punishment provides four steps for managers to achieve the goal of helping employees correct behavioral or performance-related problems. The four steps offered for discipline without punishment are (Discipline without Punishment, 2005):

1. Focusing on the problem at hand. Focus on the issue that is causing the problem and not the person. Stay away from personality related concerns or your likes or dislikes of the person. Discuss the specific work-related problem so it can be fixed. To avoid generalities and vague statements, managers should clarify the specific problem and perhaps write it down before discussing it with the employee.
2. Gaining the employee's agreement that there is a problem and that it must be changed. The employee should at least agree to change or that a change is needed. Furthermore, he or she should agree that it is his/her responsibility to correct the problem.
3. Identifying appropriate strategies for improvement jointly with the employee. These strategies should either eliminate the problem or at least improve the performance to a satisfactory level as agreed upon.
4. Following-up to make sure the problem is eliminated and the behavior is improved. Take correct action as appropriate. When the behavior is improved, this provides an opportunity to further develop the individual and the relationship.

The four steps for disciplining employees without punishment is one effective approach to correcting behavioral, work-related problems in the workplace, without causing too much stress to employees, or personally being stressed each day as the manager of the department. It is understood that the manager is running the department and not the other way around, so managers should not stress themselves. Because some discipline incidents or approaches tend to be negative and cause friction between the manager and employees due to a lack of effective communication, a number of managers simply avoid facing the problem until it becomes a huge issue and can no longer be avoided. Such tendencies and procrastination of discussing problems and performance-related issues with employees can cause much undue stress, frustration, and hostility. Discipline without punishment offers an effective approach to address most behavioral and performance-related problems immediately in a mature, professional, direct, and task-focused manner, while attempting to jointly "brainstorm" on possible solutions that the employee can use to improve the situation. It must be remembered that the problem "owner" is the employee and consequently he or she is responsible for taking care of the problem. Managers can use the situational leadership styles of telling the employee what to do, selling the employee on the solution, participating with the employee on coming up with a solution, or delegating the task to the employee as per his or her level of readiness and maturity for the specific task or issue. Just like effective leadership, disciplining is not always reserved just for poor performers; rather, it is something that managers should do consistently with all employees, when needed, in order to create an inclusive, productive, and safe work environment for all. With this mindset and paradigm, disciplining employees requires effective leadership, management, and coaching skills. Effective coaches, managers, and leaders know that solving the immediate problem or performance challenge is one immediate opportunity for improvement, while developing the employee and a good relationship with him or her is another major objective for the department's long-term success. Managers must be cautious to not always strive for gaining immediate benefits at the cost of long-term success. Managers should work as coaches to enhance long-term performance.

The Coaching Challenge

Effective coaches encourage, inform, praise, raise awareness, collaborate, set clear expectations, serve as role models, empower, help, challenge, serve as vehicles for change, remove barriers, and enable others to reach their full potential. One should remember that coaching others to higher performance can be the single most important thing one does as a leader or manager in the workplace. Also, skilled managers and coaches never let good or poor performance go unnoticed. When effective coaches and managers see good performance, they say it and praise it. One should not let poor performance go unnoticed by saying it privately to the employee and making it positively anchored toward future performance. For real personal issues and poor personal habits: first, prepare the teammate/associate; and second, be gentle and to the point in stating the problem that needs fixing. The video titled *The Practical Coach,* which has been used by many corporations to train managers, offers many insights and suggestions on coaching for all leaders. The video offers a concept called the *"Two Minute Challenge"* with the following steps:

◊   First, state what you observed.
◊   Second, wait for a response.
◊   Third, remind the person of the goal.
◊   Fourth, ask for a specific solution.
◊   Fifth, jointly agree on the solution and its implementation.

Perhaps, some of these steps from *The Practical Coach* can apply to disciplining employees without punishment in order to effectively fix problems and enhance performance. A manager's responsibility, as a coach and as a leader, is best fulfilled when he or she maximizes long-term value for his or her department, organization, and the society through the use of available resources and effective discipline management approaches. Effective managers jointly and collaboratively work with their employees to increase each worker's commitment to the job, enhance his or her performance on each task, and maximize each associate's long-term value to the organization. The discipline without punishment approach, when applied correctly, can correct most behavioral and performance-related problems in the workplace without having to resort to progressive punishment or employee discharge and employment terminations. However, when all else fails, one can resort to progressive discipline, which can lead to employee discharge and termination if the problem is not resolved correctly in the required or agreed upon time.

Summary

Human beings have communicated for thousands of years; yet miscommunications seem to happen despite so much experience with it. Most people agree that communication skills are extremely important, especially for a diverse workforce and their effective management. The chapter stated that effective communication is the process of exchanging information in ways that ensure a mutual understanding of content and feelings; this includes being understood and heard. This chapter described listening and detailed the skills of empathic listening for effective communication with one's family members, friends, as well as one's colleagues in a diverse workforce. This chapter also offered suggestions and steps for effectively dealing with conflict in a diverse work environment through coaching and a fair discipline process.

Managers who are performance-focused and developmental in their management styles characteristically are usually concerned about the well-being and success of their employees. Effective managers attempt to avoid negative conflict through effective leadership and interpersonal skills. Furthermore, these managers understand the realities of conflict in a diverse organization and use appropriate conflict management styles in order to develop an effective team in the department.

Discussion Questions

1. What is effective communication? How is "effective communication" different from "communication"?
2. What is listening? How is listening different from hearing?
3. What are some common barriers to listening? How can one overcome such barriers in order to listen effectively?
4. What is empathic listening?
5. What are some techniques or listening leads that can be used when one is listening empathically?
6. Try the skill of empathic listening with four friends and colleagues; document your results. Also, try this technique with people that you do not know and document the results.
7. Is empathic listening easy, difficult, natural, or does it require conscious focus? Describe your thoughts as per your experience with your colleagues, family members, people you meet for the first time, and professionals in the community.
8. What are some common causes of conflict in a diverse workforce?
9. What is conflict? What is conflict management?
10. What are some best methods of managing conflict in the international arena?
11. What is an effective employee discipline process?
12. How can managers best use the "discipline without management" process to develop their employees? Have you seen managers use such a process effectively? If so, discuss.

Listening Scale Survey

You can rate yourself on the listening behaviors using the Listening Scale Survey (LSS) and the following guidelines:

4= Almost always
3= Most of the time
2= Some of the time
1= Almost never

Place a check mark in the appropriate box. Multiply the rating number at the top of the columns by the number of check marks in that rating area and record the results in the sub-total columns. Add the sub-totals and place the results in the area marked "Total Overall."

	When listening I do the following:	4	3	2	1
1.	I pay attention, even though the subject may bore me				
2.	I refrain from finishing the other person's sentences				
3.	I wait for the speaker to finish before evaluating the message				
4.	I maintain eye contact				
5.	I listen for feelings as well as subject matter				
6.	I show nonverbal responses to demonstrate I'm listening: nodding, smiling, leaning forward				
7.	I give brief verbal responses: "Uh-hum, M-m-m, Oh"				
8.	I stop myself from interrupting the one speaking to me				
9.	I seek to reduce or eliminate distractions				
10.	I ask questions only to clarify something said				
11.	I demonstrate I have an open mind and do not respond negatively to the other's ideas or feelings				
12.	I often paraphrase what I hear to make sure I have heard it correctly				
13.	I work to make myself really want to listen				
14.	I listen carefully to understand the main message				
15.	I maintain emotional control, no matter what is said				
16.	*Sub-totals*				
17.	*Total Overall*				

Now that you have determined your overall total from the Listening Scale Survey (LSS), you can use the following ranges of numbers to determine your listening score area:

50-60   -Congratulations! You are an excellent listener.

40-49   -Good going! You are a good listener, and you could be even better.

30-39   -Keep working on it. Listening skills will help you solve problems. Practice the skills of active and empathic listening when you can.

15-29 -You really should get serious about learning to listen. Take classes and learn active listening skills. Try to consciously focus on hearing others and what they are trying to communicate both verbally and non-verbally. Once you have mastered active listening techniques, then, focus on using empathic listening skills when emotions are involved, when you don't understand the speaker, and when the other person does not feel understood.

Conflict Resolution Survey

Effective leadership, management, and communication require an understanding of one's dominant conflict resolution style or one's natural tendencies. To understand your conflict resolution style, use the following scale to describe your typical behavior in conflict.

0 = I never behave this way
1 = I seldom behave this way
2 = I sometimes behave this way
3 = I often behave this way
4 = I very frequently behave this way

Review the following elements and give yourself a score of 0-5, as per the above scale, to determine your natural tendencies. Be honest and candid as you complete this survey.

___1. Insult the other person.
___2. Disregard the existence of a conflict.
___3. Passively comply with the other's demands.
___4. Seek a mutually beneficial solution.
___5. Seek a quick middle ground.
___6. Use threats to intimidate the other person.
___7. Postpone dealing with the issue.
___8. Sacrifice my own wishes for the sake of the other.
___9. Give information so the other can understand my feelings.
___10. Exchange concessions.
___11. Demand to have my way.
___12. Avoid communicating with the other person.
___13. Give in to the other person for the sake of harmony.
___14. Solicit information about the other's thoughts and feelings.
___15. Split the difference with the other person.
___16. Escalate the confrontation.
___17. Sidestep the area of disagreement.

___18. Protect my relationship with the other person rather than win the conflict.
___19. Explore alternative solutions to the problem.
___20. Bargain or trade with the other person.
___21. Punish the other person.
___22. Withdraw from the situation if it becomes threatening.
___23. Yield easily to the other's positions.
___24. Attempt to negotiate so that neither person must compromise.
___25. Concede some points in order to win some other points.
___26. Lose my temper.
___27. Change the topic to avoid confrontation.
___28. Let the other person have his/her way.
___29. Cooperate to find areas of agreement.
___30. Compromise.

Conflict response orientation survey calculation. To determine your conflict response orientation (CRO), calculate your conflict scores by adding the values marked for the question items in each column. The higher you score the greater your perceived tendency or orientation to utilize that specific communication style (Adapted from Tuttle, Waveland Press, 1985).

Competing	Avoiding	Accommodating	Collaborating	Compromising
1.	2.	3.	4.	5.
6.	7.	8.	9.	10.
11.	12.	13.	14.	15.
16.	17.	18.	19.	20.
21.	22.	23.	24.	25.
26.	27.	28.	29.	30.
Total =	Total =	Total =	Total =	Total =

"While vision inspires passion, many failed ventures are characterized by passion without patience" (Peter Senge, 1999).

Training Programs:
Preparation and Evaluation

*T*raining programs in the areas of teamwork, communication, diversity awareness, cultural competency, conflict management, and other such topics can enhance a diverse team's ability to get along and synergize. Upon attending a training workshop on diversity management, Bahaudin felt as though most of the participants did not get much out of it. Some of the participants were left feeling confused and most of them felt it was unrealistic for the company and the facilitators to expect them to absorb so much legal information in a short period of time. Many of the participants did not have a good understanding of the material and they were not sold on the ideas and concepts. The trainers were asked why they were rushing through the material as fast as they did without checking for understanding or reinforcement of the concepts. They responded by passing the responsibility onto the company officials who supposedly did not give them sufficient time or money to conduct the training in a more effective and participant-centered manner. They felt pressured to pass on all the pre-planned material to the participants and assumed the rest was not their responsibility. Contrary to the beliefs of a few individuals, almost all trainers and educators agree that assessment of participant's understanding and comprehension of the material is their responsibility.

This chapter[23] focuses on the need for assessment of learning, evaluation of training programs, and techniques that facilitators can use to make their diversity training innovative and more effective. Trainers should focus on influencing the learner's thoughts (head), the learner's feelings (heart), and each learner's behaviors (habits). The more techniques and strategies that trainers can use to impact the head, heart and habits of the audience, the more effective the session is likely to be in terms of the learner's participation with the activities, involvement with the exercises and long-term retention and application of the concepts presented. This chapter also emphasizes relevant concepts, thoughts and techniques that trainers can use in all their educational activities to increase the audience's involvement as well as their long-term retention and application of the training objectives.

---

[23] - This chapter is co-authored with Donovan A. McFarlane, St. Thomas University.

Training: its Need and Modality

Employees usually want relevant and effective training that can help them do their jobs better and so they can be prepared for future contribution opportunities to their respective fields. Minton-Eversole (2005) reports that of the 1,674 U.S. employees who responded to a poll conducted by Hudson in 2005, about 60 percent reported that the last training program was a good or great use of their time...however, 12 percent said their most recent training session was a total waste of time. While most training programs are very valuable, professional designers and facilitators need to continually make sure all of their sessions are productive and audience-centered.

There are a number of different goals for diversity training sessions. One prevalent goal is to minimize discrimination and harassment lawsuits. Other goals focus on improving acceptance and understanding of people with different backgrounds, experiences, capabilities, and lifestyles. Facilitations expectations and approaches to training vary based on the needs of the audience, but diversity related sessions often include at least three components (Kimberly Caleb, Personal Communication; May 20, 2006):

- *Legal awareness.* The initial step and most common component of diversity training. This training focuses on the legal implications of discrimination. A limited approach to diversity stop with these legal "dos and don'ts."
- *Cultural awareness.* Employers hope to build greater understanding of the differences among people. Cultural awareness training assists all participants to see and accept the differences in people with widely varying cultural backgrounds.
- *Sensitivity training.* This is more difficult. The aim is to "sensitize" people to the differences among them and show how their words and behaviors are seen by others. Some diversity training programs include exercises containing examples of harassment and other behaviors.

Legal awareness, cultural awareness, and sensitivity training topics are geared toward improving attitudinal and behavioral reactions toward diversity dimensions in the workplace. Training is a necessary activity in most organizations that deal with more than few employees, new technology or knowledge each and every day. The term "training" is synonymous with development, instruction, teaching, educating, guiding, coaching, preparing, developing, instructing, and other such words that deal with knowledge creation, acquisition, and transfer. Training can often deal with the transfer, guiding, development, coaching, and creation of certain technical skills to new or existing employees. Training can be from a father to son, from teacher to a student, from a colleague to another colleague, from an expert to an apprentice, from a trainer to a trainee, or from a manager to an employee. Training has been part of society since the beginning of time and now it is a formal part of most organizations. Training is both an art and a science as it requires knowledge, intuition, and skill. In the workplace, training often refers to activities which are strategically designed for the acquisition of knowledge and skills that are needed for immediate use and application (Cascio and Aguinis, 2005). While the term training is associated with skills that are used for short-term application, the term development usually implies the acquisition of qualities and attributes that help an employee become more competent in the long-term. It is important for trainers and managers to determine both the short and long term learning needs of their employees. As it has been said, if one does not know where he or she is going, then any road will be fine; however, if one knows where to go, then he or she is likely to get their faster and more efficiently. Furthermore, trainers should assess the trainee's readiness and trainability level. Cascio and Aguinis (2005) mention that the term "trainability" refers to the trainee's ability to learn the required skills, knowledge and behaviors for performing a job at a given level, and within the allotted time period.

While training is an important and often a mission-critical activity, many firms and senior leaders tend to think of it as a cost center, especially when they are not doing well compared to their competitors. Such thinking and paradigms are not effective conditions for innovation and creativity. Innovation in training requires time for creativity and experimentation which cannot be done when trainers are not certain whether they will have a job in the coming months or years. Ironically, these are the times when some firms reduce the training department's budget when in fact they should be increasing their investment on their people's development. When the times are tough, organizational leaders and trainers can clearly identify the benefits of training and demonstrate its return on investment. Trainers can demonstrate the value of training and learning within the organization by measuring hierarchical progress of employees, enhancement of morale, satisfied employees and customers, effective management, higher sales and profits, reduction of employee and customer complaints, and other tangible and intangible results. Furthermore, they should make sure that the training objectives are fully aligned with the company's strategic goals. Cascio and Aguinis emphasize that firms which provide sufficient opportunities for employee learning and growth tend to have a distinct advantage when they are competing for the recruitment and retention of superior talent in the industry (2005, p. 380). While training and development are critical, there are limits for their use and it is not always the solution to a company's structural or systems-related problems. Researchers have found various characteristics that differentiate successful firms in training and development practices from others and some of them are (Cascio and Aguinis, 2005):

1. Top management is committed to training and development as it becomes part of the culture.

2. Training is tied to business strategies and objectives. Training is linked to the bottom-line results.
3. Organization is flexible and can change accordingly to meet the developmental needs of its employees.
4. Organizational environments are "feedback-rich"; they stress continuous improvement, promote risk-taking, and afford opportunities to learn from the successes and failures of one's decisions.
5. There is commitment to invest the necessary resources, to provide sufficient time and money for training.

Companies should be investing in the development of their employees if they are to keep up with the competition in today's global and diverse environment of business. The best way to capture new sales, new markets, and higher profits is often through continuous innovation and creativity in delivering superior value to one's employees, the end-users and customers. The best way to achieve such superior results in today's competitive work environment is to invest an appropriate amount of a company's budget in employee training and development. Companies need to be innovative and keep up with their competitors by training their employees and developing their employee's minds, positively impacting their feelings, and making their behaviors more service-oriented. In other words, companies need to impact their employees' heads, hearts and habits if they are to remain innovative, productive and competitive in the twenty-first century's work environment. Companies that don't continually invest in employee training, creativity and development practices can suffer in the long-term. Studies have shown that creativity and innovation programs can help foster a culture of risk-taking, collaboration, out-of-the-box thinking, team synergy, and teamwork. Leaders must understand that innovation through an empowered and creative workforce is essential for a company's survival and long-term success in a competitive industry.

While training can be conducted in many formats and delivery modalities, today's employees can receive instruction and training without having to leave their offices. The virtual online classrooms have made learning and training easier both for trainers and trainees. Online training that is geared toward the needs of the audience can reduce costs since there is often no travel expense, buying of books, printing of workbooks, or ever having to leave the office at a specific time. Virtual training can take place asynchronously at one's own free time, at one's own preferred pace, and it can be conducted at the office, library or home. American firms from the United States tend to spend about $40 to $50 billion each year on training; furthermore, it is estimated that about 70% of the learning in the workplace is acquired through informal means (Cascio and Aguinis, 2005). In 2003, many of the large firms offered about 146 hours of training for their employees. The training comes both in formal and informal modalities through on-ground and virtual platforms. While about 60 to 70% of training is still conducted using regular or traditional modalities, more and more organizations are using the electronic media to conduct much of their training through web-based instruction, computer-based training, CD-ROMs, virtual classrooms, and video cassettes. One of the most impressive aspects of virtual or online training is that people learn at their own pace and time. Some employees learn faster than others and such innovative training techniques can make allowance for individualized learning preferences. Just like online academic classes, web-based training sessions can involve interactive activities with the trainer or instructor using virtual chatrooms, voice café, and teleconferencing. So, online or virtual training can be in real time and collaborative as needed according to the complexity of the material and the readiness of the trainees.

Some online software programs for virtual training can allow trainers to provide real-time audio instruction to the trainees. The trainers can be connected to the trainees' computers via intranet or the world-wide-web. In a real time virtual training scenario, trainers can point to or call on a trainee using the computer as do faculty members who hold synchronized chat sessions with their classes in the academic environment. The trainers can privately communicate to a trainee while the virtual session is being conducted or make the interaction public so others can benefit from what is being said or communicated. Most virtual training programs are set up to support various diverse teaching tools such as blackboard, e-university, WebCT, whiteboard, a training resource, proctored or real-time quizzes, Microsoft Word or Power-Point applications, and HTML files. Since there are many tools and options for various training sessions, facilitators should be careful in choosing the right platforms and software for their needs. Selecting the right virtual training option depends on the training activity and objectives as well as the skill level of the audience. Furthermore, each trainee's readiness level and competency with the software must also be considered. Most updates, policy changes, and dissemination of new information can easily be completed through virtual collaboration software. However, for training new employees or passing on complex information to existing employees, trainers should use a software program that offers interactive collaboration opportunities between the facilitator and learner. Trainers should also be aware that some skills such as driving a car, operating on a patient, running a new machine to manufacture products, and other such complex devices that need hand-on experience cannot be mastered through virtual platforms. However, most knowledge-based and routine training sessions can successfully be completed using web-based applications and modalities.

Assessment of Learning

Training and development of employees almost always imply behavioral changes in terms of their skill, knowledge, attitude toward work or the organization, and interpersonal relations with colleagues and co-workers. Since training and development take a trainee's valuable time away from his or her job, it is best that such sessions are planned and specific objectives are linked to desired performance for each position.

It is believed that both the company and the facilitators have the responsibility to make the participants' time worthwhile for them by giving them material that will help them personally and professionally. Of course, the facilitators can do their part by being better prepared and by teaching the material in such a way that is interactive, reflective, humorous, and pleasurable for everyone, including the trainers / facilitators.

Some corporate training programs are geared toward passing on the information to the participants in the most efficient manner, while the measuring instrument to determine efficiency is time. It is like trying to make each participant eat an entire loaf of fresh-baked, hard crusty Italian bread, which is not sliced, by shoving it down their throat from one end to the other. Of course the elimination of slicing, portioning, chewing, and adding other liquids or entrees of food would save time, money, aggravation, and accomplish the results without messing things up or having to wash a number of dishes after a full meal. People don't do this in real life to eat more "efficiently," then why should trainers facilitate too much information in a short period of time without allowing a few sufficient moments for the participants to understand, comprehend and reinforce the material through various activities that involve more of their senses.

The goal of some corporate training programs, especially large corporations, is to train as many participants as possible in the shortest period of time and at minimum cost. So, often the trainers lecture and pass on as much information as possible during the allotted time and hope that participants can make sense of it when they go back to their workstations. This might be analogous to the goal of teaching people how to fish by giving them more fish than they can carry at one time or eat in a week. Of course, by the end of the week they will be so tired of looking at fish that they would not even want to go near it, let alone find out how they can get more fish by themselves and the purpose behind learning how to fish. This is why most corporate training programs fail to accomplish its results and most often they are perceived to be factitious corporate attempts to build their public image. For example, companies that are introducing diversity or ethics training programs because of lawsuits or public image may have difficulty convincing their associates because most often the associates perceive the situation as a fake. Also, deceitful corporate attempts can create many more dissatisfied associates and customers who in turn can become highly litigious. So, fighting fires may not produce the same results as eliminating the root causes, which is where the focus should be.

Call it an aberration in the authors' level of thinking, but shouldn't the goal of any training program be to help participants learn, think, and even act differently than they did prior to attending the training session? This is a totally different view as opposed to passing on information as if the participants were tape recorders or video recorders retaining everything for replay or reproduction at a later date. If we want them to learn, think, and act differently, then we would need to examine the participant's level of new knowledge and how they are planning to use this new knowledge in their workstations. Therefore, the new level of knowledge and its application should be the measuring devise or instrument as opposed to simply passing on information in the shortest period of time at a minimum cost.

So, trainers should appropriately "feed" participants what they can "chew" at a given period of time and each "bite" should be measured and flavored to the participant's taste and preference. Even then one should consider the digestion process and the time required between the feeding periods because everyone likes eating good food, but too much of a good thing can make a person very sick. Corporate training programs should be based on the concepts of andragogy which focuses on the art and science of teaching adults. Great emphasis should be placed on the involvement of adult learners in the process of self-diagnosis of needs for learning. The concept of andragogy assumes that people will experience greater learning if they see the need for it. People also want their past experiences integrated into the new learning so it makes perfect sense for them. Otherwise, they will not be supportive of the new material. The following are some hints for corporate trainers to keep participants awake and make the training worth their time:

1. Training should be a hands-on experience, involving participants.
2. Assist participants to develop their own answers. Life is a do-it-yourself process.
3. Help participants convert ideas and theories into action which increases learning.
4. Make the session pleasurable and fun for everyone because humor can help reduce stress and anxiety and increases learning.
5. Training should be designed to meet the objectives of all stakeholders.
6. Training should increase knowledge, get participants emotionally involved, and provide opportunities for using the new knowledge.
7. People cannot always be motivated for long periods through extrinsic incentives. Everyone is intrinsically motivated to accomplish worthwhile things. People take action because they *personally* feel strong about it. Have personal contact with participants and be aware of their needs.
8. Get participants involved and keep their interest high in the session by telling them what is in it for them.
9. Give specific examples, to keep their interest, that everyone can relate to and understand.
10. Encourage, welcome, and thank people for participation and for sharing their life experiences to make the content more relevant.
11. Make everyone feel as though they are the owners of the company and create a sense of personal responsibility where people are intrinsically motivated by their feelings and actions.

12. Be excited about the session and show enthusiasm.
13. The average person speaks about 110 to 160 words per minute and thinks at a rate of 400 to 500 words per minute. So, use visual presentations which can help participants learn more while keeping their attention focused on the content as opposed to daydreaming on the beach.

As a trainer, one should aim to express, not impress, by only feeding what the participants are able to take-in during a given period of time. The feeding should be based on a need to satisfy their hunger and not to shut people up by keeping their mouths busy. So, as per the concept of situational leadership, trainers should "feed" participants as per their level of hunger for knowledge and readiness to absorb, digest, retain, and apply the new material to their current work environment.

Techniques for Effective Training

The traditional rule of thumb for training people has been a five step process, which is: tell them (trainees or learners) what needs to be done, show them how it needs to be done, let them tell you how the job should be done, let them show you how they are doing the job, and collaboratively set goals for further development and/or the next session's objectives as needed. While the traditional five step process seems easy, it can be very complex as the "telling" and "showing" can be conducted in may different varieties and modalities. Cascio and Aguinis (2005, p. 16) discuss that training and development techniques fall into the three general categories of information presentation, simulation methods, and on-the-job training.

1. *Information presentation* techniques can include lectures, conference methods, correspondence sources, videos, compact disks, reading lists, interactive multimedia, intranet and internet, systematic observations, and long-range organizational development plans such as succession planning and development programs.
2. *Simulation methods* can include case studies, analysis of various incidents, role-playing, experiential exercises, task models, in-basket techniques, business games, assessment centers, and behavior or competency modeling.
3. *On-the-job training* methods can include orientation programs, apprenticeships, on-the-job training, near-the-job training, job rotation, understudy assignments, executive coaching, and performance management techniques.

Many innovative trainers and organizations have integrated some of the aforementioned techniques with computer-based training programs. Computer-based training, as explained by Cascio and Aguinis (2005), is the "presentation of text, graphics, video, audio, or animation via computer for the purpose of building job-relevant knowledge and skills" of trainees. Whatever modality trainers use to transfer knowledge or skill to learners, they should use a formal training process to document the process for consistency and learning accumulation. Figure 15.1, the Training Model and Process, provides one process that trainers can adapt for their usage. As can be seen from the model, identification of the training needs and objective is the initial starting point, and learning from the process through formal evaluation of the results for continuous improvement purposes is the last step.

Regardless of the modality used for training, professionals should become aware of and involve different teaching techniques and facilitation methods to enhance the learning process for their adult audience. In other words, trainers should use as many mediums and approaches as possible to impact the thoughts (head), feelings (heart), and behaviors (habits) of their learners. As advocated by facilitators and trainer at Publix Super Market's Education and Training Development Department in the late 1990s, every educator should have a *Multiple Intelligence Toolbox* that lists possible activities that could be incorporated into the training program or activity. The purpose of such a list is to get trainers to think about how they might vary the activities within a training session to optimize learning through audience-centered sessions.

In an effort to make training more effective and satisfying, educators should evaluate the learning strategies that they incorporate into the programs and activities that they develop. If educators understand how the brain works and the way people learn, they can develop activities that will engage the learner and help them to learn better (Publix Training, 1999). The analysis and design of a course are crucial, but if the intended learning is to actually take place, the learning experience has to address multiple intelligences and different learning styles. The goal is to meet associates' training needs in the most effective way applying the most current brain research. The following thoughts and suggestions come from experts, trainers, and educators (such as Eric Jensen and his book entitled *Brain Compatible Strategies, 1997*).

One task of trainers and educators is to help associates grow out and not necessarily fill up with information. The traditional method of training for some trainers has been to plan the content. The traditional method could be considered backwards or upside down. According to experts, the brain-based way for training and education is simple; it's planning for learning by adding outward to expand existing knowledge. Trainers can extend natural knowledge, re-frame knowledge, or change the context of the application. This approach is more audience-centered, customer-based, learner-compatible, and user-friendly. Learners can't know a trainer's experience base, the details, the emotions, or his or her depth of information and intentions. So the best and only place for learners to start learning is from what they already know, their current knowledge and experiences. Innovative trainers can change the traditional model of training from a "fill up" their brains approach to "grow out" their brains concept.

Innovative trainers and facilitators can use multiple strategies to help the audience be involved in the learning process and have better recall of the information for possible future applications. Research suggests that one's memories are not stored in any picture form. We tend to simply recreate them on the spot, each time one wants to recall something. There's no memory center in the learner's brain, but the learner can recall things with an impromptu composition by all the triggered experiences. This means that one's existing memories will change with new knowledge, experimentation and more information. People's experiences, values, beliefs, and biases can alter their memories. One assumption is that the greater the variety of learning input, the more accurate the recall will be both in the short and long-terms. Sights, smells, sounds, and touch all create (as a whole) more complex and rich memories than a workbook or a multi-media CD. The learners, even under the best of conditions, need continual opportunities to share, discuss, map, journal, teach, and reorganize the learning; this reinforcement process not only keeps information and new knowledge fresh, but it encourages deeper meaning and reflections.

Figure 15.1 – Training Model and Process

Participants tend to get a deeper and greater meaning from multiple contexts. Experts explain that when learning occurs, cells grow branch-like extensions called dendrites (Publix Training, 1999). Each dendrite provides another pathway with which to make connections. What is called "greater depth of meaning" simply means cells making more connections and new pathways to other cells. The secret for educators and trainers are to provide multiple contexts for learning the same concepts over an extended period of time. That means the more ways people learn something, in more situations, with more intelligences, emotions, and forms of media, the better. This allows learners to access their learning far easier, at a later time for application in the workplace.

Experts recommend teaching in such a way that make learners reflect and think. In other words, it is best to get their head (thoughts and knowledge), heart (feelings) and habits (behaviors) involved in the training process. Research suggests that feelings are critical to the learning process in many ways. Feelings help determine:

- If a learner wants to learn a subject,
- How one feels about a subject,
- Whether one wants to learn about a subject,
- If one believes whether the information is true,
- Whether one is able to apply the information to his or her daily activities, and
- How long one remembers the information.

Learners can understand a topic without having feelings about it, but it may not mean as much to them until an emotion is attached to it. It simply is not real to the brain until one feels it is real. Learning without feelings is incomplete as it may not last for long nor be applied into the workplace. Perhaps the brain is analogous to a box packed with emotions. So, the question for a trainer becomes, "How can one integrate emotions more productively into the learning process?"

Regardless of the current techniques used by trainers to make their sessions more innovative and more effective, it is always best to understand and become aware of new strategies and terminologies applied in facilitation activities. Some of the more unfamiliar terms and techniques for learning activities with new trainers are as follows (as presented by facilitators at Publix based on the work of experts such as Jenson, 1997).

- *Active imagination* is using one's mind to discover pictures, shapes and designs. It can also create visual relationships and intuitive connections which transform apparent chaos and confusion into a place of creativity and imagination.
- A *classifying matrix* is a way of classifying things on a chart with certain categories across the top and others down the side of the chart; items in the chart must meet the criteria of both the top and side category.
- A *cognitive organizer* is a visual aid that helps learners order and patterns their thinking in ways that are both logical and that promote higher order reasoning.

- *Cross laterals* are body movements that involve the right side of the body interacting with the left side of the body. *Cross laterals* force the brain to talk to itself and use both hemispheres. The purpose is to activate the brain through movement. For example, touching hands to opposite knees is a *cross lateral* movement.
- *Each one teach one* is an interactive group strategy in which each person in a group learns something and then teaches it to the others in the group. This is similar to a three-person teaching process where each person takes turn teaching his or her learning to the other two group members.
- *Empathy practices* develop sensitivity to another person's perspective and feelings. We work on ourselves and then transfer this skill to real situations with other people
- *Forced relationships* are finding connections between things that normally would have no relationship. However, when forced together, they make perfect sense. For example, how is a radio like an apple?
- *Guided imagery* is a thinking process that activates one's imagination and capacity to pretend. The facilitator *guides* the imagery.
- A *human graph* is a thinking strategy that asks people to physically stand along a spectrum that indicates how they feel or think about an issue. Privilege walk exercise, which is often conducted in diversity training workshops, is one example.
- *KWL (*what do you *know,* what do you *want* to know, what have you *learned) goal setting* is a graphic organizer that helps one assess prior knowledge and current questions for a learning task, and then to assess what was actually learned after the task is completed.
- The literal meaning of *metacognition* is "thinking about thinking"; the ability to step back from a situation in which you are involved and watch yourself.
- *Mindfulness* is the ability to observe your thoughts, feelings, actions, and sensations in a detached, objective way without getting caught up in emotions, opinions, intellectual ideas or theories, and immediate reactions.
- *Multi-tracking* is any physical exercise that involves performing several different actions simultaneously (i.e., rubbing the stomach and patting the top of the head while jogging in place).
- A *syllogism* is an argument or form of reasoning in which two statements or premises are made and a logical conclusion drawn from them. For example, all mammals are warm-blooded; whales are mammals; therefore whales are warm-blooded.
- *Turn to your partner and...*is an interactive strategy in which two people who are seated next to each other discuss and/or process information, share feelings and thoughts, and explore ideas.

The Four Levels of Training Evaluation

Training programs must be a constant and vibrant part of organizational structure, development and settings in order to attain growth, effective transition, and achieve strategic goals. The success of training programs in today's organizations will dictate the failures and successes along the path of performance and market vitality. Training programs are the most effective, subtle and passive method of overcoming resistance to change and represent the most viable approach to cultivating new philosophies and values in employees. The development of effective training programs has seen successful invention and implementation over the last few decades, especially with the available technological and training tools we have amassed. The most pressing need therefore lies in the effective evaluation of implemented training programs to ensure organizational success in a high-culture learning environment. Kirkpatrick and Kirkpatrick (2006) have provided the most comprehensive, extensive and widely used approach to evaluate training programs in corporate, government, academic and other business and institutional areas.

Kirkpatrick and Kirkpatrick's book entitled *Evaluating Training Programs: the Four Levels* is an indispensable tool; a guide for developing a reliable method of evaluation suitable within the business, institutional or organizational context. Kirkpatrick and Kirkpatrick's Four Level Model focuses on four fundamental elements of effective evaluation: reaction, learning, behavior, and results. The authors outline ten simple factors which should be taken into consideration when planning and implementing an effective training program. These steps or factors are:

- Determine needs,
- Set the objectives,
- Determine the subject content,
- Select the participants,
- Determine the best schedule,
- Select the appropriate facilities,
- Select and prepare the audiovisual aids,
- Coordinate the program, and finally,
- *Evaluate* the program. Evaluation is the last step in the process of planning and implementing an effective training program in any organizational setting. It is the tenth step that will ultimately spell success or failure as far as training programs are concerned, and thus Kirkpatrick and Kirkpatrick (2006) see the evaluation process as critical.

According to Kirkpatrick and Kirkpatrick (2006) it is extremely critical that professionals evaluate training programs for the following three main reasons: to justify the existence and budget of the training department by showing how it contributes to the organizational objectives and goals; to decide whether to continue or discontinue training programs; and to gain information on how to improve future training programs. The second reason to decide whether to continue or discontinue training programs, is extremely important in today's changing business environment. Only effective training programs will produce organizational value on any level by increasing people value and complementing the other facets or value drivers. Therefore, evaluation becomes a source of measuring several things: effectiveness, potential success, resistance level, workability-applicability, progress, and even quality along a continuum.

In defining the four levels which constitute the Four Level Model of Evaluating Training Programs, Kirkpatrick and Kirkpatrick (2006) identify and describe *reaction* as a process where evaluation at this stage measures how well those who participate in the program react to it. This reiterates the need to ascertain levels of organizational resistance, adaptability to change and the change process. Level two; *learning*, is defined as the extent which participants change their attitudes, improve knowledge, and/or increase skill as a result of attending the program. The change in behavior brought about by the training program will communicate the effectiveness of the training as far as its ability to contribute to organizational and people value, eliminate and change aversive behaviors, and help foster and engrain the new approaches, methods or operations management is putting into place. According to Kirkpatrick and Kirkpatrick, *behavior* is simply the extent to which behavior change occurred because the participants attended the training program. Kirkpatrick and Kirkpatrick emphasize the importance of this third level in the model by stating that in order for change to occur, the following four conditions must be met: persons must have a desire to change; persons must know what to do and how to do it; persons must work in the right climate; and persons (employees) must be rewarded for change, that is, positive change. On this same level, the authors state that the right climate for effective training programs and eventual success of such programs must be present. By the "right climate" Kirkpatrick and Kirkpatrick refer to the positivity or negativity of the training environment, that is; the environment will be either preventing, discouraging, neutral, encouraging, or requiring. The final level in the model is *results*, which the authors define as the final results such as increased production, improved quality, decreased costs, reduced frequency and/or severity of accidents, increased sales, reduced turnover, and higher profits that occurred because the participants or employees attended the training program. So according to Kirkpatrick and Kirkpatrick, the four levels of evaluation for any training program are reaction, learning, behavior, and results.

Organizational Training Programs (OTPs) are long-term value investments (LVIs) which companies must see as part of their essential strategies and plans for future success in the global village or future society, where keeping up with technological and corporate developments in a competitive arena will be the absolute norm. The evaluation of training programs is the most significant factor underlying their testimony as worthwhile corporate investments. The cost-center approach to training program development and evaluation that is the traditional typical perspective of today's organizational leaders and managers will not facilitate positive organizational attitude towards the implementation of effective training programs. Management must view training programs as part of organizational growth, expansion and adaptive learning. Thus, the evaluation of training programs must be based upon the critical factors Kirkpatrick and Kirkpatrick advocate in the Four Levels Model, along with other organizationally-specific criteria. Organizationally-specific criteria are of utmost importance in the process, and as such, must be very clear in terms of their alignment with the training program goals and those of the entire organization. When leaders and managers are developing and evaluating implemented training programs, they must always keep the organizationally salient considerations parallel across the board. If organizational training programs are incongruent with organizational goals, vision, and mission, they are strategically useless and a waste of time, money and other resources.

The management of a diverse workforce is better facilitated by effective training programs which identify the needs of employees from every angle with regards to their differences and how these invariably add to organizational innovativeness and capacity building. As such, training programs cannot be standardized. Each organization will require critically developed programs which reflect the nature of their current and future needs, the needs of the diverse workforce, and the utilization of the resources they have on hand. When training programs are diversity-based they can pose more difficult challenges for managers and consultants to evaluate, especially if organizationally-specific goals are based on diversity integration with significant structural assessments developed around diversity issues and concepts such as affiliations, gender, ethnicity or the like. The best advice we would offer is not to develop and evaluate training programs with these physical factors at heart, but to concentrate on the four factors: reaction, learning, behavior, and results in terms of employees without emphasis on differential cohorts. When evaluation is aimed at any specific group or groups of employees however, such evaluation is usually relevant to assess integration into organizational corporate culture, and are relevant in assessing the needs of such a group or groups.

Training programs should reflect critical organizational needs and issues, especially in today's environment where change in the external environment of the organization have greater effects than they did in the past. For example, the ongoing wars; major political changes bringing about consequential economic and legal problems is affecting MNCs (multinational corporations) and all other organizations on all levels in different nations and regions. Thus, training programs must be developed and likewise, evaluated according to the firm's or organization's and employees' needs along the line of changes and the responses to them. Effective training programs when evaluated will reveal themselves as those that effectively address changes and the resistance to them, and Kirkpatrick and Kirkpatrick's reaction and learning factors in the Four Levels Model of evaluating training programs will effectively assess the foregoing.

The evaluation of training programs should take place on a continuous basis, and like all operations in business should be controlled and monitored with established standards or against established criteria. Many organizational leaders make the error of not evaluating training programs. In many organizations, even when professional consultants are hired to develop effective and superior training programs to improve organizational success and performance, such programs fail, and often for one major reason: such programs are left unmonitored after the consultants do their part and leave the organization. Sometimes the current management lacks the proper skills and techniques to effectively evaluate such training programs, especially to determine their pros and cons in terms of costs and benefits in accurate financial or measurable terms. When training programs go unevaluated they can become dormant and useless, and result in a loss of valuable time and other organizational resources. The importance of evaluating training programs along the line of organizational-wide performance measurement standards and criteria cannot be overemphasized. In fact, an added dimension is that of contingency planning striving out of the results of evaluation which will help in strategy formulation and program improvement or redesign.

While Kirkpatrick and Kirkpatrick (2006) advocate reaction, learning, behavior, and results as the four key components of evaluation in training programs, it is important to know that training programs should be evaluated along the following lines and with these factors as major considerations:

1. Organizational goals, mission and vision.
2. Corporate culture convergence and social integration.
3. Employees' and organization's needs.
4. Task-specific functional needs, goals and processes.
5. Goal-strategy formulation and implementation.
6. Establishment and measurement of performance standards.
7. Total quality concepts and process improvement.
8. As a part of competitive strategy and response to internal and external organizational forces and problems.
9. As part of the organizational SWOT (strengths, weaknesses, opportunities, threats) approach to developing or enhancing competitive advantage through human resources development.
10. Human resources development planning and workforce efficiency.
11. Productivity considerations and targets.
12. Value constraints planning and innovation responses.
13. As an alternative method to outsourcing because of lack of internal labor specialization and strength in specific area.
14. As a long-term cost-saving strategy, and
15. To foster effectiveness and efficiency at all levels in the organization.

When training programs are evaluated solely within narrow confines, that is, only with the intention of assessing the worth or value of the program itself rather than its results and overall effects based on long-term perspectives and organizational directives, such programs can be easily mistaken by impatient managers lacking proper assessment skills to be useless and hence discarded before they prove their worth.

Training programs take time to yield benefits, and thus, reaction, learning, behavior and results might not be readily observable, and most are only identifiable in processes and tasks where employees have the opportunities to apply their training. This brings an important consideration with it. Some organizational leaders and managers implement excellent training programs, often for the wrong reasons or wrong purpose. Not every problem that appears to require training as a solution requires it. Sometimes all that is needed is employee motivation from the top down. Often, in many organizations there are qualified employees who are hired to work, and this is more of a fact today than before since more and more people are getting college degrees and great formal training in the fields they end up working in. When such qualified individuals seem to have job-task problems, it could simply be that they are dissatisfied with work, the work environment, the rewards and other internal organizational factors, or simply personal and other problems. Hence, a training program might not cut it for such individuals, but rather high motivation and work-employee value ethics from a caring and socially friendly organizational culture. There are cases where individual employees can be very well skilled in their professional work ethics, abilities and tasks, but their performance does not indicate this. In such a case, rather than rapidly implementing training, an industrial psychologist might be a very good consultant to deal with issues on a person-to-person basis. Often, training programs are for teams, groups or departments, and not for individuals.

The individualization of employee training programs is a difficult task and can represent high costs to firms. Therefore, training programs are often designed without individually-specific needs and problems in mind. Managers and leaders are often more concerned with synergy, and thus the specific effects on a department, branch, or group's performance, than on that of a particular individual. This lack of attention to individual effects in training program development, implementation, and evaluation can be a costly error. Often when these training programs fail to yield expected results, managers are perplexed and troubled by the costs and waste of resources, including time. Many times, training programs fail to meet individual-specific needs, and hence, are of no significance to such individuals and their reaction, learning, behavior, and results remain the same, worsen or are dramatically different from expectations and those of their team members. In such a case, synergy may not take place and managers discard an effective training program rather than modify or improve its elements to cater to unique individuals. In addition, not all employees can be trained into proficiency. Some employees will have limitations in tasks, while others will be slow in developing skills, and training programs which are short-term will not really help such individual employees.

Training programs are very valuable tools and do have their pros and cons. The biggest disadvantage of training programs is the level of resistance and resentment they can cause to develop in some employees with negative attitudes towards training. For example, employees who are very formally qualified and those who have been in the organization for a long time and performing a specific task or job function for a long time might feel that training is a waste of time, and even an insult to their years of education and work expertise and experience. It is important in this case to educate employees about the need for training and training evaluation in order to encourage participative attitudes and motivation. In educating employees about the need for training, managers and organizational leaders should let employees know that training purpose is three-fold: it helps develop physical skills, cognitive skills and social-motivational skills. When most employees hear the word training they think only about the development of either physical or cognitive skills. However, training can be a powerful tool for modifying employees' behavior as far as their social skills and levels of motivation affect organizational goals and outcomes. Many employees are highly skilled at their job tasks, but fail to meet productivity goals and targets because of their social attitudes stemming from:

1. Failure to adjust to work environment.
2. Failure to adjust to corporate culture.
3. Personality problems and issues.
4. Inability to handle work load because of social unrest.
5. Personal problems which interfere with work performance.
6. Lack of motivation.
7. Inability to work as part of team or group.
8. Resistance to work ethics and policies.
9. Medical or health problems which cause mood changes, and
10. Lack of a supportive, caring and rewarding work environment.

Organizationally productive training programs are those that do not fall short of managerial expectations, they live up to performance expectations, evaluation criteria standards, improve employees' performances in all areas; social, cognitive, and physical, by positively affecting behavior, bringing about learning, developing the appropriate reaction and producing expected results even above what they have been implemented to yield. Organizationally productive training programs produce synergy within teams, groups and departments, and appropriately respond to the issues they are designed to address; both individual and organizational.

Managers should be very keen on eliminating prejudices when evaluating training programs. Training program evaluation should be an objective process. When using Kirkpatrick and Kirkpatrick's (2006) Four Levels of evaluation, managers should objectively evaluate training programs to identify those behaviors, reactions, results, and learning that are specific to and stem from the implemented and current training program as opposed to those which stem from other factors within or outside of the organization. Sometimes employees' reactions and behaviors are not the result of the implemented training program. One of the ideals that organizations must embrace is that of constant development and monitoring to ensure that the training program is modified or expanded to address issues arising constantly. Change invariably affects all the four factors Kirkpatrick and Kirkpatrick propose. They however fail to provide sufficient detail on how this constant change will affect the evaluation process as change affects the degree to which each factor becomes relevant at any point in time in evaluating programs. For example, when should managers specifically emphasize reaction over behavior and vice versa? Another issue is that the four levels are too closely interrelated to work with for some programs and to be effectively used in some settings. In fact, reaction, learning, and behavior all seem to stress the affective or social aspect of training, and results is a very broad area encompassing these along with the physical outcomes such as productivity measures of performance and change. Learning is often defined as a relatively permanent change in behavior as a result of experience. Thus, Kirkpatrick and Kirkpatrick's four levels can prove complicated and repetitive when the definitional perception of each level is broadened. Moreover, the level of knowledge required to apply these training evaluation factors effectively will vary according to situation and organization, as well as individual evaluator skills and understanding of these. This is perhaps the greatest criticism of the four levels proposed by these experts. However, the applicability and usage have been very widespread over the years.

Because organizations are so varied in their structures and processes and individuals are unique, there is no one best method to evaluate a training program. Even though the Four Levels Model has been used most widely and extensively by many corporate, government, academic and other business institutions and fields, there are several other methods and recommendations by other experts. We will take a look at some of the other possible methods and approaches for evaluating training programs in organizations.

According to Gibson, Ivancevich, Donelly, and Konopaske (2003), the structuring of training programs along with their performance evaluation are relevant steps in effective accommodation socialization. As such, training programs are invaluable in the break-in-stage for instructing new employees in proper techniques, and to help them develop requisite skills. Gibson et al. argue that effective training programs [and effective evaluation of such programs] provide frequent feedback about progress in acquiring relevant skills. These writers seem to emphasize training programs from the traditional viewpoint of skills development. Training programs must appropriately address social-behavioral skills, and not just "proper techniques" in task functionality and progress. For the evaluation aspect of training programs Gibson et al. focus on both the individual and non-individual aspects. Unlike many writers they see the value of evaluation from an individual rather than a group-based perspective. However, both methods should be combined effectively if the true worth or value of training programs is to be ascertained. Evaluation must be a managerial process according to Gibson and colleagues, hence, the use of management by objectives and behaviorally anchored rating scales must be employed as important training program evaluation tools.

The authors earlier communicated the idea that most training programs are designed for groups and with groups rather than individual considerations in mind. Gibson et al. (2003) seem to support this as they state the rationale for training and training programs. According to Gibson et al. (2003), training is a team or group oriented act because individuals are being asked to put aside personal concerns and contribute to a group's effort. Thus, they argue that members usually need training in the following areas: team building, listening, and communication that will counteract attitudes and habits left over from previous work environments [and individual behavioral and personal social values].

Wheelen and Hunger (2000) see training and its evaluation relevant as strategic requirements in an organization. This is in agreement with the necessity of evaluating training along strategic dimensions; formulation, development and considerations as stated above by the authors much earlier. According to Wheelen and Hunger staffing requirements are likely to follow a change in strategy, whether in the form of promotions or new hires, and therefore, training and evaluation will become relevant. They further identify training as a retentive tool in organizations as new strategic initiatives are put into action and require new skills and talents. Wheelen and Hunger mainly see training and training evaluation from a strategy perspective and a productivity perspective, and rightly so, since they are well-known experts in the area of strategy.

Bahaudin has long been a management trainer and has amassed a good body of knowledge on training programs and their evaluation over the years. The authors of this chapter firmly believe that the goals of any established and implemented training program should be centered upon individual needs – helping the individual participant to develop new or better thinking methods, learning, and behavior which reflect the effectiveness of the training session when one compares individual values, behavior, reaction, learning, and even results prior to such a session. This should be the case since a relatively permanent change in behavior or attitude as a result of training will communicate the program's effectiveness in effectuating change at some levels. Whatever philosophy one holds about training programs and their evaluation, today's diverse multicultural and competitive global business environment is one where change is the only moderator of performance effectiveness and success. Training programs designed and evaluated with this perspective in mind are those that will yield the highest results and become valuable to organizational survival and employees' motivation.

Encouraging Training Innovation

Trainers and organizational leaders should take sufficient time to determine what innovative learning and development activities they want to initiate and integrate at their organizations. Training leadership is sometimes about successfully navigating organizational politics and drumming up the necessary support for innovative employee development approaches to make the needed activities available for the company's most important asset, their human resources. Brandon Hall's 2005 article, entitled *Training*, provides a look at three examples in training and development and how they used innovative thoughts, ideas and concepts in their organizations. Hall discussed innovative training approaches from General Mills, Lockheed Martin, and Intel.

Getting Things Done at General Mills. Kevin Wilde is Vice President and Chief Learning Officer at Minneapolis-based food manufacturer, General Mills. The company doubled in size after acquiring its competitor Pillsbury. Generally speaking, after a company completes an acquisition employees often seem to have two jobs: they continue to do their usual jobs or tasks, and they need to learn to integrate with the newly combined organization. But after the acquisition of Pillsbury, some of General Mills workers struggled with the second task (learning to integrate with the newly combined organization). Many employees at General Mills were concerned about how they were going to get everything done. Eventually, one senior manager saw his workload spinning out of control and hired an outside coach to help him change his workflow. The coach helped him focus on the priorities (big projects) rather than simply processing work from his in-basket. When others in the firm noticed these improvements, they wanted similar coaching, and soon demand for such coaching outpaced capacity. So, the team worked with the coach to create a custom training program that incorporated this "Getting Things Done" approach. Day one focused on training the concepts, ideas, and principles behind this new methodology so managers can focus on the "big projects." On day two, participants were required to go on a field trip to their own offices and put into action the procedures they learned on the previous day. From one executive coaching session, within one year, the program has grown to over 500 attendees and is expected to draw about 3,000 participants over a two-year period.

Preparing Internal Coaches at Lockheed Martin. It was determined that one of Lockheed Martin's strategic priorities for the organization was talent development. They wanted to identify and groom high performers who can take on future leadership positions. As a result, Marilyn Figlar, Vice President of Learning and Organizational Development at the defense and aerospace technology company in Bethesda, MD, began to focus on the talent development mandate. Figlar decided to go beyond the usual leadership development activities. The organization had successfully used outside coaches for executive level senior managers in the past. Now, they wanted to extend this coaching and development opportunity to high potentials as well. However, they also understood that outside coaches can be expensive, especially when it is being offered to a large group of potential participants. Consequently, instead of using outside coaches, Figlar created a certification program to train their own human resource employees to become certified coaches. Within a short period of time, nearly 200 HR professionals completed the required training and became certified coaches. This was an excellent employee development program for the human resource professionals in the company as they learned new skills and competencies. Furthermore, these internal coaches in human resources can now serve the coaching needs of the company for the years to come much more efficiently than outside coaches.

Pockets of Excellence at Intel. Ron Dickson is the knowledge and learning research strategist at Intel Corp., which manufactures semiconductors in Santa Clara, Calif. Dickson's innovation is an annual internal awards program to recognize excellence among the training professionals at Intel. This awards function is more than a recognition program because their practices can also serve as best practices and models for others within the firm. When candidates submit their paperwork of new practices, they are capturing valuable project ideas which are made available to others inside the firm. The 130 entrants over a two-year period indicate that interest is high. They want to locate pockets of excellence in the organization and encourage others to freely benchmark these techniques and adapt them to their own work practices. With about 1,000 trainers at Intel, this is a way to stand out and be recognized because the entries are posted internally and winners are highlighted on the corporate Web site.

Innovation and creativity take time, courage, expertise, and out-of-the-box thinking. As such, leaders and managers should encourage such initiatives as they contribute to new approaches for productivity and best practices in the field. In the twenty first century's competitive work environment, there is a strong need for professional trainers to be involved in best practices as well as in integrating various web-based virtual sessions and appropriate brain-based learning approaches into their the classrooms and employee development activities. Experts and organizational should encourage all training professionals to stay updated through personal development programs, think outside-of-the-box, take calculated risks, challenge the status quo, and make something significant happen in their organizations and industries each year.

Summary

Training is an important activity as it can increase a learner's knowledge, the person's productivity and change his or her behavior in the workplace. This chapter focused on the need for assessment of learning, evaluation of training programs, and techniques that facilitators can use to make their training more effective. Trainers should focus on influencing the learner's thoughts (head), the learner's feelings (heart), and each learner's behaviors (habits) for long-term retention and application of the material. The more techniques and strategies that trainers can use to impact the head, heart and habits of the audience, the more effective the session is likely to be in terms of the learner's participation with the activities, involvement with the exercises and long-term retention and workplace application of the concepts presented.

Discussion Questions

1. Have you ever attended a diversity training program or any other training program that you thought was a "waste of time"? What could have the facilitators done differently to make sure the workshop was more effective? Discuss.

2. What is assessment? What can trainers do to effectively assess their workshops and training programs?

3. What is learning and how can a workshop result in learning? How would one know that learning has taken place? Discuss.

4. What are some innovative training techniques that you have seen in the last few years? What made them innovative?

5. Discuss two techniques that trainers and facilitators can use to involve the learners.

6. What should a diversity training program include? Discuss the content and how it could be assessed.

7. Can organizations use mentoring and coaching programs to bring about behavioral changes in their new employees? Discuss and provide examples.

8. Discuss and describe specific examples of the four levels of evaluation that are described by Kirkpatrick and Kirkpatrick.

9. What can trainers do to assess the reaction of workshop participants? Discuss.

10. There are many firms and organizations with comprehensive and documented diversity programs. Several of the companies that offer comprehensive diversity program include Publix Super Markets, American Express, Bank of America, Coca Cola, Allstate, Deloitte & Touche, Cracker Barrel, and Denny's Restaurants. Some of these companies created these programs proactively and some created them reactively to make sure their people are treated with respect and dignity. Go to these companies' corporate offices or Internet websites and see what unique programs they have for diversity initiatives and trainings. Document your findings.

11. Using the training model presented, design a training program for a specific aspect of diversity. The training program could be two hours, four hours, one day, or several days as per the needs of the audience. Provide an outline of the topics that must be covered and then discuss each step in the design process.

Diversity: the Engine for Success

E mployee discipline, terminations and retention are facts of life in both homogeneous and heterogeneous places of work. However, these processes do not have to be negative as they can be objectively used for an employee's developmental needs. Similarly, terminating employees, who are not the right match for the job, are very important elements of organizational capacity building as well as a manager's responsibility in the institution. Managers, who are performance-focused and developmental in their leadership and management styles, usually are concerned about the well-being and success of their employees. They attempt to avoid employee termination, discipline, and discharge by recruiting and retaining the right individuals from the outset, while developing and assisting them to achieve the stated objectives through situational leadership styles and appropriate management skills. Along with appropriate interviewing, hiring, and training practices, managers also need to learn effective skills for coaching employee performance to retain successful and committed employees. This chapter provides a summary of diversity concepts, an overview of diversity philosophy, and the science of employee success and retention.

Diversity: The Poster Child of Social Progress and Change[24]

Diversity is having a long reign as the 'New Social Movement' of the twenty-first century. Diversity talks have become a large portion of our everyday language, strategies, and actions, in both the corporate and regular social settings. To embrace diversity and have a disparate view is the new positivism of most developed nations. As a civilization, diversity as a philosophy and practice of tolerance and acceptance regarding various cultural, social and physical issues has been long overdue; especially when we look back at our historical events and records to recognize where a lack of diverse views and socially-open environments led to many wars, conflicts and hostility among individuals, nations, and groups. We have traveled far despite the fact that diversity appreciation is still lacking in many corners of the globe, especially where issues of religion and culture still produce rifts between peoples.

Diversity is a highly ideological and philosophical perspective underlying human understanding, and is in fact a method of wide-scale conflict resolution which attempts to find a common ideal among people of varied social and

---

[24] - This material is co-authored with Donovan A. McFarlane, St. Thomas University.

cultural, racial and ethnic, as well as economic, political, and religious origins, and backgrounds. Thus, as an ideology it is also resisted and shunned as much as any other philosophical movement or view and must live up to change and opposition to yield its maximum benefits for the greater number as a greater good. Diversity is not an imposition when we consider how varied we are in our beings and social makeup as individuals; we are inherently diverse as intended by nature or the peculiar sway of nature. Hence, embracing diversity might be a natural intent of evolutionary design or creationism according to whichever one believes.

There are theoretical, ideological and philosophical dilemmas that undermine harmonious diversity, including Darwinism, Segregationism, Fundamentalism, Religionism, and Existentialism, and many others. These movements along with their highest ideals survive on advocating self-efficacy and narcissism, which might be discriminatory or even exclusionary as far as the issues which envelop themselves around diversity are concerned.

There have been countless events and issues in history, some brutal and some plainly ignorant that have provided the rationale for diversity studies and programs, integration, education, and awareness today. Slavery and racial segregation in the Americas were of particular importance, as these two echoed the human plight far beyond their times and ending. Race has been the most formidable and commonplace diversity issue in most modern societies and the United States is of particular interest when it comes to such a discussion. In the event one had to account for the most diversity initiatives and programs across the globe, the United States would be the dominant leader on that issue, stemming from democracy and the fact that the Civil Rights Movement was rooted in this nation. Diversity is inherently a part of many modern movements, including democracy, liberalism, regional integration, internationalization, globalization and relativism. With an increase in technology, global communications, transportation, and networking, we will see even more diversity in our social institutions and societies.

Overall, diversity has one universal meaning, despite the fact that individuals often apply the term according to their own relativistic views. As mentioned in the initial chapter, diversity simply refers to the variety of human traits and ideals, both physical and social that characterizes us as a species. With regards to diversity, there are many dimensions ranging from sexual orientation and religious beliefs, to social and cultural values, physical appearance, among other things. Diversity in any society or group should be examined from the point of view of the prevailing perspectives, religious, social, and cultural practices, and the degree of tolerance and acceptance existing between the individuals and institutions, groups and communities holding differing views. Diversity thus refers to both internal and external concepts of variety as far as perspectives, traits and characteristics are concerned. Similarly, diversity is also seen as important elements of democracy and liberalism so everyone can be free to voice their opinions and thoughts.

Modern democracy as well as the concept of having a democratic society seems to go hand in hand with diversity. The acceptance of democracy is ultimately the acceptance of a society and values which are multiple and vastly different from our own. The success of modern democratic expansion across the globe brings with it increased diversity in all aspects of society. The characteristics of democracy as a political-social system make it the most prevalent atmosphere in which diversity initiatives, practices, policies and programs strive. Modern democracy through its embracement of equal justice, treatment, representation, and laws protecting against racial and social injustices has made diversity a virtually irresistible ideology. To democratize is to essentially make a person, group or nation diverse; affording a fair chance for the recognition of differential needs, customs, rights, privileges, freedom, among other things.

Democracy and the spread of its social, economic, and political ideology are vital to the growing diversity and the progress, which diversity movements have made in modern society. As democracy spreads beyond western borders and into the Middle East and Southeast Asia, we will see more and more nations embracing various aspects of civilization with regards to race, sexuality, gender, ethnicity, nationality, creed, class, and many other diversity dimensions. While democracy offers diversity great chances to flourish, it also has a very long way to go as far as many economic and political issues are concerned. The majority rule, by which democracy seems to flourish as an expression of societal needs, does not often provide a broad avenue for the expression of minority values and traits.

Similar to democracy, impartial thoughts and liberalism are vital to the existence and growth of diversity and a diverse society. Liberalism simply refers to the political tradition, ideology and the philosophy where liberty becomes or is seen as the central political value in any social system, social institution or society. Liberalism as such, offers a latitude for tolerance and acceptance more extensive than any other socio-political view. One of the strong points of liberalism is the relativistic perspectives underpinning many mundane social issues, which are otherwise controversial points of grave conflicts in other social ordering systems. Liberalism seeks a society characterized by all values and elements, which constitute a truly diverse society where freedom of thought for individuals, limitations on the power of government and religion and the rule of law, the free exchange of ideas, a market economy supporting private enterprise or liberal entrepreneurism, and a transparent political arm exist. Most importantly, in a liberal society the rights of minorities are guaranteed.

The rights of minorities, the degree to which this exists determines in full, how diverse a society is, since historically a minority has always been subject to majority rule and control. Liberalism offers this, and the new trend in many westernizing and formerly non-democractic monarchial societies is that of going towards a liberal democracy where a republican or contitutional monarchy is the rule. The current uprisings, for example, in Nepal seem to be reflecting this process. Liberalism is not without numerous disadvantages. In fact because of the aim of liberals there are often many conflicts emerging pertaining to rights and priveleges, especially where human rights and civil justice are concerned. Liberalism takes four major forms that engender principles and concepts vital to the creation and progress of diversity. These forms include:

- *Political liberalism*; the belief that individuals are the basis of law and society, and that society and its institutions exist to further the purpose of individuals, without showing favor to any particular individuals or groups.
- *Cultural liberalism*; the rights of individuals with regards to right and wrong, morality or conscience and lifestyle surrounding issues of sexual freedom, religious freedom, mental freedom, and protection from government intervention into private life (this is similar to the concept of cultural relativism).
- *Economic liberalism*; where freedom of contractual relations and property rights are the basis of business and economical survival and free enterprise and laissez-faire capitalism are advocated.
- *Social liberalism*; this form is often referred to as welfare liberalism, reform liberalism, or New Liberalism, where basic necessities such as education, economic opportunity, and protection from harmful events beyond individual control are part of the role of society through its political arm.

Liberalism is a very controversial theory of politics and philosophy despite the obvious need for the diversity perspectives which it engenders. Liberals are often seen as too controversial, extreme and even chaotic by the conservative and even ultra-conservative groups in society. However, what liberalism means for diversity is greater acceptance of minorities, their cultures, values, and all other social issues. Diversity strives most in liberal environments and among individuals with a liberal perspective.

Diversity and Regional Integration

The prosperity of many of the world's regions will depend on integration at all levels: social, cultural, economic, religious, and political. This will only be effectively achieved through having diverse perspectives. Regional planners must integrate diversity programs and initiatives into their economic plans for regional development. This will break the social barriers, which are often obstacles preventing individual nations and people with vastly different religious, political, social and cultural beliefs, history and lifestyles from working in cooperative groups. This is especially true in regions where disunity on all matters prevail, because of the inability to accept adjacent nations' and peoples' cultural and social values. One of the interesting issues has been that of political diversity lacking between many regions, especially where both democratic and communist nations exist in the same region experiencing developmental issues. There are often different political aims and goals, and political and social systems often fail to overlap.

While regional integration defines a process by which countries remove barriers to free trade and the free movement of people across their national borders in order to reduce the problems that can lead to international conflict, there are many underlying social-cultural issues which must be addressed. Often, issues of racism, cultural superiority and cultural differences get in the way of political and economic integration. Some type of understanding and acceptance must exist between the nations which are in the process of integrating. For example, the Caribbean nations of CARICOM and the European nations of the EU have certain common social systems, historical similarities, acceptance of each other's cultures and a significant understanding of their common needs and goals. The lack of diverse understandings existing between nations in the process of regional integration can make or break the process. Often nations with opposing views on important social and political issues find it diffiuclt to work together, and this often leads to a fall-out among them. Diversity initiatives and programs should be the underlying processes which establish the consensus needed for nations and peoples of different cultures, social class, race, lifestyles, consciences and ethnicity, among other factors to work together effectively to eliminate poverty, diseases, oppression, war and crimes as they aim to improve living standards, life expectancy, and health.

Diversity and Internationalization

Internationalization can be defined in two ways: internationalization as a process of internationalizing business and economic activities by expansion across borders and into new nation areas; and internationalization as in 'internationalization and localization' which are essentially processes of adapting products and services for non-native environments, i.e. other nations and cultures. As such, internationalization requires cultural and social understanding, and the endorsement of diversity on which it must strive to essentially achieve product and organizational goals. To adapt products and services to non-native environments there must be cultural and social understanding of the people whose nation is being patronized. Many organizations make the error of entering new and unfamiliar markets without carefully considering socio-cultural factors and how they impact product success and marketing strategies. This can often result in failure. In addition, the inability to embrace diversity and not adapting to the social lifestyles, values and cultures of hosts countries can prove unprofitable for business. For example, car dealers entering the Chinese automobile market and failing to recognize the cultural factors impacting car buying decisions, and hence failing to adapt their cars to the needs and beliefs, customs and perpectives of the people often experience failure. One example of this is a scenario where a car dealer in the Chinese market has a lot of mostly white cars. In such a market sales would be extremely low because white in China is closely associated with death, and hence white cars are not popular or appealing.

In many Caribbean countries such as Jamaica, where drivers' steering wheels and controls are to the right side of the vehicle, cars being built by a foreign or specifically an American car manufacturer must be specially built or adapted to meet this criteria, for where as we drive on the left in the United States, is the opposite in most Caribbean countries. Internationalization and localization therefore, entail cultural and social understanding with economic implications for individuals and businesses. Companies that cherish, practice, and embrace diversity are more likely to be successful in different environments. Diversity as such allows for adaptation through understanding and awareness, education, tolerance, and acceptance. Furthermore, diversity facilitates diversification and innovation at all levels. Internationalization and localization in turn bring further diversity to societies in which they are taking place.

Diversity and Globalization

Globalization is similar to regional integration, with one distinction; globalization takes place among countries around the world from all major regions as a process of political, cultural, social, economic, and technological integration. Increased trade and migrations resulting from this global process of integration can lead to societies and regions becoming more and more diverse. Globalization and diversity are thus complimentary processes; each one facilitating the growth of the other. Furthermore, globalization leads to more diversity and attempts of diversify and facilitate the growth and success of global initiatives. Globalization and increased diversity have been both facilitated by a number of factors: technological advances, increased communications capabilities; transnational and regional, increased travel and advances in transportation capabilities, international trading, and increased competition.

As we become more global in our practices and perspective, we will also become diversified with issues of culture, religion, nationality, politics, social values, beliefs, among other things are concerned. A society that wholly accepts the idea that we are living in a global networking world will be more open to diverse issues, which invariably are parts of the globalization process. Globalization is not without problems for societies and peoples, and this is evident in anti-globalization protests and movements. Often, many people who are conservatives will feel compelled to oppose diversity initiatives and programs which seem to eradicate old values or beliefs, for example, many Caribbean nations are still very opposed to the issue of homosexuality, and globalization in the form of politics that asks for and regulates flexibility on such issues that can be a cause for resistance. There are countries, which henceforth, oppose western wealthy nations in which such social lifestyle is a regular and protected part of the constitutions. In addition, the resistance to change which naturally becomes a part of any new movements and processes or ideologies is present within the atmospheres where globalization is unfolding. Diversity from a global perspective is very healthy for our world. Only with diversity can we truly see the benefits of globalization in each nation, region and society.

Diversity and International Management

The growth of international management over the past two decades has pushed diversity initiatives and programs to the forefront of management thought and practices. Organizational leaders and managers, theorists and practitioners now recognize the importance of applying management concepts and techniques in multinational environments, and adapting home-country practices and methods to different socio-cultural, economic and political environments. This means success in the global business environment, where internationalization and localization processes ensure product adaptability. With international management practices built on recognizing differences in socio-cultural environments, expatriate managers and leaders are better equipped to become successful in non-native environments. Negotiations and other international agreements demand diversity understanding and recognition. For example, American business leaders negotiating with Chinese business leaders must know a variety of cultural and social practices, which will be essential in bringing a successful negotiation process.

Multinational corporations (MNCs) are very important in promoting diversity as they often carry out business activities in several countries and possess a mix of nationality and culture in terms of managers and owners making up the entire corporation. The acceptance of diversity in such large corporations ensure that diversity initiatives and programs become successful parts of management practices and strategies, eventually becoming part of each society in which these corporations are located, and parts of the individual employees through integration into the corporate culture.

Diversity and Culture

Cultural diversity is one of the most prolific changes taking place in our society today. The United States has been referred to as one of the most culturally diverse nations on earth, due to the number of different people from various nations and cultures living in this country. Cultural differences affect us at all levels; social, political, economic and religious. Culture is a very difficult issue to deal with when it comes to diversity, even as difficult as religion, which itself cannot be separated from culture. Culture, which usually refers to the way of life of a group of people, and the beliefs and practices they share, is often characterized by the following: it is learned, shared, generational, symbolic, and adaptive. Cultural adaptation is the most important characteristic when it comes to diversity. The ability of people to adapt to new and vastly different practices, values, beliefs and other social elements than their own, essentially defines diversity of perspective.

The degree to which a particular culture is "open" will affect the degree to which individuals of that particular culture accept and embrace diversity stemming from cultures and individuals with practices unparallel to their own. Cultures are the main social building blocks of nations and people, and this becomes evident in the values and attitudes towards certain social issues. The merging of culture and acceptance of differences which remain unmixed are what diversity seeks; integration or tolerance in society and the organizations and institutions where we play, live and work. Cultures often vary not only between individuals, but nations and regions as well. One of the most significant digressions is observed in the cultural differences and practices among nations of the western hemisphere and the eastern hemisphere. For example, the differences existing between Japanese and U.S. culture are often explained from a hemispheric viewpoint; east versus west. National and regional cultures vary according to political and historical factors; which become part of the obstacles and problems when diversity initiatives and programs are pursued in many diverse settings.

Diversity and Religion

Diversity is seen in religious beliefs more than in any other social practices in society. Even within one single social group, there can exist many varied beliefs regarding issues of religious nature. Human beliefs, while collective by definition, of culture, are often individual by definition of faith. There are hundreds of religions around the world, each holding its own rituals and beliefs regarding human purpose and destiny. The conflicts that exist in religion however, mainly stem from those religions that are mainstream and large: Christianity, Islam, Hinduism, and Buddhism. The attempt to foster religious diversity has been totally unsuccessful in many nations, especially where one dominant religion prosecutes others.

Religious pluralism is the widest attempt at encouraging universality and the acceptance of diversity in beliefs. It is simply an ideology of religious relativism meant to foster equality of religion and religious beliefs. Encouraging religious diversity has been a very difficult issue, especially where monotheism is concerned. Furthermore, even among Christians there are religious differences existing, which are often the cause of conflicts and disagreements. For example, the differences of the conception of the God-head existing between Protestants and Catholics, Pentecostals and non-Pentecostals, etc. In addition, there are sub-cultural religions and religious beliefs that add to the diverse systems of faith existing in societies, for example, the differences in the religious beliefs of Rastafarians and other individuals in Jamaican society concerning the definition and identification of "God."

Religious diversity is very important if we are to live peacefully and prosperously in any society. The lack of religious diversity in many eastern nations has been the cause of conflicts and individual oppression. Being tolerant of another's religious beliefs is the ultimate display of human respect, since an individual's belief is a vital part of his or her being. Diversity in religions certainly exists in many societies, as it is the acceptance of this diversity that is the real issue. Accepting others' religious beliefs and respecting them will foster cooperative human understanding. We are distinct as individuals, therefore, why can't our beliefs in faith and religion be just as unique? Religious diversity can be the source of peace for many societies, especially those currently undergoing religious conflicts and troubles across the globe.

Diversity and Relativism

Relativism is the philosophical view that human value and beliefs are only meaningful in cultural or historical contexts. As such relativism denounces the existence of absolutes as far as human values and social, religious, cultural, political and other views are concerned. Relativism is an ideology of diversity and tolerance. We will often hear the concept of cultural relativism, which refers to the process of interpreting cultural values and beliefs only from the viewpoint of the culture and history of the group, society or nation in which they exist. This is a good practice which ensures that individuals and groups are not discriminated against because of ethnic origin, nationality, social and sexual orientation, and most profoundly as a cause of any behavior, value or attitudes originating from historical or cultural contexts.

While relativism promotes diversity and its ideologies are dependent on one accepting diversity, it is has some drawbacks which have become very apparent in today's society. These include the destruction of some values and principles within frameworks of ethics. The growth of relativism has been aided by a large population of young people who are more liberal than their predecessors. Hence, liberalism and relativism are complimentary processes in many ways. Relativism ensures that individuals who would otherwise be oppressed because of their values, beliefs, lifestyles and perspectives are tolerated in mainstream societies. It advocates acceptance and tolerance with the rationale that human understanding should be based on contexts and history – human learning and experience thus far, rather than on prejudgments that lead to hostility and discrimination. As a philosophy, relativism has done much for diversity and its growth and continues to be more prevalent as we move further into becoming a truly global society.

Diversity and Competition

Competition is fueling rapid growth and integration, networking and collaboration in our economies and societies of the twenty-first century. This competition has led to the growth of MNCs, global logistics, offshoring, increased migration and emigration, cultural mixing and social integration on all levels. The advent of economic and financial competition has led us to come closer together as a civilization as we interact to exchange our goods and services for survival.

We are competing for the same resources, the same jobs, the same material rewards, and are forced beyond our basic needs, through the distribution of resources, specialization of labor, technological and human capabilities to interact more than ever before. As such, we must learn each other's languages, values, beliefs, strategies and methods to best supply our own needs. Competition forces us to learn and acquire knowledge about our neighbors both near and afar. In fact, to survive and compete successfully, we must often adapt to the cultures, values and practices of each other.

We are competing in a world where resources are limited and wants are unlimited. Often we must combine our resources; both human and technological to solve issues and meet challenges, which threaten and endanger the existence of our civilization and our world. This forces us to become cooperative societies adapting standards, methods, tools, techniques, beliefs and knowledge from each other on a daily basis. Thus competition means learning diverse strategies and applying them for human survival.

Diversity and Change

The changes taking place in all sectors of twenty-first century society are unprecedented. There are vast changes taking place in the political, religious, economic, social, and cultural arenas that are direct and indirect results of the need for diversity and universal perspectives in responding to the issues, problems and challenges of our time. Change is definite and often embracing diverse perspectives is our only weapon against change, especially where outdated methods and beliefs, values and practices jeopardize human safety, rights, and the achievement of societal and organizational goals. Social change is the most powerful proponent of diversity because our values, behaviors, and attitudes are the most measurable and predictable variables of variety as far as beliefs and practices, values and perspective are concerned.

Heartily embracing change often means the acceptance of diversity, since change brings along with it new and innovative methods, peoples, practices and paradigms which often are different from the pre-existing ones. Change management in the twenty-first century must be built around diversity initiatives and programs and with strategies to overcome the resistance to diversity elements, factors and consequences of change since most changes are often interpretive of social adaptation and adjustments.

Diversity Program Examples

There have been numerous cultural theories and studies attempting to categorize and explain human behaviors, values and attitudes in terms of variety or diversity. For example, Trompanaar's Research, which over a decade ago examined human diversity from a cultural viewpoint using cultural group and factors such as individualism and communitarianism (equivalent to Hofestede' individualism and collectivism), specific relationship, diffuse relationship, universalism, particularism, neutral relationship, emotional relationship, achievement and ascription. Hofestede used factors or dimensions such as individualism and collectivism, power distance, uncertainty avoidance, masculinity and femininity among other variables. These are prime examples of how we have attempted to explain and bring to the forefront awareness of diversity in the human species.

While these theories and the numerous others which exist offer us great insight into understanding cultural and social differences that are a part of human diversity, there is no one theory that can communicate wholly just how diverse we are. We need to recognize the role of socialization and culture and how these program us to grow and become who and what we are. More importantly however, we need to recognize the need to rationally examine our own values and attitudes when we come face to face with others different from our own, and in doing so, put ourselves in the place of the other individuals - the historical and cultural contexts of relativism – in order to be fair in our evaluations and conclusions. As human beings we are born into socialization and culture and these are inescapable facts of life from which we emerge to be who we are.

Various nations, cultures, and people have different practices, beliefs, and values which must be respected regardless of our own over-imposing views. Here are some examples of diversity between various cultures, nations, and peoples regarding gestures:

A. *The Chinese*: the Chinese are not too fond of gestures and many facial expressions. Touching is not appreciated, especially between unfamiliar persons among whom no relationships have been established.

B. *The Japanese*: unlike the Chinese, the Japanese are more open to facial expressions. However, the slightest of facial expressions can carry strong meanings and dramatic or strange facial expressions make them uncomfortable. Touching is an issue, especially slapping one's back, particularly among men. Pointing with less than the entire hand and direct eye contact can be taken as disrespectful gestures.

C. *The Russians*: firmness in bodily composure and gestures are appreciated. For example, when sitting, legs should be firm and together. There is strictness regarding gestures and the shaking of the fist is seen as vulgar.

D. *The Italians*: among the Italians touching while talking is accepted and very common. In fact, gestures are very much a part of communication, especially accentuating gestures. Facial expressions are not offensive in particular, and being a very expressive group of people with a vivid language, the Italians have less rigid rules regarding gestures.

E. *The Jamaicans*: like many Caribbean people, Jamaicans are very expressive; and speaking with gestures of hand and facial expression is common. However, pointing at or towards a senior or elderly person is offensive, and so are winking and rolling the eyes. In some rural areas, looking an elderly person directly in the eyes is seen as ill-mannered and contemptuous.

F. *The Afghans*: like most other Islamic nations, men in Afghanistan often do not touch women in the workplace. However, it is common for men to shake hands or kiss each other on the cheeks when close friends see each other after many weeks or months. Afghans are relationship-oriented and value loyalty. Global business managers are encouraged to build a high level of trust with their Afghan partners before negotiating business deals.

The above are just a few examples of diversity existing between different cultures and people regarding gestures and in no way remain definite since societies are rapidly changing both culturally and socially. Thus, in many areas in such cultures, these commonly identified practices or rules of social engagement are being altered. People are now adapting universal approaches towards communication and other forms of social exchanges, and this becomes more the case as we embrace diversity and become more tolerant and accepting on all levels.

Diversity and the Future

Diversity should not be seen as an artificially designed imposition. By nature we are diverse as a species, and the physical world in which we live holds to the law of diversity as well. We all cannot think the same, look the same, behave the same, or have the same beliefs, values and attitudes. This would be a dull world indeed. Our future depends on how much we embrace diversity as societies in turmoil. The society of today and tomorrow will be vastly different in terms of its composition and outlook, provided that we have not experienced any drastic changes or revolutions that reverse the course in diversity movements and programs. The tyrannies of the past which kept various groups oppressed on the grounds of race, nationality, ethnicity, creed, class, and religious beliefs among other things, have fallen for most part. There are still mental and ideological aspects of such systems and social rules which exist in our society today. Hopefully, while embracing diversity as a social movement we will be able to fully integrate every aspect of human beliefs into whatever settings we will live in the near and far future so that we will have a peaceful existence and civil progress.

Our societies of today and tomorrow are vastly different from those of yesterday. Today we are constantly experiencing technological advances, increasing integration, advances in telecommunications and networking capabilities, logistics, dissolution of political, social and cultural boundaries, the elimination of barriers to trade and travel, increased trade in the forms of exporting and importing, and unification of territories and regions. With all of these taking place, there comes the growth of diversity; we are not only growing in numbers, but also in beliefs, attitudes, values, lifestyles, practices, and "oneness." Diversity will continue to increase as Darwinianism, existentialism, narcissism, fundamentalism, and many self-centered philosophies along with ethnocentrism become less popular in our social systems. Diversity is vital to our future and progress since we as a civilization, are still examining our purpose and trying to solve the most fundamental problems of life and existence. May we all grow healthfully and prosperously, accepting each other regardless of race, color, creed, class, sex, sexuality, ethnicity, and all factors which so mundanely separate us.

Retaining a Competent and Diverse Workforce

As can be seen from the aforementioned content, diversity concepts directly relate to society in many aspects, including the outcome of attracting highly qualified employees and retaining them. High employee turnover can be very costly, especially when they involve high recruitment costs, extensive training and orientation, exit interviews, outplacement programs and assistance, counseling, incentive benefits, severance pay, and other administrative and clerical support. During this new millennium, the cost of turnover may range anywhere from $10,000 to $150,000 per person. In some foreign countries the turnover cost may be higher because many governments mandate extensive benefits for employees who are terminated, laid off or simply discharged. According to a study reported by Michelle Laque Johnson, entitled *"Look Before You Leap into European Labor Market"* and published in Investor's Daily Business (April 1992), the turnover of a 45 year-old European worker with 20 years of service earning about $50,000 per year can cost the company high amounts in different countries, as demonstrated in Table 16.1.

Employee turnover can also negatively affect productivity, customers, sales, suppliers, morale of the retained workforce, and the overall survival of the firm. Many employers during the last few decades have strategically reduced their workforce for various reasons and simultaneously increased their workforce diversity to retain a competitive advantage. For example, AT&T downsized their workforce by 58,000 associates from 1984 to 1992 and increased their minority managers from 3 to 9 percent. Similarly, they increased their proportion of female managers from 2.5 to 9 percent. Major companies like American Express, Disney World, Publix Super Markets, AT&T, Wal-

Marts, and other such successful firms have strategically designed diversity development programs to proactively recognize, value, celebrate, and retain a diverse workforce as well as a diverse value chain of suppliers, vendors, and customers or end-users.

Table 16.1 – Termination Costs around the World (US Dollars)

Country	Statutory Termination Benefits
Italy	$130,000
Spain	125,000
Belgium	94,000
Portugal	83,000
Greece	67,000
Germany	25,000
United Kingdom	19,000
Ireland	13,000

The key to retaining a productive workforce is to focus on who is attracted to the firm, and who is retained, how they are being retained, what is retaining them, and how the competent employees can be kept indefinitely for the years to come. The employee retention strategy directly affects diversity, efficiency, effectiveness, and the overall productivity. The employee retention programs as well as recruitment programs have a continual impact on the productivity, diversity and competitive advantage of firms. A firm's workforce diversity initiatives are highly affected by the firm's ability to effectively recruit and retain employees.

It is extremely important to retain highly qualified women and men of various minority backgrounds, experiences and cultures. Generally speaking, women have a tendency to be more process-oriented and can intuitively make decisions more quickly. On the other hand, most men are goal or result-oriented and tend to want all the facts in order to reach logical conclusions. While men can have a tendency to be more business focused, women are likely to consider the people involved and the impact of business decisions on all stakeholders. While men often focus on the destination women determine how to get there through a fair process. These are mere speculations and generalizations, which means that both men and women are equally capable of seeing the process and the destination. The goal is to understand that we tend to become like those we interact with, and if we only have men in the department then we may focus more on the destination as opposed to on the process and vice versa. Minority men of various backgrounds can also bring much needed perspectives and ideas into the team or company. Men from various cultures, countries and backgrounds can prevent managers and companies from making huge and costly mistakes while dealing with others whose customer, norms, mores, beliefs and values may be different. This dimension becomes even more important when firms are competing nationally or internationally in a global market. It can help firms to harmoniously shift from a perspective of ethnocentricity, polycentricity and centocentricity to a paradigm of geocentricity where firms are viewed as global markets with no geographic centers and where people think globally and act locally. A *geocentric* firm integrates an interdependent network of decentralized and specialized companies throughout the world with no single gender, nationality, race or group of people dominating the firm. In order to encourage geocentricity, managers need to become aware of their mental tapes or stereotypes about people of different skin color, religion, education, culture, language, national origin, race, as well as other traits and disabilities, prevent them from affecting their managerial decisions. Fairness is the key. All decisions must be based on the performance as well as the character of individuals as opposed to character traits which are not job related. This can serve as the first steps toward insuring equality, fairness and productivity while maintaining a diverse workforce.

Another dimension of a diverse workforce is to attract and hire highly qualified individuals who are *differently-abled*. Differently-abled individuals bring new perspectives to the organization and can help attract new customers as well as new markets. There are over sixty five million people in the United States of America that are considered to be either physically, emotionally or mentally disabled to one extent or another. Since a majority of a firm's employees are likely to have not dealt with such disabilities, it may be very difficult for one to satisfactorily predict the demands and needs of differently-abled associates, suppliers and customers. Attracting and retaining highly qualified differently-abled associates requires specific strategies, flexibility, and accommodations that transcend the minimum requirements imposed by local, state or federal laws. Many individuals still view differently-abled individuals as persons who may not have much to contribute to the company. This is a myth and not a fact. In order to have a productive and successful workforce, managers need to treat every individual as an individual and not prejudge the person based on physical appearances that may not say much about his/her job performance. Just because a person has a disability does not mean that he or she cannot fully perform the tasks. Differently-abled or individuals with various disabilities can fully perform many jobs without any accommodations when they are given the opportunity. In some cases firms need to remain flexible and make some accommodations for those who are able to perform the job differently by restructuring the job, the process or simply the system.

Age is also a very important part of diversity initiatives for a competitive organization. Attracting and retaining people of different ages can be a vital part of any successful operation. Retaining both older workers and younger workers is another way of preserving heterogeneous workforce that can lead to successful competitive advantage. Age discrimination seems to be more difficult to pinpoint and very subtle when compared to either racial or gender discrimination. Nonetheless, age discrimination is very much a part of the corporate world which tends to discourage highly qualified and productive employees from staying with the company. Age discrimination needs to be prevented if firms are to have a satisfied and productive diverse workforce. Based on the author's years of management experience, older workers tend to be more loyal, more productive, better communicators, more experienced, and are likely to have less absenteeism rates.

Both solid retention as well as downsizing strategies should consider maintaining a productive, highly qualified, diverse workforce that is extremely competitive in expertise, experience as well as knowledge, and a workforce that is open-minded, resilient and flexible to the many ubiquitous vicissitudes of a changing global market. Retention of a diverse and competent workforce can lead individuals and their organizations to both happiness and success in today's global marketplace.

Employee Retention through "DIVERSITY" Training

Racial biases cost the U.S. economy about 4 percent of the gross domestic product during some years. Therefore, its elimination from the workforce becomes imperative not just morally, but also economically. Understanding and executing the ideas included in the acronym "DIVERSITY" (as presented in Table 16.2) can be a starting place.

Table 16.2 – DIVERSITY Model

Define "diversity."
Implement diversity training.
Value individuality.
Enforce equal opportunity.
Require behavior alignment.
Support artistry and openness.
Involve everyone synergistically.
Transcend tolerance to a win / win paradigm. And
Yearn for peace and sensitivity.

Define the term "diversity" and develop a strategic diversity training program. People define diversity in different ways and some of them might even be counterproductive. Therefore, it is essential to create and communicate a common definition and shared understanding for the term diversity in order to gain the most from any multicultural education program one wishes to implement or initiate. Any diversity definition should include both similarities and differences. Many diversity programs attempt to increase awareness by placing emphasis on current laws and policies. Other programs focus on the cultural differences and similarities of individuals and seek to develop better relationships among teams as well as to provide skills that make diverse teams more productive thereby creating a competitive advantage through the human resource asset. The human resource asset is the only asset which can be long lasting and difficult for competitors to duplicate.

Implement a strategic diversity training program to create and maintain an inclusive work environment. This requires eliminating prejudiced, exclusivity, and all unfair forms of professional discrimination in the workplace. Initiating and creating an inclusive work environment requires an absence of unfair professional discrimination. *Professional discrimination,* stemming from prejudice, is defined as the politically correct patterns of double standard in judgments, promotions, assessments, evaluations, assignments, rewards, perks, benefits, compensation, and other decisions that limit or hinder the progress of individuals who are different from the norm. Prejudice and "inclusivity" are mutually exclusive and cannot happen simultaneously. An inclusive work environment requires the absence of prejudice. It is the elimination of unfair and professional discrimination that will encourage and allow individuals to interconnect effectively. Human beings have been interconnected through the explosive nature of the information super highway, the communication innovations and revolution, high speed trains, jets and planes, satellites, and telecommunications. It is now time for everyone to interconnect mentally and/or spiritually by creating an inclusive society where the global brain can function synergistically.

Value individuality as well as similarities and differences. Many companies talk about valuing their greatest asset, which is their people, but too few demonstrate it. Individuals are people with emotions and should not be treated as numbers. Each individual must be treated fairly and exclusively based on his/her likes, dislikes, character, competence, lifestyle, communication style, and learning style. The "one size fits all" mentality does not respect individuality nor cultural differences, and furthermore it can be offensive when dealing with individual anomalies. Therefore, it needs to be changed to "one size fits one" with a caveat stating that it may not be suitable for any other; or it can be changed to "all sizes can accommodate one," which focuses on flexibility and adaptability. Managers should seek to capitalize on each associate's unique talents and strengths. Employees should retain their individual identities…similar to a fruit salad where the ingredients compliment one another, while maintaining their original flavors, to form something very appetizing for one to enjoy.

Enforce equal opportunity employment practices. Then, educate, expect and encourage associates to become "cultural allies." Expect everyone to not only obey the laws, but to go above and beyond the laws in order to create an inclusive work environment where all individuals can be successful in what they want to achieve. Individuals often do what is expected of them especially if they value "the means and the ends." Reward good behavior and effectively correct poor behavior or performance. Constantly model the good behavior through action, newsletters, video training, workshops, quarterly publications, and weekly paychecks. Encourage and empower everyone to take personal responsibility for their actions and to become cultural allies in the workplace.

Require behavior alignment with organizational values. Every organization has certain values and beliefs, which help to form its organizational culture. The sum of these values and beliefs make up the character of the organization and what it stands for as a company. The employees of each company should align their behaviors with the values and character of the organization. While top executives cannot require individuals to change their personal set of beliefs and values they can make sure individual behaviors are representative of company values as stated in their corporate credo, vision, mission or strategic objectives.

Support creativity and openness to reduce groupthink. Sponsor and encourage attendance to both formal and informal corporate and local community events that are culturally unique and different. Many individuals feel uncomfortable and apprehensive in ceremonies or events, which are unfamiliar to them. Participation in such events could be one way of eliminating some of their phobias which might be based on lack of understanding, misinformation and/or societal conditioning.

Involve everyone to achieve synergy. Research has shown that the heterogeneous teams tend to be more productive in complex jobs and decisions than homogeneous teams. When heterogeneous team members seek to understand each others' perspectives, value and appreciate each others' differences, develop good work relationships, and work synergistically productivity increases. Remember, there is no "I" in team and **T**ogether **E**veryone **A**chieves **M**ore. However, as mentioned before, people need to be encouraged to maintain their individuality just like a fruit in a fruit salad bowl which maintains its own unique flavor. Discourage individuals from maintaining the status quo and encourage them to challenge and change discriminatory and archaic systems that are not achieving synergy.

Transcend tolerance to create win-win situations for all stakeholders. While tolerance is a way of living peacefully in a diverse society where beliefs and values vary greatly, transcendence is about going beyond tolerance and actually working synergistically. It means understanding, appreciating, and valuing individuals for who they are, what they stand for and giving them a fair chance to achieve their goals within a team-oriented structure. In the business world, transcendence is about eliminating win/lose, win, lose-lose, and lose/win mentality be replacing it with a win/win paradigm as well as continuously thinking win/win. Remember, hurt feelings don't just vanish and may surface and riposte at an unexpected time in a treacherous way.

Yearn for justice and cultural sensitivity. The best way to yearn for justice and cultural sensitivity is to make sure current systems and processes in the workplace support cultural diversity. These systems and processes should be able to support the needs and demands of a diverse workforce. Organizations that are proactive in the area of managing diversity will be prepared and appropriately positioned to satisfy the changing needs of a diverse workforce. Effectively managing diversity will be one of their long lasting competitive advantages in the global economy.

While the mission (destination) is having a peaceful world, the strategy (means) is cultural sensitivity as we embrace the prospective and intense global competition based on race, culture and ethnicity during the twenty-first century. Remember, the ability to achieve exists in each and every person. As David Pomeranz's song says, "Its in everyone of us"; and each person has to discover that ability intrinsically through reflective and/or spiritual intrapersonal communication. Life can be a very busy crowded way that needs to be traveled on with caution, understanding and appreciation for all of its palpable and incorporeal beauty. So, take the time and encourage others to do the same in order to discover the inherent yearning desire for peace and joy that flows from within.

Any discrimination lawsuit will more than likely cost firms money in legal fees, loss of productivity, loss of morale, bad public image, and talented employees regardless of whether the lawsuit goes to court or not. Legal fees alone can run up to tens of millions of dollars each year in large organizations. Discrimination suits can last as long as four to six years, which can be very costly to the firm and its stakeholders. So, let us take the moral challenge of eliminating prejudice from one's professional decisions in the workplace, and providing a fair playing field for all participants through "DIVERSITY" training programs. Remember, fairness, justice and equality promotes long lasting and genuine feelings of joy, pride and commitment, none of which can be bought or sold but they must be earned through good leadership and integrity. Great leadership through diversity training can be a great source of motivation and employee empowerment which will improve employee retention.

The Science of Success

As discussed in the initials chapters, success should be defined by each person based on his or her desires, abilities, competencies, goals, and efforts. It is not the place of managers to determine how successful a person can or should be, based on his/her first impression of the employee or on the associate's physical/personality characteristics. Ralph Waldo Emerson said:

> "What is success? To laugh often and much; to win the respect of intelligent people and the affection of children; to earn the appreciation of honest critics and endure the betrayal of false friends; to appreciate beauty; to find the best in others; to leave the world a bit

beauty; to find the best in others; to leave the world a bit better, whether by a healthy child, a garden patch, or a redeemed social condition; to know even one life has breathed easier because you have lived."

Simply put, success can be practicing what you preach, progressively realizing predetermined goals/ideals, and doing one's best to make worthwhile contributions to society. It is a moral imperative and obligation for managers and organizational leaders to (assume and) proceed as though limits to employees' abilities do not exist; thus, each employee should be given fair opportunities to perform as per his or her desires, abilities, competencies, and dreams.

The book entitled "*Social Intelligence: the New Science of Success*[25]," written by Karl Albrecht in 2006, discusses some basic tenets of human relations that should be practiced by each professional and managers in the workplace. Albrecht's goal is to help professionals, managers and leaders see the beauty in human behaviors and at the same time to let people understand those behaviors that differentiate effective leaders from ineffective ones. Effective leaders, according to Albrecht (2006), are those leaders who exhibit nurturing behaviors: behaviors that make people feel valued, capable, loved, respected, and appreciated.

Some people feel that leadership and success is only about financial wealth. According to one of the author's colleague, Ikwukananne I. Udechukwu from Georgia State University, in the past six years, business executives and in some instances employees, have become targets of unethical behavior expressed in immense greed and organizational theft. More recently, stakeholders have even sought to tightly tie executive compensation to organizational performance. Thus, according to Professor Udechukwu, some aspects of business research has focused on individual behaviors that have led to such unhealthy outcomes. As such, Albrecht (2006) notes that the basis for social intelligence is built on the principle of S.P.A.C.E. (situational awareness, presence, authenticity, clarity, and empathy). The situational awareness dimension highly relates to the concept of situational leadership which, among many factors, takes into consideration the psychological and task readiness of the follower in terms of his or her development and responsibility delegation.

The book recognizes other forms of intelligence such as abstract intelligence, practical intelligence, emotional intelligence, aesthetic intelligence, and kinesthetic intelligence. Albrecht (2006) defines emotional intelligence as self-awareness and self-management, while social intelligence is defined as the way to deal with people. The idea is that one has to know the self first before one can improve the situation of others. Professor Udechukwu states that the interesting and powerful thought about Albrecht's book is that it does not

[25] This material is co-authored with Raimi Abiodun, University of Phoenix.

focus on teaching about different human traits or personalities, rather, and more practically, it focuses on the natural principles or fundamentals that partly lead to or form those individual traits and behaviors that are readily observable on either routine or continuous basis in various contexts. Another interesting observation of social intelligence is that at some level the concept ties into the theory of ethical behavior and leadership, which also advocates methods of dealing with individuals, groups, and organizational activities on a fair, consistent, and sound basis. Professor Udechukwu concludes that the implication of social intelligence using S.P.A.C.E. is that executives and employees may be socially smarter about how their actions and behaviors shape their immediate and future life and work situations as well as the immediate and future life and work situations of their work subordinates and loved ones.

According to Albrecht, the global working environment of the twenty-first century has changed, as have the expected behaviors from managers and employees. Successful organizations must develop a better mechanism to recruit and retain good and knowledgeable workers from diverse backgrounds. Promoting a caring culture will depend on leaders' behaviors. The author draws on his long time experiences in human relations and organizational development to challenge organizational leaders to institute a nurturing behavioral culture within the organization. The author specifically defines social intelligence (SI) as "the ability to get along well with others and to get them to cooperate with you." These abilities are the most important ingredients in our efforts to develop successful relationships. Albrecht hypothesizes five dimensions of basic interaction skills that can be used to develop, assess, and describe social intelligence on a personal level. The various chapters of the book are divided according to these competencies, and each gives full and due consideration to all aspects of the dimensions. The chapters contain useful quotations and short stories that illustrate each dimension. Albrecht also uses some actual experiences and examples to aid the readers' comprehension.

The "S" factor represents *situational awareness* or the individual's situational radar and ability to understand and empathize with people in different situations. Situational awareness, similar to situational leadership skills, could be tied to a manager's ability to sense people's readiness to successfully complete as task as well as their feelings and intentions. How well can a leader study the environment, the culture, the social rules, and norms, and use these differences to appreciate the various points of view without being judgmental? Good situational radar demonstrates the leader's concern for people, his or her deep respect for others and his or her ways of thinking. Situational awareness includes the leader's belief in multiple ways to solve problems as well as the leader's belief that he or she is not self-centered. A self-centered individual will find cooperation by others difficult to accept; he or she will find it difficult to get people to accept him/her or share themselves with him/her.

"P" stands for *presence,* or the way the leader affects others through his or her physical appearance, mood and demeanor, body language, and approachability. Albrecht states that leaders' behaviors must communicate a sense of confidence, professionalism, kindness, and friendliness to the followers. The leader's presence in the mind of his or her followers must not be seen as depressing, indifferent, or insecure. As a leader, one must pay special attention to the sense of presence he or she is communicating to others in order to be accepted and taken seriously.

"A" stands for *authenticity,* which measures how honest and sincere a leader is both to him or herself and to the followers. According to the author, "authenticity is about the desire and ability to let yourself be real, not phony or contrived. It's how you connect with other people so you become worthy of their trust." Leaders must be seen as straight up, someone who believes in doing the right thing, and stands up for what he or she believes in. Authenticity means a solid, trustworthy person with a positive attitude and an upstanding character.

The "C" in S.P.A.C.E. means *clarity.* Clarity is the leader's ability to make him or herself known and clear to his or her followers. Clarity measures your ability to express your thoughts, opinions, ideas, and intentions clearly to your audience or listeners. Albrecht argues that managers must examine their communication skills and ask: do you say what you mean and mean what you say? Do you speak too fast, too much, or not at all? Does your voice pitch, rate, volume, and inflection inspire confidence or disrespect? Do you use language skillfully? Can you frame concepts and issues for others in an articulate, compelling way? Do you listen attentively and skillfully? These questions should be tied to the organization's behavioral model and should be expected of every leader in the organization. The author makes it clear that awareness of one's mode of communication makes communication better and puts more clarity into one's intention or purpose. Albrecht states that, "Certain patterns of language, either aggressive, dogmatic, or restrictive in their implications, can alienate others, contaminating the process of understanding." To influence other people with our ideas and thoughts, leaders must present the information in a way that makes it easy and fast for people to understand.

Finally, "E" stands for *empathy,* which addresses how considerate the leader is to people's feelings. The leader must be able to show people that he or she can identify with and appreciate them for who they are. It is this sense of connectedness that establishes a condition of rapport between two people and inspires followers to cooperate with their leaders. The author provides two ways for leaders to ensure that they are perceived as caring. Albrecht urges leaders to avoid or abandon toxic behaviors and increase the use of nourishing behaviors. Empathy, according to the author, is a long-term investment and not an episodic application of charm. Albrecht believes that leaders cannot expect followers to respect and accept their leadership if they constantly abuse, insult, and make them feel insignificant or unworthy. The road to complete acceptance, according to the author, is to get them to share a feeling of connectedness with you as a leader, making them closer, rather than farther from you.

It is a fact that inappropriate behaviors by managers and employees make employee retention difficult and makes effective relationships a difficult objective to achieve in an organization. However, effective interpersonal relationships are an important tool for quality leadership and productive organizations. Furthermore, developing a positive relationship with a diverse workforce could come from a corporate culture that institutes better corporate behaviors through education and training in the area of workforce diversity management.

Summary

Leading, managing, developing, and retaining employees are realities of life in all organizations, and they are all very important elements of a manager's responsibility and his or her level of success in the workplace. Effective managers attempt to avoid employee termination, discipline, and discharge by recruiting and retaining the right individuals from the outset. Furthermore, they develop and assist employees to achieve the stated objectives through effective leadership and diversity management skills. Effective managers are always concerned about the creation of an inclusive workplace and the progressive development of their employees; thus they utilize a standardized performance management processes when expectations and standards are not going as desired. Coretta Scott King, civil rights leader, said "It doesn't matter how strong your opinions are. If you don't use your power for positive change you are, indeed, part of the problem." Keep in mind that as an effective manager and an advocate of an inclusive workplace, "It is literally true that you can succeed best and quickest by helping others to succeed," said Napoleon Hill.

Effective managers and professionals work strategically to make sure all their employees are as successful as they would like to be based upon each employee's qualifications, goals, abilities, and competencies. Effective managers are enablers and empower their people to make great contributions. Furthermore, effective managers and leaders of a diverse workforce are open-minded and continuous learners themselves. Remember, as stated by Michael E. Gerber, "The difference between great people and everyone else is that great people create their lives actively, while everyone else is created by their lives, passively waiting to see where life takes them next. The difference between the two is the difference between living fully and just existing." While society's ills, biases and discriminatory practices must be reduced or eliminated, one should also be active and take personal responsibility for creating the life one has envisioned for him or herself. So, go out there and live a full life for yourself, your family, and your friends and colleagues in a fair and fruitful way.

Private institutions, academics, governments, and communities are now recognizing the necessity of valuing diversity to remain competitive in today's complex global world. Since the current workforce is indeed demographically diverse, leadership and management techniques of inclusion are imperative. Creating an inclusive environment (and eliminating the exclusive world of bias and stereotypes) is necessary for an effective learning environment with all employees. As a role model for current and future leaders and managers, you must create an inclusive working environment and educate all of your followers/peers in this direction as well.

Leaders and managers need to understand that valuing diversity requires the creation of an open, supportive, and responsive environment where differences are accepted, valued, and managed effectively toward organizational learning and synergy. Creating such an open atmosphere is the responsibility of the leader and each professional. Valuing diversity means the management of a group of people with differences so that all individuals perform at their maximum potential for the achievement of organizational goals by using their unique skills, competencies, and talents. "For remember, my friend, the son of a shepherd who possesses knowledge is of greater worth to a nation than the heir to the throne if he be ignorant. Knowledge is your true patent of nobility, no matter who your father or what your race may be" (Kahlil Gibran, 20th-century Syrian-American mystic poet and painter; "The Words of the Master," viii, in The Treasured Writings, 1980).

It is best to realize that there are many things that people can worry about, but one should focus only on those things that one can actually do something about. Always remember that there are two forms of worries in this world; the first are those worries and concerns that you can do something about, and the second are those that you cannot really influence or change. The key to success is to not spend too much time on the latter and focus on those worries and concerns that are within your control or circle of influence. As Stephen Covey in 1989 emphasized, highly effective people focus on their circle of influence. *Circle of influence* includes things, situations or circumstances over which you have direct or indirect control or influence. *Circle of concern*, on the other hand, includes those things, situations or circumstances over which you have no control or influence. In other words, your decisions or choices do not affect or change things that are in your circle of concern. So, separate your worries and work on those things that fall within your circle of influence. Remember the "Serenity Prayer" which states that "God grant me the serenity to accept the things I cannot change, the courage to change the things I can, and the wisdom to know one from the other."

As human beings, it is always best to keep hope alive for a better future as writer Helen Keller said "Optimism is the faith that leads to achievement; nothing can be done without hope and confidence." Vaclav Havel, writer and President of the Czech Republic, said that "Hope is a state of mind, not of the world; hope, in this deep and powerful sense, is not the same as joy that things are going well, or willingness to invest in enterprises that are obviously heading for success, but rather an ability to work for something because it is good." Hope requires patience, persistence and goal-oriented action as stated by Frank Tibolt, author, "We should be taught not to wait for inspiration to start a thing; action always generates inspiration; inspiration seldom generates action." With regard to persistency and sticking with one's goals, know that "The great thing and the hard thing is to stick to things when you have out-lived the first interest, and not yet got the second, which comes with a sort of mastery" said Janet Erskine Stuart, educator and writer. Abraham Lincoln, former U.S. President, stated that "You can have anything you want -- if you want it badly enough; you can be anything you want to be, do anything you set out to accomplish if you hold to that desire with singleness of purpose." So, stick to your dreams and goals while remaining flexible to learn and ad-just as appropriate in getting there. Author H.G. Wells said, "I see knowledge increasing and human power increasing; I see ever-increasing possibilities before life, and I see no limits set to it at all; existence impresses me as a per-petual dawn; and our lives, as I apprehend, are great in expectations." Part of success in life is about knowledge acquisition, knowledge generation, and experience as "Experience shows that success is due less to ability than to zeal; the winner is he who gives himself to his work body and soul," said Charles Buxton, author. Confucius said that you should "Acquire new knowl-edge whilst thinking over the old, and you may become a teacher of others."

Try new things, take calculated risks, and continue in the road of your dreams. John Glenn, astronaut and U.S. Senator, said that "People are afraid of the future, of the unknown; if a man faces up to it and takes the dare of the future he can have some control over his destiny." So, be persistent and always remember to "Work joyfully and peacefully, knowing that right thoughts and right efforts will inevitably bring about right results," said James Allen, novelist. When things are not clear, ask the right questions and remember that you don't have to always have the answers. Rudyard Kipling, writer, said that "I keep six honest serving-men (They taught me all I knew), their names are What and Why and When and How and Where and Who." Using these six "honest serving-men," explore and continue working toward your dreams and aspirations. Dr. David M. Burns, author, encourages us to always "Aim for success, not perfection. Never give up your right to be wrong, because then you will lose the ability to learn new things and move forward with your life."

Charles Dickens, author, once stated "I never could have done what I have done without the habits of punctuality, order, and diligence, without the determination to concentrate myself on one subject at a time." Despite good habits and careful planning, know that human beings are bound to make mis-takes which can lead to learning. Wang Yang-Ming, philosopher, writes that "The sages do not consider that making no mistakes is a blessing; they be-lieve, rather, that the great virtue of man lies in his ability to correct his mistakes and continually make a new man of himself." Without taking chances, trying new things or attempting the impossible, one may not always be able to make a positive difference. Tom Peters, author and management guru, states that "Unless you walk out into the unknown, the odds of making a profound difference are pretty low." People make mistakes, but people always make many good contributions and one should remember and celebrate these successes. David Niven, actor and author, states that:

> "Which is more important, good or bad? Regardless of which you consider to be the right answer, bad is often the bigger part of our thoughts. The traffic jam that bogs down our day stays in our thoughts longer than the open road that sped us on our way. The rude clerk is memorable long after the nice clerk is forgotten. Remind yourself to see the good, to think about the good, to remember the good. The good is out there just as much as the bad, but we are often prone to miss it."

So, decide to look for the book, to be positive, and to try new things in hopes of creating a better world and leaving the world better than you found it. When it comes to decision-making, author and minister Robert H. Schuller tells us to "Never cut a tree down in the wintertime; never make a negative decision in the low time; never make your most important decisions when you are in your worst moods; wait; be patient; the storm will pass and the spring will come." With each season, change and adapt as needed and try to see its positive side. Author Thomas Crum suggests that "Instead of seeing the rug being pulled from under us, we can learn to dance on a shifting carpet." Norman Vincent Peale, author and minister, states that "Any fact facing us is not as important as our attitude toward it, for that determines our success or failure." Of course, having a positive attitude and planning proactively can make a great difference in the achievement of one's dreams and goals. Richard I. Winword writes that "Life offers two great gifts --time, and the ability to choose how we spend it; planning is a process of choosing among those many options; if we do not choose to plan, then we choose to have others plan for us." So, create your immediate personal goals, envision your contributions to the society, plan for yourself, and continue on the road to success.

Above all, keep your eyes and mind open since such activities can increase your knowledge, wisdom, productivity, and enhance your behavioral contributions to the society. As an effective manager, professional or leader in your field, you should consciously focus on your thoughts, on your feelings, and on your behaviors as they can make a huge difference to you, your family, your colleagues, your profession, and this world. Think positively and be positive; have a clear vision of your future and this world, then take one step at a time toward making it come true. Dr. Deepak Chopra, medical doctor and author, once said that "The way you think, the way you behave, the way you eat, can influence your life by 30 to 50 years." One could further say that the way human beings think and behave can influence the lives of many others for hundreds of years and several generations to come. As stated by Lee

Iacocca, "No matter what you've done for yourself or for humanity, if you can't look back on having given love and attention to your own family, what have you really accomplished?" The goal should be to make a positive impact on individuals around you and thereby to society. Such an impact can be seen from the thoughts, feelings and behaviors of thousands of individuals including Mother Teresa, Mahatma Gandhi, Dr. Martin Luther King, Jr., and many others around the world. So, determine what your identity and contributions to this society will be and make these dreams and goals a part of your thoughts, feelings and behaviors.

Discussion Questions

1. What is employee retention? Why would employee retention be important in today's workplace? Discuss.
2. Why are employees terminated? What are some of the common reasons for employee terminations? Discuss some common examples or reasons.
3. What are some common reasons for why firms cannot retain a qualified diverse workforce? Why do employees leave organizations for better organizations?
4. Can there be a relationship between stereotypes and negative employee performance appraisals? Discuss.
5. What can managers do to make sure their personal biases and stereotypes are not impacting the employee's performance appraisal process?
6. Have you ever seen managers or heard of managers who have terminated an employee in a totally wrong manner as the manager allowed his or her emotions to drive the decision? Discuss your personal examples. What could have been done to terminate the employee in a dignified and respectful manner?
7. What can a firm's managers do to respect all of their employees from the beginning (hiring) to the end (retirement or dismissal)?
8. What are some strategies that firms have used or can use to attract, hire, develop, and retain a highly qualified diverse workforce? Discuss actual examples.
9. How is diversity related to internationalization and globalization? Discuss recent examples.
10. How is diversity related to religion, competition, and democracy?
11. Discuss the future of diversity and this world! Present your thoughts and your philosophy regarding diversity.

Part IV

Cases and Exercises on Culture and Diversity

Cases

*C*ulture and diversity related cases can serve as laboratories for the application of theoretical concepts and long-term retention. The following pages provide a number of diverse cases, dilemmas and scenarios for individual and group discussion purposes. Read each case and answer the questions factually based on your understanding of the concepts and based on your further research on each topic. You can look at relevant textbooks, articles and relevant websites for the definition of the terms and understanding of the concepts. Always support your thoughts and answers with recently published articles and examples from the workplace. In your analysis and discussions with colleagues (face-to-face and online), please use constructive criticism for reflective thinking and development purposes. A colleague, by the name of Saber Stanakzia, said that "Constructive criticism is the process of offering valid and well-reasoned opinions about the work of others, usually involving both positive and negative comments, in a friendly manner rather than an oppositional one" (Personal electronic communication through Afghan Newsgroup, June 14, 2006) In collaborative work, this kind of constructive criticism is often a valuable tool in raising and maintaining performance standards in the department, institution and/or society. Constructive criticism includes a balance of analysis and feedback. Critical thinking and constructive criticism can help identify relevant issues to focus on during team discussions. One must use logic, patience and objective data to support one's point of view. Unfortunately, due to the overuse of poorly written negative and nagging comments, some people can easily become defensive even when constructive criticism is given in a spirit of good will. Keep in mind that constructive criticism is more likely to be accepted if the comments are objective and focused on the work or agenda rather than a person's personality or background. That is, attacking personality issues and cultural traditions must be avoided in order for effective collaborations to take place among diverse teams.

Culturally sensitive individuals can adopt a passive, nonviolent attitude if they view a situation as personal, pervasive, or permanent in order to effectively collaborate with others on the team or group. Other individuals may adopt an aggressive response, but such aggression must be professional, objective and to the point. One must keep in mind that constructive criticism can be easily misinterpreted and aggressive exchanges often spiral out of control, resulting in "flaming" responses. Effective interpersonal communication skills can be helpful to assess a responder's frame of mind or paradigm. During initial exchanges or when encountering defensive individuals, effective criticism calls for softer language and inclusion of positive comments. It is best to remember that when a speaker strongly identifies with contentious areas (such as politics or religion), non-offensive criticism can become challenging. So, be careful in your discussions and use constructive criticism to get your points across to diverse team members and colleagues.

For a standardized and formal process, unless suggested otherwise, you can use the following suggestions for analyzing each case:

1. Review and thoroughly read the case and several other recently published articles related to this topic. Provide a brief summary of the case (or topic). Discuss the dilemma, the challenge or problems that are apparent.
2. Next, clearly state one main Problem or Opportunity Statement facing you in this case. Remember that the Problem or Opportunity Statement must be in the case or in its questions.
3. Provide at least one good alternative to solve the problem, enhance performance (capitalize on the opportunity) or enhance the work environment. Justify your alternative.
4. Offer an implementation plan and relevant steps for the stated alternative (preferably using a table or Gantt chart).
5. Provide an overall summary and discuss what employees, managers, and firms can learn from the lessons offered in this case?

Overall, the analysis can be in the American Psychological Association (APA) format. If relevant, you can include data, tables, figures, models, and graphs as such visuals make the material easier to read and more interesting. Make sure to label your visuals appropriately. Make sure to provide full references at the end of your analysis.

Case 1: The Truth about Diversity

The term diversity can mean different things to different individuals. As such, the term "diversity" is often misunderstood and at times despised or feared. Of course, diversity itself is neither good nor bad. Everyone is diverse and unique as a human being. This diversity does not necessarily make a person good or bad, inferior or superior. It is what people do with various dimensions of diversity or have done with it through their responses that have left a good or bad impression on many individuals' minds. Diversity is not about females or blacks; yet, many workshops in the United States have traditionally made their content solely about these two dimensions of the term. Diversity is not about quotas and reverse discrimination; yet, some managers and corporations have established quotas (as goals) and some males and Caucasians may have been victims of such unfair practices. Furthermore, as a male, if I think that diversity is about gender, then I might feel that I am at a disadvantage since females are likely to get promoted before me because there is a greater need for female managers and executives in most firms. Therefore, I might associate diversity with reverse discrimination toward qualified males in the workplace. On the other hand, if I feel that diversity is about people of different cultures and multinationals, then I might feel that the government or the corporation owes me certain privileges simply because I am multicultural. Of course, such thoughts and thinking are not the realities of diversity or cultural competency. Therefore, it is important to get a clear understanding of what the term "diversity" actually means and how it applies to EVERYONE in the workplace.

While diversity is not advocating any form of unfair discrimination, it is not just about gender and skin color as it is inclusive of every unique trait that makes a person special or different from others. As Dr. Preston Jones would say, who is the Executive Associate Dean of the business school at Nova Southeastern University, 'diversity is about being truthful, searching for the truth and celebrating the truth.' The truth about diversity is that it is a reality of life in this universe. Diversity is a broad concept and workforce diversity management skills enable managers to effectively capitalize on everyone's strengths and knowledge to create synergistic results.

Discussion Questions

1) What does the term "diversity" mean to you and your workplace?
2) Is diversity something that is mandated or created by law or a government? Explain.
3) Can diversity be avoided in the workplace? Explain.
4) Why are some people fearful of the term "diversity"?
5) What can leaders and human resource management experts do to remove people's fear of the term "diversity"?
6) Discuss at least three benefits of diversity and diversity management that apply to your workplace, employees, colleagues, and/or customers.

Case 2: Diversity and Profiling[26]

There are many concerns that one is constantly faced with on a daily basis, including how to do one's hair, when to go workout or simply what to eat each night! However, there lies greater concerns around the world, concerns that are larger and more important than simply deciding what to have for dinner! On the national level, the greatest concern lies in the notion of how even the most educated persons in the United States as well as other nations can be largely ignorant. It seems that after the 9/11 attacks, preconceived notions and stereotypes were reinforced, where the most diverse nation in the world was faced with a blind diversion. It seems that on the external front, there was unification, yet internally there was bitterness, strong dislike and most importantly hate for not only people of Middle Eastern descent, but more so for any brown colored person. It seems that Bina, as a Hindu, was faced with discriminatory remarks; her parents' businesses were broken into during the late hours of the night, where messages of "Get out of our country" were written almost

---

[26] Co-authored with Bina Patel, Nova Southeastern University.

throughout their walls. Even today, along with other minorities, the "brown colored" individuals face discriminatory remarks. The 2006 movie entitled "*The Inside Man,*" with Denzel Washington, Jodie Foster, Clive Owen, Willem Dafoe, and Christopher Plummer showed one realistic scenario where the police officers labeled a Hindu worker from the bank as an Arab from the Middle East. The Hindu worker continued to say that he is not an Arab but the officers were not willing to believe him at first. Yes, many Hindus do wear a turban which is very different from the turbans that people wear in some Asian countries such as Afghanistan. So, a turban or other wardrobes do not necessarily make one a Hindu, a Jew or a Muslim. One must not assume and associate wardrobes with religious affiliations or ethnicity.

Perhaps the greatest concern lies in how uneducated "the educated" really are! The 9/11 attacks have left a permanent imprint in everyone's minds, which can not only lead to societal discrimination, but discrimination within the workplace. Profiling has been and continues to be a national concern in the United States. The key to preventing its negative impact on innocent individuals is more education, awareness and fact-based decision-making.

Discussion Questions

1) What is profiling? How has it impacted minorities in the United States over the past 100 years?

2) "Educated persons" refers to what kind people? What qualifications would be needed in order to be considered educated? Historically speaking, have "educated" and "bright" individuals discriminated against minorities?

3) What is meant by preconceived notions and stereotypes?

4) Will these preconceived notions and stereotypes hold true within ten or twenty years from now?

5) Discuss the statement "It seems that on the external front, there was unification, yet internally there was bitterness…" What is referred to as the external front?

6) How would the situation differ if the 9/11 attacks had taken place in another country? Would this affect the judgment of individuals on 'brown colored' people? If so, how and why?

7) Is profiling a real solution to some of the challenges this world faces in the twenty-first century environment?

Case 3: Harassment in the Workplace[27]

Jodi is a twenty-two year old undergraduate student at one of the local universities pursuing a degree in business. She has several interests, including politics, journalism, working in hospitals, etc., but has no idea what she would like to pursue as a career. So one day, she decides to visit the career services center located at the university. At career services, Jodi discovers that there is an internship offered by the

---

[27] Co-authored with Bina Patel, Nova Southeastern University.

local government; they are looking to hire a college student to write departmental polices and procedures. She realizes that internship will not count as course credit, but it does pay a substantial amount of money. She realizes that more than anything, the experience should be worth it.

A few days later Jodi decides to fill out the application and within a couple of weeks she is asked to come in for an interview. On the day of the interview, Jodi meets with a supervisor, Diana, of the Recreation and Parks Department. She is asked several questions in regards to her writing and communication skills, as well as her ability to work with people and in teams. The interview finally comes to an end and the supervisor tells Jodi that she will be given an answer within three business days.

Three days later, Jodi hears the good news and takes the offer. The following week she begins her internship and throughout several weeks, she conducts research on how to write policies for the department. Jodi and Diana conduct several meetings in order to put the manual together. Throughout these meetings the director of the department, Mr. Finely, is also present. Mr. Finely, who is also fairly new to the department, is in his early fifties, and appears to be more of a father figure to Jodi. His work within the department, as well as the local government, is highly regarded.

Within two months of her internship, Jodi has completed the final draft of the policies and procedures for the department. With nothing to do and still having a month left before the completion of her internship, the director asks her to assist him with several of his projects. Feeling honored, Jodi eagerly helps and soon realizes that Mr. Finely is always asking her to help him with his presentations. Jodi constantly thinks to herself how an educated man, such as the director, cannot seem to get down the basics to putting together a presentation. She finally concludes that he may just not remember due to his busy schedule. During the course of the projects, Mr. Finely comments on how well dressed Jodi always is and how well she maintains her posture. Jodi feels that his compliments are very friendly and takes them in a light and innocent manner.

Finally her internship comes close to the end and the director asks her out to lunch and leaves it up to her to decide when and where to go. Jodi finally thinks to herself and decides to go to a local restaurant nearby the following day. Later that afternoon, Jodi sends the director an email confirming their lunch appointment for the following day. She waits for an answer from the director, but does not get one; so she assumes that lunch may or may not be on for tomorrow. Later that evening, Jodi receives a phone call from the director. Surprised to hear from him at her home, Jodi confirms the lunch appointment and asks why other interns were not invited. The director claims that since they will be working there on a full time basis, they will be treated to lunch another day. While Jodi continues to think, the director begins to ask her several questions, such as "what kinds of movies do you like?", "what is your family like and how many siblings do you have?" Before Jodi begins to answer, she realizes that his questions are becoming more and more personal. She feels that he is interested in her, specifically when he states that he "would like to spend more time with her." The situation becomes very uncomfortable for Jodi, who quickly makes an excuse to hang up. She decides to tell Diana about the conversation the following day, as well as deciding to quit her internship. Diana asks Jodi to file a formal compliant as this becomes a sexual harassment case. Months later, Jodi receives news from Diana that the director has been forced to resign.

Discussion Questions

1) Often people are confused about the terms harassment, sexual harassment and a hostile work environment. Based on your research and understanding, what is harassment? What is sexual harassment? What is the definition of a "hostile work environment"?

2) Is the director's behavior in this case sexual harassment? Explain.

3) If the director had continued to call Jodi several times in the coming weeks, how would your answer change for the second question?

4) Should Jodi have quit her internship? Could Jodi have avoided the situation? How? What should one do when faced with this situation?

5) Were the director's comments towards Jodi's dress attire innocent?

6) What necessary steps could have been taken by Jodi in order to avoid the situation from arising?

7) Did Mr. Finely really need Jodi's help with the presentations? Or was it a reason for him to spend more time with her?

8) Are the director's actions justifiable? Did he act in a professional manner?

9) Should the director be fired based on his comments towards Jodi? Discuss the actions taken against the director. Should he have been forced to resign based on this incident? Could there have been other reasons for this resignation?

Case 4: Black History Facts

There are many achievements and accomplishments from various diverse groups of people that need to be remembered and celebrated. Also, proper credit needs to be given to the right individuals, their communities, and ethnicities. In the United States, now there is much information about African-Americans and Blacks being mentioned and taught in diversity and history related textbooks. However, historically, such achievements about minority groups in the United States were not emphasized as much since most textbooks were written about the dominant groups and their achievements. As such, many are not fully aware of certain achievements and facts from individuals of diverse backgrounds. The following list is provided by AMANA (2006) to create awareness throughout the various communities about the various historical facts (such as birth dates, dates when famous people died, and other such events) about Black History in the month of April on a day-by-day basis. Review each historical fact and see how many of these should be promoted a bit more in the popular media or through education. Put a checkmark next to the ones you think should receive more coverage in school textbooks or in other specific fields.

1. April 1, 1950 - Charles R. Drew developed techniques for processing and preserving blood.
2. April 2, 1984 - Georgetown coach John Thompson becomes first Black coach to win NCAA basketball tournament.

3. April 3, 1826 - Poet-orator James Madison Bell, author of the Emancipation Day poem "The Day and the War."
4. April 4, 1968 – Dr. Martin Luther King, Jr. assassinated.
5. April 5, 1951 - Washington, D.C. Municipal Court of Appeals outlawed segregation in restaurants.
6. April 6, 1909 - Matthew A. Henson reaches the North Pole, 45 minutes before Commandeer Peary.
   April 7, 1885 - Granville T. Woods patents apparatus for transmission of messages by electricity.
7. April 8, 1974 - Atlanta Braves slugger Hank Aaron hits 715 home run, surpassing Babe Ruth as the game's all-time home-run leader.
8. April 9, 1898 - Paul Robeson, actor, singer, and activist.
9. April 10, 1947 - Brooklyn Dodger Jackie Robinson becomes first African-American to play major league baseball.
10. April 11, 1966 - Emmett Ashford becomes first Black umpire in the major leagues.
11. April 12, 1983 - Harold Washington becomes first African American mayor of Chicago.
12. April 13, 1950 - Historian Carter G. Woodson, author of The Miseducation of the Negro.
13. April 14, 1775 - First abolitionist society in U.S. is founded in Philadelphia.
14. April 15, 1964 - Sidney Poitier becomes first Black to win an Academy Award for Best Actor for *"Lilies of the Field."*
15. April 16, 1862 - Slavery abolished in the District of Columbia.
16. April 17, 1983 - Alice Walker wins Pulitzer Prize for Fiction for "The Color Purple."
17. April 18, 1864 - More than 200 Black Union troops massacred by Confederate forces at Ft. Pillow, Tennessee.
18. April 19, 1972 - Stationed in Germany, Major Gen. Frederic E. Davidson becomes first Black to lead an army division.
19. April 20, 1894 - Dr. Lloyd A. Hall, pioneering food chemist.
20. April 21, 1966 - Pct. Milton L. Olive III awarded the Medal of Honor posthumously for valor in Vietnam.
21. April 22, 1922 - Jazz bassist and composer Charles Mingus born.
22. April 23, 1895 - Clatonia Joaquin Dorticus patents photographic print wash.
23. April 24, 1944 - United Negro College Fund Incorporated.
24. April 25, 1918 - Ella Fitzgerald, "First Lady of Song."
25. April 26, 1888 - Sarah Boone patents ironing board.
26. April 27, 1968 - Vincent Porter becomes first African American certified in plastic surgery.
27. April 28, 1839 - Cinque leads mutiny off the coast of Long Island, NY.
28. April 29, 1899 - Duke Ellington, jazz musician and composer.
29. April 30 1952 - Dr. Louis T. Wright honored by American Cancer Society for his contributions to cancer research.

Discussion Questions

1. How many of the above facts should be covered more heavily in school systems in the United States or around the world? Which specific two and why?
2. Do you think some people would be surprised to hear some of these facts? Which ones might surprise people and why?
3. Check out the following website and find one more fact about Blacks that might be interesting for others to know: http://www.theblackmarket.com.
4. What are some facts about females and their contributions to society?
5. What are some facts about individuals with various disabilities and their contributions to society?
6. What are some facts about Europeans and their contributions to society?
7. What are some facts about Bahamians and their contributions to society?
8. What are some facts about Jamaicans and their contributions to society?
9. What are some facts about the Russians and their contributions to society?
10. What are some facts about Arabs and their contributions to society?
11. What are some facts about Japanese and their contributions to society?
12. What are some facts about Bahaudin and his contributions to society? I am only kidding about this question, just skip it but do think about your up-coming contributions to your immediate family, relatives, friends, colleagues, community, and the society at large. You can go beyond simply thinking about your contributions and write them down; then strategically work on actually achieving them in the years to come.
13. What are some facts about _____ (*choose a country, people group based on one diversity characteristic, etc.*) and their contributions to society?

Case 5: Clustering of Nations: Are All Caribbean Cultures[28] Alike?

The Caribbean region is made up of several small island nations, which often have been romanticized as a singular Caribbean, assuming that they all share the same culture and values. The romantic ideal of the region as one dates as far back as late nineteenth century when the first colonial proposals of a unified Caribbean were proposed, albeit as a measure of having effective management of the region. The Caribbean today promotes itself in the tourism and leisure market as a place where, while it may have been culturally plural in the past, today the manifestations of culture is singular – a Caribbean culture.

The forces of globalization has once again caused the Caribbean region to look at individual island nations' competitiveness as well as combined regional competitiveness. The aspect of a successfully combined Caribbean will bring into sharp focus the need for understanding of the cultures of the region. Understanding of the various islands' cultures will not only show the diversity of the cultures that make up the re-

---

[28] - Co-authored with Reccia N. Charles, St. George's University.

gion, but also identify the similarities and differences that exists among them. The island nations have a basic understanding of the various historical contextual dramas that shaped their realities of today, however there is still a dearth of information on the basic underlying cultural values that shape the various peoples of the region.

The economies of the region are diverse. Trinidad is based on oil and manufacturing in contrast to other islands' economies, which are based on agriculture, tourism and offshore banking in varying degrees. Given that Jamaica was included in the Hofstede's 1980 study on cultural dimensions, and that the other islands were not; brings into the question the validity of using the Jamaican cultural values as a measure for the entire region. Within the region, there are fundamental historical differences that may cause deviations in the dimensions of culture.

The Caribbean has a unique history of colonization by the European nations: England, Spain, Portugal, France, and the Netherlands. A history that also involved African slavery and Asian indentured labor created a situation where the cultural identity of today has become blurred and very fluid even by anthropological and social standards. Most of the Caribbean's written history begins with the so-called discovery of the Caribbean by Columbus in 1492. The discovery is one that Columbus believed to be the beginning of the East Indies and Asia that he had set out to find, and so the region also became known as the Indies, today the West Indies.

For the majority of Caribbean islands, independence from the colonial powers only occurred in the sixties, seventies and eighties, leaving on average only thirty-five years of free thinking and the search for a cultural and even national identity. The only three exceptions being Haiti 1804, Dominican Republic 1844 and Cuba 1902, that gained independence from their respective colonial masters. In the case of Haiti, independence was a result of the successful slave revolution led by Toussaint Louverture and ultimately declared by Jean-Jacques Dessalines, who became Haiti's first dictator. The fight for independence had left the country ravaged beyond recognition; the plantations and infrastructure were destroyed in the years of fighting.

The Caribbean is also influenced by the immigrant labor that entered the region during that five hundred year period. The Spaniards met the native 'Indians,' the Tianos (Arawaks) and Kalinas (Caribs) who inhabited the region prior to the arrival of the European nations. These natives served as the first laborers in the region and were soon replaced by white indentured laborers from the European nations in the seventeenth century. The white servants were later replaced by the African slaves and shortly after the end of slavery, the Asians (Indians, Chinese, and Japanese) transposed the African slaves as the last indentured laborers in the region. The last wave of indentured labor forever changed the ethnic makeup of the Caribbean people. There was also a growing Creole population which was a result of the miscegenation of the various settlers. Experts conclude that the resulting interrelationship of class, ethnicity, sex, color, religious, rural/urban, and language divisions in the region makes the social structure and culture even more difficult to analyze.

Caribbean culture tends to be analyzed through the class structures that emerged after the gain of independence. As with most post-colonial countries, a class structure emerged that had a distinct ruling and servant class, as well as other intermediary classes. With the class system there is usually some avenue in which to move up the social ladder, however what existed under the feudal-colonial system, seemed more like a caste system since there was no avenue for mobility.

The political climate of the Caribbean has been stable in comparison to Central and South America. The Caribbean's long history of colonialization and the subsequent interests of first the powerful planters, landowners and today, the foreign corporation created a legacy bias that ultimately favors capitalism; and the private sector involvement in the public sector and formation of public policy. It should also be noted that today there are still thirteen territories which remain under the colonial rule of Britain, France, Netherlands, and the United States. Experts note that one of the main characterizations of the Caribbean has been the change from colonial to liberal-democratic states and the subsequent shift to leftist-socialist one party states (Grenada, Guyana and Suriname). Grenada's venture was one of a military coup, while Guyana and Suriname being one of political decide via racial lines, including blacks and East Indians.

The majority of studies on culture tend to look at the outwardly manifestations of it, or rather the most obvious and recognizable parts of culture; or what experts define as the aesthetics, until Hofstede's 1980 study of the cultural dimensions which included the island of Jamaica. The Caribbean represents itself as a culturally plural place and rightly so, but the very virtue of being culturally plural means that a study of one island's national culture does not define the culture of the other islands. The spheres of colonialist influence mixed with pervasive and unceasing movement across geographical, social and linguistic boundaries contributes further to the complexity of the region. It is based on this fact that a study of each island's national culture is warranted in order to fully understand the region and its challenges. Cultural understanding of the various islands using Hofstede's five dimensions can lead to further studies that can be of value to marketers, politicians and businesses, because the impact of each dimension can then be tested in relation to other factors.

Discussion Questions

1. What are some of the commonalities that the people of various nations in the Caribbean share?

2. What are some common factual characteristics that the people of Jamaica share as a people group? Which characteristics are also shared by some individuals in other Caribbean nations?

3. Why do people assume that all Caribbean nations share similar characteristics with regard to their cultures? What are some of the major differences among people of different nations in the Caribbean?

4. Why do people assume that all Middle Eastern nations share similar characteristics with regards to their cultures? What are some major differences among people of different countries in the Middle East?

5. Why do people assume that all Asian nations share similar characteristics with regards to their cultures? What are some major differences among various nations in Asia?

6. Why do people assume that all Latin American countries share similar characteristics with regards to their cultures? Are there major differences among Latin American countries? What are some of them?

Case 6: No Place for Hate: Clashes of Values

Values theory states that what you value drives your behavior. Furthermore, the stronger and more deeply one believes in a specific value, the more faithful and loyal he or she is going to be to that value. Many individuals claim that they are honest or truthful at all times; yet, some people are not always honest if it is going to hurt them personally, professionally or hurt one of their close friends or family members since they don't want to see a loved one suffer. In other words, their level of honesty depends on the outcome or consequence of the situation. At the same time, many other individuals who strongly believe in this value of honesty will decide to be truthful regardless of the consequence. For example, most people value life. However, to what extent each person values life might vary. A person may value life and limit the extent of this belief to human life; therefore, he or she would have no problem going hunting to kill a deer, birds, rabbits, or other wild animals. On the other hand, other persons may value life, yet will have no problem killing humans who cause harm to the community, because they might be soldiers in the military or police officers protecting a community. However, Mohandas "Mahatma" Gandhi said that he valued life in all of its forms. Therefore, he probably avoided hurting insects, animals, birds, and human beings. People like Mohandas Gandhi, Dr. Martin Luther King and Mother Theresa were willing to die for good causes through non-violence and they strongly believed on this non-violence belief being the best solution toward equality and peace. Gandhi has said that he was willing to die for causes of equality and justice, but there was no cause for which he was willing to kill another living being. So, values can drive a person's behavior depending on how much reflection has been put into what that value means to him or her. Strongly held values can be consistent drivers as well as predictors of behavior. This is why many individuals are willing to die for their religious values.

For thousands of people around the world, religious values tend to be a strong driver of behavior since they have given religious values much thought, reflection, and reinforcements over the years living in the community. For these individuals, religion is a way of life as they are living according to its guidelines, and for causes that often have more meaning than their own lives, thoughts, and material properties. These are some reasons why people respond very strongly to movies, television sitcoms, Hollywood shows, radio talk show hosts, newspapers, and/or cartoons that paint a negative or inappropriate picture of their faith or religious figures. This was the case with regard to the cartoons which portrayed Prophet Mohammad inappropriately. The following commentary was forwarded to various newsgroups in South Florida on March 31, 2006 and it is written by Moiez A. Tapia. Read the commentary and then see the discussion questions.

I begin with the name of the Lord, the Creator and the Sustainer of the universe, the Most Gracious, Merciful and Almighty God of all mankind.

For many decades in the recent times, the behavior of the Western world towards Islam and Muslims has angered the Muslims all over the world. The Danish caricatures insulting Prophet Muhammad [Peace Be Upon Him -PBUH] and distorting his highly ethical, merciful and loving character and his teachings of love, charity and forgiveness were the last straw that broke the camel's back. Islam advocates freedom of speech and worship. But this freedom does not permit, among other things, insulting God's prophets, communities and their sacred symbols. All prophets from Adam to Moses, Jesus and Muhammad [PBUH] were sent not only to give Laws but also to serve as models showing how to practice the Laws they were sent with. Whenever such a model sent by God is distorted, it disturbs Muslims very much. Movies that distort the noble character of Prophet Jesus [PBUH] and depict it to be weak such as THE LAST TEMPTATION OF CHRIST were banned in Pakistan. Such movies and pictures of so called artists painting a jar of urine with a picture of Jesus in it are a deplorable statement accomplishing nothing but hurting of the feelings of Muslims and Christians.

Journalist Sarwat Husain recently wrote, "The anger shown by some of the Muslims around the world in response to the provocative cartoons of our beloved Prophet Muhammad (PBUH) published in some of the Western media, is not the way prophet Mohammad himself would have reacted. All the Western Muslim organizations, leaders and mosques unequivocally denounced the violent reaction from some of the Muslims in those countries." It should be noted that many of the individuals that demonstrated violently are among the nations that have a high rate of illiteracy. Such obscene expressions in any form must be protested against—but they must be protested against peacefully in non-violent ways.

Several countries have anti-blasphemy laws. Denying the Holocaust is a crime in some places. Pornography is not allowed in public expressions in many places. Why not have laws against insulting prophets, sacred books and symbols and religions of the world? I would like to emphasize that the Danish caricatures were the last straw that broke the camel's back and Muslims have been angry at the West for many decades for many reasons that we do not have time today to discuss fully. I will touch upon them merely briefly:

1. Muslims are very happy and grateful that the European scientist continued the tradition of scientific research and exploration that Muslims started. However, some people in the West, including the USA, are ignorant about the Muslim contributions to science and technology that the Muslims pioneered when Europe was in darkness.

2. Muslims are grateful to the Americans for lots of aid that they gave to many poor countries in the world, including Muslim countries, in various ways. However, they are very angry and sad about the foreign policy of U.S. government, which is based on friendship and material interests and does not hesitate to violate justice and international laws in order to achieve goals based on friendship and material interests, and has thus hurt millions of innocent Muslims unfairly and unjustly.

3. Until 1992, when communism collapsed, our government gave unyielding support for the right of Kashmiris for self-determination. But after 1992 we dropped that sacred principle to please India. This unjust switch on our part has angered Muslims and freedom-loving people throughout the world.

4. The permanent segment of the Security Council of the United Nations consists of 4 Western nations. 1.3 billion Muslims, 1 billion Hindus, and hundreds of millions of Latinos, Africans and hundreds of millions of native Indians in the USA and South America are not represented in it. By what divine right have these four western nations and China secured veto power and dictate the world to their wishes?

5. An effort by many Western media to distort the image of Islam and Muslims has contributed significantly towards prejudice and hatred towards Muslims. Journalist Sarwat Husain wrote, "Long before publishing these particular cartoons of the prophet Mohammad, in April 2003, Danish illustrator Mr. Christopher Zieler submitted a series of cartoons dealing with the resurrection of Christ to Jyllands-Posten, the same newspaper that published prophet Mohammad's cartoons. But the paper refused to run these drawings of Jesus, according to UK's Guardian newspaper." This shows a double standard.

The best response to the Danish cartoons is the statement of the French writer, poet and politician Alphonse de Lamartine, who wrote the following about Prophet Muhammad, whom the cartoons insulted:

> "If greatness of purpose, smallness of means and astounding results are the three criteria of human genius, who could dare to compare any great man in modern history with Mohammad? The most famous men created arms, laws and empires only. They founded, if anything at all, no more than material powers, which often crumbled away before their own eyes. This man moved not only armies, legislations, empires, people and dynasties, but millions of men in one third of the then inhabited world; and more than that, he moved altars, gods, religions, ideas, beliefs and souls."

Let us pray to God of the entire mankind that He May continuously remind us that we all are children of Adam and Eve and show us how to live like brothers and sisters of the same family with justice, peace, tolerance, harmony and mutual love and respect, Amen!

Discussion Questions

1. Have you ever met people who have strong values? Which ones? How do such values drive their behavior at home, community or workplace? Discuss examples.

2. In what ways do religious people demonstrate their values which are associated with their faith? Discuss at least two specific examples.

3. Can extremism in any faith lead to discrimination, violence and hatred? What are some actual examples of extremism that are seen throughout the world across various beliefs and faiths?

4. Should governments consider anti-blasphemy laws?

5. What is "freedom of expression" and how far should people go to express themselves? What are some thoughts or variables that people should consider before they choose to express themselves or their thoughts in public?

6. Should comedians be allowed to make fun of religions in their acts to make people laugh? Discuss and be specific.

Case 7: The Relevance of Values

What are values?[29] According to Steven A. Beebe, Susan J Beebe and Mark V. Redmond in their 2002 book *"Interpersonal Communications: relating to others,"* values can be seen as enduring concepts of good and bad or right and wrong. Values are more resistant to change than ones attitudes and beliefs. They are also more difficult for most people to identify. Values are so central to who you are that it is difficult to isolate them. According to William D. Guth and Renato Tagiuri, in their 1965 publication, a Harvard Business Review article, "Values are such an intrinsic part of a person's life and thoughts that he tends to take them for granted, unless they are questioned or challenged." So, how are values acquired? Our values are instilled in us by our earliest interpersonal relationships. According to Scott Reeves (2006), personal finance writer for *"Forbes Magazine"*, in his article *"The Fiscal Facts of Life,"* he said that if you teach your child the difference between needs and wants, how to budget and how to save, your child will know more than many adults. Guth and Tagiuri state that "Values are acquired very early in life." Values are transmitted to a child through his/her parents, teachers, coaches, mentors, and other significant persons in his/her environment who, in turn, acquire their values in similar fashion from their role models and family members. Experts state that child rearing practices are expressions of a family's values, the community, and of the values of the social group or society to which the family and its members belong.

Values are powerful as they are central to one's behavior and concept of self. Reeves (2006) went on to explain that if you teach your child about spending limits and help him/her develop the discipline needed to stick to them, trouble with credit can be avoided because interest payments will not take a significant bite out of the monthly budget. Guth and Tagiuri wrote that by using knowledge about personal values, a CEO can identify differences between him or herself and others to modify possible strategies for future growth.

How are values used? Values are used to determine what we believe to be true or false. We are what we see, we are what we do, and we are how we behave. Guth and Tagiuri wrote that, it is believed that the modified strategy would match the values of the group better than any individual strategy. A CEO who is armed with a modified strategy from his/her group of executives based on their personal values could lead the group toward a consensus which everyone would be very satisfied with. They further wrote that few of us make the effort to study our own values to the point of being able to be explicit and articulate about them.

Of course, values can change over time. As a child grows, so does his/her capacity to absorb more information as well as differing beliefs and values. In his article, Reeves (2006) said that the sooner parents start with their children; the easier it is to pass on both mechanical skills about managing money and your financial values. An allowance is a good way to introduce children to money management. A piggy bank will do for a young child, followed by a savings account. As the child grows, consider opening an investment account. Parents will have to make the trades, but the child will learn the importance of diversification. Do not forget to teach the child about giving back to the community – a religious cause, a civic organization or some educational program about a disability or a physically challenged group.

Why are values important? Personal values are important because by spending time to identify them, people in general and top-level managers will have an explicit

---

[29] -Co-authored with Macie E. Dawkins-Hanna, Nova Southeastern University.

and useful way of thinking about them and about the influence these have on the strategic decisions in general.

Each person has his or her own personal and professional group of values that guide him or her through life and its major events. The following, for example, are one group of values:

1.   I value myself as a Person.
2.   I value self Respect.
3.   I value Family.
4.   I value Friends.
5.   I value Life.
6.   I value Truth.
7.   I value Honesty.
8.   I value Community.
9.   I value Education.
10. I value Faith.
11. I value Leadership.
12. I value Excellence.
13. I value Timeliness.
14. I value Professionalism.

These values are important to individuals who take ownership of them for their own reasons of existence, dreams and goals. These values can be motivational to those who take ownership of them through personal reflections and what they mean to his or her life or "way" of living. The more meaningful such values are to one's life, the more likely that they will drive a person's behavior and the choices one makes in his or her daily activities

Discussion Questions

1.   What do values mean to you?
2.   Are values capable of driving one's behavior? If so, how and according to what theory or examples?
3.   What are your values? Explain your top five professional values that apply to the workplace.
4.   Imagine you are the President of the World for this year. What would be five values that you would want everyone to internalize? In other words, what should be the top five universal values in society?

Case 8: Discrimination Lawsuit and Cracker Barrel

Unfortunately, discrimination and discriminatory practices are everywhere in the workplace. There are all types of discriminations including racial, sexual, and age discrimination. One such a case is the discrimination that Cracker Barrel Restaurants were involved in during the early 1990's against homosexual employees (Howard, 2005). Dan Evins in Lebanon, Tennessee founded Cracker Barrel Restaurants in 1969. In 1991 they operated over 100 stores around the country, with revenues exceeding $300 million and with about 10,000 non-unionized workers. In 2005, Cracker Barrel's annual net sales were $2.2 billion. About 77.4% of Cracker Barrel's revenue comes from restaurant sales and around 22.5% of their revenue comes from retail sales. The following are some of the historical dates and milestones for Cracker Barrel as presented in their online website (Cracker Barrel, 2006):

- 1969: On September 19, 1969, Cracker Barrel Old Country Store opens in Lebanon, Tennessee.
- 1970: Cracker Barrel incorporates and a second store is opened in Manchester, Tennessee.
- 1977: About 13 stores in Tennessee and Georgia. Cracker Barrel stops selling gasoline to focus on restaurant and retail operations.
- 1980: 20th location opens. Stock goes public, named one of the top 12 US stock picks by Money magazine.
- 1982: The first store in Alabama opens.
- 1986: Cracker Barrel has a total of 3100 employees.
- 1987: Cracker Barrel opens its 50th store, located in Savannah, GA.
- 1990: 88th location opens after expanding in Southeast states.
- 1990: *Restaurants & Institutions* magazine names Cracker Barrel "Best Family Dining Restaurant." Cracker Barrel wins the award for the next 13 years {1990-2003}.
- 1991: Cracker Barrel reaches 100 stores when Lexington, NC opens. The first stores in Mississippi, Missouri and Michigan open.
- 1993: *Destinations* magazine poll ranks Cracker Barrel as the "Best Restaurant Chain." Cracker Barrel wins top honor 10 consecutive years {1993-2003}.
- 1995: Cracker Barrel expands into Colorado and New Mexico.
- 1997: Stores open in Arizona, Connecticut, Maryland, New York and Utah. The Cracker Barrel web site makes its debut.
- 1998: Cracker Barrel opens its first "off-interstate" location in Dothan, Alabama. Cracker Barrel moves into Idaho, Montana, Nebraska, and New Jersey.
- 2000: The 431st location opens.
- 2005: For 4th year in a row, The Good Sam Club names Cracker Barrel as "The Most RV Friendly Sit-Down Restaurant in America."

During the early part of 1991, through their headquarters in Lebanon, Tennessee, William Bridges, Vice President of Human Resources, issued a policy that stated that it would no longer employ those people whose sexual orientation fail to demonstrate normal heterosexual values. As per this policy the store managers were forced to interview employees and ask them if they were in violation of the new policy that was set.

There was a cook in the Douglasville, Georgia store that had been working for them for over three years by the name of Cheryl Summerville and she answered the questions truthfully. Her official paperwork stated the reason why she had been dismissed. She was being terminated for violation of the company policy because she was gay. Management proceeded with their interviews and fired about 16 other employees in different stores across the United States. They were being fired without any severance pay. These employees did not have any legal recourse. Federal civil rights laws did not cover discrimination based on sexual orientation.

In February of 1991, management issued a statement, which stated that they were going to continue and employ homosexual individuals. They would handle the situation on a store-to-store basis. The previously fired employees, because of the original policy, had not been rehired. People were unconvinced of their new statement and intentions. Lesbian and gay activists called for a nationwide boycott of Cracker Barrel restaurants. This was coordinated by the Atlanta Chapter of Queer Nation, which was co-chaired by Cheryl Summerville and Lynn Cothren. Lynn Cothren was an official with the Dr. Martin Luther King, Jr. Center for Non-Violent Social Change. The activists staged various picket demonstrations and sit-ins. They would sit in various Cracker Barrel restaurants during peak hours and only order coffee. These demonstrations continued throughout the summer of 1991. Several people were arrested at these demonstrations including Summerville and Cothren. Summerville was hailed by reporters and politicians, as the Rosa Parks of the movement. The boycott organizers accused the company of racism and sexism. Many of their stores at that time sold confederate flags, black mammy dolls, and other offensive items.

Elizabeth Holtzman, New York City comptroller, and Carol O'Cleiracain, finance commissioner, wrote a letter to Dan Evins (on March 12, 1991) which stated their concern on the negative impact on the company sales and earnings, since they were trustees of various city pension funds that owned about $3 million in stock. They asked for a clear statement of the company's policy regarding employment and sexual orientation. They also wanted to know what steps had been taken in regards to the dismissed employees. About one week later, Dan Evins wrote back saying that the policy had been cancelled and that it had not impacted the sales. The officials were not satisfied and wrote back again asking for the status of the fired employees. The officials also asked if the company had established a policy that would communicate clearly that discrimination based on sexual orientation was not allowed. Dan Evins never replied to this letter.

In a campaign launched by Queer Nation, activists bought single shares of Cracker Barrel common stock. They did this so the company could suffer from the expense involved in the processing of paperwork. In buying a share of stock, they could also attend the annual stockholders meeting. Company officials, in November 1991, prevented these new stockholders from participating in the meeting and also blocked protesters at the corporate offices with a court injunction. The boycott did not impact the company's sales up 33% in 1992, increasing their revenue to $400 million, and expanding to 127 restaurants. Their stock, traded on NASDAQ exchange, and appreciated 18%. All the media attention significantly increased the national awareness of the lack of protection for homosexuals on the job. Many states, counties, and municipalities passed legislation designed to prevent discrimination on employment based on sexual orientation.

The boycott continued against the Cracker Barrel's restaurants. The Cracker Barrel's board of directors and their upper management, with one exception, remained all white male dominated. The NAACP and a group of employees and former employees filed a class action lawsuit against Cracker Barrel alleging discrimination against African-Americans in hiring, promotion and termination practices. Along with 42 customers and over 400 witnesses, the class lawsuit accused Cracker Barrel of repeatedly offering whites segregated, better and faster seating.

Despite such successes and growth history as that of Cracker Barrel's, many firms seem to have a difficult time in dealing with various dimensions of diversity. It surprises most people that there is so much discrimination, both subtle and blatant, among people in this twenty-first century work environment. Cracker Barrel's company philosophy, according to their online website is: "To serve the finest quality, reasonably priced home-style country food and quality gift items in a comfortable and friendly atmosphere." Of course, management's challenge is to make sure ALL of their customers are being served in a "comfortable and friendly atmosphere", and that ALL of their employees are working in a "comfortable and friendly atmosphere."

Discussion Questions

1. What can management of Cracker Barrel do to make sure all of their employees and customers are offered a "comfortable and friendly atmosphere" regardless of their race, gender, or sexual orientation?

2. Is it difficult to determine sexual discrimination patterns in the workplace? Why or why not? Explain.

3. Why are so many successful firms getting themselves into so much negative publicity with regard to various dimensions of diversity? Discuss.

4. Should restaurants and retailers be concerned about the race, religion, sexual orientation and other such dimensions of diversity? Why or why not? Discuss.

Case 9: Afghan-English Beauty Queen

When one hears about Afghanistan, due to the years of war with and by foreign forces, the thought of peace, centuries of civilization, art, and history does not always come to the minds of many individuals from new generations around the globe. As an Afghan scholar (Ehsan Naji) once stated, it is time to make the identity of Afghans clear from behind the "cloud of war" which has been blocking the sun from making it shine. Gun is not an Afghan identity; Afghan identity is in their ancient civilization; the Afghan identity is written thousands of years before Christ and Prophet Mohammad in the forehead of Buddha in Bamyan, and in the best values of Zoroaster, along the Road of Abrisham (Silk Road). While many leaders are working hard to clarify Afghanistan's identify in today's global world, Afghans are getting involved in many aspects of the international community, including competing to become beauty queens.

This case is a story about the Afghan-English Beauty Queen which was emailed to the author and it is written by Katy Guest (December 04, 2005). Read the story and then reflect on the questions.

Who says I can't be English, Muslim and a beauty queen? Hate mail and clerical condemnation will not stop her from competing for Miss World. She couldn't care less about working with animals and children. She has already traveled the world.

She doesn't appear in a bikini. And she speaks six different languages. Miss England is a lot more than just a pretty face.

Hammasa Kohistani was born in Uzbekistan and is the first Muslim to win the Miss England title. On Saturday she will represent her country against 103 other women, all competing to become Miss World. The pageant means that China is the 26th country she has explored. And she is prouder to be English than anyone in the world.

But it has not been an easy journey from Uzbekistan to evening wear: when Miss Kohistani was chosen as Miss England, she and her family were subjected to threats and abuse, and Muslim "leaders" condemned her. Rumors reached her that her A-level classmates were grumbling that she should not represent the English. Hammasa, whose name means "ambition", was born in Uzbekistan because her parents were studying in the country. They returned to their native Afghanistan when she was one year old. Her memories of her childhood home are vague and few. "Once, when Kabul was being attacked, Mum sat me on the window sill and I could see bombs dropping and shooting," she recalls. "Mum started screaming because bullets began flying past our faces, so we all had to spend the night in the corridor as that didn't have windows or doors."

It was for their daughter's sake that the Kohistani family - a law lecturer and a government administrator - decided to leave Afghanistan in 1996, as the Taliban were rising to power. "Conditions had always been quite bad, but they became too bad to stay," she says. "My parents decided it was safer to leave, especially having a first-born girl: those are not good conditions for girls." Her parents both have master's degrees and have always encouraged her academic achievements, and though she is only 18, she knows what she wants. She is taking a break from her four A-levels while she tours the world as Miss England, but when she finishes school she wants to work in advertising design - "on the other side of the lens."

She would like to go back to Afghanistan, but only to visit. "My parents talk about it quite a lot, but it would never be safe for me there," she says, sadly. Both her parents had studied in the former Soviet Union, so before Hammasa started school the family fled to Moscow, where they had friends. They lived in Uzbekistan, Ukraine and Dubai before settling in Southall, west London. "I have lived in four countries and traveled in 25 - that's why I can speak so many languages," she says. "I speak Persian, Russian, Dari [spoken in Afghanistan], French ... And I had to learn English when I was nine years old."

Her knowledge will be coming in handy now. Miss Kohistani and finalists from 103 other countries are in China, where Miss World will be chosen on Saturday. "This is my first trip as Miss England, and probably the biggest of my life," she says. There were those back in London who were not entirely supportive of their new representative when she was awarded the Miss England title in September. Message boards carried spiteful discussions saying Miss Kohistani was not truly English and should not be representing the country. She barely acknowledges the slights. Instead, she is thrilled by the support she has received from Muslims and non-Muslims. She says she feels no pressure to be a role model for her co-religionists. "I am proud to be what I am regarding background, religion and what I represent," she says. "So many Muslim people have contacted me to say that they are proud of me and are supporting me. I have letters from Jewish people who have congratulated me, too."

As for Englishness, she knows who she is. "The color of your skin or your hair does not make you English," she says. "What you believe makes you English. I probably consider it more of a home than many other people because I have traveled more to get here. I have been chosen as an ambassador for England, and that says it all for me."

Discussion Questions

1. Hammasa Kohistani has lived in many countries and visited even more. Is Miss Kohistani Afghan or English? Should she have dual citizenship and dual ethnicities?

2. What are some of the values that Miss Hammasa Kohistani has gained from living in diverse countries and cultures? What are some of the values that she is currently cherishing?

3. The case mentions that Hammasa Kohistani does not wear a bikini by choice, why? Discuss. Can this choice be an advantage or a disadvantage for her as a contestant? Explain.

4. Are there others like Miss Hammasa Kohistani that were born in one country, have parents from another, and have lived in many different countries? Who? What do they consider themselves in terms of ethnicity?

5. Can a person who was born in one country, be raised in another and yet live somewhere else, call this third country his or her home?

6. Miss Kohistani said "The color of your skin or your hair does not make you English. What you believe makes you English." What does she mean by this statement? Aren't all English people supposed to be white, all Africans black, all Italians romantic, and all Afghans covered with hijabs or turbans? Comment on why such misperceptions have become so common in the minds of some individuals around the world.

Case 10: Education and Taliban Spokesman at Yale

The country of Afghanistan has suffered great tragedies in the last twenty five years, and the "downward trend" began with the invasion of the country by the Russian soldiers in 1979. Once the Russian soldiers were "defeated" at the closure of the "Cold War" and they left Afghanistan in 1989, the country began experiencing further destruction from the decade or so of internal animosity and civil war. Perhaps, some of the animosity and ineffective leadership of various governments could be linked to the lack of proper education and development for the people of Afghanistan prior to, during and after the war eras. Luckily, this is changing as the leaders and people of Afghanistan are now more focused on providing the young generation a fair education opportunity. Ambassador Sayed Tayeb Jawad, in June 2006, said that "Afghans were more absorbed with the struggles of surviving their present agonies...Many crimes were committed in Afghanistan over the last twenty years, but robbing an entire generation of boys and girls of their childhood and depriving them of the joy of going to school rank among the worst transgressions" (Embassy of Afghanistan Newsletter, June 2006). Ambassador Jawad further stated that "Those of you who have {recently} visited Afghanistan know how dramatically our country has changed. Boys and girls have returned to schools and their parents are determined to rebuild their country...In Afghanistan we have learned the hard way that the best way to invest in peace and security is to invest in education. By investing in education, we are writing the history of the future; a future of hope, prosperity, peace, love, and unity."

Due to the "brain drain" from Afghanistan in the last twenty five years, many Afghan expatriates are now serving as leaders, managers and educators throughout the world. Some Afghans are major leaders in the corporate arenas, some are in government sector, and others are professors, directors, deans, and university presidents in Europe, Russia, and/or the North American countries. Some of these prominent Afghans are returning home or are making various "roadways" available for Afghans to receive a good education, whether they are in Afghanistan or other part of the world. As a result of such efforts along with the international community, not only are more Afghans receiving a better education in Afghanistan, many are getting the opportunity to travel and study abroad. In the last two years, there have been nearly 80 Afghan exchange students who completed one year of their high school studies in the United States and then returned home. Seven of these high school students lived with various host families in South Florida. Similarly, many Afghans are attending prestigious colleges and universities around the globe now. John Kasich, in his article entitled "*Yale Must Wake Up*" (March 06, 2006), stated that the former Taliban spokesperson is now receiving an education from Yale University. The following are some of what John Kasich wrote in his article.

How did he get a visa? To apply for a visa you must answer a question about belonging to a terrorist organization. While the Taliban may not be an officially recognized terrorist group, they are certainly our enemy in Afghanistan and Hashemi was their spokesman, even appearing on the Yale campus in 2001 defending many of the Taliban's actions. Why is our government allowing this man to live within our borders? Every day many people are denied entry to the United States, yet he continues on at Yale, lending credibility to the Taliban. Sometimes we get it right, and sometimes we get it wrong.

Yale University in their drive to promote diversity and tolerance, has gotten it very wrong. Their decision to admit the former deputy foreign secretary of the Taliban is both puzzling and worrisome.

The spokesman for the Taliban, a regime known for their disregard for human rights and their oppression of women and non-Muslims, should not be given a platform at one of our nation's top universities. The dean of undergraduate admissions disagrees saying that Sayed Rahmatullah Hashemi is "a person to be reckoned with and who could educate us about the world." The dean also explained that they were eager to have Hashemi as a student because they lost another student with similar credentials to Harvard. Since when does academic competition trump principle? And what are we supposed to learn about the world from the atrocities of the Taliban? And where is the outrage on the Yale campus? While Hashemi has been attending classes at Yale for eight months, the university continues to ban other students from organizing a ROTC chapter on campus and has sought to deny military recruiters access to students on campus. I look forward to the women's groups, the human rights advocates and others standing up, speaking out and clamoring against Hashemi's presence on campus and the extreme views of the Taliban.

Both Yale and those within our government who approved this visa must wake up and right this wrong. While diversity may be a noble ideal, tolerance and understanding end where torture and oppression begin. Continuing to allow this man to stay in the United States studying at Yale is a mistake and sends the wrong message to other students, the American people and the world about our values and our commitment to defending them.

Discussion Questions

1. Why is education important for economic development? How can people of third world countries and nations that have been destroyed due to years of civil war or poverty provide a better education for their young children? Discuss.

2. Visit the Embassy of Afghanistan's Website in the United States (at: www.embassyofafghanistan.org) and discuss what Afghan leaders are doing to provide educational opportunities for their youth. Discuss.

3. What are your thoughts about Yale University admitting Mr. Sayed Rahmatullah Hashemi as one of their students?

4. Why do some schools encourage controversy and debate? Discuss the benefits of such a policy.

5. Should schools of higher education grant access to their educational opportunities for people of diverse countries and views? Discuss and explain your thoughts.

6. Just because Mr. Sayed Rahmatullah Hashemi worked for the Taliban government, does that mean that he accepts or represents the views of Taliban?

7. Should people who work for a government that is in charge be denied access to education when that government is no longer functioning?

Case 11: Workplace Policies and Behavior Alignment

As presented by Cavico and Mujtaba (2005), Eastman Kodak fired an employee who criticized a company initiative on behalf of gay workers. The termination has caused an angry debate between proponents of corporate diversity and free expression. This dispute echoes other recent ones at various companies, including AT&T and Verizon Communications, in which employees alleged that they were disciplined for opposing policies advocating gay acceptance. Some of these employees have sued, claiming violations of their rights to religious expression.

In the AT&T situation, a former employee has sued the company in federal court, alleging she was fired for refusing to sign the company's handbook, which had a provision about respecting and valuing differences in sexual orientation, due to her strongly held religious beliefs. Similarly, in the Verizon case, an employee was suing the firm, claiming she was punished for her religious beliefs because she refused to sign the company's code of conduct, which required the employees to respect gays.

Discussion Questions

1. Sexual orientation is one aspect of diversity that managers and employers face every day. Some managers and employees are likely to have different orientations than their colleagues. How should managers deal with the issue of sexual orientation in their departments and workforce?
2. Should sexual orientation policies be documented in employee manuals?
3. Can employers expect behavior alignment with their organizational policies and practices in the workplace?
4. Does behavior alignment with organizational practices mean that one has to change his or her personal beliefs and values?
5. How can "professionalism" be used to make sure one's behavior in the workplace is aligned with the organizational values and policies? Provide an example.
6. There is likely to be a combination of personal, organizational, and professional values in a given department or firm. What should managers do when an employee's personal values are contradictory to the organizational values or the views of others in the department? How can manager use "professionalism" or "professional values" to overcome such differences?

Case 12: Cross Dressing Away from the Workplace

As presented by Cavico and Mujtaba (2005), a federal judge ruled that the Winn-Dixie grocery store chain did not violate any federal law when it terminated a long-time employee, a truck driver, who dressed as a woman when he was away from work. The case was brought as a sex discrimination case pursuant to federal anti-discrimination law. The employee, an employee-at-will, worked for Winn-Dixie for twenty years. The employee crossed-dressed on his own time as a way to relieve stress and express his feminine side. The issue was brought to Winn-Dixie's attention by the employee himself, who mentioned his feminine proclivity during an annual employment review. The terminated employee contended that his employer discriminated against him because of his sexual orientation. Winn-Dixie claimed it acted in its own best interest as a business, and fired him in the belief that, if word got out, some customers would shop elsewhere. The terminated employee eventually got another job hauling stock for a pet store chain. He asked the American Civil Liberties Union to represent him with his appeal to the U.S. Court of Appeals.

Discussion Questions

1. In the United States, is it illegal for a male to dress like a woman? Should cross-dressing be illegal in the workplace, in the community or in one's home?
2. Should employees be fired for cross-dressing on their own time or when they are away from the workplace? Discuss.

3. Should managers be concerned about what employees wear when they are not in the department or in the workplace? Discuss.

4. Do you agree with the decision of Winn-Dixie's management to terminate this employee? Why or why not?

Case 13: Peer Pressures and Accusation of Acting like Others

As reported on most news reports, many celebrities (such as Johnny Carson, Marlin Brando, Jennifer Anniston, Lisa M. Presley, and others) have at times felt "lonely" as it might be difficult for others to understand them when they are actually on "top of their game" or at the apex of their professions. Perhaps the statement which says that "it is lonely at the top" is somewhat true. Maybe, due to "expectations" from celebrities and for their own security reasons they do act differently than the normal person.

Most people would agree that when a person is acting like someone else, then he or she is probably wasting the life of the person that he or she is. Therefore, one should be the best he or she can be without turning him or herself into somebody else. Of course, while attempting to become the best one can be, some individuals are wrongly accused of acting like someone else. For example, some African American or Black teenagers who study hard and earn good grades in school are at times accused of "Acting White." Famous celebrities like Kareem Abdul Jabar (basketball star and actor) and Will Smith (actor and singer) have had to deal with such pressures as being accused of "Acting White" when they were seen reading books or going to libraries. A survey of 90,000 students (as reported on ABC's 20/20 Show on April 14, 2006 which was focused on Freak-economics) showed that black students who got good grades had fewer friends. The results of the survey showed that for white students, a higher GPA often meant more friends. Acting White to some people means that one desires to become like a white individual (from Anglo Saxon or Caucasian background); for girls "acting white" may mean acting like or desiring to become "Barbie," the doll.

According to the 20/20 report on ABC, when White teenagers improve their grades to A and B, they tend to also increase the number of their friends. In other words, White teenagers who get better grades tend to have more friends. However, this is not true for Black or African American teenagers in the United States. When a Black or African American teenager's grades improve from an average of C to A and B grades, he or she is likely to have fewer friends, at least based on some statistics presented by the ABC report. One possible reason for these statistics and conclusions could be the peer pressure associated with the smart kids "Acting White." Of course, it is best to avoid such labels as studying is not a "White" phenomenon. Everyone should strive to become the best he or she can be without losing his or her identity. In an inclusive society, everyone can be a professional and retain his or her cultural identity.

According to a colleague from Nassau, let us call her Carletha, "In the Bahamas acting white is not really a term used." However, she went on to say, that the term white in the Bahamas is associated with persons who are "mango," skinned color, or "Kunky Joe," a mixed breed when one is bright/white in color but one of his/her parents is Black. Carletha also mentioned that some members of The Rastafarian beliefs and traditions consider reading a book, making a professional career, and being successful as being associated with "whiteness." As she was growing up, she had noticed many young teenagers and adults from the Bahamas who went off to college in the United States and the Caribbean Islands and returned home as Rastafarians with dreadlocks and smoking habits, saying that education is for the "white man not them." According to some of these individuals, Blacks were supposed to work with their hands and be self-employed instead of becoming slaves for the "white man." If one worked in a bank or insurance company, just to name a few, that was considered being a slave for the White man. As a result, many of the Rastafarians sold fruits, peanuts, homemade juices such as carrot, eggnog and peanut juices which they produced manually. They also sold Bob Marley paraphernalia and Rasta color belts, sandals, hats, and other products. The parents of these individuals were often ashamed, embarrassed and hurt to see their educated children return home and refuse to work in professional positions, calling them "White man" jobs. According to Carletha, at one time, the Rastafarians were popular and on the rise in The Bahamas, but now the culture has changed to being a proud Bahamian. Besides that, Bahamians encourage everyone to read, get advanced degrees, and get an education because the world is a competitive market and the best way to compete is if you have appropriate credentials, skills, experiences, and relevant knowledge that can produce a better outcome than others.

Carletha does not think that the focus of becoming competitive is associated with whiteness, because in order to get new knowledge you have to read; and in order to be successful you need a good education. To get a good job, which in return will make you more successful from an economic perspective, one needs to read and learn. Carletha said that she remembers a story told by one of her history teachers, which said that "the white man used to hide books and knowledge from the Black slaves to keep them down and to keep them dependent upon their masters." She continued to say that "I do not know if this was true....but this is probably where the Rastafarian got their beliefs from in regard to the jobs which supposedly belonged to the White man."

Another colleague, let us call her Betty, said that some of the pressures children face today are acceptance, clothing and body appearance. The term "acceptance," according to Betty, refers to a sense of belonging to a group, like the most popular kids, Hispanics, football team, the rockers, gang members, so forth. Such behaviors increase the separation of the student body as a whole and in many situations create differences that may escalate to conflict for not accepting others in one's group. Additionally, Betty states that clothing is another pressure kids experience in many schools. As absurd as it sounds, one's clothes may help one gain or lose friends. If a student can not afford brand name clothes, then he or she may join a different group of friends than those who can actually afford it. Sadly enough this pressure can create distractions at any age for youth can be very vulnerable. Betty stated that her niece is in kindergarten and the first couple of days in school she literally came home crying because she could not make friends claiming that they were "mean" to her. One student (6 years old) told her that she couldn't be her friend because she did not dress cool and she was not popular. Again in the same pattern, the body figure or appearance also has a lot to do with friends and acceptance both for girls and boys. Many kids can be cruel, calling each other names and creating rumors and stories to damage other children's self esteem. A recent example, according to Betty, in a local high school is that somebody took a picture of a student and downloaded it into "Myspace.com" and entered it in his profile that he is bisexual since he "appears" as one. As a result, this poor student's reputation is damaged due to normal peer pressure as many of his friends want to know if he truly is bisexual. Such intentional or unintentional jokes can hurt other teenagers, especially when the victim is not very confident or sociable with his or her peer groups.

It has been said that if I am I because you are you and you are you because I am I, then I am not and you are not. However, if I am I because I am I and you are you because you are you, then I am and you are. Everyone should be himself or herself.

Discussion Questions

1. What is meant by "Acting White"? Which generations of minorities are often associated with this accusation?
2. What types of other peer pressures do children face today in their primary or secondary education?
3. Why are many teenage individuals accused of "Acting White"? Is this "peer pressure"? If so, how can one effectively deal with it?
4. Why is reading a book, making a professional career, and being successful associated with "Whiteness"?
5. What is oppression (or cycle of oppression) and how can this cycle be broken?
6. How have minority celebrities (African-Americans, Hispanics, Native Americans, those with disabilities, females, Asians, etc.) overcome major obstacles in their lives or communities to become successful in their fields, professions or industries? Discuss one or two specific examples that you are aware of in the last few decades.
7. Does success change one's cultural identity, race or ethnicity?
8. Can people achieve high levels of success based on their performance amid major stereotypes, biases and discriminatory practices? If so, who are some examples and role models?

Case 14: Assimilation and Integration into a New Culture

Harvey and Allard (2005) state that assimilation is treating everyone the same (they should adjust to our way and be like us), and integration is appreciating the differences and respecting uniqueness. According to many experts, assimilation is the process of re-socialization that seeks to replace one's original worldview with that of the host culture. The concept of assimilation was generally focused on ethnicity and is now primarily on linguistic issues. In most cases, in this process of assimilation, the minority group or culture may disappear by losing its members to the larger and more dominant cultural group. For example, consider the case of an immigrant Spanish-speaking Mexican woman who is Catholic marrying an English-speaking Anglo-American Protestant male. If the woman learns English, changes her maiden name and religion, and later becomes a U.S. citizen, she will have assimilated into mainstream American culture (The Gale Corp Inc., 2002). Another example can be a white woman who marries a black man, and the woman learns the way the black families' value religion, food, and household responsibilities. The woman conforms herself to abide by these different black family's norms, she has then assimilated into the mainstream of African- American culture.

Integration is the transition where people see themselves as inter-culturalists or multi-culturalists in addition to their national and ethnic backgrounds. According to some people, integration expresses a complex concept whose meaning can differ according to the country considered as well as political and historical circumstances. Concepts of integration can range from multiculturalism to full assimilation and even segregation. Generally, integration refers to the broader context of legal access to resources, rights, goods and services, whereas social inclusion also includes a foreigner's individual choice to be part of the host community's social life (Medda-Windischer, 2004). According to Medda-Windischer, integration policies strive to bring immigrants into mainstream, society while simultaneously protecting minorities' ability to develop and express their socio-cultural features. This conception is based on two elements: reciprocity and socio-cultural diversity (Medda-Windischer 2004). Integration brings changes to policies and practices such as flex time, mentoring job assignments, broader strategies, recruitment career development, upward mobility, and global computer networks just to name a few. Even though diversity is the new frontier for the global market today, it is not celebrated by every organization. Some organizations find the focus of diversity too limiting and others object to managing diversity. Further, it is important to prepare, train and inform employees of diversity benefits in the workplace because companies have to deal with it anyway since it is part of our world today.

Some people are very focused on not assimilating with others. For example, the Chinese entrepreneurs in most foreign countries tend to only hire people of their own nationality. If they hire people from the local culture or any other nationality they are often hired for limited tasks and responsibilities. Otherwise they run their own businesses, and they hire their own people for major positions, such as chefs in their restaurants. While private entrepreneurs do not like others assimilating with them, the situation is very different for most large and public organizations. Often in public institutions such as schools and hospitals, one can find a diversity of nationalities being integrated into the workplace. Most often, these professionals from around the globe, having diverse cultural backgrounds, are able to easily integrate into completing the job in an inclusive work environment. Furthermore, local people should understand that forcing the dominant culture on others is not effective for the creation of an inclusive work environment. For example when immigrants come over from their various countries, the best method of integrating them is trying to keep the immigrants' own cultures and practices separate from those of the host country, but at the same time teaching them the language, culture, and social behavior of the host country. For example, when a Mexican immigrant comes over to the United States to live and work, Americans should make sure the immigrant understands the local language, culture, and accepted norms, but at the same time allow immigrants to keep a good sense of their own language, culture, and social behavior.

Discussion Questions

1. What are some typical challenges associated with assimilation and integration into a new culture? Discuss specific examples.

2. Is assimilation into a new culture a desirable trait? Discuss its advantage and disadvantages.

3. How can one best integrate into a new nation's culture or a new organization's culture? Is integration into the new culture a necessity? Does integration imply losing one's identity? Discuss.

Case 15: Religious Discrimination[30] in the Workplace

Religion is a very important influence in the lives of many workers today. Many individuals would believe they would never do such a thing as religious discrimination. However, a survey conducted in 2001 by the Tanenbaum Center discovered much about religious discrimination in the workplace. For example, the center conducted a survey of 675 individuals and about 20% had either been victims of religious discrimination or knew someone who had. Additionally, it was discovered that about 15% of employers provide space or time for religious observance, study or discussion, and only 13% accommodate the needs of different religions. In a country such as the United States which is founded on religious freedom, this is not acceptable to most people. Religious discrimination may send a message to others of religious freedom being a privilege to some elite group, but not everyone.

The simple example provided by Georgette Bennett and others provides a situation where an employer hosts an employee recognition lunch on a Friday afternoon. The menu consists of ham, roast beef, or salami and cheese sandwiches, julienne meat salads, some champagne to start the celebration with a prayer, and soda. This may sound like a wonderful meal for some. It may also be thought by the employer to be a wonderful way of showing appreciation. What is wrong with this picture? The employer is trying to say thank you.... right? They have clearly purchased all the food. The employees should be appreciative and thankful for this.... right? Wrong! The problem with this particular situation is that the Christian employees cannot participate because the event is held during Lent and they cannot eat meat. The Hindu employee cannot eat meat at all. The Jewish employees cannot participate because meat and cheese eaten together are not kosher. And, the Muslims are not even present due to the event being held during a prayer time and furthermore, the Muslim employees would not be able drink the champagne since it has alcohol or to eat ham, salami or julienne meat salads. The luncheon sounded like a good idea. The best of intentions are now an arena of exclusion. Furthermore, the employer is now perplexed and cannot figure out what the problem is, or why morale and performance will decline. This is a simple example of how easily an employer can have a good intention and manage to unintentionally discriminate against, and offend a number of their diverse employees. What then is the solution?

Initially, employers must explore a few relevant facts. According to Ms. Bennett, in 1970, less than five percent of the U.S. workforce was foreign born. By the year 2000, foreign-born employees in the workforce doubled to 10.4%. Therefore, the workforce is now more diverse with immigrants from Latin America, Africa, Asia, and the Middle Eastern countries. This adds millions of Muslims, Buddhists, and other non-Judeo/Christians to the U.S. workforce. Billions of dollars have been spent in the United States since the 1960's to correct racial, ethnic, and sexual discrimina-

---

[30] Co-authored with Michelle Newton, Nova Southeastern University.

tion in the workforce. However, many employers remain extremely reluctant to address or discuss religious issues. Since 1992, complaints to the Equal Employment Opportunity Commission (EEOC) have risen 30%. This is a very volatile situation. Discrimination issues do not go away by ignoring them or through ignorance; in fact they often grow very big, very fast and can cause low morale and lawsuits.

The survey conducted by Tanenbaum included workers from across 47 states in the U.S. and a wide spectrum of religions, with over half being college educated management, and skilled technicians. These are often the employees in greatest demand, and whom most companies want to retain. The survey revealed that many had faced religious discrimination. They also discovered over two thirds believed some form of religious bias had occurred in their workplace. Nearly half of those surveyed said their performance suffered after they felt they had been discriminated against, and nearly 45% considered changing jobs. And with recruitment and retention being the most critical employment issues facing employers today, these results should be of concern to any employer and diversity trainer. Some examples of religious discrimination the respondents reported were as follows (Tanenbaum, 2004; Bennett, 2004):

1. Employees are told they are not allowed time off from work to observe their particular religious holidays;
2. Employees are afraid to ask for time off from work to observe their particular religious holidays;
3. Employees are told that they are not allowed any breaks for prayer time;
4. Employees' personal property has been destroyed or damaged because of their religious beliefs or faith;
5. Employees are told that they cannot wear any type of beard or facial hair even those worn for religious reasons;
6. Employees are told that they cannot wear any form of head covering even though it may be a part of that person's religion;
7. Employees who wear clothing that express their particular faith do not get promotions or advance as quickly as other employees;
8. Employees are dismissed for expressing their faith through the way they dress; and
9. Employees who wear clothing that express their particular faith are made fun of or talked about by other employees.

So then, what is the answer? What should employers do to ensure they manage religious diversity within the workplace? If a religious discrimination complaint is made, employers must show that they have complied with three requirements. They must be able to prove they have educated themselves, been reasonable by not relying on stereotypes, and have considered all alternatives for accommodation. The Tanenbaum study also proves companies could substantially benefit from employing flexible policies, attentiveness to and respect for religious and racial diversity. Additionally, they should enforce intolerance to all forms of bias and prejudice, as well as maintain a proactive stance toward hearing and addressing the concerns of all workers. But above all, employers should listen to the concerns of its employees and seek their suggestions.

More specifically, the Tanenbaum Center suggests employers create a mechanism allowing all to step outside of their established comfort zone and discuss religious issues. Most persons are willing to discuss their religious practices. Employers should also create a safe space where everyone can effectively deal with religious problems. And, the employer should also focus on the small things, since that is where most issues begin. It should be noted the mission of the Tanenbaum Center is to combat the verbal and physical violence that people do to each other in the name of religion. They implement their mission by bridging the gap between analysis and action. On the analysis side, they focus on the theological roots of prejudice and conflict. On the action side, they create pragmatic programs that reach people where they live and impact everyday life. One of their core programs is religious diversity in the workplace (for more information, see their website at: www.tanenbaum.org).

In conclusion, managing workplace religious diversity is clearly no simple task. It requires education of oneself, empathy for others and becoming "other oriented", as well as being willing to communicate with others on sensitive issues. American employers should stop running from diversity, and embrace the various theories, with hope for a more healthy, happy, and productive tomorrow. Employers should strive to create an environment where both the employer and employee can be satisfied and proud of everyone's accomplishments; and where all employees can work in an environment free of discriminatory practices.

Discussion Questions

1. What are some common beliefs that most religions tend to share? How do these beliefs impact people's behaviors?
2. What is religious discrimination?
3. Have you heard of or seen religious discrimination in your industry, community or workplace? If so, what are some typical examples of such discrimination?
4. What should employers and managers do to accommodate their employees' religious needs?
5. Should employees be able to promote their religious values and philosophies in the workplace? Why or why not? Explain.

Case 16: Communication with the Hearing Impaired[31]

The American with Disabilities Act (ADA) was singed into law in 1990 by the President of the United States. The law protects people with disabilities from being discriminated against in the workplace. Hard-of-hearing people are included in this law, which not only protects them from discrimination in employment, but also requires employers, public facilities, government agencies, and telecommunications companies to make provisions to accommodate people that suffer from a hearing loss. According to U.S. government estimates, almost 55-60 million Americans have some kind of disability. Their ages range from 16 and 64 and many of them are unemployed. They would like to work if they were given the opportunity to do so. According to statistics, about twenty-two million Americans are hearing impaired.

---

[31] Co-authored with Bebe T. Frisbie, Nova Southeastern University.

Experts estimate that about ten million of these hearing-impaired people could be added on to the workforce if certain accommodations are made.

Managers have their work cut out for them in order to get ready for the influx of retirees that will be looking for jobs who are experiencing hearing loss. One particular group of people that are coming of retirement age is the "baby boomers." Many of them will continue to work because of the cost of health care and not saving enough money for their retirement or simply because they would like to keep busy. Some of these "baby boomers" may have a problem when they are forced to go out and look for a new job because their employers force them into retirement. Some experts have said that the "baby boomers" as well as the generations of today have two strikes against them when it comes to their hearing. Even though aging is the most common cause of hearing loss, the second most common cause is noise-induced. Rock and roll music came out in the 50s with its loud sounds. Every year since, the sounds used to make music have become louder and louder. During the baby boomer years, as well as today, people have been listening to loud music not realizing that it is damaging their hearing.

Employers always look to find workers that are knowledgeable and have the skills and abilities to perform jobs, but they often neglect to look at a great source, individuals with disabilities. Some employers who have hired individuals with disabilities were concerned at first about hiring them, but they soon found out that these individuals could provide valuable contributions to their companies because they are loyal and productive workers. Managers soon realized that they had to adjust the structure of the work for the rest of the employees who did not have any disabilities, and think about those with disabilities in order for all of the employees to be able to work well with one another for the good of the company. In order to do this, managers started developing programs that would prepare their current employees for the interaction they would soon have with workers that have various forms of disabilities. In order to be able to work with a hearing impaired person, we first have to understand what their world is like. Can you imagine what it would be like not to be able to hear? Try stuffing cotton balls in your ears for a day just to see what it would be like. It can be a very lonely feeling. Furthermore, one of their greatest challenges is communication.

How we perceive something plays a big role in whether or not we are going to accept it with open arms. A major problem that people with a hearing loss have is that it is a hidden disability. If you see someone in a wheelchair or walking with a cane, you are more likely to help that person. People do not understand that hearing loss is a disability also even though you cannot see it. If a person has a real bad vision problem, they wear glasses, which are visible to everyone else. Hearing aids are not always visible so you cannot tell whether a person is experiencing a hearing loss. Employers need to determine whether or not a deaf or hard-of-hearing person applying for a job is capable of performing the functions that the job requires. They also need to know whether or not the applicant can follow detailed instruction, work together with a team, if they are able to adapt to change, and how they interact with co-workers and supervisors.

When dealing with the hearing impaired in the selection process, the manager must go through two steps. The first step is to screen their written job applications and the second step is to interview them. In order to be able to go through these steps, the manager must make appropriate accommodations. If the hearing-impaired person has someone to help him or her fill out the application, the manager should accommodate them. Also, if the hearing-impaired person needs more time to fill out the application or would like an interpreter, the manager should accommodate him/her. The best way for a manager to handle a hearing impaired person is to ask them what accommodations are needed beforehand. The manager should also accommodate the hearing impaired during the interview process. Some accommodations may include: Conducting the interview in a quiet, well lighted setting; using whatever devices the hearing-impaired may have; talk normally at a normal pace and pitch; be willing to repeat any questions if asked; and obtain a professional sign language interpreter if one is needed. If group interviews are given, the manager should also accommodate the hearing-impaired person in this type of interview setting as well by: speaking to one person at a time; and make sure the hearing-impaired person knows the interviewer is speaking before the others in the room speak.

With the right training and accommodations, people who are deaf or hearing-impaired can perform most jobs that are available. Screen actors as well as politicians have been successful in their high profile jobs even though they suffer from hearing loss. The success of a deaf or hard-of-hearing person really depends on everyone's attitude and willingness to help resolve communication barriers in the workplace. Being able to communicate with the hard-of-hearing seems to be the strongest barrier to their success in the workforce. Co-workers who are not hard of hearing must be willing to help them in order for them to succeed. Some things co-workers can do to help when dealing with a hearing-impaired person is: to make sure that the hearing-impaired person is able to see their lips by standing in good light, if they are aware that the hard-of-hearing person has a better ear, they need to be closest to it. Similarly, the hearing-impaired person needs to make co-workers aware if they have a good ear. Furthermore, managers and co-worker needs to avoid background noise when talking to the hearing-impaired person.

According experts, some methods to help a hearing-impaired person would be to: get their attention before talking to them and face them directly when talking to them; speak as clearly as possible and do not shout; if the hearing-impaired person does not understand what you say, rephrase it, and ask the person if they understood what you said. Also, make sure that your mouth is not hidden from the hearing-impaired person and do not chew gum or smoke while talking to them. And remember, facial expressions are important to the hearing impaired; to them, feelings are expressed better non-verbally than verbally. Experts further advice that supervisors and coworkers need to control their attitude when working with the hearing-impaired. Some tips would be: do not become impatient with them; stay relaxed and positive; talk to the hearing-impaired person not about them; treat them with respect and help them build their confidence; and ask them what you can do to make communication better. People with disabilities are subject to the same stereotyping, prejudices and discrimination as minority groups. Many individuals may feel uncomfortable around people with disabilities because they are not used to being around them and have not learned how to deal with them. Every workplace needs to have some type of diversity training so employees can learn to deal with individuals with disabilities. It is easy to get agitated with someone if one does not understand what they are feeling. Everyone has a right to work if they want to. We all need to get along together and help each other to succeed in whatever endeavors we are pursuing.

Discussion Questions

1. Name five disabilities that you are aware of and mention how such disabilities can be accommodated in the workplace.

2. What are some common disabilities that impact one's communication in the workplace?

3. Do you know someone who has a hearing disability? How do people communicate with this person?

4. Do you know of people with various forms of disabilities that perform their jobs very effectively? Discuss one example.

5. What are some common forms of discrimination that people with disabilities face in the workplace? What can be done to make sure discrimination is prevented?

6. Who are some celebrities, politicians, professionals, and mentors that have had a form of a disability, but have pursued their goals despite societal challenges? Mention their names, disabilities, and achievements.

Case 17: Global Management Orientations and Strategies

Global managers and leaders know that there are four different ways that most international professionals lead their operations. As such, an understanding of ethnocentric, polycentric, regiocentric, and geocentric management orientations are a necessity for global management. Ethnocentric orientation is one in which the individual is home country centered. Polycentric orientation is one that the individual is host country centered. *Regiocentric* is one in which the individual is focused on regional headquarters or regional basis. And in the geocentric orientation, the individual is world oriented.

In *ethnocentric* management orientation, the approach is basically "what works at home, will work here." One example of this is individuals who choose to open restaurants that are successful in the U.S., in a foreign country. Due to cultural differences, a company that mandates particular work shifts may not be successful in Mexico or other Hispanic cultures with a polychronic time orientation where a linear view of time is not such a high priority. If a manager was successful with this approach in the U.S., and then began operations in Mexico, mandating employees to arrive at 7 a.m. for example, may result in discharge or termination if the employee does not comply. The Mexican worker may arrive to work at eight or so, due to this polychronic view of time, the company would not be successful. In fact, in this situation, the culture believes this way and people are conditioned toward this orientation. Therefore, it would not be one individual who would arrive late; all employees of the culture may arrive very early or a few minutes late. This would occur due to cultural differences conflicting with the ethnocentric orientation. The manager would be wise to reconsider the approach in this particular example.

In *polycentric* management orientation, managers believe the foreign market to be too difficult to understand. They remain host country centered. An example is Pepsi Cola. They operate in joint ventures in other countries. Basically, they bring individuals from other countries to the U.S., train them, and then allow them to work however they choose to accomplish the goals of the company. In this orientation, the company probably finds this approach easier and safer, but they fail to learn much about other cultures, or grow in their knowledge of world diversity.

In *regiocentric* management orientation, the company believes the regional managers are best able to organize operations within the region. Regional offices are located at various locations, and report to a regional headquarters, and then to headquarters. An example may be an automobile manufacturer. Foreign automakers establish companies within the U.S., and they do not generally micromanage these foreign facilities, located in U.S. areas. They rely on the regional offices to monitor production of the cars, and then report back to headquarters.

In *geocentric* management orientation, the management style focuses on both local and worldwide objectives. The management style is interdependent. An example of such a company is Whirlpool; they were able to create a refrigerator from European insulation technology, U.S. manufacturing and design, and Brazilian affiliates. Therefore, in the geocentric management style, resources can come from virtually anywhere locally, or in the world.

Though these four types of management orientation, companies can clearly change from one orientation to another, depending on the needs of the company. A company's main objective is to ensure success and survival of the organization. Therefore, a successful company would utilize whichever style of management orientation offered the greatest potential for success.

These four different strategies of ethnocentric, polycentric, regiocentric, and geocentric orientations are further emphasized as follows:

1. *Ethnocentric management* is where the home country management style is imposed on the host country. The assumption is that what works at home should also work overseas. This style of management is not well suited or applicable to the global world today. The management team has to diversify and adjust in being flexible to accommodate the host country's culture and employees' norms and social relation in the workplace.

2. In *polycentric management*, the foreign market is "too hard to understand," so host-country managers are relatively free to manage their own way. Competition is focused on a market-by-market basis. This type of management style is used by such franchises as McDonald's, Domino's Pizza, Kentucky Fried Chicken, and Burger King.

3. *Regiocentric management* is the style most parent organizations use when they feel that the regional insiders best coordinate operations within the region. The assumption is that the regional workers know the market, and know it better than others. Similarly, these employees can serve an entire region for economies of scale purposes instead of having many representatives in various countries.

4. *Geocentric management* is a highly interdependent system that speaks in terms of the global village. The focus is at once both worldwide and on local objectives. Some franchises operate based on the geocentric management orientation. They focus on being a world-wide business first and then they regionalize in groups.

One should remember that the four management orientations discussed above are not mutually exclusive. Therefore, they can all take place one at a time within the same organization for its different departments or product lines. Many organizations often begin with the ethnocentric mindset or polycentric and gradually develop a more regiocentric or geocentric framework.

Discussion Questions

1. What is an ethnocentric mindset and how can it apply to employee staffing?
2. What is a polycentric mindset and how can it apply to employee development and promotions?
3. What is a regiocentric mindset and how can it apply to promotions and marketing?
4. What is a geocentric mindset and how can it apply to management and leadership of a company?
5. Which management orientation best matches a new company entering a new country?
6. What are the advantages and disadvantages of each management orientation for hiring staff?
7. Can a company be ethnocentric and polycentric at the same time? Explain with a specific example.
8. Which style of global management orientation best matches the concept of an inclusive workplace?

Case 18: High and Low Context Cultures

According to anthropologists and experts on cutlure, a *high context* culture is one in which much of the information in communication is in the context or in the person rather than explicitly coded in the verbal messages (Devito, 2005). On the other side, a *low context* culture is one that derives much information from the words of a message and less information from nonverbal and environmental cues. High context cultures have a greater amount of shared knowledge. Low context cultures, on the other hand, deliver messages which are highly explicit, assuming much less previous knowledge. These differences in communication styles can lead to major misunderstandings.

According to previous studies and research, common characteristics of high context cultures are:

-   Less verbally explicit communication, less written/formal information.
-   More internalized understandings of what is communicated.
-   Multiple cross-cutting ties and intersections with others.
-   Long term relationships.
-   Strong boundaries- who is accepted versus who is considered an outsider.
-   Knowledge is situational; relational.
-   Decisions and activities focus around personal face-to-face relationships, often around a central person who has authority.

According to previous studies and research, common characteristics of low context cultures are:

- Rule-oriented; people play by external rules.
- More knowledge is codified, public, external, and accessible.
- Sequencing, separation of time, of space, of activities, of relationships.
- More interpersonal connections of shorter duration.
- Knowledge is more often transferable.
- Task-centered; decisions and activities focus around what needs to be done, division of responsibilities.

High context cultures can be difficult to enter if you are an outsider (because you don't carry the context information internally, and because you can't instantly create close relationships). Low context cultures are relatively easy to enter if you are an outsider (because the environment contains much of the information you need to participate, and because you can form relationships fairly soon, and because the important thing is accomplishing a task rather than feeling your way into a relationship). Every culture and every situation has its high and low aspects. Most cultures are somewhere in between in the continuum of high and low contexts. Often one situation will contain an inner high context core and an outer low context ring for those who are less involved.

Discussion Questions

1. What are some typical cultures or countries that might serve as examples of low context cultures? Why are these nations considered to be low context cultures?

2. What are some typical cultures or countries that might serve as examples of high context cultures? Why are these nations considered to be high context cultures?

3. What are some of the advantages of a manager from a high context culture going to another country that is a high context culture?

4. What are some of the disadvantages of a manager from a high context culture going into a low context culture?

5. What are some things that a manager should be aware of if he or she is going from a low context culture to a high context culture? Discuss specific examples.

Case 19: Islam and Ihsan-Doing what is Good!

Each religion has its beliefs, philosophies and values. However, religious values are often misinterpreted or used for personal agendas. Islam, one of the major religions in the world, is a way of life for nearly two billion people around the globe and there are stereotypes about it. First of all, one of the most common stereotypes about Islam is that it encourages violence and terrorism. In reality, however, one of the greatest sins in Islam is the taking of an innocent life, which is the definition of terrorism. Even in a state of war, there are strict rules, which include not targeting rorism. Even in a state of war, there are strict rules, which include not targeting women, children, elderly, and the clergy, or the ecosystem or infrastructure, specifically, mentioned in a saying of the Prophet Muhammad prohibiting the destruction of even fruit trees. Islam also forbids taking one's own life. The term "*Jihad*" is often mistranslated as "holy war," a word which supposedly does not exist in Arabic. The term "*Jihad*" means "striving" with one's tongue or pen against oppression. Jihad can be declared by a legitimate head of state. Jihad cannot and should not be used to justify acts which contradict the teachings of Islam.

Second to the stereotype about Muslims and violence is the perception that Muslim women are oppressed. This perception is due in great part to stereotypical representations in the media and Hollywood, where the portrayal of Muslim women is often negative. Rarely are images of the many millions of strong, educated Muslim women in the diverse cultures where Islam is practiced given the spotlight or even mentioned. If we look at the basic principles laid down by the Qur'an, we find that men and women are described as having the same nature, duties, and hope for reward, a fact taken for granted today, but not even imagined 1,400 years ago. Similarly we find that Islam gave women rights that have only recently been acquired by Western women, such as the right to earn, keep, and inherit money, and the right to take part in politics, economics, and even the military. While many in the West view the prescribed Muslim dress, which includes a head scarf, known as hijab, as oppressive; in reality, the purpose of this modest dress, similar to the dress of nuns or Orthodox Jewish women is protection and dignity, and to raise her above being valued for her physical aspects.

Many individuals in the Western world tend to have an incomplete view of Islam due to stereotypes and misinformation that is offered through various sources of information in the society. Islam has many important elements and dimensions that are emphasized in one's daily actions and overall purpose in life. The three dimensions, as discussed by many Islamic scholars and writers, for a Muslim are the concepts of Islam, Iman, and Ihsan.

1. *Islam*: The first element or dimension is entering into submission to God, implying obedience to His laws and following the acts of worship that are prescribed for Muslims.
2. *Iman*: The second is attaining faith in God, and other beliefs, that are based on faith, rather than reason or intellect and involve what is known as "the realm of the Unseen," such as God and the angels.
3. *Ihsan*: The third and highest level is ihsan, or doing what is good. This level is attained by the one who lives his/her life as if he or she can actually see God, in accordance with the saying of the Prophet Muhammad (p) that *"Ihsan is to worship God as if you can see Him, because while you cannot see Him, He can see you."*

Ihsan is a level of moral character of the highest caliber in which one has overcome egotistical desires and promptings, such as envy, jealousy, rivalry, deceit, and other characteristics which bring one down. Under the dimension of Ihsan, or doing good deeds, Muslims are asked to perfect their faith. This involves different levels, including:

- One's spiritual relationship with God, improving and refining it to bring alive the saying about Ihsan as "worshipping God as if one sees Him."
- Intention is extremely important in Islam, and a Muslim should strive constantly to purify his/her intention.
- One of the main purposes of religion is the perfection of moral character, especially when interacting with others. This can be summarized by the basic precept of *"doing unto others as you would have them do unto you."*
- Part of perfecting moral character is of course avoiding wrongdoing, as prescribed by all religions, and doing good deeds. Under the first category one finds the same general precepts of most faiths such as, avoiding such vices as back-biting, lying, cheating, envy, in addition to the major sins such as stealing, killing, etc., and conversely encouragement for such recommended acts or qualities as generosity, kindness, honesty, forbearance, etc. Cultivating such qualities is the true goal of all faiths and is often, unfortunately the greater challenge for adherents to any religion.

Ihsan, or doing what is good, can be achieved through focused and thoughtful actions as discussed by another Islamic concept known as Ijtehad. According to Professor Maqsood Jafri, *Ijtehad* means intellectual endeavor to seek the solutions of day-to-day matters (electronic communication through Afghan Newsgroup on April 18, 2006). It is a rational and analytical approach, based on the Quran and on the teachings of the Sunnah, for interpreting religious matters. Time and again the Quran says that its verses are for thinkers. It stresses the exercise of the rational mind. Professor Maqsood Jafri states that in The Heifer Sura, the Quran says: "Do not treat Allah's signs as a jest, but solemnly rehearse Allah's favors to you, and the fact that He sent down to you the Book and wisdom, for your instruction" (2:231). This verse shows that the words of God and wisdom are prerequisites to keep human beings on the right track and a progressive and just path. The Creator has put the human brain in the skull not in the ankle. Perhaps this is a symbol and Professor Maqsood Jafri states that the place of the brain at the top of the human body signifies the value and importance of the mind. The Book has laid down the foundations, but each person has to be wise in taking appropriate steps to build his or her life upon it through the course of time by chiseling a character for him or herself that stands the test of time.

Discussion Questions

1. What are some misconceptions and misunderstandings about various religions of the world?
2. Can people use religious beliefs and statements to guide people in the wrong path? If so, how? Discuss using any religious views that you are aware of in the modern times.
3. What are two facts about Islam? What are some facts about Christianity, Hinduism, Judaism, and other major faiths in the world?
4. What does the term Jihad mean? How is this term portrayed in the media?

5. Do religions encourage the oppression of women? Discuss. Do you know a Muslim female? How does she live and work in the society? Discuss.

6. What are Ihsan and Ijtehad? Are you aware of other religions that have similar philosophies (as Ihsan and Ijtehad) in guiding human beings in the "right" path toward justice, fairness, and equity for all? Discuss and explain.

Case 20: Globalization and its Origin

Let us think about the diversity of different cultures, organizations, contributions of different countries and regions to modern society, and various practices that today's global firms use to achieve their objectives by understanding the origins of globalization. The key is to reflect upon what has caused globalization. Globalization has impacted people both positively and negatively throughout the world. Globalization has been spread, to some extent, by many of today's large multinational corporations in their drive to maximize profitability and their stockholder's wealth. The more risk that multinational corporations take as they serve new markets around the globe, the more rewards they are likely to enjoy when they are successfully serving an emerging base of prospective customers. So, multinational corporations are one driver of globalization. Is globalization a Western or an Eastern phenomenon? How did it get started and who should claim credit for its innovation or rise? Contrary to the popular perceptions, many claim that such questions do not have a simple answer as globalization has many sources of origin. Some writers claim that popular sentiments against globalization have often been directed at one of its "perceived" vehicles or engines — a Western consumer culture of fast food, gadgetry and cinema imposed on the entire world. But is globalization itself truly a creation of the West to benefit the West? Amartya Sen, Nobel Prize Winner in Economics, argues that "globalization's fruits — and even its origins — can be claimed by East and West alike" (Sen, 2002).

Experts, such as Amartya Sen and other economists, agree that "Globalization is often seen as global Westernization. On this point, there is substantial agreement among many proponents and opponents. Those who take an upbeat view of globalization see it as a marvelous contribution of Western civilization to the world." On the other side, experts also state that "Western dominance — sometimes seen as a continuation of Western imperialism — is the devil of the piece. In this view, contemporary capitalism, driven and led by greedy and grabby Western countries in Europe and North America, has established rules of trade and business relations that do not serve the interests of the poorer people in the world" (Sen, 2002). Globalization is not necessarily a Western phenomenon since for thousands of years, "globalization has contributed to the progress of the world through travel, trade, migration, spread of cultural influences and dissemination of knowledge and understanding (including that of science and technology)" (Sen, 2002). So there are many roads and avenues that have led to what is today termed as globalization.

Discussion Questions

1. What is globalization? Define it as you or other experts see it.
2. What are the main drivers, vehicles or engines of globalization? What forces are impacting or driving the trend toward globalization?
3. Is globalization good or bad? First, give a specific example from your perspective (or your culture) and then provide one more point of view (from another expert or culture).
4. Will globalization speed up the divergence or convergence of cultures around the world? How and why? Discuss.

Case 21: Promotional Journey through the Hierarchy[32]

Most Americans know how the race issue plays itself out in the United States today. It is a sensitive issue. Even in our families, race is used as a card to either uplift or depress our esteem. In 2001, John Artund was made to believe by a member of his family that he could not get certain jobs because he was of a certain race. This family member believed only people of a certain other race had the potential to obtain certain jobs, especially an administrative job like a Human Resource Specialist. After 5 months of job searches and job applications for various positions, he was finally called for an interview at a state agency. He was eventually offered a position in the human resources department. The family member was perplexed because this went against traditional beliefs. However, John had a bachelor's degree in business and recently completed a master's degree in public administration right before he was offered the job. This was the beginning of John's journey into the world of race, perceptions, and disparate treatment, all connected to the topic of workplace diversity.

In John's first job, he quickly realized that he was the only black male in the human resource department. He also happened to be one of the youngest. Over a few months, John noticed that some staffers treated him differently than others. He asked why and he was told because he was selected ahead of other staff members who had higher tenure on the job in the department. Those who treated him differently appeared to be of another race. After a few months, John decided to leave the agency. He got a promotion into another state agency's human resource department.

Surprisingly, in this new agency, once again, John realized he was the only black male in the department. At that moment, he realized, how racially different he was from the norm. Yet, he continued to work for that department for 3 years. In one instance, the director had asked John to avoid writing academically, but to write professionally and keep the content in a "simple-to-read" format for the average person. Remember, John was still the only black male in the new department and believed he was being singled out for such "non-existing" issues because he looked different from the others. Eventually, John was offered another job with another state agency's human resource department as the only black male in that department. In each case, as he moved, his pay rose.

After a few months on this job, John once again, moved to another state agency, making more money, where he finally met another black male, in a lower paying job, after five years of working in several human resource departments. Furthermore, John noticed some statistics that show how black males are not attending higher education

---

[32] - Co-authored with Ike Udechukwu, Georgia State University.

institutions as the same rate as white males. Consequently, the challenge of not having enough qualified black makes in human resource management departments are likely to continue for the coming years.

Discussion Questions
1. How did John achieve this higher status given the challenges he had faced in his previous jobs?
2. Why did John's perception of his ability and self overwhelm stereotypes fed to him by relatives?
3. Has the oppression cycle in the United States been internalized by some family members in the minority groups? If so, what can people do to overcome or effective deal with such deeply held conditioning?
4. Was John successful at moving to different jobs because he was the only black male available, and by having a degree, was selected for diversity purposes?
5. Was John the best candidate selected for each interview or do you believe John was a token to fill diversity needs in his previous and current place of employment?
6. Do you think John was treated fairly enough in all his previous and current places of employment, such that he would not have moved so often? Or, do you think John was after making more money for himself?
7. What do current statistics show about black and white males in higher education? Do you see any patterns of decrease or increase? Are the percentages of each race or ethnicity rising or decreasing when compared to ten or twenty years ago?
8. Search various sources of data (government or human resources departments for public firms or institutions) on the internet or websites regarding the gender of HRM employees. Are there more females in HRM departments than males? What are your results and why are the trends as such? Discuss.

Case 22: Diversity and Group Morale[33]

Sunlight Bay Agency, a recruiting and search start-up, has some of the most talented and experienced recruiters in the New England area. In addition they have a well thought out business plan and financial backing from its owner, Tom. He initially hired ten recruiters placing three in executive positions. However, after the initial excitement of opening a new firm, morale began to decline. The major problem seems to stem from the top recruiters' inability to process discussions. No matter how large or small the issues are, the group has difficulty making or staying committed to the decisions.

---

[33] - Coauthored with Jean McAtavey, Nova Southeastern University.

Yesterday, in frustration a top recruiter resigned from her position. Tom is worried about the group, the other employees and its impact on their newly developed clients. The group of talented recruiters consists of the following individuals:

1. *Jim* is 57 and is friendly and outgoing. He likes the spotlight and tells stories from past experiences. He avoids conflicts and will shut down when discussions become too heated. However when a decision is made he is quick to work on implementing the decision.

2. *Trudy* is 27 and full of energy and likes meetings to be fun. She enjoys problem solving and focuses on getting results and making thinks happen. However, she does not like long explanations or stories and will often roll her eyes or make off handed remarks when someone does become a little too long-winded. She comes from a low-context culture and messages tend to be specific and to the point. Trudy often comes late for the 8:00 AM meetings due to childcare issues. This irks others, especially Jim who prides himself on being prompt.

3. *Tom* age 40, the founder and owner of the company, is quick and imaginative. He comes from a monochromic culture where time is considered "money" and tasks are very structured. He is able to generate many ideas and tries to quickly resolve issues and implement decisions.

4. *Carmen*, 47, is serious and reserved. She makes decisions slower than others in the group. Carmen comes from a high context culture where interpersonal communication is not always explicit. Oftentimes she agrees with the decisions that are made only to ask the group to revisit the decision days later. Once she makes up her mind, she steadily moves towards accomplishing her goal.

Discussion Questions

1. You have been hired as a consultant because of your ability to work with diverse groups. The case mentions a description of the members of the group and the behaviors they exhibit during meetings. What are the diversity and communication issues that should be addressed?

2. What can be done to improve morale and create excitement?

3. How will valuing diversity enable this group to increase innovation, productivity and decision-making?

4. During meetings it appears that a wide range of perspectives are represented. What skills are needed to enhance their communication process?

Case 23: Alleged Fraud and Grade Tampering[34]

The following is one administrator's letter that was submitted to the School President and Academic Dean about an alleged fraud and grade tampering by an institution named "ABC University." Read the case, written in the form of a letter,

---

[34] Co-authored with James Artley, Florida Metropolitan University.

stitution named "ABC University." Read the case, written in the form of a letter, and then answer the subsequent questions.

Introduction:

The purpose of this memo is to bring to your attention an ongoing fraud and theft, as well as dishonest and probably criminal, behavior at ABC University. As an officer of this fine institution, I am terribly disappointed, ashamed, and saddened to have discovered such an outrageous and inconceivable matter in such a diverse work environment. With a high diversity of adult educators and administrators at this institution from different cultures and countries, I am surprised that this incident had not already been discovered and resolved prior to this date.

Initial Discovery:

Summer of 2003, Tom Smith, the business manager of ABC University, registered to take Marketing Management (MARP 5805) via direct study. I was assigned as the instructor. On September 10th, 2003 while referring to my direct study notes, I realized that I may have omitted submitting an "I" grade for Mr. Smith. To confirm whether or not I had submitted an "I" grade for Mr. Smith, I checked Mr. Smith's transcript in the computer. To my surprise an "A" grade was reflected in the system.

It was impossible for Mr. Smith to have an "A" grade for two reasons. First, he had not commenced the complex research assignment that I was preparing for him. Second, I would not submit an "A" grade without completion of the required work. Because of this major discrepancy, I began to conduct further investigation regarding Mr. Smith's academic history. My initial investigation revealed that an "A" grade was posted for every class taken by Mr. Smith at ABC University. I also began to question if Mr. Smith was receiving help from the registrar, in that the registrar is the only person that could input grades into the computer.

Specific Findings;

Tom Smith – Business Manager

Mr. Smith is currently in the graduate program, which he started 10/14/02. Regarding this term, which began 7/14/03, his registration form shows that he was approved to take three online classes, two during the regular term and one in the mini-term. However, his schedule on the computer shows three classes during the day for the regular term and one during the day for the mini-term. A review of the online roster for all students for the term 7/14/03 was conducted; Mr. Smith's name does not appear on any class. A review of his schedule reflects that he is taking the approved classes on campus with instructors being listed as "TBA." Additionally, all classes are listed as being on Monday mornings at 8:00am. The graduate courses are only taught in the evenings and Saturday mornings.

On the previous term 4/14/03, the same process occurred, his registration form shows that he was approved to take two online classes. However, his schedule on the computer shows two classes during the day with instructors listed as "TBA". A review of the online roster for all students for the term 4/14/03 was completed; Mr. Smith's name does not appear on any class. He has since completed the class with "A" grades. The question now becomes who are the "Mystery TBA" instructors. What would Mr. Smith grade be again at the end of this current term and who will have submitted the grades?

Further research on Mr. Smith's previous transcripts when he earned his Bachelor's degree, suggests that this has been ongoing for quite some time. A close examination of his Bachelors degree transcript shows Mr. Smith completing 6 classes in 12 weeks and added 3 more in the mini-term for a total of 9 classes (36 credits) in a 12-week period. Another shows completing 4 classes in 12 weeks and added 3 more for a total of 7 classes (26 credits) in 12 weeks. In two terms Mr. Smith earned 62 credits (16 classes), and received all "A's". If this does not raise a "red flag" I do not know what will. Assuming that all these classes were taken legitimately, the stage is now set for this term. Mr. Smith is registered for 3 classes during the regular term and 1 class during the mini-term. There is no record in all the various files in the computer, on-line or in-class, as to who his instructors are. The question now becomes who will submit the grades at the end of the term (week of October 6th, 2003)? It is clear in my mind that somehow he has used his position or contacts for his benefit, which is ethically wrong to the 1000th degree.

Sly Fox - Registrar
As mentioned earlier, only the registrar can input grades. Thus I grew concerned that Mr. Fox may have been aiding Mr. Smith in exchange for silence regarding his own indiscretions. I reviewed Mr. Fox's current schedule for this term 7/14/03, and it reflected that he was registered for 3 classes using direct study: Business Law II with Prof. Roberts and Intermediate Accounting and Federal Taxation with Dr. Lord. Mr. Fox's name does not appear on any of the direct study rosters. Additionally, when I asked the instructors, without revealing the situation about them teaching the above courses, they each responded that they have never taught the respective courses. Like Mr. Smith, Mr. Fox has a 4.0 GPA or an "A" grade for every class taken at ABC University.

The question now becomes if both Instructors listed for Mr. Fox are not teaching these classes or have never taught them, which "mystery instructor" will submit grades at the end of the term (week of October 6th, 2003)? Is there a "red flag" here? Please see attach transcripts for further review.

Conclusion:
It is clear that based on these two incidences with our staff; there is a serious issue with honesty and integrity in our school. A serious violation of the Company's Code of Conduct and Ethics has occurred. There are too many unknowns; such as who paid for "dummy classes" taken and who gave "real grades." My duty is to report what I have discovered. We must conduct a complete investigation and audit of the registrar and business offices respectively. I cannot in good conscience be part of such misconduct. It is wrong, it is a disgrace; and above all it can be catastrophic to our school.

Questions:
1. Why is this administrator or staff writing this letter to his/her boss?
2. Is this case really relevant to diversity? Discuss; why or why not?
3. What can the senior administrators do and what should they do in this case? In other words, what would you do if you were the senior leader in this institution?
4. Is cheating a cultural or universal problem? Is cheating specific to certain cultures or a challenge that most faculty members and administrators face throughout most colleges and universities in various countries?

5. In this case, the names of the individuals were changed and the University's name altered to maintain confidentially. Note that this is an actual case that occurred; after complete investigations, both Mr. Smith and Mr. Fox were terminated. Why were these two individuals terminated? Were they treated in a moral manner? Are there proactive alternatives available to prevent such incidents from taking place? Discuss.

Case 24: Graduation Speaker and Insensitivity

It is hoped that each day is a good day and everyone is heard, understood and treated fairly with the highest levels of sensitivity, dignity and respect. However, the world is a very complex place, time is limited and not everyone's voices are heard at all times. Sometimes, you may have to go with the flow, but at other times, you should voice your opinion to increase awareness and sensitivity in hopes of better decision making in the future. This case is about an anonymous letter which can be seen as an example of a culturally ally in an institutional setting. An educator voices his/her opinion about a graduation speaker to the institution's leaders and administrators, while offering a solution for the enhancement or creation of an inclusive work environment. Read the letter and then reflect on the discussion questions.

Dear Administrators and Graduation Committee Members:

I, as a faculty member, always enjoy the graduation ceremonies as so many dreams are coming true and, of course, faculty members are proud of their students' achievements and are happy that they had a small part in it. However, with all due respect, I must acknowledge that this year's ceremony was not as joyous in one respect and that is the selection of and the inappropriate religious remarks made by the keynote speaker. He seemed to single out Muslims to make an "uncalled for," remark regarding the Quran, Prophet Mohammad, and inappropriately linked the Quran to women either purposely or for a "cheap" laugh. He provided a caveat that he did not write this material as he was quoting someone else...as if that would reduce the impact of this inappropriate statement. The fact of the matter is that he did say the inappropriate statement loudly and clearly at the graduation ceremony (as such, it matters not even one bit that someone else originally wrote it many years ago). He also made an inappropriate remark about stereotypes associated with "blondes" which, I believe, had no place in this graduation ceremony since he was not being honored as a comedian.

As an educator, I feel compelled to express my opinion, in hopes of future developments and progress. I am one of the faculty members who actually teach the course entitled *Managing Workforce Diversity* in the University's Undergraduate Business Program for the Human Resources Management concentration. I have taught these concepts and topics in the national as well as in the international clusters outside of the United States. Furthermore, as a certified diversity trainer by the National Multicultural Institute (NMCI) out of Washington D.C. and as a trainer and speaker on diversity topics throughout the United States and abroad, it is my firm belief that it was very inappropriate to invite him as a keynote speaker for the graduation. I have been associated with this University for the past fifteen years and this is the first time that I personally felt offended and ashamed about the school's decision to invite a person, as a graduation keynote speaker, who is offensive to millions and possibly billions of people around the globe, for making inappropriate remarks about their faith. If the school or any of its agents wanted to raise controversy for creative and critical thinking, then it may have been perfectly fine to invite him as a special guest speaker within the university for a specific topic, but not necessarily for a graduation ceremony which should be fully about students and their celebration of achievement.

As a professional and certified trainer of diversity and cultural competency facilitator for corporate executives and managers over the past decade, I have deeper concerns about the selection committee's lack of proactive response and institutionally biased decision making for such issues when they were raised by students months in advance. Wrong is wrong, regardless of which religion is being offended and the school, as an institution of higher learning, should not take any actions that encourage offensive remarks toward a group of people. The following are three areas of concern to reflect upon:

1. First of all, because the selected candidate had been offensive to millions of people for his consistent inappropriate remarks about their faith, he should have never been invited to be a graduation keynote speaker. This is especially so for a heterogeneous student population's graduation ceremony which should be a symbol of synergy to show how different people groups work together toward their common dreams and goals of higher education.

2. Second, once the students brought up this issue to the administration a few months ago, it should have been considered much more seriously in taking a positive action toward bringing another speaker for their graduation. The response that was posted at the school's newspaper about students' concerns in the April 2006 issue could basically amount to what diversity experts call a "double daily indignity" which many minority groups in the United States have gone through in the past and still experience on some occasions in today's environment. Given that the ceremony took place with this offensive speaker, some offended parties could consider this process as a "triple indignity" as the keynote speaker was given a special honorary doctorate degree by their own university...which further encourages his offensive remarks toward a billion people's religious beliefs. Daily indignities are the negative things that individuals do or say to or about one another on a consistent basis, because of their biases, differences and perceived stereotypes. The remarks made to students could also amount to what is known as a "common response" to those who say they are offended or unfairly discriminated. In other words, instead of really hearing the persons or correcting the process, the person in authority is telling the offended individual that "the remarks are not offensive...it is just a perception that it is offensive or it is only in your head or thoughts which are really faulty thinking and not based on facts." It also states to the person who brought up the issue of offensive remark or the concern that "I am right and you are wrong...so forget about it and lift you chin up or suck it up as things are not going to change." Such perceptions and messages are often communicated to others who are the recipients of the offensive remarks regardless of whether they were intended or not. If the selection committee and officials did debate the students' concerns, which I am sure they did, then, at the very least, the keynote speaker should have been "coached" to stay away from

any remarks regarding religious beliefs, especially to those about whom he has written so many negative remarks in his past documents.

3. Third, since a person's past actions are often a good predictor of future behavior, the keynote speaker lived up to this theory as he did actually bring up a billion people's Prophet as well as their religious Book into the speech in an inappropriate manner, and made a derogatory remark about women. Similarly, since institutions often create an organizational culture that encourage "the status quo" which can cause individuals to make similar decisions in the future, it is hoped that the University can take appropriate steps that would help future selection committees to invite appropriate speakers in graduation ceremonies.

It is unfortunate to see that some students chose not to attend their own graduation simply because their ceremony was partially being conducted by a person who has been offensive to their faith and/or their friends' faith and religious role models. As an educator, one should reflect upon why such institutionally inappropriate decisions take place when the school is so diverse in its student body. Perhaps one variable might be that while the student body is very diverse, the decision makers are not. A high number of top echelons and leaders at the University happen to be white males, they are typically older, and their personal beliefs and values seem to be very similar to one another. While there is nothing wrong with a leader being male, white, older, or of a certain religious philosophy, a large number of homogenous individuals from similar backgrounds can result in the existence of "The Abilene Paradox" or groupthink. As such, majority of the decision makers on selecting a keynote speaker for the graduation ceremony might have been of the same backgrounds, values and religious philosophies. Therefore, it is not difficult to see how a homogenous group could become a victim of groupthink to decide on a speaker that has made so many inappropriate religious remarks on a consistent basis. If the past is any predictor of the future, then the selection committee members should have been able to at least consider that this person might say something that could offend the student body (whether it is about their personal faith or not). This observer was pleased to see that the student body and audience members did not all laugh at the speaker's derogatory religious remarks. Once again, it should be emphasized that if changing the speaker was not an option, then, at the very least, the speaker should have been asked and/or told to stay away from religious remarks so his or her statements could be aligned with the organizational values of the University.

It is believed to be fairly clear to most people that it is not culturally sensitive to invite individuals as guest speakers to a graduation ceremony if they have made inappropriate remarks about others based on their skin color, race and/or ethnicity. It makes one wonder why the selection committee thought it would be culturally appropriate, rather than culturally insensitive, to invite a religiously offensive speaker to the graduation ceremony. He should not have been invited even if the offended religion's members were not participating at the graduation ceremony since culturally or religiously inappropriate remarks are wrong regardless of when and where they take place; this is especially so in a diverse environment. One real question to reflect upon is this: *would the school or selection committee have invited this person as a keynote speaker for graduation had he written so much offensive material about Christianity or Judaism?* The answer is likely to be a definite "no" because this would be offensive to most graduating students and their family members who value diversity and respect each other's personal religious beliefs. If the answer is yes, then there are plenty of candidates, with extremely offensive views, for future graduation ceremonies. As a matter-of-fact, and in the spirit of equal opportunity offending, there are a few popular and highly intelligent political leaders who supposedly have claimed that 'a certain country and/or faith should not exist and therefore should be eliminated from the face of this planet.' Then, logic would have it that one such individual can be invited for next year's graduation, and another person who offends millions of individuals from another faith or country should be invited as a prospective speaker for another year's graduation ceremony. One could wonder where this pattern of illogical thinking would lead an institution or society...perhaps it could lead to much despair and hatred as can be seen in the extreme views and violent behaviors that have existed in various parts of this world. Of course, it should be acknowledged that this writer is being facetious with several of the previous statements to make the reader think about the consequences of such logic or irrational thinking, because bringing individuals who have made offensive remarks about people's religious beliefs as graduation ceremony keynote speakers is NOT something an inclusive work environment or an inclusive learning environment should encourage. As a respected institution of higher learning, a University should not invite offensive individuals to be keynote speakers at graduation ceremonies of diverse students, especially when those students formally voice their thoughts and opinions in a peaceful and professional manner...well in advance once the speaker was announced.

To prevent inappropriate decision making in the future and to further create a better and more inclusive workplace as well as an inclusive learning environment for all, the University should provide everyone, including all administrators, an intensive diversity competency training program and institute relevant processes to prevent offending its own students and faculty. One institution that might be able to assist with a comprehensive diversity training program is the National Multicultural Institute (NMCI), which is a not-for-profit organization. While diversity or cultural competency training programs and processes cannot erase years of societal bias and should not focus on changing anyone's beliefs or values, it can increase diversity awareness and provide more tools to the University administrators' and employees for the enhancement and/or creation of a healthier workplace as well as an inclusive learning environment for all.

Regards!

Discussion Questions

1. What is a cultural ally? What can one do to stop insensitive remarks and decisions from taking place at the workplace?
2. Should one always take action when insensitive remarks or decisions are made? Discuss the pros and cons.
3. Should higher learning institutions invite controversial speakers to be keynote speakers at graduation ceremonies? Why or why not? Discuss the pros and cons.
4. What are the benefits of inviting controversial individuals to a school's campus as guest speakers for such events as distinguished lecture series, or other such programs (not graduation ceremonies)

where multiple or conflicting perspectives can be explored by various parties? Discuss.

5. Did the selection committee make an appropriate decision to invite a speaker for the graduation ceremony who has consistently said offensive things about a religion?

6. What is a daily indignity and how does it take place in today's workplaces? Discuss a modern example or possibility.

7. It is apparent that a good number of students did not attend their own graduation ceremony because of the selected keynote speaker who has been offensive to their faith and religion. As such, they brought up their concerns to the administration well in advance once the keynote speaker was announced. Let us say that you were part of the committee who selected this person in the first place. How would you respond to these students' concerns?

8. Let us say that you are the director of the department and one of your faculty members came and said "I cannot attend this graduation ceremony because the speaker has been insensitive regarding my religion and the speaker has consistently made offensive remarks about my faith. Consequently, I do not respect him and I think it is not right to allow him to be the keynote speaker at our diverse student population's graduation. Therefore, I respectfully request that I be granted permission not to attend the graduation ceremony." You look at the school's policy which states that "All faculty members are required to attend the graduation ceremony." What do you do? Would you grant this faculty member the opportunity not to attend the ceremony? Discuss, why or why not? Discuss.

9. This anonymous letter has started with the letter/word "I" and ended with the word "all." Is the author sending a message? If so, what might he or she be saying?

Case 25: Find What You Love and Do It

An article entitled "You've Got to Find What You Love" was published in one of Stanford's Report (June 14, 2005) about Steve Job's road to success in his speech at a commencement address. This case is the text of the Commencement address by Steve Jobs, CEO of Apple Computer and of Pixar Animation Studios, delivered on June 12, 2005. The following material comes from the Stanford Report.

I am honored to be with you today at your commencement from one of the finest universities in the world. I never graduated from college. Truth be told, this is the closest I've ever gotten to a college graduation. Today I want to tell you three stories from my life. That's it. No big deal. Just three stories!

The first story is about connecting the dots.

I dropped out of Reed College after the first 6 months, but then stayed around as a drop-in for another 18 months or so before I really quit. So why did I drop out?

It started before I was born. My biological mother was a young, unwed college graduate student, and she decided to put me up for adoption. She felt very strongly that I should be adopted by college graduates, so everything was all set for me to be adopted at birth by a lawyer and his wife. Except that when I popped out they decided at the last minute that they really wanted a girl. So my parents, who were on a waiting list, got a call in the middle of the night asking: "We have an unexpected baby boy; do you want him?" They said: "Of course." My biological mother later found out that my mother had never graduated from college and that my father had never graduated from high school. She refused to sign the final adoption papers. She only relented a few months later when my parents promised that I would someday go to college.

And 17 years later I did go to college. But I naively chose a college that was almost as expensive as Stanford, and all of my working-class parents' savings were being spent on my college tuition. After six months, I couldn't see the value in it. I had no idea what I wanted to do with my life and no idea how college was going to help me figure it out. And here I was spending all of the money my parents had saved their entire life. So I decided to drop out and trust that it would all work out OK. It was pretty scary at the time, but looking back it was one of the best decisions I ever made. The minute I dropped out I could stop taking the required classes that didn't interest me, and begin dropping in on the ones that looked interesting.

It wasn't all romantic. I didn't have a dorm room, so I slept on the floor in friends' rooms, I returned coke bottles for the 5¢ deposits to buy food with, and I would walk the 7 miles across town every Sunday night to get one good meal a week at the Hare Krishna temple. I loved it. And much of what I stumbled into by following my curiosity and intuition turned out to be priceless later on. Let me give you one example:

Reed College at that time offered perhaps the best calligraphy instruction in the country. Throughout the campus every poster, every label on every drawer, was beautifully hand calligraphed. Because I had dropped out and didn't have to take the normal classes, I decided to take a calligraphy class to learn how to do this. I learned about serif and san serif typefaces, about varying the amount of space between different letter combinations, about what makes great typography great. It was beautiful, historical, artistically subtle in a way that science can't capture, and I found it fascinating.

None of this had even a hope of any practical application in my life. But ten years later, when we were designing the first Macintosh computer, it all came back to me. And we designed it all into the Mac. It was the first computer with beautiful typography. If I had never dropped in on that single course in college, the Mac would have never had multiple typefaces or proportionally-spaced fonts. And since Windows just copied the Mac, its likely that no personal computer would have them. If I had never dropped out, I would have never dropped in on this calligraphy class, and personal computers might not have the wonderful typography that they do. Of course it was impossible to connect the dots looking forward when I was in college. But it was very, very clear looking backwards ten years later.

Again, you can't connect the dots looking forward; you can only connect them looking backwards. So you have to trust that the dots will somehow connect in your future. You have to trust in something - your gut, destiny, life, karma, whatever. This approach has never let me down, and it has made all the difference in my life.

My second story is about love and loss.

I was lucky - I found what I loved to do early in life. Woz and I started Apple in my parent's garage when I was 20. We worked hard, and in 10 years Apple had grown from just the two of us in a garage into a $2 billion company with over 4000 employees. We had just released our finest creation - the Macintosh - a year earlier, and I had just turned 30. And then I got fired. How can you get fired from a company you started? Well, as Apple grew we hired someone who I thought was very talented to run the company with me, and for the first year or so things went well. But then our visions of the future began to diverge and eventually we had a falling out. When we did, our Board of Directors sided with him. So at 30 I was out. And very publicly out. What had been the focus of my entire adult life was gone, and it was devastating.

I really didn't know what to do for a few months. I felt that I had let the previous generation of entrepreneurs down - that I had dropped the baton as it was being passed to me. I met with David Packard and Bob Noyce and tried to apologize for screwing up so badly. I was a very public failure, and I even thought about running away from the valley. But something slowly began to dawn on me - I still loved what I did. The turn of events at Apple had not changed that one bit. I had been rejected, but I was still in love. And so I decided to start over.

I didn't see it then, but it turned out that getting fired from Apple was the best thing that could have ever happened to me. The heaviness of being successful was replaced by the lightness of being a beginner again, less sure about everything. It freed me to enter one of the most creative periods of my life.

During the next five years, I started a company named NeXT, another company named Pixar, and fell in love with an amazing woman who would become my wife. Pixar went on to create the worlds first computer animated feature film, *Toy Story*, and is now the most successful animation studio in the world. In a remarkable turn of events, Apple bought NeXT, I retuned to Apple, and the technology we developed at NeXT is at the heart of Apple's current renaissance. And Laurene and I have a wonderful family together.

I'm pretty sure none of this would have happened if I hadn't been fired from Apple. It was awful tasting medicine, but I guess the patient needed it. Sometimes life hits you in the head with a brick. Don't lose faith. I'm convinced that the only thing that kept me going was that I loved what I did. You've got to find what you love. And that is as true for your work as it is for your lovers. Your work is going to fill a large part of your life, and the only way to be truly satisfied is to do what you believe is great work. And the only way to do great work is to love what you do. If you haven't found it yet, keep looking. Don't settle. As with all matters of the heart, you'll know when you find it. And, like any great relationship, it just gets better and better as the years roll on. So keep looking until you find it. Don't settle.

My third story is about death.

When I was 17, I read a quote that went something like: "If you live each day as if it was your last, someday you'll most certainly be right." It made an impression on me, and since then, for the past 33 years, I have looked in the mirror every morning and asked myself: "If today were the last day of my life, would I want to do what I am about to do today?" And whenever the answer has been "No" for too many days in a row, I know I need to change something.

Remembering that I'll be dead soon is the most important tool I've ever encountered to help me make the big choices in life. Because almost everything - all external expectations, all pride, all fear of embarrassment or failure - these things just fall away in the face of death, leaving only what is truly important. Remembering that you are going to die is the best way I know to avoid the trap of thinking you have something to lose. You are already naked. There is no reason not to follow your heart.

About a year ago I was diagnosed with cancer. I had a scan at 7:30 in the morning, and it clearly showed a tumor on my pancreas. I didn't even know what a pancreas was.

The doctors told me this was almost certainly a type of cancer that is incurable, and that I should expect to live no longer than three to six months. My doctor advised me to go home and get my affairs in order, which is doctor's code for prepare to die. It means to try to tell your kids everything you thought you'd have the next 10 years to tell them in just a few months. It means to make sure everything is buttoned up so that it will be as easy as possible for your family. It means to say your goodbyes.

I lived with that diagnosis all day. Later that evening I had a biopsy, where they stuck an endoscope down my throat, through my stomach and into my intestines, put a needle into my pancreas and got a few cells from the tumor. I was sedated, but my wife, who was there, told me that when they viewed the cells under a microscope the doctors started crying because it turned out to be a very rare form of pancreatic cancer that is curable with surgery. I had the surgery and I'm fine now. This was the closest I've been to facing death, and I hope its the closest I get for a few more decades. Having lived through it, I can now say this to you with a bit more certainty than when death was a useful but purely intellectual concept.

No one wants to die. Even people who want to go to heaven don't want to die to get there. And yet death is the destination we all share. No one has ever escaped it. And that is as it should be, because Death is very likely the single best invention of Life. It is Life's change agent. It clears out the old to make way for the new. Right now the new is you, but someday not too long from now, you will gradually become the old and be cleared away. Sorry to be so dramatic, but it is quite true.

Your time is limited, so don't waste it living someone else's life. Don't be trapped by dogma - which is living with the results of other people's thinking. Don't let the noise of other's opinions drown out your own inner voice. And most important, have the courage to follow your heart and intuition. They somehow already know what you truly want to become. Everything else is secondary.

When I was young, there was an amazing publication called *The Whole Earth Catalog*, which was one of the bibles of my generation. It was created by a fellow named Stewart Brand not far from here in Menlo Park, and he brought it to life with his poetic touch. This was in the late 1960's, before personal computers and desktop publishing, so it was all made with typewriters, scissors, and Polaroid cameras. It was sort of like Google in paperback form, 35 years before Google came along: it was idealistic, and overflowing with neat tools and great notions.

Stewart and his team put out several issues of *The Whole Earth Catalog*, and then when it had run its course, they put out a final issue. It was the mid-1970s, and I was your age. On the back cover of their final issue was a photograph of an early morning country road, the kind you might find yourself hitchhiking on if you were so adventurous. Beneath it were the words: "Stay Hungry. Stay Foolish." It was their farewell message as they signed off. Stay Hungry. Stay Foolish. And I have always wished that for myself. And now, as you graduate to begin anew, I wish that for you. Stay Hungry. Stay Foolish. Thank you all very much.

Discussion Questions

1. How did the three stories in Steve Job's life change his paradigm about life, performance and opportunities?
2. Facing obstacles is not limited to one's gender, skin color, disability, financial stability, or other most often discussed dimensions of diver-

sity. So, each person can face obstacles that are unique to him or her. What obstacles did Steve Jobs face in his journey of becoming successful in the field of computers?

3. What does it mean to "Stay Hungry" and "Stay Foolish"?

4. Are there people in your personal life, similar to Steve Jobs, who have overcome many obstacles and achieved much success as a result of their outlook on life? If so, mention their story.

Exercises

*C*ulture and diversity related exercises can serve as laboratories for the application of theoretical concepts and long-term learning. Read each exercise and follow or answer its relevant directions or questions.

Exercise 1: Group Similarities and Differences

This is an introductory exercise. You are unique in your own way; you may have some things in common with others and probably few or none in common with others who may look like you. Complete your answers first and then your objective is to match as many names on your list as possible during the few minutes allotted for this exercise with your colleagues. Only one match per person (You can use the same person's name only once in your match column). Be prepared to answer some questions with regard to your matches!

- Fill your information first for each question on the "Similarities and Differences Variables" sheet on the next page (Table 18.1). Complete all your answers first.
- Then, while meeting others in the session, your objective is to find at least one person who has a similar answer as you. The objective is to match as many answers on your list as possible during the next few minutes. So, if another person's answer matches one of your items, then write his/her name on the second column.
- Only one match per person (You can only use the same person once). Then, move on to the next person.

Be prepared to answer the following questions:

- Were you able to match all the items on the sheet? Did you match more than ten items?
- What did you learn from this activity?
- What was the most unusual match? What was the hardest thing to match?
- Did you find you had some things in common that surprised you? What are some of those things?
- How did you or others make these matches? Did some different strategies develop? You may have observed some auctions, collaborations, or various creative ways of finding matches. This can show that there are multiple ways that we can connect with each other.
- What is different about the group now that you have done this exercise?

Table 18.1 – Similarities and Differences Variables

TOPICS	YOUR ANSWER	YOUR MATCH (His or her name)
1. Month of birth		
2. Number of children		
3. Number of brothers and sisters		
4. What you like best about this city		
5. Kind of car you drive to work		
6. Favorite book you have read		
7. Favorite movie you have seen		
8. Length of time with your current company		
9. Favorite food		
10. Foreign language(s) spoken		
11. Favorite television show		
12. Favorite place for vacation visit		
13. If you could be anywhere else to-day, where would you be?		

We can and often do the same things in *real life* to help each other make our departments and company more successful. We can take time to understand each other better, know that what is important to us might be important to others, and interact and collaborate to find better strategies and means of meeting each others' needs. While we have many differences and similarities, we all have one thing in common and that is the desire to work for good organizations.

Exercise 2: Understanding and Describing Values

Each person is unique and may define himself or herself based on different dimensions of diversity and a different set of values. As such, it is important that each person takes some time to examine his or her group membership qualities and values. To get you started on this reflection process, answer the following questions.

1. How would you describe yourself to another person who does not know you at this time? Write a brief biography of yourself for a two minute introduction to a group of people which includes your peers, industry leaders, your parents, and your children. This biography will be used by the master of ceremony for your introduction.

2. For deeper reflections, discuss values, how values are acquired, where values are acquired from, the power of values, how values are used, how values can change

over time, and why values are important. You can also mention how a person's values can impact one's behavior in the workplace, society and life. Explore and determine your list of values (could be personal and/or professional), write them down and briefly discuss why these values are important to you. List your values in a prioritized order with one representing your most important value.

_____

_____

_____

_____

_____

_____

_____

_____

_____

_____

Exercise 3: Diversity in Academic Environments

Academic institutions hire staff and faculty members who come from the local community or the society general. These staff and faculty members bring with them their previously learned biases and stereotypes to the school. The following situation[35] is discussed from one student's perspective. Read the student's perspective and then complete the questions.

After completing elementary, high school and college in Jamaica and living by the motto *"out of many one people,"* one would assume that it would be easy to make the transition of attending a university in the United States of America, which is considered to be one of the most diverse nations in the world. But, I can safely say I've had very extraordinary experiences.

I attained my first degree at a university in New Hampshire (the population was 98% white at that time). However, I coped very well because my program of enrollment catered well to international students. It was an exciting experience for me, as I learnt about various cultures and backgrounds and I made many friends (everyone looked out for each other). The university was also designed to meet our needs. For example, the cafeteria would provide Jamaican food at least twice per week and most programs and courses integrated interactive programs where we would share our experiences about our traditions and way of life; professors often encouraged us to speak about work experiences that we've had in our home country.

In comparison, I am now completing my Masters' degree at a university in Florida and the experience is the total opposite. Despite the fact that most students are from varied ethnicities and the population here is very diverse; my experience is not

---

[35] - Coauthored with Simone Maxwell, Nova Southeastern University.

always positive. The warmth and friendliness that I previously experienced in the classroom and in my environment is definitely not the same. In one of my classes, a professor mentioned that he was amazed to find out that people in third world countries are smart. Originally and as a consequence of his perceptions, he had thought that he would have to lower the test standards in Jamaica and the Bahamas. This statement was very offensive to me, and many others in the class felt the same way, as most students there originated from third world countries. I told another Jamaican classmate during the break that I was in disagreement with this professor's statement. She said "I've heard professors make comments like that all the time, it's their perception and that's ok." Also, the cafeteria and lounges at my current university do not cater to a wide cross-section of cultures, and my courses, assignments and interactive sessions seem to be specifically related to companies here in the States and the dominant culture.

So, the question that comes to mind is: are universities effectively catering to their diverse student population?

Exercise Discussion Questions:
1. Are universities effectively catering to their diverse student populations? Discuss and provide examples.
2. Interview five international students from at least two different colleges or universities to find out their perceptions and thoughts about the sensitivity of the school, its staff and faculty members to their needs. Are culturally-diverse students comfortable in their school's learning environment? Do they feel that their faculty members and university staff are culturally competent? What suggestions do they have for the university staff and faculty members?
3. Should university staff and professors be given diversity and cultural competency training? If so, what type of content should be covered in such a training session? Discuss.
4. What programs can universities implement to broaden students' horizons on diversity and cultural competency?

Exercise 4: Destiny and Place of Birth

There are nearly 6.5 billion individuals on earth today and each person was born in a different place and time than many others. Some people are born in a Muslim family, some with atheists, some with Christians, some with Jews, and some with parents or families who believe in other faiths. Some people are born in developed economies while others are born in the poorest parts of the world. Some are born in financially poor families while others are born in families that are financially very wealthy. Some believe they are in charge of their own destinies while others believe that their destinies have already been determined by their Creator. Some believe in reincarnation while others believe there is life in the hereafter.

Take a few minutes and reflect upon how your life would be different if you were much different than you are. If you were to be born as a different person, in a different location, and with a different family, how would your life change in today's society? Discuss how your personal and/or professional life would be different for each of the following diversity dimensions. Would people respond to you differently because of your new diversity dimension?

Diversity Dimension	Impact on Your Life – *How would your life be different than it is today?*
Country:	
Ethnicity:	
Education:	
Values and beliefs:	
Sexual orientation:	
Profession:	
Language:	
Others:	

Exercise 5: Dreams of Business Leaders

From the formal and informal readings thus far, you probably know that *Workforce Diversity Management* is basically the study and understanding of what people think, feel, and do in and around their organizations. In other words, this is really the study of content from topics in sociology, psychology and organizational behavior. As such, each individual has her/her own desires and motivations that impact his/her behavior. Therefore, effective managers have to get to know each individual in order to maximize individual and organizational performance through individuals, groups and processes. We can start by getting to know our own motivations first.

As an exercise, you are asked "If you could sit next to any business leader on a plane, whom would you choose and why? What would you talk to him/her about? If you could be a chief executive officer (CEO) of any company for a day which one would you choose and what would you want to accomplish at the end of your day?" In other words, if you could be the top leader of any company for a day which firm would you choose and, more specifically, what would you want to accomplish at the end of your day with regard to diversity awareness and/or cultural sensitivity? Discuss your answers.

Exercise 6: Walking in Someone Else's Shoes

Being different or not being a part of the "norm" often means dealing with perceptions, responses and behaviors that are different than others. For example, left-handed people face different challenges when they face machines that are built for the "norm" than those who are pre-dominantly right handed. Similar, females experience the world differently than males. Individuals with various forms of disability may unintentionally receive different treatment from people in society than everyone else.

Your challenge is to try and be different for an hour or a day and see how people respond to you. Try to act and be a different individual personally professionally, mentally, and physically during this testing period. For example, you can choose to act as a (an):

1. Faculty (male or female), age 55, walking with a cane.
2. Female who looks extremely attractive while passing by a construction site with predominantly male employees.
3. Exchange student who does not speak the local language.
4. An applicant who is fully qualified for a job or an opening, but is not able to walk (he or she is wheelchair-bound).
5. Worker who is going to work and needs help crossing the street as he or she cannot see well.
6. Blind female student in the college building.
7. Blind male student in the college building.
8. Blond, brunette, redhead, bald, person with a mustache or beard, etc.
9. Politician in Palestine, Israel, United States, Russia, Afghanistan, or the United Nations (or other places as you specify).
10. Deaf student who reads lips and uses sign language for communication.
11. A person who talks with lisp or a heavy accent (such as Italian, Russian, European, Asian, etc.).
12. Student who wears ethnic clothes.

After completing this exercise and acting like a different person or with a different apparent characteristic for an hour or a day, how did you feel and how did others respond to you? Document your responses and notes.

_____
_____
_____
_____
_____
_____
_____
_____
_____
_____
_____
_____

Exercise 7: Diversity in the Community

Prepare a summary of a major discrimination lawsuit and/or diversity efforts for a firm in your community. You can do both or choose one of the following options:

1. The submission (for the discrimination lawsuit) should include the lawsuit along with the judgments and settlements, interview questions for the company evaluation, and any written company material used in the evaluation process. The major points of the lawsuit should be covered, including judgments and/or settlements. Also mention the lessons learned from this case. What are some things that other managers, employees and companies should be aware of and concerned with?
2. When possible, you are encouraged to visit the company, observe, ask questions, and evaluate the company's efforts towards workplace diversity. During the evaluation, consider the printed material distributed to employees, the company's mission statement, formal diversity training sessions for managers and employees, and conduct an interview with a human resource representative in the firm. Mention any items you discover.

Document your findings.

_____

_____

_____

_____

_____

_____

_____

_____

_____

_____

_____

_____

_____

_____

_____

_____

_____

_____

_____

_____

_____

_____

_____

_____

Exercise 8: "Disabled" or "Handicapped"?

Since there are so many different forms of disability, managers should become familiar with its legal definition. They should know what a "disability" is as it relates to the workplace environment. According to the official government website of the Americans with Disabilities Act (ADA), "An individual is considered to have a 'disability' if s/he has a physical or mental impairment that substantially limits one or more major life activities, has a record of such an impairment, or is regarded as having such an impairment" (ADA, para. 3). Furthermore, "The ADA prohibits discrimination in all employment practices, including job application procedures, hiring, firing, advancement, compensation, training, and other terms, conditions, and privileges of employment. It applies to recruitment, advertising, tenure, layoff, leave, fringe benefits, and all other employment-related activities" (ADA para 2).

A colleague of mine in the corporate arena always used a wheelchair due to the fact that an accident had prevented him from standing up, and managed his department very well despite the apparent disability. He did not like the term "disabled" or the perceptions that come with the term "disabled" because he managed his department very effectively and his people loved his leadership. He often joked and said most people without disabilities should be termed or labeled as "TABs" standing for "Temporarily Abled Bodies," because anyone can develop a disability at any time. When a person in wheelchair comes to your organization, s/he may prefer to be called something other than "disabled" and remember s/he is the customer and ultimately determines what the right terminology may be for him/her. A person may have a disability, but s/he may certainly be able to do thousands of functions like those who do not have the disability. Therefore, the person should not be labeled as "disabled" in the work environment when s/he is actually performing the same job as everyone else, provided that sometimes the person may do it differently. There are over 60 million Americans with some sort of a disability (and there are over 50 different legally recognized forms of disabilities) but the majority of these individuals with disabilities are working along side everyone else and often their disabilities cannot be seen.

In my many years of teaching "Cultural Competency and Diversity" to managers and leaders of corporations, the best term that I have seen and the one that seems to be most sensitive to everyone's needs is "*Differently-abled.*" Diversity articles and literature have suggested this term because of its appropriateness and the fact that a person with a disability often achieves the same results on a job as everyone else. However, the term is not widely used as of yet, but it is becoming more and more prevalent in the corporate arena every day.

My wife was working at Target during the Holidays in November - December of 2004 and she enjoyed the experience, as she was pleased with their training program for their employees. They tend to take care of all their customers (referred to as guests at Target), including those "guests" with disabilities. Target teaches employees to use the term "disability" instead of "disabled" or "handicapped" for their customers. Target, in their employee training manual entitled "*Target Corporation Guide to Helping Guests with Disabilities,*" stated that "handicap" traditionally describes obstacles or barriers that are imposed by the environment or society in general. It encourages employees to avoid terms like "handicapped parking" and "handicapped restrooms" and to instead use "accessible parking" and "accessible restrooms." They further encourage everyone to use the term "disability" when referring to a functional limitation. They also encourage employees to use the terms "Uses a Wheelchair" instead of saying someone is "confined to a wheelchair" or "wheelchair-bound," since some people only use a wheelchair to increase their mobility. Essentially, wheelchair is a mobility aid and not a part of the person.

As you know, the term "handicapped" is often used to describe a person's physical "limitations" while the meaning behind the term "disabled" could range from physical limitations, mental illness to learning barriers and so on. Some people prefer to use the word limitations to describe a person with disability because it does not seem to carry the same stigma as the word "handicapped" or "disabled." A colleague mentioned something she learned by working in the field was when she said that "I represent individuals with disabilities," some employers would automatically think of either physical or severe mental disability. Actually, many of her clients were highly functional, limited by dyslexia or a medically controlled disability or illness such as depression. You may also be surprised to find that many of the hiring personnel are still very uneducated when it comes to individuals with disabilities. Some actually blatantly discriminate, while others discriminate without really thinking about it. For example, according to my colleague, one time she brought a client to complete an application for a cleaning position, they were told the position had been filled. She called the facility five minutes later disguised as an interested applicant, and was told the same position was open. Such a blatant form of discrimination has happened and may still happen to individuals based on disabilities, skin color, gender, body size, sexual orientation, age, and other characteristics in our society. Since many people are not aware of how their actions discriminate or offend people, we need to educate the employers about different disabilities and that having a disability does not necessary make someone "handicapped", "disabled" or "low-functioning."

It is certain that we all have friends and colleagues that many say are "mentally challenged" instead of using "handicapped" or "disabled." These individuals feel the term "mentally challenged" is better because their disabilities are not physical, but on the mental level. On the other hand, a colleague's mother uses a cane because her legs do not work as well as they used to and she refers to it as a "handicap." And then there are those whose challenges are not necessarily seen, such as person who is going through chemo or radiation treatment. These individuals have a disability, even though it is temporary. So when it comes to what politically-correct term you use, one would have to use a term that will not offend that individual. Many individuals understand that the term "disabled" can certainly have negative connotations because no one wants to think they are less than whole. No one wants to sit around and have people wait on them when they can get things for themselves. So, yes the term "disabled" can be considered negative, but we put labels on everything so if you do not say "disabled" or "handicapped," then what can you use?

Questions for Discussion:

We all know that the term "handicap" is not used now as much because it is not a politically correct term. Could the term "disabled" be considered a negative term as well since many individuals that have disabilities are fully able to work and function just like the "*abled bodies*"? Interview two persons with a disability and find out their views about the terms "disability" and "handicapped." Or visit a company that has a good policy for employees and customers that may have a disability. After the interview or finding more about a company's policies regarding employees or customers with disabilities, what are your thoughts and some best practices that you have seen or observed thus far in society when it comes to individuals with disabilities? Which term should be used when describing a person with disability?

Exercise 9: Time Orientations and First Memories of Difference

Culture tends to reinforce the information or misinformation that we learned in our earlier influences. We form what we can call a "cultural filter or lens," in our heads, that all information tends to pass through. What the information is actually passing through is an accumulation of all stereotypes and prejudices; in other words, the information gets filtered through our preconceived notions. We tend to make assumptions based on these preconceived notions and then act on them as if they were fact. This is a part of what is known as being ethnocentric. That is, a belief that "our" culture is the right one and anything different is suspect. *Ethnocentricity*, as discussed before, is a trait that is especially true of members of dominant cultures. The assumptions we make are influenced by the culture we were brought up in.

Sometimes our behavior is influenced by our culture. Understanding culture can help us to keep it from being a source of conflict when we encounter people who see the world differently than ourselves. Every culture is unique and has many elements that must be considered when learning about them. Understanding culture and its importance in shaping what we believe can help us to recognize when cultural differences are the cause of our conflict. For example, there are different forms of ceremonies in each culture and, based on the nation or its typical norms, what a person is to say and do on a particular occasion can vary greatly. Other major examples of cultural differences can include religion, subsistence, and value. *Religion*, one's attitudes toward the divine and the supernatural and how they affect a person's thoughts and actions, can vary between continents and within each nation or community. *Subsistence*, one's attitudes about providing for oneself, the young, and the old, and who protects whom, can also vary greatly among various tribes and people groups. A person's general *values*, one's attitudes toward freedom, education, cleanliness, cruelty, and crime to name but a few, can also vary and change from culture to culture and from time to time.

Experts on anthropology and culture tend to explain that there are differences in time systems around the globe. For example, two major systems are monochromic and polychronic time orientations. *Monochronic time* means paying attention to and doing only one thing at a time; *polychronic time* orientation means being involved with many things at once. In monochronic cultures, time is experienced and used in a linear way. Monochronic time is perceived as being almost tangible: people talk about it as though it were money, as something that can be "spent," "saved," "wasted," and "lost." Because monochronic time concentrates on one thing at a time, people who are governed by it don't like to be interrupted. Monochronic time seals people off from one another and, as a result, intensify some relationships while short-changing others. Time becomes a room which some people are allowed to enter, while others are excluded. Monochronic time dominates most business in the United States. Polychronic time is characterized by the simultaneous occurrence of many things and by a great involvement with people. There is more emphasis on completing human transactions than on holding to schedules. Proper understanding of the difference between the monochronic and polychronic time systems will be helpful in dealing with the time-flexible Mediterranean peoples. In monochronic time cultures, the emphasis is on the compartmentalization of functions and people. In polychronic Mediterranean cultures, business offices often have large reception areas where people can wait. Polychronic people feel that private space disrupts the flow of information by shutting people off from one another. In polychronic systems, appointments mean very little and may be shifted around even at the last minute to accommodate someone more important in an individual's hierarchy of family, friends, or associates. Some polychronic people (such as Latin Americans and Arabs) give precedence to their large circle of family members over any business obligation.

Exercise directions. Use a blank sheet of paper to remember your first memories of difference from your younger years. The objectives of this exercise are to identify some of your earliest memories of when and how you first learned about personal and cultural differences; and to allow you to share the feelings you have had (or have) about those experiences, bring them to surface and analyze their impact. With regard to this exercise, try to go as far back as possible (even 5-10 years of age) and reflect on the most impactful memories you had (or have) about personal or cultural differences. Keep in mind that differences can include such things as race, ethnicity, skin color, or gender. As a matter of fact, these primary dimensions of diversity can often be major sources of difference for most minority groups. Think about who was giving you the message in the scene, where you were, and who else was present. Draw one or two pictures which depict those memories. Artistic talent is not important and you may use blocks, square boxes, lines or stick figures to express your initial experiences of personal or cultural differences.

Think about what you felt at the time of the occurrence and identify what messages you might have gotten from the experience. You may want to identify or notice some themes, occasionally, when you compare or share your experiences with others who complete the same exercise. It is important to develop an awareness of how the things we learned about cultural difference as children affect the way we deal with those differences in the workplace as adults. This exercise also points out that we learn about personal or cultural differences very early in the socialization process, people with different influences may have different beliefs and values, and the fact that some of the things we learned as children about differences are based on misinformation and stereotypes.

Exercise 10: Whites, Blacks and Mexicans

There are many stereotypes in the society that are based on misinformation. This is especially so in the United States about various groups of individuals, more specifically about Whites, Blacks, and Mexicans. Managers and professionals must not let such biases drive their behaviors. One of my colleagues (E. A. Thomas, on April 2006) said it clearly when she stated:

> Some stereotypes in the United States are that all Mexican families live together, all Black people like chicken, and all White people sleep in the same rooms as their pets or animals. Yes, most Mexican families tend to stick together; in society we often see Mexicans out together as a family and automatically assume that they all live together. Similarly, Black people are stereotyped to all eat fried chicken every day; all Black people don't eat chicken and many may not even like it. Of course, some Blacks have been heard to say that we eat chicken because it is cheap. While many White people may sleep with their pets in the same rooms or beds, they all don't do it. I know a lot of White people who do not sleep with their pets. The main thing I hear is that some White people smell like wet dogs, so people assume or think they must be sleeping with their pets. These stereotypes are all wrong;

we as Americans need to stop labeling each other, if we get to know one another, we will understand each other's cultures and know that almost all the stereotypes in America are wrong.

While stereotypes might be true of some individuals within various groups (not just Whites, Blacks or Mexicans), they do not always fit an entire people group. Managers, professionals and employees should remember that each individual is different and should initially be treated as an individual rather than Black, White or a Mexican. If a person "self identifies" with a specific group or race then he or she should be respected as such. Also, nobody should be treated with stereotypes since biased information is often based on false information or myths that do not apply to all individuals.

Question for Discussion:
Interview or think about a White person, a Black persons, and a Mexican. Then write all the facts and commonalities that they all share. What are some other stereotypes in the society that you have heard about various groups of people that are based on assumptions and misinformation? Discuss. What can one do to make sure his or her decisions are not driven by such stereotypes?

_____

_____

_____

_____

_____

_____

_____

_____

_____

_____

_____

_____

_____

_____

_____

_____

_____

_____

_____

_____

_____

_____

Exercise 11: Value Delivery through a Diverse Workforce

On January 12th 2004, I met Mr. Richard Wagoner, Jr. who is the Chairman & Chief Executive Officer of General Motors Corporation at Nova Southeastern University, as he presented his suggestions to business leaders, faculty members and business graduates. He said organizations must offer what their customers want or else they will go out of business. For example, in many European countries, people want small cars because gasoline is taxed very heavily, which discourages the use of luxury cars for most working professionals. General Motor makes small cars for their customers, but a good number of the customers in the United States want large cars instead of small cars for luxury and comfort. Therefore, they are meeting the needs and demands of their customers in the United States by producing large cars instead of all small ones. Furthermore, he said organizations need to consider the global impact of competitive forces on their business even if they are not currently doing business internationally. Globalization is a huge aspect of doing business today and all business professionals and educators must understand its forces in order to effectively meet the current and upcoming challenges. Another important area, according to Richard Wagoner, for both educators and practitioners is to consider the diversity of one's employees and customers for success in the twenty-first century. Wagoner said many firms are still suffering because their customers are becoming more diverse yet their employees are pretty much homogenous and are not able to fully understand the changing needs of their consumer market. As such, educators and practitioners must prepare people to diversify the organization's empowered workforce in order to synergistically become competitive while offering all segments of the consumer markets great value.

Understanding the customer and, more importantly, what the customer values, is vital to any business and a diverse workforce is the best way to keep one's finger on the changing pulse of diverse consumers. Part of understanding the customers is not taking anything for granted and not making any assumptions about their needs or wants.

Question for Discussion:

Interview a local manager to find out if their customers are becoming more diverse and in what ways? How are organizations diversifying their workforce to meet the needs of their current and prospective diverse customers?

Exercise 12: Religious Diversity and the Community

Religious diversity is a fact of life both in the community and in the workforce. It is important for today's managers, leaders, and professionals to understand some of the basics about the various religious beliefs of their co-workers, employees, and colleagues in the workplace. Managers must also be aware that the Civil Rights Act of 1964 prohibits employers from discriminating against an applicant or employee's religious beliefs. The Act was amended in 1972 seeking to protect all aspects of religious observance and beliefs. Under the law, employers must provide reasonable accommodations upon request to an employee that has a "sincerely held" religious believe. An employer can be exempt to this provision only by proving inability to provide reasonable accommodation to an employee or prospective employee to their religious observance or practice without "undue hardship" for the employer's business.

Experts and practitioners of diversity recommend that the best proactive measure for human resources professionals is to get educated and informed about the different practices and beliefs of followers of various religions in an effort to avoid disrespect for people's personal beliefs and discrimination in the workplace. Additionally, management in general must be neutral when it comes to making decisions about people whose beliefs may vary from their own personal beliefs by making professional decisions that are aligned with the organization's core values and mission. When it comes to accommodating diverse religious practices in the workplace, managers must be aware of and, at minimum, align their practices with the government's expectation. Reasonable accommodation under the Title VII law states:

> Employers must reasonably accommodate employees' sincerely held religious practices unless doing so would impose an undue hardship on the employer. A reasonable religious accommodation is any adjustment to the work environment that will allow the employee to practice his religion. An employer might accommodate an employee's religious beliefs or practices by allowing: flexible scheduling, voluntary substitutions or swaps, job reassignments and lateral transfers, modification of grooming requirements and other workplace practices, policies and/or procedures. An employer is not required to accommodate an employee's religious beliefs and practices if doing so would impose an undue hardship on the employers' legitimate business interests. An employer can show undue hardship if accommodating an employee's religious practices requires more than ordinary administrative costs, diminishes efficiency in other jobs, infringes on other employees' job rights or benefits, impairs workplace safety, causes co-workers to carry the accommodated employee's share of potentially hazardous or burdensome work, or if the proposed accommodation conflicts with another law or regulation (EEOC).

Exercise and Questions for Discussion:

1. How does the "reasonable accommodation" clause apply to your firm or organization?
2. What are some common religious beliefs in your organization?
3. What are some common best practices that your organization (or one that you are familiar with) has used to accommodate diverse religious practices?
4. *Exercise*. What are some common religious practices in your community? Once you have determined the common religious beliefs in your community, then determine which one you would like to know more about as per your personal interests and the needs of your workplace. Now, go and visit a place of worship about this religious philosophy in your community to familiarize yourself with their thoughts, beliefs, practices, and how their religious needs can be best accommodated in the workplace.

Exercise 13: Pregnancy Discrimination in the Workplace

Pregnancy discrimination cases in the United States seem to be on the rise over the past decade and many believe that this is because today's generation of female employees are not willing to put up with such unfair practices. CBS Evening News did a segment (May 14, 2006) entitled *"Bias Because Baby Is on the Way: Discrimination Complaints Increase,"* where one mother's story was emphasized on the rise of pregnancy discrimination over the last few years. Like many other aspiring professionals, Sarah had been working in the corporate environment when she realized that she also wanted to be a mother. Eventually, Sarah became pregnant. Sarah worked as a manager at Merisant, the maker of the artificial sweetener Equal. According to the news report, Sarah said that "As soon as I let them know, within a week or two, the demeanor of the company changed." She continued to say that "They began to exclude me from large management decisions and meetings." Furthermore, there was a promotional opportunity, which was originally promised to her, that had gone to a male candidate. According to the CBS News report, "When a promotion she'd been promised went to a man, Sarah Babb filed a pregnancy discrimination complaint with the Equal Employment Opportunity Commission." Such cases as Sarah's is not uncommon in today's workplace. CBS News (2006) reported that "The number of reported pregnancy bias cases since 1992 has risen 31 percent, even though the birthrate has dropped. Pregnancy now ranks second among the fastest growing bias categories."

Experts believe that Generation-X women have a lot to do with the increase in complaints as their needs, expectations and desires are somewhat different from their predecessors, i.e. the traditional and baby boomer generations. The Gen X category of women, who are mostly in their 20s and 30s, tend to feel entitled to be in the work environment and should not be penalized when pursuing their dreams of motherhood.

According to the CBS News report, "In recent years Google, Novartis, Kohl's — even maternity apparel retailer 'Mothers Work Inc.' — have all been accused of pregnancy bias. Soap opera actress Kari Wuhrer sued ABC claiming her character was killed off when producers learned she was pregnant" (May 14, 2006). Managers should be fully aware that Federal law, in the United States, prohibits pregnancy discrimination against employees. Such awareness can hopefully provide fair opportunities for female professionals and eliminate the biases and discriminatory practices which often are corollary of pregnancy in the work environment.

Merisant's management told CBS News "...the company has had a very successful track record of employing pregnant employees..." adding that "Sarah Babb was terminated for performance and business reasons" (May 14, 2006). Experts believe that the number of pregnancy cases and actual discrimination toward pregnant women may be much higher since some workers do not want to take legal action against their employers because they fear it could damage their current and prospective careers in the industry.

Any form of discrimination, including pregnancy discrimination, can be very stressful and devastating to mothers who rely on their existing jobs and employer for income and health insurance. Most local agencies, in various states, require that employers should not discriminate against pregnant women. More specifically, employers should not discharge, refuse to promote, refuse to hire, withhold training, or harass pregnant employees as this can be a violation of the law.

Questions for Discussion:
1. Interview five working women who have had their children while being employed. Find out how they were treated by their colleagues and managers, determine if their employers had fair policies regarding pregnancy leaves,

what can be changed regarding pregnancy leaves as per their suggestions, and what would they do differently if their employees were to take time off when they are "expecting"?

2. Review the rules and policies of two large corporations or public agencies regarding pregnancy leave. Compare these policies with the existing federal and local laws to see if they match. Report your findings and discuss whether you suggest any changes to the existing policies and guidelines for any of these organizations.

Exercise 14: Conducting an Organizational Diversity Audit

The purpose of a diversity audit is to assess what the organization is communicating to its employees, customers, vendors, suppliers, governments, third parties, unions, and the society in general through its advertisement, printed material, service to employees and customers, website material, phone messages, etc. As stated by experts in the diversity field, cultural diversity audits can be seen as the assessment of both efforts that an organization is putting forward and the actual results it is achieving from the diversity initiatives and programs.

Dr. Carol Harvey of the Assumption College (Harvey and Allard, 2005) provides excellent instructions on how to conduct a diversity audit in her article titled "*Evaluating Diversity in the Real World: Conducting a Diversity Audit.*" The goals of such audits are to achieve a comprehensive learning experience that enables learners and managers to see how various diversity concepts can be applied in the work environment. Such an audit provides best practices and some unique ways that modern organizations are working to manage diversity, or how some institutions are simply limiting their diversity initiatives to legal compliance. Dr. Harvey emphasizes the importance of understanding that all people develop criteria, whether conscious or unconscious, which they use to evaluate diverse people, places, ideas, and experiences. Dr. Harvey mentions that an effective way to communicate is to have a group discussion with your peers or colleagues on the "criteria" used to evaluate a familiar experience, such as judging a recent movie (for example, what did you think about the following movies when you first saw or heard about them: the Break Up, Pirates of the Caribbean: The Curse of the Black Pearl, Spanglish, RV, My Big Fat Greek Wedding, The Italian Job, The Last Samurai, The Legend of Zorro, The Passion of Christ, The Recruit, War of the Worlds, A History of Violence, Anger Management, Bowling for Columbine, Bruce Almighty, Catch Me if You Can, Cinderella Man, Collateral, Fahrenheit 9/11, Harry Potter and the Prisoner of Azkaban, Hidalgo, Hostage, Hotel Rwanda, Kill Bill II, Laws of Attraction, Lost in Translation, Master and Commander: The Far Side of the World, or X-Men III: The Last Stand.) The same can apply to evaluating or deciding whether to buy a piece of clothing while in the Bahamas vacationing, or waiting until one returns home. With regard to watching the latest Hollywood film, most people will give answers such as: "the movie was too violent", "the comedy movie made me laugh", "I really like Jennifer Anniston and Vince Vaughn in the Break Up", "I loved the music in the latest James Bond movie," etc. This can lead to a discussion and/or an understanding of the unconscious criteria that people use to evaluate the worth of things and diversity efforts in an organization.

You can brainstorm some potential criteria that a team of consultants could use to evaluate the diversity efforts of an institution (government or the private sector). Initially, for example, you may think of evaluating their website or the makeup of the board of trustees, and upper management (i.e. Are they really diverse in significant ways compared to their competitors?). You may ask such questions as:

1. What does the organization's website communicate about their human diversity and diversity programs?
2. What does the website communicate about their mission and commitments to customers, vendors, suppliers, government, unions, third parties, stockholders, the environment, and employees?
3. What are the current organizational values and philosophies? Does the organization "walk its talk" in terms of living their own stated values and policies?
4. Do their benefits and work scheduling practices recognize the needs of diverse employees (scheduling plans, religious accommodations, spousal health insurance for all employees, day care, flextime, job sharing, etc.)?
5. What types of diversity initiatives and training programs does the institution or organization offer? Who gets trained and how? Who conducts the training? What does the training cost? How are its outcomes measured?
6. What seems to be the motivation for diversity initiatives? (Affirmative Action, legal compliance, avoiding lawsuits, the beliefs of a strong leader, recognition of the need to have employees who relate to and understand target customers, etc.)

It is important that you develop appropriate and personalized criteria for the organization that you are auditing. As consultants and researchers, you should measure the company's performance against established criteria; and, keep in mind that the established criteria can be updated as per the new information and discoveries during your research, interviews and visits with the company.

For example, a consultant/group may find that an organization is very diverse in terms of age, race and ethnicity. However, on visiting the company, they learn that turnover and lack of innovation are mentioned as serious problems. Although the company has visible demographic diversity, it does little or nothing about addressing the need to train employees in terms of interpersonal relations, teamwork and intercultural communication among diverse employees. You may discover that the organization's benefits and policies do not support the needs of the religious diversity of its existing employees. In such a case, you may conclude that there is a total lack of recognition to capitalize on the positive aspects of diversity characteristics since an organizational diversity challenge and initiatives should involve more than just recruiting diverse employees. Modern organizations should do all they can to retain productive and experienced employees by providing teamwork and interpersonal communication training. Employee retention in modern society can be very important, especially when the unemployment rates are low and when firms are competing for the best talent. As a team of consultants, you can develop additional criteria that address how well an organization recognizes and responds to the differing needs of its diverse employees. Attracting and hiring diverse employees is a good start, but keeping them there may require a lot more than just having a few diversity initiatives.

As consultants, your job is to focus on evaluating the organization's diversity efforts against established criteria (developed specifically for this organization with the competitors in mind) rather than on a long organizational history. The consultants are required to develop a list of recommended actions that the organization can take to benefit from the existing or prospective diversity. The consultants may recommend that the organization needs to recruit more diverse employees; change their holiday and vacation policies; get diverse customers; enter into new markets to learn about diverse customers; conduct a survey of their employees as per their gender, age or religious backgrounds to see how satisfied they are at this time; provide diversity training to all managers and employees; and enhance their website to reflect a positive image of the firm. If you have a number of recommendations for the firm, try to put this into a Gantt Chart, showing how and when each task should be accomplished. Overall, provide an introduction for your project, a body for your project along with all the specifics, findings, and recommendations, and finally offer an overall summary. Some items such as surveys or standard questions for interviews and other supplementary material can be included in the appendix of the report.

Overall, as a consultant team, you may take the following steps to serve as a group of experts for completing this project on organizational diversity audit:

1. Determine which type of an organization, institution or department you would like to audit. It is best if this institution or organization is a medium-sized firm or has about 500 to 1,000 employees.
2. Call several specific firms and get an agreement from an employee, an official, or a manager who is willing to cooperate with you on this research during the allotted time.
3. As a team, conduct as much research about this firm as possible before officially meeting with anyone in the firm about the actual project. Use the firms' website and their competitors' websites to find the best practices in the industry. You can look at their published reports and training manuals. In addition, you can find material from secondary sources online or at the local library.
4. Determine your established assessment and evaluation criteria for assessing the diversity of this organization or institution. Be objective to determine if this organization should receive a grade of A (excellent), B (good), C (satisfactory or average), or D (below standard) for their organizational diversity audit when evaluated with the established criteria and compared with competitors in the industry. Provide sufficient reasons for your grading of this organization and support it with objective information.
5. Prepare your interview questions and survey instrument for your primary research.
6. Conduct the interview and visit (or distribute the surveys as per your plan).
7. Analyze your findings and debrief.
8. Find more information as needed or according to any existing gaps.
9. Prepare your final professional report, recommendations and presentation to the company officials and your colleagues.
10. Unless told otherwise, use the American Psychological Association (APA) guidelines for the formatting and referencing of this 8-12 page report.

Exercise 15: The Way We See Me

The purpose of "The Way We See Me" exercise, which is a commonly used self assessment tool by most communication experts, is to clarify how you see yourself and understand how others see you. This will help you capitalize on your strengths and create a plan to strengthen your weaknesses or areas of opportunity during your interaction with others. As a result, discuss the following questions: How can you use the results? What are you going to do to improve your communication? What can others learn from your findings? Discuss things you can do to improve your overall effectiveness with your colleagues, friends, and family members.

You may choose to use the following suggested steps to conduct your research and prepare your paper.

Step	Guidelines	Research Notes
1.	Create a purpose and plan for the study and determine your target populations. Distribute surveys to your audience and collect within the allotted time.	Discuss in the "*Introduction*" part of your research document. Guarantee confidentiality of the individual results to the target.
2.	Complete the survey on your own behalf and determine how you see yourself.	Discuss this on the "*How I See Myself*" section of your research.
3.	Analyze the data and discuss how others see you.	Discuss this in the "*Result*" section of your research.
4.	Compare your own evaluation with the evaluation of others. Discuss differences (may use the Johari Window as a guideline).	Discuss this in the "*Comparison of Results*" section of the research.
5.	Discuss the results and how you will apply the results to improve your communication and interaction with others to accomplish your goals.	Expound on this in the "*Application and Goals*" part of your research.
6.	Summarize your learning from this experience and the overall results of the survey.	Discuss this in the "*Summary / Conclusion*" section of your research.
7.	Finish your research document. Make it a good learning experience.	Tell everyone your main findings.

Directions: The Way We See Me Survey

Please take a few minutes and check (√) your understanding of how the following characteristics apply to me. The results will remain confidential - so please be honest, as the cumulative responses will be used for research and improvement purposes.

One: How well do the following words apply to me?

	Not at all	Slightly	Moderately	Rather well	Extremely well
1. Self-confident					
2. Tactful					
3. Irritable					
4. Quiet					
5. Emotionally variable					
6. Serious					
7. Energetic					
8. Well-adjusted					
9. Cooperative					
10. Prejudiced					
11. Unpredictable					
12. Selfish					
13. Leader					
14. Considerate of others					
15. Good natured					
16. Tense					
17. Open to criticism					
18. Aggressive					
19. Creative					
20. Sense of humor					
21. Responsible					
22. Ambitious					
23. Mature					
24. Open - Easy to approach					
25. Attractive					

Two: Please state three of my specific strengths and three specific weaknesses!

Exercise 16: Making Assumptions

We have a tendency to generalize and make assumptions about the words, language and the meaning of what is said often from the context in which statements are made. This shows that there might be some fallacies in one's thinking when they are based upon hidden assumptions. Answer the following questions as quickly as you can (in about five to eight minutes) and keep track of your start and end times.

Questions	Answers
1. Each country has its own "Independence Day." Do they have a 4th of July in Canada?	1.
2. How many birthdays does the average person have in the United States of America?	2.
3. Can a person living in Canada be buried in the United States?	3.
4. If you had one match and entered a room in which there was a Kerosene lamp, an oil heater and wood burning stove, which would you light first?	4.
5. Some months have 30 days, some have 31. How many have 28 days?	5.
6. If a doctor gives you three pills and told you to take one every half hour, how long would the pills last?	6.
7. If you have a red color pen and a blue color pen, is it possible to write green with them?	7.
8. How far can a runner run into the forest?	8.
9. You have two U. S. coins in your hand which total 55 cents in value. One is not a nickel. What are the two coins?	9.
10. A shepherd has 19 goats. All but nine died. How many does he have left?	10.
11. Two players played racquetball. They played five games and each player won the same number of games. There were no ties. How can this be?	11.
12. Take two oranges from three oranges and what do you get?	12.
13. Divide 30 by one-half and add 10. What is the answer?	13.
14. An archaeologist claimed she found gold coins dated 46 B.C. Do you think she did and why?	14.
15. An airplane crashed exactly on the U.S./Canada border. Where would they bury the survivors?	15.
16. How many animals of each species did Moses take aboard the ark with him?	16.
17. Is it legal in California for a man to marry his widow's sister?	17.
18. How much dirt can be removed from a hole that is five feet deep, three feet wide, and eight feet long?	18.

Making Assumptions, continued

19. If your electricity didn't work and you couldn't see anything in your room, how many socks would you need to take out of the bureau drawer, to guarantee that you have two of the same color socks, if there are 15 black socks and 20 blue socks.	*19.*
20. You have four nines (9,9,9,9). Arrange them to total 100. You may use any of the arithmetical processes (addition, subtraction, multiplication, or division). Each nine must be used once.	*20.*
21. If it takes five people five days to dig a hole, how long will take two people to dig half a hole?	*21.*
22. How can the following be true? "In my bedroom, the nearest lamp that I usually keep turned on is 12 feet away from my bed. Alone in the room, without using any special devices, I can turn out the light on that lamp and get into bed before the room is dark."	*22.*
23. A doctor refuses to operate on a patient who has been injured in an auto accident in which the patient's father was killed. The doctor refuses to operate because the patient is the doctor's son. How can this be?	*23.*
24. There are 12 one-cent stamps in a dozen, but how many two-cent stamps are there in a dozen?	*24.*
25. What four words appear on every denomination of United States coin and currency?	*25.*
26. Which is correct: 7 and 8 are 13 or 7 and 8 is 13?	*26.*
27. If 3 cats kill 3 rats in 3 minutes, how long will it take for 100 cats to kill 100 rats?	*27.*
28. Which is definitely correct: "I am a dog" or "I ain't no dog"?	*28.*

Note: Commonly agreed-upon answers will be provided by the facilitator.

DON'T QUIT

When things go wrong as they sometimes will.
When the road you are trudging seems all up hill.
When funds are low and debts are high.
And you want to smile, but you have to sigh.

When care is pressing you down a bit.
Rest, if you must, but don't quit.
Life is queer with its twists and turns.
As everyone of us sometimes learns.

And many a failure turns about
When he might have won had he stuck it out:
Don't give up though the pace seems slow --
You may succeed with another blow.

Success is failure turned inside out --
The silver tint of the clouds of doubt.
And you never can tell how close you are.
It may be near when it seems so far:

So stick to the fight when you are hardest hit --
It's when things seem worst that you must not QUIT.

(Unknown)

"Happiness is when what you think, what you say, and what you do are in harmony" (Mahatma Gandhi). May you have harmony in your head (thoughts), heart (feelings), and habits (behaviors)!

Bibliography

Alder, J. (2005, September 5). Special Report: Spirituality 2005. *NewsWeek Magazine*, 46.

Adler, N. J. and Izraeli, D.(1994) *Women managers in a global economy*. Blackwell Publishers.

Adler, Nancy J. (1991). *International dimensions of organizational behavior*. 2nd edition. Boston, MA: PWS-Kent Publishing Company.

Age and Attitude, 1994. *Age and Attitude Documentary*. ABC Prime Time with Diane Sawyer. Aired on 6/9/1994.

Ahmed, A. M., Yang, J. B., & Dale, B. G. (2003). Self-assessment methodology: The route to business excellence. *The Quality Management Journal, 10*(1), 43-57. Retrieved March 26, 2005, from ProQuest database.

Ahn, M. J., Adamson, J. S. A., & Dornbusch, D. (2004). Leaders to leadership: Managing change. *Journal of Leadership and Organizational Studies, 10*(4), 112-123. Retrieved March 28, 2005, from ProQuest database.

Albrecht, Karl (2006). *Social Intelligence: the New Science of Success*. Jossey-Bass.

Allegretti, J.G. (2000). *Loving your job, finding your passion: work and the spiritual life*. New York: Paulist Press.

AMANA, 2006. *April Black History Facts*. AMANA, American Muslim Association of North America. Received electronically AMANAvoice on April 05, 2006.

Angoujard, R. (2005). Exceeding customer expectations at Novotel. *Strategic HR Review, 4*(2), 8-9. Retrieved May 25, 2005, from EBSCOhost database.

Anson, W. (2001) Intellectual Capital Values in Liquidation. The Secured Lender, 57, 6, 52

Applebaum, S., Bartolomucci, N., Beaumier, E., & Boulanger, J. (2004). Organizational citizenship behavior: A case study of culture, leadership and trust. *Management Decision, 42*(1), 13-39. Retrieved December 4, 2004, from ProQuest database.

Argyris, R. P., Smith, D.M. (1985) Action Science. San Francisco: Jossey-Bass.

Armistead, C. (1999) Knowledge and Process Performance. Journal of Knowledge Management, 3, 2, 143

Ashmos, D.P. & Duchon, D. (2000). Spirituality at work: A conceptualization and measure. *Journal of Management Inquiry, 9 (2)*, 135-145.

Barnum, P.; Liden, D. R. And DiTomaso, N., 1995. Couble Jeopardy for Women and Minorities: Pay Differences with Age. *The Academy of Management Journal*. Vol. 38, # 3. June.

Bartlett, C.A., Ghoshal, S., and J. Birkinshaw (2004). *Transnational Management* (4th ed.). *ISBN: 0072482761*

Bass, B. M. (1990). *Bass & Stogdill's handbook of leadership: Theory, research & managerial applications*. New York: The Free Press.

Baylor, Kenneth (2005). *French and Raven: The Study of Social Power*. Unpublished manuscript. United States, Nova Southeastern University (2005).

Beck, C. E. (1999). *Managerial Communication/ Building Theory and Practice*. Upper Saddle River, NJ: Prentice Hall. ISBN 0-13-849886-5

Beck, C. E (1985). *The Open Door Policy: Communication Climate and the Military Supervisor.* Retrieved March 31, 2005 from http://www.airpower.maxwell.af.mil/airchronicles/aureview/1985/may-jun/beck.html

Becker-Reems, E. (2001). Synergy in motion: The board chair and CEO relationship, a high-performance organization needs a winning team. *Trustee,* 24-28. Retrieved March 14, 2005, from http://www.Pubmed.com.

Bedingfield, C. (2004). How assessment centers helped Energis get customer-focused. *Strategic HR Review, 3*(6), 10-11. Retrieved February 15, 2005, from EBSCOhost database.

Beebe, S. A.; Beebe, S.J. and Redmond, M.V. (2002). *Interpersonal Communication: relating to others* (3rd Ed.). Boston, MA: Allyn & Bacon.

Benner, D.G. (1989). Toward a psychology of spirituality: Implications for personality and psychotherapy. *Journal of Psychology and Christianity, 5,* 19-30.

Bielous, Gary (1995). Seven Power Bases and How to Effectively Use Them. *Supervision,* 56, 10, 14. Retrieved on August 11, 2005, from http://edelpage.the-mooseboy.com/7000/seven_power_bases.html

Bennett, G. (2004). *Religion and the Workplace.* Retrieved on April 20, 2004 from: www.diversityresources.com/rc21d/ religious_diversity_in_the_workplace.htm.

Bennett, R.H.III, Fadil, P.A., & Greenwood, R.T. (1994) Cultural Alignment in Response to Strategic Organizational Change: New Considerations for a Change Framework. Journal of Managerial Issues, 6, 4, 474

Berman-Brown, R. & Woodland, M. (1999). Managing Knowledge wisely: A Case Study in Organizational Behavior. Journal of Applied Management Studies, 8, 175-198.

Bernard, C. I., (1938). The executive functions. In Ott, S. J. (1996) *Classical Readings in Organizational Behavior* (2nd ed.): 181-183. Orlando, FL: Harcourt Brace & Company.

Berne, R. W., & Raviv, D. (2004). Eight-dimensional methodology for innovative thinking about the case and ethics of the Mt. Graham, large binocular telescope project. *Science and Engineering Ethics, 10*(2), 235-242. Retrieved March 24, 2004, from EBSCOhost database.

Berry, J. (2000). Traditional Training Fades In Favor of E-Learning – Internet Economy Demands: A Flexible Training Approach. Internetweek, Manhasset. 800, 33-34

Best, A., Moor, G., Holmes, B., Clark, P. I., Bruce, T., Leischow, S., et al. (2003). Health promotion dissemination and systems thinking: Towards an integrative model. *American Journal of Health Behavior, 27*(3), 206-216. Retrieved April 24, 2005, from EBSCOhost database.

Blair, E. (2003). Culture and leadership. *Professional Safety, 48*(6), 18-22. Retrieved March 28, 2005, from EBSCOhost database.

Brandt, E. (1996). Corporate pioneers explore spirituality. *HR Magazine, 41,* 82.

Bregman, L., and S. Thierman. (1995). *First person mortal: Personal narratives of illness, dying, and grief.* New York: Paragon.

Brown, Donald R. and Don Harvey. 2006. *An Experiential Approach to Organizational Development,* Seventh Edition. Upper Saddle River, NJ: Pearson Education, Inc.

Bruce, C. (2004). Tips for Competing Against Younger Job Candidates. Retrieved April 28, 2006, from Career Journal .com Web Site: http://http://www.careerjournaleurope.com/myc/diversity/20040723-imdiversity.html

Bruins, Jan (Spring, 1999). Social Power and Influence Tactics: A Theoretical Introduction-Social Influence and Social Power: Using Theory for Understanding Social Issues. *Journal of Social Issues.* Retrieved on August 24, 2005, from

Buckingham, M. (2005). What great managers do. *Harvard Business Review, 83*(3), 70-79. Retrieved March 31, 2005, from EBSCOhost database.

Cabrera, E. F. & Bonache, J. (1999). An expert HR system for aligning organizational culture and strategy HR. Human Resource Planning Tempe, 22, 51-60

Cameron, K.S. & Quinn, R.E. (1999) *Diagnosing and Changing Organizational Culture: Based on the Competing Values Framework.* Addison-Wesley Publishing Company, Inc.

Campbell, D. J. (2000). The proactive employee: Managing workplace initiative. *The Academy of Management Executive, 14*(3), 52-66. Retrieved November 15, 2004, from ProQuest database.

Capra, F. (1996). *The web of life.* New York: Anchor Books.

Carr, D. K., Hard, K. J., & Trahant, W. J. (1996). *Managing the change process: A field book for change agents, consultants, team leaders, and reengineering managers.* New York: McGraw-Hill.

Cascio, W. F. and Aguinis, H. (2005). Applied psychology in human resources management. (6th ed.), New Jersey: Pearson Prentice Hall.

Cathon, D. E. (2000) The Learning Organization: Adapted from The Fifth Discipline by Peter Senge. Hospital Material Management Quarterly, 21, 3, 4-10

Cavanaugh, M. B. (2001). Social security: Can the promise be kept? An introduction. *Washington and Lee Law Review, 58*(4), 1197-2002. Retrieved April 25, 2005, from ProQuest database.

Cavico, F. & Mujtaba, B., (2005). *Business Ethics: Transcending Requirements through Moral Leadership.* Pearson Custom Publications. U.S.A. ISBN: 0-536-85783-0.

CBS News, (May 14, 2006). *Bias Because Baby is on the Way: Discrimination Complaints Increase.* Retrieved on May 16, 2006 from: http://www.cbsnews.com/stories/2006/05/14/eveningnews/main1616608.shtml?CMP=ILC-SearchStories.

Center for Leadership Studies. Escondido, CA. Phone: (760) 741-6595. Retrieved on August 12th 2004 from: http://www.situational.com/leadership/green_base.html

Chandler, C.K., & J.M. Holden. (1992). Counseling for spiritual wellness: Theory and practice. *Journal of Counseling and Development, 71,* 168-176.

Chappel, T. (1993). *The soul of a business.* New York: Bantam Books.

Champion, Daryl (2003). *The Paradoxical Kingdom* (pp. 20-24). New York: Columbia University Press.

Chebat, J., & Kollias, P. (2000). The impact of empowerment on customer contact employees' role in service organizations. *Journal of Service Research, 3*(1), 66-81. Retrieved May 1, 2005, from ProQuest database.

Checkland, P. (1999). *Systems thinking, systems practice.* New York: John Wiley & Son.

Checkland, P. (1999). *Systems thinking, systems practice: A 30-year retrospective.* New York: John Wiley & Sons.

Civil Society Empowerment, (2006). *Sensitivity to others.* Retrieved on June 11, 2006 from: http://www.passia.org/seminars/99/leaders/bb.htm

Clark, Donald (2000). *Leading and Leadership.* Retrieved on August 11, 2005, from www.nwlink.com/donclark/leader/leaderled.html

Clegg, S. R., Hardy, C., & Nord, W. R. (Eds.). (2002). *Handbook of organization studies.* London: Sage.

Communicate, 1998. *Communicate: A Workbook for Interpersonal Communication.* 6th edition. Editor-in Chief: Linda A Joesting. Communication Research Associates. Long Beach City College. ISBN: 0-7872-4510-0.

Cook, J., Hepworth, S., Wall, T., & Warr, P. (1981) *The experience of work: a compendium and review of 249 measures and their use.* New York: Academic Press.

Cooperrider, D. L., Sorensen, P. F., Yaeger, T. F., & Whitney, D. (2001). *Appreciative inquiry: An emerging direction for organizational development.* Champaign, IL: Stipes.

Cooperrider, D. L., & Srivastva, S. (Eds.). (2003). *Appreciative inquiry in organizational life.* Bedford Heights, OH: Lakeshore Communications.

Cooperrider, D. L., Whitney, D., & Stavros, J. M. (2003). *Appreciative inquiry handbook.* Bedford Heights, OH: Lakeshore Communications.

Country Studies: Saudi Arabia. (2005). Retrieved February 22, 2006, from http://countrystudies.us/saudi-arabia/.

Cox, T. (2001). *Creating the Multicultural Organization: A Strategy for Capturing the Power of Diversity.* San Francisco: Jossey-Bass.

Cracker Barrel, (2006). *Cracker Barrel Old Country Store.* Retrieved on April 30, 2006 from: http://www.crackerbarrel.com/

Crum, T. F., (1987). *The Magic of Conflict: Turning a Life of Work into a Work of Art.* Touchstone; Simon and Schuster.

Cultural Differences, 2006. Retrieved on 4/30/2006 from the following URL: http://www.analytictech.com/mb021/cultural.htm

Czinkota, M.R., Ronkainen, I.A, and Moffett, M.H. (2004). *International Business* (7th ed.). *ISBN: 0324259913.*

Dale, E.S. (1991). *Bringing Heaven down to Earth. A Practical Spirituality of Work (American University Studies, Series 7, Theology and Religion, vol. 83).* New York: Peter Lang.

Daft, R. L. (2004b). Theory Z: Opening the corporate door for participative management. *Academy of Management Executive, 18*(4), 117-121. Retrieved February 19, 2005, from ProQuest database.

Daspro, E. (2004). *An evaluation of female expatriate managers' efficacy.* Retrieved on May 11, 2006 from: http://econoquantum.cucea.udg.mx/pdf/Suplemento%20An%20evaluation%20of%20female%20expatriate.pdf.

Davis, J.E. (1998). The Evolution, Development, and Future of Affirmative Action in Government.

Davis, J. H. & Ruhe, J. A. (2003). Perceptions of country corruption: Antecedents and outcomes. *Journal of Business Ethics, 43,* 275-288.

Deeny, Raymond M. and Wymer III, John f. (1993). *Avoiding Sexual Harassment Problems in the Workplace.* Video by the Institute for Applied Management and Law (IAML); Documented Employment Law Video Series. Phone: (714) 760-1700.

De Long, D.W. & Fahey, L. (2000). Diagnosing cultural barriers to knowledge management. The Academy of Management Executive, 14, 113-127.

Denison, D.R. (1996) What is the Difference Between Organizational Culture and Organizational Climate? A Native's Point of View on a Decade of Paradigm Wars. Academy of Management. The Academy of Management Review, 21, 3, 619.

Denison, D. R. (1996). What is the difference between organizational culture and organizational climate? A native's point of view on a decade of paradigm wars. *Academy of Management Review, 21*(3), 619-654. Retrieved May 1, 2005, from EBSCOhost database.

Denison, D. R. (2000). *Denison Organizational Culture Survey*. Retrieved February 28, 2005, from http://www.denisonculture.com

DePree, H. (1992). *Business as unusual: The people and principles at Herman Miller*. Zeeland, Michigan: Doubleday Books.

Deshpande, R. Farley, J. U. & Webster, F.E. (1993) Corporate Culture, Customer Orientation, and Innovativeness. Journal of Marketing, 57, 1, 23

Dessler, Gary (2001). *A Framework for Human Resource Management*. 2nd edition. Prentice Hall.

Discipline without Punishment. A CRM Learning Video. 2215 Faraday Avenue. Phone: (800) 421-0833. Also made available by the Performance Systems Corporation: The Walk the Talk Company. Retrieved on 10, 06, 2005 from: http://www.crmlearning.com/product.cwa?isbn=111472V

Dixon, N. (1996). The hallways of learning. *Strategy and Leadership, 24*(2), 52. Retrieved March 26, 2005, from ProQuest database.

Dobbs, L. (2004). *Exporting America.* Warner Business Books. p 1-160.

Doh, J. P. (2000). Entrepreneurial Privatization Strategies: Order of Entry and Local Partner Collaboration as Sources of Competitive Advantage. *Academy of Management Review*, Vol. 25, No. 3; pages 551-571.

Dometrius, N. & Sigelman, L. (1984). Assessing progress toward Affirmative Action goals in state and local governments: A new benchmark. *Public Administration Review, 44(3),* 244-245.

Dowling, P.J. (2005). Are Female Expatriates Different? *International Human Resource Management: Managing People in the Multinational Context*. 4th Ed. South-Western: Mason, Ohio.

Drew, S. A. W., Smith, P. A. C., (1995) The Learning Organization: "Change Proofing" and Strategy. The learning Organization, 2, 1, 4-14

Drogin, B. (1995). South Africa Struggles to Enforce Affirmative Action Plan. *The Detroit News.*

Drucker, P. F. (2002). *Managing the next society: The CEO in the next millenium.* New York, NY: St. Martin's Press, 10010.

Drucker, P. F. (2001). *The essential drucker.* New York, NY: Harper Collins Publishers Inc., 10022.

Dunning, J.H. (1997). *Micro and macro organizational aspects on MNE and MNE activity. International Business: an emerging vision*, Columbia, SC: University of South Columbia Press.

Dupont, Kay (1997). Handling Diversity in the Workplace. AMI Publication. Forwarded by Dr. R. Roosevelt Thomas.

Educational Kit, (1999). *Think Ability*. President's Committee on Employment of People with Disabilities. See "A message from the chairman Tony Coelho."

EEOC Publication, (2006). Wal-Mart to pay in settlement $315,000. Retrieved on June 11, 2006 from: http://wwweeoc.gov/press/6-01-06html

Eisenhart, M. (2001) Gathering Knowledge While It's Ripe. Knowledge Management, 4, 50.

Elkins, D.N., Hedstrom, L.J., Hughes, L.L., Leaf, J.A., & Saunders, C. (1988). Toward a humanistic-phenomenological spirituality: definition, description and measurement. *Journal of Humanistic Psychology, 28,* 5-18.

Elliott, S., O'Dell, C. (1999) Sharing Knowledge & Best Practices: The Hows and Whys of Tapping Your Organization's Hidden Reservoirs of Knowledge. Health Forum Journal, 42, 3, 34-37

Emblen, J.D. (1992). Religion and spirituality defined according to current use in nursing literature. *Journal of Professional Nursing, 8,* 41-47.

Emmons, G (2005). *The New International Style of Management.* Retrieved November30, 2005 from Harvard Business School website: http://hbswk.hbs.edu/item.jhtml?id=4893&t=globalization

Emmons, R.A. (2000*). Is spirituality an intelligence? Motivation, cognition, and the psychology of the ultimate concern.* International Journal for the Psychology of Religion, 10, 30-36.

English, L. M., Fenwick, T. J., & Parsons, J. (2003). An appreciative inquiry into the spiritual values of Christian higher education. *Christian Higher Education, 2*(1), 71-90. Retrieved May 26, 2004, from EBSCOhost database.

Erickson, S. G., Rothberg, H. N. (2000) Intellecutal capital and competitiveness: Guidelines for policy. Competitiveness Review , 10, 192-198.

Equal Employment Opportunity Training (1998). *Equal Employment Opportunity Training for Managers at Publix Super Markets*. Workshop format. Lakeland, Florida.

Evans, Gail, (September 2001). *Play Like a Man, Win Like a Woman: What Men Know About Success that Women Need to Learn.*

Feldman, S. (1999) The leveling of Organizational Culture; Egalitarianism in Critical Postmodern Organization Theory. The Journal of Applied Behavioral Science. 35, 228-244.

Fetterman, D. M. (2002). Empowerment evaluation: Building communities of practice and a culture of learning. *American Journal of Community Psychology, 30*(1), 89-102. Retrieved April 1, 2005, from ProQuest database.

Fiedler, F. E. (March, 1969). Style or circumstance: The leadership enigma. *Psychology Today* 2(10), 38-43.

Fitzgerald, S. P., Murrell, K. L., & Miller, M. G. (2003). Appreciative inquiry: Accentuating the positive. *Business Strategy Review, 14*(1), 5-7. Retrieved November 9, 2004, from EBSCOhost database.

Flanagan, R. (1999) Knowledge Management in Global Organizations in the 21st Century. HRMagazine, 44, 11, 54-55

Fletcher, B., Jones, F. (1992). Measuring Organizational Culture: The Cultural Audit. Managerial Auditing Journal, 7, 6, 30

Forbes Magazine, 2006. Retrieved April 26, 2006 from: http://www.forbes.com/2006/04/24/kids-and-money-cx_sr_0425money_print.html

Foley, R., & Wurmser, T. (2004). Culture diversity / a mobile workplace command creative leadership, new partnerships, and innovative approaches to integration. *Nursing Administration Quarterly, 28*(2), 122-128. Retrieved April 12, 2005, from Infotrac database.

Foster, C. & Harris, L. (2005). Easy to say difficulty to do: diversity management in retail. *Human Resource Management Journal, 15*(3). pp. 4-17.

Freedom Charter 1955 Kliptown. South Africa belongs to all who live in it.

Freshman, B. (1999). An exploratory analysis of definitions and applications of spirituality in the workplace. *Journal of Organizational Change Management, 12 (4), 318.*

Friedman, Emily. 2005. *White Coats and Many Colors—Population Diversity and Its Implications for Health Care.* An issue briefing prepared for the American Hospital Association.

Frey, H. William, (1999). Minority Majorities. *Written in American Demographics Books.* Page 6.

Fry, R., Barrett, F., Seiling, J., & Whitney, D. (2002). *Appreciative inquiry and organizational transformation: Reports from the field.* Westport, CT: Quorum Books.

Fukuda-Parr, S., et al. (2001). *Human development report 2001: Making new technologies work for human development.* New York: Oxford University Press. Available from www.undp.org/hdr2001/

Fukuda-Parr, S., et al. (2004). *Human development report 2004: Cultural liberty in today's diverse world.* Available from http://hdr.undp.org/reports/global/2004/

Gable, W., & Ellig, J. (1993). *Introduction to Market Based Management.* Fairfax, VA: Center for Market Process.

Galanti, Geri-Ann. 2004. *Caring for Patients from Different Cultures,* Third Edition. Philadelphia: University of Pennsylvania Press

Gardenswartz, L. & Rowe, A. (1995). *Diverse Teams At Work: Capitalizing on the Power of Diversity.* New York: McGraw-Hill Books.

Gardenswartz, L. & Rowe, A. (1998). *Managing Diversity: A Complete Desk Reference and Planning Guide.* (Rev.Ed.) New York: McGraw-Hill Books.

Gardenswartz, Lee and Anita Rowe. 1998. *Managing Diversity in Health Care.* San Francisco, CA: Jossey-Bass, Inc.

Geddes, R. R., (2004). *Competing with the Government: Anticompetitive Behavior and Public Enterprises.* Hoover Institution Press, Stanford University.

Geertz, C. (1973). The interpretation of Cultures. New York: Basic Books.

Gender Relations in Educational Applications of Technology (GREAT). (16 March 1998). "Special Issue: The Effect of Computers on the Gender Gap in Education—Gender Inequalities in Education: What's Been Done." Available from the Stanford University Web site, www.stanford.edu

Gergen, K. (2003). Beyond knowing in organizational inquiry. *Organization, 10*(3), 453-455. Retrieved October 30, 2004, from ProQuest database.

Geust, R. (2004). The World's Most Extreme Affirmative Action Program. *Wall Street Journal.*

Giacolone, R., & Jurkiewicz, C. (2003). *Handbook of workplace spirituality and organizational performance.* New York: Spring Books.

Gibson, C. & Jung, K. (2006). *Historical census statistics on the foreign-born population of the United States: 1850-2000.* Washington, DC: U.S. Census Bureau Population Division Working Paper No. 81.

Gibson, J.L., Ivancevich, J.M., Donelly, J.H., & Konopaske, R. (2003). Organizations: Behavior, structure, processes. (11th ed.), Boston: McGraw-Hill Irwin.

Goh, S. C. (1998) Toward a Learning Organization; The Strategic Building Blocks. Advanced Management Journal, 63, 2, 15-22

Goldhaber, G.H., Dennis, W.C. & Redding, G.H. (2000). Organizational Climate/Communication Research.

Goldstein, S. M. (2003). Employee development: An examination of service strategy in a high-contact service environment. *Production and Operations Management, 12*(2), 186-203. Retrieved March 31, 2005, from ProQuest database.

Golembiewski, R. T. (1999). Process observer: Large-system interventions, II: Two sources of evidence that O.D.ers have been there, been doing that. *Organization Development Journal, 17*(3), 5-8. Retrieved February 26, 2005, from ProQuest database.

Gomolski, B. (2001, February 13). *Managing Age Diversity in the* Workplace. Retrieved March 28, 2006, from Computerworld Web Site:

Goodman, E. A., Zammuto, R.F., Gifford, B.D. (2001). The Competing Values Framework: Understanding The Impact of Organizational Culture on the Quality of Work Life. Organizational Development Journal, 19, 3, 58-68

Goodwin, Jan (1987). *Caught in the crossfire.* E. P. Dutton, N. Y.. ISBN 0-525-24493-X

Gorritz, C. M. & Medina, C. (2000). Engaging girls with computers through software games. *Commun. ACM* 43(1), p. 42. Available from the ACM Digital Library Web site, www.acm.org

Gragnolati, B. A., & Stupak, R. J. (2002). Life and liberty: The power of positive purpose. *Journal of Health and Human Services Administration, 25*(1), 75-88. Retrieved February 4, 2004, from ProQuest database.

Greenberg, J. (1984). Affirmative Action in Other Lands: A Summary.

Greenspan, A. (2002) Testimony of Alan Greenspan: *Semiannual monetary policy report To the Congress.* 5-6. Federal Reserve Board.

Grilley, P. (2003). Yin Yoga blending Taoist principles with yoga practice. *Share Guide, 1*(67), 34-35. Retrieved April 24, 2005, from EBSCOhost database.

Gruss, V., McCann, J. J., Edelman, P., & Farran, C. J. (2004). Job stress among nursing home nursing assistants: Comparison of empowered and nonempowered work environments. *Alzheimer's Care Quarterly, 5*(3), 207-216. Retrieved April 1, 2005, from EBSCOhost database.

Gupta, B., Iyer, L.S. & Aronson, J.E. (2000) Knowledge Management: Practices and Challenges. Industrial Management + Data Systems, 100(1) 17-21

Guth, W.D. and Tagiuri, R. (1965, September-October). Personal Values and Corporate Strategies. *Harvard Business Review*, Reprint #65507, p124.

Hafkin, N. & Taggart, N. *Gender, Information Technology, and Developing Countries: An Analytic Study.* Available from the Office of Women in Development, U. S. Agency for International Development Web site, pdf.dec.org

Hall, Brandon (January 2005). Training. *Minneapolis*; Vol. 42, Issue 1, p. 36. Email: edit@trainingmag.com

Harder, J., Robertson, P. J., & Woodward, H. (2004). The spirit of the new workplace: Breathing life into organizations. *Organization Development Journal, 22*(2), 79-103. Retrieved July 17, 2004, from ProQuest database.

Harrington, W. (2004, October 7-9). Worldview resiliency of business degree graduate students – An examination of spiritual experiences and psychological attitudes. *Association on Employment Practices and Principals,* 119.

Harris, S. G., Mossholder, K. W. (1996) The Affective Implications of Perceived Congruence with Culture Dimensions During Organizational Transformation. Journal of Management, 22, 4, 527

Harvey, Carol P. and Allard, M. June, (2005). *Understanding and Managing Diversity: Readings Cases and Exercises.* 3rd ed., Pearson Prentice Hall.

Henry, N. (2004). *Public administration & public affairs* (9th Ed.). Upper Saddle River, NJ: Pearson Education.

Herbig, P. A., & Miller, J. C. (1992). Culture and Technology: Does the Traffic Move in Both Directions? *Journal of International Marketing, 6*(3), 75-105.

Hersey, P. (2000). *Management of Organizational Behavior: Leading Human Resources.* (8th ed.) Boston: Prentice Hall/Pearson Education.

Hersey, P., Blanchard, K H. & Johnson, D. *Management of Organizational Behavior: Utilizing Human Resources.* Prentice Hall, upper Saddle River, NJ, 1996

Hersey, P. & Campbell, R. (2004). *Leadership: A Behavioral Science Approach.* California: Leadership Studies Publishing.

Hersey, P.; Blanchard, K.; and Johnson, D., (2001). *Management of Organizational Behavior.* Eight edition. Prentice Hall. ISBN: 013-032518X.

Hersey, Paul (1984 & 1997). *The Situational Leader.* Escondido, CA. The Center for Leadership Studies. ISBN: 0-931619-01-7. Phone: (760) 741-6595.

Hersey, Paul & Campbell, Ron (2004). *Leadership: A Behavioral Science Approach.* Leadership Studies Publishing: Escondido, CA.

Hewitt Associates (2004). *Preparing the Workforce for Tomorrow Survey.* Retrieved September 15, 2005 from:
http://was4.hewitt.com/hewitt/resource/rptspubs/subrptspubs/publications/workforce_tomorrow.pdf

Hoecklin, L (1995). *Managing cultural differences: strategies for competitive advantages.* New York: Addison - Wesley Publishing.

Hodgetts, R. M., & Luthans, F. (2003). *International Management* (5th ed.). Boston: McGraw-Hill.

Hofsted, Geerte. (2006). Retrieved March 9, 2006, from:
http://en.wikipedia.org/wiki/Hofstede

Hofstede, G., & Hofstede, G. J. (2005). *Cultures and Organizations: Software of the Mind* (2nd ed., Rev.). New York: McGraw-Hill.

Hofstede, G. (1998) Attitudes, Values and Organizational Culture: Disentangling the Concepts. Organizational Studies, 19, 3, 477-492

Hofstede, G., Bond, M.H. & Chung-Leung, L. (1993) Individual Perceptions of Organizational Cultures: A Methodological Treatise on Levels of Analysis. Organization Studies, 14, 4, 483

Hofstede, G., Neuijen, B., Ohayv, D. & Sanders, G. (1990) Measuring Organizational Cultures: A Qualitative and Quantitative Study Across Twenty Cases. Administrative Science Quarterly, 35, 2, 286

Hofstede, G. (2001) Culture's Recent Consequences: Using Dimension Scores in Theory and Research. International Journal of Cross Cultural management, 1, 1, 11-30

Hofstede, G. (1993). Cultural Constraints in Management Theories. *The Executive*, 7(1), 81-94.

Hofstede, G. (2001). *Cultural Consequences: Comparing Values, Behaviors, Institutions, and Organizations across Nations* (2nd ed.). London: Sage Publications.

Hofstede, G., & Bond, M. (1988, Spring). The Confucius connection: From cultural roots to economic growth. *Organizational Dynamics, 16*(4), 4-21.

Hofstede, G. (1983). The cultural relativity of organizational practices and theories. *Journal of International Business Studies*, (Fall), 75-89.

Hofstede, G. (1984). *Culture's Consequences: International differences in work-related values* (Abridged Edition), Beverly Hills, CA: Sage Publications.

Hofstede, G. (1994). *Cultures and organizations: Intercultural cooperation and its importance for survival*. Hammersmith: Harper Collins Publishers.

Hofstede, G. (1997). *Cultures and Organizations: Software of the Mind*, New York, McGraw Hill.

Hofstede, G. (1980). *Culture's Consequences: international differences in work related values*. London: Sage

Hopkins, E. Willie (1997). *Ethical Dimensions of Diversity*. Sage Publications: Sage Series on Business Ethics.

Howard, John (2005). The Cracker Barrel Restaurants. Pages 302-310. Published in *Understanding and Managing Diversity*, third edition. By Carol P. Harvey and M. June Allard in 2005. Pearson Prentice Hall.

Howard, L. W. (1998) Validating the Competing Values Model as a Representation of Organizational Cultures. International Journal of Organizational Analysis, 6, 3, 231-250

Hueth, A. C. (2004). e-learning and Christian higher education: A war of the worlds, or lessons in reductionism? *Christian Scholar's Review, 33*(4), 527-546. Retrieved April 24, 2005, from ProQuest database.

Hughes, R., Ginnett, R. & Curphy, G. (2002), Leadership: Enhancing the Lessons of Experience (4th ed.). McGraw-Hill/ Irwin, New York, New York.

Hughes, Richard, Ginnett, Robert & Curphy, Gordon (2002). *Leadership: Enhancing the Lessons of Experience*. McGraw-Hill: NY.

Human, L. (1993). The Development of black and female managers in South Africa: Why many Affirmative Action programs fail.

Hutinger, P. L. (1996). Computer applications in programs for young children with disabilities: recurring themes. *Focus on Autism and Other Developmental Disabilities*, 11(2), 105-124.

IKEA-Group. (n.d.). *IKEA Group corporate site*. Retrieved October 3, 2005, from http://www.ikea-group/intro

Institute of Medicine. 2002. *Unequal Treatment: Confronting Racial and Ethnic Disparities in Health Care*. Washington, DC: The National Academies Press.

International Business Etiquette and Manners. (2003). Retrieved February 25, 2006, from http://www.cyborlink.com/

Internet Center for Corruption Research. (2002, July 6). The 1999 Corruption Perceptions Index. www.gwdg.de/~uwvw/1999Data.html

Internet Center for Corruption Research. (2005, November 15) Transparency International (TI) 2003 Corruption Perceptions Index (CPI). Available from http://www.icgg.org/corruption.cpi_2003.html

Intelligence Report, (Spring 2006). *The Year in Hate: Intelligence Report.* Issue 12. A Southern Poverty Law Center.

Irogbe, Kema (Spring 2005). Globalization and the Development of Underdevelopment of the Third World. *Journal of Third World Studies*; 22, 1; Research Library.

Jackson, K. & Tomioka, M. (2004). *The Changing Face of Japanese Management.* New York: Routledge- Taylor & Francis Group.

James. V. V and Etim (1999). The feminization of development processes in Africa – current & future perspective: Prager Publisher.

Jensen, Eric (1997). Brain compatible strategies. Brain Store Publications. ISBN: 0-96378-327-0.

Johnson, Bill & Weinstein, Art (2004). *Superior Customer Value in New Economy.* Second Edition. CRC Press.

Johnson, W. D., & Johnson, F. P. (2003). *Joining together: Group theory and group skills.* Boston, MA: Pearson Education, Inc.

Jones, C. E., Dixon, P., & Umoja, A. O. (2003). The role of service-learning in recapturing the empowerment mission of African-American studies. *Western Journal of Black Studies, 27*(3), 205-214. Retrieved May 2, 2005, from ProQuest database.

Jones, G. R., & George, J. M. (2006). *Contemporary* Management (4th ed., Rev.). New York: McGraw-Hil-Irwinl.

Jones, Gareth R., George, Jennifer M. (2003). *Contemporary Management.* Third ed: New York, NY: McGraw-Hill.

Kacapyr, E. (2001). Business as usual: Corruption and business activity. *The Journal of Social, Political, and Economic Studies, 26*(4), 671-681.

Kallio, J., Saarinen, T., Tinnila, M. & Vepsalainen, A. P. J. (2000) Measuring Delivery Process Performance. International Journal of Logistics Management, 11, 1, 75-87

Karahalios, M. (2005). A Computer-based Nutritional Intervention to Teach Adolescents with Autism How to Make Healthier Food Choices. Unpublished dissertation proposal.

Kark, R., Shamir, B., & Chen, G. (2003). The two faces of transformational leadership: Empowerment and dependency. *Applied Psychology, 88*(2), 246-255. Retrieved February 17, 2004, from EBSCOhost database.

Katzenbach, J. R. (1998). *Teams at the top: Unleashing the potential of both teams and individual leaders.* Boston: Harvard Business School.

Katzenbach, J., & Smith, D. (2005). The Discipline of Teams. *Harvard Business, Review, 83*(7), 162-170. Retrieved September 8, 2005, from ABI/INFORM Global database. (Document ID: 863429711).

Katzenbach, Jon R. & Smith, Douglas K., (1993). *The Wisdom of Teams.* Harvard Business School Press.

Kemp, D. (1998). *The Hon. Dr. David Kemp, Minister Assisting the Prime Minister for the Public Service, Workplace diversity: Innovation & Performance Conference*, Canberra, February 10, 1998.

Kennedy , M. M. (2004). *Workplace Generational Differences.* Retrieved March 28, 2006, from Career Strategies Web Site:

Kerfoot, K. (2004). Leading the leaders: The challenge of leading an empowered organization. *Urologic Nursing, 24*(3), 224-226. Retrieved April 1, 2005, from EBSCOhost database.

Kerr, B., Miller, W., & Reid, M. (1998). Determinants of female employment patterns in U.S. cities: A time series analysis. *Urban Affairs Review. 33(4),* 559-578.

Kerr, B. & Neuse, S. (2000). *Economic representation of women: Determinants of sex-based pay disparities in state governments, 1987-1997.* Presented at the annual meeting of the American Political Science Association, August 31-September 3, 2000, Washington, DC.

Kieran-Greenbush, S. (1991). Respecting diversity: designing from a feminine perspective *Proceedings of the 19th ACM SIGUCCS Conference on User Services,* pp. 171 – 175. Available from the ACM Digital Library Web site, www.acm.org

Kim, C. W. and Mauborgne, R. (August 1997). Fair Process: Managing in the Knowledge Economy. *Harvard Business Review.* Pages 65-66.

Kinjerski, V. (2004). Defining spirit at work: Finding common ground. *Journal of Organizational Change Movement, 17 (1), 26-27.*

Kirkpatrick, D. L. and Kirkpatrick, J. D. (2006). Evaluating training programs: The four levels. (3rd ed.), Berrett-Koehler Publishers, Inc. San Francisco.

Klalia, D. (2000) Knowledge Management. Executive Excellence, 17, 3, 13-14

Kletter, D. (2001). Sharing Knowledge. Executive Excellence, 18, 6, 15

Kling, K., & Goteman, I. (2003). IKEA CEO Anders Dahlvig on international growth and IKEA's unique corporate culture and brand identity. *Academy of Management Executive, 17*(1), 31-37.

Knorr, E. (Jan 2005). Looking Out; Looking In - Outsource what makes sense, but create some new internal opportunities for yourself. CIO Magazine. Retrieved from: http://www.cio.com/archive/011505/et_pundit.html

Koch, (2004). *Koch Industries.* Retrieved on December 17th 2004 from: http://www.kochind.com

Koch, M. (1994). No girls allowed. *Technos* 3(3), pp. 14-19.

Kolb, D. A. (1984). Experiential Learning: Experience as the Source of Learning and Development. Englewood Cliffs, NJ: Prentice Hall.

Kolb, D.A. & Frohman, A.L. (1970). An Organizational Development Approach to Consulting. Sloan Management Review, 12, 1, 51-65.

Kroll, F. (2003, September 17). Megachurches, megabusinesses, *Forbes Magazine.* Retrieved on October 22, 2005, from : http://www.forbes.com/2003/09/17/c2.1k.097 1megachurch.html.

Kruppa, R., & Meda, A. K. (2005). Group dynamics in the formation of a Ph.D. cohort: A reflection in experiencing while learning organizational development theory. *Organization Development Journal, 23*(1), 56-67. Retrieved January 4, 2005, from ProQuest database.

Kuczmarski, T.D. (2003) Firms mustn't Innovations as They Strive to Survive. Chicago Sun-Times, p.57

LaBonte, T. J. (2003). Building a new performance vision for results. *Industrial and Commercial Training, 35*(1), 33-37. Retrieved March 27, 2005, from ProQuest database.

Lamb, Annette & Johnson, Larry (2004). *Are You an Effective Leader?* Retrieved on September 6, 2005, from http://eduscapes.com/sms/management.html

Lambert, L. M. (1999). Intellectual Capital: A Primary Asset. Life Association News, Washington, 94, 8, 12.

Lamsa, A., & Savolainen, T. (2000). The nature of managerial commitment to strategic change. *Leadership & Organization Development Journal, 21*(6), 297-299. Retrieved May 1, 2005, from ProQuest database.

Lancaster, L., Stillman, D., & MacKay, H. (2002). *When generations collide.* New York: HarperCollins

Landsberg, B.K. (1995). Affirmative Action : What is the Law?

Lange-Fox, J., Tan, P., (1997). Images of a Culture in Transition: Personal Constructs of Organizational Stability and Change. Journal of Occupational and Organizational Psychology, 70, 3, 273-293.

Laschinger, H. K. S., Finegan, J., & Shamian, J. (2001). The impact of workplace empowerment, organizational trust on staff nurses' work satisfaction and organizational commitment. *Health Care Management Review, 26*(3), 7-23. Retrieved January 24, 2004, from ProQuest database.

Lashley, C. (2000). Empowerment through involvement: A case study of TGI Fridays restaurants. *Personnel Review, 29*(5/6), 791-815. Retrieved August 17, 2004, from EBSCOhost database.

Lassiter, Sybil M. 1995. *Multicultural Clients: A Professional Handbook for Health Care Providers and Social Workers.* Westport, CT: Greenwood Press.

Lee, F. (2001). The fear factor. *Harvard Business Review, 79*(1), 29-31. Retrieved April 24, 2005, from EBSCOhost database.

Lee, James Sr. (2000). Knowledge Management: The Intellectual Revolution. IIE Solutions, 32, 34-37.

Leedy, P.D. & Ormrod, J.E. (2001). *Practical Research: Planning and Design* (7th ed.). Columbus, OH: Prentice Hall, 71.

Lelah, L. J. (2005). *Application of an appreciative inquiry and work-out intervention: the influence on empowerment.* Dissertation completed through the University of Phoenix.

Leiter, S.& Leiter, W.M. (2002). Affirmative Action in Antidiscrimination Law and Policy : An Overview and Synthesis. SUNY Series in American Constitution.

Lowi, T. (1985). The state in politics: The relation between policy and administration. In R. Noll (Ed.), *Regulatory policy and the social sciences.* Los Angeles, CA: University of California Press, 67-104.

M'Pherson, P. K. & Pike, S. (2001) Accounting, Empirical Measurement and Intellectual Capital. Journal of Intellectual Capital, 2, 3, 246

Maccoby, M. (1996). Interactive dialogue as a tool for change. *Research Technology Management, 39*(5), 57-59. Retrieved February 28, 2005, from EBSCOhost database.

MacKenzie, D.W., (2006). Outsourcing America: What's Behind Our National Crisis And How We Can Reclaim American Jobs? Book review for *Journal of Applied Management and Entrepreneurship.* Book is written by Ron Hira and Anil Hira, AMACOM, 2005.

Mackey, S. (2002). *The Saudis: Inside the Desert Kingdom.* New York: W.W. Norton & Company, Inc.

Mansfield, S. (2004). *The Faith of George W. Bush* (1st ed.). Strang Communications Publishers. 117.

Marques, J, & Dhiman, S. (2005). Spirituality in the workplace: Developing an integral model and a comprehensive definition. *Journal of American Academy of Business, 7 (1),* p 81.

Maslow, A. H., (1970). *Motivation and Personality.* New York, NY: Harper & Row.

Maskus, K. E., and Reichman, F. H., (2004). The Globalization of Private Knowledge Goods and the Privatization of Global Public Goods. *Journal of International Economic Law*; Vol. 7, No. 2. p. 279.

Matsumoto, D. & Juang, L. (2004). *Culture and Psychology.* (3rd ed.). Belmont: Wadsworth/Thomson Learning.

Alon, I. and McAllaster, C. (June 2006). The Global Footprint. *BizEd*, vol. V, issue 4. Pages 32-35.

McCarthy, P. M., & Stein, J. (Eds.) (2002). *Agile business for fragile times.* New York, NY: McGraw-Hill Company, 10121.

McCoy, B. (2001). CRE perspective: Living beyond the boundaries. *Real Estate Issues, (2),* 47-50.

McDermott, C.M. & Stock, G.N. (1999) Organizational Culture and Advanced Manufacturing Technology Implementation. Journal of Operations Management, 17, 521-533

McDermott, R. (1999) Why Information Technology Inspired But Cannot Deliver Knowledge Management. California Management Review, Berkely, 41, 103-117

McElyea, B. (2002) Knowledge Management, Intellectual Capital, and Learning Organizations: A Triad of Future Integration. Futurics, 26 ½, 59-65

McFarlin, D.B., Coster, E.A. & Mogale-Pretorius, C. (1999). South African management development in the twenty first century. Moving toward an Africanized model. *The Journal of Management Development.* Bradford:1999.Vol. 18 Iss.1; pg. 63

McKnight, R. (1984). Spirituality in the workplace. In J.D. Adams, *Transforming work: A collection of organizational transformational readings,* (ed.), Alexandria, VA: Miles River, 138-153.

McLaughlin, C. (1998, March 17). Spirituality at work. *The Bridging Tree, 1,* 11.

McShane, S. L., & Von Glinow, M. A. (2003). *Organization Behavior: Emerging Realities for the Workplace Revolution.* McGraw-Hill/Irwin. ISBN is: 0-07-255181X. Publisher URL: www.mhhe.com/mcshane2e.

McShane, S.L., & Von Glinow, M. A. (2002). Organizational Behavior (2nd ed.). The McGraw-Hill Companies.

Medda-Windischer, Roberta 2004. *Legal Indicators for Social Inclusion of New Minorities Generated by Immigration.* Retrieved on 4/30/2006 from: http://www.eumap.org/journal/features/2004/stopracism/legalind

Megginson, William L. (2005). *The Financial Economics of Privatization.* ISBN: 0-19-515062-7. Oxford, University Press. USA.

Mellander, K. (2001) Engaging the Human Spirit: A Knowledge Evolution Demands the Right Conditions for Learning. Journal of Intellectual Capital, 2, 2, 165-171

Microsoft Corporation. (2002) Cat Family. *Microsoft Encarta.* Electronic Version (CD-ROM).

Midgley, G. (2004). Five sketches of postmodernism: Implications for systems thinking and operational research. *Journal of Organisational Transformation & Social Change, 1*(1), 47-62. Retrieved April 24, 2005, from EBSCOhost database.

Miles, R.E., Miles, G., & Snow, C.C. (2005). *Collaborative Entrepreneurship: How Communities of Networked Firms Use Continuous Innovation to Create Economic Wealth.* Stanford University Press. Stanford, California.

Miller, K. (Sept 2003). When Elephants Fly. Newsweek. Retrieved from: http://www.neoit.com/gen/news-events/news-contents/When_Elephants_Fly.pdf

Miller, M. G., Fitzgerald, S., Preston, J., & Murrell, K. (2002). The efficacy of appreciative inquiry in building relational capital in a transcultural strategic alliance. *Academy of Management*

Miller, W., Kerr, B., & Reid, M. (1999). A national study of gender-based occupational segregation in municipal bureaucracies: Persistence of glass walls? *Public Administration Review, 59(3)*, 218-230.

Milliman, J., Ferguson, J., Trickett, D., & Condemi, B. (1999). Spirit and community at Southwest Airlines: An investigation of a spiritual values-based mode. *Journal of Organizational Change Management, 12 (3)*, 221.

Minority, (2006). Overcoming biases in the nursing workplace. Retrieved on June 11, 2006 from: http://www.minoritynurse.com/features/nurse_emp/02-05ahtm

Minton-Eversole, Theresa (January 2005). Workplace training often considered 'Waste of Time,' survey shows. *Recruiting and Staffing News,* SHRM.Online. Retrieved on April 1, 2006 from: http://www.shrm.org/ema/news_published/CMS_015414.asp

Mitroff, I. I. (1992). Business not as usual: Building the organization of the future now. In Ott, S. J. (1996). *Classical Readings in Organizational Behavior* (2nd ed.): p. 264. Orlando, FL: Harcourt Brace & Company.

Mitroff, I., & Denton, E. (1999). *A spiritual audit of corporate America: A hard look at spirituality, religion, and values in the workplace* (1st ed.). San Francisco: Jossey-Bass Publishers.

Mohr, B. J., & Watkins, J. M. (2002). *The essentials of appreciative inquiry: A roadmap for creating positive futures.* Waltham, MA: Pegasus.

Morgan, J.C. & Morgan, J.J. (1994). *Cracking the Japanese Market: Strategies for Success in The New Global Economy.* New York, NY: The Free Press.

Morrison, T., Conaway, W.A. & Borden, G. A. (1994). *Kiss, Bow or Shake Hands: How To Do Business In Sixty Countries* (pp. 322-329). Avon, MA: Adams Media.

Mujtaba, B. G. (2007). *Mentoring Diverse Professionals.* Llumina Press. Coral Springs, USA. Available through www.llumina.com and www.amazon.com

Mujtaba, B.; McCartney, Cavico, F.; and DiPaolo, P. (1999). Business Ethics Survey of Managers and Their Associates in the Retail Industry. *Journal of Global Competitiveness,* Volume 7(1). Pages 427 - 440. ISSN: 1071-0736. Available on: http://www.amazon.com

Mujtaba, B. (2006). *Cross cultural change management.* ISBN: 1-59526-568-6. Llumina Press, Tamarac, Florida. Website: www.L.lumina.com

Mujtaba, Bahaudin G., (2006). *AFGHANISTAN: Realities of War and Rebuilding.* ISBN: 1-59427-0481. Aglob Publishing Inc. Hollandale, Florida USA.

_____, (November 2005). Management and Leadership Developments in Afghanistan: An Interview with Sayed Tayeb Jawad, Afghanistan's Ambassador to the United States. *Journal of Applied Management and Entrepreneurship.* Volume 10, Number 4.

_____, (2005). *The Ethics of Management and Situational Leadership in Afghanistan.* Aglob Publishing Inc. ISBN: 1-59427-047-3. Hollandale, Florida USA. Website: www.aglobpublishing.com. Phone: (954)465-1476.

Mujtaba, G. B. and Preziosi, R. (2006). Adult education in academia: Recruiting and retaining extraordinary facilitators of learning. (2nd ed.). ISBN: 1-59311-476-1. Information Age Publishing. Greenwich, Connecticut. Phone: (203) 661-7602.

Murphy, Jim (1994). *Managing Conflict at Work.* American Media Publishing.

Myers, J.E. (1990, May). Wellness throughout the lifespan. *Guideposts Magazine, 1,* 33.

National Coalition for Women and Girls in Education (NCWGE). (2002). Title IX at 30: Report Card on Gender Equity.

Newman, M. & Guy, M. (2006). *Pay inequity: The penalty of emotion work.* Paper prepared for presentation at the annual meeting of the American Society for Public Administration, Denver CO, April 1-4, 2006.

Nieves, R. and Mujtaba, B. G. (2006). The Effect of Cultural Values, Professional Engineering Cultures, and Technology on International Joint Ventures in Mexico and the United States. *International Business and Economics Research Journal,* Vol. 5, Num. 1. Ciber Institute.

Nikpai, Qadam Ali (February 2005). *Higher education in Afghanistan is expected to be revamped.* Pajhwok Afghan News, Kabul, Feb. 01.

Nimmo, C. (1994). Autism and computers. *Communication,* 28(2), 8-9.

Ninow, Martha (2002). *Partners, Not Rivals: Privatization and the Public Good.* Beacon Press, Boston.

Nonaka, I., & Nishiguchi, T. (2001). *Knowledge emergence: Social, technical, and evolutionary dimensions of knowledge creation.* New York: Oxford University Press.

Northcraft, G.B. (1983). The Stigma of Affirmative Action: An Empirical Analysis.

Nuruzzaman, M. (2004). Neoliberal Economic Reforms, the Rich and the Poor in Bangladesh. *Journal of Contemporary Asia;* Vol. 34, No. 1. Page 33.

NW Regional Education Laboratory, (2006). Cultural Ally. Retrieved on June 11, 2006 from: http://www.nwrel.org/pastfeature799.html

O'Toole, J. (1996). *Leading change: The argument for values-based leadership.* New York: Ballantine Books.

Office of Personnel Management (2005). *Federal employment statistics,* http://www.opm.gov/feddata/index.asp.

Olsson, J. (1996). *IKEA of Sweden.* Retrieved October 1, 2005, from : http://www.geocities.com/TimesSquare/1848/ikea.html

Osteen, J. (2004). *Your best life now –7 steps to living at your full potential.* New York, NY: Thomas Nelson Publishers.

Ostroff, C. & Schmitt, N. (1993). Configurations of Organizational Effectiveness and Efficiency. Academy of Management Journal. 36, 6, 1345

Ott, S. J. (1996). Leadership. *Classical Readings in Organizational Behavior* (2nd ed.): p. 163-170. Orlando, FL: Harcourt Brace & Company.

Overby, S. (Mar 2003). Bringing IT back home. CIO Magazine. Retrieved from: http://www.cio.com/archive/030103/home_claudio.html.

Overby, S. (Nov 2004). The Inner Cost of Outsourcing - When contemplating outsourcing, CIOs should first think about their people. CIO Magazine. Retrieved from: http://www.cio.com/archive/110104/interview.html

Oxbrow, N. (2000) Skills and Competencies to Succeed in a Knowledge Economy. Information Outlook, 4(10) 18-22

Pacelle, M. (2002). Chaos management: The odd job of CEO at post crash ENRON. *Wall Street   Journal.* December 3: A1

Panyan, M. V. (1984). Computer technology for autistic students. *Journal of Autism and Developmental Disorders*, 14(4), 375-382.

Parker, D. and Saal, D. (2003). *International Handbook on Privatization.* Edward Elgar. Cheltenham, UK.

Peak Experiences (2005). *Power and Influence.* Retrieved on August 11, 2005, from www.peak.ca/articles/power.html

Peak, T., & Sinclair, S. V. (2002). Using customer satisfaction surveys to improve quality of care in nursing homes. *Health & Social Work, 27*(1), 75-79. Retrieved January 12, 2004, from EBSCOhost database.

Peccei, R., & Rosenthal, P. (2001). Delivering customer-oriented behaviour through empowerment: An empirical test of HRM assumptions. *Journal of Management Studies, 38*(6), 831-857. Retrieved August 1, 2004, from EBSCOhost database.

Pemberton, J. D. & Stonehouse, G.H. (2000). Organisational Learning and Knowledge Assets – An Essential Partnership. The Learning Organization,7, 4, 184-193.

Pickersgill, Carrol J., (2005). *The impact of governance indicators on foreign direct investment to developing nations: the case of Jamaica.* Doctoral dissertation at the H. Wayne Huizenga School of Business and Entrepreneurship, Nova Southeastern University.

Pinkston, G. (1984). Affirmative Action to Open doors of Job Opportunity. A Policy of Fairness and Compassion That Has Worked.

Pohlman, R. & Gardiner, G. (2000). *Value Driven Management: How to Create and Maximize Value Over Time for Organizational Success.* New York: AMACOM.

Pohlman, R. A., Gardiner, G. S., & Heffes, E. M. (2000). *Value Driven Management.* New York: American Management

Popper, M., & Lipshitz, R. (1998) Organizational Leraning Mechanisms: A Structural and Cultural Approach to Organizational Learning. The Journal of Applied Behavioral Science, 34, 2, 161-179

Preston, David R., (2004) The enlightened leader and effective learning strategy. *Handbook of Business Strategy,* Pp, 81-84.

President J.F. Kennedy (1961). Executive Order 10925

President L.B. Johnson (1964). Civil Rights Act.

Proceedings, 1-6. Retrieved March 2, 2005, from EBSCOhost database.

Profiles in Diversity Journal. A publication for sharing diversity information. Volume 1, number 2. Summer 1999.

Progressive Discipline, (2005). *Legal and Effective Progressive Discipline.* A 23 minute video. COASTAL Human Resources. Available through Video Training, Inc.; Phone-(800) 600-1555 or (206) 682-1555.

Publix Training, (1999). Education and training development: Training activities. Workshop Presented at Publix Super Markets.

Pullen, C. (2001). Appreciative inquiry in financial planning and life. *Journal of Financial Planning, 14*(10), 52-54. Retrieved February 27, 2005, from EBSCOhost database.

Queens land University of Technology, (2006). Ally Network. Retrieved on June 11, 2006 from: http://www.equity.qut.edu.au/issues/sexuality/allynetwork.jsp

Quinn, R.E. & Rohrbaugh, J. (1983). A Spatial Model of Effectiveness Criteria: Towards a Competing Values Approach to Organizational Analysis. Management Science, 29, 3, 363-377

Quinn, R.E. & McGrath, M.R. (1985) The Transformation of Organizational Cultures: Competing Values Perspectives. Management Science, 18, 315-334.

Quinn, R.E., Hildebrandt, H.W., Rogers, P.S. & Thompson, M.P. (1991). A competing Values Framework for Analyzing Presentational Communication in Management Contexts. The Journal of Business Communication, 28, 3, 213-232

Quinn, R.E. & Spreitzer, G.M. (1991) The Psychometrics of the Competing Values Culture Instrument and an Analysis of the Impact of Organizational culture on Quality of Life. Research in Organizational Change and Development, 5, 115-142.

Quinn, R.E., Spreitzer, G. M. & Brown, M.V. (2000) Changing Others Through Changing Ourselves: The Transformation of Human Systems. Journal of Management Inquiry, 9, 2, 147-164

Ramamoorthy, N., & Flood, P. (2004). Individualism / collectivism, perceived task interdependence and teamwork attitudes among Irish blue-collar employees: A test of the main and moderating effects. *Human Relations, 57*(3), 347-367. Retrieved March 23, 2005, from ProQuest database.

Ratzburg, Wilf (2005). *Organizational Power: Power Defined.* Retrieved on September 3, 2005, from www.geocities.com/Athens/Forum/1650/htmlpower.html?20053

Rausch, E. (2003). Guidelines for management and leadership decision. *Management Decision, 41*(10), pp. 979-988. Retrieved November 18, 2004, from ProQuest database.

Ribiere, V.M. (2001) Assessing Knowledge management Initiative Successes as a Function of Organizational Culture. George Washington University. Bell & Howell Information and Learning Company.

Ricketts, M., & Seiling, J. G. (2003). Language, metaphors and stories: Catalysts for meaning making in organizations. *Organization Development Journal, 21*(4), 33-43. Retrieved August 10, 2004, from ProQuest database.

Ritchie, M. (2000). Organizational Culture: An examination of It's Effect on the Internalization Process and Member Performance. Southern Business Review, 25, 1-13

Roashan, G. Rauf, (2005). *Karzai and Triple Ms.* Article distributed to all subscribers on January 7th 2005 via AfghanServer@yahoogroups.com

Robbins, Stephen P. *Organizational Behavior.* 9th ed. Upper Saddle River, NJ: Prentice Hall, 2001.

Robbins, S. P. and Hunsaker, P. L. (2006). The book *Training in Interpersonal Skills: Tips for Managing People at Work.* Pearson Prentice Hall.

Rogers, C. R., & Roethlisberger, F. J. (1952). Barriers and Gateways to Communication. *Harvard Business Review.*

Roosevelt Thomas, Jr., R.R. (1996). *Redefining Diversity.* New York: Amacom.

Roosevelt Thomas, Jr., R.R. (2001). *Harvard Business Review on Managing Diversity.* Boston: Harvard Business School Publishing.

Rough, J. (2002). Thriving through teamwork. *Journal for Quality & Participation,* 25(1), 4-9. Retrieved July 17, 2004, from EBSCOhost database.

Rowden, R. W. (2001) The Learning Organization and Strategic Change. S.A.M. Advanced Management Journal, 66, 3, 11-16

Rubaii-Barrett, N. & Wise, L. (2006, April). Diversity Recruitment and Retention in Government, *Public Administration Times Newsletter, April 2006.*

Prewitt, E. (Dec 2004). The End of Service with a Smile? Outsourcing trends erode the commitment of top service employees. CIO Magazine. Retrieved from: http://www.cio.com/archive/120104/hs_management.html

Ryan, M., (1995). *"Personal Ethics and the Future of the World." Varied Directions International.* (800) 888-5236. Narrated by Meg Ryan.

Saba, D. S. & Zakhilwal, O. (2004). *Afghanistan National Human Development Report 2004: Security with a Human Face: Challenges and Responsibilities.* United National Development Programme 2004. Available from : http://hdr.undp.org/docs/reports/national/AFG_Afghanistan/afghanistan_200 4_en.pdf

Salner, M. (1999) Preparing for the Learning Organization. Journal of Management Education, 23, 5, 489-508

Sandholtz, W. & Gray, M. M. (2003). International integration and national corruption. *International Organization, 57,* 761-800.

Sankar, Y. (2003). Character, not charisma, is the critical measure of leadership excellence. *Journal of Leadership and Organizational Studies,* 9(4), 45-55. Retrieved December 4, 2004, from ProQuest database.

Sawicki, D. S. (2002). Improving community indicator systems: Injecting more social science into the folk movement. *Planning Theory & Practice, 3*(1), 13-32. Retrieved April 24, 2005, from EBSCOhost database.

Savas, E. S. (1987). Privatization and Public-Private Partnership.

Schein, E. H. (1997). *Organizational culture and leadership.* San Francisco: Jossey-Bass.

Schein, E. H. (1999). *The corporate culture: Survival guide.* San Francisco: Jossey-Bass.

Schein, E. (1992). *Organizational culture and leadership.* San Francisco, CA: Jossey-Bass Company.

Schein, E. H. (1985). *Organizational Culture and Leadership.* Jossey-Bass, 1986, 9.

Schein, E. H. (1993). How Can Organization Learn Faster? The Challenge of Entering the Green Room. Sloan Management Review, 34, 2, 1985

Schein, E. H. (1996) Three Cultures of Management: The Key to Organizational Learning. Sloan Management Review, 38, 1, 9

Schein, E. H. (1996) Culture: The Missing Concept in Organization Studies. Administrative Science Quarterly, 41, 2, 229

Schermerhorn, J. R., Hunt, J. G., & Osborn, R. N. (2000). *Organizational behavior* (7th ed.). New York: Wiley.

Schwartz, S.H. (1990). Individualism-collectivism: Critique and proposed refinements. *Journal of Cross-Cultural Psychology*, 21, 139-157.

Schwartz, S.H. (1992). Universal in the content of and structure of values: Theoretical advances and empirical tests in 20 countries. In M.P. Zanna (Ed.), *Advances in experimental social psychology* (Vol. 24, pp. 1-65). San Diego, CA: Academic Press.

Schwartz, S.H. (1996). Value priorities and behavior: Applying a theory of integrated value systems. In C. Seligman, J.M. Olson, & M.P. Zanna (Eds.), *The psychology of values: The Ontario symposium* (Vol. 8, 1-24). Mahwah, NJ: Erlbaum.

Schwartz, S.H. (1999). A theory of cultural values and some implications for work. *Applied Psychology: An International Review*, 84(1), 23-47.

Schwartz, S.H., & Bilsky, W. (1987). Toward a universal psychological structure of human values. *Journal of Personality and Social Psychology*, 53, 550-562.

Schwartz, S.H., & Bilsky, W. (1990). Toward a theory of the universal content and structure of values: Extensions and cross-cultural replications. *Journal of Personality and Social Psychology*, 58, 878-891.

Schwartz, S.H., & Ros, M. (1995). Values in the West: A theoretical and empirical challenge to the individualism-collectivism cultural dimension. *World Psychology*, 1, 99-122.

Schwartz, S.H., & Sagiv, L. (2000). National cultures: Implications for organizational structure and behavior. In N.N. Ashkanasy, C. Wilderom, & M.F. Peterson (Eds.), *The handbook of organizational culture and climate*, 417-436, Newbury Park, CA: Sage.

Schwarzwalder, R. (1999) Librarians as Knowledge Management Agents. Econtent, 22, 4, 63-65.

Science and Engineering Equal Opportunities Act (SEEA), Section 32(b), Part B of P.L. 96-516, 94 Stat. 3010, as amended by P.L. 99-159.

Scott, R.C., Amos, T., & Scott, J.D. (1998). Affirmative Action as seen by business majors in the US and South Africa. *S.A.M. Advanced Management Journal*. Cincinnati. Summer. Vol.63. Iss.3. pg.28

Secretaria de Economia, (2005). Direccion General de Inversion Extranjera, *www.economia.gob.mx*

Selmer, J., and Leung, A. (2003). Female Business Expatriates: Availability of Corporate Career Development Support. *Business Research Centre Papers on Cross-Cultural Management*. Retrieved on May 11, 2006 from: http://net2.hkbu.edu.hk/~brc/CCMP200106.pdf.

Semler, R. (1993). *Maverick: The success story behind the most unusual workplace.* New York: Warner Bros.

Sen, Amartya (2002). *Does Globalization Equal Westernization?* Retrieved on April 21, 2006 from: http://www.theglobalist.com/DBWeb/StoryId.aspx?StoryId=2353

Senge, P. (1998). Sharing Knowledge. *Executive Excellence*, 15, 6, 11-12

Senge, P. (1999). The discipline of innovation. *Administrator Excellence*, June issues, pages 10-11.

Senge, P. (1994). *The Fifth Discipline Fieldbook: Strategies and tools for building and learning.* New York, NY: Doubleday.

Senge, Peter (1992). *Learning Organizations and Human Resources.* American Society for Training and Development (ASTD) National Conference. New Orleans.

Senge, P. M. (1990). *The fifth discipline: The art & practice of the learning organization.* New York: Doubleday.

Setltzer, R. & Thompson, E. (1985). Attitudes towards Discrimination and Affirmative Action for Minorities and Women.

Seyoum, B. (2001). *The State of the Global Economy 2001/2002: Trends, Data, Ranking, Charts.* New York: Encyclopedia Society.

Shafranske, E.P., and R. L., Gorsuch. (1984). Factors associated with the perception of spirituality in psychotherapy. *Journal of Transpersonal Psychology, 16,* 231-241.

Shavers, V. L., PhD, and B. S. Shavers, JD. 2006. Racism and health inequities among Americans. *Journal of the National Medical Association* 98(3):386-393.

Sims, R. L. (2005, November). Culture and Human Development as Predictors of National Corruption. Paper presented at the Southern Management Association's Annual Conference, Charleston, South Carolina.

Simons, G. (1996). *Questions of Diversity.* Amherst: HRD Press.

Simons, George and Zuckerman, Amy J. (1994). Working Together: Succeeding in a Multicultural Organization. Revised edition. Crisp Publications.

Sion, B. (2006, March 34). *Awards Try to Tackle Age Discrimination.* Retrieved April 6, 2006, from http.//icwales.icnetwork.co.uk Web Site: http://www.agepositive.gov.uk

Sirat, Abdul Sattar (2004). *The Long Way for Peace in Afghanistan.* Emailed by Muhammad Kabir to the afghaniyat@yahoogroups.com on Friday, January 16th 2004.

Situational, 2004. *The Center for Leadership Studies.* Escondido, CA. Phone: (760) 741-6595. Retrieved on August 20th 2004 from: http://www.situational.com/leadership/green_base.html

Smithsonian Institution. (2001). *Animals: The definitive visual guide to the world's wild life.* New York, NY: Dorling Kindersley Publishing Inc.

Sonnenschein, W. (1999). *The Diversity Toolkit: How You Can Build and Benefit from a Diverse Workforce.* Chicago: NTC/Contemporary Publishing Group.

South African Department of Census and Statistics. Statistics 1996 and 2001.

South Australia (2002). *The Managing Diversity Workforce Profiling Project, July 2002.* South Australia: Department of The Premier and Cabinet for South Australia, The Commissioner For Public Employment, Supporting Material.

Southern Poverty Law Center (2006). Tolerance in the Workplace. Retrieved on June 02, 2006 from: www.tolerance.org. Also, on June 02, 2006, visited the hidden bias.org website at: www.hiddenbias.org.

Speer, P. W. (2000). Intrapersonal and interactional empowerment: Implications for theory. *Journal of Community Psychology, 28*(1), 51-61. Retrieved July 17, 2004, from EBSCOhost database.

Spring, T. Florence (2002). *French and Raven's Source of Power.* Retrieved on August 22, 2005, from http://profsfp.cegepsth.qc.ca/lblain/cours_management/auteurs/french_and_raven.htm

Stanford Report, 2006. Steve Job's Graduation Speech. Retrieved on April 01, 200(from: http://news-service.stanford.edu/news/2005/june15/jobs-061505.htm¹

Star, P., (1987). The Limits and Privatization. In Steve H. Hanke, Prospects ' Privatization, 37 (3). *Proceedings of Academy of Political Science,* 37 (3)

Steinhauser, S. (1999). *Successfully Managing an Age Diverse* Workforce. Retrieved March 28, 2006, from Metropolitan State College of Denver Web Site: http://http://clem.mscd.edu/~steinhas/managing_diversity.

Sumner, J. (2004). Connecting with your customer. *KM Review, 7*(3), 2-3. Retrieved March 28, 2005, from EBSCOhost database.

Swanson, J. (2000). What's the difference? Available from the Girl Tech Web site, www.girltech.com

Swettenham, J. (1996). Can children with autism be taught to understand false belief using computers? *Journal of Child Psychology and Psychiatry and Allied Disciplines*, 37(2), 157-165.

Talley, K. (2006, March 5). *Work Force: Understanding Age Diversity in the Workplace*. Retrieved April 6, 2006, from The Amarillo Globe-News Online Web Site: http://www.amarillonet.com/cgi-bin/primetime.pl

Tanenbaum Center, (2004). Retrieved on April 20, 2004 from: www.tanenbaum.org.

Tart, C. (1975). Introduction. In Tart, C. T., *Transpersonal Psychologies* (ed.). New York, NY: Harper and Row, 3-7.

Temin, T. (July, 1996). What's their game? Government Computer News. Issue; Vol. 15 No. 15. Retrieved from: http://www.gcn.com/15_15/news/31749-1.html

The Gale Corp Inc., (2002). *Concepts Regarding Assimilation*. Retrieved on 4/30/2006 from: http://heatlh.families.com/assimilation-78-85-eph

The World Factbook. (2006). Retrieved February 22, 2006, from http://www.cia.gov/cia/publications/factbook/geos/sa.html

Thornton, B., Peltier, G., & Perreault, G. (2004). Systems thinking: A skill to improve student achievement. *The Clearing House, 77*(5), pp. 222-228. Retrieved February 17, 2005, from ProQuest database.

Tichy, M. N., & Ulrich, O. D., (1984). The leadership challenge: A call for the transformational leader. In Ott, S. J. (1996) *Classical Readings in Organizational Behavior* (2nd ed.): 210-211. Orlando, FL: Harcourt Brace & Company.

Tichy, N. M. (1983). *Managing strategic change: Technical, political and cultural dynamics*. New York: John Wiley & Sons.

Tichy, N. M., & Devanna, M. A. (1986). *The transformational leader*. New York: John Wiley & Sons.

Timbrook, Laurel (2001). *High and Low Context Cultures*. Retrieved on 4/30/2006 from: http://www.colostate.edu/Depts/Speech/rccs/theory63.htm#low

Topping, K. J., Campbell, J., Douglas, W., & Smith, A. (2003). Cross-age peer tutoring in mathematics with seven- and 11-year-olds: Influence on mathematical vocabulary, strategic dialogue and self-concept. *Educational Research, 45*(3), 287-308. Retrieved April 24, 2005, from EBSCOhost database.

Trice, H. M., & Beyer, J. M. (1993). *The culture of organizations*. Upper Saddle River, NJ: Prentice Hall.

Trice, H.M., & Beyer, J.M. (1993). *The cultures of work organizations*. New Jersey: Prentice Hall.

Tripp, H. & North, P. (2003). *Culture Shock! A Guide to Customs and Etiquette*. Oregon: Graphic Arts Center Publishing Company.

Trompenaars, F. (1993). *Riding the Waves of Culture: Understanding Diversity in Global Business*, (New York: Irwin, NY).

Tuckman, B.W. (1965). Developmental Sequence in Small Groups. *Psychological Bulletin*, Pp, 384-99.

Tuller, L.W. (1993). Doing business in Latin America and the Caribbean: AMACOM.

Tworoger, L. C. (2004). *The Use of Power in Organizations: An Empirical Study of Public Bureaucratic and Private Non-Profit Organizations and the Adoption of a Market Orientation.* Doctoral dissertation, United States, Nova Southeastern University (2004).

U.S. Census Bureau (2004). U.S. interim projections by age, race, sex and Hispanic origin, http://www.census.gov/ipc/usinterimproj/. Internet release March 18, 2004.

U.S. Census Bureau (2002). *2002 Census of governments, 3(2), compendium of public employment: 2002.* Washington, DC: U.S. Government Printing Office. Retrieved from http://www.cemsis/gov/govs/www/apesfed04.html.

U.S. General Accounting Office (2000, May). *Senior Executive Service: Retirement trends underscore the importance of succession planning.* Washington, D.C.: GAO.

United States Small Business Administration, 2006. *Business Mentoring.* Retrieved on 4/30/2006 from: http://www.sba.gov/training/bizmentoring.html#Introduction

Van der Harr, D., & Hosking, D. M. (2004). Evaluating appreciative inquiry: A relational constructionist perspective. *Human Relations, 8*(57), 1017-1036. Retrieved May 12, 2004, from ProQuest database.

Vasquez, B. (1997 June). How to build a better team entrepreneurs tell which approaches work and which don't. *The Denver Business Journal, Vol. 48, Issue: 40,* 19. Retrieved September 8, 2005, from ABI/INFORM Global database. (Document ID: 12470072).

Vaughn, F. (1979). Spiritual issues in psychotherapy. *Journal of Transpersonal Psychology, 23,* 105-119.

Vengel, Alan A. (2000). *The Influence Edge: How to Persuade Others to help you Achieve Your Goals.* San Francisco, CA: Berrett-Koehler Communications, Inc.

Victorian Department of Education, (2005 April 5). *Managing Workplace Diversity.* Retrieved March 27, 2006, from Human Resources Web Site: http://https://www.eduweb.vic.gov.au/hrweb/divequity/diversity/workdiv.htm

Viswanathan, R. (1996) Getting women into business: Blackwell Publishers.

Vogl, F. (1998). The supply side of global bribery. *Finance & Development, 35*(2), 30-32.

Vogl, A. J. (2004). The anti-CEO. *Across the Board, 41*(3), 30-36. Retrieved October 27, 2004, from EBSCOhost database.

Vroom, V. (2003). Educating managers for decision-making and leadership. *Management Decision, 41*(10), pp. 968-978. Retrieved July 18, 2004, from ProQuest database.

Walker, K., & Carr-Stewart, S. (2004). Learning leadership through appreciative inquiry. *International Studies in Educational Administration, 32*(1), 35-45. Retrieved February 11, 2005, from EBSCOhost database.

Walter, B., & Walter K. (1998, July). Teams can work, if all the ingredients are provided. *Capital District Business Review: Vol. 25, Issue: 14,* 24. Retrieved September 8, 2005, from ABI/INFORM Dateline database. (Document ID: 32012546).

Wang, T. (2004). From general system theory to total quality management. *Journal of American Academy of Business, 4*(1/2), pp. 394-402. Retrieved March 22, 2005, from ProQuest database.

Ware, Lorraine C. (Sep 2003).Weighing the Benefits of Offshore Outsourcing. CIO Magazine. Retrieved from http://www2.cio.com/research/surveyreport.cfm?ID=62

Warnaby, G. (1999). Strategic Consequences of Real Acquisition: IKEA and Habitat. *International Marketing Review, 16*(4/5), 406. Retrieved October 3, 2005, from ABI/INFORM Global Database Web Site: http://0-proquest.umi

Warren, R. (2002*). The purpose-driven life*. Grand Rapids, MI: Zondervan Publishing.

Washington State (2000). *Impact of aging trends on the state government workforce.* Olympia, WA: Washington State Department of Personnel Task Force on the Changing Age Profile of the Washington State Government Workforce (June 2000).

Watkins, J. M., & Mohr, B. J. (2001). *Appreciative inquiry: Change at the speed of imagination.* San Francisco: John Wiley & Sons.

Weil, J. (2002). A CEO's candid speech may come back to haunt Lucent. *Wall Street Journal.* November 20: C1

Weinstein, Art & Johnson, Bill (1999). *Designing & Delivering Superior Customer Value: Concepts, Cases & Applications. ISBN: 1574442406.*

Welford, C. (2002). Matching theory to practice. *Nursing Management-UK, 9*(4), 7-11. Retrieved March 29, 2004, from EBSCOhost database.

Wheelen, T.L., & Hunger, J.D. (2000). Strategic management: Business policy. (7th ed.), New Jersey: Prentice Hall.

White, H. & Rice, M. (2005). *The multiple dimensions of diversity and culture.* In M. Rice (Ed.), *Diversity and public administration.* Armonk, NY: M.E. Sharpe, pp. 3-21.

Whitney, D., & Trosten-Bloom, A. (2003). *The power of appreciative inquiry: A practical guide to positive change.* San Francisco: Berrett-Koehler.

Wilhelm, P. G. (2002). International validation of the corruption perception index: Implications for business ethics and entrepreneurship education. *Journal of Business Ethics, 35,* 177-189.

Wilson, M. S., Hoppe, M. H., & Sayles, L. R. (1996). *Managing Across Cultures.* Greensboro, North Carolina: Center for Creative Leadership.

Wise, L. & Tschirhart, M. (2000). Examining empirical evidence on diversity effects: How useful is diversity research for public sector managers, *Public Administration Review,* 60(5): 386-394.

Women's Educational Equity Act Resource Center (WEEA). (November 1999). "Connecting Gender and Disability." *Gender and Disability Digest.*

Wong, P.T.P. (1998). *Implicit theories of meaningful life and the development of the personal meaning profile (PMP).* In Wong, P.T.P., and P. Fry, (Eds.), *Handbook of Personal Meaning: Theory, Research, and Practice* (ed.). Mahwah, NJ: Lawrence Erlbaum.

Wright, Barbara D., Myra Marx Ferree, Gail O. Mellow, Linda H. Lewis, Maria-Luz Daza Samper, Robert Asher, and Kathleen Claspell (Eds.). (1987). *Women, work, and technology transformations.* Ann Arbor: The University of Michigan Press.

Yoon, J. (2001). The role of structure and motivation for workplace empowerment: The case of Korean employees. *Social Psychology Quarterly, 64*(2), 195-206. Retrieved September 1, 2004, from ProQuest database.

Zeus, P. & Skiffington, S. (2003). *The Coaching at Work Toolkit: A Complete Guide to Technique and Practices.* McGraw-Hill:Sydney.

Zigurs, I., & Buckland, B. K. (1998). A theory of task/technology fit and group support systems effectiveness. *MIS Quarterly, 22*(3), 313-334. Retrieved April 28, 2005, from EBSCOhost database.

Author Biography

Dr. Bahaudin G. Mujtaba is an Associate Professor of Management, Human Resources and International Management. In the years 2003-2005, he was the Director of Institutional Relations, Planning, and Accreditation for Nova Southeastern University at the H. Wayne Huizenga School of Business and Entrepreneurship in Fort Lauderdale, Florida. As a director, he was responsible for the planning of accreditation reviews for all Huizenga School's academic programs in all locations throughout United States of America and abroad. In administrator and faculty capacities since 1996 in academia, Bahaudin has prepared for and worked with the requirements of Southern Association of Colleges and Schools (SACS), International Assembly for Collegiate Business Education (IACBE), Association to Advance Collegiate Schools of Business (AACSB), North Central Association (NCA) / Higher Learning Commission (HLC), and the University Council of Jamaica (UCJ). Bahaudin was appointed as the Director of Business Department for Undergraduate Studies at the Farquhar Center of NSU in the year 2002. As an academic Director, he was responsible for the operation of Undergraduate Business Programs. Bahaudin has been a speaker for 'The Caribbean Area Network for Quality Assurance in Tertiary Education" (CANQATE) in Jamaica, IACBE (USA), and the Association for Tertiary Institutions in the Bahamas (ATIB) in the Nassau, Bahamas.

Bahaudin has worked with various firms in the areas of management, cross-cultural communication, customer value/service, and diversity training for over twenty years. As a Management Development Specialist and Senior Management Training Specialist at Publix Super Markets, Bahaudin became a certified Cultural Diversity trainer through the National Multi-Cultural Institute (NMCI) which is based out of Washington DC. He has been involved in diversity education, awareness and management since the late 1980s. Bahaudin was born in Logar and raised in Kabul of Afghanistan. Bahaudin has been a guest speaker on conferences in the United States of America, Jamaica, Bahamas, and Afghanistan.

Author Contact Information:
Dr. Bahaudin G. Mujtaba
Office Phone: (954) 262-5045, OR (800) 338-4723 ext. 5045.
Email: mujtaba@nova.edu

Contributors' Biographies

1. **James Artley** is a Competitive Intelligence Analyst with Blue Cross Blue Shield of Florida. James is also the Academic Program Director at Florida Metropolitan University's Jacksonville Campus, were he is responsible for the University's operations in the evenings. In 2002-2003, James received the Instructor of the year's award at FMU. James is currently pursing his Doctorate degree at Nova Southeastern University. He holds an MBA from NSU and a Bachelor of Science in Health from the University of North Florida.

2. **Dr. Dan Austin** teaches graduate course at the H. Wayne Huizenga School of Business and Entrepreneurship of Nova Southeastern University. After many years of being a full-time faculty member and administrator, Dr. Austin is now working as adjunct professor at Nova Southeastern University.

3. **Fred Barron** was a graduate student at Nova Southeastern University's Masters of Management with a focus on Leadership Program at the School of Business and Entrepreneurship. Fred initially completed the degree of Masters of International Business Administration at NSU. His research topics include workforce diversity, teamwork and cross-cultural management.

4. **Frank J. Cavico** teaches Business Law and Ethics at the H. Wayne Huizenga School of Business and Entrepreneurship of Nova Southeastern University. Professor Cavico holds a J.D. degree from St. Mary's University School of Law and a B.A. from Gettysburg College. He also possesses a Master of Laws degree from the University of San Diego School of Law and a Master's degree in Political Science from Drew University.

5. **Dr. Claudette Chin-Loy** completed her doctoral degree in Business Administration at Nova Southeastern University, with a specialization in human resources management. Dr. Chin-Loy has collaborated on research and consulting projects in the USA and the Caribbean widely in Human Resources and Diversity Management. She has lived in the Caribbean, Europe and the USA for many years with extensive exposure to varying cultures and diversity issues. Dr. Chin-Loy also has family ties in China and exposure to the Chinese and eastern cultures.

6. **Reccia N. Charles** is a faculty member at St. George's University in St. Lucia. Reccia is currently completing her doctoral work in the area of International Business at the H. Wayne Huizenga School of Business and Entrepreneurship of Nova Southeastern University. Professor Charles has lived and traveled in the Caribbean Islands and the USA for many years with extensive interest in international and cultural issues.

7. **Dr. Roscoe G. Dandy** is a former Commissioned Officer in the United States Public Health Service and Associate Director of a health care facility, has worked in the Federal Sector for over 30 years in clinical, administrative, management, and policy level positions. Dr. Dandy has also served as an adjunct professor for over 25 years. Dr. Dandy is currently serving as a Senior Public Health Analyst in the United States Public Health Service and he recently volunteered for Hurricane Katrina Deployment to Gulfport Mississippi.

8. **Dr. Barbara Dastoor** is an Associate Professor of Management Science in the H. Wayne Huizenga School of Business and Entrepreneurship at Nova Southeastern University. She has a Ph.D. from U.T. Dallas Specializing in Organizational Behavior and Human Resource Management with a minor in Statistics and Research Methods.

9. ***Macie E. Dawkins-Hanna*** is completing her undergraduate degree in business administration and management at the H. Wayne Huizenga School of Business and Entrepreneurship at Nova Southeastern University's Bahamian Education Center in Nassau. Macie was born in the Grand Bahamas and currently works in Nassau. According to her friends, Macie is an excellent "listener" and a great team player. She is an advocate of cultural sensitivity and diversity education.

10. ***Dr. Peter DiPaolo*** joined Nova Southeastern University as an adjunct faculty member in 1981, a visiting professor in 1988, and a full time faculty member in 1998, teaching courses for the Business Programs. Prior to joining NSU, he served as Vice-President of Engineering/Finance for Multimedia Concepts Incorporated, a startup multimedia development company.

11. ***Denice Ford*** is completing her undergraduate degree in business administration and management at the H. Wayne Huizenga School of Business and Entrepreneurship at Nova Southeastern University's Bahamian Education Center in Nassau. Denice was born in the Grand Bahamas and is employed in Nassau. Denice is an avid reader of management topics and functions well in diverse work environments.

12. ***Bebe T. Frisbie*** is a Registered Medical Assistant and a former Licensed Hearing Instrument Specialist. She is a Placement Director and an instructor at a private community college. Bebe is continuing her education at Nova Southeastern University. She comes in contact with the hearing impaired every day as her husband suffers from hearing loss. Bebe is very passionate about eliminating unfair discrimination, especially toward those with various forms of disabilities. She is an advocate of diversity awareness, fairness, equity, and justice for all.

13. ***Regina Harris*** is currently the Director of Claims for a Professional Liability Insurance Group. She graduated from Nova Southeastern University's Masters of Management with a focus on Leadership Program at the School of Business and Entrepreneurship. She has a Bachelors of Business in Marketing from the University of Miami. She was inducted into Huizenga School's International Honors Society. She is interested in the topics of workforce diversity management, power bases, leadership, teamwork, and coaching.

14. ***Dr. J. Preston Jones*** is the Associate Dean in Nova Southeastern University's Wayne Huizenga Graduate School of Business and Entrepreneurship. In his numerous years at NSU, Dr. Jones has helped to lead the development of the Huizenga School's online distance learning education programs to business administration and accounting. Dr. Jones' professional career began in 1972 with the Johnson & Johnson Family of Companies.

15. ***Dr. Larry J. Lelah*** is a Global Customer Service Vice President with AT&T. He has worked with over 50 Fortune 500 companies, representing multiple industries and including such clients as IBM, Home Depot, JPMorgan Chase, and Lexmark. He has recently been honored by being recognized as a 2006 Distinguished Alumnus of the University of Phoenix. His research was done in the area of Appreciative Inquiry, Customer Satisfaction, and Business Process Improvement.

16. ***Dr. Terrell Manyak*** received his Bachelors of Science degree from California State University at Northridge. He went on to obtain his Masters in Public Administration degree from the Syracuse University Maxwell School of Citizenship and Public Affairs. After graduation, he worked for the Alaska Legislative Council in helping that state complete the transition from territorial status to statehood. Dr. Manyak then returned to California to pursue a Ph.D. from UCLA. As part of his graduate program, he was asked to teach public administration courses at the University of Khartoum in the Sudan

public administration courses at the University of Khartoum in the Sudan Republic and to work with Ministry of the Interior to write a new constitution for the country.

17. **Bryan P. Monaghan** is a graduate of Aurora University, located in Aurora, Illinois, and holds a Bachelor of Arts degree in Criminal Justice. He is currently completing a master's program in leadership at Nova Southeastern University. Bryan has focused his master studies on the essence of teamwork and project management. He has over 20 years of law enforcement experience, and is currently employed in a national security position. Bryan resides in South Florida with his wife Tami, and his son Nicholas.

18. **Eleanor Marschke** is currently a doctoral student specializing in Human Resource Management. Eleanor is employed at Thomas & Betts Corporation where for the last twenty years she has been a top performer in the sales department of this Fortune 500 Company which manufactures electrical construction products. Her interest in *Spirituality in the Workplace* is a focus of her dissertation work.

19. **Simone Maxwell** is a graduate student at Nova Southeastern University. Simone was born and raised in St. Mary, Jamaica. She pursued her undergraduate degree in Hospitality Administration at the Southern New Hampshire University. Simone is currently enrolled at NSU, where she is pursuing the Master's of Business Administration with a specialization in Leadership.

20. **Dr. Jean McAtavey** provides consulting to individuals and businesses in the areas of career development, leadership development, diversity and organizational development. Dr. McAtavey is a dynamic speaker and coach with a strong commitment to education. She teaches master level courses at Nova Southeastern University.

21. **Dr. Donovan A. McFarlane** is currently an Adjunct Professor in Business Studies at City College, and a Doctoral Scholar in Educational Leadership Studies and International Business at St. Thomas University. He holds an MBA, as well as a B.S. degree in Business Administration from Nova Southeastern University, a Doctor of Philosophy (PhD) from The American Institute of Holistic Theology, and a Doctor of Metaphysical Science (Msc.D.) from The University of Metaphysics. He was born in Manchester, Jamaica where he grew up and attended DeCarteret College, and Church Teachers' College.

22. **Lisa M. Mujtaba** is an educator and a medical coding specialist. Lisa is currently employed in the area of healthcare billing in North Miami. Lisa has worked as a middle school teacher in Central Florida as well as in government agencies in various administrative capacities. She holds a Bachelors of Science degree in science education from the University of Central Florida. Lisa lives in the United Sates and has traveled to the countries of Canada, Jamaica and the Grand Bahamas.

23. **Michelle Newton** is a graduate of the H. Wayne Huizenga School of Business and Entrepreneurship of Nova Southeastern University. Michelle is a resident in the town of Zephyrhills, Florida. She has worked in a variety of industries and is familiarized with distance education and has been extremely successful in online and distance education.

24. **Bina Patel** was born in Nairobi, Kenya. She moved to the United States at a very early age and was raised in Gainesville, Florida, where she attended the University of Florida for her undergraduate studies. Currently, she resides in Pembroke Pines, FL, where she is pursuing a Masters degree in International Business. Her research area include international business, international management, ethics, corruption, and cultural awareness.

25. *Nicole A. Pirone* received her B.S. degree in Psychology and is currently enrolled in Nova Southeastern University's M.S. of Management with a focus on Leadership Program. Nicole is a fitness and nutrition consultant in South Florida. Her research focus is on the topics of cultural diversity, coaching, leading change, and health administration.

26. *Dr. Robert C. Preziosi* is a professor of management education at Nova Southeastern University. He is the Chair for the Human Resource Management. In December of 2000, he was named *"Professor of the Decade."* In 1997, he received the school's first "Excellence in Teaching Award." He has been Vice President of Management Development and Training for a Fortune 50 company. In 1984, he was given the Outstanding Contribution to HRD Award by the American Society for Training and Development. In 1990, he received the "Torch Award," the highest leadership award that the Society can give. He was named HRD Professional of the Year for 1991.

27. *Dr. Abiodun Raimi* was born and raised in Nigeria to the Akinleye's family. Abiodun went to Duquesne University in Pittsburgh for higher education and graduated with a bachelors of science degree in nursing. He joined University of Maryland for advanced education in healthcare administration. While going to school, he has worked in hospitals for over a decade in the United States. Abiodun received his Doctorate of Management degree from the University of Phoenix. Abiodun is married and has three children. He loves to play tennis, basketball and golf. His research areas include hospital administration, healthcare and leadership.

28. *Dawn Rahicki* is president and founder of The Illume Group, Inc., a results-oriented marketing, advertising and coaching firm which primarily serves executives and entrepreneurs seeking growth, are in a start-up mode or are stalled in their career or business. Dawn has over 20 years experience as a marketing professional, most recently leading an award-winning creative department for a $9+ billion dollar company in Florida. She has a Bachelors degree with a concentration in Marketing from Barry University and is pursuing a Masters in Leadership from Nova Southeastern University. Dawn resides in Delray Beach, Florida.

29. *Dr. Philip Rokicki* has a Ph.D. from Saint Louis University and has worked in several universities. He has taught classes in Psychology, Sociology and Anthropology (both in physical and cultural), and Statistics. Dr. Rokicki has also worked with the Broward Workforce Development Board and in private businesses in South Florida. He also works at Rokicki and Associates, Inc. which has been providing program evaluations, development of curricula for distance education programs and grant-writing and contract development for nonprofits and for profit companies for nearly fifteen years.

30. *Jennifer Severe* is now completing graduate work in international business. She was raised in the Boston, Massachusetts's area and moved to West Palm Beach about eight years ago. Some of her hobbies are reading, writing (poetry, short stories, and plays), and helping. She works in the area of finance on Palm Beach Island. She is interested in importing/exporting.

31. *Dr. Michael Sithole* joined Nova Southeastern University as an adjunct faculty member in 2003, a later went to College of the Southwest as a full time faculty member, teaching courses for the Business and Management Programs. Prior to joining academia, he worked in various locations in the United States and abroad. Dr. Sithole completed the doctorate program at the H. Wayne Huizenga School of Business and Entrepreneurship with a focus on management and human resources management.

32. **Dr. Gerraldine Ippolito** works with the Globe Institute of Technology in the city of New York. She has worked on several projects with Dr. Michael Sithole and other colleagues. She regularly attends and presents her research at various academic conferences. She is multicultural and her research areas include culture, cultural diversity, Affirmative Action programs in the United States and South Afira, management, and technology, to name a few.

33. **Ikwukananne I. Udechukwu** received an MPA degree from Valdosta State University and a B.S. degree in Management from Park University. "Ike" is currently pursuing a Doctorate in Business Administration (DBA) at Nova Southeastern University. He has served as a Classification and Compensation Analyst for both the Georgia Department of Corrections and the Georgia Department of Human Resources. He is now a Recruitment and Employment Specialist.

You Are You & I am I!
I do my thing, and you do your thing.
I am not in this world to live up to your expectations
And you are not in this world to live up to mine.
You are you and I am I,
And if by chance we find each other,
It's beautiful...

Frederick S. Perls

Be Yourself!
If I am I because you are you,
and you are you because I am I,
then I am not and you are not.
However, if I am I because I am I,
and you are you because you are you,
then I am and you are.

Printed in the United Kingdom
by Lightning Source UK Ltd.
126759UK00001B/127/A